The Bhagat Singh Reader

Chaman Lal is professor (retired) and former chairperson of the Centre of Indian Languages at Jawaharlal Nehru University. He is honorary advisor, Bhagat Singh Archives & Resource Centre, Delhi Archives, and fellow of Panjab University, Chandigarh.

The Bhagat Singh Reader

CHAMAN LAL

HarperCollins *Publishers* India

First published in India in 2019 by
HarperCollins *Publishers*
A-75, Sector 57, Noida, Uttar Pradesh 201301, India
www.harpercollins.co.in

2 4 6 8 10 9 7 5 3 1

Copyright © Chaman Lal 2019

P-ISBN: 978-93-5302-849-7
E-ISBN: 978-93-5302-850-3

The views and opinions expressed in this book are
the author's own and the facts are as reported by him,
and the publishers are not in any way liable for the same.

Chaman Lal asserts the moral right
to be identified as the author of this work.

All rights reserved. No part of this publication may be reproduced,
stored in a retrieval system, or transmitted, in any form or by any
means, electronic, mechanical, photocopying, recording or otherwise,
without the prior permission of the publishers.

Typeset in 11.5/15 Adobe Caslon Pro at
Manipal Digital Systems, Manipal

Printed and bound at
Thomson Press (India) Ltd

MIX
Paper
FSC FSC® C010615

This book is produced from independently certified FSC® paper
to ensure responsible forest management.

Editor's dedication:
To
Narendra Dabholkar, Govind Pansare, M.M. Kalburgi and
Gauri Lankesh, who gave up their lives in their effort
to create the India of Bhagat Singh's dreams

CONTENTS

A Note on Compilation and Editing   ix
Introduction   xvii

Section – 1
Letters/Telegrams   1

Letters from School   3
Letter from College   8
Letters from Revolutionary Life   9
Letters to the Colonial Administration/Judiciary from Jail   21
Political Letters from Jail   65
Personal Letters from Jail   86
Telegrams from Jail   97

Section – 2
Posters/Notices/Leaflets   101

Section – 3
Court Statements   107

Section – 4
Essays, Articles and Sketches   121

Essays, Articles and Sketches in Various Journals   123

Sketches of Indian Revolutionaries in *Kirti*, *Maharathi*, *Pratap* and *Prabha*	245
Thirty-five Sketches from Phansi Ank of *Chand*	296

Section – 5
The Jail Notebook — 395

A Short History of the Publication of the *Jail Notebook*	397
A Martyr's Notebook	402
The Jail Notebook	416
References	541

Appendices

Manifestos Drafted in Consultation with Bhagat Singh	545
Manifesto of Naujawan Bharat Sabha	545
Manifesto of the Hindustan Socialist Republican Association	551
Language-wise Details of Bhagat Singh's Writings	554
Life Events of Bhagat Singh	560
Genealogy	564
Ordinance by Viceroy	565
Lahore Conspiracy Case Judgement	571
Privy Council Judgement	583
Newly Found Material	585
Bibliography	589
Acknowledgments and Sources of Documents	615

A NOTE ON COMPILATION AND EDITING

My interest in Bhagat Singh and other Indian revolutionaries began even before I was twenty years old. My interest was first aroused by Manmath Nath Gupta, a convicted revolutionary in the Kakori Case, who later turned into a historian of the Indian revolutionary movement during the freedom struggle and wrote the Hindi book *Bharat Ke Krantikari* (*Revolutionaries of India*) (Reference 1). I translated the book into Punjabi in the early 70s, and from there my interest was further piqued – even though I was a student of Hindi literature and worked mainly in Hindi literature and translation, revolutionary movements and the lives of revolutionaries were always on my mind. In 1985-86, *Bhagat Singh aur Unke Sathiyon ke Dastavez*, co-edited by me, was published by Rajkamal Prakashan, one of Delhi's eminent publishers. The book was an instant hit and continues to be so even today (Reference 2). Moroever, I narrowed my interest in India's revolutionaries and started searching and focussing on documents of Bhagat Singh. I found Bhagat Singh to be the most organised in his thinking about the revolution and the means to achieve it. Bhagat Singh went beyond the tradition of the early revolutionaries and gave an ideological direction to the whole movement, which had been missing earlier. After a profound study of revolutionary movements from around the world, Bhagat Singh realized that the goal of the Indian revolution should be a socialist revolution, which aims at ending not just colonial rule but class rule as well.

Before Bhagat Singh, the revolutionary movement was the study of the bravery, fearlessness, and patriotism of the revolutionaries. With Bhagat Singh, it took an entirely different turn and became a study of the ideas of the revolutionaries, and not just about their brave actions.

To study ideas, one needs documents and physical records of their thoughts and actions. Bhagat Singh became the first such Indian revolutionary, who like the socialist revolutionaries from around the world, would write and record his thoughts. Bhagat Singh was just sixteen when he wrote his first essay available to us, apart from the few letters he had written earlier to family members. His first published essay, 'The Problem of Language and Script in Punjab', was published ten years later in a Hindi journal *Hindi Sandesh* in 1933. He wrote it for a competition and won the first prize of Rs 50, which in those days would be close to Rs 5000 of today. But from his very first essay to the last, none among those discovered till now are in Bhagat Singh's own handwriting. Most essays or sketches, are found in print form and almost all are attributed to fictitious names; one hardly finds any printed essay remotely associated with his real name. For example in an essay in the Delhi-based Hindi journal *Maharathi* one finds the mention of a writer B.S. Sindhu. One can identify this as Bhagat Singh Sindhu, as his family clan title was Sindhu. But he twisted the name to Sandhu, perhaps in his strong patriotic feeling as an Indian, being a resident of 'Sindh', the ancient identity of India as 'the civilisation of Sindhu Valley'! Interestingly, when his niece, Veerendra, took to writing the family biography and edited his documents, she took the same title 'Sindhu'- Veerendra Sindhu and not Sindhu, as is popular (Reference 3)! The only documents found in Bhagat Singh's own handwriting are either letters or the *Jail Notebook*. Though not all letters are preserved well, quite a few letters are still conserved, including the oldest ones which he wrote to members of his family at the age of fourteen in 1921.

Bhagat Singh's writing life and active revolutionary life run simultaneously. He joined the revolutionary movement at the age of sixteen in 1923 and had less than seven years to achieve his goals of the revolution. During this time, he not only carried out political revolutionary acts – which are referred to in the introduction to the book – but also wrote prolifically. He travelled a lot all over India and spent a lot of time reading the best books from all over the world, be it history, politics, economics, or literature. Bhagat Singh wrote in four languages – Urdu, Hindi, Punjabi, and English. He had a good command over Sanskrit, as he had studied it in school, all the more encouraged by his grandfather, Arjun Singh. He understood Bengali very well, and could recite verses by poets such as Nazrul Islam and Tagore fluently in Bengali. At one time, he was learning Persian as well. He wrote more than 130 documents in seven years, covering nearly 400 hundred pages! He wrote more than fifty letters, apart from numerous court statements, pamphlets, essays and sketches. Yet, it is believed by many, on the basis of the accounts of one of his comrades in jail, that Bhagat Singh wrote four more books in jail – these manuscripts were smuggled out but are yet to be found!

The 59 letters available and presented in this book are in all four languages – Urdu, Punjabi, Hindi and English. Letters from his school period are in Urdu and Punjabi. Urdu was the primary medium of instruction in schools those days, and also commonly used in the socio-political life among all the three communities of Punjab – Muslims, Sikhs and Hindus. One can see from his three letters to his grandfather, Arjun Singh, which are all in Urdu, that Bhagat Singh had a good command over the language. However, in the two letters written in Punjabi to his aunt, Hukam Kaur, one can see many spelling and grammatical errors. This is perhaps, due to the fact that Bhagat Singh had learned Punjabi on his own in the year 1921, when the Nankana Sahib tragedy took place, in which innocent devotee Sikhs were killed at the hands of Mahant cohorts, supported by the British colonial government, and there was a massive movement against the Mahants and the British government. Bhagat Singh wore a black turban in protest and served food to processions passing through his village Chak No. 105, to cross over to Nankana Sahib, which was a few miles away from his village. As he left home to take part in revolutionary activities at that time, Bhagat Singh wrote his first political letter to his father in Urdu. From all his writings one can see that Bhagat Singh was most comfortable in writing Urdu and he wrote most of his letters that were of personal nature to family members in Urdu. In his first Hindi essay in 1923, which he wrote when he was sixteen years old, one can observe its literary flavour, showing how much command he had over Hindi as well. Since he had studied Sanskrit is school, two essays in Hindi – written and published in 1924 and 1925 in the Calcutta-based Hindi journal *Matwala* – 'Vishwa Prem (Universal Love)' and 'Yuvak (Youth)', are penned in such a Sanskritized form of Hindi, that it is a challenging task to translate these essays, particularly 'Yuvak'. On the other hand, his writings in the Punjabi magazine *Kirti* are in very simple language; in fact, they are written in everyday conversational style, which indicates that Bhagat Singh never became too well-versed with the highbrow literary style of writing in Punjabi. One does not know the form of language he used for these same essays in the Urdu *Kirti*, which was also simultaneously published, as Urdu *Kirti* files have still not been consulted by scholars.

Interestingly almost all his jail writings, written between 8 April 1929 and 22 March 1931, are in English; barring letters written to family and friends. Even though Bhagat Singh had not studied beyond the F.A. (Faculty of Arts) Programme of college, he had a powerful command over the English language; so much so that at a court-hearing in the Delhi Bombing Case, the judge told Bhagat Singh's counsel, Asaf Ali, that he suspected it was him and not Bhagat Singh who was drafting the 'statements' by the accused! The counsel had to clarify that he was reading whatever was handed over to him by his clients; such was the flair of Bhagat Singh's language. Historian V.N. Datta, has even speculated in his book, *Gandhi and Bhagat Singh* that perhaps Nehru was drafting or polishing the statements given by Bhagat Singh and his comrades (Reference 4).

The fact of the matter is that Bhagat Singh had put in a tremendous effort into teaching himself English; he used to keep a pocket dictionary in his pocket all the time and even during his life underground, he would read world classics voraciously in the time that was available to him. And one can see from the maturity of thought in the flawless English that Bhagat Singh wrote in his beautiful handwriting, that any task is achievable for revolutionaries once they set their mind to it – even learning a new language all by oneself. In fact, the Sessions

Court statement by Bhagat Singh can be compared to Fidel Castro's statement in the July 1953 Moncada Garrison Attack trial in Havana, with the apt title 'History will absolve me'! Both statements are now classic political statements of eminent world revolutionaries.

A note about the authenticity of documents. Whatever is available in Bhagat Singh's own handwriting – letters and the *Jail Notebook* are indisputable. But what has been available to us in a printed form needs some explanation. Very few people know that many of his documents were in fact published during his lifetime; only the names Bhagat Singh used were fictitious due to the fear of state oppression. Bhagat Singh worked as a member of the staff of many journals and papers like the Punjabi and Urdu *Kirti*, the Hindi daily *Pratap* , and the Delhi-based Hindi journal *Arjun* between 1923-1928, in the time period prior to his arrest. His writings in Hindi were published in *Arjun, Maharathi* and *Matwala* . His essays in *Kirti* were published under the name 'Vidrohi' and in *Pratap* he used the pen name 'Balwant'. He wrote nearly thirty-seven sketches on the lives of revolutionaries, out of the total forty-eight sketches published in 'Phansi Ank' (Gallows Issue) issue of the Allahabad-based Hindi monthly *Chand* in November 1928. Many of these sketches were translated from the Punjabi journal *Kirti* by Shiv Verma, who wrote a few sketches himself. Shiv Verma also improved a few sketches of the Babbar Akali movement written by Bhagat Singh. In 1977, Bhagat Singh's niece, Veerendra Sindhu, published all the sketches from the issue of 'Phansi Ank' under Bhagat Singh's name – *Mere Krantikari Saathi* (*My Revolutionary Comrades*) (Reference 5), unaware of the fact that Shiv Verma and Bhagat Singh had jointly prepared the issue in November 1928 while sitting at the home of its editor, Ramrakh Singh Sehgal, in Allahabad. But there were a lot of questions regarding the authorship, especially from Manmath Nath Gupta. In response to Manmath Nath Gupta's persistent queries regarding the authorship of these sketches, Shiv Verma finally clarified – out of a total of forty-eight sketches, Bhagat Singh was definitely the author of twenty-eight sketches relating to the Ghadar Party and Punjab, while details on authorship of the sketches on the Babbar Akali were still open to debate, which meant that Bhagat Singh and Shiv

Verma can be considered joint authors of these nine sketches, and Shiv Verma is the author of ten sketches (Reference 6). A few of his letters from jail were published in papers like the *Tribune* from Lahore. Many more published his letters immediately after his execution; papers and journals like the Lahore-based the *People*, the Urdu *Bande Matram*, the Hindi *Bhavishya*, and *Abhyuodey* from Allahabad, the Kanpur-based *Pratap*, and *Prabha* from Kanpur, the Calcutta-based *Hindu Panch*. Others published his writings through Kumari Lajjawati of the Bhagat Singh Defence Committee, or sent in by some of his family members and friends. Three of his famous documents – the 'On Harikishan Trial', 'Why I am an Atheist' and 'Letter to Young Political Workers' were published in the year 1931 itself.

It is not only in the recent times that Bhagat Singh has been described as a socialist or Marxist revolutionary; the papers in those days also described him as such! There is an interesting true story relating to 'Why I am an Atheist', which was first published in the 27 September 1931 issue in the *People* weekly, edited by Lala Feroze Chand. Comrade P Jeevanandam was asked to translate this essay in Tamil by E.V. Ramaswamy, popularly known as Periyar, as early as in 1934, which was published in his journal *Kudiyarasu*, with Periyar's own tribute to Bhagat Singh. During the 1947 Partition, issues of the *People* could not reach India for many years; this essay was banned later by the British colonial government. During those times, someone retranslated this essay from Tamil to English, which still continues to be in circulation on many websites and from this, many further translations were done! Websites like Marxist-Leninist.org continue with the retranslated version; and in Pakistan some translations in Punjabi were done from the retranslated version. The original version of the *People* is now preserved at the Nehru Memorial Museum and Library, and has been reproduced in a scanned format in my book *Understanding Bhagat Singh*, published in 2013.

Some documents were recovered and published very late. The *Jail Notebook* could not be published before 1992, when, for the first time, Bhupender Hooja serialized it in his journal *Indian Book Chronicle* and later published it in the form of a book. Later, a few more letters came to light when M.J.S. Waraich published five letters for the first time around 2007 in *Proceedings of the Lahore Conspiracy Case*. Ten letters saw the light of day only through digital records of the Supreme Court exhibition titled 'The Trial of Bhagat Singh', which were later published in the *Hindu* with a note by the editor of this volume in their 15 August 2011 issue.

The most important find among Bhagat Singh's documents is the 'lost letter' relating to the Harikishan case; Harikishan was executed on 9 June 1931 in the same Lahore jail Bhagat Singh, Rajguru and Sukhdev were earlier hanged. Bhagat Singh wrote a letter to someone on the outside, giving some suggestions and his opinion on how the Harikishan case should be fought in court. He was visibly unhappy with the concerned lawyer's approach, so much so that he had to write another letter expressing his unhappiness at 'the loss of earlier sent letter' (Reference 7)! That 'lost letter' reached this editor courtesy Dr Raghuvir Singh, who did his doctoral research on the political thought of Bhagat Singh, and Pandit Ram Sharma, a school teacher from Beena, who preserved issues of the magazine *Hindu Panch* and some other journals files dating from 1926 to 1932. The issue dated 18 June 1931 of the journal *Hindu Panch* carries Bhagat Singh's lost letter in Hindi along with the second letter sent in the same context. Both letters have been translated from English to Hindi, and so the editor of this volume has retranslated this letter into English. The same thing happened with 'Why I am an Atheist'! One can only hope that one day the original English letter also reappears. Another letter, dated 3 March 1931, is in the 'lost' category. Bhagat Singh, while writing the last letter to his brothers on 3 March gave it to his younger brother Kulbir Singh clearly mentioning that the 'accompanying letter in Hindi' may be 'given to K's sister'. It is assumed this is referring to B.K. Dutt's sister, to whom Bhagat Singh had written earlier also. That particular letter has still not surfaced from any family connections of either Bhagat Singh or B.K. Dutt.

Just before this volume was going to press, five more letters were recovered from amongst the family records of Bhagat Singh's younger brother, Ranvir Singh. His son, Major General (retd) Sheonan Singh, found these among Urdu sheets that belonged to his father. We can assume that he was probably writing the biography of his elder brother, though it could not be completed. Yet another letter, dated 8 May 1930, was found from Punjab Archives, Lahore, shared by Lahore journalist Ammara Ahmad.

While presenting Bhagat Singh's documents here in this volume, to avoid repetition, out of the essays in *Kirti* and *Chand*, the ones in *Kirti* have been preferred, and only where the *Kirti* files have not been traced have the essays been translated in English from the November 1928 'Phansi Ank' issue of *Chand*, which is available in print (Reference 8).

Many of the documents have more than one name; for example in many documents relating to the jail administration and judicial courts, the letters are signed by both Bhagat Singh and B.K. Dutt, his co-accused in the Delhi Bomb Case. One or two documents relating to the Lahore Conspiracy Case also carry the signatures of more than one person. Pamphlets and posters are issued in the name of 'Kartar Singh', the alias used by Chandra Shekhar Azad, who was also the Commander-in-Chief of the Hindustan Socialist Republican Army (HSRA). But all these documents were drafted by Bhagat Singh, though in consultation with his comrades. Out of the entire group, it was Bhagat Singh who developed a competence and flair in English writing. So, the authorship of all these documents is attributed to Bhagat Singh, who was considered the ideological leader of the revolutionary group, even when some of these had many signatories and names.

As readers will know later, Bhagat Singh's the *Jail Notebook* is not a personal diary or an account of his days in prison; it comprises notes taken from books that he read during his days of incarceration. We can even assume that he had some plan to write a book later had time permitted him.

INTRODUCTION

Reading Bhagat Singh

Bhagat Singh is a legend, but how he became the legend he is considered now needs to be understood. Born on 28 September 1907 at village Chak No. 105 at Lyallpur Bange – now in Pakistan and renamed as Faislabad. Bhagat Singh did not complete even twenty-three-and-a-half years of his life, for he was executed by the British colonial government in Lahore on 23 March 1931. Yet, his popularity soared so high that historian, activist, and member of the Congress party, Pattabhi Sitaramayya acknowledged that Bhagat Singh's popularity was equal to that of Mahatma Gandhi at one time. Mahatma Gandhi lived a long life and had enough time to leave his impact on both South African and Indian society; but Bhagat Singh, in his short life and even shorter seven years of political life, made an immense impact on Indian people.

The legend of Bhagat Singh can be divided into three phases. The first phase is from 17 December 1928 to 23 March 1931, the last two years and four months of his life. Deputy Superintendent of Lahore police, John Saunders was assassinated on 17 December 1928, in broad daylight in Lahore, in front of the Senior Superintendent of Police's office. The next day, proclamations by the Hindustan Socialist Republican Army (HSRA) were pasted all over Lahore's roads, and newspapers from around the world carried the sensational news. Another notice came up on 23 December in Lahore that saw the HSRA owning up to the assassination of Saunders. By now, the police were frantically searching for the revolutionaries responsible for this assassination, but to no avail. It would take many months to get a breakthrough in this case. In the meantime, the political atmosphere was heating up all over the country. In fact, this assassination itself was the result of the heated atmosphere all around; the visit by the

Simon Commission to India met with mass boycott and processions led by national leaders all around. In Lahore, the youth had convinced leader and freedom fighter Lala Lajpat Rai to lead the anti-Simon Commission protests. He led the procession on 30 October 1928, and became a victim of police oppression and violence when he was hits by lathis by John Saunders on the orders of Senior Superintendent of Police, James Scott. Due to that brutal lathi charge, Lala Lajpat Rai later declared in a public meeting held at Mori Gate that 'every lathi on my body would prove to be the last nail in the coffin of British rule in India!'[1] On 17 November 1928, Lala Lajpat Rai died due to the wounds he suffered at the lathi charge. Basanti Devi, widow of the radical nationalist Chittranjan Das, rallied the youth of the country and asked in anguish whether youth of the country were dead, that they could not avenge the death of the 'tallest' nationalist leader at the hands of petty police official of the colonial Raj. She touched a raw nerve and the HSRA took up the challenge, despite promising to leave the path of violence three months ago in its early September 1928 meeting at the Feroz Shah Kotla ground, Delhi. In this meeting, the Hindustan Republican Association rechristened itself to Hindustan Socialist Republican Association and decided to pursue the cause of socialist revolution in India by working with mass organisations of peasants, youth, students, and workers.

Responding to Basanti Devi's call, the HSRA decided to punish James Scott, who was responsible for ordering the attack on Lala Lajpat Rai. Bhagat Singh and Rajguru were chosen to shoot Scott. Jai Gopal was to identify him and Chandra Shekhar Azad was to provide cover to the whole team during the operation. Bhagat Singh was supposed to shoot first, but he stopped at the last minute. As Jai Gopal gave the signal identifying the British officer, Rajguru immediately took the shot; while Bhagat Singh tried to intervene by saying, 'Panditji, he is not Scott!'. But before Bhagat Singh could complete his sentence, Saunders was already shot by Rajguru. Bhagat Singh had no option but to pump more bullets into Saunders' fallen body to ensure he did

---

[1] Yashpal, *Simhavlokan* (Allahabad: Lokbharti, 1994), p. 126

not survive. The task was complete and the revolutionaries owned up to this assassination with posters all over Lahore by the next morning.

But this action also sealed the fate of Bhagat Singh, who himself was absolutely convinced that he was going to be put to the gallows whenever he was arrested for this case. So, with a razor-sharp mind and with crystal-clear perception, Bhagat Singh decided to perform as many spectacular revolutionary acts as possible in the short duration of his remaining lifetime. In fact, he drew a clear plan of his life and actions, and it involved the most powerful of the British colonial authority

But how Bhagat Singh acquired such a maturity in his perception, can be seen from his family background, who were all deeply involved in the national movement.

From his infancy, Bhagat Singh was nurtured and brought up not only on his mother's milk, but also the milk of patriotism from almost the day of his birth. The day of his birth, news arrived that his father Kishan Singh and two uncles, the revolutionary Ajit Singh and Swarn Singh, had been released from prison. However, Swarn Singh died shortly after his release and Ajit Singh, who was also the founder of Bharat Mata Society along with Lala Lajpat Rai, was forced to flee the country in 1909. Ajit Singh spent his exiled life mostly in Latin America, continuing his revolutionary activities for the freedom of the country and returned to India at the invitation of Nehru himself, who was leading the interim government in March 1947. In fact, Ajit Singh tried to get Bhagat Singh out of the country as he knew about his nephew's revolutionary activities. According to Baba Bhagat Singh Bilga, the veteran Ghadarite revolutionary who lived in Argentina in the 1930s, Ajit Singh had three letters of Bhagat Singh with him, which were later given to someone for safekeeping, but were subsequently lost.

Once, at the age of four, Bhagat Singh had told Mehta Anand Kishore, a well-known freedom fighter and a friend of his father's, that he 'would sow rifles in the fields in order to reap a fruit of fullsome crop to drive the British out of the country'.[2] Later, at the age of twelve,

---

2 Sindhu, Veerendra, *Yugdrashta Bhagat Singh aur Unke Mrityuanjay Purkhe* (Delhi: Rajpal & Sons, 2000), p. 130

Bhagat Singh visited Jallianwala Bagh in Amritsar in April 1919, after the massacre of people and brought back a fistful of the 'blood-soaked sand'. At the age of fourteen, while he was still at school in Lahore, Bhagat Singh told his grandfather about the preparations being made by railway men to go on strike.[3]

Bhagat Singh had enrolled in the F.A. class at the National College Lahore at the age of fifteen.[4] Just sometime before that, he had welcomed protesting Akali workers into his village; on 20 February 1921, more than 140 devout Sikhs were killed by Mahant Narain Dass in collaboration with the British authorities at Gurudwara Nankana Sahib. It was during this time that Bhagat Singh learnt the Gurmukhi script and Punjabi. In school, Bhagat Singh learnt Urdu, Hindi and English, along with Sanskrit, which his Arya Samajist grandfather insisted upon. Worried about Bhagat Singh's growing revolutionary tendencies, the family – his father, in particular – thought of reigning him in using marriage. But if marriage could not control Ajit Singh, who Bhagat Singh was much closer to in terms of his ideas, how it could control Bhagat Singh? Bhagat Singh was already sensitive to the sufferings of both of his aunts at home, the widow of Bhagat Singh's younger uncle Swarn Singh, and Bibi Harnam Kaur, wife of his exiled revolutionary uncle Ajit Singh. He was particularly attached to his aunt Harnam Kaur. According to an account of one of Bhagat Singh's schoolmate and close friend, Jaidev Gupta, Bhagat Singh was given to Harnam Kaur to adopt as she was childless, while her husband Ajit Singh living in exile.[5] In any case, Bhagat Singh was very much attached to his uncle and his ideas without even having lived with him. Ajit Singh was much more revolutionary in thought than the Congress and he wanted to awaken and organize the peasantry on the basis of their economic exploitation at the hands of big feudal lords and the colonial

---

3   Letter to grandfather Arjun Singh, see p. xx
4   Sindhu, Veerendra, *Ibid.*, p. 143
5   Interview by S.L. Manchanda in May 1978, Oral History Cell, Nehru Memorial Museum and Library, New Delhi

system. Bhagat Singh built on this advanced thinking and reached the logical end of adopting the Marxist ideology of liberation.

At the young age of fifteen, Bhagat Singh was already questioning his father about the withdrawal of the Non-Cooperation Movement by Mahatma Gandhi on the pretext of the Chauri Chaura incident. In fact, this withdrawal in 1922 had disillusioned the youth and revolutionaries all over India. Chandra Shekhar Azad, too, who had earlier been flogged in Benaras for shouting 'Mahatama Gandhi ki jai (All hail Mahatma Gandhi)!' was also very bitter at this development and later during his revolutionary activities would never trust Gandhi. Most of these young revolutionaries had associations with leaders like Chittaranjan Das, Motilal Nehru, Jawaharlal Nehru, Subhas Chandra Bose, Lala Lajpat Rai, Madan Mohan Malviya and many others, but none of the revolutionaries claimed a closeness to Gandhi; even though there had been some correspondence between Sukhdev and Gandhi. Gandhi had replied to Sukhdev's letter written before his execution, given to him through 'Young India'.[6] To be fair, Gandhi received the letter, though written earlier, only after Sukhdev's execution along with Bhagat Singh and Rajguru.[7]

In a way, the withdrawal of the Non-Cooperation Movement in 1922 gave a renewed impetus to the revolutionary movement throughout the country; even though pockets of the revolution already existed in Bengal in the form of groups like Anushilan and Yugantar, H.R.A in Uttar Pradesh, etc. Hence, Bhagat Singh reached Kanpur in 1923, after informing his father through a letter that his life is dedicated to the nation and so could not think of marrying.[8] His teacher at the National College, Jai Chander Vidyalankar, had given an introduction letter for Ganesh Shankar Vidyarthi, editor of *Pratap*, and also a Congress leader. Bhagat Singh not only joined the Hindi paper but also joined the underground revolutionary organization Hindustan

---

6 Paper edited by Mahatma Gandhi in English

7 Thapar, Mathuradas, *Mere Bhai Sukhdev* (Delhi: Praveen Prakashan, 1998), p. 191

8 Letter to his father Kishan Singh in 1923, see letters section

Republican Association, organized by Sachindra Nath Sanyal, the author of *Bandi Jivan*,[9] who, had already gone through one round of transportation to the Andamans. Bhagat Singh had met him at Lahore. It was at Kanpur that Bhagat Singh met Bejoy Kumar Sinha, Shiv Verma, Jai Dev Kapoor, B.K. Dutt and Ajay Ghosh, who were all revolutionary comrades of the HRA. Sukhdev and Bhagwati Charn Vohra were his comrades in Lahore. For about six months, Bhagat Singh wrote for *Pratap* under the pen name of 'Balwant', worked for flood relief and also performed the duties of a headmaster in a national school at Shadipur village near Aligarh. But he returned to Lahore after hearing the news of his grandmother's illness and getting the assurance that no one would talk to him about marriage anymore. By the age of sixteen, Bhagat Singh had matured a lot; in 1924. His Hindi essay on the language issue in Punjab won a prize in a competition. In the next two years, he wrote the essays 'Vishv Prem' and 'Yuvak' for the *Matwala*, both under the pseudonym 'Balwant Singh'. In 1926, his article, '*Holi ke din rakat ke Chhinte* (Drops of blood on Holi)', written on the execution of six Babbar Akali revolutionaries, was published under the name 'One Punjabi Youth'. Four years later, he wrote 'Why I am an Atheist', and referred to the development of his ideas by saying that he had become an atheist by the end of 1926 itself, when he was yet to be nineteen years of age and that these changes in his personality had taken place in the backdrop of a lot of Marxist literature being available at the Dwarkadas Library at Lahore, where Bhagat Singh had become a voracious reader from 1924 onwards.

Bhagat Singh was searching for the ultimate ideology of human liberation from all kinds of oppression and exploitation, he had almost become a committed Marxist through his contacts with *Kirti* group of Ghadrite revolutionaries of Punjab. He had regularly contributed articles to the Punjabi-language *Kirti* on various issues; 'Religion-oriented Riots and their Solution', 'Issue of Untouchability', 'Religion and our Freedom Struggle' were some of them. The only differences he

---

9   Sanyal, Sanchindra Nath, *Bandi Jivan* (Delhi: Atmaram & Sons, 1986), p. 284

has with his comrades was about the programme of the revolutionary party; for Bhagat Singh and his comrades were convinced that to awaken the country from slumber, the youth need to perform daring acts of revolution and make sacrifices to advance the movement.

By 1928, not only Bhagat Singh, but many other revolutionaries like Sukhdev, Bhagwati Charan Vohra, Bejoy Kumar Sinha, Shiv Verma and Jai Dev Kapoor, were all getting more and more convinced about the need of a socialist agenda for their revolutionary party. They gave their vision a practical shape by calling for an urgent meeting of the central committee of the HRA on 8-9 September 1928 at the Feroz Shah Kotla grounds in Delhi. After long deliberations, and at the proposal of Bhagat Singh, supported by Sukhdev, Bejoy Kumar Sinha, Shiv Verma and Jai Dev Kapoor, HRA was rechristened as the Hindustan Socialist Republican Association.[10] The addition of the word 'socialist' was not just ornamental as was done by Indira Gandhi during the Emergency when she added the word socialist to the preamble of the Indian constitution. For these revolutionaries, it was a well thought-out qualitative change of perception about the goal of the Indian revolution; which even had the sanction of Chandra Shekhar Azad, who was not that well-read but who trusted Bhagat Singh absolutely.[11]

Prior to the formation of the HSRA, Bhagat Singh trained himself in mass organizational work through the Naujwan Bharat Sabha (NBS), which has created on the pattern of Young Italy, a youth organization in Italy inspired by Giuseppe Mazzini and Giuseppe Garibaldi, in 1926. Though Ram Chandra, who remained the president of NBS, claimed that it came into existence in 1924.[12] Bhagat Singh was the organization's general secretary and Bhagwati Charan Vohra was the propaganda secretary. The NBS were particularly inspired

---

10 Chandra, Comrade Ram, ed., *Naujwan Bharat Sabha and HSRA* (Delhi, 2003), p. 55

11 Verma, Shiv, ed., *Samsmritiyan* (Delhi: National Book Trust, 2009), p. 18

12 Chandra, Comrade Ram, *Naujwan Bharat Sabha and HSRA* (Delhi, 1986), p. xii

by the sacrifice of Kartar Singh Sarabha, as he was executed at the young age of nineteen in 1915 at Lahore; Bhagat Singh always kept his photograph in his pocket. In all their public meetings, they would garland Sarabha's picture and place it on a dais. During this period, the Ghadarite revolutionaries, now trained in Communist theory from the Eastern University of the Toilers in Moscow, returned from the Soviet Union and set up a journal *Kirti*. Santokh Singh was first editor of *Kirti*, a journal in Punjabi and Urdu, with which Bhagat Singh was also closely associated. Bhagat Singh even formally worked on *Kirti* as a part of the editorial staff for a while, as he was in touch with the later editor of the journal, Sohan Singh Josh, in connection with the activities of the NBS. Even before forming NBS in Lahore, Bhagat Singh was in touch with Communists in Kanpur, a working-class city. He was in touch with Satyabhakat, Muzaffar Ahmad, Radha Mohan Gokulji, Hasrat Mohani and Shaukat Usmani. Bhagat Singh was literally a part of the Communist movement in India since its very inception. During this time, Bhagat Singh did not formally become a member of the Communist Party as it was still in its formative period. Bhagat Singh had met one of the founders of the Communist movement, Muzaffar Ahmad, when he had come to Lahore after his release from jail in connection with the Kanpur Conspiracy Case in 1924.[13] While Bhagat Singh had no reservations about joining the Communist Party formally, his efforts were going into trying to shape their own revolutionary organization, HSRA. He was also clear, as is evident from his jail writings, that ultimately the HSRA had to undertake and organize mass organization of workers, peasants, students and other potentially revolutionary sections of society. Bhagat Singh and his group were of the view that some spectacular revolutionary actions along with the noble sacrifice of young men would awaken the masses from slumber as was necessary to arouse an upsurge against the British. Sohan Singh Josh aptly described this in his *Bhagat Singh nal Merian Mulakatan* (*My Meetings with Bhagat Singh*), 1977. And after the formation of HSRA in September 1928, political developments took place in a way

---

13   Ahmad, Muzzafar, *Myself and Communist party of India*

that did not really allow the HSRA to transform itself into a nucleus of large mass organizations; though apart from NBS, there were organizations like the Lahore Students Union, Bal Students Union, Bal Bhart Sabha, etc. The NBS had helped form Bal Bharat Sabha, which was an organization of school students between the ages of twelve and sixteen.[14] The president of the Bal Bharat Sabha at Amritsar, Kahan Chand, who was just eleven years old, was awarded three months of rigorous imprisonment for revolutionary activities. Another young activist, Yash, who would later go on to become a renowned editor of the Urdu daily *Milap*, was the son of Mahasha Khushal Chand, the secretary of Bal Bharat Sabha. Yash, who was just ten years old, was persecuted on three counts including assisting the Lahore City Congress and Naujwan Bharat Sabha. In those days, a total number of 1192 of juveniles, all under the age of 15, were convicted for political activities. Among these, around 189 were from Punjab and 739 from Bengal. Apart from Bal Bharat Sabha, Bal Student Union was also active in those days. In fact, this shows the impact of Bhagat Singh in those days not only on the youth, but even on the Lahore city Congress. Lala Lajpat Rai was the tallest leader of the Punjab Congress, but his own family and families of other Congress party workers were drawn to his magnetic personality. Lala Lajpat Rai's own grandson, Baldev Raj, was the secretary of the Bal Student Union and Dyanat Rai was the President – such was the infectious impact of patriotic feelings generated by Bhagat Singh and his comrades in those days. Perhaps, alarmed by Bhagat Singh's impact on the youth of India, he was arrested by the Lahore police on May 1927 on the excuse of his involvement in the October 1926 Dussehra Bomb Case.

Bhagat Singh's comrades protected him during this period when he was underground after the Dussehra Bomb Case. Arjan Singh Gadgajj mentions in his memoirs that Bhagat Singh was kept at the hut of a poor Muslim labourer, Ibrahim, with the help of Lala Pahad Chand, a rich sympathiser of the movement. After a few days, just

---

14 Chandra, Comrade Ram, ed., *Naujwan Bharat Sabha and HSRA* (Delhi, 2003), p. xvi

before Bhagat Singh left, Lala Pahad Chand gifted him a diamond ring. During his stay at Ibrahim's hut, Ibrahim once mentioned that his daughter Sakeena was to be married but he was too poor to afford the marriage expenses. Feeling for his plight, Bhagat Singh handed over the diamond ring to him by saying that this was his marriage gift for his sister, Sakeena.[15]

Bhagat Singh was kept in jail for about five weeks, before being released on a bail bond of Rs 60,000, which was withdrawn a few months later. It was during this period that Bhagat Singh planned mass activities for the organization. When the Simon Commission came to India, the Naujwan Bharat Sabha was more active than ever in Punjab. During this time, the NBS had many differences with Lala Lajpat Rai, due to Lalaji's association with communal elements and an altercation led to Lala Lajpat Rai angrily shutting the doors of his house to Bhagat Singh, Sukhdev and Bhagwati Charan Vohra. Despite this, they requested Lala Lajpat Rai to lead the demonstration against Simon Commission, when he was visiting Lahore on 30 October 1928.

Many comrades of the HSRA went underground due to their involvement in the Kakori Rail Robbery Case, particularly Chandra Shekhar Azad. After that, because of their involvement in the Saunders murder, Bhagat Singh, Rajguru, and Sukhdev also went underground. Soon after, Bhagat Singh escaped to Calcutta along with Durga Bhabhi.[16] There he remained in touch with delegates of the Congress session like Sohan Singh Josh and also some Bengali revolutionaries like Jatinder Nath Das, a Bengali revolutionary who agreed to come to Lahore to train other comrades in bomb-making techniques. At this point, the HSRA was in a fix, on the one hand, while adopting a socialist perspective of Indian liberation, they wanted to focus upon organizing workers, peasants, students and youth; on the other hand,

---

15 Vidyarthi, Sudhir, ed., *Kranti ka Sakshaya: Shaheed Bhagat Singh*, Arjan Singh Gadgajj-*Sakeena Ke vivah mein Anguthi* (Delhi: Rajkamal Prakashan, 2009) p. 293

16 Manchanda, S.L., 'Interview with Durga Bhabhi', Oral History Cell, Nehru Memorial Museum and Library, 4 February 1977

the Saunders murder case and other cases against them could not allow them to work openly. Neither could they take cover of the Congress for open political work as they had serious and fundamental differences with the party. The only option Bhagat Singh could visualize in such a binding situation was to awaken the countrymen by their revolutionary activities, but with a minimum loss of life. The ultimate goal was to sacrifice their own lives in such a manner that the whole country would become aware of their goals and ideas. At the same time, Bhagat Singh also wanted to remove the terrorist tag that was attached to their organization and themselves. For this, they wanted to use platforms from where their voice could reach millions of people.

Many knew the danger Bhagat Singh's life was in. Shaukat Usmani mentions in his autobiography how during one of his visits to Moscow, Soviet supremo Joseph Stalin had asked him to send Bhagat Singh to Soviet Union. Seeing Bhagat Singh growing into a full-fledged socialist revolutionary, Jawaharlal Nehru, too, wished to send Bhagat Singh to Moscow, and was even ready to fund his trip as he told Chandra Shekhar Azad. Bhagat Singh's uncle, Ajit Singh, had also wished Bhagat Singh to come to him in South America. But Bhagat Singh and his comrades were destined to die for the country

Bhagat Singh knew that what they could not achieve by living for a long time, they would achieve by sacrificing their lives in the prime of their youth – in such a manner their sacrifices would become the focus of the attention for a large number of their countrymen. By shooting Saunders in broad daylight, HSRA had moved in this direction. This incident inspired millions of countrymen; and the consequent death of Lala Lajpat Rai, due to police brutality incited the revolutionaries. By killing Saunders, the HSRA and Bhagat Singh came into centre focus of the nation's political scene; though Bhagat Singh made it absolutely clear in one of his court statements that they 'bore no personal grudge or malice against anyone' and went on to say, 'we hold human life sacred beyond words, and would sooner lay our lives in the service of humanity than injure anyone else.'[17] Jawaharlal Nehru had very aptly underlined

---

17   See, '6 June Court statement' in Sessions Court in documents

the popularity of Bhagat Singh being responsible for 'vindicating the honour of Lala Lajpat Rai and the nation' in his autobiography in this context.[18]

When Jatinder Nath Das came to Lahore, bomb factories were set up in Agra, Lahore, Saharanpur, and Rohtak, in some rented houses. The bombs were tested in the forests in Jhansi and near the banks of the river Ravi in Lahore; incidentally Bhagwati Charan Vohra, a senior and ideologically strong member of the group, lost his life here during a bomb testing on 28 May 1930. The group had planned to get Bhagat Singh freed from jail, but the death of Vohra put a stop to this plan.[19] The bomb that was used in the Delhi Central Assembly on 8 April 1929 was put together at Agra and was ready by January 1929.[20] In another police version, the bomb thrown in the Delhi Assembly was from the Lahore factory. To further encourage the people's enthusiastic response to Saunders' murder, Bhagat Singh wanted another such equally spectacular event to take place. At that time, the British were bent upon notifying the Public Safety Bill and Trade Disputes Bill as law in spite of stiff opposition from the public and from members of the Central Assembly. And so, it was decided to throw 'harmless' bombs into the Central Assembly that would create noise, but do no damage to human lives. The idea was discussed in the central committee meeting of the HSRA; Sukhdev was absent from this meeting. Bhagat Singh's proposed his own name for it, but was rejected as everyone knew he was bound to be trapped in the Saunders' murder case and the party did not want to lose leadership in such a crucial time. When Sukhdev came to know of the decision, he became upset and angry at Bhagat Singh and taunted him for 'trying to save his life'. They met again and Bhagat Singh insisted that not only would he go for the job; he along

---

18   Nehru, Jawaharlal, *Autobiography* in *Ideology and Battle Cries of Indian Revolutionaries* (Delhi, 1989)

19   Chandra, *Naujwan Bharat Sabha and HSRA*, p. 122

20   Yashpal, ed., *Simhavlokan* (Allahabad: Lokbharti, 1994), p. 138

with his other comrade would get themselves arrested after the act.[21] B.K. Dutt was to accompany him. The members of the party wanted them to escape after the act, but reluctantly agreed to Bhagat Singh's proposals. Bhagat Singh went on to observe the entry and exit of the Central Assembly along with Jai Dev Kapoor, who was to accompany him to the building but leave before the bomb blast. Dr Saifudin Kitchlew, a member of the Central Assembly, had recognized Bhagat Singh there despite the fact that he had shaved off his beard in this period. This plan was inspired by a similar plan acted out by France's revolutionary Auguste Vaillant in the French Parliament to focus attention on the poverty of the people, which had a famous one-liner, 'It needs explosion to make the deaf hear'. Bhagat Singh was influenced by Vaillant's act, who was also put to gallows in 1893 for his actions. That famous line was also the first sentence of the pamphlet thrown by Bhagat Singh and B.K. Dutt in the Central Assembly, after they had thrown two bombs over the empty benches of the Central Assembly. But the explosion did create a commotion in the Assembly and only few members like Pandit Motilal Nehru, Madan Mohan Malviya and Muhammad Ali Jinnah could keep their calm by remaining standing on their seats. Most of the others, including the Home Secretary ran helter skelter, some even hiding under the benches; and here the two historic slogans came into existence on the Indian political horizon – 'Inqilab Zindabad (Long Live Revolution)' and 'Samrajyavad Ka Nash Ho (Down with Imperialism)'. In time these slogans, particularly Inqlab Zindabad, became a part of not only revolutionary groups but was adopted by many other organizations including the Congress. Of course, right-wing organizations such as the RSS and the Hindu Mahasabha would never touch this slogan. In fact, Inqilab Zindabad, was an international slogan of the working-class movement. There were attempts to translate it in Hindi as 'Kranti Chirjivi Ho', but it did not catch the imagination of people. Inqilab Zindabad, not only caught the imagination of the Hindi-speaking population of India but

---

21 Verma, Shiv, ed., *Samsmrityian* (New Delhi: National Book Trust, 2009), p. 25

also spread from Agartala to Chennai to Srinagar to Mumbai. Not only that, this slogan spread beyond India's borders too, as it became popular in Pakistan, Bangladesh, Nepal and many other countries. Bhagat Singh felt rightly proud that 'in his small life, he has made this slogan reach crores of Indians'.[22] The slogan, Inqalab Zindabad, finally replaced 'Vande Matram', which was a popular slogan of the nationalist movement since 1905. Though this slogan was coined by Hasrat Mohani, it became popular due to Bhagat Singh and any objective analysis of his contribution to the national movement would be giving the masses the slogan of Inqilab Zindabad.

The whole event was planned in a very meticulous manner; photographs of Bhagat Singh and B.K. Dutt were made beforehand, and copies of the statement issued on the occasion were made available to the press on the very same day of the event. The *Hindustan* published the full statement in its special edition. The British police officers on the scene were too scared to arrest Bhagat Singh and B.K. Dutt as both of them were holding loaded pistols in their hands. But while shouting out the slogans, both of them put their pistols on the table to indicate to the police that they were ready to be arrested. In the meantime, Jai Dev Kapoor had already gone out of Assembly hall. The purported target of revolutionary group was achieved and now the next task was to spread the message of revolution to the countrymen.

Bhagat Singh again had a well-thought-out plan in place – they would not defend themselves in the British courts, but rather use the courts as platforms to spread their ideas and values by making political statements. They did not hire any lawyer for their defence, but accepted the consultancy with advocates. Nationalist lawyer, Asaf Ali was made available to them for consultancy, and on 6 June 1929 he read out the historic statement at the sessions court by Bhagat Singh and B.K. Dutt. The statement is a policy document which explains the aims and objectives of revolutionary movement in most lucid terms:

We humbly claim to be no more than serious students of the history and the conditions of our country and her aspirations. We despise

---

22 See, 'Last letter to Comrades' on 22 March 1931

hypocrisy. Our practical protest was against the institution, which since its birth has eminently helped to display not only its worthlessness, but its far reaching power for injustice. The more we have pondered, the more deeply we have been convinced that it exists only to demonstrate to world India's humiliation and helplessness and it symbolizes the overriding domination of an irresistible and autocratic rule. Solemn resolutions passed by the house have been contemptuously trampled underfoot on the floor of so-called Indian Parliament.' Bhagat Singh and Dutt further clarified their aim – 'We deliberately offered ourselves to bear the penalty for what we had done and to let the imperialist exploiters know that by crushing individuals, they cannot kill ideas. By crushing two insignificant units, a nation cannot be crushed.' And they dared the colonialist power by putting forth the question, 'Can ordinances and safety bills snuff out the flames of freedom in India? Conspiracy cases, trumped up or discovered and the incarceration of all young men who cherish the vision of a great ideal, cannot check the march of a revolution. But a timely warning if not unheeded, can help to prevent loss of life and general sufferings.'

The main statement ends with the words, 'we took it upon ourselves to provide this warning and our duty is done.' Through their statement, Bhagat Singh and B.K. Dutt had explained that how they had thrown the harmless bombs in 'vacant spaces' so as not to harm anyone; the only destruction was the slight damage to the empty benches and slight abrasions to less than half a dozen people. And since they were asked in court 'what he meant by the word revolution', they explained this in their statement in the Sessions Court, explaining the concept of revolution almost in Marxist terminology. They spoke of capitalism and the establishment of dictatorship of the proletariat, of the consummation of the ideal of revolution. Yet, they also gave the message to the British using the Marxist epithet that said 'peaceful transition is also possible if timely warning is heeded by the power that be'. Their statement concluded with the slogan 'Long Live Revolution!'.[23]

---

23   See, 'Sessions Court statement' of 6 June 1929

In fact, the concept of revolution had become so all-consuming for Bhagat Singh that all his attention and energy was focused on clarifying it, to himself as well as to his comrades, countrymen, and the imperialist British. When Ramanand Chatterjee, the editor of *Modern Review,* ridiculed the slogan 'Long Live Revolution', Bhagat Singh and B.K. Dutt wrote a rebuttal which was published in the *Tribune* on 24 December 1929. In that they wrote, 'Revolution did not necessarily involve sanguinary strife. It was not a cult of bomb and pistol. They may sometimes be mere means for its achievement. A rebellion is not a revolution, it may ultimately lead to that end.' In the article, Bhagat Singh defines revolution as 'spirit of longing for change for the better' and that 'they wish that the spirit of Revolution should always permeate the soul of humanity, so that the reactionary forces may not accumulate strength to check its eternal onward march'.[24]

Shiv Verma, is his introduction to the *Selected Writings of Shaheed Bhagat Singh* has drawn attention to his article 'Ideology and Development of the Revolutionary Movement From Chapekars to Bhagat Singh'. This is a significant analysis of the Indian revolutionary movement. There had been sporadic rebellions or revolutionary activities against the British from 1757 onwards, when they had won the Battle of Plassey and started controlling India in bits and pieces through the East India Company – tribal revolts in Bihar and Jharkhand like those of Tilka Manjhi, Sido-Kanu and others took place even before the First Battle of Independence of 1857. Shiv Verma traces the entry of revolutionaries into the freedom struggle from the time of the Chapekar Brothers in Poona in 1897. It was the time when Bal Gangadhar Tilak dominated the national scene, he used to expose the British colonial state machinery's anti-people role through his Marathi newspaper *Kesri*. During that time there was outbreak of plague in Pune, and to contain the plague the British government created a Special Plague Committee (SPC), of which British officer Walter Charles Rand was appointed as Chairman. But soon, Rand enforced many oppressive measures on the Indian population. Seeing this, the Chapekar brothers shot Rand

---

24 See 'Letter to Editor', *Modern Review*

and another officer, Lt Ayers on 22 June 1897. They were sent to the gallows following the assassination. But the distinct feature of these earliest revolutionaries was that they were inspired by strong religious sentiments of Hinduism. The situation was the same in Bengal. Bankim Chandra Chatterjee's novel *Anand Math* published in 1882, contained the nationalist song *Vande Matram*, which was the war cry of the Sanyasi revolutionaries. This kind of nationalist trend continued with Savarker in Maharashtra, so was Anushilan Samiti in Bengal. Hence, between 1897 to 1913, Shiv Verma sees the first phase as a 'phase of revolutionary movement inspired by Hindu religion'. There were many who fought for the revolution. Khudi Ram Bose and Praful Chaki gave their lives for the cause in 1908 in Bihar and Bengal, while Madan Lal Dhingra, inspired by Savarkar, shot Colonel Wyle in London and got executed in 1909. Bal Gangadhar Tilak, Lala Lajpat Rai, Bipan Chandra Pal, and Aurobindo Ghosh all drew their inspiration from religion. Though Aurobindo Ghosh's brother, Barinder Kumar Ghosh, and Swami Vivekanand's brother, Dr Bhupender Nath Dutt, in their later life overstepped narrow religious vision of nationalism and adopted a more advanced and progressive socialist vision of nationalism in their later life.

At the same time there was another trend which Shiv Verma had not been able to pay due attention to – nationalist activities in foreign countries and in Punjab. Indian revolutionaries like Shyamji Krishna Verma and Madam Bhikaiji Cama were flying the flag of socialism high abroad, as early as in 1907 or so. Shyamji Krishna Verma worked through his paper the *Indian Sociologist* and Bhikaiji Cama pursued the cause through her association with the international socialist movement.

In Punjab, Ajit Singh, an uncle of Bhagat Singh, formed the revolutionary society, Bharat Mata Society, which focussed upon the exploitation of the peasants. Ajit Singh's comrade, Punjabi nationalist poet, Lala Banke Dayal, created the song '*Pagri Sambhal Jatta* (Take care of your turban, O peasant)', which would become the war cry in Punjab. First sung in March 1907, Banke Dayal was imprisoned for writing this song. Ironically, even now, the peasants of Punjab are facing the same problem of indebtedness that they did in the early twentieth century, with farmer suicides being reported every so often.

Their plight was brought into focus by Malcolm Darling in 1928 in his classic book, *The Punjab Peasant in Prosperity and Debt*, which Bhagat Singh probably read as he asked for it to be sent to the Lahore jail for another friend Dr Alam.[25]

Shiv Verma had rightly focused upon the formation of the Ghadar Party in America as the beginning of the secular nationalist movement from 1914 onwards; although the process of the party's growth was on from 1909 itself when Ajit Singh was forced to leave the country and go into exile. Revolutionaries like Lala Hardyal, Tarak Nath Das and G.D. Kumar were either writing pamphlets or bringing out papers in India and abroad; which finally led to the formation of Ghadar Party. Earlier known by the popular name of the Hindi Association of Pacific Coast, the Ghadar Party came into being on 21 April 1913 under the presidentship of Baba Sohan Singh Bhakna and Lala Hardyal as the general secretary, and its paper *Ghadar* was started from 1 November 1913. *Ghadar* was initially in Urdu, but later editions came out in many more languages like Punjabi, Hindi, and Gujarati. The organization was named as the Ghadar Party to appropriate the legacy of the 1857 Ghadar Movement and to give new respectability to the word 'Ghadar' after being discredited by British colonialists. The party's headquarters was in San Francisco and was named as Yugantar Ashram; again to appropriate the Yugantar revolutionary movement of Bengal. The organization, and the movement at large, had a large number of Punjabis, followed by Bengalis, and a few members from Uttar Pradesh and southern India. The Ghadar Party gave a call to liberate India from the British through armed struggle and even gave a date of liberation 21 February 1915; later changed to 19 February.

That the movement did not succeed was due to various factors, but the Ghadar Party revolutionized the tradition of revolutionary movements in India, which for the first time after 1857 was inclusive of people from all religious communities. There was not only Kartar

---

25   See Letter to Jaidev Gupta of 24 July 1930

Singh Sarabha, the youngest martyr and hero of the movement, but also martyrs and activists from different parts of the country like Vishnu Ganesh Pingle, Rehmat Ali Wajidke, Tarak Nath Das, Champak Raman Pillai, D Chenchiah and Maulvi Barkatullah. The movement had a true pan-India character and a modern secular perception. The movement later reorganized itself and took the shape of the first Communist groups in Punjab, to which Bhagat Singh was directly related. In fact, Bhagat Singh's personality and ideas were majorly shaped by the tradition of his uncle Ajit Singh and by the Ghadar Party.

Even though the Ghadar Movement had taken place prior to the 1917 Soviet Revolution, it was first among the organizations worldwide which were deeply impressed by it. By 1922 or so, Ghadarite revolutionaries had started reaching Soviet Union and getting ideological training from the Eastern University of the Toilers, which was established in 1921. Maulvi Barkatullah, secretary of the Ghadar Party after Lala Hardyal had left the USA, was in the Soviet Union even before important Ghadarites like Rattan Singh and Santokh Singh came to the Soviet Union. Santokh Singh later started the Punjabi journal, *Kirti*, with which Bhagat Singh was deeply associated. Apart from the Ghadarites, there were many other Indian revolutionaries in the Soviet Union in those days. Bhagat Singh was also in touch with Radha Mohan Gokulji, Satyabhakat, Hasarat Mohani and Shaukat Usmani, who were a group of Communists from Kanpur. He had also met Muzaffar Ahmad in Lahore earlier. Satyabhkat even wrote a small book on Bhagat Singh in Hindi, *Krantiveer Bhagat Singh*, after he was executed.

Shiv Verma has discussed the growth of Bhagat Singh's thoughts toward scientific socialism through his writings and also through his close personal interaction with him in jail. He opined that in Bhagat Singh, the ideological development of the revolutionaries' movement in India climaxed with the perception of a socialist revolution. This has been an objective assessment, yet some later movements also need mention here. The Chittagong Revolt of 1932 was one such revolutionary movement which is comparable to the earlier Ghadar Movement. Led by the legendary Master Surjya Sen, inclusive of both

Anushilan and Yugantar factions, the Chittagong Revolt had given the call of 'Do and Die', much before Gandhi had given call of 'Do or Die' in 1942. The Chittagong Revolt led to the martyrdom of the young revolutionary Preeti Lata Wadedar, apart from other martyrs. Another distinctive feature of the surviving Chittagong revolutionaries was that they joined Communist group in jail, and while serving their sentence; legendary Chittagong revolutionaries like Ganesh Ghosh and Anant Singh became committed Communists under the influence of renowned Ghadarite Baba Gurmukh Singh.

In 1940, Udham Singh, inspired by Bhagat Singh shot dead Michael O'Dwyer, who was responsible for the Jallianwala Bagh massacre and of other oppressions in Punjab in 1919. Udham Singh was hanged in London in 1940. The Quit India movement of 1942 also freed certain areas of Ballia from British yoke for few days. Netaji Subhas Chandra Bose's Azad Hind Fauj's march towards India's freedom and the 1946 Navy revolt are all a part of the glorious legacy of India's revolutionary movements. But the distinctive feature of all revolutionary movements was that was after Bhagat Singh and the HSRA, all movements have been secular and democratic to the core and broadly leftist in thought. Netaji Subhas Chandra Bose was helped out of India by none other than Bhagat Ram Talwar in Kabul, a Ghadarite sympathizer and brother of martyr Harikishan.

Returning to Bhagat Singh's story, there were two things on his agenda while in jail; to expose British colonialism by using the courts as a platform for spreading their ideas to a wider audience and to expose the brutalities of the British in jail by resorting to hunger strikes in jail, and thus drawing public attention. Bhagat Singh was successful in achieving both these ends. The third thing on his agenda was his own ideological development. It was amazing to see a man who was about to go to the gallows immersing himself deep into the most serious study of world revolutionary history, that too in such trying circumstances. Bhagat Singh did not have the privilege to go to library or bookshops, or to buy books at will and then visit coffee houses to discuss new ideas. He was instead always preparing court statements, in which his serious study of Marxism helped, or organizing hunger strikes for months together, spending time with his comrades, being brutally beaten up in courts by police and then nursing his wounds in jail, alongside studying and taking notes from the books he read in prison.

He was also writing during that time, as mentioned by Shiv Verma in his preface. There are mentions of four manuscripts drafted by Bhagat Singh while he was in jail; the first was *The Ideal of Socialism,* second one was an autobiography, third was *History of Revolutionary Movements in India,* and the last, *At the Door of Death.* According to Shiv Verma, these manuscripts were smuggled through Kumari Lajjawati, who then handed them over to Bejoy Kumar Sinha in 1938 after his release from the Andaman jail. Sinha passed these manuscripts on to a friend for safe custody, who destroyed the manuscripts in fear of a police raid at some stage.[26] However, the manuscript of *Jail Notebook* was collected by Kulbir Singh or some other member of Bhagat Singh's family. Kumari Lajjawati, who was the secretary of the Bhagat Singh Defence Committee and a Congress activist, frequently visited the Lahore Jail to discuss legal aspects of the case. In an interview to the Nehru Memorial Museum and Library, and to the library's Oral History Cell, she said that that she had handed some papers given to her by Bhagat Singh to Feroze Chand, editor of the *People*, which was a paper established by Lala Lajpat Rai. Feroze Chand was told to select whatever he wanted to publish; and having done so he returned the remaining to Lajjawati. Kumari Lajjawati then handed these papers to Bejoy Kumar Sinha in 1938. Feroze Chand published the essay 'Why I am an Atheist' *in* the issue dated 27 September 1931, which also happened to be Bhagat Singh's first birthday after his execution on 23 March. Prior to that, the *People* published extracts from the now famous 'Letter to Young Political Workers' in its issue dated 29 March, just days after Bhagat Singh's execution. It looks like that Feroze Chand had selected some other papers too, including Bhagat Singh's letter on the death sentence given to the young revolutionary Harikishan, which was also published by the *People*. Bhagat Singh's father was also keen to acquire or at

---

26 Verma, Shiv, *Selected Writings of Shaheed Bhagat Singh* (Delhi: National Book Centre, 1986), p. 4

least see the papers written by his son, but he was strictly refused by Lajjawati, purportedly on the instructions of Bhagat Singh himself. The strange part of this whole saga of indifference to the documents, considered so valuable now, is that neither Kumari Lajjawat nor Feroze Chand, or even Bejoy Kumar Sinha, who was given the custodianship of those papers at the instructions of Bhagat Singh himself, took the trouble to take a serious look through the papers and at least note down their contents. What seems certain is that Bhagat Singh's thought had come to light broadly through the papers and that an evaluation of his thought process can be made on the basis of the retrieved documents, which are quite substantial.

However, Bhagat Singh did plan to write a full-fledged book, *The Science of the State*, for which he had taken detailed notes which are included in his *Jail Notebook*. In this proposed book, Bhagat Singh was trying to trace the growth of the State from primitive Communism to the modern Socialist State. Had he got the time to write this book, it would probably have been a major contribution in the field of Marxist study and in the concept of the State.

The manuscript of the *Jail Notebook* was first published in 1994, edited and annotated by Bhupender Hooja, is a significant document in its own right. It is not a notebook like the prison notebooks of Antonio Gramsci or the philosophical notebooks of Lenin, not even like Che Guevara diaries. It is not diary at all; this notebook is unique in its own way as it includes the notes of the books read by Bhagat Singh in jail before his execution. Apart from being significant in its selection, these notes are an objective reflection of the development of Bhagat Singh's ideology. These are also reflective of his aesthetic sensibilities as a large number of quotes are from classic literary pieces of world literature. These quotes show that Bhagat Singh was a revolutionary with rare sensitivity. During his student days and after, his fondness for films has been mentioned by many of his close friends and comrades. He was a fan of Charlie Chaplin films and also of films like *Uncle Tom's Cabin* and *The Three Musketeers*. He was also a good singer in college and acted in college dramas; all this showed his deep involvement with literature and other art forms. That is why elder revolutionary, L Ram Saran Das asked for Bhagat Singh to write an introduction for his poetry collection, *Dreamland*. Some of his favourite books mentioned by almost all of his teachers, friends, and comrades were *Cry for Justice* edited by Upton Sinclair, *Les Misérables* and *Ninety-Three* by Victor Hugo, books on Urdu poetry, and more. Every memoir underlines his habit of voracious reading; even mere minutes before going to the gallows he was reading a book on Lenin.

It is also interesting to note that much before Bhagat Singh's *Jail Notebook* came into focus in India, it was discussed in detail by Soviet Indologist L.V. Mitrokhin in his 1981 book *Lenin and India*; a Hindi translation of the book was published in 1990. In this book, one full chapter is devoted to Bhagat Singh under the title, 'The Last Days of Bhagat Singh'. References have been made to even earlier documents, such as A.V. Raikov's 1971 article 'Bhagat Singh and his Ideological Legacy' and Mitrokhin's own earlier book '*The Books Read by Bhagat Singh*', included in the 1971 publication of *India on Lenin*, etc. In these Russian publications, assessment of Bhagat Singh's ideological development has been made quite objectively and he had been placed firmly within the tradition of Marxist thought.

The *Jail Notebook* should be read in relation to Bhagat Singh's other significant documents like 'Why I am an Atheist', 'Court Statements', 'Letter to Young Political Workers', etc., which by now have acquired the status of classic documents of the revolutionary movement. In fact, in the *Jail Notebook*, the quotes taken from books, other than literary, are a sort of reference to the significant books about the development of democratic political thought, which include books from ancient Greek thought to the latest Marxist classics of that time. In a way the *Jail Notebook* is also a mirror of the ideological development of Bhagat Singh's personality, which concluded with the partially read book on Lenin on 23 March 1931, when he was hanged to death. The Punjabi revolutionary poet Paash, had paid apt tribute to Bhagat Singh on his last moments by saying, 'The Indian youth need to read the next page of Lenin's book, folded by Bhagat Singh on the last day of his life'.[27]

---

27 Lal, Chaman, ed., *Vartman Ke Rubaru-Pash* (Delhi: Vaani Prakashan, 2000), p. 18

Bhagat Singh's story continued in jail through indefinite hunger strikes along with his comrades, in which one of their dear comrades Jatinder Nath Das lost his life on 13 September 1929 on the sixty-third day of his fast unto death. Jatinder Nath Das' health was beyond redemption, the forcible feeding of milk had burst his lungs, and despite appeals to break his fast by his other colleagues few days earlier, he had refused to give up, with the clear understanding and declaration that he was consciously giving up his life for the nation. Bhagat Singh, B.K. Dutt and a few more of their comrades had continued their fast even after his death, breaking it only in the first week of October, making at that time, a record of a 111-days long fast. Bhagat Singh undertook another hunger strike against the tribunal hearing in the Saunders Murder Case when they were brutally beaten up on the orders of Presiding Judge Coldstream.[28] The second hunger strike observed in February 1930 lasted for sixteen days. The third and last hunger strike was done by Bhagat Singh from 28 July to 22 August; this information only came to light after his new letters were discovered in the Supreme Court exhibition titled 'The Trial of Bhagat Singh'. These letters were first published by me in the 15 August 2011 issue of the *Hindu*. Bhagat Singh and B.K. Dutt cumulatively almost observed five months of hunger strike in less than two years of imprisonment.

The political weapon of hunger strike was used by Bhagat Singh and his comrades in a most effective manner. In fact, it needs to be emphasized that the moral strength of observing a self-sacrificing hunger strike has always been effective in all societies and it still carries that strength. The difference between a suicide bomber and a person on a hunger strike is that while a suicide bomber gives his life for a cause dear to him and also takes away the lives of others, losing the sympathy of people in the process, a person on a hunger strike only harms himself or herself and even sacrifices his or her life, in the process pricking the conscience of the nation. Bhagat Singh and his comrades were aware of this fact and they used it to the hilt, all the while erasing the impression

---

28 Noorani, A.G., *The Trial of Bhagat Singh: Politics of Justice* (Delhi: Konark Publishers, 1996) p. 146

of themselves being killers or terror creators. This realization also shows the political maturity of Bhagat Singh. The weapon of the hunger strike is quite effective even today, provided it carries the moral strength of the cause and person undertaking this step.

Bhagat Singh and his comrades boycotted the trial of the Saunders Murder Case, and the way the tribunal handed the death sentence to Bhagat Singh, Rajguru and Sukhdev is thoroughly exposed in A.G. Noorani's book *The Trial of Bhagat Singh*. It was nothing but murder committed by British colonialists through judicial drama, and as Bhagat Singh had befittingly written to the Governor Punjab three days prior their execution about how they were to be treated as war prisoners, as they were waging war against British imperialism and as such 'they should be shot dead' rather than being hanged to death like common criminals. But the British proved to be so cowardly, that they even flouted international norms of the timing of the hanging, i.e., 6-7 a.m.; Bhagat Singh, Rajguru and Sukhdev were hanged to death at 7 p.m. on 23 March itself. That day a huge rally was held at Lahore by the NBS, which had apprehended that the execution would take place instead on the morning of 24 March. As a last act of defiance, not only did the three revolutionaries refuse to cover their face with a black mask as is the practice, but they also put the noose around their neck themselves while addressing the magistrate who came to watch the execution process and said to him, 'Mr Magistrate, you are lucky to watch our execution and to see how Indians kiss the gallows cheerfully.'

Scared of the huge gathering at the Lahore Central Jail, the British jail officials executed them at 7 p.m. on 23 March (As per execution notifications issued by British authorities, which were displayed for the first time by Punjab Archives Lahore in March 2018 in an exhibition). But the news could not be withheld from the people of Lahore. The rally was about to end when the news of executions came out and the people rushed to the gates of jail. Scared, the British officials cut the still-warm bodies of the martyrs in pieces and after filling these in sacks, took these away from the back exit of the jail towards the Sutlej River bank near Ferozepur. This was all done under the cover of the night. The British officials got a Granthi and a pandit from Ferozepur town to perform the religious rituals. The bodies were burnt with kerosene in an alarming hurry in the jungle near Ganda Singh Walla village. People from Ferozepur and Lahore came searching for the bodies and before the dawn of 24 March, they were able to locate the place, out of which some unburnt and half-burnt bones, the smell of kerosene, and stains of blood came out. In anguish and anger, the people collected these body parts and reached Lahore, and the three martyrs were given a proper cremation on the banks of the river Ravi, where earlier Lala Lajpat Rai had been cremated.[29] Thousands of people joined the funeral procession and memorial meeting that was held later in Minto Park near the river bank. The Congress party in Punjab at that time formed a fact-finding committee to enquire after the mistreatment of the dead bodies of the martyrs. Newspapers in those days, particularly *Bhavishya* from Allahabad, had highlighted the committee's hearing but the report was either not released or remain dumped in the Congress papers. While the Kanpur riots, report of the Congress, which took place after the execution had drawn national attention and its reprint has even been published by the National Book Trust, it is strange that no one ever even remembers the Congress party's fact-finding report about the mistreatment of the bodies by the British colonial authorities. The Kanpur riots, which started after the execution of Bhagat Singh and his comrades, unfortunately took on a communal colour and tragically took the life of Congress leader, nationalist journalist and admirer of Bhagat Singh, Ganesh Shankar Vidyarthi.

This was also the condition of the martyr's memorial. The Naujwan Bharat Sabha had formed a memorial committee to build a suitable memorial for the martyrs, which was sabotaged by the Congress party through Bhagat Singh's father, Kishan Singh, with the promise that the Congress party would build a grander, national memorial for the martyrs.[30] That later a memorial near Ferozepur called Hussainiwala

---

29 Thapar, Mathuradas, *Mere Bhai Sukhdev* (Delhi: Praveen Prakashan, 1998), p. 185

30 Chandra, Comrade Ram, *Naujwan Bharat Sabha and HSRA* (Delhi, 1986), p. 164

was built had no relevance at that time to the national movement. Lahore was the hub of the national movement, it was the place where Bhagat Singh and his comrades had spent their lives in political action, and it was where they were executed and cremated. The most logical thing would have been to build a memorial in memory of Lala Lajpat Rai, Bhagat Singh, Sukhdev and Rajguru at the banks of the river Ravi, which would had been a source of inspiration for the youth of Punjab; perhaps, this could have even proved as a deterrent to the division of Punjab.

Looking back, more than eight decades later, one can only wonder that how come no memorial was built to these martyrs in Lahore or in Lyallpur, the birth place of Bhagat Singh and Sukhdev, which is now called as Faislabad in Pakistan. Bhagat Singh is the one and perhaps only symbol which evokes respect among both Indian and Pakistani people. Bhagat Singh is the common thread between the now-divided Punjabis – a symbol of resistance against colonialism and imperialism. He can still become a common symbol of resistance against the new colonial corporate regime as well. It is heartening to see that civil groups in Lahore are now demanding the naming of Shadman Chowk – built after demolishing the Lahore Jail, where the three revolutionaries were hanged – to be named as Bhagat Singh Chowk and a statue of Bhagat Singh be installed there. In the same way, the people of Chak no. 105, Lyallpur Bange, have started holding a mela in memory of the martyrs, and the primary school of the village, where Bhagat Singh was a student, has been renovated to commemorate the great revolutionary. The Bhagat Singh Foundation, led by Imtiaz Rashid Qureshi, who is fighting a case in the Lahore High Court to get the death sentence given to the revolutionaries upturned posthumously, claims that the village has been named as Bhagatpura.

There are some other interesting aspects about Bhagat Singh, for instance he had an excellent rapport with national leaders, be it Subhas Chandra Bose, Jawaharlal Nehru, Motilal Nehru, Lala Lajpat Rai, Madan Mohan Malviya, or others. Subhas Chandra Bose and Nehru were both much appreciative of Bhagat Singh's personality, even though Congress leaders and the young revolutionaries were at crossroads many times due to their different perceptions and way of working. Seeing Lala Lajpat Rai working with communal forces, Bhagat Singh and his comrades attacked him openly. Yet, they did not break contact with him. In fact, Lala Lajpat Rai's grandson was the secretary of the Bal Students Union, which was inspired by Bhagat Singh. Motilal Nehru, Madan Mohan Malviya, Dewan Chaman Lal had all condemned the Central Assembly bomb-throwing by Bhagat Singh and his comrades in rather strong words. Gandhi even declared it 'a mad act of two young men'. Bhagat Singh described Dewan Chaman Lal as a 'pseudo socialist' in his famous Sessions Court statement and accused Tej Bahadur Sapru as being no different from the British if the system remains same. Yet, the same leaders, from Motilal Nehru, Dewan Chaman Lal, Madan Mohan Malviya, even Tej Bahadur Sapru, apart from Jawaharlal Nehru, Subhas Bose and Jinnah, stood up for these revolutionary youth in courts and when they were on hunger strikes went to every possible extent to save their lives. Advocates like Asaf Ali, Kailash Nath Katju, Chander Bhan Gupta, Mohan Lal Saxena, all stood by the youth. It was the spirit of nationalism which bound these national leaders and the revolutionary youth. Even though both factions criticized each other bitterly, yet they stood together at the time of crisis, particularly against the British empire – something which needs to be learnt by present-day national leaders and the youth of India.

Another aspect of Bhagat Singh and his brand of the revolutionary movement was the total opposition of the caste system and communalism. Dalit movements of today, after Dr Ambedkar, accept Bhagat Singh as their genuine supporter. Bhagat Singh's writings and his conduct earned him the love and support of the Dalit masses. Periyar and Ambedkar's tributes to Bhagat Singh have come to light decades after they first appeared in Tamil and Marathi. In jail, before going to the gallows, Bhagat Singh was not only reading Lenin, he asked for food from Bebe, a name given to a Dalit jail employee, Bogha, in affection by Bhagat Singh, with the logic that the mother too cleanses the defecation of her children, just as the Dalit woman had to for grown-up people. In that sense, Bhagat Singh treated and respected the manual scavenger in jail just like his mother. And when Bhagat Singh, Sukhdev and Rajguru were going to gallows, arm in arm, laughing and singing, it was jail warder Charat Singh and the prisoners, who were crying and shouting 'Inqilab Zindabad', with the three revolutionaries. Having great affection for Bhagat Singh, the deeply religious jail warder had requested Bhagat Singh to recite the Gurbani before going to the gallows. Bhagat Singh told him politely and affectionately that if he did so, the coming generations would think of him as a coward, who could not remain true to his convictions in the face of death. Written six months before his execution and two days before his death sentence was announced, Bhagat Singh had underlined this spirit in his now-celebrated essay 'Why I am an Atheist', that he will not remember 'God', while going to the gallows, even if he was dubbed as vain, something he was sure of even before the judgement came.

It must be underlined that none of the communal organizations, be it the Hindus, Muslims or Sikhs, had spoken a word in favour or in defence of these revolutionaries. Ironically, now all communal organizations want to give a religious colour to these national martyrs, despite Bhagat Singh being a committed atheist and had refused to perform any religious rituals before going to gallows. This also needs to be noted that it is only the Leftist movement in the country which has truly tried to uphold and imbibe the spirit of revolutionary movement of our country, while the Right, whether inside or outside the Parliament, have always tried to appropriate the legacy of the revolutionaries and the movement. Whether it is the issue of NCERT books or the so-called controversy about the national song *'Vande Mataram'*. In fact, the political Right in India, during and after the freedom struggle, have always tried to divide Indians on narrow, communal lines and always played the role of agents for the neo-colonial forces. Hence, the Left are the true inheritors of the legacy of the freedom struggle, though ironically they were dubbed as 'traitors' for not supporting the Quit India Movement of 1942.

In this whole saga, two people and an institution knew how the whole scenario would end. Mahatma Gandhi and Bhagat Singh both knew that nothing could stop the execution of the revolutionaries – Gandhi due to his own beliefs and Bhagat Singh due to his own equally (or perhaps much stronger) convictions. The British empire in India, of course, knew the end best as it was hell-bent upon finishing these young men, particularly Bhagat Singh, in whom they saw the traits of a growing 'Indian Lenin'. The British could afford to deal with the Gandhian Congress party, shedding its political power but protecting its economic interests. But it could not afford to have Bhagat Singh, who, if allowed to live, would have worked towards the complete overthrow of the system of imperialist and capitalist exploitation they had brought upon India.

In a way, Bhagat Singh had what it took to take on the British colonial power his way. With a group of less than hundred people all over the country, he could unnerve and rattle the most powerful empire on earth, could chalk out a path to glory and martyrdom, and stir up millions of people at the same time; Pattabhi Sitaramaya, the Congress historian and Gandhi's candidate against Subhas Chandra Bose in the Tripura Congress even admitted that Bhagat Singh was no less popular than Mahatma Gandhi. This was no small achievement for a young man of less twenty-four years with just six to seven years of active political career behind him.

After the pronouncement of his death sentence, Jai Dev Kapoor asked Bhagat Singh 'if he regretted dying so young'. Bhagat Singh first laughed at the question, then replied seriously, 'Stepping up on the path of revolution, I had thought that if I could spread the slogan of Inqilab Zindabad throughout the country by giving away my life, I would feel that I have received the full value of my life. Today, sitting behind the bars of the gallows barracks I hear the sound of the slogan from crores of people. I believe that this slogan of mine would attack imperialism as the driving force of freedom struggle till the end. What more value can be of such a small life?'[31]

---

31 Interview by S.L. Manchanda on 3 October 1974 for Oral History Cell of Nehru Memorial Museum and Library, New Delhi

Shiv Verma had mentioned an incident that happened in jail in July 1930 when Bhagat Singh had come to the Lahore Burail Jail from the Central jail to meet them on the excuse of discussing their court case. Everyone pronounced judgements on each another in jest except for Rajguru and Bhagat Singh – everyone knew they will be hanged. Bhagat Singh then said that they all were afraid to face the reality as the pronounced sentence would be, 'To be hanged by the neck till we are dead'. Shiv Verma recounts, 'He was in form that day; he was speaking in a low pitch that was his style. Showing off was not his habit, that was perhaps his strength also.' Verma quotes Bhagat Singh's own words, 'This is the highest award for patriots and I am proud that I am going to get it. They may kill me, but they cannot kill my ideas. They may crush my body, but they will not be able to crush my spirit. My ideas will haunt the British like a curse till they are forced to run away from here.' Speaking with passion, he continued, 'Bhagat Singh dead will be more dangerous to the British enslavers than Bhagat Singh alive. After I am hanged, the fragrance of my revolutionary ideas will permeate the atmosphere of this beautiful land of ours. It will intoxicate the youth and make him mad for freedom and revolution, and that would bring the doom of British imperialists nearer. This is my firm conviction. I am anxiously waiting for the day when I will receive the highest award for my services to the country my love for my people.'[32]

In this first phase of understanding Bhagat Singh's personality, it is important to know that his publications and actions during the last two years of his life took him to the skies of popularity among the Indian masses. He became popular, but he also got the status of the thinking revolutionary because of his published letters, statements, and essays. An intellectual like Jawaharlal Nehru would not have admired Bhagat Singh if he had not seen the spark of intellectual quest in him for socialist ideas. However, a few years after his death, he has been limited to the figurehead of a 'brave hero and martyr', while knowingly or unwittingly suppressing his ideas. Popular images like the one where

---

32 Verma, Shiv, *Selected Writings of Shaheed Bhagat Singh* (Delhi: National Book Centre, 1986), p. 41

he is a young gun-toting man with a turned-up moustache in a yellow turban, make him look like a fearsome and reckless person. In fact, Bhagat Singh in real life never wore a yellow or saffron turban, he was always dressed in a white khadi kurta and pyjama and a white turban. There are just four 'real' photographs of him; in two he is wearing a white turban, in one he is sitting on a cot with his hair open, and in the fourth and most famous photograph, clicked just before he went on to throw a bomb in the Assembly in April 1929, he is wearing a hat and looking straight into the camera. The photographer from Kashmiri Gate had later appeared in court as a prosecution witness. The photograph was published for the first time in the 12 April 1929 issue of the Lahore-based *Bande Matram* and then in the 18 April 1929 issue of the *Hindustan Times* of Delhi; both of these are now part of the National Archives of India at New Delhi. All other photographs available, including the one with the yellow turban, are either fake or paintings. Unfortunately, even the Central and State governments keep promoting these fake photographs.

Bhagat Singh's ideas on socialism, ending exploitation, and bringing total revolution in society were either ignored, distorted or suppressed. This continued for quite a long period of time, despite the fact that his comrades like Ajoy Ghosh, Sohan Singh Josh, Shiv Verma, Bejoy Kumar Sinha, and others, had been writing about his ideas. But all their writings were ignored dismissing them as 'Communist writing'. And later, trash biographies were created, which made Bhagat Singh look like either a narrow and sectarian nationalist, fitting him into either the Hindutva agenda or the gun-toting Khalistani warrior trope. The credit of retrieving his socialist ideas goes to Professor Bipan Chandra, which he did through his publication of Bhagat Singh's article 'Why I am an Atheist' along with an erudite introduction in the 1970s which brought Bhagat Singh's ideas into focus again.[33] Later, many of Bhagat Singh's writings came out in multiple publications in many Indian languages, some brought out by me as well in Hindi.

---

33 Singh, Bhagat, 'Why I am an Atheist', (Delhi: People's Publishing House, 1994)

The third phase of understanding Bhagat Singh began in his birth centenary year, 2007, when seminars, conferences, public meetings were held throughout the country focussing on his ideas. It now became impossible to distort Bhagat Singh's image after his publications became easily available in almost all Indian languages, and many students, youth and other Left-oriented organizations appropriated the legacy of Bhagat Singh's ideas in earnest. In this third phase, many eminent historians, political scientists and other scholars apart from Prof. Bipan Chandra, Prof. Irfan Habib of AMU, Prof. J.S. Grewal, Prof. K.M. Panikkar, Prof. S Irfan Habib, Prof. Sabyasachi Bhattacharya, and Prof. Mubark Ali from Pakistan, started writing on his role in the freedom struggle. Even scholars based abroad, like Chris Moffat, Neeti Nair, and Kama Maclean focussed their research on Bhagat Singh, thus bringing him into international spotlight as a revolutionary thinker.

This third phase of understanding Bhagat Singh was mainly through studying his ideas through his writings, which include his ideological writings. This cleared the false perceptions and labels about him like 'terrorist', which was coined by the British. Bhagat Singh too, had been able to clear the tag of terrorist pinned onto him when he wrote in his politically and ideologically most significant writing 'Letter to Young Political Workers' on 2 February 1931, 'Apparently I have acted like a terrorist, but I am not a terrorist. I am a revolutionary who has got such definite ideas of a lengthy programme as is being discussed here. Let me announce with all the strength at my command, that I am not a terrorist and I never was, except perhaps in the beginning of my revolutionary career. And I am convinced that we cannot gain anything through these methods. I do not mean to say that bombs and pistols are useless, rather the contrary. But I mean to say that mere bomb throwing is not only useless but sometimes harmful.'[34]

It may be underlined here that the term 'terrorism' was not that damned a term in the 1930s as it is today. In countries like Asia, Africa, and other areas who were struggling against colonial occupation,

---

34   See, Letter to Young Political Workers, 2 February 1931

revolutionary terrorism was a respectable concept adopted by anti-colonial struggles and thinkers like Franz Fanon, who has defended it in context of Algerian and African anti-colonial struggles. The so-called nationalists who attack scholars like Prof. Bipan Chandra or Professor Mohammad Tajuddin (in November 2018, quoting him out of context and blaming him for calling Bhagat Singh 'a terrorist') are either ignorant of history of anti-Colonial struggles or are doing it with certain communal and anti-Communist mischief in mind, as these people themselves never participated in the anti-colonial freedom struggle of India.

Till now, while almost all his complete writings have been available in languages like Hindi, Urdu and Marathi in single volumes. Few other Indian languages and English have only some of his selected writings available. For the first time, all his available documents and writings are being made available through this HarperCollins edition of *The Bhagat Singh Reader*. In fact, this volume is more comprehensive than all other previous editions of Bhagat Singh's writings, some of which are not available even in earlier published 'complete' documents in Hindi or Punjabi. Of course, translations done by Bhagat Singh of some books in Hindi or Punjabi are not included here. Bhagat Singh translated *Bandi Jivan* of Sachindra Nath Sanyal in Punjabi and also translated Dan Breen's *My Fight for Irish Freedom* in Hindi. He probably got Veer Savarkar's *First Indian War of Independence* reprinted in Hindi, which was earlier banned by the British regime. Savarkar's book was originally written in Marathi and it was non-controversial at that time as it even recognized the role of Muslims in its text. Savarkar became controversial in his later writings, after he adopted extremism through the lens of Hindutva. Though, there is no reference of Veer Savarkar writing a tribute on to Bhagat Singh on his death, whereas other national leaders like Mahatma Gandhi, Jawaharlal Nehru, Sardar Patel, Maulana Azad, Subhash Bose, Periyar, and Dr Ambedkar, all paid their tributes to these revolutionaries, even while disagreeing with his views. Mahatma Gandhi, for instance, clearly expressed his opinion and said, 'The youth should not follow Bhagat Singh's path', but Periyar eulogised him unconditionally.[35]

Some of the writings have been recovered, thanks to the efforts and help from many sources, acknowledged later in this volume. For academia, this volume is just basic material to pursue further research on the vastly unexplored area of the revolutionary aspect of the Indian freedom struggle. While some research has been done on the Chittagong Revolt of 1932, on the Ghadar Party of 1913-47, and a bit on Bhagat Singh, there still remains vast scope of exploration, not only from 1857, but from 1757 onwards itself, when the East India Company took large parts of India under its control. I hope this book will make the task of academia easier in terms of understanding, analysing, and evaluating Bhagat Singh's ideas and his role in the cause of liberation of India from all kinds of oppression. Moreover, since scholars abroad are now showing keen interest in studying Indian movements of resistance as subaltern study, this volume may serve as a contribution towards that goal.

---

35   Ramaswamy, E.V., Periyar, editorial, *Kudiyarasu*, 29 March 1931

SECTION – 1

LETTERS/TELEGRAMS

LETTERS FROM SCHOOL

1. Letter to grandfather Arjun Singh; 22 July 1918 (Originally in Urdu.)[1]

This is Bhagat Singh's first available letter, written when he was in Class VI and less than eleven years old. Bhagat Singh received his primary education at the village of Chak no. 105, Lyallpur Bange (now in present-day Pakistan). For further studies, he went to Lahore to stay with his father. This letter, written in Urdu, is addressed to his paternal grandfather, Arjun Singh, who was in their ancestral village, Khatkar Kalan at the time.

Lahore, 22 July 1918

Respected Dadaji,[2]
Namaste.[3]

I received your letter. Reading it made me happy. The reason I didn't write earlier about the examinations is that we were not told about them. Now we have been told about English and Sanskrit. I have passed these; I have scored 110 out of 150 in Sanskrit. I've got 68 out of 150 in English; the passing marks are 50 out of 150. So with 68 marks, I have passed comfortably. Please don't worry at all. The rest hasn't been told to us, and

---

1   Editor's note: The formatting of letters written by Bhagat Singh in his own hand have been kept as close to the original as possible.

2   Paternal grandfather

3   Greetings

about the holidays–8 August is the first holiday. Please write when you will be making a trip here.

Yours obediently,
Bhagat Singh

2. Letter to grandfather; 27 July 1919 (Originally in Urdu.)

This is the second letter written by Bhagat Singh to his grandfather, Arjun Singh, in Urdu when the former was aged 12. This letter was written almost a year the first one.

Om[4]

Lahore, 27 July 1919

Respected Dadaji,
Namaste!

I am well here and pray for your health to Shri Narayanji.[5] Further news is that we have had our half-yearly exams, which began in July. Many students have failed the Maths paper, so we'll have a retest in Maths in August. Rest all is fine. When will you come? Tell Bhaiyaji that I have passed in all the subjects in the half-yearly exams. Namaste to Mataji[6] and Chachiji.[7] Kultar Singh had fever on the night of 24 July, till the evening of 25 July. Now he's all right; don't worry at all.

Yours obediently,
Bhagat Singh

---

4   Hindu invocation
5   Invoking the Hindu god Narayan
6   Mother, but here he is referring to his paternal grandmother
7   Aunt, or father's younger brother's wife

3. Letter to grandfather; 14 November 1921 (Originally in Urdu.)

Bhagat Singh was little more than fourteen years old when he wrote this third and last available letter to his grandfather on 14 November 1921. This letter hints at Bhagat Singh's growing political awareness; he refers to a railway workers' strike that was happening at that time in a scrutinising manner.

Lahore, 14 November 1921

My respected Dada Sahibji,[8]
Namaste!

Things are fine here and I pray to God for your health. I haven't received your kind letter for a very long time. What is the reason? Please let me know how Kulbir Singh and Kultar Singh are doing. Bebey Sahiba[9] has not returned from Moranwali yet. The rest is fine.

[on the other side of the card]

Namaste to Mataji.[10] Namaste to Chachi Sahiba.[11] Mangu Chamar has not come till now. I bought a second handbook, which I got at a very reasonable price.
[In inverted characters between the lines on the card]
The railway people are planning to go on a strike these days. One hopes that it would begin immediately after next week.

Yours obediently,
Bhagat Singh

---

8   Paternal grandfather
9   Mother
10   Mother, but here the reference is to his paternal grandmother
11   Aunt, or father's younger brother's wife

4. Letter to aunt Hukam Kaur; October 1921 (Originally in Punjabi.)

This was the first letter to be written in Gurmukhi script by Bhagat Singh. He wrote this to his uncle's wife; his uncle, twenty-three-year-old Swaran Singh, had died after coming out of prison. Later, Bhagat Singh would write several essays in Punjabi, but this letter shows his growing political awareness, as well as his growing interest in attending processions and protests meetings.

Omkar[12] ...

Lahore, October

My dear Chachiji,
Namaste!

I went to Lyallpur to see the procession (meeting). I had planned to come to the village, but Bapuji[13] had forbidden me to do so, so I didn't come. Please forgive me for any mistake. Chachaji's[14] portrait is almost ready, I was supposed to bring it along, but it could not be completed by then; so please forgive me. Do write back soon. Please pay my respects to older Chachiji and to Mataji, and namaste to Kulbir and Kultar.

Your son,
Bhagat Singh

---

12   Gurbani word
13   Paternal grandfather
14   Father's younger brother or uncle

5. Letter to aunt Hukam Kaur; November 1921 (Originally in Punjabi.)

Bhagat Singh wrote another letter to his younger aunt, Hukam Kaur, the widow of his chacha (uncle), Swaran Singh, in Punjabi in the Gurmukhi script. This letter was written a day after he wrote to his grandfather in Urdu. Out of all available letters of Bhagat Singh, only these two addressed to his aunt are in Punjabi. Other letters are written in Urdu, English and Hindi. It is clear from these letters that Bhagat Singh has yet not completely mastered the Punjabi language, as there are many spelling errors in these postcards.

November 1921

My dearest Chachiji,
Namaste.

I've got delayed in writing the letter. I hope you'll forgive me. Bhaiyaji[15] has gone to Delhi. Bebey has gone to Moranwali. Rest is all fine. Please pay my respects to elder Chachiji. Please pay my respects to Mataji,[16] and Sat Sri Akal[17] or Namaste to Kultar, Kulbir Singh.

Yours obediently,
Bhagat Singh

---

15   Father
16   Mother, but here the reference is to his paternal grandmother
17   Greetings

LETTER FROM COLLEGE

6. Letter to father, Kishan Singh; 1923 (Originally in Urdu.)

In 1923, Bhagat Singh was studying at the National College, Lahore. He had joined forces with revolutionary teachers and friends; he would have intense debates and discussions with them on how to achieve freedom for India. He even participated in the drama club of the college to help spread awareness.

It was during this time that his Dadiji[18] had initiated talks for her grandson's marriage at home. When Bhagat Singh realized that his arguments had no effect on her, he left this letter for his father and left college for Kanpur to meet Ganesh Shankar Vidyarthi, a well-known Congress leader. He began working with Vidyarthi and edited the Hindi newspaper, *Pratap*. There, he also encountered other revolutionaries like B.K. Dutt, Shiv Verma, and Bejoy Kumar Sinha. His arrival in Kanpur was an important part in Bhagat Singh's life and with this, he was on the path to revolution.

Respected Pitaji,[19]
Namaste.[20]

My life has been dedicated to the noblest cause of attaining freedom for Hindustan. That is why worldly desires and comfort hold no attraction for me.

You would remember that when I was a kid, Bapuji[21] had announced at the time of my yagyopavit[22] ceremony that I would be dedicated to the service of my nation. Therefore, I am fulfilling the vow taken at that time.

I hope that you will be magnanimous and forgive me.

Yours obediently,
Bhagat Singh

---

18   Paternal grandmother
19   Father
20   Greetings
21   Paternal grandfather
22   Hindu thread ritual ceremony

LETTERS FROM REVOLUTIONARY LIFE

7. Letter to Postmaster, Lahore; 1 November 1926 (Originally in English.)

Recently, five more letters of Bhagat Singh have been discovered among the papers of his younger brother, Ranvir Singh (1924–1998). Ranvir Singh's son, retired Major General Sheonan Singh found these letters among his father's Urdu sheets, which are perhaps a part of a manuscript of an intended biography of Bhagat Singh in Urdu, but remained incomplete and covers only Bhagat Singh's childhood years. Among these sheets, five letters written by Bhagat Singh and two written by British officials addressed to Bhagat Singh were found. The latter refer to the interception of Bhagat Singh's post in 1926, when he was just nineteen years old.

Bhagat Singh wrote all the letters on his father's letterhead and got the postal certificate from the post office at Lahore on the same letterhead. At least one initial letter by Bhagat Singh is missing, as the first letter found in this series of correspondence is dated 1 November 1926, and seems to be in response to a letter from the postmaster at Lahore, dated 30 October 1926, while the postmaster had written the letter to Bhagat Singh on 26 October; and it still remains untraced.

**First letter by Bhagat Singh to postmaster of Lahore;
1 November 1926**

To
The Postmaster
Lahore
Sir,

I thank you for your favour dated 30 October 1926, No. D2850. In reply to the same, I may request that I tore off all the envelopes whenever I received them. Yet this one referred in my last letter was preserved and is being enclosed herewith. This was posted at Bombay on 13 October:

Two days before the other one, but was delivered on 23, along with that one. The circumstances were quite normal. The letter box contained few letters at first delivery. The letter box was emptied by myself. When at 12 or so, at noon I again opened the letter box, I found these two and another letter there. The circumstances were quite ordinary.

But I have been marking since one or two months that all the letters addressed to me were stamped and then stamped again. Cut exactly at the same place. This of course did arouse suspicion in my mind. I had no desire to write at first, but at the receipt of these two letters, I was anxious to know the real cause. This envelope will help you to some extent to prove the truth of allegation.

But may I request you to write a definite answer to my first letter – are any letters opened or intercepted? If so, why?

I am certain about one thing and that is this, that they were not delivered to me by first delivery but were detained for a day or two. This envelope will help you in this matter also.

Sd/- Bhagat Singh

8. Second letter to the Secretary, Punjab Government; 17 November 1926 (Originally in English.)

The next two letters refer to the interception of Bhagat Singh's post, addressed by him to the to the Punjab Government, Lahore. The first letter was written on 17 November, and the second on 28 November. The letters written to officials in the Punjab Government were responded to by no less that the Chief Secretary of Punjab, HD Craik, on 27 November 1926. Craik informed Bhagat Singh that it was the Governor of Punjab himself who gave orders for interception and censoring of all of Bhagat Singh's mail.

C/o The Himalaya Ass: Co: Ld:
Loharigate
Lahore, 17 November 1926

To
The Secretary,
The Punjab Government
Lahore
Sir,

I enclose, herewith, a copy of the letter of Postmaster Lahore GPO dated 16, instant addressed to me. In reply to my letter dated 1 November, instant addressed to him, he wrote to me that my letter(s) were detained by that department under the orders of the Punjab Government.

May I ask you whether any such orders have been issued to that department? If so, when and why? And are there any letters that were intercepted and never delivered to me?

I would request you to kindly give a direct, plain and detailed reply to it. Moreover, will you please let me know what led you to issue such orders?

Awaiting an early reply

Yours obediently,
Sd/- Bhagat Singh

9. Letter to Secretary, Punjab Government; 26 November 1926 (Originally in English.)

C/o The Himalaya Ass: Co: Ld:
Loharigate
Lahore, 28 November 1926
To
The Secretary,
Lahore
Sir,

I beg to draw your kind attention towards my last letter dated 17 November sent under registered cover, which was received by you the very next day. It is more than a week since, and I have altogether failed to receive any reply to the same.

I had sent a copy of the Post Master's letter dated 16 November addressed to me telling me that my letters were being intercepted under the order of the Punjab Government. Naturally, I was very anxious to know what led the Punjab Government to issue such orders. I think that as an honest citizen I have a right to enquire such a question relating to myself. But I have not received any reply to that letter. Will you kindly send a reply to the same at an early date and also let me know the cause of this delay?

Hoping to be favoured soon

Yours obediently,
Sd/- Bhagat Singh

10. Letter to SSP, Lahore; 1927 (Originally in English.)

Bhagat Singh was arrested on 29 May 1927 by the Lahore police in a false case, related to the Dussehra bomb blast that took place in October 1926 at Lahore. He was detained for five weeks before being released on a bail of sixty thousand rupees, a very high amount in those days. After his release, he wrote to the SSP (superintendent of police) of Lahore, demanding the return of his personal belongings that had been taken away by the police at the time of arrest. This had its echo in the Punjab assembly, Lahore, when the matter was raised in the assembly by MLA (member of Legislative Assembly) Gopi Chand Bhargav, who later became CM (Chief Minister) of Punjab, post-Partition. Finally, the bail amount and conditions were removed and the case was also closed. This letter was written on the letterhead of his father, Kishan Singh, and was produced as evidence by the prosecution in the Lahore Conspiracy Case.

CHIEF AGENT FOR Tele {gram:- "Himmassure" Lahore
The UPPUNJAB & N.W.F Province phone:-
The HIMALYA ASSURANCE CO. LTD

Punjab Chief Agency
Ref. No.------- Dated-------------1927
Sir,

I was arrested on 29 May 1927 under section 302 IPC, and was detained in police custody for five weeks. I was released on bail on 4 July 1927. Since then, I have never been called by the police or any court to stand my trial under the *said section* (written in hand), and so I presume that you have completed your investigation and found nothing against me *and* (written in hand) have practically withdrawn the case. Under the circumstances, I request you to kindly return all the things that were taken from my body at the time of my arrest and to inform me when and where to see you for the said purpose.

An early favour will highly oblige.
Your etc. (written in hand)
Sd/ Sadiq Ali Shah
S.I.
D/ 2-5-29 (written in hand)

Read out, admitted in evidence and added to Special Tribunal Lahore Conspiracy Case File.
J Coldstream, Judge Special Tribunal

11. Letter to friend Amar Chand; 1927 (Originally in Urdu.)

This is Bhagat Singh's only letter to Amar Chand, written in 1927, though not much is known about Amar Chand. This letter was written after Singh's release from the Lahore police station, where he was detained for five weeks in May–June 1927. This letter depicts Bhagat Singh's interest in books and his desire to go abroad for higher studies, which he suppressed due to his revolutionary activities. He refers to the harassment faced by him at the hands of the police and also his concern for his uncle Ajit Singh, who was living in exile since 1909. The extent to which Bhagat Singh valued knowledge and education can be seen from his last letter to his younger brother Kultar Singh on 3 March 1931. Even in this letter, this emotion is seen when he tells his friend to 'study with heart and soul'.

My dear brother Amar Chandji,
Namaste.

This time, I came here as my mother fell ill suddenly and I also happened to meet your respected mother. I read your letter. I wrote the other letter on her behalf. I also got an opportunity to pen down a few words. What should I write about? Karam Singh has gone abroad; I'm sending his address to you. He has written that he wishes to study law, but God knows how he is managing; it is very expensive.

Brother, if you ask me, my desire to go abroad to pursue my studies proved to be very ruinous. Anyway, I wish you people all the best. Whenever you get an opportunity, I'd be obliged if you would take the trouble to send me some good books. After all, America has a lot of literature. Though I know you must be very busy with your studies these days.

Perhaps you may hear something about Sardarji [Ajit Singhji] from San Francisco etc. Please make an effort to find out about him. At least we will be reassured that he is alive. I'm going to Lahore. Please do take out some time to write to me if you get a chance to. Please address it to Sutra Mandi, Lahore. What else shall I write? There is nothing to say. I have been in quite a state. I have constantly been facing a lot of problems. Finally, the case was withdrawn. Later I was arrested again. I have been released on a bail of rupees sixty thousand. So far they have not been able to concoct a case against me, and God willing nor will they be able to. Now it is nearly a year, but the condition of my bail hasn't been reversed. Whatever God wills! They are harassing us unnecessarily. Brother, study with all your heart and soul.

Yours sincerely,
Bhagat Singh

What else should I write about myself; that I've been a target of suspicion needlessly? My mail is being checked. Letters are opened. I wonder why they have begun to regard me with so much suspicion. Anyway, Brother, finally the truth will surface and prevail. [1927]

12. Letter to the Editor, *Maharathi*; 27 February 1928 (Originally in Hindi.)

Maharathi, a Hindi journal from Delhi, published sketches on revolutionaries. Bhagat Singh contributed a life sketch of Namdhari Guru Ram Singh to this journal. The letter refers to a photograph of Guru Ram Singh. This letter, which is dated 27 February 1928, was written in Hindi. Singh's sketch of Guru Ram Singh, accompanied with photographs, was published in the February 1928 issue of *Maharathi*. Till date, this is the only handwritten letter written by Bhagat Singh in Hindi which has been found.

Shehanshahi Kutia
Soot Mandi, Lahore
27.2.1928

Dear Editor,
Saadar Vande![23]

I received your kind letter dated 17.2.1928, and a copy of the February issue of *Maharathi*. Please accept my heartfelt gratitude. Did you get a photograph of Guru Ram Singh, made out of the picture in three colours or not? I've only got to know that the photo at least hasn't been published by you so far. I feel that the significance of these essays gets diminished without the photos. The rest of the essays, that I shall send for your perusal very soon, should only be published with the pictures. Blocks for several of these are already available. Only the mailing charges and some money will need to be paid. If you deem fit, please write to me and I shall make arrangements for it. I'm enclosing another photograph of Guru Ram Singhji. A gentleman told me that he had the block for it. If you like, he can get that published as well and send it. Kindly write

---

23   Greetings

how many photos will be required. This will depend on the total number of copies of *Maharathi*.

Essay after essay remains pending but here arrangements are being made to observe 'Shaheedi Divas'[24] in the National Week. So if I'm not able to send the essay in time, please forgive me. I'll send the first essay in a weeks' time if it is possible. When will the next issue of *Maharathi* be published? Till when should the essay and the photos reach you? Please do write. I shall be grateful for a prompt reply.

Yours faithfully
Bhagat Singh

13. District Magistrate, Lahore, dated 9 May 1928 (Originally in English.)

These two letters by Bhagat Singh (from Ranvir Singh files referred above) addressed to British officials are part of the correspondence relating to his first arrest on 29 May 1927 and his release on bail bonds on 4 July 1927. Interestingly, Bhagat Singh refers here to a question put forward in a session of the Punjab Assembly regarding his arrest and bail bonds by Dr Gopi Chand Bhargava MLC (Member of Legislative Council), who would later become the first Chief Minister of East Punjab after the 1947 partition of India. A letter dated May 1929 was already available, referring to this incident, and now two earlier letters from May and June 1928 have also been found.

Shahanshahi Kutia,
Sutarmandi,
Lahore, 9.5.28
To the District Magistrate
Lahore
Sir,

---

24   Martyrs' Day

Kindly let me know the exact date on which my personal bond for Rs. 20000/ and bail bonds and sureties for Rs. 20000/-each (In the case Crown vs. Bhagat Singh section 302 IPC) were cancelled as stated by the honour Sir Geoffrey De-Montmousery in reply to starred question no. 1380(d) put by Dr Gopi Chand Bhargwa M.L.C. on the 8th instant in Punjab Legislative Council.

An early reply will highly oblige.

Yours etc.

(In the hand of Bhagat Singh. No Signature.)

14. Superintendent of C.I.D., Lahore, dated 19 June 1928 (Originally in English.)

Shahanshahi Kutia
Sutar-Mandi
Lahore,

To
The Superintendent
Punjab C.I.D. (Political)
Lahore
Dear Sir,

I am sorry to say that I have not received any reply to my last letter requesting to return all my clothes and papers that were taken from my body at the time of my arrest on May 29 1927, and the clothes and books that were sent by my father while I was in police custody. Will you kindly let me know by the return when and where I can get the same?

Hoping to be favoured soon.

Yours etc.
Shahanshahi Kutia
Sutarmandi, Lahore

15. Letter to Sukhdev; 5 April 1929 (Originally in Hindi.)

This letter, dated 5 April 1929, to Sukhdev was delivered by Shiv Verma personally. It was written in the context of their group, Hindustan Socialist Republican Association's (HSRA) decision to send two other comrades to throw bombs in the Delhi Assembly on 8 April 1929, despite Bhagat Singh's plea to send him. Sukhdev was not present in that meeting. Despite knowing about decision made by the group, Sukhdev later accused Bhagat Singh of escapism, due to his 'fascination' for a certain woman! This allegation hurt Bhagat Singh a lot, and, at his insistence, a group meeting was reconvened and the decision was reversed. Bhagat Singh and B.K. Dutt were chosen for the cause and Bhagat Singh wrote this letter to Sukhdev, who was personally very close to him, to clear his doubts and spell out the revolutionaries' approach towards the issue of 'love'!

Dear Brother,

By the time you get this letter, I would have travelled far away towards my destination. Believe me, these days I am happier than ever before and am prepared for my final journey. Despite all the joys and sweet memories in my life, one thing has continued to prick my heart. This is that my own brother misunderstood me and levelled a very serious charge of weakness on me. Today I am more satisfied than ever before. Today, I feel that this was nothing more than a misunderstanding. His (your) doubt was ill-founded. I was considered to be talkative because of my gregarious nature and my confession was seen as a weakness. But today I feel that there is no misunderstanding, I am not weak; rather not weaker than any one of us.

My dear brother, I will bid goodbye with a clear heart and will erase your doubt as well. I shall be very grateful to you for this. But you must be careful; you must not take any hasty step. Think carefully; you have to carry forward the task seriously and calmly. Don't try to force an opportunity. As you have some obligations towards the people, you must carry on with your work cautiously. As a word of advice, I'd like to say that I think Shastri appeals to me more now. I would try to bring him to the field, provided he is willing to offer himself to a dark future clear-sightedly. Let him get closer to the comrades so that he can imbibe their behaviour and thinking. If he works in the correct spirit, he will prove to be very useful and valuable. But don't rush anything. You are yourself a good judge of character; see if he satisfies you. And my brother, let us celebrate now.

In this happy moment, I can say that as far as the issue of debate is concerned, I cannot help but present my side of the case. I can aver with complete confidence that I am fully immersed in all the colours of a fulfilling life, suffused with all hopes and aspirations, but I can renounce everything at the appropriate time. And that is sacrifice in the true sense of the word. These things never hinder a person's path, provided that he is a human being. You will get evidence of this very soon. In the context of discussing someone's character, one thing that is worth thinking about is if love has ever proved to be helpful to any person. Let me answer this today-yes it did, for Mazzini. You must surely have read that he was not able to endure the first unsuccessful rebellion, the grief of a heart-wrenching failure, and the memory of martyred comrades. He could have either gone mad or committed suicide, but with a letter from his beloved, he became not only as strong as the others, but stronger than everybody else.

As far as love is concerned at the ethical plane, I can say that this is nothing more than an emotion; and not a beastly but a very sweet human emotion. Love is never a bestial passion. The character of a person is always elevated by love; it never shows one in a bad light provided that the love is true love. You cannot call these girls mad – as we see them in films, always playing into the hands of bestial passions. True love can never be created. It wells up by itself when, no one can predict.

I can say that a young man and woman can love each other and on the basis of their love, they can rise above their passions. They can continue to maintain their purity. I want to state clearly here that when I had called love a human weakness, then I had not said it with reference to any normal person, as far as they are normal at an ordinary level. That would be the ultimate, ideal situation when human beings will be able to conquer and control love, hate, and all other emotions, when a human being will able to base his actions as per the directions of his conscience. It is not bad in modern times; rather, it is good and beneficial for man. I have criticized the falling in love of one individual with another, and that too when the situation is at an ideal level. A person must have a deep feeling of love that is not limited to only one individual, but encompasses all humanity.

In my opinion, I have made my position quite clear. But there is one thing that I particularly want to say to you – despite revolutionary thought, we cannot adopt the Arya Samaj model of puritan morality. We can hide this weakness very easily by talking loudly, sprouting revolutionary ideas, but in real life, it makes us shudder.

I beg you to give up this weakness. Without giving rise to any misgiving in my mind, may I beg you most humbly to temper the extreme idealism that you have. Don't be cold to those who lag behind and fall prey to a disease like mine; don't heighten their pain by scolding them, because they need your sympathy. May I hope that without holding a grudge against any one particular individual, you would sympathize with them; that is what they really need. But you cannot understand these things till you yourself fall prey to this. But why am I writing all this? Actually, I want to speak my mind frankly. Now I have unburdened my heart.

With best wishes for your success and happy life.

Yours,
Bhagat Singh

LETTERS WRITTEN TO THE COLONIAL ADMINISTRATION/JUDICIARY FROM JAIL

16. Letter to the District Magistrate, Delhi; 25 April 1929 (Originally in English.)

Bhagat Singh wrote to the District Magistrate in Delhi through jail officials for a supply of daily newspapers and books on 25 April 1929.

To,
The District Magistrate,
Delhi
Sir,

I will be obliged if you will kindly allow me the use of daily newspapers and books.

Yours etc.
Bhagat Singh

25.4.29
Bhagat Singh accused wrote this in my presence at the Delhi jail.
Ghulam Rasul

---

17. Letter to father, Kishan Singh, 26 April 1929 (Originally in Urdu.)

Bhagat Singh wrote this letter to his father from the Delhi Jail after he was arrested for throwing a bomb in the Assembly Hall.

Respected Pitaji Maharaj,[25]
Vande Mataram,[26]

---

25   Father
26   Greetings

We people were transferred to the Delhi Jail on 22 April from the police lockup and are in the Delhi Jail at the moment. Proceedings will begin on 7 May in the jail premises itself. The whole drama should be over in approximately a month's time. There is no need to worry too much. I heard that you had come here and consulted some lawyer, and someone even tried to meet me. But the arrangements could not be made then. I got my jail dress the day before yesterday. Now you can meet me whenever it is convenient for you to come. There is no need for any lawyer or anyone. I wish to take some advice on a couple of issues, but nothing very important. Don't put yourself through unnecessary stress. Please do not bring respected Mataji[27] with you. She will cry unnecessarily and this will definitely cause me anguish as well. I will get to know how everyone at home is doing once I meet you.

If possible, please bring *Gita Rahasya* and *The Biography of Napoleon*, which you will find among my books and some good novels in English. My respectful greetings to dear mother, Bhabhi Sahiba,[28] Mataji, Dadiji, Chachi Sahiba. Namaste to Ranvir Singh and Kultar Singh. Please pay my respects to Bapuji. Right now we are being treated extremely well in the police lockup and jail. Don't worry about anything. I don't know your address, so I'm sending the letter to this address (the Congress office).

Yours obediently,
Bhagat Singh

18. Letter to the Superintendent, Criminal Investigation Department (CID), Lahore; 31 May 1929 (Originally in English.)

This letter to the Superintendent of Lahore is marked by the jail staff on 31 May 1929. It seems that Bhagat Singh was not allowed meetings

---

27 Mother
28 Brother's wife

with his father in the Delhi Assembly Bomb Case trial without the permission of the Punjab CID, so he wrote to seek permission to meet his father. It is also possible that Bhagat Singh was taken to Lahore during the Delhi Assembly Bomb Case trial by the Punjab police, for investigation of the Lahore Conspiracy Case since many of the other accused – Sukhdev, Shiv Verma, Jaidev Kapoor and Gaya Prasad Katiyar – were already arrested and Bhagat Singh's name may have come up in that case. However, as of today, all the details are not available. Bhagat Singh and B.K. Dutt remained incarcerated in Delhi Jail till 14 June 1929, when they were convicted and shifted to Punjab Jail.

The Superintendent (Special Duty)
C.I.D. (Political Branch), Lahore
Dear Sir,

I will feel much obliged if you will kindly allow me to have an interview with my father, as I have got some very important instructions to give him for my defence counsel in connection with the Delhi case.

I hope you will not disallow it on the grounds that I have already had an interview, because the matter is very urgent.

Hoping to be favoured

Yours etc.
Sd/ Bhagat Singh

Noting in Urdu by officials, dated 31/5/29.

Stamp in English on upper-left corner of the letter – admitted into evidence and added to Special Tribunal Lahore Conspiracy Case.

Sd/ Judge
Special Tribunal, date not mentioned.

19. Letter to the Inspector General, Jails; 17 June 1929
(Originally in English.)

Letters 19–21, written between 17 and 19 June, relate to Bhagat Singh's demand for a transfer to the Lahore jail and the hunger strike undertaken by him and B.K. Dutt to secure 'Political Prisoner' status for them, which would mean access to better facilities.

Inspector General,
Punjab Jails, Lahore
Through: Superintendent Mianwali Jail
Dear Sir,

I have been transferred from Delhi to Mianwali District jail, in spite of the fact that I am going to be tried along with other young men arrested in connection with the bomb factory and Mr Saunders shooting case. The case is coming up for hearing on 26 June 1929. I have utterly failed to understand the intention behind this transfer of mine to this place.

Anyhow justice demands that an undertrial must be furnished with all the facilities to prepare and fight his case. But how can I arrange for a counsel, while detained here, without getting any opportunity to see my father or any relative, this place being quite remote, out of the way and far off from Lahore.

I request you, therefore, to order my transfer at once to Lahore Central Jail, so that I may get a fair chance to fight my case.

Hoping to be favoured soon.
17.6.1929

Yours
Bhagat Singh
Life Prisoner, Mianwali Jail

20. Letter announcing the hunger strike; 17 June 1929 (Originally in English.)

The Inspector General
Punjab Jails, Lahore
Through-Superintendent, District Jail, Mianwali
Dear Sir,

I have been sentenced to life imprisonment in connection with the Assembly Bomb Case, Delhi and am obviously a political prisoner. We got special diet in Delhi Jail, but since my arrival here, I am being treated as an ordinary criminal. Therefore I have gone on a hunger strike since the morning of 15 June 1929. My weight has decreased by 6 lbs than my weight at the Delhi Jail in these two or three days.

I wish to bring to your kind attention that I must get special treatment as a political prisoner.

My demands being

1. Special diet (including milk and ghee, rice and curd etc.)
2. No forcible labour
3. Toilet (soap, oil, shaving etc.)
4. Literature of all kinds (History, Economics, Political Science, Science, Poetry, drama or fiction, newspapers.)

I hope you will very kindly consider what I have said and decide favourably.

17th June 1929

Yours
Sd./ Bhagat Singh
Life Prisoner, Mianwali Jail

The superintendent of Mianwali jail wrote to Bhagat Singh on 18 June 1929, replying to some queries regarding his demands. To this, Bhagat Singh replied on 19 June, defining the term 'Political Prisoner' lucidly.

21. Letter to the Superintendent, Mianwali Jail; 19 June 1929 (Originally in English.)

To,
The Superintendent
District Jail, Mianwali
Dear Sir,

With reference to the inquiries you have made as regards my application, I would like to say:

1. I am a political prisoner. I do not know what privileges the Special Class prisoners enjoy. As a right I would like to say that we ought to be treated as State prisoners. But the very term "State Prisoner" might seem to be too much. Hence I say I must be treated specially; meaning, I must get special diet, as I used to get at Delhi jail, both as an undertrial and for two days after my conviction. Along with that, I want freedom to study literature. Because we are convicted for our ideas, and are generally called 'misguided' or so. Hence we must get a chance to study and form sober opinions, and views. Anyway, books on subjects like History, Economics, we must be allowed to get without restrictions as they are allowed to Special Class prisoners.
2. In Delhi Jail, we got a special diet and literature both as undertrial and after conviction.
3. By forcible labour I mean that we political prisoners must not be forced to do labour as a part of punishment. We might do the labour at our will.
4. I did not feel the necessity of asking the judge for special rights or privileges, as we already enjoyed there.
5. Well, as regards your fifth question, I would simply like to request that I am asking for rights which we as political prisoners, are

entitled to. Any law that will violate our rights cannot be supposed to be respected by us. I do not want to begin any quarrel without reason. I think I have made the most reasonable demands. And if my behaviour so far which I think is most reasonable indicates that I have trespassed any law, then I am sorry to say, I cannot help and am prepared for any hardships I may have to bear for the same.

I request you to kindly consider what I have said without bearing any sort of prejudice in mind, and do the needful.

Lahore, Through Superintendent
19-6-1929

Bhagat Singh,
Prisoner no. 1119

22. Letter to Home Member, Government of India; 24 June 1929 (Originally in English.)

Letter numbers 22 and 23 were written on 24 July and 6 September, to different authorities regarding Bhagat Singh and his comrades' hunger strike in the Lahore Jail, which continued till 4 October 1929. Though there was a short break for two days on the assurance of their demands being met, the strike was resumed immediately after the British administration refused to honour the Jail Enquiry Committee report. Motilal Nehru had assured them that British officials would meet their demands, but officials later refused to accept them. During the hunger strike, Jain Das died after 63 days, on 13 September 1929. The letter written to the Home Member is referred to on different dates by the editors. While Shiv Verma refers to it as 24 June, Jagmohan Singh gives the date of 14 July, and Veerendra Sindhu mentions 24 July, probably because this letter was published in the 25 July 1929 issue of *The People*.

Central Jail, Lahore
24.6.29

WE, BHAGAT SINGH AND B.K. DUTT, WERE SENTENCED to life transportation in the Assembly Bomb Case, Delhi, 8 April 1929. As long as we were undertrial prisoners in Delhi Jail, we were accorded a very good treatment from that jail to the Mianwali and Lahore Central Jails respectively, we wrote an application to the higher authorities asking for better diet and a few other facilities, and refused to take the jail diet. Our demands were as follows:

We, as political prisoners, should be given better diet and the standard of our diet should at least be the same as that of European prisoners. (It is not the sameness of dietary that we demand, but the sameness of standard of diet.)

We shall not be forced to do any hard and undignified labours at all.

All books, other than those proscribed, along with writing materials, should be allowed to us without any restriction.

At least one standard daily paper should be supplied to every political prisoner.

Political prisoners should have a special ward of their own in every jail, provided with all necessities as those of the Europeans. And all the political prisoners in one jail must be kept together in that ward.

Toilet necessities should be supplied.

Better clothing.

We have explained above the demands that we made. They are the most reasonable demands. The Jail authorities told us one day that the higher authorities have refused to comply with our demands.

Apart from that, they handle us very roughly while feeding us artificially, and Bhagat Singh was lying quite senseless on 10 July 1929, for about 15 minutes after the forcible feeding, which we request to be stopped without any further delay.

In addition, we may be permitted to refer to the recommendations made in the UP Jail Committee report by Pandit Jagat Narain and KB Hafiz Hidayat Hussain. They have recommended the political prisoners to be treated as "Better Class Prisoners".

We request you to kindly consider our demands at your earliest convenience.

By "Political Prisoners", we mean all those people who are convicted for offences against the State, for instance the people who were convicted in the Lahore Conspiracy Cases, 1915-17, the Kakori Conspiracy Cases, and Sedition Cases in general.

Yours
Bhagat Singh
B.K. Dutt

(Taken from *Selected Writings of Shaheed Bhagat Singh*, edited by Shiv Verma.)

23. Letter to the Chairman, Jail Inquiry Committee; 6 September 1929 (Originally in English.)

This letter written on 6 September 1929, is important to underline that Bhagat Singh and his comrades had suspended their hunger strike on 2 September on the assurance of the Congress Committee, but on 4 September, a statement in the *Civil and Military Gazette* from the committee upset them so much that they resumed the hunger strike from that very day, which continued till 4 October. Despite the Congress's Jail Committee's recommendations, the British Government did not release Jatinder Nath Das unconditionally and insisted on releasing him on bail only. He died on 13 September, a week after this letter was sent. This letter has since been retranslated from Hindi, as the original in English cannot be located.

The Chairman, Punjab Jail Inquiry Committee,
And Members of the Hunger Strike Sub-Committee, Simla
(Through – Superintendent, Borstal jail, Lahore)

Dear Sirs,

We seek permission to place the following points for your consideration –

1. That we did not give up the hunger strike, rather we postponed it only till the government's decision. We think that we had made it clear to you and repeatedly requested you to clarify the same to the public and also to the government.

   We were shocked that in the press release by the members of the Hunger Strike Sub-Committee in the *Civil and Military Gazette*, dated 4 September, there was no mention of this fact. Still we hope that you will clarify this as soon as possible.

2. We did not postpone our hunger strike merely on the assurance that you and the rest of the members of the Inquiry Committee would accede to all our demands and recommend the same. One among us even told you that the government did not pay heed to the recommendations of the Inquiry Committee in the past, because this does not serve their purpose; an earlier committee was cited as an example.

   They apprehended that the recommendations of this committee would also meet the same fate. In response to that, you had said that before coming to us, you had spoken to the local government and that you were in a position to offer us an assurance that the government would not act in the same manner this time.

   Only on this explicit and necessary assurance, after a nine-hour-long debate, did we agree to postpone our hunger strike.

   Apart from this, you had assured us that as per our firm resolve, Jatinder Nath Das would be released, in view of his precarious health.

   Also, that as undertrial prisoners, our demands, the most important of which is that all of us (including Bhagat Singh and Dutt) be kept together in a common barrack, would be accepted by the government within a day or two.

   But our doubts proved to be true, when, despite the strong and unanimous recommendation of the Sub-Committee, the government neither agreed to release Das nor allowed Bhagat Singh and Dutt to stay with us.

   So we have received immediate proof of this fact that the government pays no heed to your recommendations and we hope that you will forgive us for saying that the government just wanted to use your honourable position of people's leaders to break our hunger strike. And we may also add that before postponing our hunger strike, we had given careful consideration to the question that how far we could trust the Inquiry Committee. In this regard, Bhagat Singh and Dutt had advised that it would be tested on this occasion. Now we see that when the government hasn't paid attention to even two insignificant demands of yours, we are compelled to resume our hunger strike immediately.

3. Jatinder Nath Das's death is extremely disturbing and if the government thinks that after his death, all of us would shirk our duty, then it is a fatal mistake on their part. All of us declare that each one of us is prepared to follow Das's footsteps. Even so, keeping the continuing struggle in mind, we are dividing ourselves into two groups, out of which the first is beginning the hunger strike with immediate effect.

It has been decided that when one member of the first group dies, then a member from the second group would step forward.

We have taken this decision with the full seriousness of the issue in mind. We are left with no other honourable or simple option, except to follow our comrade Das's footsteps.

We consider our cause to be just and honourable, which any government would have accepted without forcing us to take such extreme steps. Let us reiterate that in this struggle, we have firm resolve that nothing is more honourable and glorious than to struggle till death, for a just and pure cause.

Finally, we feel that we would not be fulfilling our duty if we don't express our heartfelt gratitude for your sincere concern and undertaking great hardships, in supporting our cause before the government.

Yours
Lahore Conspiracy Case hunger strikers
Friday, 6 September 1929
10:00 A.M.

24. Letter to the Special Magistrate by the sixteen accused regarding Prem Dutt; 21 October 1929 (Originally in English.)

On 11 December 2014, Professor S Irfan Habib tweeted a page signed by the sixteen accused who faced trial in the Lahore Conspiracy Case. It seems to be a two-page letter dated 21 October 1929. The first page's side is visible in the second clear page, which has the fifth point raised by the signatories. The letter regretted the action of their youngest comrade, Prem Dutt Verma, who could not control himself, provoked by approver Jai Gopal, and threw a slipper at on him, while he was giving evidence in the court. The last paragraph of the letter reads as:

'That we are considerably surprised and grieved to note the attitude taken up by the learned magistrate in not giving us the opportunity of clearing our position in spite of our repeated requests.'
    Signed by

1. Bhagat Singh 2. Bejoy Kumar Sinha 3. Des Raj 4. Ajoy Kumar Ghosh 5. Jitender Nath Sanyal 6. B.K. Dutt 7. Kamal Nath Tewari 8. Sukhdev 9. Jai Dev Kapur 10. Kishori Lal 11. Shivram Hari Rajguru (Signed in Marathi) 12. Gaya Prasad (Signed in Urdu) 13. Surender Pandey (Signed as Supande) 14. Agya Ram 15. Mahavir Singh 16. Shiv Verma

The letter, as usual, is drafted in Bhagat Singh's handwriting, and he has inserted the names of Rajguru and Gaya Prasad, in brackets in English on their Marathi and Urdu signatures. This is a rare document found with such clear signatures of Bhagat Singh and his comrades. The next representations, again, found partially in the Supreme Court records, is in context of this very incident and a continuation of their protestation of not being heard properly.

25. Letter to the Special Magistrate, Lahore; October end/November 1929 (Originally in English.)

On 21 October 1929, during the hearing of the case, approver Jai Gopal provoked the revolutionaries in court with an indecent remark that the youngest of the accused, Prem Dutt, could not tolerate. So, he threw a slipper at Jai Gopal. Later, much hostility was meted out on all the accused for many days inside the court, despite the others disassociating themselves from Prem Dutt's act and expressing regret. Bhagat Singh addressed this letter to the Special Magistrate around October-end, but the second page of this typed letter in the Supreme Court's digital records is not available. More details about this are found in Bejoy Kumar Sinha in Sreerajyam Sinha's book (Reference 9). Letter numbers 24 and 25 should be read together. It is thought that letter number 24 is the second page of the same letter.

In the Court of the Special Magistrate, Lahore
Crown versus Sukhdev, etc.
It is submitted as follows:-

That on 21 [October 1929] instant an unhappy incident occurred in the court. While an approver named Jai Gopal was giving his evidence standing in the dock, he adopted such a provocative posture that apart from twisting his moustaches, he addressed the accused: Janab ye sab ap ke kartut hain. Sachchi batein keh raha hun. [Sirs, these are all your misdeeds, I am telling you the truth.] In these most provocative circumstances, the youngest of all the accused, Prem Dutt, who was just eighteen years old at that time, got excited and threw a slipper at the approver. All the accused disapproved of his act and disassociated themselves from it. They wanted to make a statement in connection with that affair. But their statement was not recorded. They then submitted a joint statement (posted above) In spite of their statement to that effect, orders were passed against all the accused, and all were subjected to undergo humiliation and brutal statement for the fault of one person, which was against the principle of Justice.

Comrade Bijoy Kumar Sinha has already submitted a statement about what happened in the Borstal Jail on 22. On 23 October Bhagat Singh and B.K. Dutt were brought to the gate of the court by the Jail authorities. But the notice wanted to handcuff them on both hands, which they refused. Then a large number of policemen and a few sub-inspectors and inspectors pounced upon them. A few sat on their bodies and others [word erased] continued violently kicking and beating them. These blows were dealt with mercilessly on their heads and chests. Then both of them were dragged to the courtroom. They asked if the police officials were acting under his orders and if he would ask for explanation from their officials for such brutal and illegal conduct. But no attention was paid to these.[29]

26. Letter to the Special Magistrate, Lahore; 4 November 1929 (Originally in English.)

In this letter, written on 4 November to the Special Magistrate, Bhagat Singh demands to visit the locality and location of the Saunders' murder to prepare his defence. This letter is taken from the Supreme Court's digital records.

In the Court of the special magistrate, Lahore.
Crown V S Sukhdev & Others
Charged under section 121N 302+120 B.

---

[29] Editor's note: The second page of this statement is not found in the Supreme Court digital records. Many of the accused, including Bijoy Kumar Sinha and Kamalnath Tiwari, had submitted written statements on police brutalities after this incident to the court, some of which were not recorded faithfully and distorted by court officials. This statement also seems to be part of the same records, which probably was submitted on behalf of Bhagat Singh and B.K. Dutt. Most of the jail statements were drafted by Bhagat Singh.

This humble petition of the accused Bhagat Singh most humbly shweth**
(states)—

1. That the petitioner is going unrepresented in the case.
2. That evidence has been produced in this court entangling the petitioner in the murders of Mr Saunders and Sardar Chanan Singh,
3. That the petitioner may be able to effectively cross-examine the witnesses, that (as in Bhagat Singh's own handwriting) it is necessary that the petitioner may be given an opportunity to visit the spot and see the roads and other surroundings in connection with the alleged incident.
4. That the petitioner therefore prays that proper facilities to be afforded him for the said Purpose and that the production of further witnesses regarding the particular incident may be postponed till the petitioner has been able to examine the locality.

D/ 4th Nov.29 Sd./ Bhagat Singh
Petitioner

27. Letter to the Special Magistrate, Lahore; 16 December 1929 (Originally in English.)

Another incomplete letter is found in the Supreme Court's digital records, which focuses on the revolutionaries' mistreatment in jail. They had sent a telegram to the Government of India on 20 January indicating they were resuming their hunger strike, which had continued for fifteen days. This letter to the Special Magistrate Lahore could be prior to the said hunger strike notice and could have been sent on 16 December; a reference to this is made in the next letter to the Home Member, Government of India, highlighted in bold letters.

In the court of the Special Magistrate, Lahore
Crown vs Sukhdev & Others

Charged under sections 120B+302, 121A the petitioners respectfully submit the following:

1. That majority of the petitioners have been in confinement for the last nine months in the above case and the rest have been so confined for terms varying from two to six months, and the case will yet take a very long time.
2. That the charges against the petitioners are of a very serious nature.
3. That the petitioners are being deprived of the fundamental right of being defended by a counsel as they are not permitted to see their attorneys and friends, a matter which the learned court has delegated to the jail authorities who have refused to allow their interview with their attorneys and friends.
4. That although the police and other officials are permitted to come freely into the court room, the petitioners friends are not even permitted to enter the court room.
5. That the dock in which the petitioners are kept in the course of the inquiry is always surrounded by police and jail officials and even those petitioners who are represented by counsel feel handicapped in communicating with and giving full instructions to them.
6. That an unprecedented practice of keeping an assistant jailor and some jail officials present always around the dock is being daily pursued.
7. That the petitioners have been deprived of the right of having access to newspapers which they need very badly in connection with the defence.
8. That they are being persecuted and punished by the jail authorities for matters which have occurred in the court.
9. That the petitioners are unable to take legal steps in respect of the illegal punishment inflicted on them and the illegal treatment meted out to them by the jail authorities.
10. That definite complaints filed by some of the petitioners in respect of the ill treatment and assault by the police officials have not been attended to by the authorities and while in custody the petitioners are unable to prosecute them—

The first page of the petition ends here, and the second, and likely final, page is not in the digital records of the Supreme Court. It seems the second page may contain one or two more submissions and comments from jail authorities, if at all they had forwarded the petition. The petition could be dated January–February 1930, when the trial was in progress. Presided over by Special Magistrate Rai Saheb Pandit Sri Kishan, a lot of unpleasant incidents had taken place during its course.

28. Letter to the Government of India; 28 January 1930 (Originally in English.)

Since the Government of India did not respond to the 20 January telegram sent by the revolutionaries, Bhagat Singh, B.K. Dutt and others, sent a detailed letter to the government, reiterating their resolve to resume their hunger strike in absence of their concerns being addressed.

The Home Member,
The Govt. of India
Delhi
Through
The Special Magistrate,
Lahore Conspiracy Case,
Lahore
SIR,

With reference to our telegram dated 20 January 1930, reading as follows, we have not been given any reply.
    Home Member Government.
    Delhi undertrials, Lahore Conspiracy Case, and other Political Prisoners suspended hunger-strike on the assurance that the India Government was considering the Provincial Jail Committee's reports.

All Government Conference over, no action yet taken. As vindictive treatment to political prisoners still continues, we request we be informed within a week final Govt. decision. Lahore Conspiracy Case under trials.

As briefly stated in the above telegram, we beg to bring to your kind notice that the Lahore Conspiracy Case undertrials and several other political prisoners confined in Punjab jails suspended hunger strike on the assurance given by the members of the Punjab Jail Enquiry Committee that the question of the treatment of political prisoners was going to be finally settled to our satisfaction within a very short period. Further, after the death of our great martyr Jatindra Nath Das, the matter was taken up in the Legislative Assembly and the same assurance was given publicly by Sir James Crerar. It was then pronounced that there has been a change of heart and the question of the treatment of political prisoners was receiving the utmost sympathy of the government. Such political prisoners who were still on hunger strike in jails of the different parts of the country then suspended their hunger strike on the request being made to this effect in an AICC resolution passed in view of the said assurance and the critical condition of some of the prisoners.

Since then all the local governments have submitted their reports. A meeting of Inspectors-General of Prisons of different provinces has been held at Lucknow and the deliberations of the All-India Govt. Conference have been concluded at Delhi. The All-India Conference was held in the month of December last, over not carried into effect any final recommendations. By such dilatory attitude of the government we no less than the general public have begun to fear that perhaps the question has been shelved. Our apprehensions have been strengthened by the vindictive treatment meted out to hunger strikers and other political prisoners during the last four months. It is very difficult for us to know the details of the hardships to which the political prisoners are being subjected. Still the little information that has trickled out of the four walls of the jails is sufficient to furnish us with glaring instances. We give below a few such instances which we cannot but feel, are not in conformity with the govt. assurance.

1. B.K. Banerji, undergoing 5 years imprisonment in connection with Dakshineshwar Bomb Case in Lahore Central Jail, joined the hunger strike last year. Now as a punishment for the same, for each day of his period of hunger strike, two days of the remission so far earned by him have been forfeited. Under usual circumstances his release was due in December last, but it will be delayed by full four months. In the same Jail similar punishment has been awarded to Baba Sohan Singh, an old man of about seventy, now undergoing his sentence of life transportation in connection with the (first) Lahore Conspiracy Case. Besides, among others, Sardar Kabul Singh and Sardar Gopal Singh confined in Mianwali Jail, Master Mota Singh confined in Rawalpindi Jail have also been awarded vindictive punishments for joining the general hunger strike. In most of these cases the periods of imprisonment have been enhanced while some of them have been removed from the Special class.

2. For the same offence, i.e. joining the general hunger strike, Sachindranath Sanyal, Ramkishan Khattri and Suresh Chandra Bhattacharya, confined in Agra Central Jail, Rajkumar Sinha, Sachindranath Bakshi, Manmathnath Gupta and several other Kakori Case prisoners have been severely punished. It is reliably learnt that Mr. Sanyal was given bar-fetters and solitary cell-confinement and as a consequence there has been a break-down in his health. His weight has gone down by eighteen pounds. Mr. Bhattacharya is reported to be suffering from tuberculosis. The three Bareilly Jail prisoners also have been punished. It is learnt that all their privileges have been withdrawn. Even their usual rights of interviewing with relations and communication with them were forfeited. They have all been considerably reduced in their weights. Two press statements have been issued in this connection in September 1929 and January 1930 by Pandit Jawaharlal Nehru.

3. After the passing of the AICC resolution regarding hunger strike, the copies of the same, which were sent to different political

prisoners, were withheld by the jail authorities. Further, the govt. refused a Congress deputation to meet the prisoners in this respect.

4. The Lahore Conspiracy Case under trials were assaulted brutally on 23 and 24 October 1929, by orders of high police officials. Full details have appeared in the press. The copy of the statement recorded by the Special Magistrate, Pandit Sri Kishan, has been duly forwarded to you in a communication dated 16 December 1929. Neither the Punjab Government nor the Government of India felt it necessary to reply or even acknowledge receipt of our communication praying for an enquiry. While, on the other hand, local government has felt the imperative necessity of prosecuting us in connection with the very same incident for offering "violent" resistance!

5. In the last week of December 1929, Kiran Chandra Das and eight others confined in the Lahore Borstal Jail, when being taken to and produced in the Magistrate's Court, were found handcuffed and chained together in flagrant breach of the unanimous recommendations of the Punjab Jail Enquiry Committee and also of Inspector-General of Prisons, Punjab. It is further noteworthy that these prisoners were under trials, changed for a bailable offence. A long statement issued by Dr Mohd Aslam, Lala Duni Chand of Lahore and Lala Duni Chand of Ambala in this connection, was published in the *Tribune*.

When we learnt these and other sufferings of the political prisoners we refrained from resuming our hunger strike, though we were much grieved as we thought that the matter was going to be finally settled at an early date, but in the light of the above instances, are we now to believe that the untold sufferings of the hunger strikers and the supreme sacrifice made by Jatin Das have all been in vain? Are we to understand that the govt. gave its assurance only to check the growing tide of public agitation and to avert a crisis? You will agree with us if we say that we have waited patiently for a sufficiently reasonable period of time. But we cannot wait indefinitely. The government, by its dilatory attitude and the continuation of vindictive treatment to political prisoners, has left us no other option but to resume the struggle. We realize that to go on hunger strike and to carry it on is no easy task. But let us at the same time point out that India can produce many more Jatins, Ram Rakhas and Bhan Singhs. (The last two named laid down their lives in the Andamans in 1917 – the first breathed his last after 63 days of hunger strike while the other died the death of a great hero after silently undergoing torture for a full six months.)

Enough has been said by us and the members of the public (inquiry committee) in justification of the better treatment of political prisoners and it is unnecessary here to repeat the same. We would however like to say a few words as regards the inclusion of motive as the basis and the most important factor in the matter of classification. Great fuss has been created on the question of criteria of classification. We find that motive has altogether been excluded so far from the criteria suggested by different provincial governments. This is really strange attitude. It is through motive alone that the real value of any action can be decided. Are we to understand that the Government is unable to distinguish between a robber who robs and kills his victim and a Kharag Bahadur who kills a villain and saves the honour of a young lady and redeems society of a most licentious parasite? Are both to be treated as two men belonging to the same category? Is there no difference between two men who commit the same offence, one guided buy selfish motive and the other by a selfless one? Similarly, is there no difference between a common murderer and a political worker, even if the latter resorts to violence? Does not his selflessness elevate his place from amongst those of ordinary criminals? In these circumstances we think that motive should be held as the most important factor in the criteria for classification.

Last year, in the beginning of our hunger strike, when public leaders including Dr Gopi Chand and Lala Duni Chand of Ambala–the last named being one of the signatories to the Punjab Jail Enquiry Committee Report–approached us to discuss the same thing and when they told us that the government considered to treat the political prisoners convicted of offences of violent nature as Special Class prisoners, then by way of compromise we agreed to the proposal to the extent of excluding those actually charged with murder. But, later on, the discussion took a different turn and the communiqué containing the terms of reference for the Punjab Jail Enquiry Committee was so worded that the question of motive seemed to be altogether excluded, and the classification was based on two things:

(1) Nature of Offence; and
(2) Social Status of "Offender".

These criteria, instead of solving the problem, made it all the more complicated.

We could understand two classes amongst the political prisoners, those charged for non-violent offences and those charged for violent offences. But then creeps in the question of social status in the report of the Punjab Jail Enquiry Committee. As Chaudhary Afzal Haque has pointed out and rightly too, in his note of dissent to this report, what will be the fate of those political workers who have been reduced to pauper's conditions due to their honorary services in the cause of freedom? Are they to be left at the mercy of a magistrate who will away try to prove the bonafide of his loyalty by classifying everyone as an ordinary convict? Or, is it expected that a non-cooperator will stretch his hand before the people against whom he is fighting as an opponent, begging for better treatment in jail? Is this the way of removing the causes of dissatisfaction, or rather intensifying them? It might be argued that people living in property outside the jails, should not expect luxuries inside the prison when they are detained for the purpose of punishment. But, are the reforms that are demanded, of a nature of luxury? Are they not the bare necessities of life, according to the most moderate standard of living? In spite of all the facilities that can possibly be demanded, jail will ever remain a jail. The prison in itself does not contain and can never contain any magnetic power to attract the people from outside. Nobody will commit offences simply to come to jail. Moreover, may we venture to say that it is a very poor argument on the part of any government to say that its citizens have been driven to such extreme destitution that their standard of living has fallen even lower than that of jails? Does not such an argument cut at the very root of that government's right of existence? Anyhow, we are not concerned with that at present. What we want to say is that the best way to remove the prevailing dissatisfaction would be to classify the political prisoners as such into a separate class which may further be subdivided, if need be, into two classes - one for those convicted of nonviolent offences and the other for persons whose offences include violence. In that case motive will become one of the deciding factors. To say that motive cannot be ascertained in political cases is hypocritical assertion. What is it that today informs the jail authorities to deprive the 'political' even of the ordinary privileges? What it is that deprives them of the special grades or 'nambardaries', etc.? What does make the authorities to keep them aloof and separated from all other convicts? The same thing can help in the classification also.

As for the special demands, we have already stated them in full in our memorandum to the Punjab Jail Enquiry Committee. We would however particularly emphasize that no political prisoner, whatever his offence may be, should be given any hard and undignified labour for which he may not feel aptitude. All of them, confined in one jail, should be kept together in the same ward. At least one standard daily newspaper in vernacular or English should be given to them. Full and proper facilities for study should be granted. Lastly, they should be allowed to supplement their expenses for diet and clothing from their private sources.

We still hope that the government will carry into effect without further delay its promise made to us and to the public, so that there may not be another occasion for resuming the hunger strike. Unless and until we find a definite move on the part of the government to redeem its promise in the course of the next seven days, we shall be forced to resume the hunger strike.

Yours, etc.
Bhagat Singh,
Dutt,
Others
28 January 1930
Undertrials, Lahore Conspiracy Case

29. Letter to the Superintendent, Lahore Jail; 11 February 1930 (Originally in English.)

On 11 February 1930, Bhagat Singh and his comrades wrote to the Special Magistrate again, citing the reasons for the boycott of the court, and demanding proper and judicious trial conditions. This letter was published in the 13 February 1930 issue of *Hindustan Times*. The second hunger strike of the LCC (Lahore Conspiracy Case) accused was also suspended after twenty-one days on the assurance given by the government. But there were so many minor issues and complaints which the Magistrate was not prepared to listen to. The accused thereupon refused to attend the court. The *Civil and Military Gazette* (an Anglo-Indian daily from Lahore) commented that the accused had boycotted the British court. However, this was factually incorrect. Bhagat Singh contradicted it and explained the reasons for refusing to attend the court.

MISTER MAGISTRATE

After going through your order dated 4 February 1930, which was published in the *Civil and Military Gazette*, it appears necessary that we explain to you the reason of our boycott of the court.

It is wrong to say that we have boycotted the courts of the British government. Today, we are going to the court of Mr. Louis who is hearing the case initiated against us under Section 22 of the Jail Act. We had presented our problems and difficulties in our bail application before you, but it still remains unconsidered.

Our under-trial comrades belong to different and distant corners of the country. Therefore, they should be given the facility of meeting their well-wishers and sympathizers. B.K. Dutt gave an application to meet Miss Lajjawati, and Kamal Nath Tewari also wanted to meet someone, but were neither their relatives nor their lawyers. Even after securing their authorization, they were not allowed to meet. It is quite clear from this that the under trials are not given the facilities for their defence. Not merely this, Comrade Kranti Kumar, who was doing very useful work for our defense committee and was also providing us with things of daily use, has been imprisoned on a fabricated charge. It has come to our knowledge that when the fabricated charge of bringing bullets in the sauce, could not be proved against him, under Section 124 A in Gurdaspur which is distant from Lahore.

I myself cannot keep a whole-time lawyer: therefore I wanted that my trusted friends should observe the court proceedings by being present there, but they were denied permission without any explicit reason, and only Advocate Lala Amardas has been given a seat.

We can never like this drama acted out in the name of justice, because we do not get any facility or benefit for defending ourselves. One more serious complaint is against non-available of newspapers. Under trial prisoners cannot be treated like convicted prisoners. We should be given at least one newspaper regularly. We want one newspaper also for those who do not know English; therefore, as a protest, we are returning even the English daily *Tribune*. We decided to boycott the court on 29 January, 1930, because of these complaints. We will rejoin the proceedings when these inconveniences are removed.

Yours
etc. etc.

(Taken from *Selected Writings of Shaheed Bhagat Singh*, edited by Shiv Verma.)

30. Letter to the Government of India, Shimla; 2 May 1930 (Originally in English.)

On 2 May 1930, Bhagat Singh and his comrades wrote to the Government of India, condemning the appointment of the Special Tribunal to hear their case. The strategy of the Lahore Conspiracy Case accused was to prolong the case and use the court as a platform for propagating the aims and objects of the revolutionary party. The government saw through this and, to expedite the proceedings, withdrew the case from the lower court, and promulgated an ordinance known as the LCC Ordinance No.3 of 1930. Equipped with the ordinance, it appointed a Special Tribunal consisting of three High Court judges, handed over the case to it and empowered it to dispense with the witnesses and proceed with the case even in the absence of the accused. The Governor General, while justifying the step, said that the accused were resorting to hunger strikes over and over again, and were making it impossible for the court to proceed. It was in this context that Bhagat Singh wrote this letter to the Governor General.

His Excellency
The Governor General of India

Simla,
2 May 1930

Sir,

The full text of the special Ordinance to expedite our trial has been read over to us. To Tribunal has also been appointed by the Chief Justice of the Punjab High Court of Judicature. We welcome the news. We could have kept silent, had you not referred to our attitude adopted so far in this case, and thus tried to throw the sole responsibility on our shoulders. In the present situation, we feel it necessary to make a statement to clear our position.

We have been marking from the very beginning that the Government authorities have always been trying to deliberately misrepresent us. After all, this is a fight, and the misrepresentation is and has always been the best instrument in the hands of the Government to meet their enemies. We have absolutely no grudge against this mean tactic. However, there are certain things the consideration of which is forcing us to make the following counter.

You have mentioned your statement issued along with the Lahore Conspiracy Ordinance, our hunger strike. As you have yourself admitted, two of us had begun the hunger strike weeks before the commencement of the inquiry into this case in the court of RS Pandit Sri Kishan, Special Magistrate. Hence any man with the least common sense can understand that the hunger strike had nothing to do with the trial. The Government had to admit the existence of these grievances. When the Government made some gesture as to making certain arrangement for the settlement of this question, and Provincial Jail Enquiry Committees were appointed for the same purpose, we gave up the hunger strike. But at first we were informed that the question would be finally settled in November. Then it was postponed till December. But January also passed and there was not the least to indicate as to whether the Government was going to the do anything in this connection at all, or not. We feared that the matter was shelved. Hence the second hunger strike on 4 February 1930, after full one week's notice. It was only then that the Govt. tried to settle this question finally. A Communiqué was published and we again gave up the hunger strike and did not even wait to see the final decision, in this connection, carried into effect. It is only today that we are realizing that the British Government has not yet given up the policy of telling lies even in such ordinary matters as this. This Communiqué is in specific terms, but we find something quite contrary in practice. Anyhow, this is not the proper place to discuss that question; we might have to deal with it later on, if the occasion arises. But what we want to emphasize here is that the hunger strike was never directed against the proceedings of the court. Such great sufferings cannot be invited and such great sacrifice cannot be made with that ordinary motive. Das did not lay down his life for such a trivial cause. Rajguru and others did not risk their lives simply to protract the trial.

You know thoroughly well, and everybody concerned knows it, that it is not hunger strike that has forced you to promulgate this Ordinance. There is something else the consideration of which confused the heads of your Government; it is neither the protraction of the case nor any other emergency which forces you to sign this lawless law. It is certainly something different.

But let us declare once and for all that our spirits cannot be cowed down by ordinances. You may crush certain individuals but you cannot crush this nation. As far as this Ordinance is concerned, we consider it to be our victory. We had been from the very beginning pointing out that this existing law was a mere make-believe. It could not administer justice. But even those privileges to which the accused were legitimately and legally entitled and which are given to ordinary accused, could not be given to the accused in political cases. We wanted to make the Govt. throw off its veil and to be candid enough to admit that fair chances for defence could not be given to the political accused. Here we have the frank admission of the Government. We congratulate you as well as your Government for this candour and welcome the Ordinance.

In spite of the frank admission of your agents, the Special Magistrate and the Prosecution Counsels, as to the reasonableness of our attitude throughout, you had been confused at the very thought of the existence of our case. What else is needed to assure us of our success in this fight.

31. Letter to the Commissioner, Special Tribunal, Lahore; 5 May 1930 (Originally in English.)

On 5 May, Bhagat Singh and five other revolutionaries wrote to the Special Tribunal, terming it as a 'farcical' trial and boycotted the proceedings. For propaganda purposes, the Lahore Conspiracy Case's accused had divided themselves into three groups. The first group consisted of comrades who were represented through a lawyer. This was a small group of comrades against whom there was not much evidence and who had chances of getting acquitted. The second group consisted of the unrepresented accused; Bhagat Singh belonged to this group. Comrades of this group were generally vocal in the court. They cross-examined the prosecution witnesses, challenged the prosecution, challenged the rulings of the court, delivered political speeches, and made every effort to prolong the proceedings. The third group consisted of the undefended accused. They were to challenge the bona fides of the court and the government. It consisted of five comrades.

On the very first day, they submitted a written statement before the Tribunal, saying that they did not recognise the alien government and the court appointed by it, and that they did not expect any justice from the enemy court. The statement was prepared by Bhagat Singh and was read in the court by Jitendra Nath Sanyal. The other four signatories were Mahabir Singh, Gaya Prasad Katiyar, Kundan Lal, and Batukeshwar Dutt. The Tribunal declared it as seditious, banned it and refused to record it as part of the proceedings. This statement's first page is found in the Supreme Court's digital records, but the second page is nowhere to be found.

The Commissioner,
The Special Tribunal
Lahore Conspiracy Case, Lahore.
Sirs,

On behalf of the five of my comrades, including myself, I feel it necessary to make the following statement at the very commencement of the trial and wish that it be retained on the record.

We do not propose to take any part in the proceedings of this case because we do not recognise this Govt. which is said to be based on justice or established by law.

We believe and do hereby declare that

"Man being the source of all the authority, no individual or government can be entitled to any authority unless and until it is directly derived from the people."

Since this Government is an utter negative of these principles, its very existence is not justifiable. Such governments, which are organized to exploit the oppressed nations, have no right to exist except by the right of the sword (i.e., brute force) with which they try to curb all the ideas of liberty and freedom and the legitimate aspirations of the people.

We believe all such governments., and particularly this British Government thrust upon the helpless but unwilling Indian nation, to be no better than an organized gang of robbers, and a pack of exploiters equipped with all the means of carnage and devastation. In the name of "law and order", they crush all those who dare to expose or oppose them.

We believe that imperialism is nothing but a vast conspiracy organized with predatory motives. Imperialism is the last stage of development of insidious exploitation of man by man and of nation by nation. The imperialists, with a view to further their piratical designs, not only commit judicial murders through their law courts but also organize general massacres, devastations and other horrible crimes like war. They feel no hesitation in shooting down innocent and unarmed people who refuse to yield to their depredatory demands or to acquiesce in their ruinous and abominable designs. Under the garb of custodians of 'law and order', they break peace, create disorder, kill people and commit all conceivable crimes.

We believe that freedom is an undeniable birth-right of all people, that every man has the inalienable right of enjoying the fruits of his labour, and that every nation is indisputably the master of its resources. If any govt. deprives them of these primary rights, it is the right of the people – nay, it is their duty – to destroy that government. Since the British Govt. is a negation of these principles for which we stand, it is our firm conviction that every effort made, every method adopted to bring about a revolution and to destroy this Govt. is morally justified. We stand for a change, a radical change in the existing order of affairs in social, political and economic spheres, and the complete replacement of the existing order by a new one rendering the exploitation of man by man impossible and thus guaranteeing full liberty to all the people in all the spheres. We feel that unless the whole social order is changed and socialistic society is established, the whole world is in danger of a disastrous catastrophe.

As regards the methods, peaceful or otherwise, to be adopted for the consummation of the revolutionary ideal, let us declare that the choice rests with those who hold power. Revolutionaries, by virtue of their altruistic principles, are lovers of peace – a genuine and permanent peace based on justice and equality, not the illusory peace resulting from cowardice and maintained at the point of bayonets. If the revolutionaries take to bombs and pistols, it is only as a measure of terrible necessity, as a last recourse.

We believe that "Law and Order is for man, and not man for Law and Order."

As the supreme juris council of Revolutionary France has well expressed:

"The end of law is not to abolish or restrain but to preserve and enlarge freedom. The legitimate power is required to govern by promulgated laws established for the common good alone and resting ultimately on the consent and the authority of the people, from which law no one is exempted – not even the legislators."

The sanctity of law can be maintained only so long as it is the expression of the will of the people. When it becomes a mere instrument in the hands of an oppressing class, it loses its sanctity and significance, for the fundamental preliminary condition for administration of justice is the elimination of every interest. As soon as the law ceases to correspond to the popular social needs, it becomes the means for perpetration of injustice and tyranny. The maintaining of such a law is nothing but a hypocritical assertion of a special interest against the common interest.

The law of the present Government exist for the interest of the alien rulers, against the interest of our people, and as such they have no moral binding whatsoever. It is therefore incumbent duty of all Indians of defy and disobey these laws. The British law courts, as part and parcel of the machinery of exploitation, cannot administer justice – especially in political cases where there is a clash between the interests of the Government and the people. We know that these courts are nothing but the stages for the performance of mockery of justice.

For these reasons we decline to be a party to this farcical show and, henceforth, we shall not take any part in the proceedings of this case.

Yours,
Drafted by Bhagat Singh
Signed by:

JN Sanyal, B.K. Dutt, Dr Gayal Prasad, Kundan Lal, Mahabir Singh
May 5, 1930

(Taken from *Selected Writings of Shaheed Bhagat Singh*, edited by Shiv Verma.)

32. Letter to the Special Tribunal, Lahore; 19 June 1930 (Originally in English.)

This letter by Bhagat Singh, to the Special Tribunal, dated 19 June 1930, is to demand some court documents. This letter has been taken from the Supreme Court's digital records.

To
The Registrar,
The Special Tribunal
Lahore Conspiracy Case
Lahore
Sir,

Kindly supply me with an attested copy of the order of the Special Magistrate, dated 3 May 1930, according to which the inquiry proceedings in that court were stayed.

Thanking you in anticipation
Yours etc.
D/ 19th June 1930
Sd./ Bhagat Singh
Undertrial, Lahore Conspiracy Case, Lahore

To,
The Registrar,
Special Tribunal, Poonch House Lahore
Through
The Superintendent,
Central jail, Lahore
Noting—No. 7 by D/20th June 1930
Forwarded to the Registrar, Special Tribunal Poonch House, Lahore, for favour of necessary action as he deems fit.

Signatures, etc. Sd./ Major Ims,
Superintendent, Central Jail, Lahore

33. Letter to the Special Tribunal, Lahore; 25 June 1930 (Originally in English.)

This letter to the Special Tribunal by Bhagat Singh and his comrades, is to reject the reorganized Special Tribunal with Justice Hilton as part of it. The Lahore Conspiracy Case opened on May 5 1930 before the Special Tribunal. On May 12, the presiding judge lost his temper when the revolutionaries started singing a song in court. He ordered that the accused be handcuffed. When they resisted, they were removed from the court forcefully and sent back to the jails. The accused boycotted the court the next day onwards, and demanded that the presiding judge must apologize, or he should be removed.

On June 21, the presiding judge was removed, but along with him the Government removed Justice Agha Haider, also who was the next senior judge and was sympathetic towards the accused.

On June 23, the accused went to the court to find Justice Hilton, who was a party to the order, presiding over the court. The accused objected to it and demanded that Justice Hilton should dissociate himself from the order or he should apologize, failing which he should also be removed from the Tribunal. It was in this context that Bhagat Singh wrote this letter.

To
The Commissioner,
The Special Tribunal,
Lahore Conspiracy Case,
Lahore
Sir,

Whereas two judges of the Tribunal have withdrawn or have been made to withdraw themselves from the Tribunal and two new judges have been appointed in their place, we feel that a statement is very necessary on our part to explain our position clearly so that no misunderstanding may be possible.

It was on 12 May 1930, that an order was passed by Mr Justice Coldstream, the then President, to handcuff us in asking the court to inform us as to the cause of this sudden and extraordinary order was not thought worth consideration. The police handcuffed us forcibly and removed us back to jail. One of the three judges, Mr Agha Haider, on the following day, dissociated himself with that order of the President. Since that day we have not been attending court.

Our condition on which we were prepared to attend court was laid before the Tribunal on the next day, namely that either the President should apologize or he should be replaced; by this we never meant that a judge who was a party to that order should take the place of the President.

For more than five weeks no heed was paid to the grievances of the accused.

According to the present formation of the Tribunal, both the President and the other judge who had dissociated himself from the order of the President have been replaced by two new judges. Thus the judge who was a party to that order - as the President gave the order on behalf of the majority - has now been appointed the President of the Tribunal. In these circumstances we want to emphasize one thing that we had absolutely no grudge against the person of Mr. Justice Coldstream. We had protested against the order passed by the President on behalf of the majority and the subsequent maltreatment meted out to us. We have every respect for Mr. Justice Coldstream and Mr Justice Hilton that should be expected from man to man. And as our protest was against a certain order we wanted the President to apologize, which meant apology by the President on behalf of the Tribunal who was responsible for that order. By the removal of the President the Position is not changed because Mr Justice Hilton, who was a party to the order, is presiding in place of Mr Coldstream. All that we can see is that the present position has added an insult to injury.

Yours, etc.
Bhagat Singh, B.K. Dutt
25 June 1930

(Taken from *Selected Writings of Shaheed Bhagat Singh*, edited by Shiv Verma.)

34. Letter to the Special Tribunal, Lahore; 11 August 1930 (Originally in English.)

The next seven letters, written between 11 and 30 August 1930, to the Special Tribunal and Punjab High Court, came to light for the first time through the Supreme Court's exhibition, 'The Trial of Bhagat Singh', held in the year 2008. These letters indicate a third hunger strike which lasted for almost a month, beginning from 28 July to 22 August; this hunger strike was never known before. It seems that there was very strict surveillance on the revolutionaries' meeting with their relatives, and since the revolutionaries were boycotting the court and not going out, none of their letters got leaked to the media in this period. These letters, thus, only came to light 78 years later, in 2008, through Supreme Court records. The editor got a digital copy from the Supreme Court of India with permission to publish it with acknowledgement, which was duly done with these and some more letters that had been published in *The Hindu* on 15 August 2011.

In the court of the Special Tribunal, Lahore Conspiracy Case, Lahore
Constituted under the Lahore C.C. Special ordinance
Crown VS. Bhagat Singh & Others
Charged under sections121, 121A, 302, 120B etc.
Most Respectfully Shweth:

1. That the petitioner is an accused in the above case.
2. That he is not attending the court, due to the account given in a previous letters, submitted by him before this court.
3. That he went on hunger strike in protest against certain Rules and regulations of jail department and that the hunger strike had nothing to do with the trial whatsoever.
4. That according to the provisions of the special ordinance, accused still have the right to be represented by a counsel if so desired.
5. That the case is entering a new stage i.e. the prosecution evidence is going to be closed and the accused shall be called upon to produce defence or to make statement if so desired.

6. That at this delicate moment the petitioner wants the help of his relatives and legal advisers.
7. That all the interviews with relatives and legal advisers have been stopped by the jail authorities due to the so-called breach of jail discipline caused by his hunger strike.
8. That the purely executive affair is hampering the cause of justice.
9. That it is prayed in the interests of justice and fair play that the court be pleased to issue orders to the jail authorities to allow him all these interviews which are very essential for defence purposes.

D/ 11/8/30 Sd./

Bhagat Singh
Convict-Undertrial
Central Jail, Lahore

No. 488-p D/ 11.8.30
Forwarded to the Registrar, Hon'ble Special Tribunal Lahore Conspiracy Case, Lahore for favour of disposal.

Lahore / 11.8.30 Sd./ Supdt. Central Jail, Lahore

35. Letter to the High Court, Lahore; 11 August 1930 (Originally in English.)

Charged under sections 302, 121, 121A etc. of I.P.C

Most respectfully Shweth:

1. That the petitioner is an accused in the Lahore Conspiracy Case, being tried by the Special Tribunal constituted under the Lahore Conspiracy Ordinance.
2. That the petitioner and his coaccused refused to attend the court in protest of certain order passed and treatment meted out to the accused.

3. That the petitioner went on hunger strike on July 28th 1930 in protest against certain regulations of the jail department.
4. That the trial is entering in new stage i.e. the Prosecution evidence is about to be closed and the petitioner is to be called upon to make his statement and to offer any defence if desired.
5. That the jail authorities have altogether stopped all the interviews of the petitioner with his relatives and legal advisers.
6. That the purely executive affair is hampering the cause of justice and these orders of the executive are highly illegal.
7. That the petitioner wants the help of his relatives and legal advisers in deciding the most delicate questions of defence.
8. That there is a special provision in the Lahore Conspiracy Case Ordinance to the effect that if any accused voluntarily disables himself by hunger strike or otherwise or resists his production before the court, he still has the right to be represented by a counsel in his absence.
9. That in the present circumstances, the accused feels quite handicapped due to the above-mentioned order of the jail authorities.
10. That it is prayed that in the interest of justice and fair play, the court be pleased to issue such instructions to the authorities concerned, as would be necessary to give full and proper facilities for arranging defence adequately in a case where the petitioner is being tried for such serious offences as may bring extreme penalty of law.
11. That it is prayed that the court be pleased to issue urgent orders for allowing interviews etc. at the earliest convenience.

D/ 11/8/30 Sd./

Bhagat Singh
Convict-undertrial
Lahore Conspiracy Case, Lahore

Through the Suptdt. Central Jail, Lahore
Central Jail, Lahore

No. 127-Sd./ 11/8/30
Forwarded to the Registrar of the High Court of Judicature for favour of disposal
Sd./

36. Letter to High Court, Lahore; 16 August 1930 (Originally in English.)

In the Hon'ble High Court of Judicature (Punjab) Lahore
Crown VS. Bhagat Singh & Others
(Lahore Conspiracy Case)
Charged under sections 302, 121, 121A etc. of I.P.C.
Most respectfully Shweth:

1. That the petitioner submitted a petition on 11th August 1930 to this learned court through the supdt. Central jail, Lahore, praying the court to intervene in the matter of interviews essential for defence purposes, with concerned relatives and legal advisers, which have been stopped due to his resorting to hunger strike as a protest against certain jail rules.
2. That a full week has elapsed since and no orders have been received by the petitioner.
3. That the defence is being unnecessarily handicapped and he is suffering simply due to high handedness of the executive authorities.
4. That it is prayed that immediate orders be passed to this effect and the petitioner be informed of that.

D/ 16/8/30

37. Letter to the Special Tribunal, Lahore; 18 August 1930 (Originally in English.)

To,
The Special Commissioners
Lahore Conspiracy Case Tribunal, Lahore
Sir,

I have just been informed by the jail authorities that the learned court was pleased to pass orders on my application dated 11 August 1930, to the effect that interviews with legal adviser alone may be allowed. I was at a loss to understand the reason of such an order. Why should I not be allowed to see my relatives, when the said interviews are very essential for defence purposes? If the order is meant simply to make a show that the accused are given proper facilities regarding their defence, though in reality nothing of the sort is done, on the contrary the defence is hampered at every step, then all my petitions and representations are useless.

My legal adviser, L. Duni Chand Bar-at-Law is in jail. I want to engage a new one, which I can not do without the help and advice of my father. Therefore the interview is very essential. I have to consult my father about offering the defence. I want to ascertain how far he can help me in this respect. If interviews will not be allowed, the court and jail authorities shall stand responsible for the serious consequences that I might have to bear for this high-handedness.

With no stretch of imagination can I understand as to why should the court of law join hands with the executive in such matters as are immediately concerned with the administration of justice and be a party to the unnecessary harassment of the accused.

I most earnestly request the court to reconsider their order passed on my said application and to issue instructions to the jail authorities to allow my interviews so long as the trial is going on. They shall have time enough to treat us as they like after conviction.

Hoping to be forwarded with an early decision.

Yours etc.
D/ 18th Aug. '30 Sd./ Bhagat Singh
Convict-Undertrial

38. Letter to the Special Tribunal, Lahore; 22 August 1930
(Originally in English.)

In the Court of the Special Tribunal,
Lahore conspiracy Case Lahore
Crown VS. Sukhdev & Others
Charged Under sections 121, 121 A, 302 & 120 B
Most Respectfully Shweth-

1. That the petitioner has today, on 22 August 1930, been supplied with the copies of the orders of the learned court bearing the dates 11 August and 22 August 1930.
2. That in spite of the order of 11 August, no interview has so far been allowed to him.
3. That it is impossible for the petitioner to represent his case personally before the court on 25 August due to the weakness caused by hunger strike.
4. That unless and until he is allowed to see his relatives he is not in a position to engage any counsel.
5. That unless and until he is allowed to consult his co accused, he can not decide about other matters concerning the defence.
6. That it is for the court to see that their orders are carried into effect properly.
7. That it is prayed that the court be pleased to issue immediate orders to the jail authorities to allow these interviews without any further delay.

D/ 22nd Aug'30 Sd/

Bhagat Singh
Central Jail, Lahore

This application was handed over to me by Bhagat Singh at the Central Jail on the 22 August 1930.

Sd/ Fatebuhan Reg (Not Clear)

39. Letter to the Special Tribunal, Lahore; 26 August 1930
(Originally in English.)

In the Court of the Special Tribunal
Lahore Conspiracy Case, Lahore
Crown VS. Sukhdev & Others
Charged under sections 302, 120B, 121, 121A etc. of I.P.C.
Most Respectfully Shweth:

1. That the petitioner has just been furnished with a copy of the learned court regarding the close the prosecution evidence.
2. That since the accused-petitioner has not been given any opportunity to interview the relatives and particularly his father, who is the only person interested in his defence, he is not in a position to engage any counsel or legal adviser, and without whose help he can not decide anything regarding such a delicate matter as the defence.
3. That it is preyed that the court be pleased to see if it is proper in these circumstances to deprive a man of all facilities of defence; and to do whatever is thought proper to meet the ends of justice.

D/ 26/8/30

Sd./ Bhagat Singh
Petitioner
Central Jail, Lahore

Seen by all the members of Tribunal.
Placed on the record.
Sd. / ... d. 27/8/30

40. Letter to the Special Tribunal, Lahore; 30 August 1930
(Originally in English.)

In the court of the Special Tribunal
Lahore Conspiracy Case, Lahore

Crown VS. Sukhdev & others
Charged under sections 121, 121A, 302, 120B etc.
Most Respectfully Shweth:

1. That yesterday on 29 August 1930 the petitioner was informed by the jail authorities that orders have been received from the local government to allow him interviews with the legal advisers, relatives and coaccused for discussing and deciding finally about our defence in this case on 29, 30 and 31 August 1930.
2. That father of the petitioner who is at Ludhiana standing his own trial, has been sent for and is expected today.
3. That the petitioner shall have an interview with his coaccused tomorrow viz 31 August 1930.
4. That in the present circumstances, the petitioner shall be able to decide about his defence and will inform the court about the same on Monday i.e. 1 September 1930.
5. That it is therefore prayed that the learned court be pleased to postpone the passing of any final orders on the question of defence till Monday when the petitioner shall be in a position to inform the court of his final decision regarding the same.

D/ 30th August 30

Sd./ Bhagat Singh
Petitioner

No. 182-c D/ 30.8.30 Forwarded to the Registrar to the court of Special Tribunal Lahore Conspiracy Case Lahore for favour of disposal.

Lahore Central Jail Sd./
30.8.30 Supdt. / Central Jail

41. Letter to the Governor of Punjab, Shimla; 20 March 1931 (Originally in English.)

The last letter to the British Government in India was addressed by Bhagat Singh, Rajguru and Sukhdev to the Governor of Punjab on 20 March 1931, three days prior to their hanging, demanding that 'being war prisoners', they should be shot and not 'executed'.

To
The Punjab Governor
Sir,

With due respect we beg to bring to your kind notice the following:

That we were sentenced to death on 7 October 1930 by a British Court, L.C.C Tribunal, constituted under the Sp. Lahore Conspiracy Case Ordinance, promulgated by the H.E. The Viceroy, the Head of the British Government of India, and that the main charge against us was that of having waged war against H.M. King George, the King of England.

The above-mentioned finding of the Court pre-supposed two things:

Firstly, that there exists a state of war between the British Nation and the Indian Nation and, secondly, that we had actually participated in that war and were therefore war prisoners.

The second pre-supposition seems to be a little bit flattering, but nevertheless it is too tempting to resist the desire of acquiescing in it.

As regards the first, we are constrained to go into some detail. Apparently there seems to be no such war as the phrase indicates. Nevertheless, please allow us to accept the validity of the pre-supposition taking it at its face value. But in order to be correctly understood we must explain it further. Let us declare that the state of war does exist and shall exist so long as the Indian toiling masses and the natural resources are being exploited by a handful of parasites. They may be purely British Capitalist or mixed British and Indian or even purely Indian. They may be carrying on their insidious exploitation through mixed or even on purely Indian bureaucratic apparatus. All these things make no difference. No matter, if your Government tries and succeeds in winning over the leaders of the upper strata of the Indian Society through petty concessions and compromises and thereby cause a temporary demoralization in the main body of the forces. No matter, if once again the vanguard of the Indian movement, the Revolutionary Party, finds itself deserted in the thick of the war. No matter if the leaders to whom personally we are much indebted for the sympathy and feelings they expressed for us, but nevertheless we cannot overlook the fact that they did become so callous as to ignore and not to make a mention in the peace negotiation of even the homeless, friendless and penniless of female workers who are alleged to be belonging to the vanguard and whom the leaders consider to be enemies of their utopian non-violent cult which has already become a thing of the past; the heroines who had ungrudgingly sacrificed or offered for sacrifice their husbands, brothers, and all that were nearest and dearest to them, including themselves, whom your government has declared to be outlaws. No matter, it your agents stoop so low as to fabricate baseless calumnies against their spotless characters to damage their and their party's reputation. The war shall continue.

It may assume different shapes at different times. It may become now open, now hidden, now purely agitational, now fierce life and death struggle. The choice of the course, whether bloody or comparatively peaceful, which it should adopt rests with you. Choose whichever you like. But that war shall be incessantly waged without taking into consideration the petty (illegible) and the meaningless ethical ideologies. It shall be waged ever with new vigour, greater audacity and unflinching determination till the Socialist Republic is established and the present social order is completely replaced by a new social order, based on social prosperity and thus every sort of exploitation is put an end to and the humanity is ushered into the era of genuine and permanent peace. In the very near future the final battle shall be fought and final settlement arrived at.

The days of capitalist and imperialist exploitation are numbered. The war neither began with us nor is it going to end with our lives. It is the inevitable consequence of the historic events and the existing environments. Our humble sacrifices shall be only a link in the chain that has very accurately been beautified by the unparalleled sacrifice of Mr

Das and most tragic but noblest sacrifice of Comrade Bhagawati Charan and the glorious death of our dear warrior Azad.

As to the question of our fates, please allow us to say that when you have decided to put us to death, you will certainly do it. You have got the power in your hands and the power is the greatest justification in this world. We know that the maxim "Might is right" serves as your guiding motto. The whole of our trial was just a proof of that. We wanted to point out that according to the verdict of your court we had waged war and were therefore war prisoners. And we claim to be treated as such, i.e., we claim to be shot dead instead of to be hanged. It rests with you to prove that you really meant what your court has said.

We request and hope that you will very kindly order the military department to send its detachment to perform our execution.

Yours,
Bhagat Singh, Rajguru, Sukhdev

(Taken from *Selected Writings of Shaheed Bhagat Singh*, edited by Shiv Verma.)

POLITICAL LETTERS FROM JAIL

42. Message to the Punjab Students' Conference; 19 October 1929 (Originally in English.)

Bhagat Singh sent a message for the Punjab Students Conference, which was held on 19 October 1929 at Lahore with Netaji Subhas Bose as the chair. This letter was read out in the conference and was later published in the *Tribune* on 22 October 1929.

COMRADES,

Today, we cannot ask the youth to take to pistols and bombs. Today, students are confronted with a far more important assignment. In the coming Lahore Session the Congress is to give call for a fierce fight for the independence of the country. The youth will have to bear a great burden in this difficult time in the history of the nation. It is true that students have faced death at the forward positions of the struggle for independence. Will they hesitate this time in proving their same staunchness and self-confidence? The youth will have to spread this revolutionary message to the far corner of the country. They have to awaken crores of slum-dwellers of the industrial areas and villagers living in worn-out cottages, so that we will be independent and the exploitation of man by man will become impossible. Punjab is considered politically backward even otherwise. This is also the responsibility of the youth. Taking inspiration from the martyr Yatindra Nath Das and with boundless reverence for the country, they must prove that they can fight with steadfast resolve in this struggle for independence.

(Taken from *Selected Writings of Shaheed Bhagat Singh*, edited by Shiv Verma.)

43. Letter to the Editor, *Modern Review*; 22 December 1929 (Originally in English.)

Ramanand Chatterjee, editor of the *Modern Review*, ridiculed the slogan of 'Long Live Revolution' in one of his editorials. Bhagat Singh wrote a reply to the note and handed it over to the trying magistrate to be sent to the *Modern Review*. The reply was subsequently published in the *Tribune* on 24 December 1929. Ramanand Chatterjee wrote the following in his editorial: According to a free press message, at a meeting of the Naujawan Sabha (Youth League) of Gujranwala in the Punjab a resolution was passed protesting against the arrest of students on the ground of their shouting "Long Live Revolution" and "Down with Imperialism", before the Court of the Special Magistrate of Lahore. The resolution states that everyone has the right to utter these cries. It is difficult for laymen to say what cries are or are not legal, when even High Court judges have differed in their interpretation of the law of sedition. But young enthusiasts will pardon an old cynical journalist for confessing that the cry of "Long Live Revolution" has sometimes appeared to him to be a bit funny. A revolution may now and then have been a necessity in the world history, and we should personally like an early non-violent social, economic and political revolution in India. But, what is the exact meaning of "Long Live Revolution"? To be at work is a sign of life. When a desire is expressed for revolution to live long, is it desired that the revolutionary process should be at work every hour, day, week, month and year of our lives? In other words, are we to have a revolution as often as possible? Such ceaseless revolution may make for change, but scarcely for progress, improvement and enlightenment. What one revolution offered must have time to settle down and take root and bear fruit. A ceaseless revolutionary process would make India like what James Russel Lowell called "the Catherine-while republics of South America", of his day. No doubt, no revolution can produce a final state of improvement; there must be changes even after a revolution. But these should be brought about by evolution. There may again be a revolution after several generations, if not centuries, have passed. But that is not what is implied in the shout "Long Live Revolution".

The following was Bhagat Singh's response:

THE EDITOR,
MODERN REVIEW

You have, in the December (1929) issue of your esteemed magazine, written a note under the caption "Long Live Revolution", and have pointed out the meaninglessness of this phrase. It would be impertinent on our part to try to refute or contradict the statement of such an old, experienced and renowned journalist as your noble self, for whom every enlightened India has profound admiration. Still we feel it our duty to explain what we desire to convey by the said phrase, as in a way it fell to our lot to give these "cries" a publicity in this country at this stage.

We are not the originators of this cry. The same cry had been used in Russian revolutionary movements. Upton Sinclair, the well-known socialist writer, has, in his recent novels *Boston* and *Oil*, used this cry through some of the anarchist revolutionary characters. The phrase never means that the sanguinary strife should ever continue, or that nothing should ever be stationary even for a short while. By long usage this cry achieves a significance which may not be quite justifiable from the grammatical or the etymological point of view, but nevertheless we cannot abstract from that the association of ideas connected with that. All such shouts denote a general sense which is partly acquired and partly inherent in them. For instance, when we shout "Long Live Jatin Das", we cannot and do not mean by that shout is that the noble ideal of his life, the indomitable spirit which enabled that great martyr to bear such untold suffering and to make the extreme sacrifice for that ideal, should ever live. By raising this cry we wish that we may show the same unfailing courage in pursuance of our ideal. It is that spirit that we allude to.

Similarly, one should not interpret the word "revolution" in its literal sense. Various meanings and significances are attributed to this word, according to the interests of those who use or misuse it. For the established agencies of exploitation it conjures up a feeling of blood-stained horror. To the revolutionaries it is a sacred phrase. We tried to clear in our statement before the Sessions Judge, Delhi, in our trial in the Assembly Bomb Case, what we mean by the word "Revolution".

We stated therein that Revolution did not necessarily involve sanguinary strife. It was not a cult of bomb and pistol. They may sometimes be mere means for its achievement. No doubt they play a prominent part in some movements, but they do not - for that very reason - become one and the same thing. A rebellion is not a revolution. It may ultimately lead to that end.

The sense, in which the word "Revolution" is used in that phrase, is the spirit, the longing for a change for the better. The people generally get accustomed to the established order of things and begin to tremble at the very idea of a change. It is this lethargical spirit that needs be replaced by the revolutionary spirit. Otherwise degeneration gains the upper hand and the whole humanity is led astray by the reactionary forces. Such a state of affairs leads to stagnation and paralysis in human progress. The spirit of Revolution should always permeate the soul of humanity, so that the reactionary forces may not accumulate (strength) to check its eternal onward march. Old order should change, always and ever, yielding place to new, so that one "good" order may not corrupt the world. It is in this sense that we raise the shout "Long Live Revolution."

Yours sincerely
(Sd.) Bhagat Singh
B.K. Dutt

(Taken from *Selected Writings of Shaheed Bhagat Singh*, edited by Shiv Verma)

44. Letter to Sukhdev, on suicide; September 1930 (Originally in Hindi.)

Judgement in the Lahore Conspiracy Case was expected in September-October, when Sukhdev expressed the view that he would rather commit suicide than spend a long time being incarcerated in jail. That time, Bhagat Singh wrote to him on the conceptual philosophy of suicide. The letter was written sometime in September 1930, and the judgement was delivered on 7 October. The ideas that Bhagat Singh was using as a medium to fight his entire battle are clear from the letter that he wrote to Sukhdev in the context of an ongoing debate about their ideas. It is unfortunate that Sukhdev's letter, in response to which Bhagat Singh wrote the following letter, is not available to us today. Even so, all the points arising during the exchange of ideas and arguments are clear here. What Bhagat Singh mentions in the letter very bitterly, that if at all Sukhdev was to think of suicide, he should have executed that idea at the time of his arrest, because, in the police's trap, he had narrated the whole story of the group's activities which harmed the group as well as their court case. However, Sukhdev redeemed himself for not seeking any pardon in lieu of that, rather, he became a bigger victim of the British justice system when he was given death sentence despite not being part of Saunders' murder. Both of Bhagat Singh's letters are significant as, in one letter he discusses the concept of 'love' and in the second, the concept of 'suicide'. Both these issues are relevant to the youth.

It is cowardice to run away from hardships

Dear Brother,

I have perused your letter carefully several times. I feel that the changed circumstances have affected both of us differently. The things that you hated outside the jail have now become essential for you. Similarly, the things that I especially espoused outside the jail don't have much meaning for me now. For example, I firmly believed in individual love, but now this emotion has no special place in my heart or head. Outside, you were a firm critic of this, but there is a great change and revolution in your feelings regarding this now. You consider it to be an extremely important and essential part of human life and this perception has also imparted a kind of joy to you.

Perhaps you remember that one day I spoke to you on the topic of suicide. I told you at that time, that in certain circumstances, suicide could be appropriate, but you had opposed my viewpoint. I well remember the time and place of that discussion. We had this talk in the Shehanshahi Kutia in the evening. You had laughingly said in joke, that such an act of cowardice could never be considered appropriate. You had said that such an act was horrible and despicable, but even on this topic I see that your opinion has undergone a change. Now in certain circumstances, you consider it not only appropriate, but also important and essential. Now my opinion about this is what you held earlier; that is, suicide is a despicable crime; this is completely an act of cowardice. Not only for revolutionaries, but it can also not be considered appropriate for any human being.

You say that you cannot understand how one can serve the nation merely by enduring suffering. Such a question from someone like you is surprising, because in the Naujawan Bharat Sabha we had become devoted to the concept of 'Endurance of suffering through service and sacrifice' after careful consideration. I think that you have done the maximum service possible for one to do. Now the time has come to accept the consequences of that action and undergo suffering. The other thing is that this is the time, when you have to lead the entire people.

A human being acts only when he believes it to be right, just as we committed an action of throwing a bomb in the Legislative Assembly. After committing an action comes the turn of its result and suffering its consequences. Do you believe that our action would have been right if we had begged for mercy, to escape punishment? No, it would have had the opposite effect on people. Now we have achieved complete success in our mission.

When we were taken prisoners, the condition of political prisoners of our organization, was extremely wretched. We began to try to improve it. Let me tell you in all seriousness that we believed that we would die within a very short time. We neither knew about force feeding, during fasting, nor did this thought occur to us. We were prepared to die. Do you think that we wanted to commit suicide? No, to be a striver and to give up one's life for a noble and superior ideal can certainly not be called suicide. The death of our friend (Jatinder Nath Das) was an enviable one. Would you call it suicide? Our enduring of agony bore fruit. A massive and all-pervading agitation has begun all over the country. We succeeded in our aim. To die in a struggle like this is an ideal death.

Apart from this, those of us who are certain to get the death sentence should wait patiently for the day when this sentence would be pronounced, after which they will be hanged. Even that death will be beautiful, but to commit suicide, to put an end to one's life, to escape some suffering – that is cowardice. I wish to tell you that it is hardship that make a person complete. You and I, I would say, have not endured the least problem. This part of our life is now beginning.

Perhaps you recall that we have talked several times about the fact that the realism that one finds in Russian literature everywhere is not seen at all in our literature. We really admire the painful and sorrowful situations in their stories, but do not feel the sensation of going through that pain. We praise their intense passion and their characters to unprecedented heights, but never trouble to ponder over their reasons. I would say that it is the delineation of suffering in their literature that gives sensitivity, a sharp pang of pain and nobility to their characters and literature. Our condition becomes pitiable and laughable when we introduce mysticism into our life without a reason, unless there is a natural and solid base for it. People like us, who take pride in being revolutionaries from every angle, should always be prepared to go through those hardships, anxieties and pain that we invite upon ourselves through the struggle we ourselves begin, and due to which we call ourselves a revolutionary.

Let me tell you that in jails, and only in jails, can a person get an opportunity to study intensely important social subjects like crime and sin. I have read some literature on these subjects and jails are the most suitable place to practically experience such subjects. The best part of self-experiment is – endure agony oneself.

You well know, that in Russia the suffering endured by political prisoners in jails was the biggest reason for them to bring about a revolution in the administration of the jails after overturning the Tsar's dictatorship. Does India not need such people who are fully aware about this subject and have personally experienced this problem? Just to say that someone else would do this, or that there are plenty of people to do this, cannot be called right in any manner. So those who consider putting the onus of revolutionary work on others to be dishonourable and despicable must themselves begin the struggle against the present conditions with complete dedication. They need to violate those practices, but they must observe propriety, because unnecessary and unjustifiable efforts can never be considered just. This kind of movement will reduce the time frame of the revolution to a great extent. I am unable to understand all the reasons that you have given to stay aloof from all the movements that begun till now. There are some friends who are either foolish or immature. They consider your behaviour (that they themselves admit to not understand at all, because you are far greater in stature and beyond their comprehension) different and strange.

In fact, if you feel that life in imprisonment is really humiliating, then why don't you agitate against it and try to reform it? Possibly you would answer that this struggle cannot succeed, but this is the same logic that usually weak people employ to escape every movement. This is the logic that we have heard from those who want to avoid associating with the revolutionary activities outside jail. Will I hear the same words from your lips today? What can our party, based on a handful of workers, had done compared to its aims and ideals? Shall we conclude from this that we have committed a grave error in starting this work? No, it would not be right to come to this conclusion. This exposes the inner weakness of a person – of one who thinks like this.

You go on to write that after spending fourteen years of suffering in jail no person can be expected to retain the same ideas as he had before he went to jail, because the environment of the jail will trample all the ideas to dust. May I ask you if the environment outside the jail was favourable to us? But could we abandon it because of lack of success? Do you mean to say that had we not entered this arena, no revolutionary work could ever have been done? If that is so, you are making a mistake. Though it is true that we have succeeded to a large extent in changing the environment, yet we are just product of the need of the hour.

I will go to the extent of saying that Marx, the father of Communism, was not really the originator of the idea. In fact, the industrial revolution in Europe had given rise to people with a certain kind of ideas. Marx was one of them. Yes, in his own place, Marx undoubtedly proved to be essentially helpful to some extent in moving the wheel of time in a particular direction.

I (and you as well) have not given birth to the ideas of socialism and communism in this country; rather, it is the impact of our times and circumstances upon us. Undoubtedly, we have done some simple and small things to propagate these ideas; so I say that when we have taken such a difficult task upon our hands, then we must continue it and take it forward. To commit suicide to escape calamities would not show the right path to the people; in fact, it would be a reactionary act.

As per the rules of the jail, we continued to work to protest against the extremely challenging environment of disappointments of life, repression and violence. When we carried out this work, we were made targets of a variety of hardships. So much so that those who felt great pride in calling themselves great revolutionaries also left us. Were those circumstances not challenging? Then what reasons and logic did we have to continue with our movement and efforts?

Does this same logic not give strength to our ideas? And do we not have examples before us of people who returned from jail after completing their sentence and are still involved in the movement? If Bakunin (Mikhail) had thought like you he would have committed suicide right at the beginning. Today you see countless such revolutionaries who are occupying offices of responsibility in the Russian state, who have spent a major portion of their lives in jail to undergo punishment. A person must try to stay firm on his beliefs with conviction. No one can predict what will happen in the future.

Do you remember that when we were discussing the issue of keeping an extremely fast-working and powerful poison in our bomb factories, you had opposed it very firmly? You had hated this idea. You had not believed it. Then what happened now? Here the circumstances are also not so terrible and complicated. For me, it is odious to even consider this issue. You had detested even that mentality that permitted suicide. Please forgive me for saying that if you had acted as per these thoughts while you were arrested (that is, if you had committed suicide by consuming poison at that time) then it would have been a great service to the revolutionary cause, but now to even think about such an option is very detrimental to us.

Another important thing that I wish to draw your attention to is that we people do not repose any faith in God, reincarnation, heaven and hell, punishment and reward; that is, the accounts of life being settled by God. That is why we must ponder over the topic of life and death from a completely materialistic viewpoint. One day when someone was brought from Delhi to identify me, then some officers of the secret service spoke to me about this in the presence of my father. They said that since I was not prepared to reveal any secret and save my life, it proves that I was very unhappy with my existence. Their logic was that my death would be like a suicide but I answered them that a person with my beliefs and convictions would never assent to die in such a pointless manner. We wish to get the highest possible value for our lives. We wish to serve humanity to the maximum extent. Especially simple people like me, whose life has not been unhappy or anxious in any manner; who, let alone commit suicide, does not even think it proper to have its idea in mind. That is what I want to say to you.

I hope you will not mind my telling you what I think of myself. I am totally certain of being given the death sentence. I have no hope whatsoever of receiving a pardon or a mitigation of my sentence. Even if there is any pardon, it would not be for everyone, and that too would be very limited and conditional for people other than us. For us there can be no pardon, nor will there be any. Even then I wish that the resolution for our release should be united and spread worldwide; and along with it is my desire that when this movement reaches its peak, we should be hanged. I want that if it is ever possible to have an honourable and just compromise, then our matter should not become an obstacle or create a hurdle in that. When the destiny of the country is being decided, then individual destinies should be disregarded completely. Being revolutionaries, we are completely aware of all the experiences of the past. So we cannot believe that there would be such an astonishing transformation in the feelings of our rulers, especially the British. This kind of transformation cannot be possible without revolution. Revolution can be achieved only by continuous struggle, effort, suffering and sacrifice, and will be done.

As far as my viewpoint is concerned, I can welcome facilities and pardon for everyone only on the condition that its impact is permanent and our hangings etch some enduring imprints on the hearts of the people of this country. That is all, nothing more than this.

45. Letter to father, Kishan Singh; 4 October 1930 (Originally in Urdu.)

Bhagat Singh's father, Kishan Singh, sent a petition to the Special Tribunal Lahore in September, when the Tribunal had closed the proceedings and was to announce its verdict in a few days. He wanted to bring somehow delay the decision by saying that Bhagat Singh was not being present in Lahore on the day of assassination of Saunders, and so deserves a chance to defend himself. Bhagat Singh was very upset at knowing this and thus, wrote a very strong letter to his father on 4 October 1930, denouncing him. Bhagat Singh took strong exception to it and made his father realize his mistake, and insisted that this letter be published at the earliest in all major newspapers. Accordingly, the letter was published the very next day, before the judgement was pronounced on 7 October. In this letter, Bhagat Singh went as far as proclaiming his political independence from his father.

4 October 1930

My Dear Father,

I was astounded to learn that you had submitted a petition to the members of the Special Tribunal in connection with my defence. This intelligence proved to be too severe a blow to be borne with equanimity. It has upset the whole equilibrium of my mind. I have not been able to understand how you could think it proper to submit such a petition at this stage and in these circumstances. In spite of all the sentiments and feelings of a father, I don't think you were at all entitled to make such a move on my behalf without even consulting me. You know that in the political field my views have always differed with those of yours. I have always been acting independently without having cared for your approval or disapproval.

I hope you can recall to yourself that since the very beginning you have been trying to convince me to fight my case very seriously and to defend myself properly. But you also know that I was always opposed to it. I never had any desire to defend myself and never did I seriously think about it. Whether it was a mere vague ideology or that I had certain arguments to justify my position, is a different question and that cannot be discussed here.

You know that we have been pursuing a definite policy in this trial. Every action of mine ought to have been consistent with that policy, my principle and my programme. At present, the circumstances are altogether different, but had the situation been otherwise, even then I would have been the last man to offer defence. I had only one idea before me throughout the trial, i.e., to show complete indifference towards the trial in spite of the serious nature of the charges against us. I have always been of the opinion that all the political workers should be indifferent and should never bother about the legal fight in the law courts and should boldly bear the heaviest possible sentences inflicted upon them. They may defend themselves, but always from purely political considerations and never from a personal point of view. Our policy in this trial has always been consistent with this principle; whether we were successful in that or not is not for me to judge. We have always been doing our duty quite disinterestedly.

In the statement accompanying the text of Lahore Conspiracy Case Ordinance the Viceroy had stated that the accused in this case were trying to bring both law and justice into contempt. The situation afforded us an opportunity to show to the public whether we were trying to bring law into contempt or whether others were doing so. People might disagree with us on this point. You might be one of them. But that never meant that such moves should be made on my behalf without my consent or even my knowledge. My life is not so precious, at least to me, as you may probably think it to be. It is not at all worth buying at the cost of my principles. There are other comrades of mine whose case is as serious as that of mine. We had adopted a common policy and we shall stand to the last, no matter how dearly we have to pay individually for it.

Father, I am quite perplexed. I fear I might overlook the ordinary principle of etiquette and my language may become a little bit harsh while criticizing or rather censuring this move on your part. Let me be candid. I feel as though I have been stabbed at the back. Had any other person done it, I would have considered it to be nothing short of treachery. But in your case, let me say that it has been a weakness – a weakness of the worst type.

This was the time where everybody's mettle was being tested. Let me say, father, you have failed. I know you are as sincere a patriot as one can be. I know you have devoted your life to the cause of Indian independence; but why, at this moment, have you displayed such a weakness? I cannot understand.

In the end, I would like to inform you and my other friends and all the people interested in my case that I have not approved of your move. I am still not at all in favour of offering any defence. Even if the court had accepted that petition submitted by some of my co-accused regarding defence, etc., I would have not defended myself. My applications submitted to the Tribunal regarding my interview during the hunger strike were misinterpreted and it was published in the press that I was going to offer defence; though in reality I was never willing to offer any defence. I still hold the same opinion as before. My friends in the Borstal Jail will be taking it as a treachery and betrayal on my part. I shall not even get an opportunity to clear my position before them.

I want that the public should know all the details about this complication, and, therefore, I request you to publish this letter.

Your loving son
Bhagat Singh

46. Letter regarding the Harikishan Trial; January 1931 (Originally in English.)

Bhagat Singh wrote two letters, no. 46 and 47, in reference to the young revolutionary Harikishan's case, who had thrown a bomb at the Governor of Punjab on 23 December 1930, during the Punjab University convocation in Lahore. Despite being the son of a rich and influential father, Gurdas Ram Talwar from Mardan, now Pakistan, he was bound to receive a death sentence, which Bhagat Singh knew. But

Harikishan's lawyers, in order to defend him, made some averments in his petition, which did not enhance the respect of a revolutionary. Bhagat Singh was very upset about this and wrote to some of his unnamed contacts about it. The first of his letters did not reach its destination and was 'lost', as Bhagat Singh himself mentions in his second letter, which repeated the arguments made in first letter. The first letter, till now considered lost, was published in the 18 June 1931 issue of *Hindu Panch* from Calcutta in a Hindi translation, which was sent to the editor, courtesy of Dr Raghuvir Singh from Palwal and Ram Sharma from Beena. Since the original English letter is yet to be found, here, the retranslation from Hindi to English has been done by the editor of this volume. Harikishan was hanged on 9 June 1931 in Lahore jail. The *Hindu* carried these letters in its issue of 22 March 1914.)

Dear Brother,

I was surprised to know that Sh. Harikishan wants to present the same arguments for defence in the court that were used in the Assembly Bomb Case. I was no less surprised to know that Sh. Asaf Ali was called for arguing the case from Delhi and, apart from charging a fat fee for the case; he was paid double first-class rail fare. Though any good lawyer from Lahore would have agreed to take up the case, at a much lower fee. But anyhow, the second aspect is not the main reason for writing this letter. I mean here, the first aspect.

Possibly I have no right to intervene or meddle with the matter of a young man, who is certain to get the highest punishment in law, that is the death sentence. Seeing that it is certain that he would be sentenced to death, I am daring to speak on the political aspect of the matter, leaving behind the issue of personality. At the moment I am writing this letter to you at a personal level, though I don't know for sure whether you can do something about it or not. I hope that before taking any final decision in this matter, my views will be taken into account.

The incidents of the case are clear, and the consequence is also clear. The accused himself understands this most clearly. He has accepted his crime in the lower court, can give his statement in the session court and he should give the statement.

Whatever I have heard that defence lawyer is advising him to state:

1. He had no intention to kill the Governor.
2. He only wanted to hurt him.
3. And this he wanted to do it as a warning.

I request you to please think calmly over this issue. Would not such statements be ridiculous? What would be the meaning of such statements on this occasion? Would it not be repeating the same thing, which has already been stated in an appropriate manner and which has no meaning at present?

After a long, careful consideration, I have come to the conclusion that there is no person who could understand and appreciate the complete individual efforts, even if these efforts may be much scattered and disconnected. No one tries to ensure that each such occasion is used to strengthen the movement. Because of a lack of vision in political matters, the defence lawyer has dared to give such advice, or due to his personal ambition, the lawyer has thought of getting such a statement. I don't mean that people should not offer defence in the cases, rather my opinion is the reverse. But this also does not mean that lawyers, without understanding the real problems, should intervene to put revolutionaries in confusion and discourage them. Despite participating in public causes, these lawyers – and I am referring to Punjab alone – have not adopted revolutionary thinking at all. They neither understand the viewpoint of the revolutionaries nor their mentality.

Rather than talking in general terms, let me come to the point. In this matter, to state that the aim of Harikishan was only to issue a warning is absolutely inadequate. Just ponder over it; this incident has occurred after the Assembly Bomb Case, the attempt to blow up the Viceroy's train, the Chittagong revolt and many such incidents. It is foolishness to say that the accused just wanted to hurt the Governor as a form of protest. For him, a more appropriate statement would be:

1. That, despotic use of power like the lathi charge in Bombay and Amritsar, the arrest of women, beatings and the unprovoked firing on people (here the reference is to the one-sided proceedings of the tribunal in the Lahore Conspiracy Case and the award of death sentences, which can link this incident to a continuous chain of actions of the entire revolutionary movement), motivated him to act in that manner.
2. This is just the beginning; the accused has only given an indication of the resentment prevalent among people, which, if it explodes, will bring destruction.
3. This is standard government policy to take the country towards bloodshed.
4. People can become impatient anytime and take to violent methods by renouncing non-violence.
5. The accused does not want the government to stop this policy as it would encourage people to rise against it.
6. The government has already stopped following the rule of law in general.
7. And the aim of the revolutionary movement is to show the people that the British rule is here only through military power, and so this government should be overthrown through political action.

After this he can define the socialist programme. He can make an appeal to Lahore students that they should shed their laziness and join the people's movement. Under the circumstances this is the best statement he can give.

He can state like an idealist that he has not come to kill an individual; he rather wanted to destroy the system. He feels anguished at the killing of a man, but there is no other way. Individuals have to be sacrificed at the altar of revolution. After all he is also an individual.

He can express sorrow at the killing of the senior inspector, whom he had not wanted to kill. He can also congratulate the Governor for surviving the attack. He can also add that to liberate the oppressed people, loss of individuals cannot matter much.

He should say all these things. Does the lawyer think that by saying that he did not want to kill the Governor, he can be saved? This is sheer childishness. It has no advantage but the harm it causes is immense. If an incident is detached from a movement, it loses its significance. When a sacrifice has to be made, then it should be fully utilized for the best purpose. In future also, all such incidents should be linked to the revolutionary movement and other such efforts; the revolutionary movement should be linked to mass movements. The best way in such matters is to invite a panel of lawyers...[30]

47. Another letter regarding Harikishan; February 1931 (Originally in English.)

I am very sorry to note that my last letter in this connection did not reach its destination at the proper time and therefore could be of no use, or failed to serve the purpose or which it was written. Hence, I write this letter to let you know my views on the question of defence in the political cases in general and the revolutionary cases in particular. Apart from certain points already discussed in that letter, it shall serve another purpose too, i.e., it shall be a documentary proof that I am not becoming wise after the event.

Anyhow, I wrote in that letter that the plea that the lawyer's line of defence should not be adopted. But it has been done in spite of your, and mine, opposition. Nevertheless, we can now discuss the matter in a better light and can formulate definite ideas about the future policy regarding defence.

You know that I have never been in favour of defending all the political accused. But this does not imply that the beauty of the real struggle should be altogether spoiled (Please note that the term beauty is not used in the abstract sense, but it means the motive that actuated a particular action). When I say that all the radicals should always defend

---

30 Editor's note: A few words and sentences left out.

themselves, I say it with certain reservations. It can be cleared by just one explanation. A man does an act with a certain end in view. After his arrest the political significance of the action should not be diminished. The perpetrator should not become more important than the action itself. Let us further elucidate it with the help of the illustration. Mr. Hari Kishan came to shoot the Governor. I don't want only to discuss the ethical side of the action. I want only to discuss the political side of the case. The man was arrested. Unfortunately, some police official had died in the action. Now comes the question of the defence; well, when fortunately the Governor had escaped there could be a very beautiful statement in his case, i.e., the statement of actual facts as was made in the lower court. And it would have served the legal purpose too. The wisdom and ability of the lawyer depended on his interpretation of the cause of the Sub-Inspector's death. What did he gain by saying that he did not intend to kill the Governor and only wanted to warn him, and all that sort of thing? Can any sensible man imagine even for a moment the possibility of such a design? Had it any legal value? Absolutely none; then, what was the use of spoiling the beauty of not only the particular action but also the general movement? Warning and futile protests cannot go on forever. The warning has once been given long ago. The revolutionary struggle had begun in right earnest so far as the strength of the revolutionary party allowed. Viceroy's train action was neither a test nor a warning. Similarly, Mr. Hari Kishan's action was part of the struggle itself, not a warning. After the failure of the action, the accused can take it in purely sportsman-like spirit. The purpose having been served he ought to have rejoiced in the lucky escape of the Governor. There is no use of killing any one individual. These actions have their political significance in as much as they serve to create a mentality and an atmosphere which shall be very necessary to the final struggle. That is all. Individual actions are to win the moral support of the people. We sometimes designate them as the "propaganda through deed".

Now, the people should be defended but subject to the above consideration. This is after all a common principle that all the contending parties always try to gain more and to lose less. No general can ever adopt a policy in which he may have to make a greater sacrifice than the gain expected. Nobody would be more anxious to save the precious life of Mr. Hari Kishan than myself. But I want to let you know that the thing which makes his life precious should by no means be ignored. To save the lives at any cost, is not our policy. It may be the policy of the easy-chair politicians, but it is not ours.

Much of the defence policy depends upon the mentality of the accused himself. But if the accused himself is not only afraid of shirking but is as enthusiastic as ever, than his work for which he risked his life should be considered first, his personal question afterwards. Again, there may be some sort of confusion. There may be cases where the action is of no general importance in spite of its tremendous local value. There the accused should not be sentimental as to admit the responsibility. The famous trial of Nirmal Kant Rai would be the best illustration.

But in cases like this, where it is of such political importance, the personal aspect should not be attached greater value than the political one. If you want to know my frank opinion about his case, let me tell you frankly that it is nothing short of the political murder of an incident of historic importance at the altar of professional (legal) vanity.

Here I may point out one thing more, that the people responsible for this strangulation of the case, having realized their blunder and having become wise after the event in not daring to shoulder their responsibility, are trying to belittle the beauty of the marvellous character of our young comrade. I have heard them saying that Mr. Hari Kishan shirked to face it boldly.

This is a most shame-faced lie. He is the most courageous lad I have ever come across. People should have mercy upon us. Better ignored than demoralized and degraded but well looked after.

Lawyers should not be so unscrupulous as to exploit the lives and even deaths of young people who come to sacrifice themselves for so noble a cause as the emancipation of the suffering humanity. I am really ...[31] otherwise, why should a lawyer demand such an incredible fee as has been paid in the above case?

---

31   Editor's note – Some words missing

In the sedition cases, I may tell you the limit to which we can allow the defence. Last year when one comrade was prosecuted for having delivered a socialistic speech and when he pleaded not guilty to that charge, we were simply astounded. In such cases we should demand the right of free speech. But where such things are attributed to one as he has not said and are contrary to the interests of the movement, deny. Thought in the present movement the Congress has suffered for having allowed its members to go to jail without defending themselves, in my opinion that was a mistake.

Anyhow, I think if you read this letter along with my previous one, you will come to know very clearly my ideas about the defence in political cases. In Mr. Hari Kishan's case, in my opinion, his appeal should be filed in the High Court without fail and every effort should be made to save him.

I hope both these letters indicate everything I want to say on this subject.

(Taken from *Selected Writings of Shaheed Bhagat Singh*, edited by Shiv Verma.)

48. Last letter to comrades; 22 March 1931 (Originally in Urdu.)

The last letter Bhagat Singh wrote was to his comrades on 22 March 1931, a day before his execution. Some of Bhagat Singh's comrades thought that he could still be saved from the gallows by helping him escape from the jail. While appreciating his comrades' concern, Bhagat Singh underlines the significance of his own execution for the country, which indicates his farsightedness and political maturity.

Comrades!

It is natural that the desire to live should be in me as well, I don't want to hide it. But I can stay alive on one condition that I don't wish to live in imprisonment or with any binding.

My name has become a symbol of Hindustani revolution, and the ideals and sacrifices of the revolutionary party have lifted me very high – so high that I can certainly not be higher in the condition of being alive.

Today my weaknesses are not visible to the people. If I escape the noose, they will become evident and the symbol of revolution will be tarnished, or possibly be obliterated. But to go to the gallows with courage will make Hindustani mothers aspire to have children who are like Bhagat Singh and the number of those who will sacrifice their lives for the country will go up so much that it will not be possible for imperialistic powers or all the demoniac powers to contain the revolution.

And yes, one thought occurs to me even today – that I have not been able to fulfil even one thousandth parts of the aspirations that were in my heart to do something for my country and humanity. If I could have stayed alive and free, then I may have got the opportunity to accomplish those and I would have fulfilled my desires. Apart from this, no temptation to escape the noose has ever come to me. Who can be more fortunate than me? These days, I feel very proud of myself. Now I await the final test with great eagerness. I pray that it should draw closer.

Your comrade
Bhagat Singh

PERSONAL LETTERS FROM JAIL

49. Letter to Jaidev Gupta; 24 February 1930 (Originally in English.)

Bhagat Singh wrote four letters, no. 49 to 52, to Jaidev Gupta, between 24 February 1930 and 24 July 1930. He was one of Bhagat Singh's close friends, from whom he demanded not only books, but even sweets, shoes, cigarettes, etc., for himself, as well as for other comrades. One can see from these letters, Bhagat Singh's concern for B.K. Dutt, as well as his humorous nature, which made him so dear to his comrades.

Very Urgent
No. 103, Condemned Cell
Central Jail
Lahore

My Dear Jai Deo!

I hope you would have heard of our abandoning the fast after 16 days, and you can guess how greatly we feel the necessity of your help at this stage. We received a few oranges yesterday but no interview was held. Our case has been adjourned for a fortnight. Therefore kindly arrange to send a tin of 'Craven Cigarettes - A' and a tin of ghee immediately. And a few oranges along with a few rasgullas will also be welcome. Mr. Dutta is facing hard times without cigarettes. Now you can understand the urgent nature of our needs.

Thanking you in advance.
Yours Sincerely
Bhagat Singh

Address - To, Mr. Jai Deo Prasad Gupta, c/o the provincial Congress Committee

Bradlaugh Hall, Lahore

50. Letter to Jaidev Gupta; 28 May 1930 (Originally in English.)

This letter was written to Jaidev Gupta on 26 May 1930 in English. The stamp of the Lahore post office dates it at 28 May 1930 on the post card.

937 D/ Lahore Central Jail
26/5/30 (jail no.) Lahore

Dear Brother Jai deo,

Today again I am writing this letter to give you some trouble, which I hope you will not mind. Please see if you can arrange to send one fleet shoe for me. I think No. 9-10 will do. Chapli[32] is too uncomfortable. Also please try to send it on Friday or Saturday through Kulbir when he will be coming for an interview. Really it is very sad that I have not so far been allowed any interview with you. Had this impasse in our trial not occurred I will have repeatedly reminded the authorities to sanction your interview. Anyhow by the time this question is settled I will again try to get the interview sanctioned. Well I hope you will send the shoe without fail and without delay. These days I have got only one book with me—a very dry one. Please see if you can send a couple of recent interesting novels. Please remember me to all friends.

Yours Sincerely
D/ 26/5/30 Bhagat Singh

Address--- Mr. Jai Deo Prasad Gupta c/o S. Kishan Singh Bradlaugh Hall, Lahore

51. Letter to Jaidev Gupta; 30 June 1930 (Originally in English.)

Central Jail
Lahore
30 June 1930

My dear Jai Deo,

Please accept my best thanks for sending "Victory" fleets and white polish bottle. I am writing again to ask for certain other things. Please see if you can arrange to send another pair of fleet-shoes for Mr Dutt (size no. 7), but ensure with the shop-keeper for its return, if it does not fit his feet. I would have written for this along with mine, but Mr Dutt was not in a good mood at that time. It is difficult for me alone to wear shoes. So I hope in the next interview we will find another pair of shoes lying here.

Also please send one white shirt, chest 34, with a Shakespearean collar and half sleeves. This is also for Mr Dutt. You should not think that even

---

32   Slipper

in jail we have not been able to check with our expensive mode of living. But these are after all, necessities and not luxuries. Send two 'langots'[33] for bathing and exercise, made of some soft cloth, a few soap cakes for washing clothes, also some badams[34] and one swan ink bottle.

How about Sardarji[35] Has he returned to Ludhiana? These days, the court will be closed and the trial won't proceed. If he is not coming, then please send someone to fetch him here. After all, his as well as mine[36] are nearing the end. Can't say whether we will get any other opportunity to see each other again. Hence call him at once, so that he may have two interviews with me this week. And if he is not coming soon, then please send Kulbir and sisters to interview me tomorrow or at the latest the day after. Remember me to my friends.

By the way can you send me one Persian Primer with Urdu translation.

Yours
Bhagat Singh

52. Letter to Jaidev Gupta; 24 July 1930 (Originally in English.)

Lahore Central Jail
24.7.30

MY DEAR JAIDEV,

Please take following books in my name from Dwarkadas Library and send them through Kulbir on Sunday:

Militarism (Kari Liebknecht)
Why Men Fight (B. Russel)
Soviets at Work

---

33   Loincloth underwear
34   Almonds
35   Father
36   Cases

Collapse of the Second International
Left-Wing Communism
Mutual Aid (Prince Kropotkin)
Fields, Factories and Workshops
Civil War in France (Marx)
Land Revolution in Russia
Spy (Upton Sinclair)

Please send one more book from the Punjab Public Library: *Historical Materialism* (Bukharin). Also, please find out from the librarian if some books have been sent to Borstal Jail. They are facing a terrible famine of books. They had sent a list of books through Sukhdev's brother, Jaidev. They have not received any book till now. In case they have no list, then please ask Lala Firoze Chand to send some interesting books of his choice. The books must reach them before I go there on this Sunday. This work is a must. Please keep this in mind.

Also send Punjab *Peasants in Prosperity and Debt* by Darling and 2 or 3 books of this type for Dr Alam. Hope you will excuse me for this trouble. I promise I will not trouble you in future. Please remember me to all my friends and convey my respect to Lajjawati. I am sure if Dutt's sister came she will not forget to see me.

With regards
Bhagat Singh

(Taken from *Selected Writings of Shaheed Bhagat Singh,* edited by Shiv Verma.)

53. Letter to B.K. Dutt's sister, Promila; 17 July 1930 (Originally in English.)

A postcard written by Bhagat Singh to B.K. Dutt's sister, Promila, was given in a scanned form by the Nehru Memorial Museum and Library, Delhi, to the editor, which is included here. Perhaps he wrote more post cards, a reference can be found to one in the letter Bhagat Singh wrote to Kulbir Singh on 3 March 1931, where Bhagat Singh mention's an 'accompanying letter in Hindi may be given to 'K's sister'.

Dear Sister,

Yesterday Batu himself wrote a letter informing you to not to come here till you receive his letter. Batu was transferred yesternight to some other jail. Up to this time, we are quite in dark about his destination. Anyhow I earnestly request you not to leave Benaras for Lahore unless you received his letter. His separation is unbearable for me too. It is only today that I feel quite perplexed and every minute has been a burden. Really it is very hard to be separated with a friend, more dear than my own brothers. Anyhow we must bear all patiently. I would request you to keep courage. Don't ... stress, something good will come out of it.

Yours
Bhagat Singh

(One postal mark of 17 July and other 19 July of Benaras.)

54. Letter to B.K. Dutt; November 1930 (Originally in English.)

This letter to B.K. Dutt, written in November 1930, gives an idea about what Bhagat Singh expected and hoped from those comrades who would escape capital punishment.

Central Jail,
November 1930

DEAR BROTHER,

The judgement has been delivered. I am condemned to death. In these cells, besides myself, there are many other prisoners who are waiting to be hanged. The only prayer of these people is that somehow or other they may escape the noose. Perhaps I am the only man amongst them who is anxiously waiting for the day when I will be fortunate enough to embrace the gallows for my ideal.

I will climb the gallows gladly and show to the world as to how bravely the revolutionaries can sacrifice themselves for the cause.

I am condemned to death, but you are sentenced to transportation for life. You will live and, while living, you will have to show to the world that the revolutionaries not only die for their ideals but can face every calamity. Death should not be a means to escape the worldly difficulties. Those revolutionaries who have by chance escaped the gallows for the ideal but also bear the worst type of tortures in the dark dingy prison cells.

Yours
Bhagat Singh

(The original in English, now lost, was published in the *New Era*. A re-translation from Hindi has been picked up from *Selected Writings of Shaheed Bhagat Singh*, edited by Shiv Verma.)

55. Letter to younger brother Kulbir; 16 September 1930 (Originally in Urdu.)

Three letters, no. 55–57, to younger brother Kulbir Singh, have been found so far. Two were written in September 1930, on September 16 and 25, and the last one was in 3 March 1931, a parting letter. Kulbir Singh was more grown-up at that time.

Central Jail, Lahore
16 September 1930

Dear brother Kulbirji,

Sat Sri Akal!

As you know that as per the order of the administrative officer, I have been barred from meeting anyone. In the circumstances, we won't be able to meet at the moment and I think that the verdict will be given out very soon. So come to the jail one of these days, and take away my books and some documents from the office of the Jail Superintendent. The verdict and the challan will come within a month's time at the most. In these circumstances, we may meet in another jail, but it doesn't seem possible to meet here.

Send the advocate if possible. I wish to make an important query regarding the Privy Council. Reassure respected mother; tell her not to worry.

Your brother,
Bhagat Singh

56. Letter to younger brother Kulbir; 25 September 1930 (Originally in Urdu.)

25 September 1930
Central Jail, Lahore

Dear brother Kulbir Singhji,

Sat Sri Akal!

I was very sorry to hear that one day you brought dear mother, but were not allowed to meet me and had to return empty-handed. At least you had come to know that the jail authorities would not permit a meeting. Then why did you bring mother along? I know that she is very anxious at the moment, but what's the use of this worry and anxiety? In fact, it causes more harm because ever since I've learnt that she's been crying constantly, I myself feel restless. There is nothing to worry about and it serves no purpose. Everyone must face the situation with courage. After all everyone in the world is beset with a great many problems; moreover when one has not been satisfied even after meetings over an entire year, then how will a few more meetings satisfy one? I have a feeling that after the verdict and the challan, this ban on meeting anyone will be lifted, but supposing that permission to meet anyone is not given even then, what's the use of worrying?

Yours,
Bhagat Singh

57. Letter to younger brother Kulbir; 3 March 1931 (Originally in Urdu.)

3 March 1931
Central Jail, Lahore

Dear Kulbir Singh,
You have done a lot for me. During the meeting, you asked me to write something in response to the letter. Let me write just a few words. Look, I have not done anything for anyone; not even for you. I'm leaving you in a difficult situation. What will happen to you? How will you manage? All these things cause a shudder to run down my spine, but dear brother, take heart; never be afraid to endure hardship. What else can I say? If you could go to America, it would have been good, but now it seems impossible. Work hard at your studies, diligently and patiently. If you can learn a trade, it would be very good, but do everything with Pitaji's[37] advice. As far as possible, live a life of loving each other. What else should I say?

 I know that today a sea of sorrow is welling in your heart. Brother, I think of what you said, and tears fill my eyes, but what can be done; keep courage! My beloved, my very, very dear brother, life is very tough and the world very uncaring. People are very merciless. Only love and courage can take one through. You have to take care of Kultar's education as well. I feel very ashamed that I can do nothing except express my regrets. The

---

37 Father

other letter is written in Hindi. Give this letter to K's sister. All right, namaskar, dear brother, Alvida[38]... Rukhsat.[39]

Your well-wisher,
Bhagat Singh

58. Letter to younger brother Kultar; 3 March 1931 (Originally in Urdu.)

The day the family members had their last meeting with him, Bhagat Singh wrote a touching letter to his younger brother Kultar Singh. On 3 March 1931, at the meeting, Kultar Singh, who was very young at that time, was in tears. Bhagat Singh, too, was overcome with emotion while writing the letter and asked him to be strong and put his heart in his studies.

3 March 1931
Central Jail, Lahore

Dear Kultar,

I was extremely sorry to see tears in your eyes today. There was a lot of pain in your words today; I cannot bear your tears.

Young man, acquire your education with courage and take care of your health. Keep your strength; what else can I say.

Unhe ye fiqr hai hardam naya Tarze zafa kya hai,
He frets about the form the next torture can take

Hamen ye shauq hai dekhen sitam ki inteha kya hai.
And we are impatient to test the limit of cruelty.

---

38   Goodbye

39   Departure; used here in the sense of 'I take your leave'

Dahar se kyon khafa rahen, charkh ka kyon gila karen
Why be displeased with depths, why reproach the sky

Sara Jahan Adu sahi, aao muqabla karen.
Let the entire world be our enemy, come let us face it.

Koi dam ka mehman hun ai ahle-mehfil,
I am but a fleeting visitor, oh sweet company

Charage-sehar hoon bujha chahta hoon.
A lamp of the morning am I, ready to be put out.

Hawa men rahegi mere khyal ki bijli,
The current of my thought will be carried on the breeze

ye mushte-khak hai fani, rahe na rahe.
This body is but mortal; here today, gone tomorrow

All right, bye now! May you be happy, my country; we have to set forth on our journey. Keep your courage. Namaste.

Your brother,
Bhagat Singh

From the proceedings of the trial of the Lahore Conspiracy Case, it seems that some of the letters may still be in the police files of the case, which are still in the custody of the Government of Pakistan. From the letters recovered at Bhagat Singh's father Kishan Singh's house in Lahore, there are references to a letter from Rio De Janeiro (Brazil) in 1928 signed 'AS', taken away by the police, which indicates that Bhagat Singh was in touch with his uncle in exile at that time. Ghadarite revolutionary and late President of Desh Bhagat Yadgar Committee, Jalandhar, Baba Bhagat Singh Bilga, who spent some time with Ajit Singh in Brazil during his exile period, where he himself was Ghadar Party activist said that Bhagat Singh wrote three letters to Ajit Singh, his uncle in exile.

TELEGRAMS FROM JAIL

59. Telegram to Home Member, Government of India; 20 January 1930 (Originally in English.)

Bhagat Singh and some of his comrades had ended their 110 days of hunger strike on 4 October 1929 after concrete assurances from the Government and Congress leaders. However, the British Government officials, not only dishonoured the assurances, but also resorted to oppressing the revolutionaries inside jail, and even in court. Bhagat Singh, and many more, were badly beaten up between 21–24 October in court and in jail; the details of which are available in Srirajyam Sinha's book, *A Revolutionary's Quest for Sacrifice* (Reference 9). A telegram in this regard to the Government of India was followed by the 28 January letter, mentioned above.

20 January 1930

To
Home Member,
Govt. Of India
From Bhagat Singh and other accused

On the assurance of Committee that the issue of treatment with political prisoner is being solved to our satisfaction shortly, we had suspended our hunger strike. Copies of resolutions of All India Congress Committee regarding hunger strike, have been withheld by jail authorities. Congress delegation has been refused permission to meet the accused. Conspiracy accused were badly attacked on 23-24 October at the orders of police officers.

60. Telegram to the Third International on Lenin Day; 24 January, 1930 (Originally in English.)

On 21 January 1930, the accused in the Lahore Conspiracy Case appeared in court wearing red scarves. As soon as the magistrate took his chair, they raised slogans of 'Long Live Socialist Revolution', 'Long Live Communist International', 'Long Live People', 'Lenin's Name Will Never Die', and 'Down with Imperialism'. Bhagat Singh then read the text of this telegram in court, and asked the magistrate to send it to the Third International.

On Lenin day we send hearty greetings to all who are doing something for carrying forward the ideas of the great Lenin. We wish success to the great experiment Russia is carrying out. We join our voice to that of the international working class movement. The proletariat will win. Capitalism will be defeated. Death to Imperialism.

(Taken from *Selected Writings of Shaheed Bhagat Singh*, edited by Shiv Verma.)

61. Telegram to the prisoners indicted in the Kakori Case; 1930 (Originally in English.)

In 1930 itself, Bhagat Singh and his comrades sent a telegram to the prisoners arrested in connection with the Kakori Case, who were on a hunger strike in the Bareilly jail, appealing to them to suspend their hunger strike.

The Special Magistrate
Lahore
Sir,

Kindly transmit the following telegram immediately to Kakori prisoners, who are on hunger strike in Bareilly jail and are said to be in precarious condition, and oblige.

Yours
Bhagat Singh & Dutta

Telegram
Gupta-Bakshi-Sinha and Mukandi Lal
Central Jail, Bareilly

Greatly alarmed and pained to learn of your precarious condition. We apprehend our last telegram has not reached you. We earnestly request you to terminate your struggle in view latest govt. Communiqué re: classification prisoners. As afar enforcement new rules let us all wait together.

Bhagat Singh-Dutta.

(Typed from the original handwritten telegram in Bhagat Singh's handwriting.)

62. Telegram to Berlin Indian Independence Committee; 5 April 1930 (Originally in English.)

On 5 April 1930, Bhagat Singh and his comrades sent a telegram to the Hindustani Committee, Berlin, expressing their grief at the passing of the great revolutionary, Shyamji Krishan Verma. This telegram was published in the 8 April 1930 issue of the *Tribune*. Shyamji Krishan Verma, born in 1857 at Mandvi in Gujarat, spent most of his life abroad, founded India House and the journal *Indian Sociologist* from London in 1905. He moved to Paris in 1907 to avoid prosecution, and died on 30 March 1930 in Geneva, Switzerland.

Please convey our heartfelt condolences to your comrades on the passing away of Shyamji Krishan Verma, one of the flag bearers of Socialist revolutionary movements in India.

His life is a national treasure in the long struggle of Indian liberation which will always inspire the activists of freedom struggle.

5 April 1930

Lahore Conspiracy Case accused

(Published in *The Tribune*, Lahore, on 8 April 1930)

SECTION – 2

POSTERS/NOTICES/ LEAFLETS

1. (63). Poster on the Saunders Killing; 18 December 1928 (Originally in English.)

Two notices-cum-posters, no. 1 and 2, were pasted on the walls of Lahore after Saunders' murder on 17 December 1928. The first one was pasted on 18 December and the second on 23 December, which proclaimed that 'Lala Lajpat Rai's murder at the hands of petty British police officials has been avenged' and thus 'national honour has been protected and will be protected in future too!'

POSTER – AFTER SAUNDERS' MURDER
'Notice'
By Hindustan Socialist Republic Army.
'Bureaucracy Beware'

With the death of J.P. Saunders the assassination of Lala Lajpat Rai has been avenged.

It is a matter of great regret that a respected leader of 30 crores of people was attacked by an ordinary police officer like J.P. Saunders and met with his death at his mean hands. This national insult was a challenge to young men. Today the world has seen that the people of India are not lifeless; their blood has not become cold. They can lay down their lives for the country's honour. The proof of this has been given by the youth who are ridiculed and insulted by the leaders of their own country.

'Tyrant Government Beware'

Do not hurt the feelings of the oppressed and suffering people of this country. Stop your devilish ways. Despite all your laws preventing us from keeping arms and despite all your watchfulness, people of this country would continue to get pistols and revolvers. Even if these arms are not adequate in numbers for an armed revolution, they would be sufficient for avenging the insult to the country's honour. Even if our own people condemn us and ridicule us and if foreign government subjects us to any amount of repression, we shall be ever ready to teach a lesson to foreign tyrants who insult our national honour. Despite all opposition and repression, we shall carry forward the call for revolution and even if we go to the scaffold for being hanged, we shall continue to shout: "Long Live Revolution!"

"We are sorry to have killed a man. But this man was a part of cruel, despicable and unjust system and killing him was a necessity. This man has been killed as an employee of the British Government. This Government is the most oppressive government in the world.

"We are sorry for shedding human blood but it becomes necessary to bathe the altar of Revolution with blood. Our aim is to bring about a revolution which would end all exploitation of man by man.

"Long Live Revolution!"

Sd/- BALRAJ
18 December 1928. Commander-in-Chief, HSRA

2. (64). Another Poster on the Saunders Killing; 23 December 1928 (Originally in English.)

The Hindustan Socialist Republican Army

Notice
No more secrets No more Special Guess
About
The incident of 17 December
JP Saunders is dead!

Lala Lajpat Rai is avenged!!

Under the rules and regulations of the H.S.R.A. (Rule 10th B.R.C) it is hereby notified that it was retaliatory action of none but a direct political nature. The most dastardly attack made on the great old man of India Lala Lajpat Rai that caused his death was greatest insult hurled down on the head of nationhood. And hereby is it avenged!

Further on everybody is hereby requested to abstain from offering any sort of assistance to our enemy the police in finding out our clues. Anybody acting contrary will be severely dealt with.

Long Live Revolution
Balraj
Commander-in-chief
Dated 23 December 1928

3. (65). Leaflet Thrown in the Central Assembly, Delhi; 8 April 1929 (Originally in English.)

'To Make the Deaf Hear' became a catchphrase after Bhagat Singh and B.K. Dutt threw harmless bombs in the Delhi Central Assembly, now the Indian Parliament, on 8 April 1929, quoting Auguste Vaillant, a French anarchist martyr who performed a similar act in the French Parliament in 1893. This leaflet, which was thrown in the Assembly with the bombs and the shouting of slogans 'Inqilab Zindabad'[40] and 'Samrajyavvad ka Nash Ho',[41] became a turning point in the Indian freedom struggle.

"It takes a loud voice to make the deaf hear", with these immortal words uttered on a similar occasion by Vaillant, a French anarchist martyr, do we strongly justify this action of ours.

---

40 Long Live Revolution
41 Down with Imperialism

Without repeating the humiliating history of the past ten years of the working of the Reforms (Montague-Chelmsford Reforms) and without mentioning the insults hurled at the Indian nation through this House the so-called Indian Parliament – we want to point out that, while the people are expecting some more crumbs of reforms from the Simon Commission, and are ever quarrelling over the distribution of the expected bones, the Government is thrusting upon us new repressive measures like the Public Safety and the Trade Disputes Bill, while reserving the Press Sedition Bill for the next session. The indiscriminate arrests of labour leaders working in the open field clearly indicate whither the wind blows.

In these extremely provocative circumstances, the Hindustan Socialist Republican Association, in all seriousness, realizing their full responsibility, had decided and ordered its army to do this particular action, so that a stop be put to this humiliating farce and to let the alien bureaucratic exploiters do what they wish, but they must be made to come before the public eye in their naked form.

Let the representatives of the people return to their constituencies and prepare the masses for the coming revolution, and let the Government know that while protesting against the Public Safety and Trade Disputes Bills and the callous murder of Lala Lajpat Rai. On behalf of the helpless Indian masses, we want to emphasize the lesson often repeated by history, that it is easy to kill individuals but you cannot kill the ideas. Great empires crumbled while the ideas survived. Bourbons and Czars fell.

We are sorry to admit that we who attach so great a sanctity to human life, we who dream of a glorious future, when man will be enjoying perfect peace and full liberty, have been forced to shed human blood. But the sacrifice to individuals at the altar of the 'Great Revolution' that will bring freedom to all, rendering the exploitation of man by man impossible, is inevitable.

Long Live Revolution."

Sd/-
BALRAJ Commander-in Chief

SECTION – 3

COURT STATEMENTS

Two statements made by Bhagat Singh and B.K. Dutt in the Delhi Assembly Bomb Case have now become classical political documents; particularly, the statement made on 6 June 1929 in the session court of Delhi, which on 12 June convicted both of them to transportation for life. After that, they were moved immediately to the Punjab jails on 15 June and, on the way, both of them decided to begin a hunger strike, demanding the status of political prisoners. During the trial, they were provided certain facilities, which were withdrawn after conviction. Bhagat Singh had worked on this statement, so as to make their revolutionary credentials clear to the Indian public and the world at large. He was even asked about the meaning of 'revolution', in reference to the statement, which they themselves wanted to give a more clear explanation for. This session court statement can be compared to Fidel Castro's court statement made in 1953, after the attack on Moncada Garrison on 26 July 1953. That statement is now known as 'History will absolve me' worldwide. In a similar way, Bhagat Singh and Dutt's statement on 6 June 1929 is regarded as the most significant political statement from the Indian revolution and revolutionaries, who claim that they are not just fighting to replace 'white rule' with 'native rule', but are fighting against the exploitative system in general. A.G. Noorani has also referred to this statement with Asaf Ali's claim (Reference 10).

1. (66). Statement in the Sessions Court, Delhi; 6 June 1929 (Originally in English.)

In the court of the Sessions Judge, Delhi
Crown versus Bhagat Singh & B.K. Dutta
Charges S.S.307 I.P.C & 3 & 4 Explosive Substance Act
The written statement of accused Bhagat Singh & B.K. Dutta.

(Read out in the court on 6 June 1929 by Mr Asaf Ali on behalf of Bhagat Singh and B.K. Dutt.)

We stand charged with certain serious offences, and at this stage it is but right that we must explain our conduct.

In this connection, the following questions arise.
1. Were the bombs thrown into Chamber, and, if so, why?
2. Is the charge, as framed by the Lower Court, correct or otherwise?

To the first half of first question, our reply is in the affirmative, but since some of the so-called 'eye witnesses' have perjured themselves and since we are not denying our liability to that extent, let our statement about them be judged for what it is worth. By way of an illustration, we may point out that the evidence of Sergeant Terry regarding the seizure of the pistol from one of us is a deliberate falsehood, for neither of us had the pistol at the time we gave ourselves up. Other witnesses, too, who have deposed to having seen bombs being thrown by us, have not scrupled to tell lies. This fact had its own moral for those who aim at judicial purity and fair play. At the same time, we acknowledge the fairness of the Public Prosecutor and the judicial attitude of the Court so far.

Viceroy's Views Endorsed

In our reply to the next half of the first question, we are constrained to go into some detail to offer a full and frank explanation of our motive and the circumstances leading up to what has now become a historic event.

When we were told by some of the police officers, who visited us in jail that Lord Irwin in his address to the joint session of the two houses described the event as an attack directed against no individual but against an institution itself, we readily recognized that the true significance of the incident had been correctly appreciated. We are next to none in our love for humanity. Far from having any malice against any individual, we hold human life sacred beyond words. We are neither perpetrators of dastardly outrages, nor, therefore, a disgrace to the country, as the pseudo-socialist Dewan Chaman Lal is reported to have described us, nor are we 'Lunatics' as the *Tribune* of Lahore and some others would have it believed.

Practical Protest

We humbly claim to be no more than serious students of the history and conditions of our country and her aspirations. We despise hypocrisy, our practical protest was against the institution, which since its birth, has eminently helped to display not only its worthlessness but its far-reaching power for mischief. The more we have been convinced that it exists only to demonstrate to the world Indian's humiliation and helplessness, and it symbolizes the overriding domination of an irresponsible and autocratic rule. Time and again the national demand has been pressed by the people's representatives only to find the waste paper basket as its final destination.

Attack on Institution

Solemn resolutions passed by the House have been contemptuously trampled underfoot on the floor of the so-called Indian Parliament. Resolution regarding the repeal of the repressive and arbitrary measures has been treated with sublime contempt, and the government measures and proposals, rejected as unacceptable by the elected members of the legislatures, have been restored by mere stroke of the pen. In short, we have utterly failed to find any justification for the existence of an institution which, despite all its pomp and splendour, organized with the hard-earned money of the sweating millions of India, is only a hollow show and a mischievous make-believe. Alike, have we failed to comprehend the mentality of the public leaders who help the Government to squander public time and money on such a manifestly stage-managed exhibition of Indian's helpless subjection.

No Hope for Labour

We have been ruminating upon all these matters, as also upon the wholesale arrests of the leaders of the labour movement. When the introduction of the Trade Disputes Bill brought us into the Assembly to watch its progress, the course of the debate only served to confirm our conviction that the labouring millions of India had nothing to expect from an institution that stood as a menacing monument to the strangling of the exploiters and the serfdom of the helpless labourers.

Finally, the insult of what we consider, an inhuman and barbarous measure was hurled on the devoted head of the representatives of the entire country, and the starving and struggling millions were deprived of their primary right and the sole means of improving their economic welfare. None who has felt like us for the dumb driven drudges of labourers could possibly witness this spectacle with equanimity. None whose heart bleeds for them, who have given their life-blood in silence to the building up of the economic structure, could repress the cry which this ruthless blow had wrung out of our hearts.

Bomb Needed

Consequently, bearing in mind the words of the late Mr. S.R. Das, once Law Member of the Governor General's Executive Council, which appeared in the famous letter he had addressed to his son, to the effect that the "Bomb was necessary to awaken England from her dreams", we dropped the bomb on the floor of the Assembly Chamber to register our protest on behalf of those who had no other means left to give expression to their heart-rending agony. Our sole purpose was "***to make the deaf hear***" and to give the heedless a timely warning. Others have as keenly felt as we have done, and from under the seeming stillness of the sea of Indian humanity, a veritable storm is about to break out. We have only hoisted the "danger-signal" to warn those who are speeding along without heeding the grave dangers ahead. We have only marked the end of an era of Utopian non-violence, of whose futility the rising generation has been convinced beyond the shadow of doubt.

Ideal Explained

We have used the expression Utopian non-violence, in the foregoing paragraph which requires some explanation. Force when aggressively applied is "violence" and is, therefore, morally unjustifiable, but when it is used in the furtherance of a legitimate cause, it has its moral justification. The elimination of force at all costs in Utopian, and the new movement which has arisen in the country, and of that dawn we have given a warning, is inspired by the ideal which guided Guru Gobind Singh and Shivaji, Kamal Pasha and Riza Khan, Washington and Garibaldi, Lafayette and Lenin.

As both the alien Government and the Indian public leaders appeared to have shut their eyes to the existence of this movement, we felt it as our duty to sound a warning where it could not go unheard. We have so far dealt with the motive behind the incident in question, and now we must define the extent of our intention.

No Personal Grudge

We bore no personal grudge or malice against anyone of those who received slight injuries or against any other person in the Assembly. On the contrary, we repeat that we hold human life sacred beyond words, and would sooner lay down our own lives in the service of humanity than injure anyone else. Unlike the mercenary soldiers of the imperialist armies who are disciplined to kill without compunction, we respect, and, in so far as it lies in our power, we attempt to save human life. And still we admit having deliberately thrown the bombs into the Assembly Chamber. Facts however, speak for themselves and our intention would be judged from the result of the action without bringing in Utopian hypothetical circumstances and presumptions.

No Miracle

Despite the evidence of the Government Expert, the bombs that were thrown in the Assembly Chamber resulted in slight damage to an empty bench and some slight abrasions in less than half a dozen cases, while

Government scientists and experts have ascribed this result to a miracle, we see nothing but a precisely scientific process in all this incident. Firstly, the two bombs exploded in vacant spaces within the wooden barriers of the desks and benches, secondly, even those who were within 2 feet of the explosion, for instance, Mr. P. Rau, Mr. Shanker Rao and Sir George Schuster were either not hurt or only slightly scratched. Bombs of the capacity deposed to by the Government Expert (though his estimate, being imaginary is exaggerated), loaded with an effective charge of potassium chlorate and sensitive (explosive) picrate would have smashed the barriers and laid many low within some yards of the explosion.

Again, had they been loaded with some other high explosive, with a charge of destructive pellets or darts, they would have sufficed to wipe out a majority of the Members of the Legislative Assembly. Still again we could have flung them into the official box which was occupied by some notable persons. And finally we could have ambushed Sir John Simon whose luckless Commission was loathed by all responsible people and who was sitting in the President's gallery at the time. All these things, however, were beyond our intention and bombs did no more than they were designed to do, and the miracle consisted in no more than the deliberate aim which landed them in safe places.

We then deliberately offered ourselves to bear the penalty for what we had done and to let the imperialist exploiters know that by crushing individuals, they cannot kill ideas. By crushing two insignificant units, a nation cannot be crushed. We wanted to emphasize the historical lesson that *lettres de cachets* and Bastilles could not crush the revolutionary movement in France. Gallows and the Siberian mines could not extinguish the Russian Revolution. Bloody Sunday, and Black and Tans failed to strangle the movement of Irish freedom. Can ordinances and Safety Bills snuff out the flames of freedom in India? Conspiracy cases, trumped up or discovered and the incarceration of all young men, who cherish the vision of a great ideal, cannot check the march of revolution. But a timely warning, if not unheeded, can help to prevent loss of life and general sufferings. We took it upon ourselves to provide this warning and our duty is done.

(Bhagat Singh was asked in the lower court what he meant by word "Revolution". In answer to that question, he said:) "Revolution" does not necessarily involve sanguinary strife nor is there any place in it for individual vendetta. It is not the cult of the bomb and the pistol. By "Revolution" we mean that the present order of things, which is based on manifest injustice, must change. Producers or labourers in spite of being the most necessary element of society are robbed by their exploiters of the fruits of their labour and deprived of their elementary rights. The peasant, who grows corn for all, starves with his family, the weaver who supplies the world market with textile fabrics, has not enough to cover his own and his children's bodies, masons, smiths and carpenters, who raise magnificent palaces, live like pariahs in the slums. The capitalists and exploiters, the parasites of society, squander millions on their whims. These terrible inequalities and forced disparity of chances are bound to lead to chaos. This state of affairs cannot last long, and it is obvious, that the present order of society in merry-making is on the brink of a volcano.

The whole edifice of this civilization, if not saved in time, shall crumble. A radical change, therefore, is necessary and it is the duty of those who realize it to reorganize society on the socialistic basis. Unless this thing is done and the exploitation of man by man and of nations by nations is brought to an end, sufferings and carnage with which humanity is threatened today cannot be prevented. All talk of ending war and ushering in an era of universal peace is undisguised hypocrisy.

By "Revolution", we mean the ultimate establishment of an order of society which may not be threatened by such breakdown, and in which the sovereignty of the proletariat should be recognized and a world federation should redeem humanity from the bondage of capitalism and misery of imperial wars.

This is our ideal, and with this ideology as our inspiration, we have given a fair and loud enough warning.

If, however, it goes unheeded and the present system of Government continues to be an impediment in the way of the natural forces that are swelling up, a grim struggle will ensure involving the overthrow of all obstacles, and the establishment of the dictatorship of the proletariat to pave the way for the consummation of the ideal of revolution. Revolution is an inalienable right of mankind. Freedom is an imperishable birth right of all. Labour is the real sustainers of society, the sovereignty of the ultimate destiny of the workers.

For these ideals, and for this faith, we shall welcome any suffering to which we may be condemned. At the altar of this revolution we have brought our youth as incense, for no sacrifice is too great for so magnificent a cause. We are content; we await the advent of Revolution.

"Long Live Revolution."

(National Archives Records)

2. (67). Statement in the Delhi High Court; January 1930 (Originally in English.)

This High Court statement was made in reference to the appeal against the conviction of transportation for life. Bhagat Singh, through this brilliant statement, demolished the basis of the Sessions Court judgement and emphasized the importance of their motives. He argued that the motive of action should be the main consideration while judging the offence of an accused.

My Lords,

We are neither lawyers nor masters of English language, nor holders of degrees. Therefore, please do not expect any oratorical speech from us. We therefore pray that instead of going into the language mistakes of our statement Your Lordships will try to understand the real sense of it.

Leaving other points to our lawyers, I will confine myself to one point only. The point is very important in this case. The point is as to what were our intentions and to what extent we are guilty. This is a very complicated question and no one will be able to express before you that height to mental elevation which inspired us to think and act in a particular manner. We want that this should be kept in mind while assessing our intentions, our offence. According to the famous jurist

Solomon, one should not be punished for his criminal offence if his aim is not against law.

We had submitted a written statement in the Sessions Court. That statement explains our aim and, as such, explains our intentions also. But the leaned judge dismissed it with one stroke of pen, saying that "generally the operation of law is not affected by how or why one committed the offence. In this country the aim of the offence is very rarely mentioned in legal commentaries."

My Lords, our contention is that under the circumstances the learned judge ought to have judged us either by the result of our action or on the basis of the psychological part of our statement. But he did not take any of these factors into consideration.

The point to be considered is that the two bombs we threw in the Assembly did not harm anybody physically or economically. As such the punishment awarded to us is not only very harsh but revengeful also. Moreover, the motive of the offence of an accused cannot be found out without knowing his psychology and no one can do justice to anybody without taking his motive into consideration. If we ignore the motive, the biggest general of the world will appear like ordinary murderers; revenue officers will look like thieves and cheats. Even judges will be accused of murder. This way the entire social system and the civilization will be reduced to murders, thefts and cheating. If we ignore the motive, the government will have no right to expect sacrifice from its people and its officials. Ignore the motive and every religious preacher will be dubbed as a preacher of falsehoods, and every prophet will be charged of misguiding crores of simple and ignorant people.

If we set aside the motive, then Jesus Christ will appear to be a man responsible for creating disturbances, breaking peace and preaching revolt, and will be considered to be a "dangerous personality" in the language of the law. But we worship him. He commands great respect in our hearts and his image creates vibrations of spiritualism amongst us. Why, because the inspiration behind his actions was that of a high ideal. The rulers of that age could not recognize that high idealism. They only saw his outward actions. Nineteen centuries have passed since then. Have we not progressed during this period? Shall we repeat that mistake again? If that be so, then we shall have to admit that all the sacrifices of the mankind and all the efforts of the great martyrs were useless and it would appear as if we are still at the same place where we stood twenty centuries back.

From the legal point of view also, the question of motive is of special importance. Take the example of General Dyer. He resorted to firing and killed hundreds of innocent and unarmed people. But the military court did not order him to be shot. It gave him lakhs of rupees as award. Take another example. Shri Kharag Bahadur Singh, a young Gurkha, killed a Marwari in Calcutta. If the motive be set aside, then Kharag Bahadur Singh ought to have been hanged. But he was awarded a mild sentence of a few years only. He was even released much before the expiry of his sentence. Was there any loophole in the law that he escaped capital punishment? Or, was the charge of murder not proved against him? Like us, he also accepted the full responsibility of his action, but he escaped death. He is free today. I ask Your Lordship, why was he not awarded capital punishment? His action was well calculated and well planned. From the motive end, his action was more serious and fatal than ours. He was awarded a mild punishment because his intentions were good. He saved the society from a dirty leech who had sucked the life-blood of so many pretty young girls. Kharag Singh was given a mild punishment just to uphold the formalities of the law.

This principle (that the law does not take motive into consideration) is quite absurd. This is against the basic principles of the law which declares that "the law is for man and not man for the law". As such, why the same norms are not being applied to us also? It is quite clear that while convicting Kharag Singh his motive was kept in mind, otherwise a murderer can never escape the hangman's noose. Are we being deprived of the ordinary advantage of the law because our offence is against the government, or because our action has a political importance?

My Lords, under these circumstances, please permit us to assert that a government which seeks shelter behind such mean methods has no right to exist. If it exists, it is for the time being only, and that too with the blood of thousands of people on its head. If the law does not see the motive there can be no justice, nor there can be stable peace.

Mixing of arsenic (a poison) in the flour will not be considered to be a crime, provided its purpose is to kill rats. But if the purpose is to kill a man, it becomes a crime of murder. Therefore, such laws which do not stand the test of reason and which are against the principle of justice should be abolished. Because of such unjust laws, many great intellectuals had to adopt the path of revolt.

The facts regarding our case are very simple. We threw two bombs in the legislative Assembly on April 8, 1929. As a result of the explosion, a few persons received minor scratches. There was pandemonium in the chamber, hundreds of visitors and members of the Assembly ran out. Only my friend B.K. Dutt and myself remained seated in the visitor's gallery and offered ourselves for arrest. We were tried for attempt to murder, and convicted for life. As mentioned above, as a result of the bomb explosion, only four or five persons were slightly injured and one bench got damaged. We offered ourselves for arrest without any resistance. The Sessions Judge admitted that we could have very easily escaped, had we had any intention like that. We accepted our offence and gave a statement explaining our position. We are not afraid of punishment. But we do not want that we should be wrongly understood. The judge removed a few paragraphs from our statement. This we consider to be harmful for our real position.

A proper study of the full text of our statement will make it clear that, according to us, our country is passing through a delicate phase. We saw the coming catastrophe and thought it proper to give a timely warning with a loud voice, and we gave the warning in the manner we thought proper. We may be wrong. Our line of thinking and that of the learned judge may be different, but that does not mean that we be deprived of the permission to express our ideas, and wrong things be propagated in our name.

In our statement we explained in detail what we mean by "Long Live Revolution" and "Down with Imperialism". That formed the crux of our ideas. That portion was removed from our statement. Generally a wrong meaning is attributed to the word revolution. That is not our understanding. Bombs and pistols do not make revolution. The sword of revolution is sharpened on the whetting-stone of ideas. This is what we wanted to emphasize. By revolution we mean the end of the miseries of capitalist wars. It was not proper to pronounce judgement without understanding our aims and objects and the process of achieving them. To associate wrong ideas with our names is out and out injustice.

It was very necessary to give the timely warning that the unrest of the people is increasing and that the malady may take a serious turn, if not treated in time and properly. If our warning is not heeded, no human power will be able to stop it. We took this step to give proper direction to the storm. We are serious students of history. We believe that, had the ruling powers acted correctly at the proper time, there would have been no bloody revolutions in France and Russia. Several big powers of the world tried to check the storm of ideas and were sunk in the atmosphere of bloodshed. The ruling people cannot change the flow of the current. We wanted to give the first warning. Had we aimed at killing some important personalities, we would have failed in the attainment of our aim.

My Lords, this was the aim and the spirit behind our action, and the result of the action corroborates our statement. There is one more point which needs elucidation, and that is regarding the strength of the bombs. Had we had no idea of the strength of the bombs, there would have been no question of our throwing them in the presence of our respected national leaders like Pandit Motilal Nehru, Shri Kelkar, Shri Jayaker and Shri Jinnah. How could we have risked the lives of our leaders? After all we are not mad and, had we been so, we would have certainly been sent to the lunatic asylum, instead of being put in jail. We had full knowledge about the strength of the bombs and that is why we acted with so much confidence. It was very easy to have thrown the bombs on the occupied benches, but it was difficult to have thrown them on unoccupied seats. Had we not of saner mind or had we been mentally unbalanced, the bombs would have fallen on occupied benches and not in empty places. Therefore I would say that we should be rewarded for the courage we showed in carefully selecting the empty places. Under these conditions, My Lords, we think we have not been understood properly. We have not come before you to get our sentences reduced. We have come here to clarify our position. We want that we should not be given any unjust treatment, nor should any unjust opinion be pronounced about us. The question of punishment is of secondary importance before us.

(Taken from *Selected Writings of Shaheed Bhagat Singh*, edited by Shiv Verma.)

SECTION – 4

ESSAYS, ARTICLES AND SKETCHES

ESSAYS, ARTICLES AND SKETCHES IN VARIOUS JOURNALS

1. The Problem of Language and Script of Punjab; 1923 (Originally in Hindi.)

It was the year 1923. A debate on language was raging in Punjab – the issue being discussed was what the script of Punjabi language should be? Bhagat Singh, who was just sixteen years old at that time, was formulating his views on this topic. He wrote the essay 'Punjab ki Bhasha aur Lipi ki Samasya' (The Problem of Language and Script of Punjab) at the invitation of the *Punjab Hindi Sahitya Sammelan*. The organizers judged it as the best essay and awarded him a sum of Rs 50.

The secretary of the convention, Bhimsen Vidyalankar, preserved the essay and published it in the 28 February 1933 issue of *Sandesh* after Bhagat Singh's supreme sacrifice.

"It is of the utmost importance to be acquainted with the literature of a society and a nation to understand that society and nation, because the consciousness of the life of the society is reflected in the literature of the times."

History bears witness to the above statement. A country moves forward in exactly the same direction in which the literature of the country flows. Literature of a high standard is essential for the rise of any race. As the literature of a country evolves, so does the country's progress. Patriots pay the greatest attention to the literature of the country, whether they are social workers or political leaders. If they do not create new literature, keeping the social conditions and problems in mind, then all their efforts will come to naught and their work would not gain permanence.

Garibaldi may not have got his vast armies, had Mazzini not spent thirty years in creating literature and the literary consciousness of his nation. The resurrection of the Gaelic tongue was done with the same enthusiasm as the resurgence of Ireland. The rulers had thought it necessary to smother the Gaelic language to suppress the Irish, so much so that even small Irish children were punished for keeping a poem or two in Gaelic. The French Revolution would not have happened but for the writings of Rousseau and Voltaire. If Tolstoy, Karl Marx and Maxim Gorky had not spent years producing new literature, then the Russian Revolution wouldn't have taken place, let alone the dissemination and practice of communism.

Similar conditions can be seen in the context of our social and religious reformers. Kabir's literature demonstrates the enduring effect of his teachings. People are entranced even today by his sweet and lucid poetry.

Exactly the same thing can be stated in the case of Guru Nanak Devji. When the Sikh Gurus tried to bind the new religious community together with their teachings, they felt the need for a new literature, and it was with this intention that Guru Angad Devji evolved the Gurmukhi script. There was a paucity of literature in Punjab due to the centuries spent in a constant state of war and the raids by the Muslims. Even the Hindi language had all but disappeared. At this point of time, he adopted the Kashmiri script to espouse a script that was at least Indian. After this, with the efforts of Guru Arjun Devji and Bhai Gurdasji, the *Adi Granth* was compiled. They took this very significant and useful step of creating their script and literature to give permanence to their ideas.

After that, as the situation changed, the impact of literature also kept changing. The conditions continued to vary due to the constant sacrifices made by the Gurus and the suffering they underwent. Whereas we hear the note of devotion and self-oblivion in the teachings of the first Guru, and the emotion of wonderful self-effacement in the following lines –

Nanak nanhe ho rahey, jaisi nanhi doob,

Aur ghaas jari jaat hai, doob khoob ki khoob.

Nanak asks all to be humble as the humble doob[42]
All other grass gets burnt down, what flourishes is doob.

In the same way, in the teachings of the ninth Guru, Shri Teg Bahadur, we find sympathy for the oppressed and a desire to help them –

Baa(n)hi jinhan di pakariye, sir deejiye baa(n)hi na chhodiye,
Guru Teg Bahadur boliya, dharti pai dharm na chhodiye.

Forsake not those you protect; sacrifice yourself but do not forsake them,
Guru Teg Bahadur has said; don't give up your faith on this earth.

After his sacrifice, we suddenly find a militant note in the teachings of Guru Gobind Singhji. When he realized that mere bhakti would not serve the purpose, he began to pray to the Goddess Chandi and turned the Sikh community into a community of worshippers and warriors by synthesizing spiritualism and fighting. We see a new note in his poetry. He writes:

Jey tohi prem khelan ka chaav, sir dhar tali gali mori aav,
Jey it maarg paer dhareejey, sir deejey kaan ne keejay.

If you want to play the sport of love, come to my lane with your head on your palm,
If you have stepped on this path, sacrifice your head but don't fall back.

And again –

Soora so pahichhaniye, jo larey deen ke heit,
Purza kut marey, kabhu(n) ne chhaadey kheit.

---

42   Type of grass

The mark of a warrior is one, who fights for the poor,
Hacked to pieces, yet he never leaves the field.

And then suddenly the worship of the sword begins –

Khag khand vihand, khal dal khand ati run mand prakhand,
Bhuj dand akhand, teij prachand joti abhand bhaanuprambh.

The sword hacks and hews down evil – bough and root; destroys Satan's armies; it holds sway over evil in life's battlefield,
The sword is the extension of the arm; unbreakable, swift; its awesome splendour overshadows even the sun.

Baba Banda, etc. waged constant battles against the Muslims with these feelings, but later we see that when the Sikhs were reduced to being an anarchist band and declared as outlaws, they were forced to keep to the jungles. And at this time, no new literature could be written. No new passion could be infused into the community. Combative capability, courage, the will to sacrifice themselves and an abiding desire to wage a war against the Muslim rulers were instilled into them, but they were not able to envision their future beyond it. That is the reason these warrior groups of people, the 'misals', began to fight among themselves. This lack of a contemporary spirit is sorely felt here. Had a brave warrior and shrewd ruler like Ranjit Singh not been born, there was no noble ideal or thought left to hold the Sikhs together.

There is also something else that has to be kept in mind along with this. The entire body of Sanskrit literature could not resurrect Hindu society, so a new literature was created in a contemporary language. We still feel the effect of this new literature in this modern language. Erudite Sanskrit mantras and ancient Arabic aayats cannot be so powerful for an intelligent person as simple ideas presented in a simple language of his own.

A brief history of the Punjabi language and literature has been presented above. Now we come to the present situation. Swami Vivekananda in Bengal and Swami Rama Tirtha in Punjab were born just about the same time. Both were great men and enjoyed similar stature. Both of them became famous abroad and established the supremacy of Indian philosophy; and though Swami Vivekananda's mission became a permanent institution in Bengal, no memorial of Swami Rama Tirtha is visible in Punjab. Despite a great difference in their ideology, we see deep-rooted connections in the two. While Swami Vivekananda propagated the theory of 'Karma yoga', Swami Rama Tirtha was singing –

Hum rookhey tukde khaaiyenge, bhaarat pur vaare jaaiyenge,
Hum sookhey chane chabaaiyenge, bhaarat ki baat banaaiyenge,
Hum nangey umar bitaaiyenge, bhaarat par jaan mitaaiyenge.

We shall eat dry crumbs, sacrifice ourselves for India,
We shall chew hard grain, accomplish things for India,
We shall spend our lives naked, give up our lives for India,

Tears would often well up in his eyes when he beheld the sunset in America and he would say, 'Now you are going to rise in my beloved India. Give my tears as dewdrops to the beautiful moisture-laden fields of India.' Such a great patriot and God-fearing man was born in our region, but not a single memorial is seen! What but literary backwardness could be its reason?

We experience this at every step. Several great leaders of the stature of Shri Devendra Thakur and Shri Keshav Chandra in Bengal, were born in Punjab, but they were not accorded similar respect and were soon forgotten after they passed away; people like Guru Gian Singh, for example. If we probe into this, then one reason that stands out is the total lack of awareness about, and interest, in literature.

It is quite clear that no nation or race can progress without literature, but the first thing required for it is language and Punjab does not have that. Despite suffering from the lack of a language for such a long time, we have still not managed to reach any decision regarding it. The main reason for this misfortune of our region is that the language issue has been turned into a religious problem. In other regions, we see that the Muslims have completely adopted the provincial language. The poet Nazrul Islam is a shining star in the firmament of Bengali literature. Latif Hussain 'Natwar' is an eminent personality among Hindi poets. The same is the case in Gujarat, but Punjab is unfortunate. Let alone Muslims, here even the Hindus and the Sikhs cannot see eye to eye with each other.

The language of Punjab, like other states, could only have been Punjabi; and the question that is naturally raised is why this did not happen? But the Muslims here adopted Urdu. There is an utter lack of a sense of Indianness in the Muslims; that is why, rather than appreciate the importance of Indianness, they wish to propagate the Arabic script and Persian language. They fail to understand the significance of having one language – and that too, Hindi – for the entire country. That is why they refuse to budge from their stand of Urdu and have taken an isolationist stance.

Then came the turn of the Sikhs. All their literature is in the Gurmukhi script. There is a big smattering of Hindi in the language, but it is chiefly Punjabi. That is the reason the Sikhs have adopted Punjabi written in the Gurmukhi script as their own. They could not let it go under any circumstances. They have turned it into a religious language and have clung to it.

And in the meantime, the Arya Samaj was established. Swami Dayanand presented the idea of the propagation of Hindi all over India. Hindi language became a religious element of the Arya Samaj. One way in which this was beneficial was that the fanaticism of the Sikhs saved Punjabi language, and Hindi carved a space for itself due to the fanaticism of the Arya Samajis.

In the initial days, the religious meetings of the Sikhs and the Arya Samaj used to be conducted in the same place. At that point, there was not much difference between the two, but later, a great deal of misgivings rose between the two due to a couple of sentences in *Satyarth Prakash*, and the two communities began to detest each other. Swayed by this emotion, the Sikhs began to view Hindi with a prejudiced eye. No one paid any attention to this.

It was said later that Mahatma Hansraj, an Arya Samaj leader, held discussions with some people regarding a proposal to adopt Hindi script, saying that he would be able to get the Punjabi language accepted at the University level; but unfortunately, due to a narrow vision and lack of literary awareness people were unable to understand the significance of this proposal and it could not come about. Anyway! At this present moment, there are three opinions in Punjab. The first is the staunch support for Urdu by the Muslims, the second is the support to Hindi by the Arya Samajis and some Hindus, and the third, regarding Punjabi.

It would not be inappropriate if we ponder over each language. Let us first present the viewpoint of the Muslims. They are unyielding supporters of Urdu. And at the moment this is the language that holds sway in Punjab. This is the language of the court; and moreover, Muslims claim that more can be written in less space in the Urdu script. That may be so, but at this moment, the issue of paramount importance is to unite the whole of India. To create one nation it is important to have one language, but this cannot happen overnight. We have to take one step at a time for that. If we cannot decide on one language for the entire country, at least we can adopt a single script. The Urdu script cannot be called complete in all respects, and a major point is that it is based on the Persian language. The imagination of Urdu poets, even if they are Hindi (Indian), soars towards the wines of Iran and the date palms of the Arabs. Kazi Nazrul Islam refers repeatedly to Lord Shiva, Vishwamitra, and Durvasa in his poetry, but our Punjabi Hindi–Urdu poets have not even mentioned them in passing. Is that not an unfortunate thing? The main reason for this is their lack of knowledge of Indianness and Indian literature. They cannot absorb Indianness within themselves, so how can we become Indian through the literature written by them? Learners of just the Urdu language cannot attain the knowledge of ancient Indian literature. This is not to say that these treatises cannot be translated into a literary language like Urdu, but the translation would just about be adequate for a Persian to get an idea of Indian literature.

Regarding these above-written words, we shall only say that when a simple 'Arya' or 'Swarajya' words are written and read as 'Aryaa' or 'Swarajiyaa'[43] then what discussion can there be about profound metaphysical subjects? Just the other day, an Urdu book *Kaumein kis turah zinda reh sakti hain?* (*How can Nations Survive?*) written by Lala Hardyal

---

43 The former words have an unaccented 'a' at the end, whereas the latter words have a long 'aa' sound

M.A. was mistranslated by the official translator who interpreted Rishi 'Nachiketa' in Urdu as 'neechi kutia' (low bitch) and translated it as 'a bitch of low origin'. Neither Lala Hardyal, nor the translator was at fault in this. The fault was of the Urdu script, and the difference in Urdu language and Hindi language and literature.

Indian languages and scripts are used in the rest of India. In such circumstances, should we cut ourselves off completely from India by propagating Urdu in Punjab? No. And the biggest issue is that the writings of the Muslim writers, who are staunch supporters of Urdu, have a preponderance of Persian words. In Muslim newspapers like *Zamindar* and *Siyasat* there is an emphasis on Arabic, which a layperson cannot understand. How can one propagate such a language under these circumstances? We want our Muslim brothers to be Indians even while holding fast to their faith, just like Kemal Ataturk. Only then can India be redeemed. Rather than communalizing the questions of language, we need to see everything from a broad perspective.

After this, we shall consider problem of Hindi-Punjabi languages. Many idealistic souls wish to see the entire world as one nation, a world-nation. This is a beautiful ideal. We must keep this ideal in mind. It cannot be assumed to be attainable as of today; but every step that we take, every action of ours must be guided by a desire to see all races, countries and nations united in an unbreakable bond to create happiness and prosperity. Before that, we need to establish the same ideal in our own country. One language, one script, one literature, one ideal and the idea of one nation in the entire country. But before all these unities can be achieved, it is essential to have one language so that we can all understand each other very well. A Punjabi and a man from Madras need not just stare askance at each other, but try to understand each other's ideas and emotions. And this should not be in a foreign language, English, but rather in Hindi, the language of Hindustan. This ideal, too, will take a long time to be accomplished. The first thing that is required to be done is to create a literary awareness. Not just for a select few, but for the masses. To do this among the common people it is necessary to use their own language. On the basis of this very argument, we can also say that in Punjab, only Punjabi language can make one successful in achieving this target.

Punjabi has not yet succeeded in becoming a literary language and it is not the only language of the entire region of Punjab. The language spoken in central Punjab, written in Gurmukhi script, is what is known as Punjabi. It has not become especially popular as yet and nor has it been able to become a literary or a scientific language. At first, no one paid any attention to it; but now even those who are paying attention to it are frustrated by the deficiencies of the script. The lack of compound alphabets and the inability to use half alphabets, etc., makes it difficult to write all the words properly. Not only that, even compound words cannot be written. This script is even more incomplete than Urdu, and when we have a fully accomplished Hindi script, based on scientific principles, then why this hesitation in adopting it? The Gurmukhi script is only a distorted form of the Devanagri script. Both scripts begin with 'a', 'u' and the 'm', 't', 'tth', etc. All the rules are the same, so how very useful it would be to adopt it at once. Punjabi language will begin to flourish immediately upon adopting a fully accomplished script, and what is the difficulty in popularizing it? The Hindu women of Punjab are familiar with this script. D.A.V. schools and Sanatan Dharma schools teach Hindi. So what could be the difficulty? Those in favour of Hindi would be told that Hindi would definitely become the language of the entire country finally, but it would be very useful to begin to popularize it right away. Only by adopting the Devanagri script does Punjabi become like Hindi. Then there would be no difference, and this is required to educate the common people. This can be done through one's own literature in one's own language. Look at this poem in Punjabi –

O raahiya raahe jaandeya, sun jaa gull meri,
Sar te pagg tere valait di, ihnu phook muataraa laa.

O wayfarer, listen to me as you pass by,
The turban on your head is foreign, burn it; put a match to it.

And the great beautiful poems of Hindi will not be able to make any impact when compared to the impact of this, because these have not still been able to find a place in the hearts of the common people. They still seem somewhat unfamiliar. The reason is that Hindi's base is

Sanskrit. Punjabi has travelled a great distance away from it. Persian has greatly influenced Punjabi. That is, the word for a plural of 'cheez'[44] is not 'cheezein' but 'cheezaan'[45] as in Persian. We see this rule apply right through and through. The point I'm trying to make is that even though Hindi is close to Punjabi, it is quite distant from Punjabi hearts. Yes, to write the Punjabi language in Hindi script and in the attempt to make it literary, it will definitely come closer to Hindi.

Anyway, all major issues have been debated. Now, only one thing remains to be said. Many people feel that Punjabi lacks sweetness, beauty and feeling. This is utterly baseless. Just the other day, the sweetness of the song *'Lachhiye jiththe tu paani doliyaa ugg gaye sandal de bootey'* enchanted even the poet laureate, Rabindra, and he immediately began to translate it into English –

O, Lachhi, wherever you spilled water, sandalwood saplings sprout...

Many other examples can be given. Is the following sentence inferior to the poems in any other language?

Piple de pattyaa ve kehi khadkhad laayi ei
Patte jhade puraane hun rutt naveyaan di aayi aa.

O peepal leaf! Why do you rustle so loudly?
Old leaves have fallen, now the season for new ones is here.

And when a Punjabi sits alone or in a group, then the impact of these lines by Gauhar would be greater than any other language.

Laam Lakhkhaan te karoda dey Shah vekhey ne musafiran koi udhaar denda,
Diney raatin jinhon dey kooch derey, na unhaan dey thhaayin koi aitbaar denda.
Bhaurein behnde gulaan di vaashna tey, na sappa dey muhaan te koi pyaar denda,

---

44 Thing
45 Things

Gauhar samay salook han jyoondya dey, moyaan gayaan noon har koi visaar denda.

I have seen people who have lakhs and crores; no one lends to passers-by,
Those who travel day and night; shift camps, are not trusted.
Butterflies hover on the scent of flowers, no one kisses the hoods of serpents,
O Gauhar, good things are for those alive, those dead are forgotten.

And then,

Jeem jyoondiyaan noon kyon maarna ain, jeikar nahin toon moyaan nu jiyon joga,
Ghar aaye savaali noon kyon ghoorna ain, jeikar nahin toon haththin khair paun joga,
Miley dilaan noon kyon bichhodna ain, jeikar nahin toon bichhadiyan noon milaun joga,
Gauhara badiyaan rakh bund khaane, jeikar nahin toon nekiyaan kamaun joga.

Why kill the living, if you can't bring the dead to life,
Why stare at the mendicant at your door, if you can give him no alms,
Why separate lovers, if you cannot unite separated hearts
O Gauhar, keep your evil indoors, if you cannot earn good deeds.

And now Dard, Mastana, Diwana and several other good Punjabi poets are enriching Punjabi poetry.

It is such a pity that Punjabis have not adopted such a sweet, such an enchanting language. The problem is that they still refuse to adopt it. Each one stands with a religious stick to support his argument. The problem of the Punjabi language and script is how to resolve this tangle. The only hope is that literary awareness is increasing among the Sikhs, as it is rising among the Hindus. Why don't sensible people sit down and resolve this issue? This is the only solution to this problem. Rising above sectarian concerns, the issue can be discussed, and should be discussed; and then amending the language of the periodical *Prem* from Amritsar to make it a bit more literary; Punjab University should bestow recognition upon the Punjabi language. All these issues can be resolved in this way. And as soon as this issue is resolved, such beautiful and noble literature will be born in Punjab, that Punjabi will begin to be recognized as one of the best languages of India.

2. Universal Love; 1924 (Originally in Hindi.)

Bhagat Singh wrote the essay 'Vishwa Prem' (Universal Love) under the alias of Balwant Singh, and it was published in two issues of Calcutta's weekly *Matwala*, (Year 2, issues no. 13 and 14). The two issues were published on 15 November 1924 and 22 November 1924.

It is impossible for humanity to describe the greatness of the king of poetry who envisioned the invaluable idea of 'Vasudev Kutumbakam!'[46] it is the aspiration of one who has experienced such Universal Love.

'World fraternity!' I take it to mean equality in the world (Communism, Worldwide Equality in the true sense).[47]

How noble is this ideal! Let everyone be one's own. No one should be a stranger. How beautiful would that time be when alienation in the world is forever destroyed; the day this ideal is brought into practice - that day one can claim that the world has reached its zenith. How will the day look like when each individual is able to internalize this ideal in his heart? Just imagine!

That day there will be so much strength that even shouting 'Peace! Peace!' will not be able to break the peace. That day no hungry soul will need to scream for food. Trade will be at the zenith of progress, but France and Germany will no longer go to horrible war in the name of

---

46   The whole earth is a family.
47   The words, 'Worldwide Equality in the true sense' are originally in English.

trade. Both America and Japan will be there, but there will be no East, no West. Black and white races will be there, but the Americans will not be able to burn the native black people[48] alive. There will be peace but no need for the Penal Code. There will be the British and the Indians, but there will be no division of master and slave. That day, Mahatma Tolstoy's principle of 'Resist not the Evil'[49] will not need to be shouted from the rooftops, but there will be no evil in the world. That is when we shall have complete freedom. What will such a time be like? Just imagine!

Looking at the present situation, who can believe that such a day will dawn when no one will be afraid of anyone; in fact, people will desist from committing sins because of the voice of their own conscience. If even on such a day we yearn for some imaginary heaven, then we shall say that such a heaven does not exist. Can such a day dawn? This is a problem – a big problem. It is not easy. But what I wish to know is if people are really interested in bringing about such a day? Are the people who talk so stridently about 'Universal Brotherhood'[50] or 'Cosmopolitanism',[51] really concerned about this? It is not enough to say 'Yes'. This is not the proposal that Congress has. This issue needs serious consideration. Are people prepared to offer a sacrifice for it? For such an imagined future, we will have to have an extreme present. For such imagined peace, we will have to spread discord. We will have to sacrifice everything for such castles in the air. We will have to spread total anarchy to establish such a peaceful rule. To draw that blissful world towards us, we will have to inflict tyranny. For that happy time; no, no, for the mere hope of it, we will have to lay down our lives. Are people prepared for that?

We will have to spread the word of equality and egalitarianism. We will have to inflict oppression on those who oppose this. We will have to spread anarchy in those places where rules and empires have been blinded by power and are causing misery to crores of people. Are people prepared for that?

---

48   Red Indians
49   The words, 'Resist not the Evil' are originally in English.
50   Originally in English.
51   Originally in English.

We will have to prepare the entire world to be ready to welcome this ideal. To reap such a promising harvest, we shall have to weed out everything from the fields. The thorny bushes will have to be consigned to the pyre of peace. Stones, pebbles will have to be crushed. We will have to toil very hard. We will have to help the poor to rise. The crushed will need to be shown the path of progress. These false powers will have to be dragged and compelled to stand with us. The arrogance of the arrogant will have to be crushed and they will have to be taught the lesson of humility. We will have to give strength to the weak, freedom to the slaves, education to the illiterate, a ray of hope to the despairing, food to the hungry, homes to the homeless, faith to the unbelievers, vision to the superstitious. Will people be willing to do all this? O Votaries of Universal Brotherhood! Are you prepared to do this? If not, then stop your pretence. We will have to offer you as sacrifice at the feet of the Goddess of Universal Brotherhood, because you are deceivers. If you are prepared, then step into the 'karmkshetra', the field of action, and you shall be tested. Don't hide behind this noble principle, sitting at home, crouching in corners, trembling at the mere thought of the terrible images of the battlefield, avoiding the light of the truth. If you truly desire to bring about this imagined time, then come forward. The first task will be to raise this fallen Bharat. The shackles of slavery will have to be shattered. Tyranny will have to be destroyed. Lack of freedom will have to be trampled into the dust because it lures humanity that the Almighty moulded in His own image, away from the path of justice because of its own weakness.

If the fear of being jailed or hanged still prevents you from following this path despite acknowledging the truth of it, then give up this pretence henceforth.

If the fear that this revolution will lead to great anarchy and great bloodshed, and total strife prevents you from taking this path, even then you are craven, weak, and cowardly. Abandon this pretence.

If discord spreads, so be it; at least there won't be any subjugation. If anarchy spreads, so be it, at least slavery will be abolished. Ah! This conflict will crush the weak. The daily whining will come to an end. No weak shall remain; the mighty will become friends. There will be amity among the strong people. They will feel love for each other and the message of Universal Love will be carried forward.

Yes! Yes! The weak will have to be crushed in one blow. They are accountable to the entire world. They are the ones who are responsible for the spread of conflict. Let everyone be strong, or else they will be ground in the millstone.

Oh! Who is the true son of the soil who wants Universal Brotherhood with his whole heart? Who is willing to give up his happiness for the sake of the entire world?

No slave race has the right even to mention this noble ideal. These words lose their significance the moment they are uttered by the lips of a slave. If a disgraced man, crushed under feet, ground in the dust, says, 'I am a follower of Universal Brotherhood, a believer in this ideal, so I do not avenge these tyrannies', what value can his words have? Who will heed his cowardly words? Yes, if you have strength, if you have energy, if you have the power to trample the great and mighty underfoot, if you are able to lift a finger and grind the arrogance of people to dust, can put to sleep great ruling powers, can crush them into the dust, and then you say, 'We believe in Universal Love so please don't do this', then your words will hold weight – then each sentence that you utter will have value. Then the words *'Vasudev Kutumbakam'* (the whole earth is a family) will also become significant.

Today, you are enslaved, under foreign rule, not free, and your words seem a sham, pretence, rubbish. Do you want to propagate them? If yes, they you will have to follow the one who said, 'He who loveth Humanity loveth God',[52] 'God is love and love is God'[53], who embraced the gallows under crime of sedition; are you prepared to propagate Universal Love as courageously as he did? The day you become a true propagator of this unique ideal, then you will have to step into the battlefield like the true son, Guru Gobind Singh. Who, like a true devotee of Universal Love, saying 'All are the sons of the same Father', like the great soul who sacrificed all of his four beloved sons for the nation, and upon being

---

52 Originally in English.
53 Originally in English.

questioned by the mother, replying simply this; you will have to show patience like him. Can you bear to see someone sacrifice him or herself, or endure unspeakable torture, someone you hold the dearest to your heart, thinking of whom makes your heartbeat race, which you want to keep hidden in your heart? And can you climb onto a burning pyre with a smile before the same dear one, and be able to bid goodbye to the world with a compassionate look? If yes, then come forward for the test; it is time. If there is the slightest hesitation in your hearts, then for God's sake, give up this pretence.

How can Universal Brotherhood and Universal Love flourish till the time this vocabulary of black-white, civilized-savage, ruler-ruled, rich-poor, high caste-untouchable, etc. continues to be used? This message can be delivered only by a free people. An enslaved people like the Indians cannot even mention it.

Then how will the message spread? You will have to muster power. To muster power, you will have to spend all the strength you have earned till now. You will have to endure a lifetime of obstacles like Rana Pratap, only then may you pass the exam. Don't you see a true propagator of Universal Brotherhood, Mazzini, who stays incarcerated at one place on his own for twenty years? Lenin was his supporter; he endured untold hardships. George Washington – the giver of freedom to America – was a believer in Universal Brotherhood; the revolutionaries of France were staunch believers – how much blood they shed! The idealistic Brutus was a follower of Universal Brotherhood, who even assassinated his beloved Caesar because of his love for his motherland, and committed suicide afterwards. Happily and skilfully fighting wars was Garibaldi, who can also get credit for a belief in Universal Love.

A lover of Universal Love is the brave individual whom we have no hesitation in calling an awesome rebel, an uncompromising anarchist – the same Veer Savarkar, who pacing in his lawn thinking about Universal Love, would stop walking on the grass, lest he crushed the tender grass under his feet.

The brave MacSwiney who passed away after 75 days of fasting can take the credit for treading this path; who used to say:

'It is the love of the country that inspires us and not the hate of the enemy and the desire for full satisfaction for the past.' (Originally in English.)

A devotee of the Goddess of Universal Love was the author of *Gita Rahasya* (*The Secret of the Gita*), the revered Lokmanya Tilak. Do you want more? That thin, scrawny man in the loincloth (Gandhi) who could give a delighted chuckle upon being sentenced and say, 'The punishment given to me is too mild and I cannot hope for more courteous behaviour that I have met with', whose poignant tale will have no effect on your stony hearts – a believer in the ideal, he is a Mahatma.

And Lord Rama, who destroyed Ravan and Bali, demonstrated Universal Love by eating the berries which were first tasted by the Bhil woman, demonstrated Universal Love. The one who brought cousins to fight a war with each other, who completely erased the injustice from the world – Lord Krishna – demonstrated his Universal Love by gobbling up the uncooked rice that Sudama had brought for him.

Do you also assert Universal Love? First, learn to stand on your feet. Develop the capability to stand with your head held high with pride among the people of the free nations. Till the time unfortunate incidents like the Komagata Maru Ship keep on happening, till the time you continue to be called 'damn black man', till the Jallianwala Bagh-like horrible tragedies keep happening in your country, till the time you don't react to brave women being dishonoured, till then this pretence has no meaning. What peace, what happiness and what kind of Universal Love is it?

If you truly desire to propagate the ideal of peace and happiness in the entire world, then first learn to react to the insults thrown at you. Be ready to die in order to cut loose the shackles of your motherland. Be prepared to serve a life sentence at the Cellular Jail across the black seas, if you want to set your mother free. Be ready to die to keep your sobbing mother alive. Only then our country will be free. We shall be strong. We shall be able to proudly proclaim the ideal of Universal Love; will be able to compel the world to follow the path of peace.

(November 1924)

3. Youth; 1925 (Originally in Hindi.)

This essay, titled 'Yuvak (Youth)', was published in *Matwala* (Year 2, issue no. 38) on 16 May 1925 under the pseudonym Balwant Singh. This essay is also mentioned in the diary of the editor of *Matwala*, Acharya Shiv Poojan Sahai (Reference 11).

Youth is the spring season in human life. A person can go berserk during this time. He feels the intoxication of a thousand bottles. All the powers bestowed by the Creator spring in this time like a thousand streams. As uncontrollable as an elephant gone amok, as uncontainable as the dark clouds of the monsoon season, as furious as a strong hurricane in an age of annihilation, as tender as a jasmine bud of a new spring, as ungovernable as a volcano, and as sweet as a morning song is the age of youth. The splendour of a radiant dawn, the lustre of a silken sunset, the sweet warmth of the full moon of autumn and the awful midnight of a hot moonless night in the sixth month of the year are contiguous in youth. The season of youth in a human body is like the bomb in the revolutionary's pocket, the loaded revolver under the conspirator's belt, the sword in the hand of a lover of war. God fills in all possible tumult in a skin-and-bone box from sixteen to twenty-five years. For ten years, this tumultuous boat tosses in the middle of a tempest. To look at, the age of youth appears to be more attractive than the dark passionate earth, but it is filled with the horror of an earthquake. That is the reason there are only two paths available to a human being in youth – he can either ascend the highest peak of progress or fall into the deepest abyss. He can be an ascetic if he wants to, or he can become a philanderer. He can become a devta/angel or a demon. He can destroy the world, and he can offer it an assurance of shelter. The world is ruled by the young. History is full of the exploits of the youth. The youth is the lines on the forehead of the war goddess. The youth is the excited war cry of drums proclaiming the glory of a free nation. The youth is the stuff of the banner of victory of freedom. He is as obstinate as the soaring waves of the ocean. He is as dreadful as the first war cry in the Bhishma chapter of the *Mahabharata*, as ardent as the rich kiss of a first union, as fearless as Ravana's arrogance, as steadfast and unflinching as Prahlad's Satyagraha. If you desire a brave man willing to sacrifice himself, ask the youth. It is to his share that the lusciousness of life has fallen. He holds sway over emotions. Despite being ignorant of poetics, he is a gifted poet. The poet too is the honeybee hovering over the secrets of his heart. He doesn't know the definition of the Rasas, but has a truly insightful understanding of it. The youth is a special problem of creation. He is an excellent example of the glory of God's creation. He can sit for hours by the banks of a river at sunset. He can go on gazing, enchanted, at the sun journeying with its crimson rays towards the horizon. He becomes immersed in the soft melody wafting across from beyond. Strange is his life. Marvellous is his courage. Unfailing is his enthusiasm.

He is free of worries; he is careful. If he gets involved in something, to keep awake the entire night is child's play to him, the sunlight in a summer afternoon is the moonlight of spring for him, the rains in the monsoons are showers of flowers in celebration, the stillness of the cremation grounds is the warbling of birds in a garden. If he desires, he can enlighten society and the community, keep the honour of the country, brighten the face of the nation, and even overset big imperial powers. The upliftment of the downtrodden and the redemption of the world are in his hands. He is the most skilled player of this vast stage of this world.

If the sacrifice of blood is needed, who but a youth can give it? If you want a sacrifice, then you will have to look to a youth for it. It is a youth who is the shaper of the destiny of any community. A western scholar has rightly said, 'It is an established truism that young men of today are the countrymen of tomorrow, holding in their hands the high destinies of the Land. They are the seeds that spring and bear fruit.'[54] It means that the youth of today is the maker of a country's destiny. The young are the seeds of the success of the future.

Open the pages of the history of the world; it is full of immortal messages written in the blood of the young. Sift through the descriptions of revolutionary transformations in the world, and one will find only such young people, whom the wise have called 'mad' and 'misguided'. But

---

54   Originally in English.

what cynics can understand, what men of steel those Japanese youths were, who, fired by patriotism, build bridges over moats of forts with their corpses! A true youth embraces death without hesitation, digs in his feet with this chest thrust out in front of rifles, smiles even as he sits on the mouth of cannon, bursts into the national song to the jangle of iron cuffs, and swings on the gallows with a mocking laugh. It is the youth who gains weight on the day he is to be hanged, it is the youth who hums an inspiring mantra as he grinds the millstone in the jail, and he lifts his country out of darkness only by sinking in the darkness of the jail cell. Patrick Henry, the leader of the American youth, once said in one of his passionate speeches, 'Life is a dearer within the prison cell, where it is the price paid for the freedom's fight.' (Originally in English.) He meant that though life outside the jail was precious, life within the four walls of a jail was priceless, because there it is paid as the price of the freedom struggle.

Since the leader is so inspiring, the youth of America has the courage to give this rousing declaration, 'We believe that when a government becomes destructive of the natural right of man, it is the man's duty to destroy that Government.' (Originally in English.) This means that the youth of America believe that it is mankind's duty to destroy a government that denies fundamental rights to people.

O, the youth of India! Why do you lie slumbering in this haze of ignorance? Wake up, open your eyes, look around, the sun is ready to dawn in the eastern sky. Now don't keep sleeping. If you have to sleep, then sleep in the arms of eternal sleep. Why sleep in the bosom of cowardice? Renounce worldly ties of love and affection, and declare:

Farewell! Farewell my true Love
    The army is on the move
And if I stayed with you Love
    A coward I shall prove. (Originally in English.)

Your mother, worthy of your reverence, the most adored, Goddess Durga, giver of food and nourishment, your goddess with a trident, your goddess on a lion, the verdant deity of abundance is weeping bitterly today. Does her distress not disturb you even a tiny bit? May your supineness be damned! Even your ancestors bow their heads in shame at this impotence. If there is any shame in any part of your body, then get up and honour your mother's milk, pick up the challenge of redeeming her honour, take a pledge for every teardrop that she sheds, address her sorrow, and with a free throat, utter – Vande Mataram!

4. The Religious Riots and Their Solution; 1927 (Originally in Punjabi.)

The essay 'Dharmvar Fasad Te unha de ilaj (The Religious Riots and Their Solution)' was published in the June 1927 issue of *Kirti*. After the Jallianwala Bagh tragedy in 1919, the British began a huge propaganda to incite communal riots. This resulted in riots between the Hindus and Muslims in 1924 in Kohat. After this, there was considerable debate on communal riots in the national political arena. Everyone felt the need to end these, but it was the Congress leaders who made an attempt to get Hindu and Muslim leaders to sign a pact to stop the riots.

The condition of Bharatvarsha/India is indeed pitiable today. The devotees of one religion are sworn enemies of the devotees of another religion. Merely to belong to one religion is now considered enough reason to be the enemy of another religion. If we find this difficult to believe, let us look at the fresh outbreaks of violence in Lahore. How the Muslims killed innocent Sikhs and Hindus, and how even the Sikhs did their worst when the opportunity came. This butchering was not done because a particular man committed a crime, but because a particular man is a Hindu or a Sikh or a Muslim. Just the fact of a person being a Sikh or a Hindu is enough for him to be killed by a Muslim, and in the same way, merely being a Muslim is sufficient reason to take his life. If this is the situation, then may God help Hindustan!

Under these conditions the future of Hindustan seems very bleak. These 'religions' have ruined the country. And one has no idea how long these religious riots will plague Hindustan. These riots have shamed

Hindustan in the eyes of the world. And we have seen how everyone is carried on the tide of blind faith. It is a rare Hindu, Muslim or Sikh who can keep a cool head; the rest of them take sticks and staffs, swords and knives and kill each other. Those who escape death either go to the gallows or are thrown into jail. After so much bloodshed, these 'religious' folk are subjected to the baton of the English government, and only then do they come to their senses.

As far as we've seen, communal leaders and newspapers are behind these riots. These days the Indian leaders exhibit such a shameful conduct that it is better not to say anything. The same leaders who have taken upon themselves the challenge of winning independence for their country and who don't tire of shouting slogans of 'Common Nationality' and 'Self Rule... Self-Rule...' are hiding themselves and are flowing on this tide of religious blindness. The number of people hiding themselves is much less. But leaders who join communal agitations can be found in hundreds when one scratches the surface. There are very few leaders who wish for the welfare of people from the bottom of their hearts. Communalism has come like such a great deluge that they are not able to stem it. It appears as if the leadership of Bharat has gone bankrupt.

The other people who have played a special role in igniting communal riots are the newspaper people.

The profession of journalism that at one point of time, was accorded a very high status has become very filthy now. These people print prominent, provocative headlines and rouse the passions of people against one another, which leads to rioting. Not just in one or two places, but in many places riots have taken place because the local papers have written very outrageous essays. Few writers have been able to maintain their sanity and keep calm on such days.

The real duty of the newspapers was to impart education, eradicate narrow-mindedness in people, put an end to communal feelings, encourage mutual understanding, and create a common Indian nationalism. But they have turned their main business to spread ignorance, preach narrowness, create prejudice, lead to rioting and destroy Indian common nationalism. This is the reason that tears of blood flow from our eyes at Bharat's present state and the question that rises in our heart is, 'What will become of Hindustan?'

The people who are familiar with the enthusiasm and awakening of the times during the Non-Cooperation movement feel like crying at this present state. What days they were when they could glimpse independence in front of them – and today! The idea of Home Rule seems like a mere dream now. That is the advantage that the tyrants have got from communal riots. The bureaucracy that had begun to fear for its very existence has now dug in its roots so deeply that it is not an easy task to shake it.

If we look for the roots of these communal riots, the reason seems to be economic. Leaders and journalists went through untold sacrifices during the days of the Non-Cooperation Movement. They suffered financially as well. When the movement ebbed, it led to a lack of confidence in the leaders, which led to the collapse of the business of a lot of these religious leaders. The question of filling one's belly is at the bottom of whatever work is done in this world. This is one of the three principal maxims of Karl Marx. It is due to this maxim that practices like the Tablig, Tanzeem, Shuddhi (Hindu-Muslim communal practices), etc., were initiated, and it is because of this that we are in such a terrible state; in this mess.

If there is to be any lasting solution to all these communal riots, it lies only in the improvement of the economic condition of Hindustan; because the economic condition of the common people is so degraded in Hindustan, that anyone can pay four annas to get another person insulted. Tormented by hunger and sorrow, a person can abandon all principles. It becomes a matter of survival.

But economic reforms are too difficult in the present circumstances because the government is a foreign one and it does not allow any improvement in the condition of the people. That is why people must concentrate all their energy on attacking it and not rest till it is completely transformed.

Class-consciousness is crucial to stop people from fighting each other. The poor workers and peasants should be made to clearly understand that their real enemies are the capitalists, so they must be careful not to fall into their trap. All the poor people of the world – whatever their caste, race, religion or nation – have the same rights. It is in your interest that all discrimination on account of religion, colour, race, and nationality is eliminated and the power of the government be taken in your hands. These efforts will not harm you in any way, but will one day cut off your shackles and you will get economic freedom.

The people who are familiar with the history of Russia know that similar conditions prevailed there during the rule of the Tsar. There were several groups who kept dragging each other down. But from the day the Workers' Revolution took place, the very map of the place changed. Now there are never any riots there. Now everyone is considered to be a 'human being' there, not 'a member of a religious group'. The economic condition of the people was very pathetic during the times of the Tsar and this led to rioting. But now when the economic condition of the Russians has improved and they have developed class-consciousness, there is no news from there about any riots.

Though one hears very heart rending accounts of such riots, yet one heard something positive about the Calcutta riots. The workers of the trade unions did not participate in the riots nor did they come to blows with each other; on the other hand, all the Hindus and Muslims behaved normally towards each other in the mills and even tried to stop the riots. This is because there was class-consciousness in them and they fully recognized what would benefit their class. This is the beautiful path of class-consciousness that can stop communal rioting.

We have received this bit of happy news that the youth of Bharat are now tired of religions that teach mutual hatred and war, and are washing their hands off such religions; and there is so much progressiveness in them now that they look upon the people of Bharat, not from the point of view of religion – as Hindu, Muslim or Sikh – but human beings first, and then as citizens of one country. The birth of such feelings in the youth of Bharat gives us hope for a golden future and the people of Bharat should not worry about these riots; they should rather hold themselves in a state of readiness and always attempt to ensure that such an environment is not created; there are no riots ever.

In 1914-15 the martyrs separated religion from politics. They believed that religion was an individual's personal matter and no one else should interfere in it. Nor should one let religion push itself into politics because it does not unite everyone or make them work together. That is the reason movements like the Ghadar Party were strong and had a single soul in which the Sikhs were in the forefront for going to the gallows, and even the Hindus and the Muslims didn't lag behind.

At present, some Indian leaders also want to separate religion from politics. This is also a beautiful remedy to eliminate quarrels and we support it.

If religion is separated from politics, then we can all come together in politics, even if we belong to different religions.

We think that the real sympathizers of Hindustan will ponder over our prescribed remedy and that we will save India from self-destruction.

We hope that class-consciousness shall also emerge among the workers and peasants of organizations that the Congress party has adopted, because this will hasten the elimination of communal riots.

5. Religion and Our Freedom Struggle; 1928 (Originally in Punjabi.)

The essay 'Mazhab Te Sadi Azadi di jang (Religion and Our Freedom Struggle)' was published in the May 1928 issue of *Kirti*. A political conference of the Naujawan Bharat Sabha was held in Amritsar, in which there was an intense debate on religion among Bhagat Singh and his friends. This essay throws light on this issue. The outlines of the idea of an independent India had begun to be more clearly delineated. The essay makes some concrete suggestions for unity among the people of India.

A political conference was held in Amritsar from 11 April to 13 April along with the conference for the youth. A great deal of debate and discussion centred around two or three points. One of the issues was religion. Though no one would have raised the question of religion, but a resolution was proposed against communal organizations, and those who were supporting these communal organizations under the pretext of religion wanted to protect themselves. This question could have remained buried a little longer; but once it was brought to the public arena, discussion regarding it could take place and the concomitant question of solving the issue of religion also arose. Even in the subject committee of the regional conference when Maulana Zafar Ali Sahib uttered 'Khuda, Khuda!' a few times, the President, Pandit Jawaharlal, asked him to refrain from doing so on that platform. 'If you are a missionary of religion, then I am a preacher of irreligion'. Later even in Lahore a meeting of Naujawan Bharat Sabha was held. Several speeches were made and advice dispensed by some gentlemen who used religion for their benefit and also by those who were afraid to discuss this divisive issue, lest it led to tension.

The most important thing that was reiterated repeatedly and upon which Shriman Bhai Amar Singhji Jhabaal laid special emphasis was that the question of religion should not be touched at all. This was very good advice. If anyone's religion is not creating an obstacle in another person's happiness and peace then why should anyone have a reason to raise a voice against it? But the question that arises is this: what has experience taught us up till now? Even in the last agitation, the same question of religion had arisen and every one had been given complete freedom. So much so that mantras and aayats began to be read from the Congress dais as well. Those days anyone lagging behind in religion was not considered to be good. As a result, narrow-mindedness was on the rise.

The ill effects of this are not hidden from anyone. Now the nationalist people and lovers of freedom have grasped the truth behind religion and think of it as an obstacle in their path.

The moot point is that even if one keeps one's religion a private matter, does it not heighten a feeling of alienation in people's hearts? Does it not affect the aim of attaining complete freedom for the country? At this time, the worshippers of complete freedom call religion a kind of mental slavery. They also feel that telling a child that God is omnipotent and man nothing but a mere statue of clay, is to make the child weak forever. It is to destroy the strength of his heart and his sense of self-confidence. But even if we don't discuss this and go straight to the direct questions before us, even then we see that religion is an obstacle in our path. For example, we want everyone to be equal. There should be no division of class among the capitalists, nor of touchable and untouchable. But Sanatan Dharma is in favour of this discrimination. Even in the twentieth century, if a low-caste boy garlands people like the Pandit or the Maulvi, they have a bath with their clothes on and refuse to grant the 'janeyu', the sacred thread, to the untouchables. Either we pledge to say nothing against this religion and sit silently at home, or we must oppose it. People also say that we must reform these ills. Very good! Swami Dayanand abolished untouchability but he could not go beyond the four *varnas*. Discrimination still remained. If the Sikhs go to the Gurudwara and sing 'Raj Karega Khalsa (May the Khalsa rule!)' and then come out and talk of a Republic, what meaning does it have?

Religion says that the kafirs that don't follow Islam should be hacked down; what would be the result if an exhortation of unity is given here? We are aware that chanting some higher order aayats and mantras can be used to draw different interpretations but the question is why should we not rid ourselves of this entire problem? Religion stands before us like a mountain. Suppose a freedom struggle spread all over the country, armies with guns standing face-to-face, shots are about to be fired and if at that moment someone does what Mohammed Gauri did – as the story goes – and even today places cows, pigs, the *Granth Sahib*, *Veda–Quran*, etc., before us, then what will we do? If we are staunchly religious, we will roll up our beddings and go back home. While there is religion, Hindus and Sikhs will not shoot at cows or Muslims at a pig. Staunch believers would keep rolling in front of their idols like the thousands of priests at the Somnath Temple, while the others, atheists or the irreligious, will get the task done. So what conclusion do we reach? One is forced to think against religion. But let us even consider the argument offered by those in favour of religion, who say that the world would become a land of darkness and sin will increase if religion is absent. All right, let us look at this.

The Russian Mahatma, Tolstoy, writing about religion in his *Essays and Letters* has divided it into three parts:

1. Essentials of Religion, that is, the main tenets of religion – to speak the truth, not steal, help the poor, stay in harmony with others, etc.

2. Philosophy of Religion, that is, the philosophy of birth and death, reincarnation, the creation of the world, etc. In this, a person tries to think and understand things according to his own will.
3. Rituals of Religion, for example the rites and conventions, etc.

This means that in the first part, all religions are alike. All believe in speaking the truth, not lying, living in harmony with others. Some people have called these things *Individual Religion*. There is no question of dissent here. In fact, every human being should follow such noble principles. The second is the question of philosophy. One has to accept that '*Philosophy is the outcome of human weakness* (Originally in English)'. Where people can see, there is no trouble. When things are not clearly visible, then one's brain works overtime and some specific results are dug out. Philosophy is undoubtedly a very important thing because we cannot progress without it, yet peace is equally important. Our elders have said that there is reincarnation, but the Christians and Muslims don't believe in it. Very well, to each his own! Come, let us sit down and discuss this calmly. Learn each others' views. But when there is a debate on the question of transmigration of soul, then the Arya Samajis and the Muslims come to blows. The thing is that both parties lock up their intelligence, and abandon their power to think and debate. They believe that God has written this in the *Veda* in this manner – and that is the ultimate truth. The others believe that in the *Quran Sharif*, God has written this – and that this is the only truth. These people have abandoned all powers of reasoning. If philosophy had no greater power than the personal opinion of an individual and no separate groups are formed due to a belief in a particular philosophy, what is there to complain about?

Now we come to the third thing – the rituals. On the day of Saraswati Pooja, it is necessary to take Goddess Saraswati's idol in a procession and it is also necessary that a band be brought to play music before the idol. But en route there is a mosque on Harrison Road. Islam says that there should be no music in front of a mosque. Now what should be done? (*Civil Rights of a Citizen*) Civil rights decree that one can go through the market playing music, but religion says no. In one religion, cow sacrifice is prescribed and in the other, cow worship. What to do under the circumstances? If religion undergoes a change as soon as a bough of a peepal tree is cut, what should be done? And these minor differences in philosophy and rituals and customs later grow into a *National Religion* and become the reason for the making of separate organizations. The result is before us to see.

So if religion is to mix superstition with the above-written third and second thing, then there is no need for religion. Not tomorrow, rather it should be blown up today itself! If free thought can be mixed with the first and second then may such a religion flourish! But it is necessary to do away with factionalism and discrimination in the serving and sharing of food; words like untouchable will have to be uprooted entirely.

Till the time we let go of our narrow-mindedness and become one, true unity cannot be achieved. So only by following the above-mentioned things can we move towards freedom. Our freedom does not mean merely to escape the hold of the British; it means complete independence – when people will intermingle with each other freely and be rid of mental slavery as well.

6. The Issue of Untouchability; 1928 (Originally in Punjabi.)

At the Congress session in Kakinada in 1923, Mohammed Ali, in a presidential address suggested that those who were referred to as 'untouchables' (the scheduled castes), should be divided into missionary institutions of Hindus and Muslims. The rich from both communities were prepared to donate money to fortify this caste division, and these 'friends' of the untouchables tried to divide them on the basis of religion. Due to all this, untouchability was a hotly-debated issue and Bhagat Singh, too, wrote an essay 'Achhoot da Sawaal (The Issue of Untouchability)' during this period. In this essay, he makes an assessment of the power and the limits of the working class and gives concrete suggestions for the progress of the community. The essay was published in *Kirti* in June 1928 under the pen name of 'Vidrohi'.

In no other country except ours does such a bad state of affairs prevail. Strange and peculiar questions keep arising here. One crucial question is that of the untouchables. The problem is that in a population of 30 crore, there are 6 crore people who are called 'untouchable', i.e., their mere touch will pollute the dharma of the rest. Their entry into temples would displease the Gods. Drawing water from wells would make the water of these wells impure. These questions are being raised in the twentieth century and one is ashamed even to listen to these questions.

Our country is very spiritual, yet we hesitate to give the status of a human being to a person, while the West, referred to as completely materialistic, and has been raising the banner of oneness for centuries. They declared equality as a principle in the American and French Revolutions. Today Russia has resolved to eradicate every kind of discrimination, fulfilling the ideals of first May. We are forever bothered about the being of soul and God, and involved in a strident debate about whether we should grant the janeyu, the sacred thread, to the untouchable or do they have the right to study the Vedas and the scriptures or not? We complain that we are not treated well in other countries. The English government does not consider us at par with the English, but do we have the right to make this complaint?

A Muslim gentleman from Sindh, Shri Noor Mohammed, a member of the Bombay Council has spoken at length about this in 1926:

"If the Hindu Society refuses to allow other human beings, fellow creatures so that, to attend public schools, and if... the president of local board representing so many lakhs of people in this house refuses to allow his fellows and brothers the elementary human right of having water to drink, what right have they to ask for more rights from the bureaucracy? Before we accuse people coming from other lands, we should see how we ourselves behave toward our own people.... How can we ask for greater political rights when (we ourselves) deny elementary rights to human beings?" (Originally in English.)

What he says is absolutely right, but because it has been said by a Muslim, the Hindus will say, 'Look! He wants to convert the untouchables to Islam and assimilate them in their fold.'

If you consider them worse than beasts, then certainly they will embrace other religions where they will be given better rights and where they will be treated like human beings. Then to lament, 'Just see, the Christians and the Muslims are harming the Hindu community!' would be futile.

How true is this statement but everyone is enraged at it. Exactly this anxiety gripped the Hindus as well. Even the Sanatan Dharam scholars have begun to ponder over this problem. At times, those who are known as great revolutionaries joined in. In the conference of the Hindu Mahasabha in Patna, which was held under the aegis of Lala Lajpat Rai as President – an old supporter of the untouchables – a sharp debate began. There were lot of clashes. The problem was whether the untouchables had the right or not to perform yagyopavit, the Hindu ceremony of wearing the sacred thread. And did they have the right to study the scriptures and the Vedas or not? Great, well-known social reformers were incensed but Lalaji made everyone concur; and redeemed Hindu dharma by accepting both these things. Otherwise, just think how shameful it would have been. A dog can sit in our lap. He can roam freely in our kitchen but we become polluted if a human being touches us! Now a great social reformer like Pandit Malviyaji, a great champion of the untouchables, and what not, can be garlanded by a scavenger but considers himself to be impure unless he has a bath with his clothes on afterwards. What a great swindle! Make a temple to worship the God who loves everyone; but if an untouchable enters it, it becomes defiled. God becomes angry. If this is the state of affairs at home, is it seemly to fight for equal rights abroad? Then our behaviour reveals only an extremity of ingratitude. We shun the very people who do the lowliest of work to provide us with facilities. We can worship beasts but cannot make a human being sit next to us.

Today there is a great deal of hue and cry over this issue. Those ideas are being especially discussed these days. The communal feelings may or may not have done any good to enhance freedom struggle in the country, but at least it has given one advantage. Everyone is anxious to increase the numbers of their community to ask for better rights. The Muslims made a little extra effort. They converted the untouchables to Islam and gave them equal rights. This hurt the pride of the Hindus. Hostility grew, which even led to riots. Gradually even the Sikhs thought that they should not be left behind. They also began to baptize them. Hindus and Sikhs fought over the taking off of the janeyu and the cutting of hair. Now all three communities are drawing the untouchables into their fold. So there is a lot of hue and cry. On the other side, the Christians are quietly enhancing their status. Anyway, all this activity is erasing this slur on the country.

And when the untouchables saw how everyone was fighting over them and thought of them as fodder, they reflected on why they should not unite by themselves. Whether the English had any hand in this idea or not is not clear, but it is certain that there was considerable use of government machinery in the propagation of this idea. Organizations like Adi Dharma Mandal are a result of this idea.

Now another question that arises is what the correct solution to this problem should be. The answer to this is very simple. First of all, it should be decided that all human beings are equal and no one is different either at birth or through division of labour. That is, just because a man has been born in the house of a poor sweeper, he will end up spending the rest of his life cleaning the toilets of others and have no right in the world to progress – all this is rubbish. This is the cruel manner in which our Aryan ancestors treated them, stigmatizing them as low-caste and making them do lowly tasks. Along with this there was an anxiety, lest they revolt. Then the philosophy of reincarnation was propagated to show that it was the fruit of their sins in past lives. So what can be done? Spend your days quietly. By preaching patience to them in this manner, they managed to silence the unprivileged for a long time. But they committed a grave sin. They erased humanity from human beings. A lot of oppression and cruelty was inflicted. Now is the time to atone for our sins.

Another problem arose along with this. Abhorrence for essential tasks arose in the minds of the people. We spurned the weaver. Today even weavers are considered untouchables. In the region of the United Provinces, even pallbearers are considered untouchable. This has led to a lot of mess being created. This is proving to be detrimental to the process of progress.

Keeping these communities in mind, we need to neither call them untouchable nor think of them as being so. And the problem would be solved! The strategy that Naujawan Bharat Sabha and the youth conference has adopted is quite a good one. We should ask for forgiveness of those who have been called untouchables and consider them to be equal human beings like us, without being given amrit, without reciting the kalma or being purified, and count them among ourselves, to take water from their hands; that is the right course. And to fight amongst ourselves and not to give any rights to them is not the correct approach.

When the propagation of labour-rights began in villages, the government officials tried to mislead the Jat peasants by saying that pampering the low castes would affect their work adversely. And that was enough! The Jat peasants were incensed. They must remember that their condition cannot improve till the time they want to keep these poor people by terming them as low born and mean, under their thumb. It is often said that they are not clean. The answer is clear – they are poor. Treat poverty. The poor in the high castes also don't stay clean. Even the pretext of doing dirty work cannot be taken because mothers clean the shit of children and don't become untouchable or of low caste.

But this cannot be accomplished till the time the untouchables organize themselves. We consider it to be a very positive movement that they are organizing themselves voluntarily or because they are equal in numbers to the Muslims and thus asking for equal rights. Either end this problem of communal discrimination or give them their separate rights. The duty of the Councils and the Assemblies is to ensure complete freedom to these people to use schools and colleges, wells and roads. Not just by lip-service, but actually take them to the wells. Get their children admitted to schools. But in the Legislature where the Bill against child marriage and religion creates such public outrage, how can they muster the courage to assimilate the untouchables within the community?

So we say that they must have their representatives. They must demand more rights for themselves. We clearly say – Rise, brothers who are called Untouchables and are the real servants of the people! Rise, look at your history. You were the real strength of Guru Gobind Singh's army. It was due to you that Shivaji was able to do so much; due to you that his name lives on today. Your sacrifices are etched in golden letters. You are doing us a great favour by rendering your services daily, adding to the comfort of the life of the public and making life possible, and we people do not understand that. According to the Land Alienation Act, you cannot even buy land by saving money. You are so oppressed that American Miss Mayo describes you as *less than man*. Rise, recognize your strength. Get organised. In reality, without making your own efforts, you will get nothing. Those who would be free must themselves strike the blow. (Originally in English). Those who want freedom must fight for independence. Gradually human beings have developed a habit of wanting greater rights for themselves, but to keep those under them, to remain suppressed. So those who understand the language of punches don't understand words. That is, organise and stand on your own feet and challenge the entire world. Then you will see that no one will dare to deny you your rights. Don't become fodder for others. Don't look at others for help. But beware, don't be trapped by bureaucracy. They don't want to help you at all but to make you their pawns. This capitalist bureaucracy is the real reason behind your slavery and poverty. So make sure that you never join them. Be wary of their wiles. Everything will become all right then. You are the real working class. Workers unite. You have nothing to lose except chains. Rise and rebel against the present system. Gradual, slow reforms will lead you nowhere. Create a revolution with a social agitation and tighten your belts for a political and economic revolution. You are the foundation of the country; the real strength. Awake the sleeping lions! Rise and revolt!

7. Satyagraha and Strikes; 1928 (Originally in Punjabi.)

Bhagat Singh was on the editorial board of *Kirti* and he often used the magazine to air his views on various topics. In June 1928, he wrote on satyagraha and strikes.

Satyagraha

Life again seems to have been infused into Hindustan in 1928. On the one hand there are general strikes and on the other, preparations are underfoot for Satyagraha. These are very good signs. The biggest Satyagraha is being held by the peasants of Bardoli (in Gujarat). After every thirty years taxes are revised and every time the tax on the land is raised. The same thing happened this year as well and the tax has been hiked. What are people to do? The poor peasant in any case is not able to fill his belly and how can he pay 22% tax more than before? Preparations were made for Satyagraha. Mahatma Gandhi corresponded with the Governor of Punjab to try and get the tax reduced, but Sir, this government is not about to bend only through letters. It had no effect. The people had to go on a Satyagraha. Even earlier, on a few occasions, the peasants had gone on a Satyagraha in Gujarat and defeated the government. Earlier, in 1917-18 the crop had rotted due to excessive rains and was not even worth one fourth of the price of the normal crop. The law stated that tax would not be collected if the crop was less than six annas worth in a rupee and it would be collected along with the next year's tax. That year when the people protested that they did not have even four annas worth of crop, the government did not heed their word. Then Mahatma Gandhiji took the matter into his hands and held a meeting. He explained to the people that if they refused to pay the tax their land would be confiscated, and asked them if they were prepared for that. The people kept quiet and the Satyagraha leaders from Bombay became upset and got up to leave. But then an old farmer got up and said that they would endure everything, and then the others also began to concur with him. Satyagraha began. The government began to confiscate the land and property, but after two months, the government was forced to blink first and accede to the conditions set by the landlords.

The second Satyagraha took place in 1923-24, when Mahatmaji was in jail. The first time 600 villages had taken part. This time the tax of 94 villages was raised and these villages went on Satyagraha. A punitive tax was imposed on them. There was a law that no property could be attached after sunset and the peasants would lock up their houses early in the morning and leave, so the police would not find a single person as a witness. Finally, the government got fed up and revoked the tax. This time the Satyagraha has begun in Bardoli. In 1921-22 intense preparations had been made in Bardoli to Satyagraha for freedom. All a game of chance! All preparations went to naught.[55] Anyway, why brood over the past now? Now the government fixed the tax in that area. The poor farmers! Land tax was raised by 22 percent. A lot of protests took place, but was the government about to listen? Work began under the leadership of Shri Vallabh Bhai Patel and the farmers refused to pay the tax. Now all the Recovery Officers and government officials have gathered together in Bardoli area. They are doing whatever they can to misguide these people. Property is being attached; orders are being given to confiscate land. But there is no one to carry the stuff. These days there is a lot of activity there but one interesting thing is that everything is being done very peacefully. The officers, who had come to trouble the farmers, are being dealt with very cordially. Earlier they did not get food and water, now the Headman said that they must be given food and water. One day four containers were impounded from the liquor shop, but there was no one to carry them. When the officer said, "I'm very thirsty; at least give me some water," then immediately a volunteer satyagrahi brought a bottle of soda for him. So the action is on at great speed, but very peacefully. There are high hopes that the government will bow down finally.

The other place where the Satyagraha is to take place is Kanpur. There were Hindu–Muslim riots in the last few days in Kanpur. Later a disciplinary force was put on duty. A few days ago, Shri Ganesh Shankarji Vidyarthi, a member of the Kanpur Council and the editor of the newspaper *Pratap*, received a letter from a magistrate that he should prepare a list of all employees with details of their designations and salary, because punitive tax was to be collected. But Vidyarthiji wrote back to say that he was not prepared to pay any tax; nor would he render any assistance in this task because it was the police that was responsible for the riots. The people should not be punished for the police's crime. The people asked Vidyarthiji, 'What should we do?' and he answered,

---

55   Reference seems to be on the withdrawal of the 1921 Non-Cooperation movement by Mahatma Gandhi after the Chauri-Chaura incident.

'There will be trouble, a lot of damage will be done, but we should not pay this unreasonable tax.' Processions were held. 7000 people signed a petition that they would not pay the tax and sent it to the government. Preparations are being made.

The third place is Meerut. There also the land tax was revised and the tax was raised. Satyagraha has been proclaimed there as well.

Even in Punjab signs of something similar are visible. The crops in Sheikhupura and Lahore districts have been ruined due to hailstorms. There is hardly any harvest, so how can they pay the tax? But the wise and intelligent people of this region are speaking a different language – 'Let not the "disreputable" people of the Congress give speeches to the farmers, lest the government gets annoyed.' Such things are happening, but it should be remembered that 'those who understand the language of punches, don't understand words'. The British understand only the language of money and to expect that they would voluntarily take back the tax! Till when will this illusion remain?

Strikes

On the one hand Satyagraha is making waves, and on the other, strikes are playing a no less important role. It is a very happy thing that there is life again in the nation and the war of the peasants and the workers has begun for the first time. This will impact the forthcoming movement. These are really the people who deserve freedom. The peasant and the worker demand food and their demand will not be met till one has attained complete freedom. They cannot stop at the Round Table Conference or any other such thing. Anyway!

These days, the Liluah Railway Workshop, the Tata Mills in Jamshedpur, the sweeper class in Jamshedpur and the textile mills in Bombay have gone on strike. In fact, the main demands of most people are the same. Low wages, gruelling work and bad treatment. The poor eke out an existence as best they can under the circumstances, but it finally becomes unendurable. Today there are about a lakh and a half people on strike in Bombay. Only one mill is functioning. The fact is that new looms have been bought; in which one person has to work on two looms and thus has to put in double the effort. The demands include raising the wages of such workers specially, but also ask for an increase in the salaries of all the workers and a stipulation of not more than 8 hours of work. These days, strikes are popular. The Jamshedpur mill workers have similar demands. The strikes are on the rise there as well. The scavengers are on strike and the entire city is in a mess. If we do not allow these brothers who serve us the maximum to come close to us, cast them off calling them 'scavenger-scavenger' and take advantage of their poverty, and make them work for very low wages, and even without wages! Great! Finally these people too would finally rise against this. They can bring the people, especially in the cities, to their knees in just a couple of days. Their awakening is a happy development. Some people were fired from the Liluah Workshop and there was some issue regarding wages, so they went on strike. Later it was declared that the posts of several thousands of workers would be abolished and they would not be taken back even after the end of the strike. This created a sensation. But the strike is going strong. Gentlemen like Spratt are working very hard. People should support them in every way and put an end to the efforts being made to break the strike. We want that all the peasants and workers should unite and fight for their rights.

8. Students and Politics; 1928 (Originally in Punjabi.)

In July 1928, Bhagat Singh wrote this article 'Students and Politics' in Punjabi in *Kirti*.

A lot of noise is being made saying that students should not take part in political activities. The Punjab government's stand is most peculiar. Students are being made to sign an agreement that as a condition for admission in the college, they would not engage in political activities. On top of this, it is our misfortune that Manohar Lal, elected by the people, is now the Education Minister, who sends a circular to schools and colleges, decreeing that anyone studying or teaching shall not participate in political activities. A few days ago in Lahore, where the Students Union was celebrating the Student Week, Sir Abdul Qadir and Professor Ishwar Chandra Nanda emphasized that students should not get involved in politics.

Punjab is known in the political field as the most negative *politically backward*. What is the reason for this?

Have the sacrifices made by Punjab been too few? The reason is clear that our educated people are complete fools. Today, after reading the proceedings of the Punjab Council meeting, one has no doubts about the fact that our education system is rotten and useless, and young students, uncaring about the world around them, do not participate in national events. Nor do the students have any knowledge about such things. After completing their college education, only a few of them study further, but they talk in such an immature manner that one has no option but to bemoan such childishness. An attempt is being made today itself to make idiots out of the youth who will hold the reins of the country in the future. We should be able to understand the consequence of this. We agree that the main purpose for a student is to gain an education; they should direct all their energies to it, but is it not a part of education to develop the capacity to reflect upon the conditions in the country and think of ways to improve it? If not, then we consider such education as useless, which should be acquired only to get a clerical job. What is the use of such education? Some over-clever people say,

'Kaka, you may certainly study and think about politics, but don't take any practical part in it. You will prove to be more beneficial to your nation by getting greater competence.'

This sounds beautiful but we tell you, this is only superficial talk. The following anecdote makes it clear. One day a student was reading a book, *An Appeal to the Young* by Prince Kropotkin. A learned Professor asked, "Which book is this? And this seems to be some Bengali name." The boy answered, 'Prince Kropotkin is very well known. He was a scholar in Economics.' It was very essential for every Professor to be familiar with this name. The student even laughed at the Professor's lack of knowledge. And then he added, "He was a Russian." That was enough. "Russian!" Catastrophic! The Professor said, "You are a Bolshevik because you read political books. I will immediately report to the Principal!"

Look at the Professor's ability. Now what is there for those poor students to learn from such people? What can those youths learn in such a situation?

The other thing is – what is practical politics? To welcome and listen to the speeches of Mahatma Gandhi, Jawaharlal Nehru and Subhas Chandra Bose is practical politics, but what about welcoming the Commission or the Viceroy? Is that not the other side of politics? Anything concerned with governments and nations would be considered a part of the political field. Would this be politics or not? Will it be said that the government would be pleased with this but displeased with that? Then the question is of the pleasure or displeasure of the government. Should students be taught the lesson of sycophancy right from birth? What we think is that till the time Hindustan/India is ruled by foreign thugs, the loyal are not loyal but traitors, not human beings, but beasts, slaves to their bellies. So how can we say that the students should learn the lesson of loyalty?

Everyone agrees that at this time Hindustan needs people who will sacrifice everything they have – body, mind and soul – to the country and shower everything in life like madmen upon their country. But can we find such people among the older people? Will people entangled in family and worldly affairs be able to come out? Only those young people can get involved who are not caught in any webs and students and young people can think of this before getting entangled, only if they have acquired some practical knowledge. If they have done more than just cramming for the Maths and Geography exams.

Was it not politics, when all the students in England left colleges to fight against Germany? Where were our advisors then to instruct them – 'Go, go and get an education.' Today, will the students of National College Ahmedabad who are helping the Bardoli satyagrahis remain immature? Let us see how many competent people Punjab University produces as compared to them? It is the youth in all countries, who win freedom for their country. Can the youth of Hindustan save their identity and that of their country by staying indifferent? The youth cannot forget the tyrannies inflicted upon the students in 1919. They also understand that there is a need for a great revolution. Let them study; certainly let them study. But let them also acquire knowledge about politics and jump into the fray and devote their lives to it, when the need arises. Offer their lives to this cause. There seems to be no other way.

～

9. New Leaders and their Different Ideas; 1928 (Originally in Punjabi.)

In this essay published in *Kirti* in July 1928, Bhagat Singh compares the ideas of Subhas Chandra Bose and Jawaharlal Nehru, appreciating the rationality of Nehru more than the emotionality of Subhash Chandra Bose.

A great deal of disappointment and despair spread among the people after the failure of the Non-Cooperation Movement. Hindu–Muslim riots broke their remaining courage. But when awareness spreads in the countries once, the countries don't sleep. After a few days, they rise with great enthusiasm and launch an attack. Today, Hindustan is energized once again. Hindustan is gaining strength again. India is awakening again. Though a great movement is not visible, the foundations are definitely being strengthened. Several new leaders with new ideas are coming forward. This time it is the young leaders who are gaining visibility in the eyes of the patriotic, and there are active youth movements in the country. Eminent leaders are being pushed behind, despite being well-known. At the moment, leaders who have come forward are Bengal's revered Shri Subhas Chandra Bose and the respected Pandit Jawaharlal Nehru. These are the only two leaders who are visible today in Hindustan and are especially participating in the movements of the youth. Both of them are staunch supporters of freedom for Hindustan. Both are sensible men and true patriots. But there is a great deal of difference in their ideas. One of them is called a votary of Bharat's ancient culture, and the other is known as a true pupil of the West. One is called a soft-hearted sensitive man and the other a staunch revolutionary. In this essay we shall present to the people their differing ideas, so that the people can appreciate the difference between them and can reflect upon them for themselves. But before elucidating the viewpoints of both of them, it is also important to present another person who is a lover of freedom as much as they are, and a special personality in youth movements – Sadhu Vaswani; even if he's not as well-known as the more popular names in the Congress, even if he has no special place in the country's political field, he exerts influence on the youth of the country, who have to take the reins of the country in their hands tomorrow. 'Bharat Yuva Sangh',[56] a movement begun by him, has a powerful impact on the youth. His ideas are completely novel. His ideas can be summed up in a few words – 'Back to the Vedas'.[57] Arya Samaj was the first to raise this slogan. The basis for this ideology is that God has poured in all the wisdom of the world into the Vedas. There can be no further evolution. So the world hasn't gone beyond, nor can it go beyond whatever progress our Hindustan had made in various fields. Anyway, people like Vaswani had faith in this. That's why at one place he says:

"Our politics, until now, sometimes cites the examples of Mazzini and Voltaire as our ideals or has occasionally learnt lessons from Lenin and Tolstoy. Although they should know that they have even greater ideals before us – our ancient rishis." He believed that our country had reached the pinnacle of progress at least once, and today we have no need to go any further, in fact we need to return to that.

He is a poet. His poetic expression is evident everywhere in his thoughts. Moreover he is a great devotee of religion. He wishes to propagate the religion of 'Shakti' or power. He says, Our "urgent" need is Shakti![58] At this stage we desperately need power." He does not use the word 'Shakti' only for power; he has faith in a kind of Devi; a faith in divine attainment. He says like a very passionate poet –

"For in solitude have communicated with her, our admired Bharat Mata, and my aching head has heard voices saying... The day of freedom is not far off. ... Sometimes indeed a strange feeling visits me and I say to

---

56 Originally written in English as 'Order of the Young'.

57 Originally in English.

58 Originally in English.

myself, 'Holy, holy is Hindustan.' For still is she under the protection of her mighty Rishis and their beauty is around us, but we behold it not."[59]

This is the lament of a poet; he bursts out like a madman or a devotee – "Our Mother is great. She is very powerful. Who has been born who can defeat her?" In this vein, he carries on flowing on a tide of emotion –

"Our national movement must become a purifying mass movement if it is to fulfil its destiny without falling into class war – one of the dangers of Bolshevism."[60]

Just by mouthing words that one should go to the poor, or towards the villages, give them free medical aid, etc., they think that their job is done. He is a romantic poet. No specific meaning can be attributed to his poetry, but it can enthuse the heart. Apart from the cacophony of our ancient civilization he has no other programme. He offers nothing for the minds of our youth. He only wants to fill the hearts with emotion. He has a great influence over the youth; and this is on the rise. These are his summarized and conservative thoughts that we have described above. Despite his ideas not having a direct effect in the political field, they wield considerable influence. Especially because these thoughts are being propagated among the youth; the young people who are to move ahead to the future.

Now we come to the thoughts of Shri Subhas Chandra Bose and Shri Jawaharlal Nehru. In the past few months, he has been made president of several conferences, and he presented his views before the people. The government considers Subhas Babu to be a member of a revolutionary group, and that is why he was kept in confinement under the Bengal Ordinance. He was released and became the leader of a radical faction. He considers complete freedom to be the ideal for India and in his presidential address at the Maharashtra Conference he promoted this proposal.

Pandit Jawaharlal Nehru is the son of Pandit Motilal Nehru, the leader of the Swaraj Party. He has cleared his Barrister's degree. He is very learned. He has toured Russia. He is also a member of the radical

---

59   Originally in English.
60   Originally in English.

group, and it is with his support and that of his friends, that a resolution for 'Complete Independence' was passed in the Madras Conference. Even in the Amritsar Conference, he emphasized the same thing. But even then, there is ample difference in the views of both these gentlemen. The difference in their views became plain to us from their speeches during the Amritsar and Maharashtra Conference. But a lecture in Bombay later made it absolutely clear. Pandit Jawaharlal Nehru was the president of this conference and Subhas Chandra Bose delivered a speech. He is a very emotional Bengali. He began the speech by saying that Hindustan has a special message for the world. It will give the world spiritual education. Anyway, he began in a very enthused manner, 'Look at the Taj Mahal in the moonlight and imagine the greatness of the heart, whose vision resulted in this.' Think, a Bengali novelist has written that they are our teardrops frozen into stone. He also exhorts one to return to the Vedas. In his speech in Poona, he spoke about 'Nationalism' and said that internationalist's think of nationalists as narrow-minded, but this is an error. The idea of Hindustani Nationalism is different. It is neither narrow-minded, nor motivated by selfish interests, nor is it tyrannical because its base is 'Satyam Shivam Sundram', that is, 'Truth, Goodness and Beauty'.

This is the same romanticism. Sheer emotionalism. And along with it, he too has a great deal of faith in our ancient civilization. In every little thing he glimpses the greatness of the ancient age. In his view, Republicanism is not a new concept. He says that Republics and Democracy[61] are old concepts in Hindustan. He goes to the extent of saying that even (Communism) is not a new thing in Hindustan. Anyway, the thing that he emphasized the most in his speech that day was that Hindustan has a special message for the world. Pandit Jawaharlal's ideas are completely different. He says–

'Whichever country one visits, believes that she has a special message for the world. England claims to be the custodian to teach civilization to the world. I don't see anything special about my country. Subhas Babu has a lot of faith in such talk.' Jawaharlal says–

---

61   Originally in English.

"Every youth must rebel. Not only in the political sphere, but in the social, economic and religious spheres also. I have not much use for any man who comes and tells me that such and such thing is said the Koran. Everything unreasonable must be discarded even if they find authority for it in the Vedas and Koran."[62]

These are the views of a revolutionary and Subhas's views are that of a rebel. In the views of one of them, our ancient heritage is very good and, in the views of the other, one should revolt against it. One is called emotional, and the other, a revolutionary. At one point, Panditji says –

To those who still fondly cherish old ideas and are striving to bring back the conditions which prevailed in Arabia 1300 years ago or in the Vedic age in India. I say, that it is inconceivable that you can bring back the hoary past. The world of reality will not retrace its steps; the world of imagination may remain stationary.'[63]

And that is why he feels the need for a revolution.

Subhas Babu is in favour of complete independence because he says that the English inhabit the West and we, the East. Panditji says that we have to establish our rule and change the social system. For that we must strive to win complete and total freedom.

Subhas Babu has sympathy for the workers and wishes to improve their condition. Panditji wants to bring about a revolution and change the entire system. Subhas is sensitive – for the heart. He's giving a lot to the youth, but only for the heart. The other is a revolutionary, who is giving plenty for the head along with the heart.

"They should aim at Swaraj for the masses based on socialism. That was a revolutionary change which they could not bring about without revolutionary methods ... Mere reform or gradual repairing of the existing machinery could not achieve the real proper Swaraj for the General Masses."[64]

This is an accurate picture of their views. Subhas Babu considered it necessary to pay attention to international politics only till world

---

62 Originally in English.
63 Originally in English.
64 Originally in English.

politics was concerned with the question of the security and development of Hindustan. But Panditji has traversed beyond the narrow circle of nationalism and entered a wider field.

Now the issue is that we have both points of view before us. Which side should we bend towards? A Punjabi newspaper has eulogized about Subhas and, about Panditji it says that such revolutionaries beat their heads against stone walls and die. One should keep in mind that Punjab has always been a very emotional region. People become enthused very quickly and fall flat like froth equally swiftly.

Perhaps Subhas is not offering any mental stimulus, apart from some food for the heart. Now the need is that the youth of Punjab should ponder and reflect upon these revolutionary ideas and reinforce them in their minds. At this point in time, Punjab is in dire need of mental stimulus and this is available only with Pandit Jawaharlal. This does not mean that we should follow him blindly. But as far as ideas are concerned, at this time the Punjabi youths should follow him so that they can learn the true meaning of revolution, the need for revolution in Hindustan, the place of revolution in the world, etc. After proper reflection, the young people should evolve their own ideas so that even in times of disappointment, despair and defeat, they should not get shaken and can stand alone if need be, to face the world. Only such people can make the revolution succeed.

10. Lala Lajpat Rai and the Youth; 1928 (Originally in Punjabi.)

Lala Lajpat Rai has, for some reason, from the very beginning been against the youth movements. He imbibed his ideal of patriotism from the great Giuseppe Mazzini of Italy. Mazzini was a great admirer of the youth and used to say that it is the youth that carries the burden of great tasks; their voice carries magic. He felt that they are able to prepare the public for freedom struggle instantly. It is surprising that someone who professes such a personality as his ideal, then acts completely contrary to it. Why dig up the past of 1907–08? Some contemporary incidents are sufficient.

In the last Council Elections, Lalaji abandoned the Congress and began to oppose them and his talk during this period did not behove him. At this, some sensitive young men voiced their opinion against him. To avenge that, Lalaji openly declared in his lectures that these young men were very dangerous and supporters of a revolution and wanted a leader like Lenin. He said that he didn't have the strength to become Lenin. He also said that if these young men got a job for even Rs 50, they would subside flat like froth. What does this mean? Did Lenin have only such young people with him who would desert him for a paltry sum? Was this Lenin's status? Otherwise why was something like this said? Only because Lalaji, on the one side, was inciting the government to take strong action against these men and, at the same time, he was also trying to demean these men in the eyes of the public.

Every person has a right to criticize another person or an activity or a thought with good intentions. But to deliberately misrepresent someone's views, spread canards and try to harm someone is inappropriate for everyone. It may be Lala Lajpat Rai or some anonymous youth. Many such opportunities came after that election, but there is no need to enumerate them.

Lalaji has recently written another essay. Actually it was written in the context of 'Country League' that we have mentioned in the previous issue; but it referred to the youth. Lalaji expounds that people should be wary of the movements led by the hot-headed youth of today. They are supporters of an epoch changing revolution and their publicity is dangerous for property! Since they propagate communist ideas, this is dangerous for the national movement because this can cause class war. Finally he says that this has begun due to incitement by some mischievous foreign elements. These foreigners want to sow seeds of discord in our national movement, which is why they are very dangerous. Along with this he also believes that this kind of propaganda will make the propertied sections join the government. Referring to these propagandist young men as misguided, incited by foreign elements, mischievous, and greedy, he concludes by saying that he had complete faith in Pandit Jawaharlal Nehru. Whatever he is doing or saying is only out of a good intention and astuteness. Wonderful! Pandit Jawaharlal Nehru, whose thoughts were greatly influenced by Russia, who began to propagate these ideas after returning from there; there is no doubt about his intentions. He is not speaking the language of a foreign element, in fact, it is considered well-intentioned; but those poor souls who have never been out of the country are in the grip of foreign propaganda! Great! Very great! The truth is that Jawaharlal Nehru's status has gone up considerably. His name is under consideration for the post of President of the Congress, and it is hoped that he would take over as President very soon. There is a danger of getting a smarting answer back if one writes anything against him, but for anonymous young men, one can say whatever one likes.... What shall we say about this attempt to trap them into difficulties? This is not seemly for Lalaji. Anyway, let him do what he pleases. Now we would like to answer some of the issues raised by him.

First of all, we want to state that no foreign element is misguiding us. The youth is not talking in this manner because they have been incited by anyone but because they have begun to experience these things within the country. Lalaji himself is a great man. He travels by the first or the second class. How would he know the people who travel in the third class? How would he know who endures kicks in the third class waiting rooms? He sits in a motor car and passes through thousands of villages, laughing and joking with his friends. How would he know what thousands of people go through? Shall we today tell the author of the book *Unhappy India* the miserable condition of crores of starving people? After seeing those crores of people who toil with blood and sweat night and day and yet remain hungry, is there still a need for someone to come from outside and tell us to find a way to fill their bellies? When we see the peasants work in the heat, cold, rain, sun, hot loo winds and foggy day and night. But those poor people make do with dry crumbs – and are burdened by debt. Don't we burn with agony then? Does not a fire rage in our hearts? Do we still need someone to come and tell us that we should try to change this system? When we daily watch the workers die of hunger and the parasites sit and gorge on food, can we not feel the ills of this economic and social system? When we see that day by day the crime rate is on the increase, the condition of the people is deteriorating every day, then do we need outside preachers who can come and tell us that we need a revolution... crores of people whom we have set apart from us calling them untouchables, does their miserable condition not evoke anger? These crores of people could bring so much progress to the world, they could have served the people, but today we treat them as a burden. Is not a revolution needed for amelioration of their condition, to make them fully human and to get them to wells for water? Was there no need to bring them to a state that they become capable of living a decent life like us? So is not a revolution necessary to change the socio-economic system? Have the young people of Punjab and Hindustan no feeling left in them to feel anything? Doesn't a heart beat in their breast? Is there no humanity in their hearts? Otherwise why should it be said that outsiders come and incite them. Yes, we agree that the Russian Revolution has presented completely novel ideas before the world. We say that Russian scholars have presented their views before the world regarding issues that we have not found solutions to as yet after enduring great hardships, by dying bit by bit. Should they not benefit us? Is even the similarity of their thoughts an incitement? In that case, had Mazzini misled Lalaji into patriotism and working for the country!

The question is if today, in 1928, should we learn any lesson from, and make our ideal, the French Revolution or the Russian Revolution, replete with new ideas in this new environment? Does Lalaji want that now we should rebel against only the English rulers and hand over the reins into the hands of the rich? Crores of people should stay not just in this condition, but in an even worse one, die and then after hundreds of years of bloodshed again arrive at this path and then rebel against the capitalists all over again? This would be first rate folly.

A couple of times, Lalaji, upon hearing my words, talked about organizing the people in the villages. Lalaji has no time to go to the villages. How would he know what the views of the public are? The people ask frankly of what use this revolution would be to them. 'If we will still eke out as miserable an existence as ever and the Nambardar, Tehsildar and the Thanedar continue to oppress us, then why should we sacrifice our meal today; now? Why should we throw our dear ones into trouble for someone else? What shall we tell them in inspiring speeches about their ancestors so that they are prepared to sacrifice their lives?'

All right, let us assume that this revolution happens, then according to Lalaji, who should get the reins of the government? To Maharaja Vardhman or the Maharaja of Patiala? Or a bunch of capitalists? Are crores of workers in America and France not dying of hunger? Why should we fall into this well with eyes wide open?

Lalaji says that our socialist ideas will cause the capitalists to join forces with the government. Great! And where were they earlier? How many capitalists have become harbingers of change? In a revolution, anyone who fears his wealth and property may be harmed will always oppose it. In such a situation, to abandon one's principles to appease them and damage our own cause is not appropriate. Another thing is that the capitalists should ponder which situation is gainful for them? Today the English will certainly use them for their own selfish gain, but gradually they will snatch away all their wealth and transfer them into the hands of their own capitalists. Then these destitute [erstwhile wealthy] people will join the ranks of the crores of labourers and eke out a miserable life. They will again find injustice in the social system. If they participate in a socialist revolution, not only will their parasitical temperament be curtailed but they will find real happiness by participating in the prosperity that will certainly spread through the entire world. Let the Hindustani capitalists reflect on what is really in their best interest.

But the revolution of the workers cannot stop for them, nor can it wait for them. The youth need not worry. There are a lot of teething troubles at the beginning of a task; one must face them with fortitude. Lalaji and the other kinds of leaders with capitalist values are gradually withdrawing from the field as Surendranath Bannerjee did first; as Sapru and Chintamani are doing now. In the end it is the revolution of the working class that will emerge victorious. Hail the Socialists! May the Revolution endure!

11. What is Anarchism – I; 1928 (Originally in Punjabi.)

Today, there is a lot of unrest in the world. Well-known scholars are engaged in establishing peace in the world; however the peace that is sought to be established is not a temporary one, but something that can be everlasting. Several great souls have sacrificed their lives to achieve it, and people continue to do so. But today we are slaves. Our eyesight is weak; our brains are dull. Our heart is weak and weeping over its weakness. How can we worry about world peace when we are not able to do anything for our own country? We can only call it our misfortune. We are being ruined by our own conservative ideas. We are trapped in the illusion of finding God and heaven, and seek redemption for our souls. We don't take more than an instant to refer to Europe as materialistic. We pay no attention to their great ideas. Because we are more inclined towards spiritual thought! Because we believe in renunciation! We should not even speak of this material world! We have come to such a pass that one wants to weep at the condition of the world, but the situation is improving in the twentieth century. European thought is beginning to make an impact on the youth's thinking. And the youth that wants to progress in the world should study the great and noble ideas of the modern age.

A person's knowledge is incomplete without understanding fully what voices are being raised in society today against oppression, or the ideas are being born for the establishment of permanent peace in the world. Today we are listening to summarized versions of many ideas of communism and socialism etc. Anarchism is thought to be the highest ideal among all these. This essay is being written regarding anarchism.

The people fear the word 'anarchist'. When a person rises to fight for his freedom, armed with a pistol or a bomb, then all the 'bureaucrats' and their underlings scream 'Anarchist-Anarchist!' and try to frighten the world. An anarchist is considered to be a very terrible person, who has no mercy in his heart, who sucks blood, who is delirious with joy at destruction and ruin. The word 'anarchist' has been given such a bad name that even the revolutionaries of India are referred to as anarchists to make people hate them. Dr Bhupindra Nath Dutt has mentioned this in the first part of his Bengali book *Unpublished Political History* saying that even if the government called them 'anarchist' to defame them, in truth they were a group of people who sought to usher in a new order. And anarchism is a very noble ideal. How was it possible for our common people to think of such a noble ideal, because they could not think of being revolutionaries beyond rebelling;[65] of ushering in a new age. These people were merely rebels. Anyway!

As we mentioned earlier, the word 'anarchist' was given a bad name. This word was slandered in the same way that selfish capitalists slandered words like 'Bolshevik', 'Socialist', etc. Yet, anarchists are the most sensitive and ardent well-wishers of the entire world. Even if we disagree with their views, their sobriety, their love for the people, spirit of sacrifice and their genuineness cannot be doubted.

The word 'anarchist' for which Hindi word 'araajk' is used, is derived from a Greek word which literally means (an = not, arche = rule),[66] that is, no government of any kind.[67] Human beings always had a desire to be as free as possible, and from time to time, the idea of complete freedom, which is the principle of anarchism, has been mooted. For example, a long time ago, a Greek philosopher said, 'We wish neither to belong to the governing class nor to the governed.'[68]

I consider that the feeling of world-fraternity in India and the Sanskrit phrase 'Vasudev Kutumbakam' conveys the same sense. Even if we are unable to reach any conclusive proposition based on our ancient beliefs, we still have to believe that these thoughts were placed before, and openly propagated in the world at the beginning of the nineteenth century (i.e.

---

65   For both the Punjabi words 'Raj-paltau' and 'Jug-paltau', we use the English word 'Revolutionary'. Though Jug-paltau alludes largely to the spirit of revolutionary, and Raj-paltau are the people who try to overthrow the government and state only. But the Jug-paltau follow the ideal of a societal revolution. For now, readers should understand the meaning of the word 'revolutionary' in this context, so that in the future they don't misunderstand the meaning of the word.

66   Originally in English.

67   Negation of government

68   Originally in English.

the last century) by a French philosopher Proudhon. That is why he is called the father of anarchism. He began to propagate anarchism and later, one Russian brave man Bakunin did lot of work to propagate and make it successful. Later, several anarchists like Johann Most and Prince Kropotkin were born. These days, Mrs Emma Goldman and Alexander Berkman propagate this in America. About anarchism, Mrs Goldman writes:

"Anarchism – The philosophy of a new social order based on liberty unrestricted by man-made law. The theory that all forms of Government rest on violence, and are therefore wrong and harmful, as well as unnecessary."[69]

This tells us that anarchists do not wish for any kind of government and this is true. But such a thought scares us. Several bogies are raised in our minds. We should remain fearful of the ghosts of the preceding English rule even after setting up our own government, and keep on trembling in fear – this is the policy of our rulers. Under such circumstances, how can we think even for one moment that such a day will dawn when we will be able to live happily and freely without a government? But this is, in fact, our own weakness. The ideal or the feeling is not to be blamed.

The ideal freedom that is imagined in anarchism is a complete liberation, according to which neither God nor religion should oppress our minds, nor should the temptation of money or the material world overtake us, or the body could be shackled or controlled by any kind of governmental structure. This means that broadly, they wished to completely eradicate three things from this world:

1. The Church, God (and religion),
2. The State (Government)
3. Private Property

This subject is very interesting and vast and much can be written about it, but we cannot stretch this essay too much due to paucity of space. So we shall discuss the issues only broadly.

---

69   Originally in English.

God and religion

Let us first consider God and religion. Now, even in Hindustan, voices are being raised against both these demons, but in Europe a revolution had risen in the last century itself. They begin with a reference to the age when people were ignorant; in those times, they were afraid of everything, especially supernatural powers. They completely lacked self-confidence and called themselves 'puppets of dust'. They say that religion, the supernatural and God are the result of the same ignorance, and that is why the illusion of their entity must be eliminated. Also that from their very childhood, children are taught that God is everything- man is nothing. (Originally in English.)

Man is merely a statue of clay. Such thoughts crowding a person's mind erode his self-confidence. He begins to feel that he is very feeble. In this way, he is always fearful. Till the time this fear remains, complete happiness and peace cannot be attained.

In Hindustan, it was Gautam Buddha who first denied the existence of God. He had no belief in God. Even now there are a few ascetics who do not believe in the existence of God. Sohom Swami of Bengal is one such example. These days is Niralamba Swami. Recently, a book by Sohom Swami called *Common Sense* has been published in English. He has written robustly against the existence of God, trying to prove his proposition, but he does not become an anarchist. He does not wander about aimlessly using 'renunciation' and 'yoga' as pretexts. In this manner, the existence of God is being brought to an end in this scientific age, which will eradicate the very name of religion. In fact, the leader of the anarchists, Bakunin has thoroughly insulted God in his book *God and the State*. He placed the Biblical story and said that God made the world and man in his own image. Thank you very much! But he also warned against tasting the fruit of the forbidden tree of knowledge. Actually God did create Adam and Eve for his own amusement, but he wanted them to remain his slaves forever and to never raise their head before him. So he gave them the gifts of the entire world but no intelligence. This state of affairs encouraged Satan to move forward – 'but here steps in Satan, the eternal rebel, the first free thinker and the emancipator of the world'.[70] He stepped forward, taught man to rebel and offered the fruit of the forbidden tree of knowledge. And that was enough for the omnipotent, omniscient God to lose his temper with a low-class, mean-minded mentality and he began to curse the world he himself had created. Wonderful!

The question that arises is why God made a world full of such sorrow. To enjoy the spectacle? In that case, he is more cruel than the Roman tyrant Nero. Is that his miracle? What is the need for such a miraculous God? The debate is growing. So we'll conclude it right here by stating that religion has always been used by the selfish, the capitalists for their personal good. History bears witness to that. "Have patience!" "Look at your own deeds!" The havoc that such a philosophy has brought to mankind is evident for all to see.

People ask what would happen if we deny the existence of God? Sin would grow in the world. Chaos would reign. But the anarchists say that man would then grow to such a stature that without the greed of heaven and the fear of hell, he would shun bad deeds and begin to do good things. In actual fact, the reality is that in Hindustan, in the *Gita*, a world famous book, Shri Krishna, even while inspiring Arjuna to work selflessly without expectation of fruit lures him with visions of heaven after death and the crown of a king after victory in the battle. But today when we look at the sacrifices made by the anarchists, one wishes to kiss their feet. Sacco and Vanzetti's stories have been read by our readers. There is neither any desire to flatter God nor any avariciousness to enjoy the pleasures of heaven, nor any expectation of the bliss of reincarnation. To sacrifice one's life for the people and for truth with a smile on one's face is no small thing. The anarchists say that once people become completely liberated, their character will become very noble. Anyway, there can be long debates on each and every question, but we do not have enough space.

---

70   Originally in English.

12. What is Anarchism – II; 1928 (Originally in Punjabi.)

The next thing they wish is to do away with the government. If we look for the roots of political power, we arrive at two conclusions. Some people believe that the caveman's intelligence evolved gradually, and people began to live together in groups. Political power was born in this way. This is called the theory of evolution. The other theory is that people needed to get together and to organize in order to fight off wild animals and to fulfil other needs. Then these groups began to fight with each other and each one of them was afraid of the more powerful enemy. So people cooperated to establish a political order. This is called Utilitarianism. We may pick both. The evolutionists can be asked why only now evolution has come to an end. Panchayati Raj is followed by anarchism, and the answer to the others is that now there is no need for any government. This debate has taken place earlier. Even if we pay little attention to this or other such things, we shall have to agree that the people had agreed to a contract, which the famous French thinker Rousseau called a *Social Contract*. According to the contract, a person would surrender a part of his freedom, a part of his income, in return for which he would be provided with security and peace. After all this, what is worth considering is whether this contract was fulfilled. After establishing the government, the State and the Church hatched a conspiracy. People were told that these persons, the rulers, had been sent by God (*Theory of Divine Rights of Sovereignty*). People were afraid of God and the king was able to carry out wilful oppression. The Tsar in Russia and Louis in France are good examples to reveal the truth of this matter, because this conspiracy could not be carried out for too long; Pope Gregory and King Henry fell out with each other. The Pope incited the people against King Henry's rule and Henry shattered the bogey of religion. The meaning is that selfish people fought and these misconceptions were destroyed. Anyway, people rose in rebellion again and killed the cruel Louis. The entire world was in a state of chaos. Democratic governments were established, but complete freedom was still not won. On the one side, the Austrian minister, Metternich was oppressing people and thus disillusioning them through autocratic royal rule, and on the other side in America, the poor slaves were in a miserable condition in democracy. The French masses were struggling time and again to raise themselves from the morass of poverty. Even today, France has democracy, but people do not have complete freedom. That is the reason the anarchists say that no government is required. In every other thing, they are similar to the communists, but one or two things differ. The eminent communist Karl Marx's well-known friend Fredrick Engels has written about his own and Marx's Communism; and it is our ideal as well: 'Communism also looks forward to a period in the evolution of the society when the State will become superfluous and having no longer any function to perform, will die away.'[71]

This means that political power should disappear and people should have a sense of fraternity. Italy's famous political thinker Machiavelli believed that some form of rule should always prevail, whether it is a democracy or a monarchy. He believed in strong rule, like an iron fist. But the anarchists ask what is soft or hard. They want neither a soft nor a strong government. They say–

> Undermine the whole conception of a State and then and then only we have Liberty worth having."[72]

People would say that that is absurd; if there is no government, there would be no law, no police to enforce the law, and this would lead to chaos. But they say this view is also wrong. The famous political philosopher Henry David Thoreau said, 'Law never made a man whit more just, and by means of their respect for it even the well-disposed are daily made gents of injustice.'[73]

There doesn't seem to be any untruth in this. We can see that as law becomes more rigid, corruption also increases. It is an ordinary complaint that earlier without any written agreement, thousands of rupees would be exchanged and no one would cheat. Now agreements have signatures,

---

71   Originally in English.

72   Originally in English.

73   Originally in English.

thumb impressions, witnesses, and are registered. But fraud is on the rise. Then the solution they suggest is that the needs of every person should be met, everything should go according to his wish, and there would be no sin or crime.'

'Crime is naught but misdirected energy. So long as every institution of today, economic, political, social and moral conspires to misdirect human energy into wrong channels, so long as most people are out of place doing the things they loathe to do, living a life they hate to live, crime will be inevitable and all the laws on the statutes can only increase but never do away with crime.'[74]

If a person has complete freedom, then he would be able to do things according to his own will. There would be no injustice. If the exploitation by the capitalists does not end, even the most stringent of laws would not help. People say that human nature is such that it cannot survive without some government. Human beings can cause a great deal of harm if they are not kept on a leash. Commenting on human nature in his book *The Principles of Politics*, the author A.R. Lord says that ants can live in a group, animals can live in a group, but not human beings. Man is greedy, inhuman and idle by nature. Hearing such talk, Emma Goldman lost her temper and in *Anarchism and Other Essays*, she wrote, 'Every fool from king to policeman, from a flat-headed person to the visionless dabbler in science presumes to speak authoritatively of human nature.'[75] She says that the bigger a fool a person is, the more stridently his opinion in this matter is expressed. Have human beings ever been tested by giving them complete freedom, that one is forever crying over their flaws? She feels that small elected bodies should be made and the work be carried out freely.

Private Property

The third most important thing is Private Property. In fact, it is the question of filling one's belly that makes the world goes around. It is for this that sermons preaching patience, contentment, etc., are crafted. Till now, everything in life was done for the sake of property; now, the

---

74   Originally in English.

75   Originally in English.

anarchists, communists, socialists are all against property. As Emma Goldman says, "'Property is robbery' (Proudhon) but without risk or danger to the robber.'[76]

The notion of amassing property makes a person greedy. Then he becomes increasingly more stony-hearted. Mercy and humanity begin to fade from his heart. A government is required for the security of property. This again leads to an escalation of greed and the ultimate end of that is – first, imperialism, and then, war, bloodshed and a lot of destruction. There would be no greed if everything becomes common property. Everyone would work together. There would be no fear of theft or robbery. There would be no need for the police, jail, court, or army. And those with fat bellies and the parasites would also work. Production will be more even with fewer hours of work. People can have good education as well. There would be spontaneous peace, and prosperity would increase. That is, they emphasize how very important it is to eradicate ignorance from the world.

In fact, property is the most important issue; that is why another essay is required to debate this issue. The real issue arises from bread; Karl Manning averred clearly, 'Ask for work and if they don't give you work, ask for bread and if they do not give you work or bread, then take bread.'[77] Meaning that if one doesn't get either work or food, then steal food. What right does one have to gorge on cakes when others may not even get dry crumbs of bread? He also asked why a person born in a destitute household should be forced to scrimp and save, whereas a person born in a prosperous household should grow fat on idleness. The precept 'Let riches add to riches' should be stopped. It is for these reasons that they shattered the illusion of the sanctity of private property for the sake of the principle of equal opportunity. They say that property is attached to corruption, and law is needed to protect it which in turn requires government. In fact, this is at the root of all evil. As soon as this is removed, everything will be all right. What do they really want; how will it really work? This is a vast question.

---

76   Originally in English.

77   Originally in English.

It has been stated above that anarchists are anti-God and religion because these cause mental slavery. Secondly, they are against the government, because this is physical slavery. They say that it is wrong to inspire human beings to do good by the lure of heaven or fear of hell, or by wielding the stick of law. And it is an insult to the nobility of man. One should attain knowledge freely and then work according to one's will and spend one's life happily. People say that this would mean that we wish to keep mankind in a state of wildness; as we were at the beginning. This is a false interpretation; in olden days, due to ignorance, people could not go far away. But now, with full awareness, establishing mutual relations in the world, man should live free. There should be no greed for money. And the issue of money should be eradicated.

In the next essay, we shall write about some other things regarding this philosophy, different viewpoints, history and the reasons for its unpopularity, and the reason for the inclusion of violence in this.

13. What is Anarchism – III; 1928 (Originally in Punjabi.)

In the previous two essays, we have presented the popular notions regarding anarchy. The curiosity of the public cannot be assuaged merely with these two essays about such an important topic that has recently emerged before the world as a reaction to the world's trite thoughts and traditions. Several doubts raise their heads. Even so, we are placing the broad principles before the readers so that they may understand the main ideas. Now, similarly, we shall write about the ideology of Communism, Socialism and Nihilism, so that Hindustan becomes familiar with the ideologies currently prevalent in the world. But before writing about any other topic, the intention is to write down several important and interesting facts about Anarchism, which also touches upon the history of Nihilism; that is, what have the Anarchists done so far? How did they acquire such an unsavoury reputation?

We have presented their thoughts above. Now we want to discuss what they did to give a practical shape to their ideas and how they confronted very powerful governments with the use of force and even staked their lives in that conflict.

The fact is that when oppression and exploitation crosses a certain limit, when peaceful and free movement is crushed, then those who are always doers begin their work secretly and are ready to fight oppression as soon as they see it. When the poor working class was being exploited appallingly in Europe, all their efforts were crushed or were being crushed, at that time, Mikhail Bakunin, who belonged to a prosperous family in Russia and was a top officer in an arms factory, was sent to Poland to deal with the revolt. There, the manner in which the rebels were being brutally crushed brought about a change in his mindset and he became a revolutionary. Ultimately, his thoughts turned towards anarchism. He resigned from his job in 1834. Subsequently, he reached Paris through Berlin and Switzerland. Those days, most of the governments were against him due to his views. Till 1864, he evolved his beliefs and propagated them among the working class.

Later, he gained control over the International Workingmen's Association and, from 1860 to 1870, he consolidated his group. On 4 September 1870, an announcement was made to establish a third Republic in Paris. There was unrest and riots in several places in France against the capitalist government. Bakunin was involved in these. They were the stronger side. But, in a few days, they lost and left the place.

In 1873, there was a revolt in Hispania. He joined in and fought. For some time, the matter was really hot, then it finally ended in a defeat. When they returned from there, a fight was raging in Italy. He went there and took the reins of the battle in his hands. After some initial differences, Garibaldi also joined him. After a few days of opposition, they lost there as well. In this manner, his entire life was spent waging battles. When he grew old, he wrote a letter to his compatriots saying that he would relinquish the leadership, so that their work did not suffer. Finally, in 1876, he died due to an illness.

Later, four very strong people got ready for this task with great determination. They were Carlo Cafiero, an Italian belonging to quite a prosperous family. The second was Malatesta; he was a great doctor. But he renounced everything to become a revolutionary. The third was Paul

Brousse, who was also a famous doctor. The fourth was Peter Kropotkin. He was from a Russian royal family. It was often said jokingly that he was to become the Tsar. They were all devotees of Bakunin. He said that they had propagated enough with the tongue, but it had had no effect. They were tired of hearing about new-fangled ideologies. These hadn't had any effect on the public. So now it was time to propagate action. Kropotkin said,

> A single deed makes more propaganda in a few days than a thousand pamphlets. The Government defends itself. It rages pitilessly, but by this it only caused further deeds to be committed by one or more persons and drives the insurgents to heroism. One deed brings forth another, opponent's join the mutiny, the Government splits into factions, harshness intensifies the conflict, concessions come too late, the revolution breaks out.[78]

Peter Kropotkin was one of the Russian revolutionaries. After being arrested, he was incarcerated in the Peter and Paul Fortress. He escaped from this very strongly guarded prison and began to disseminate his ideas in Europe. These things tell us his state of mind in those days.

First of all, he celebrated the anniversary of the establishment of the rule of the workers in Berne city in France. This was the 18 March 1876. He took out a procession of workers on that day and got into a scuffle with the police in the streets. A riot ensued when policemen tried to uproot their red flag. Several policemen were seriously injured. In the end, all these people were arrested and sentenced for ten to forty days in jail.

In the month of April, they incited the peasants of Italy and set off riots in several parts of the country. Even there their companions were arrested, out of whom several were released. Now their strategy was a kind of publicity. That is why they used to say, 'Neither money nor organizations nor literature was needed any longer (for their propaganda

---

78 Originally in English.

work). One human being in revolt with torch or dynamite was off to instruct the world.'[79]

From the next year onwards, in 1868, such activities were on the rise. An attempt was made to assassinate the Italian emperor Umberto when he was travelling in a motorcar with his daughter. Emperor Wilhelm I of Germany was shot at by an ordinary youth. After three weeks, Dr Karl Nobiling also tried to shoot at the Emperor from a window. In those days in Germany, the movements of the poor working classes were silenced brutally. After that, it was decided in a meeting that the corrupt capitalist class and the government, and the police that colluded with it, should be frightened in whatever way it was possible.

On 15 December 1833, a notorious police officer by the name of Ulubek was killed in Willirid Floridsdorf. On 23 June 1884, Rouget was hanged for this crime. The very next day, Blatik, a police officer, was killed to avenge the hanging. The Austrian government was enraged, and in Vienna, the police besieged several people and arrested them; and two of them were hanged. There were strikes in Leon. One of the striking men, Fournier, shot his capitalist owner. He was awarded a pistol in a ceremony held to honour him. In 1888, there was a lot of unrest there and the silk workers were starving. At that time, the capitalist's newspaper-owning friends and other rich friends were busy living it up elsewhere. A bomb was thrown there. The rich were terrified. Sixty anarchists were held. Only three were acquitted. But still, the search for the actual bomb thrower did not come to an end. He was finally caught and hanged. And, in this way, this line of thinking gained momentum. And then, wherever there were strikes, murders would take place. The anarchists were blamed for all this, and as a result, people would shudder at the very mention of them.

A German anarchist, Johann Most, who had worked in an office, went to America in 1882. He also began to place his ideas before the people. He was a very good orator and impressed his audience in America. In 1886, several strikes were called in Chicago and other places. In one paper factory, an anarchist called Spies was giving a speech. The owners tried

---

79 Originally in English.

to shut the factory; a riot erupted. The police were called in and they began firing as soon as they came. Six men were killed and several were injured. Spies were furious. He himself composed a notice and decreed that the workers should unite to avenge the murder of their innocent comrades. The next day, on 4 May, 1886, the Hay Market procession was to be taken out. The President of the city had come to watch it. He saw nothing objectionable going on. So he went there. Later, the police came and without any provocation, began to beat up people and asked them to stop the procession. Just then a bomb was thrown at the police and many policemen were killed. Several people were arrested and hanged. As he was leaving, one of them said, 'I repeat, I am a sworn enemy of this present state of affairs. I want this political establishment to be destroyed and we should be able to wield political power ourselves. You may laugh that I shall no longer be able to throw bombs, but let me tell you that your oppression has forced every worker to handle and throw a bomb. You should know that after I am hanged, another one will be born. I see you with revulsion in my eyes and want to trample your State. Hang me.' Anyway, several such incidents happened. But there are a couple of other famous incidents. The American President McKinley was shot at and then there was a strike in Carnegie steel company. The workers were being brutalized here. The owner, Henry C. Frick, was injured by an anarchist, Alexander, who was sentenced for life. Anyway, this is how anarchism spread to America and began to be practiced.

In Europe, too, things were bad. The anarchists' feud with the police and the government had intensified. Finally, a youth named Vaillant threw a bomb in the Assembly, but a woman caught his hand and stopped him; as a result of which nothing much happened, except that some Deputies were injured. He offered an explanation in a ringing voice, 'It takes a loud voice to make the deaf hear.[80] Now you will punish me, but I have no fear because I have struck at your hearts. You, who oppress the poor and those who work hard, starve, and you suck their blood and take pleasure in life. I have hurt you. Now it is your turn.'

---

80   Originally in English.

Several appeals were made on his behalf. Even the most seriously injured member of the Assembly requested the jury to show mercy to him, but the jury, presided over by a person named Carnot, refused to pay any attention and sentenced him to death by hanging. Later, an Italian boy stabbed Carnot with a knife with the name Vaillant written on it.

In this manner, unable to endure any more oppression, bombs were set off even in Spain and finally an Italian killed a minister. In a similar manner, the Emperor of Greece and the Empress of Austria were also attacked. In 1900, Gaetano Bresci killed the Emperor of Italy, Umberto. In this manner, these people smilingly gave up their lives for the sake of the poor ... kissed the gallows joyfully. That is why, even those opposed to them could do nothing against them. Their last martyrs, Sacco and Vanzetti, have been hanged only last year. The courage with which these people went to the gallows is known to everyone.

And this is the brief history of anarchism and its activities. Next time we shall write an essay about Communism.

14. The Revolutionary Nihilists of Russia; 1928 (Originally in Punjabi.)

Linked to his article on Anarchism, Bhagat Singh also introduced his readers to the subject of the Revolutionary Nihilists of Russia by writing about it in *Kirti*, in both Punjabi and Urdu. Lenin's own brother was part of the Nihilist movement in Russia and was hanged. Bhagat Singh depicts an objective picture of Russian Nihilists in this essay published in August 1928.

Russia has given birth to a very great novelist – Ivan Turgenev. In 1862, he wrote a novel *Fathers and Sons*. There was a great hue and cry over the publication of this novel because it depicted the modern views of the youth. It was Turgenev who first used the word 'nihilism'. Nihilism means not to believe in anything (*nihil* – nothing); the literal meaning is – one who believes in nothing. Though, in reality, these people were the opponents of the traditional rituals, customs and bad practices. These people were fed up of the country's mental slavery, so they protested against it. They not only spoke against it, but practiced what they preached. Turgenev says that the hero of his novel is not a fictional character; on the other hand, he was a real person with such ideas and these ideas had become quite common. He says that the idea of the novel occurred to him one day while he was lazing in the sun. And he wrote the book by expanding the ideas a bit. The hero is Bazarov. He is a kind of an atheist; completely opposed to conventional rituals. He does not find verbal sycophancy very attractive. He is blunt. What he says, he does. He says everything to one's face, immediately and clearly; so much so that at times, he appears to be very brash. He is an opponent of poetry. He does not like music. But he is a lover of freedom. He is a big supporter of freedom for the common people. He fights the prevailing mindset of the people.

The picture of a real nihilist is a little different from this because the hero of the novel has some fictional elements along with reality. The true picture of nihilism is delineated in quite another manner.

"The Nihilism of 1861 – a philosophical system especially dealing with what Mr Herbert Spencer would call religious, governmental and social fetishism." (Originally in English.)

The Russian revolutionary prince Kropotkin uttered these words while referring to nihilism in 1861, which means that nihilism, was just one of the philosophies of those times which was in relation to religious superstition, social injustice, narrow-mindedness, and the excesses of the government, and preached against the superstitions created to perpetuate such things. The fact is that the youth had jumped into the fray to protest against the conditions of the times. They believed that it was necessary to destroy every existing thing completely. Even without a complete answer to what would happen later or should happen, they believed that they would be able to build a beautiful world.

"Nihilism was destructive because it wanted a wholesale destruction but with a pleasure of building up." (Originally in English.)

Gradually these ideas became more popular and a large number of young people became enamoured of them. They wanted 'to liberate the people from the chains of tradition and autocracy of the Tsar.' (Originally in English.)

These were the kinds of things being propagated those days. Conditions changed. In those days, a large number of slaves had been freed, but most of them had not been given any land to till and earn, or at least, escape starvation. Whatever little land had been allotted to them was taxed so heavily that people starved and there was a terrible famine in 1867. Those days, the Government arrangements were unspeakably bad. There was so much oppression that the public could bear it no longer. Harassed by official excesses, even big government officials became revolutionaries. Ossinsky and Kviatkovsky, who were hanged in 1880, had been government servants earlier. Similarly, many other well-known officers, even judges, became revolutionaries.

The oppression on the people became unbearable. Good books were not allowed to be propagated among the youth. There were some associations that would pick up good books from the publishers and distribute them free of cost or at cost price. All these books were censored by the government. But when the government realized that they were being used for propaganda, they decided to destroy all book publishers and distributors, and began to repress these people. From 1861 to 1870, every possible and appropriate way to improve the condition of the people and show the right way to the government was tried, but it had no impact.

In such a situation, a lot of people would sit twiddling their thumbs, waiting for times to change by themselves. How they would improve – nobody knew. People remained passive, just placing trust in God. But a fire had been lit in the hearts of the youth. There was no trust in God in their hearts. It had become difficult for them to sit quietly, without doing anything.

Prince Kropotkin writes in an essay –

"There are periods when some generations are penetrated with the noblest feelings of altruism and self-sacrifice, when life becomes utterly impossible – morally and physically impossible – for the man and woman who feels that he is not doing duty; and so it was with the youth in Russia." (Originally in English.)

In 1871, a large number of young men and women ran away to Western Europe. They studied there. Most of them were in Switzerland. They got permission to return to their country. They returned with new ideas of community and unity. They began propaganda immediately upon their return, and the Tsar got all of them arrested and they were exiled to Siberia. Their movement then assumed a covert shape.

At that time, three parties were working. Their leaders were Chernyshevsky, Ishutin, and Nechaif. Earlier the slogan was that they should be with the public, that is, they should sympathize with the public and try to uplift them, but now a new voice was heard that said that they should all become the public; that is, blend with it. As soon as this voice was heard, people were inspired to set such amazing examples of sacrifice that, till date, the world cannot find anything to match them.

But first it is necessary to discuss why this voice rose? Prince Kropotkin writes –

"Until of late – however the Russian peasant has always regarded the man who wears broad cloth and neither ploughs, nor hews, nor hammers, nor digs side by side with him, as an enemy. We wanted faith and love from him; and to obtain them it was necessary to live their life." (Originally in English.)

Ah! Today we make exaggerated claims to liberate Hindustan, but how many people are ready to make such sacrifices? How many will leave their cities and be prepared to go to the villages and live in unhygienic conditions like peasants? There a unique situation had been created.

"Young men left their classrooms, their regiments and their desks, learned the smith's trade, or the cobbler's or the ploughman's, and went to work among the villages. Highborn and wealthy ladies betook themselves to factories, worked fifteen or sixteen hours a day at machine, slept in dog holes with peasants, went barefoot as our working women go, bringing water from the river for the house." (Originally in English.)

Just one passion. One obsession. To make those poor workers aware of their miserable condition and to offer a solution. What a big sacrifice it is! The young women did a marvellous job. Madam Catherine Breshkovsky, the woman known as the grandmother of the Russian Revolution was a wealthy and beautiful lady. She also joined them. First she threw acid on herself to destroy her beauty so that it did not hinder her work among the common people. Oh! How many people would have the courage to do that in Hindustan today? In Russia, young men and women run away from home and spend their lives in this kind of work. But how many young people in Hindustan have this yearning to liberate their country? One sees quite intelligent people around but everyone is concerned only with his or her individual life and happiness. How can we then hope to improve our condition and that of our country? The youth of Russia spent the last part of the previous century in this kind of propaganda work. There are several beautiful anecdotes about women being inspired to come out of their homes.

Sonia was a priest's daughter. Revolutionary women had just joined her school as teachers. Listening to their teachings, Sonia was inspired to do patriotic work. One day she ran away from home. But her father caught her after a few days. Then the party made arrangements to liberate her from home. A young man posed as her boyfriend and went to her house. He convinced her father and married her. The story is very interesting and has been published in *The Heroes and Heroines of Russia*. We shall present the story to our readers if we get a chance. Anyway, readers shall get an idea about the kind of work underfoot in Russia through this brief description.

At first, the work was done openly but then the government cracked down brutally on them and several thousands of people were sent to Siberia. Thousands were arrested without warrants. They were locked in dark cells for four or five years. Later cases were filed against about a hundred people. Some were sentenced. One among these thousands of cases became famous by the name of 'The Trial of the Hundred and Ninety Three'. To be brief, as per the government figures, thousands of people were arrested and kept in dark, dingy cells for four to five years. Three hundred were kept in jail for a very long time out of which eleven died of tuberculosis, four slashed their own throats and many others also tried to kill themselves like this. Cases were filed against 193 people. An extremely unjust court sentenced them to ten years imprisonment just because they were the propagators even though there was very little evidence against them. 90 were acquitted and the rest were given rigorous punishment from 7 to 10 years and then exiled to Siberia for the rest of their lives. In a related matter, a woman was given 9 to 10 years of rigorous punishment only for giving a communist pamphlet to a worker.

Faced with this level of oppression, the work took a more covert and prudent form. And the feeling of revenge grew. More often than not, some wicked secret service officer would arrest and exile anyone he wished to. He would be given a reward but this endangered the life of the youth. Harassed by this, these people also thought of eliminating these tyrants.

It is said that on the 16 April 1866, when Karakozoff shot at the Tsar, it was the work of nihilists. And the shooting at the Tsar the next year in Paris by a Polish gentleman, Berezovsky was also a party action. But about the present situation, Kropotkin has written that the Tsar was never more secure as he was in the initial stages of their work. They thought of using force only in the end when they had exhausted other avenues. At first they always tried to protect the Tsar. Once when some young man reached St. Petersburg to kill the Tsar, the members of the party prevented him from doing so.

But later the work started with gusto. In 1879, one of the arrested persons, who still had been charge-sheeted formally, was caned because he did not rise and greet the police officer, and the rest of the arrested people who supported him were beaten badly on the orders of General Trepov. At this, a young woman, Vera Zasulich shot General Trepov. He did not die and a case was filed against the young woman. She was acquitted. The police tried to arrest her again but the public snatched her away.

When the Russian revolutionaries realized that no one helped them; and that there was no law to protect them, they began to take care of their own protection. The police would encircle the houses of people early in the morning; they even stripped the women of their clothes to search them. The people were harassed. Murmuring began that this did not happen in other countries. They would also not let it happen. Kovalsky was the first one to do this in Odessa. He confronted the police. The oppression grew more intense. And then, the taking of revenge began. The use of force for self-protection began to be considered appropriate. First five spies, then three officers were murdered, in return for which seventeen young people were hanged. Then this chain reaction continued – revenge, then gallows, then ...

In 1879, the word 'nihilism' came to connote only the bursting of bombs and the shooting of guns. The Tsar also finally lost his patience and decided to teach them a lesson.

And this was the catalyst needed to set all of them to complete this task. On the 14 April 1879, Solovioff had shot at the Tsar, but the Tsar escaped. The same year the Winter Palace of the Tsar was bombed with dynamite but the Tsar still escaped. The next year, when the Tsar was going from St. Petersburg to Moscow, the train in which he was travelling was bombed. Several compartments were destroyed, but the Tsar escaped yet again. On the 13 March 1881 when the Tsar was returning with his special squad after inspecting the parade of his horses and platoon, a bomb was hurled at him. The carriage was smashed and the Tsar got off to take a look at the servant, saying, "Thank God, I'm saved." But another young man, Grinevizky moved forward, and said as he hurled another bomb, "Tsar, it is too early to thank God." The bomb exploded and the Tsar was killed. Thousands of people were arrested. Many were sent to the gallows. Five people were hanged publically. The most famous among them was a woman called Sophia Perovskya.

The party was suppressed at that time. Then several other parties rose. But the history of the Nihilist Party is just this much. The Nihilists were judged unfairly by the people and given a bad name like the anarchists. An English newspaper drew a cartoon in which two nihilists stand with bombs and dynamite amid destruction. One asks, 'Brother, does anything remain?' and the other answers, 'Just the globe of the earth.' The first says, 'Let me put dynamite on that too.' This is complete misrepresentation. Oscar Wilde wrote a play titled *Vera the Nihilist* which depicted the nihilists in a positive light, but there are several errors. Another book *The Career of a Nihilist* was published. This is a readable account. It is an accurate book about nihilists. In Hindi, *Bolshevikon ki Kartoot* (*The Action of Bolsheviks*) and *Nihilist Rahasya* (*Mystery of the Nihilist*) have been published. The first has been written by the martyr of Kakori, Shri Ram Prasad Bismil. He has delineated a very pitiful picture of Nihilists. But they have been shown as being only destructive, which is not accurate.

They were sincere servants of the people. They were very sacrificing and loved the common people. They were great souls.

---

15. Ideal of Indian Revolution; 1930 (Originally in English.)

The essay, ' Ideal of Indian Revolution: A Synopsis', was found in Bhagat Singh's jail papers by the British authorities and was produced in the court during the trial of the Lahore Conspiracy Case. It is part of the Supreme Court's digital collection of 'The Trial of Bhagat Singh', and was exhibited in the court. This essay again seems to be a plan for a book and Bhagat Singh's views on the future society of India is shown. From the synopsis itself, it seems that Bhagat Singh was thinking of 'the ideal of world revolution' going beyond the national boundaries, perhaps under the influence of the famous Marxist vision of 'Workers of the world unite'!

Ideal of Indian Revolution

1. (1). Ideal of Indian Revolution:

    (a) The History of the Revolution's struggle in British India. Open and Secret.
    (b) The Ideal of Republic
    (c) 1914-15. Rising and the Ideal of Equality, Liberty and Fraternity
    (d) Indian Princes and Revolutionaries-Sarkar's pamphlet
    (e) Turkish message to Indian Muslim rulers
    (f) Berlin Committee and German plot
    (g) 1919 rising and riots
    (h) Non-Cooperation

Swaraj without clear definition

    (i) Failure of N.C.O movement and revolutionary parties

(j) Thin manifesto 1925
(k) Present Schools of thought:
　1. Sarkar's school of (Communalist) thought.
　2. Bengal School of thought (Nationalists)
　3. Chandernagar School of thoughts. Moti Lal (Spiritualists)
　4. Advanced thought. (Socialist) Dr. Bhupen Dutt
　5. Communist school of thought
　6. Bourgeoisie

　7. Nehru report
　8. P.G.
　　1. Methods
　　2. Terrorists
　　3. Mass revolutionaries
　　4. Non-violent civil disobedience
　　5. Anarchism
　　6. Socialism
　　7. Communism
　　8. Syndicalism
　　9. Collectivism

1. Ideal of the Indian Revolution
The Revolution: or the ideal of world revolution. Marriage?

∽

16. Why I am an Atheist; 1930 (Originally in English.)

The essay 'Why I am an Atheist' is a classic document from Bhagat Singh's pen. The background of writing this essay was the case of Bhai Randhir Singh, a convict who was jailed in Lahore Jail for the 1915 Ghadar Party revolt. Bhai Randhir Singh refused to accede to Bhagat Singh's request for a meeting with him as Bhagat Singh had 'cut his hairs and got shaved'. Being a devoted Sikh, Bhai Randhir Singh did not want to see a 'patit' (degenerated Sikh). Bhagat Singh sent him an emotional message, saying that 'it was mere hair he got cut for the country, he won't mind even if his whole body was cut into pieces for the cause of national liberation!' The message melted Bhai Randhir Singh's resistance and the two met. Bhai Randhir Singh tried to convince Bhagat Singh to renounce atheism and return to the fold of 'devoted ritualistic Sikhism, who follows all the tenets including not cutting hair'. Bhai Randhir Singh had claimed in his autobiography, *Jail Letters*, written in Punjabi, that at his bidding 'Bhagat Singh repented and returned to the fold of Sikhism and grew a beard.' However, Bhagat Singh was astute enough to know that his ideas can be distorted after his execution and he took extra care to put his clear ideas on paper immediately after meeting Bhai Randhir Singh. He did that in an essay written in the first week of October 1930 and handed it over to Kumari Lajjawati, Secretary of the Bhagat Singh Defense Committee, along with his other writings. Lajjawati handed over the bag with his writings to Lala Feroze Chand, editor of the Lahore-based socialist weekly the *People*. Chand published this essay on Bhagat Singh's first birth anniversary after his execution in the 27 September 1931 issue. The essay carries a brief editorial note ascribing the copyright of this essay and other writings published by the *People* to his father, S Kishan Singh.

By special arrangement, the *People* is permitted to print some of Bhagat Singh's writings in jail. The things placed at our disposal are mostly non-political in nature. Copyright vests with S Kishan Singh – Editor, *The People*.

A new question has cropped up. Is it due to vanity that I do not believe in the existence of an omnipotent, omnipresent and omniscient God? I had never imagined that I would ever have to confront such a question. But conversation with some friends has given me a hint that certain of my friends – if I am not claiming too much in thinking them to be so – are inclined to conclude from the brief contact they have had with me, that it was too much on my part to deny the existence of God and that there was a certain amount of vanity that actuated my disbelief. Well, the problem is a serious one. I do not boast to be quite above these human traits. I am a man and nothing more. None can claim to be more. I also have this weakness in me. Vanity does form a part of my nature. Amongst my comrades I was called an autocrat. Even my friend Mr B.K. Dutt sometimes called me so. On certain occasions I was decried as a despot. Some friends do complain, and very seriously too, that I involuntarily thrust my opinions upon others and get my proposals accepted. That this is true up to a certain extent, I do not deny. This may amount to egotism. There is vanity in me in as much as our cult as opposed to other popular creeds is concerned. But that is not personal. It may be, it is only legitimate pride in our cult and does not amount to vanity. Vanity, or to be more precise 'Ahankar', is the excess of undue pride in one's self. Whether it is such an undue pride that has led me to atheism or whether it is after very careful study of the subject and after much consideration that I have come to disbelieve in God, is a question that I intend to discuss here. Let me first make it clear that egotism and vanity are two different things. In the first place, I have altogether failed to comprehend as to how undue pride or vain gloriousness could ever stand in the way of a man in believing in God. I can refuse to recognise the greatness of a really great man, provided I have also achieved a certain amount of popularity without deserving it or without having possessed the qualities really essential or indispensable for the same purpose. That much is conceivable. But in what way can a man believing in God cease believing due to his personal vanity? There are only two ways. The man should either begin to think himself a rival of God or he may begin to believe himself to be God. In neither case can he become a genuine atheist. In the first case, he does not even deny the existence of his rival. In the second case as well, he admits the existence of a conscious being behind the screen, guiding all the movements of nature. It is of no importance to us whether he thinks himself to be that Supreme Being or whether he thinks the supreme conscious being to be somebody apart from himself. The fundamental is there. His belief is there. He is by no means an atheist. Well, here I am. I neither belong to the first category nor to the second. I deny the very existence of that Almighty Supreme Being. Why I deny it, shall be dealt with later on. Here I want to clear one thing, that it is not vanity that has actuated me to adopt the doctrines of atheism. I am neither a rival nor an incarnation, nor the Supreme Being Himself. One point is decided, that it is not vanity that has led me to this mode of thinking. Let me examine the facts to disprove this allegation. According to these friends of mine I have grown vainglorious perhaps due to the undue popularity gained during the trials – both Delhi Bomb and Lahore Conspiracy Cases. Well, let us see if their premises are correct. My atheism is not of so recent origin. I had stopped believing in God when I was an obscure young man, of whose existence my above-mentioned friends were not even aware. At least a college student cannot cherish any short of undue pride which may lead him to atheism. Thought a favourite with some professors and disliked by certain others. I was never an industrious or a studious boy. I could not get any chance of indulging in such feelings as vanity. I was rather a boy with a very shy nature, who had certain pessimistic dispositions about his future career. And in those days, I was not a perfect atheist. My grandfather under whose influence I was brought up is an orthodox Arya Samaji. An Arya Samaji is anything but an atheist. After finishing my primary education, I joined the D.A.V. School of Lahore and stayed in its Boarding House for one full year. There, apart from morning and evening prayers, I used to recite Gayatri Mantra for hours and hours. I was a perfect devotee in those days. Later on, I began to live with my father. He is a liberal in as much as the orthodoxy of religions is concerned. It was through his teachings that I aspired to devote my life to the cause of freedom. But he is not an atheist. He is a firm believer. He used to encourage me to offer prayers daily. So this is how I was brought up. In the Non-Cooperation days I joined the National College. It was there that I began to think liberally and discuss and criticise all the religious problems, even God. But still I was a devout believer. By that time I had begun to preserve the unshorn and unclipped long hair but I could never believe in the mythology and doctrines of Sikhism or any other religion. But I had a firm faith in God's existence.

Later on, I joined the Revolutionary Party. The first leader with whom I came in contact, though not convinced, could not dare to deny the existence of God. On my persistent inquiries about God, he used to say: 'Pray whenever you want to.' Now this is atheism less courage required for the adoption of that creed. The second leader with whom I came in contact with was a firm believer. Let me mention his name – respected

Comrade Sachindra Nath Sanyal, now undergoing life transportation in connection with the Kakori Conspiracy Case. From the very first page of his famous and only book, *Bandi Jivan* (Incarcerated Life), the Glory of God is sung vehemently. On the last page of the second part of that beautiful book, his mystic – because of vedantism-praises showered upon God form a very conspicuous part of his thoughts. *The Revolutionary* distributed throughout India on 28 January 1925, was according to the prosecution, the result of his intellectual labour. Now, as is inevitable in the secret work the prominent leader expresses his own views which are very dear to his person, and the rest of the workers have to acquiesce in them, in spite of differences which they might have. In that leaflet one full paragraph was devoted to praise the Almighty and His rejoicings and doing. That is all mysticism. What I wanted to point out was that the idea of disbelief had not even germinated in the Revolutionary Party. The famous Kakori martyrs – all four of them – passed their last days in prayer. Ram Prasad Bismil was an orthodox Arya Samaji. Despite his wide studies in the field of socialism and communism, Rajen Lahiri could not suppress his desire of reciting hymns of the Upanishads and the Gita. I saw only one man amongst them, who never prayed and used to say: 'Philosophy is the outcome of human weakness or limitation of knowledge.' He is also undergoing a sentence of transportation for life. But he also never dared to deny the existence of God.

Up to that period I was only a romantic idealist revolutionary. Up till then we were to follow. Now came the time to shoulder the whole responsibility. Due to the inevitable reaction, the very existence of the party seemed impossible for some time. Enthusiastic comrades – nay, leaders – began to jeer at us. For some time I was afraid that someday I might also be convinced of the futility of our own programme. That was a turning point in my revolutionary career. 'Study' was the cry that reverberated in the corridors of my mind. Study to enable yourself with arguments in favour of your cult. I began to study. My previous faith and convictions underwent methods alone which was so prominent amongst our predecessors, was replaced by serious ideas. No more mysticism, no more blind faith. Realism became our cult. Use of force justifiable when resorted to as a matter of terrible necessity: non-violence as policy indispensable for all mass movements. So much about methods. The most important thing was the clear conception of the ideals for which we were to fight. As there were no important activities in the field of action I got ample opportunity to study various ideals of the world revolutions. I studied Bakunin, the anarchist leader, something of Marx, the father of communism, and much of Lenin, Trotsky and others – the men who had successfully carried out a revolution in their countries. They were all atheists. Bakunin's *God and State*, though only fragmentary, is an interesting study of the subject. Later still I came across a book entitled *Common Sense* by Nirlamba Swami, It was only a sort of mystic atheism. This subject became of utmost interest to me. By the end of 1926 I had been convinced of the baselessness of the theory of existence of an Almighty Supreme Being who created, guided and controlled the universe. I had given out this disbelief of mine. I began discussion on the subjects with my friends. I had become a pronounced atheist. But what it meant will presently be discussed.

In May 1927 I was arrested at Lahore. The arrest was a surprise. I was quite unaware of the fact that the police wanted me. All of a sudden, while passing through a garden, I found myself surrounded by the police. To my own surprise, I was very calm at that time. I did not feel any sensation, nor did I experience any excitement. I was taken into police custody. Next day I was taken to the Railway Police lock-up where I was to pass one full month. After many days of conversation with the police officials I guessed that they had some information regarding my connection with the Kakori party and my other activities in connection with the revolutionary movement. They told me that I had been to Lucknow while the trial was going on there, that I had negotiated a certain scheme about their rescue, that the after obtaining their approval, we had procured some bombs, that by way of test one of the bombs was thrown into the crowd on the occasion of Dussehra in 1926. They further informed me, in my interest, that if I could give any statement throwing some light on the activities of the revolutionary party, I was not going to be imprisoned but on the contrary set free and rewarded, even without being produced as an approver in the court. I laughed at the proposal. It was all humbug. People holding ideas like ours do not throw their bombs on innocent people.

One fine morning Mr Newman, the then Senior Superintendent of C.I.D., came to me. And after much sympathetic talk with me, imparted to him the extremely sad news that if I did not give any statement as demanded by them, they would be forced to send me up for trial for conspiracy to wage war in connection with Kakori Case and for brutal murders in connection with Dussehra bomb outrage. And he further informed me that they had enough evidence to get me convicted and hanged. In those days I believed – though I was quite innocent – the police could do it if they desired. That very day certain police officials began to persuade me to offer my prayers to God regularly, both the times. Now I was an atheist. I wanted to settle for myself whether it was in the days of peace and enjoyment alone that I could boast of being an atheist or whether during such hard times as well, I could stick to those principles of mine. After great consideration I decided that I could not lead myself to believe and pray to God. No, I never did. That was the real test and I came out successful. Never for a moment did I desire to save my neck at the cost of certain other things. So I was a staunch disbeliever; and have been ever since. It was not an easy job to stand that test. 'Belief' softens the hardships, and can even make them pleasant. In God, man can find consolation and support. Without Him, man has to depend upon himself. To stand upon one's own legs amid storms and hurricanes is not a child's play. At such testing moments, vanity, if any, evaporates and man cannot dare to defy the general beliefs. If he does, then we must conclude that he has got certain other strengths than mere vanity. This is exactly the situation now. Judgement is already too well known. Within a week it is to be pronounced. What is the consolation with the exception of the idea that I am going to sacrifice my life for a cause? A God-believing Hindu might be expecting to be reborn as a king, a Muslim or a Christian might dream of the luxuries to be enjoyed in paradise and the reward he is to get for his suffering and sacrifices. But, what am I to expect? I know that the moment the rope is fitted around my neck and the rafters removed from under my feet, will be the final moment, the last moment. I, or to be more precise, my soul as interpreted in the metaphysical terminology, shall all be finished there. Nothing further. A short life of struggle with no such magnificent end, shall in itself be the reward, if I have the courage to take it in that light. That is all. With no selfish motive or desire to be awarded here or hereafter, quite disinterestedly, have I devoted my life to the cause of independence, because I could not do otherwise. The day we find a great number of men and women with this psychology, who cannot devote themselves to anything else than the service of mankind and emancipation of the suffering humanity, that day shall inaugurate the era of liberty. Not to become a king, nor to gain any other rewards here, or in the next birth or after death in paradise, shall they be inspired to challenge the oppressors, exploiters, and tyrants, but to cast off the yoke of serfdom from the neck of humanity and to establish liberty and peace shall they tread this – to their individual selves perilous and to their noble selves the only glorious imaginable – path. Is the pride in their noble cause to be misinterpreted as vanity? Who dares to utter such an abominable epithet? To him I say either he is a fool or a knave. Let us forgive him for he cannot realise the depth, the emotion, the sentiment and the noble feelings that surge in that heart. His heart is dead as a mere lump of flesh, his eyes are weak, the evils of other interests having been cast over them. Self-reliance is always liable to be interpreted as vanity. It is sad and miserable but there is no help.

You go and oppose the prevailing faith, you go and criticise a hero, a great man who is generally believed to be above criticism because he is thought to be infallible, and the strength of your argument shall force the multitude to decry you as vainglorious. This is due to the mental stagnation. Criticism and independent thinking are the two indispensable qualities of a revolutionary. Because Mahatamaji is great, therefore none should criticise him. Because he has risen above, therefore everything he says, may be in the field of Politics or Religion, Economics or Ethics, is right. Whether you are convinced or not you must say: 'Yes, that's true.' This mentality does not lead towards progress. It is rather too obviously reactionary.

Because our forefathers had set up a faith in some Supreme Being, the Almighty God, therefore, any man who dares to challenge the validity of that faith, or the very existence of that Supreme Being shall have to be called an apostate, a renegade. If his arguments are too sound to be refuted by counter-arguments and spirit too strong to be cowed down by the threat of misfortunes that may befall him by the wrath of the Almighty, he shall be decried as vainglorious, his spirit to be denominated as vanity. Then, why waste time in this vain discussion? Why try to argue out the whole thing? This question is coming before the public for the first time, and is being handled in this matter of fact way for the first time, hence this lengthy discussion.

As for the first question, I think I have cleared that it is not vanity that has led me to atheism. My way of argument has proved to be convincing or not, that is to be judged by my readers, not me. I know in the present circumstances my faith in God would have made my life easier, my burden lighter, and my disbelief in Him has turned all the circumstances too dry, and the situation may assume too harsh a shape. A little bit of mysticism can make it poetical. But I do not want the help of any intoxication to meet my fate. I am a realist. I have been trying to overpower the instinct in me by the help of reason. I have not always been successful in achieving this end. But man's duty is to try and endeavour, success depends upon chance and environments.

As for the second question that if it was not vanity, then there ought to be some reason to disbelieve the old and still prevailing faith of the existence of God. Yes, I come to that now. Reason there is. According to me, any man who has got some reasoning power at his command always tries to reason out his environments. Where direct proofs are lacking philosophy occupies the important place. As I have already stated, a certain revolutionary friend used to say that philosophy is the outcome of human weakness. When our ancestors had leisure enough to try to solve out the mystery of this world, its past, present and the future, its whys and wherefores, they having been terribly short of direct proofs, everybody tried to solve the problem in his own way. Hence we find the wide differences in the fundamentals of various religious creeds, which sometimes assume very antagonistic and conflicting shapes. Not only the Oriental and Occidental philosophies differ, there are differences even amongst various schools of thought in each hemisphere. Amongst Oriental religions, the Muslim faith is not at all compatible with Hindu faith. In India alone Buddhism and Jainism are sometimes quite separate from Brahmanism, in which there are again conflicting faiths such as Arya

Samaj and Sanatan Dharma. Charwak is still another independent thinker of the past ages. He challenged the authority of God in the old times. All these creeds differ from each other on the fundamental question; and everybody considers himself to be on the right. There lies the misfortune. Instead of using the experiments and expressions of the ancient Savants and thinkers as a basis for our future struggle against ignorance and to try to find out a solution to this mysterious problem, we lethargic as we have proved to be, raise the hue and cry of faith, unflinching and unwavering faith to their versions and thus are guilty of stagnation in human progress.

Any man who stands for progress has to criticise, disbelieve and challenge every item of the old faith. Item by item he has to reason out every nook and corner of the prevailing faith. If after considerable reasoning one is led to believe in any theory or philosophy, his faith is welcomed. His reasoning can be mistaken, wrong, misled, and sometimes fallacious. But he is liable to correction because reason is the guiding star of his life. But mere belief and blind faith are dangerous: they dull the brain and make a man reactionary. A man who claims to be a realist has to challenge the whole of the ancient faith. If it does not stand the onslaught of reason it crumbles down. Then the first thing for him is to shatter the whole down and clear a space for the erection of a new philosophy. This is the negative side. After it begins the positive work in which sometimes some material of the old faith may be used for the purpose of reconstruction. As far as I am concerned, let me admit at the very outset that I have not been able to study much on this point. I had a great desire to study the Oriental philosophy but I could not get any chance or opportunity to do the same. But so far as the negative study is under discussion, I think I am convinced to the extent of questioning the soundness of the old faith. I have been convinced as to the non-existence of a conscious Supreme Being who is guiding and directing the movements of nature. We believe in nature and the whole progressive movement aims at the domination of man over nature for his service. There is no conscious power behind it to direct. This is what our philosophy is.

As for the negative side, we ask a few questions from the 'believers'. (1) If, as you believe, there is an almighty, omnipresent, omniscient and omnipotent God, who created the earth or world, please let me know why he created it. This world of woes and miseries, a veritable, eternal combination of numberless tragedies: Not a single soul being perfectly satisfied. Pray, don't say that it is His Law. If he is bound by any law, he is not omnipotent. He is another slave like us. Please don't say that it is his enjoyment. Nero burnt Rome. He killed a very limited number of people. He created very few tragedies, all to his perfect enjoyment. And, what is his place in history? By what names do historians mention him? All the venomous epithets are showered upon him. Pages are blackened with invective diatribes condemning Nero, the tyrant, the heartless, the wicked. One Genghis Khan sacrificed a few thousand lives to seek pleasure in it and we hate the very name. Then, how are you going to justify your almighty, eternal Nero, who has been, and is still causing numberless tragedies every day, every hour and every minute? How do you think to support his misdoings which surpass those of Genghis every single moment? I say why did he create this world – a veritable hell – a place of constant and bitter unrest? Why did the Almighty create man when he had the power not to do it? What is the justification for all this? Do you say, to award the innocent sufferers hereafter and to punish the wrongdoers as well? Well, well: How far shall you justify a man who may dare to inflict wounds upon your body to apply a very soft and soothing ointment upon it afterwards? How far the supporters and organisers of the Gladiator institution were justified in throwing men before the half-starved furious lions to be cared for and well looked after if they could survive and could manage to escape death by the wild beasts? That is why I ask: Why did the conscious Supreme Being create this world and man in it? To seek pleasure? Where, then, is the difference between him and Nero? You Mohammadans and Christians: Hindu philosophy shall still linger on to offer another argument. I ask you, what is your answer to the above-mentioned question? You don't believe in previous birth. Like Hindus, you cannot advance the argument of previous misdoings of the apparently quite innocent suffers. I ask you, why did the omnipotent labour for six days to create the world through word and each day to say that all was well? Call him today. Show him the past history. Make him study the present situation. Let us see if he dares to say: "All is well."

From the dungeons of prisons, from the stores of starvation consuming millions upon millions of human beings in slums and huts, from the exploited labourers, patiently or say apathetically watching the procedure of their blood being sucked by the capitalist vampires, and the wastage of human energy that will make a man with the least common sense shiver with horror, and from the preference of throwing the surplus of production in oceans rather than to distribute amongst the needy producers - to the palaces of kings built upon the foundation laid with human bones ... let him see all this and let him say: "All is well." Why and wherefore? That is my question. You are silent. Alright then, I proceed.

Well, you Hindus, you say all the present sufferers belong to the class of sinners of the previous births. Good. You say the present oppressors were saintly people in their previous births, hence they enjoy power. Let me admit that your ancestors were very shrewd people; they tried to find out theories strong enough to hammer down all the efforts of reason and disbelief. But let us analyse how for this argument can really stand.

From the point of view of the most famous jurists, punishment can be justified only from three or four ends, to meet which it is inflicted upon the wrongdoer. They are retributive, reformative and deterrent. The retributive theory is now being condemned by all the advanced thinkers. Deterrent theory is also following the same fate. Reformative theory is the only one which is essential and indispensable for human progress. It aims at returning the offender as a most competent and a peace-loving citizen to the society. But, what is the nature of punishment inflicted by God upon men, even if we suppose them to be offenders? You say he sends them to be born as a cow, a cat, a tree, a herb, or a beast. You enumerate these punishments to be 84 lakhs. I ask you: what is its reformative effect upon man? How many men have met you who say that they were born as a donkey in previous birth for having committed any sin? None. Don't quote your Puranas. I have no scope to touch your mythologies. Moreover, do you know that the greatest sin in this world is to be poor? Poverty is a sin, it is a punishment. I ask you how far would you appreciate a criminologist, a jurist or a legislator who proposes such measures of punishment which shall inevitably force men to commit more offences. Had not your God thought of this, or he also had to learn these things by experience, but at the cost of untold sufferings to be borne by humanity? What do you think shall be the fate of a man who has been born in a poor and illiterate family of, say, a chamar or a sweeper? He is poor hence he cannot study. He is heated and shunned by his fellow human beings who think themselves to be his superiors having been born in, say, a higher caste. His ignorance, his poverty and the treatment meted out to him shall harden his heart towards society. Suppose he commits a sin, who shall bear the consequences? God, he or the learned ones of the society? What about the punishment of those people who were deliberately kept ignorant by the haughty and egotist Brahmans, and who had to pay the penalty by bearing the stream of being led (lead) in their ears for having heard a few sentences of your Sacred Books of learning – the Vedas? If they committed any offence, who was to be responsible for them and who was to inventions of the privileged ones; they justify their usurped power, riches and superiority by the help of these theories. Yes, it was perhaps Upton Sinclair that wrote at some place that just makes a man a believer in immortality and then rob him of all his riches and possessions. He shall help you even in that ungrudgingly. The coalition among the religious preachers and possessors of power brought forth jails, gallows, knouts and these theories. I ask why your omnipotent God does not stop every man when he is committing any sin or offence. He can do it quite easily. Why did he not kill warlords or kill the fury of war in them and thus avoid the catastrophe hurled down on the head of humanity by the Great War? Why does he not just produce a certain sentiment in the mind of the British people to liberate India? Why does he not infuse the altruistic enthusiasm in the hearts of all capitalists to forego their rights of personal possessions of means of production and thus redeem the whole labouring community, nay, the whole human society, from the bondage of capitalism? You want to reason out the practicability of socialist theory; I leave it for your almighty to enforce it. People recognise the merits of socialism in as much as the general welfare is concerned. They oppose it under the pretext of its being impracticable. Let the Almighty step in and arrange everything in an orderly fashion. Now don't try to advance round about arguments, they are out of order. Let me tell you, British rule is here not because God wills it, but because they possess power and we do not dare to oppose them. Not that it is with the help of God that they are keeping us under their subjection, but it is with the help of guns and rifles, bomb and bullets, police and militia, and our apathy, that they are successfully committing the most deplorable sin against society - the outrageous exploitation of one nation by another. Where is God? What is he doing? Is he enjoying all these woes of human race? A Nero, a Genghis! Down with him!

Do you ask me how I explain the origin of this world and origin of man? Alright, I tell you, Charles Darwin has tried to throw some light on the subject. Study him. Read Soham Swami's *Common Sense*. It shall answer your question to some extent. This is a phenomenon of nature. The accidental mixture of different substances in the shape of nebulae produced this earth. When? Consult history. The same process produced animals and, in the long run, man. Read Darwin's *Origin of Species*. And all related progress is due to man's constant conflict with nature and his efforts to override it. This is the briefest possible explanation of the phenomenon.

Your other argument may be just to ask why a child is born blind or lame if not due to his deeds committed in the previous birth? This problem has been explained away by biologists as a mere biological phenomenon. According to them the whole burden rests upon the shoulders of the parents who may be conscious or ignorant of their own deeds which led to mutilation of the child previous to its birth.

Naturally, you may ask another question, though it is quite childish in essence. If no God existed, how did the people come to believe in him? My answer is clear and brief. As they came to believe in ghosts and evil spirits; the only difference is that belief in God is almost universal and the philosophy is well developed. Unlike certain of the radicals I would not attribute its origin to the ingenuity of the exploiters who wanted to keep the people under their subjection by preaching the existence of a supreme being and then claiming an authority and sanction from him for their privileged positions, though I do not differ with them on the essential point that all faiths, religions, creeds and such other institutions became in turn the mere supporters of the tyrannical and exploiting institutions, men and classes. Rebellion against king is always a sin, according to every religion.

As regards the origin of God, my own idea is that having realised the limitation of man, his weaknesses and shortcoming having been taken into consideration, God was brought into imaginary existence to encourage man to face boldly all the trying circumstances, to meet all dangers manfully and to check and restrain his outbursts in prosperity and affluence. God, both with his private laws and parental generosity, was imagined and painted in greater details. He was to serve as a deterrent factor when his fury and private laws were discussed, so that man may not become a danger to society. He was to serve as a father, mother, sister and brother, friend and helper, when his parental qualifications were to be explained. So that when man be in great distress, having been betrayed and deserted by all friends, he may find consolation in the idea that an ever-true friend was still there to help him, to support him and that he was almighty and could do anything. Really that was useful to the society in the primitive age. The idea of God is helpful to man in distress. Society has to fight out this belief as well as was fought the idol worship and the narrow conception of religion. Similarly, when man tries to stand on his own legs and become a realist, he shall have to throw the faith aside, and to face manfully all the distress, trouble, which the circumstances may throw him. That is exactly my state of affairs. It is not my vanity, my friends. It is my mode of thinking that has made me an atheist. I don't know whether in my case belief in God and the offering of daily prayers which I consider to be most selfish and degraded act on the part of man, whether these prayers can prove to be helpful or they shall make my case worse still. I have read of atheists facing all troubles quite boldly; so am I trying to stand like a man with an erect head to the last, even on the gallows.

Let us see how I carry on. One friend asked me to pray. When informed of my atheism, he said: "During your last days you will begin to believe." I said: "No, dear Sir, it shall not be. I will think that to be an act of degradation and demoralisation on my part. For selfish motives I am not going to pray." Readers and friends: Is this "vanity"? If it is, I stand for it.

(From *The People*, Lahore; 27 September 1931)

17. The First Rise of Punjab in the Freedom Struggle; 1931 (Originally in Urdu.)

Bhagat Singh wrote the history of the rise of political consciousness in Punjab under the title, 'The First Rise of Punjab in the Freedom Struggle'. This account was serialized in the weekly, *Bande Mataram*, in 1931. The original Urdu text has not yet been discovered; this translation is from the available Hindi text of the same.

In his book,[81] the erstwhile Governor of Punjab, Sir Michael O'Dwyer has revealed a very unpalatable but extremely significant truth. He has said that Punjab is the most backward in political upheaval. Those who have even the slightest knowledge of Punjab's political struggle can appreciate the truth of this statement.

Look at the history until now. This state has made the maximum number of sacrifices for the freedom of the country. For this, terrible calamities have been endured by the people of this state. In political, religious etc. agitations, Punjab has been ahead of other regions of India, and it has given the largest number of sacrifices of life and property for the country, but even so, we have to accept with bowed heads that in the political sphere, Punjab is the most backward.

The reason for this is only that political agitation has not become an essential part and parcel of the personal lives of the public here. Even in the field of literature, this region has not achieved its true place. For the educated class, till O'Dwyer's book came out – the question of the country's slavery had not become the most immediate and important one, so it is generally held that this region was very backward. There are many other regions in India that are far more backward than Punjab but it is unfortunate that this ill-fated region remained backward despite such allegations.

Punjab has no specific language of its own. Due to the lack of a language, it has not been able to progress in the creation of literature. That is the reason the educated class had to remain dependent upon Western

---

81 India as *I Knew It*

literature. The unfortunate consequence of this was that the educated class remained aloof from the political turmoil. That is why politics has not been able to become a part of Punjab's literature and field of culture. That is the reason there are only a handful of people who have devoted their entire lives to politics. It is on this basis that such allegations are made against this state. This essay intends to draw attention of the local leaders and of the society to this drawback.

From the Kuka Revolt under the leadership of Guru Ram Singh, to all the agitations that have taken place in Punjab till date, and the way political consciousness rose among the public, the people became prepared to sacrifice all they had at the altar of freedom. The way in which these people laid down their lives, their biographies and history would give courage to every man and woman, so that they can manage even future movements better in light of their study and experiences. It is certainly not my aim in penning down this history those revolts would succeed only in the future. My aim is only that the public should be inspired by the sacrifices of these martyrs and their lifelong service to the country and be able to follow them. How they would have to work when the time comes, the activists may themselves decide, keeping in mind the prevailing conditions.

How did political agitations begin in Punjab?

In 1907, there was complete quiet in eastern Punjab. After the Kuka Revolt, no such political agitation was unleashed that could shatter the slumber of the rulers. In 1908, a Congress Session took place in Punjab for the first time, but at that point, the basis of the activities of Congress was to express loyalty towards the rulers, so it did not have much effect in the political arena. The powerful agitation that had arisen following the partition of Bengal in 1905-06, and the propaganda of Swadeshi and the shunning of all foreign things had a great influence on Punjab's industrial life and the common man. In those days, the question of making objects indigenously was alive even in Punjab, especially the question of preparing sugar, and soon a couple of mills were opened. Although it did not much impact the political life of the region, yet the government tried to destroy this industry by raising the tax on the harvest of sugarcane three times. Earlier the tax for approximately 2000 square yards of land was only Rs 2.50, but now they had to shell out Rs 7.50. So, suddenly a huge burden came upon the farmers and they were paralysed.

New Colony Act

On another front, the government had got a number of new canals dug in Lyallpur etc. and lured a large number of people residing in Jalandhar, Amritsar, Hoshiarpur there by promising them many facilities. These people gave up their old lands and property, and spent their sweat and blood to make this jungle arable. But they had not even been able to breathe a sigh of relief when the New Colony Act was thrust upon them. This Act was nothing but a ploy to destroy the very existence of peasants. According to this Act, only the eldest son of a person could inherit the property. The younger sons were given no share in it. Upon the death of the eldest son, that piece of land or property would not go to the younger sons and would revert to the government.

No man could fell the trees standing upon his land. He couldn't even break off a twig to brush his teeth. They had got those lands but they could only farm on that land. They could not build any kind of house or hutment, so much so, that even troughs to put animal fodder in could not be made. The slightest infringement of the laws could lead to a 24 hour notice being issued and then lands could be confiscated. It is said that the government wanted the entire land to come into the hands of a few foreigners through this law and keep the Indian tenant farmers dependent on them forever. Apart from this, the government also wanted that as in other regions, there should only be a small number of big landowners, and the rest should be extremely poor tenant farmers. In this manner, the people should be divided into two classes. The rich would never, under any circumstances whatsoever, be ready to support the opponents of the government; and the poor farmers, who would not be able to fill their bellies even after hard labour, would not get an opportunity to do so. In this manner, the government would be able to do whatever it wished.

Seeds of Unrest

In those days, the condition of Uttar Pradesh and Bihar etc. was similar, but the people of Punjab prepared themselves more quickly. They started a powerful agitation against this policy of the government. In the Rawalpindi region also, this new state of affairs had only recently been accomplished and the tax had been raised. Thus at the beginning of 1907 itself, conditions were ripe for unrest. Even the Governor of Punjab, Sir Denzil Ibbetson, had said at the beginning of this year itself that though there was apparent peace at that time, agitation in the minds of the people was growing.

These days, a kind of quiet was spread all over the country. The people were in a state of 'wait and watch'. This was the lull before the storm. All the causes of unrest were present; especially in Punjab, conditions were ripe and necessary for unrest to be caused.

The Congress of 1906

In 1906, the annual Congress convention was held in Calcutta. Dadabhai Naoroji was the President. For this first time, he uttered the word 'Swarajya' (Home Rule) in his speech in this convention. Based on their personal experience, the members of the British Parliament had themselves told Dadabhai that if we wanted to achieve anything, we would first have to acquire inner strength. We would have to stand on the strength of our own two feet; it was not enough to stare ahead with a stony glance.

Lala Lajpat Rai

Exactly this thing was said by 'Punjab Kesari' Lala Lajpat Rai one year previously in the Banaras Congress Convention. The revered Lalaji had been sent with the Congress President, the late Gokhale, as part of a deputation to England. He had delivered a stinging speech after his return from there.

Lokmanya Tilak

Lokmanya Tilak was very popular in the Congress Convention of 1906; the youth population had become devoted to him due to his honest and frank talk. His fearlessness, his desire to do something, and his being prepared every moment to endure the greatest of hardships attracted the youth towards him. Apart from speaking during the Congress Convention, Lokmanya Tilak delivered several speeches outside the ambit of the Congress convention at this time.

Sardar Kishan Singh and Sardar Ajit Singh

There were a few Punjabi youths among the men who were especially drawn towards the Lokmanya. Two such Punjabi youths were Kishan Singh and my respected uncle, Sardar Ajit Singhji.

The periodical Bharat Mata and Mehta Nand Kishore

Sardar Kishan Singh and Sardar Ajit Singh returned to Lahore and started publishing a monthly magazine called *Bharat Mata*. Taking the respected Mehta Nand Kishore along, they began to disseminate their views. They had neither any money nor any contacts amongst the wealthy. They were not even the leader or priest of any community, so they had to muster all the resources for dissemination themselves. One day they collected some people together in the bazaar by ringing a bell and began to deliver a speech on the topic of how the foreigners had destroyed Indian industry and trade. They also announced that the following Sunday, an important meeting would take place near the office of *Bharat Mata* which was situated midway between the Lahori and the Shalimar gateways. The first meeting was held in the Papad Mandi, and the second in the Lahori Mandi. Before the speeches in the third meeting, a Punjabi youth read out a very touching poem that was steeped in patriotism and came in for much praise by the people. Now this young man also joined this group. This young man was a popular poet of Punjab, Lala Lalchand 'Falak', who had been rousing the country with his stirring poetry. The same week several others like Lala Pindi Dasji and Dr Ishwari Prasadji etc. also joined the group. With all these people joining the group, an institution by the name of 'Anjuman Muhabbatane Vatan' was established, which later became famous under the name of 'Bharat Mata Society'.

Another public meeting was to be held the following Sunday as well. The same day, Mrs Annie Besant was to speak in Lahore. Some friends suggested that Bharat Mata Society be dissolved that day, but this suggestion was not accepted, nor was it considered appropriate to postpone the meeting. Finally when the meeting took place, there was adequate attendance. It was declared that a meeting would be held every Sunday, and Sardar Ajit Singh was elected as the President and Mehta Nand Kishore as its Secretary.

The Jat Sabha

This propaganda continued to be disseminated for a month or so. One day, the Jat peasants of the Lahore and Amritsar region decided to hold a meeting to protest the raise in the tax. This meeting was organized in the Ratan Chand Sarai outside the Ajmeri gateway, but when the Jats mustered there, the Deputy Commissioner summoned Ratan Chand's son and threatened to confiscate his property. So Ratan Chand's son threw out all the Jats from the inn. In such a situation, the peasants established contact with the influential members of the society of that city but they only received a cold response. Meeting with disappointment on all sides, the peasants finally went to sit in the Municipal Garden. In the meantime, the members of the Bharat Mata Society received information regarding this and they took these people to their place. Apart from a room, the Society had a large ground. Durries were spread on the ground, a large tent was erected and arrangements were made to provide food to these peasants. This energized the peasants and then for an entire week, daily meetings were held there and fearless speeches were made. The enthusiasm of the peasants in these meetings also emboldened the members of the Bharat Mata Society.

Then a schedule was drawn to make trips to the rural areas so that they could prepare the peasants to shun taxes. This was a battle cry against the government and there was so much zeal among the people that they were willing to sacrifice everything in this struggle.

Sufi Amba Prasad

Right at this time, a great patriot, statesman and writer joined Bharat Mata Society. He was Shri Sufi Amba Prasad. Sufiji was born in 1858 in Moradabad. He was a powerful Urdu writer, a strong supporter of Hindu–Muslim unity and a fearless champion of freedom. He published a weekly and after a year, was sentenced to two-and-a-quarter years of jail for treason. Within a year of completing this sentence, another case was lodged against him and he was sentenced for six years this time. In those days, people convicted of treason were considered to be dangerous criminals and they were treated very badly in jail. He was released in 1906 and, finding a new political awareness in Punjab, he came here. Here he became the co-editor of the weekly, *Hindustan*. His stinging articles and his name on the editorials gave sleepless nights to the owners of the newspaper. So he had to resign from the job. He had first come to participate in the meeting of the Jats and stayed here. Later, he became so close to Sardar Ajit Singh that it was impossible to separate the two.

A huge rally was to be held in Lyallpur during these days. This was popularly known as Mandi Maveshiyan (Animal Fair). People used to gather in large numbers to buy and sell animals. This year the owner of the daily *Zimindar*, Mian Siraj-ud-din, and a few other gentlemen decided to hold a meeting on the occasion. They were going to pass a resolution against the New Colony Act. Lalaji was a special invitee to deliver a lecture at the meeting. The members of the Bharat Mata Society also decided to hold a meeting. The Bharat Mata Society was a very overzealous lot, so the gentlemen who thought of running an agitation according to constitutional means were a little uncomfortable with it. Two workers were sent by the Bharat Mata Society in advance with the aim of first preparing the ground, so that after a day or two, Sardar Ajit Singh and his comrades could reach there and disseminate their ideas more successfully.

The workers of the Bharat Mata Society were able to deliver some lectures in the tents that had been put up by the Zimindar Sabha and garner considerable sympathy of the public. And when Lalaji set off from Lahore, Sardar Ajit Singh also set off the same day. Lalaji got someone to ask Sardar Ajit Singh what his projected programme was. He also gave information about his own programme, saying that he would thank the government for the minor alteration they had made to the Colony Act and request the government to repeal the law.

Sardarji replied that their programme was that they would try and prepare the people to resist the payment of the tax. Moreover, they could give no space to thanking the government in their programme.

Both Lalaji and Sardarji arrived in Lyallpur. A huge procession was taken out for Lalaji, due to which he was able to reach the venue only after two hours. But there were people who did not participate in the procession and reached the dais directly and began to deliver speeches. After a couple of short speeches, it was Sardar Ajit Singh's turn to speak. He was a powerful orator. The people became enamoured of his fearless oration, and the public also became enthusiastic. By the time the organizers of the procession reached the dais, the public was completely with the Bharat Mata Society. A couple of moderate leaders tried to prevent Sardar Ajit Singh's speech but the public rebuked them so much that they could do nothing. This emboldened the crowd further. One peasant got up and announced that he had 10 squares of land, which he was bestowing upon the struggle; and he was ready, along with his wife, to serve his country.

Lala Lajpat Rai rose to deliver his speech after Sardar Ajit Singh. Lalaji was an incomparable orator of Punjab, but the fearlessness, magnificence and determination with which he spoke that day was something out of the ordinary. Every line of Lalaji's speech fetched applause and slogans of 'Jai' rent the air. After the meeting, a large number of people declared their desire to serve their country.

The Deputy Commissioner of Lyallpur was also present there. The activities of the meeting made him conclude that the entire organization was a conspiracy. Lala Lajpat Rai was their leader and the young man, Sardar Ajit Singh, was his pupil. The government carried this impression for a long time. This was probably the reason for the house arrest of Lalaji and Ajit Singh.

After Lalaji's speech, Shri Banke Dyal read a very powerful poem, which became very popular later on. This was *Pagri sambhaal, O Jatta* (Protect your turban, O peasant!)'.

Lala Banke Dyal was a Sub-Inspector of Police, and he resigned from his job and joined the agitation. That day when he came down from the dais after reciting his poem, the workers of the Bharat Mata Society embraced him.

After the riots in Lahore, the Municipal Board passed a resolution that the principals of all the colleges in the city would be asked to stop the students from participating in political agitations and not be allowed to leave their hostels. The students who did not follow orders would be given the severest punishment.

Lokmanya Tilak had written a sharp essay regarding this resolution in his Marathi paper, *Kesri*. Lokmanya wondered who would not be sad and regret the riots. 'Who says that young men should not act with more patience? But what did the resolution of the Municipal Board mean? Today, after fifty years, the youth of this country have shown some awareness. Why should there be a proposal to destroy that because of normal turbulence? Today, if the youth are being filled with feelings of patriotism and are impatient for freedom, they should be dealt with affectionately and told that they must not waste their energies like this.'

When the public does something in the heat of the moment then this is the policy of the radical group. The leaders of the radical groups know that when awareness is spread among the people then enthusiasm and impatience are a normal part of it. They also knew that those overcautious people who weigh every step before taking it do not stay long in the freedom struggle. The builders of the nation are always the youth. Someone has said truly, "It is not the old who can bring about improvement because they are very wise and intelligent. Improvement is brought about by the labour, courage, sacrifice and selflessness of the youth who don't know the meaning of fear and who think less and do more."

It seems that at that time, the youth of this region were influenced by such emotions and jumped into the freedom struggle. Whereas three years ago, there was complete silence, now the Swadeshi and Swarajya agitation was so powerful that the bureaucracy took fright. On the other hand, agitation against the New Colony Act in Lyallpur districts and others was raging. The railway workers also went on strike in sympathy for the peasant struggle and funds began to be collected to help them. The result was that at the end of April the Punjab government became afraid. The Governor at that time, apprising the Indian government of the entire situation in a letter said, 'The new ideas are limited to only the educated class, and especially the lawyer and student groups in the northern districts of the region, but as we proceed towards the middle of the region it is evident that dissatisfaction and unrest are spreading rapidly.' Further in the letter he noted, 'These people (the leaders of the agitation) have got special success in Amritsar and Ferozepur. They have been able to spread disaffection even in Rawalpindi and Lyallpur. And the situation in Lahore is for all to see.' At the end of the letter, he writes, 'Some leaders are making plans to compel the English to leave the country. They want to do it either forcibly or by creating an atmosphere of non-cooperation between the public and the government, and create hatred and ill will against the English in an irresponsible manner. The present situation is very delicate and we must do something to deal with it as soon as possible.'

18. Introduction to Dreamland; 1931 (Originally in English.)

Lala Ram Saran Das was convicted for life in 1915 in the first Lahore Conspiracy Case. While at Salem Central Prison in the Madras Presidency, he wrote a book in verse titled *Dreamland*. After his release in the mid-twenties, he contacted Bhagat Singh and Sukhdev, and became an active member of the HSRA. He was arrested again in connection with the second Lahore Conspiracy Case. This time he wavered and accepted the king's pardon. Soon he realized his mistake and retracted his statement. He was charged with perjury and convicted for two years, which was subsequently reduced to six months in appeal. It was during this conviction that he passed on his manuscript to Bhagat Singh for an introduction. In this article, Bhagat Singh, while appreciating the spirit behind Ram Saran Das' work, has criticized his utopian approach to the problems of revolution. He has also expressed himself on subjects such as God, religion, violence, non-violence, spiritualism, literature, poetry, etc. Bhagat Singh wrote the introduction, which is now known as an important document, 'Introduction to Dreamland', which reflects Bhagat Singh's thoughts on literature and art. As an older revolutionary, Ram Saran Das's wish to get Bhagat Singh's introduction also indicates to Bhagat Singh's status among revolutionaries as their ideological mentor and an intellectual of repute.

My noble friend, L Ram Saran Das, has asked me to write an introduction to his poetical work, *The Dreamland*. I am neither a poet nor a litterateur, neither am I a journalist nor a critic. Hence, by no stretch of imagination can I find the justification of the demand. But the circumstances in which I am placed do not afford any opportunity of discussing the question with the author arguing back and forth, and thereby do not leave me any alternative but to comply with the desire of my friend.

As I am not a poet I am not going to discuss it from that point of view. I have absolutely no knowledge of metre, and do not even know whether judged from metrical standard it would prove correct. Not being a litterateur I am not going to discuss it with a view of assigning to it its right place in the national literature.

I, being a political worker, can at the utmost discuss it only from that point of view. But here also one factor is making my work practically impossible or at least very difficult. As a rule the introduction is always written by a man who is at one with the author on the contents of the work. But, here the case is quite different. I do not see eye to eye with my friend on all the matters. He was aware of the fact that I differed from him on many vital points. Therefore, my writing is not going to be an introduction at all. It can at the utmost amount to a criticism, and its place will be at the end and not in the beginning of the book.

In the political field, *The Dreamland* occupies a very important place. In the prevailing circumstance it is filling up a very important gap in the movement. As a matter of fact all the political movements of our country that have hitherto played any important role in our modern history, had been lacking the ideal at the achievement of which they aimed.

Revolutionary movement is no exception. In spite of all my efforts, I could not find any revolutionary party that had clear ideas as to what they were fighting for, with the exception of the Ghadar Party, which, having been inspired by the USA form of government, clearly stated that they wanted to replace the existing government by a Republican form of government. All other parties consisted of men who had but one idea, i.e., to fight against the alien rulers. That idea is quite laudable but cannot be termed a revolutionary idea. We must make it clear that revolution does not merely mean an upheaval or a sanguinary strife. Revolution necessarily implies the programme of systematic reconstruction of society on new and better adapted basis, after complete destruction of the existing state of affairs (i.e., regime).

In the political field the liberals wanted some reform under the present government, while the extremists demanded a bit more and were prepared to employ radical means for the same purpose. Among the revolutionaries, they had always been in favour of extreme methods with one idea, i.e., overthrow the foreign domination. No doubt, there had been some who were in favour of extorting some reforms through those means. All these movements cannot rightly be designated as revolutionary movement.

But L Ram Saran Das is the first revolutionary recruited formally in the Punjab by a Bengali absconder in 1908. Since then he had been in touch with the revolutionary movements and finally joined the Ghadar Party but retaining his old ideas that people held about the ideal of their movement. It has another interesting fact to add to its beauty and value. L Ram Saran Das was sentenced to death in 1915, and the sentence was later on commuted to life transportation. Today, sitting in the condemned cells myself, I can let the readers know as authoritatively that the life imprisonment is comparatively a far harder lot than that of death. L Ram Saran Das had actually to undergo fourteen years of imprisonment. It was in some southern jail that he wrote this poetry. The then psychology and mental struggle of the author has stamped its impressions upon the poetry and makes it all the more beautiful and interesting. He had been struggling hard against some depressing mood before he had decided to write. In the days when many of his comrades had been let off on undertakings and the temptation had been very strong for everyone and for him, too and when the sweet and painful memories of wife and children had added more to the work. Hence, we find the sudden outburst in the opening paragraph:

'Wife, children, friends that me surround
Were poisonous snakes all around.'

He discusses philosophy in the beginning. This philosophy is the backbone of all the revolutionary movement of Bengal as well as of the Punjab. I differ from him on this point very widely. His interpretation of the universe is teleological and metaphysical, which I am a materialist and my interpretation of the phenomenon would be causal. Nevertheless, it is by no means out of place or out of date. The general ideals that are prevailing in our country are more in accordance with those expressed by him. To fight that depressing mood he resorted to prayers as is evident that the whole of the beginning of the book is devoted to God, His praise, His definition. Belief in God is the outcome of mysticism which is the natural consequence of depression. That this world is 'Maya' or 'Mithya', a dream or a fiction, is clear mysticism which has been originated and developed by Hindu sages of old ages, such as Shankaracharya and others. But in the materialist philosophy, this mode of thinking has got absolutely no place. But this mysticism of the thinking has got absolutely no place. But this mysticism of the author is by no means ignoble or deplorable. It has its own of them are doing very productive labour. The only difference that the socialist society expects is that the mental workers shall no longer be regarded superior to the manual workers.

L Ram Saran Das's idea about free education is really worth considering, and the socialist government has adopted somewhat the same course in Russia.

His discussion about crime is really the most advanced school of thought. Crime is the most serious social problem which needs a very tactful treatment. He has been in jail for the better part of his life. He has got the practical experience. At one place he employs the typical jail terms, 'the light labour, the medium labour and the hard labour', etc. Like all other socialists he suggests that, instead of retribution, i.e., retaliation, the reformative theory should form the basis of punishment. Not to punish but to reclaim should be the guiding principle of the administration of justice. Jails should be reformatories and not veritable hells. In this connection the readers should study the Russian prison system.

While dealing with militia he discusses war as well. In my opinion war as an institution shall only occupy a few pages in the Encyclopaedia then, and war materials shall adorn the no conflicting or diverse interests that cause war.

At the utmost we can say that war shall have to be retained as an institution for the transitional period. We can easily understand if we take the example of the present-day Russia. There is the dictatorship of the proletariat at present. They want to establish a socialist society. Meanwhile they have to maintain an army to defend themselves against the capitalist society. But the war-aims would be different. Imperialist designs shall no more actuate our dreamland people to wage wars. There shall be no more war trophies. The revolutionary armies shall march to other lands not to bring rulers down from their thrones and stop their blood-sucking exploitation and thus to liberate the toiling masses. But, there shall not be the primitive national or racial hatred to goad our men to fight.

World-federation is the most popular and immediate object of all the free-thinking people and the author has well dilated on the subject, and his criticism of the so-called League of Nations is beautiful.

In a footnote, under stanza 571 (572), the author touches, though briefly, the question of methods. He says: 'Such a kingdom cannot be brought about by physical violent revolutions. It cannot be forced upon society from without. It must grow from within.... This can be brought about by the gradual process of Evolution, by educating the masses on the lines mentioned above', etc. This statement does not in itself contain any discrepancy. It is quite correct, but having not been fully explained, is liable to create some misunderstanding, or worse still, confusion. Does it mean that L Ram Saran Das has realised the futility of the cult of force? Has he become an orthodox believer in non-violence? No, it does not mean that.

Let me explain what the above quoted statement amounts to. The revolutionaries know better than anybody else that the socialist society cannot be brought about by violent means, but that it should grow and evolve from within. The author suggests education as the only weapon to be employed. But, everybody can easily realise that the present government here, or, as a matter of fact, all the capitalist governments are not only not going to help any such effort, but on the contrary, suppress it mercilessly. Then, what will his 'evolution' achieve? We, the revolutionaries, are striving to capture power in our hands and to organize a revolutionary government which should employ all its resources for mass education, as is being done in Russia today. After capturing power, peaceful methods shall be employed for constructive work; force shall be employed to crush the obstacles. If that is what the author means, then we are at one. And I am confident that it is exactly what he means.

I have discussed the book at great length. I have rather, criticised it. But, I am not going to ask for any alteration in it, because this has got its historical value. These were the ideas of 1914-15 revolutionaries.

I strongly recommend this book to young men in particular, but with a warning. Please do not read it to follow blindly and take for granted what is written in it. Read it, criticise it, think over it, try to formulate your own ideas with its help.

19. To Young Political Workers; 2 February 1931 (Originally in English.)

'Letter to Young Political Workers', published on 2 February 1931, has now become a major political document, and through this Bhagat Singh presents his socialist revolutionary ideas in an organized manner. Jotted down on 2 February 1931, it was written in in the form of a letter but is actually a major policy programme and an ideological message to the young political workers of India. At that time, there were talks of some sort of compromise between the Congress and the British Government. Through this document, Bhagat Singh explained as to when a compromise is permissible and when it is not. He also made out that the way Congress was conducting the movement it was bound to end in some sort of compromise. After analysing the conditions then, he finally advised the youth to adopt Marxism as an ideology, work among the people, organize workers and peasants, and form the Communist Party to not just change rulers from white to brown but to liberate the country from the exploitative system in general. Due to its significance, it has been included in this essays section, rather than in the section that outlined his letters. Extracts from this document were published in Hindi and English journals immediately after Bhagat Singh's execution, however, this document was published as a secret report in 1936 by British officers, as referred by Shiv Verma in his book, *Selected Writings of Shaheed Bhagat Singh* in 1986. But, Verma concludes that this document was dated as 2 February 1931. However, the website, shahidbhagatsingh.org, managed by Professor Jagmohan Singh, who is also the nephew of Bhagat Singh, carries a complete note by CES Fairweather, in which a few more pages from this document are found after the mentioned date of 2 February. The additional pages from the website are posted here in italics after the text that is taken from Shiv Verma's *Selected Writings of Shaheed Bhagat Singh*.

Dear Comrades,

Our movement is passing through a very important phase at present. After a year's fierce struggle some definite proposals regarding the constitutional reforms have been formulated by the Round Table Conference and the Congress leaders have been invited to give this *(words missing)... think it desirable in the present circumstances to call off their movement. Whether they decide in favour or against is a matter of little importance to us. The present movement is bound to end in some sort of compromise. The compromise may be effected sooner or later. And compromise is not such ignoble and deplorable thing as we generally think. It is rather an indispensable factor in the political strategy. Any nation that rises against the oppressors is bound to fail in the beginning, and to gain partial reforms during the medieval period of its struggle through compromises. And it is only at the last stage - having fully organized all the forces and resources of the nation - that it can possibly strike the final blow in which it might succeed to shatter the ruler's government. But even then it might fail, which makes some sort of compromise inevitable. This can be best illustrated by the Russian example.

In 1905, a revolutionary movement broke out in Russia. All the leaders were very hopeful. Lenin had returned from the foreign countries where he had taken refuge. He was conducting the struggle. People came to tell him that a dozen landlords were killed and a score of their mansions were burnt. Lenin responded by telling them to return and to kill twelve hundred landlords and burn as many of their palaces. In his opinion that would have meant something if revolution failed. Duma was introduced. The same Lenin advocated the view of participating in the Duma. This is what happened in 1907. In 1906 he was opposed to the participation in this first Duma which had granted more scope of work than this second one whose rights had been curtailed. This was due to the changed circumstances. Reaction was gaining the upper hand and Lenin wanted to use the floor of the Duma as a platform to discuss socialist ideas.

Again after the 1917 revolution, when the Bolsheviks were forced to sign the Brest-Litovsk Treaty, everyone except Lenin was opposed to it. But Lenin said: 'Peace. Peace and again peace: peace at any cost – even at the cost of many of the Russian provinces to be yielded to German War Lord'. When some anti-Bolshevik people condemned Lenin for this treaty, he declared frankly that the Bolsheviks were not in a position to face to German onslaught and they preferred the treaty to the complete annihilation of the Bolshevik Government.

The thing that I wanted to point out was that compromise is an essential weapon which has to be wielded every now and then as the struggle develops. But the thing that we must keep always before us is the idea of the movement. We must always maintain a clear notion as to the aim for the achievement of which we are fighting. That helps us to verify the success and failures of our movements and we can easily formulate the future programme. Tilak's policy, quite apart from the ideal i.e. his strategy, was the best. You are fighting to get sixteen annas from your enemy, you get only one anna. Pocket it and fight for the rest. What we note in the moderates is of their ideal. They start to achieve one anna and they can't get it. The revolutionaries must always keep in mind that they are striving for a complete revolution. Complete mastery of power in their hands. Compromises are dreaded because the conservatives try to disband the revolutionary forces after the compromise from such pitfalls. We must be very careful at such junctures to avoid any sort of confusion of the real issues especially the goal. The British Labour leaders betrayed their real struggle and have been reduced to mere hypocrite imperialists. In my opinion the diehard conservatives are better to us than these polished imperialist Labour leaders. About the tactics and strategy one should study the life-work of Lenin. His definite views on the subject of compromise will be found in *Left Wing Communism.*

I have said that the present movement, i.e. the present struggle, is bound to end in some sort of compromise or complete failure.

I said that, because in my opinion, this time the real revolutionary forces have not been invited into the arena. This is a struggle dependent upon the middle-class shopkeepers and a few capitalists. Both these, and particularly the latter, can never dare to risk its property or possessions in any struggle. The real revolutionary armies are in the villages and in factories, the peasantry and the labourers. But our bourgeois leaders do not and cannot dare to tackle them. The sleeping lion once awakened from its slumber shall become irresistible even after the achievement of what our leaders aim at. After his first experience with the Ahmedabad labourers in 1920 Mahatma Gandhi declared: 'We must not tamper with the labourers. It is dangerous to make political use of the factory proletariat' (*The Times*, May 1921). Since then, they never dared to approach them. There remains the peasantry. The Bardoli resolution of 1922 clearly defines the horror the leaders felt when they saw the gigantic peasant class rising to shake off not only the domination of an alien nation but also the yoke of the landlords.

It is there that our leaders prefer surrender to the British than to the peasantry. Leave alone Pt. Jawaharlal. Can you point out any effort to organize the peasants or the labourers? No, they will not run the risk. There they lack. That is why I say they never meant a complete revolution. Through economic and administrative pressure they hoped to get a few more reforms, a few more concessions for the Indian capitalists. That is why I say that this movement is doomed to die, maybe after some sort of compromise or even without. The young workers, who in all sincerity raise the cry 'Long Live Revolution', are not well organized and strong enough to carry the movement themselves. As a matter of fact, even our great leaders, with the exception of perhaps Pt. Motilal Nehru, do not dare to take any responsibility on their shoulders; that is why every now and then they surrender unconditionally before Gandhi. In spite of their differences, they never oppose him seriously and the resolutions have to be carried for the Mahatma.

In these circumstances, let me warn the sincere young workers who seriously mean a revolution that harder times are coming. Let them beware lest they should get confused or disheartened. After the experience made through two struggles of the Great Gandhi, we are in a better position to form a clear idea of our present position and the future programme.

Now allow me to state the case in the simplest manner. You cry 'Long Live Revolution.' Let me assume that you really mean it. According to our definition of the term, as stated in our statement in the Assembly Bomb Case, revolution means the complete overthrow of the existing social order and its replacement with the socialist order. For that purpose our immediate aim is the achievement of power. As a matter of fact, the state, the government machinery is just a weapon in the hands of the ruling class to further and safeguard its interest. We want to snatch and handle it to utilise it for the consummation of our ideal, i.e., social reconstruction on new, i.e., Marxist, basis. For this purpose we are fighting to handle the government machinery. All along we have to educate the masses and to create a favourable atmosphere for our social programme. In the struggles we can best train and educate them.

With these things clear before us, i.e., our immediate and ultimate object having been clearly put, we can now proceed with the examination of the present situation. We must always be very candid and quite business-like while analysing any situation.

We know that since a hue and cry was raised about the Indians' participation in and share in the responsibility of the Indian government, the Minto–Morley Reforms were introduced, which formed the Viceroy's council with consultation rights only. During the Great War, when the Indian help was needed the most, promises about self-government were made and the existing reforms were introduced. Limited legislative powers have been entrusted to the Assembly but subject to the goodwill of the Viceroy. Now is the third stage.

Now reforms are being discussed and are to be introduced in the near future. How can our young men judge them? This is a question; I do not know by what standard are the Congress leaders going to judge them. But for us, the revolutionaries, we can have the following criteria:

1. Extent of responsibility transferred to the shoulders of the Indians.
2. Form of the Government institutions that are going to be introduced and the extent of the right of participation given to the masses.
3. Future prospects and the safeguards.

These might require a little further elucidation. In the first place, we can easily judge the extent of responsibility given to our people by the control our representatives will have on the executive. Up till now, the executive was never made responsible to the Legislative Assembly and the Viceroy had the veto power, which rendered all the efforts of the elected members futile. Thanks to the efforts of the Swaraj Party, the Viceroy was forced every now and then to use these extraordinary powers to shamelessly trample the solemn decisions of the national representatives under foot. It is already too well known to need further discussion. Now in the first place we must see the method of the executive formation: Whether the executive is to be elected by the members of a popular assembly or is to be imposed from above as before, and further, whether it shall be responsible to the house or shall absolutely affront it as in the past?

As regards the second item, we can judge it through the scope of franchise. The property qualifications making a man eligible to vote should be altogether abolished and universal suffrage be introduced instead. Every adult, both male and female, should have the right to vote. At present we can simply see how far the franchise has been extended.

I may here make a mention about provincial autonomy. But from whatever I have heard, I can only say that the Governor imposed from above, equipped with extraordinary powers, higher and above the legislative, shall prove to be no less than a despot. Let us better call it the "provincial tyranny" instead of "autonomy." This is a strange type of democratisation of the state institutions.

The third item is quite clear. During the last two years the British politicians have been trying to undo Montague's promise for another dole of reforms to be bestowed every ten years till the British Treasury exhausts.

We can see what they have decided about the future.

Let me make it clear that we do not analyse these things to rejoice over the achievement, but to form a clear idea about our situation, so that we may enlighten the masses and prepare them for further struggle. For us, compromise never means surrender, but a step forward and some rest. That is all and nothing else.

Having discussed the present situation, let us proceed to discuss the future programme and the line of action we ought to adopt.

As I have already stated, for any revolutionary party a definite programme is very essential. For, you must know that revolution means action. It means a change brought about deliberately by an organized and systematic work, as opposed to sudden and unorganised or spontaneous change or breakdown. And for the formulation of a programme, one must necessarily study:

1. The goal.
2. The premises from where were to start, i.e., the existing conditions.
3. The course of action, i.e., the means and methods.

Unless one has a clear notion about these three factors, one cannot discuss anything about programme.

We have discussed the present situation to some extent. The goal also has been slightly touched. We want a socialist revolution, the indispensable preliminary to which is the political revolution. That is what we want. The political revolution does not mean the transfer of state (or more crudely, the power) from the hands of the British to the Indian, but to those Indians who are at one with us as to the final goal, or to be more precise, the power to be transferred to the revolutionary party through popular support. After that, to proceed in right earnest is to organize the reconstruction of the whole society on the socialist basis. If you do not mean this revolution, then please have mercy. Stop shouting "Long Live Revolution." The term revolution is too sacred, at least to us, to be so lightly used or misused. But if you say you are for the national revolution and the aim of your struggle is an Indian republic of the type of the United State of America, then I ask you to please let known on what forces you rely that will help you bring about that revolution. Whether nationalist or socialist, peasantry or the labour, the Congress leaders do not dare to organize those forces. Congress leaders do not dare to organize those forces. You have seen it in this movement. They know it better than anybody else that without these forces they are absolutely helpless. When they passed the resolution of complete independence – that really meant a revolution - they did not mean it. They had to do it under pressure of the younger element, and then they wanted to use it as a threat to achieve their hearts' desire – Dominion Status. You can easily judge it by studying the resolutions of the last three sessions of the Congress. I mean Madras, Calcutta and Lahore. At Calcutta, they passed a resolution asking for Dominion Status within twelve months, otherwise they would be forced to adopt complete independence as their object, and in all solemnity waited for some such gift till midnight after the 31 December 1929. Then they found themselves "honour bound" to adopt the Independence resolution, otherwise they did not mean it. But even then Mahatmaji made no secret of the fact that the door (for compromise) was open. That was the real spirit. At the very outset they knew that their movement could not but end in some compromise. It is this half-heartedness that we hate, not the compromise at a particular stage in the struggle. Anyway, we were discussing the forces on which you can depend for a revolution. But if you say that you will approach the peasants and labourers to enlist their active support, let me tell you that they are not going to be fooled by any sentimental talk. They ask you quite candidly: What are they going to gain by your revolution for which you demand their sacrifices, what difference does it make to them whether Lord Reading is the head of the Indian government or Sir Purshotamdas Thakordas? What difference for a peasant if Sir Tej Bahadur Sapru replaces Lord Irwin! It is useless to appeal to his national sentiment. You can't "use" him for your purpose; you shall have to mean seriously and to make him understand that the revolution is going to be his and for his good. The revolution of the proletariat and for the proletariat.

When you have formulated this clear-cut idea about your goals you can proceed in right earnest to organize your forces for such an action. Now there are two different phases through which you shall have to pass. First, the preparation; second, the action.

After the present movement ends, you will find disgust and some disappointment amongst the sincere revolutionary workers. But you need not worry. Leave sentimentalism aside. Be prepared to face the facts. Revolution is a very difficult task. It is beyond the power of any man to make a revolution. Neither can it be brought about on any appointed date. It is brought about by special environments, social and economic. The function of an organized party is to utilise any such opportunity offered by these circumstances. And to prepare the masses and organize the forces for the revolution is a very difficult task. And that required a very great sacrifice on the part of the revolutionary workers. Let me make it clear that if you are a businessman or an established worldly or family man, please don't play with fire. As a leader you are of no use to the party. We have already very many such leaders who spare some evening hours for delivering speeches. They are useless. We require - to use the term so dear to Lenin - the 'professional revolutionaries'. The whole-time workers who have no other ambitions or life-work except the revolution. The greater the number of such workers organized into a party, the great the chances of your success.

To proceed systematically, what you need the most is a party with workers of the type discussed above with clear-cut ideas and keen perception and ability of initiative and quick decisions. The party shall have iron discipline and it need not necessarily be an underground party, rather the contrary. Though the policy of voluntarily going to jail should altogether be abandoned. That will create a number of workers who shall be forced to lead an underground life. They should carry on the work with the same zeal. And it is this group of workers that shall produce worthy leaders for the real opportunity.

The party requires workers which can be recruited only through the youth movement. Hence we find the youth movement as the starting point of our programme. The youth movement should organize study circles, class lectures and publication of leaflets, pamphlets, books and periodicals. This is the best recruiting and training ground for political workers.

Those young men, who may have matured their ideas and may find themselves ready to devote their life to the cause, may be transferred to the party. The party workers shall always guide and control the work of the youth movement as well. The party should start with the work of mass propaganda. It is very essential. One of the fundamental causes of the failure of the efforts of the Ghadar Party (1914-15) was the ignorance, apathy and sometimes active opposition of the masses. And apart from that, it is essential for gaining the active sympathy of and of and organising the peasants and workers. The name of party or rather,*(words missing) a Communist party. This party of political workers, bound by strict discipline, should handle all other movements. It shall have to organize the peasants' and workers' parties, labour unions, and kindred political bode. And in order to create political consciousness, not only of national politics but class politics as well, the party should organize a big publishing campaign. Subjects on all proletarians enlightening the masses of the socialist theory shall be within easy reach and distributed widely. The writings should be simple and clear.

There are certain people in the labour movement who enlist some absurd ideas about the economic liberty of the peasants and workers without political freedom. They are demagogues or muddle-headed people. Such ideas are unimaginable and preposterous. We mean the economic liberty of the masses, and for that very purpose we are striving to win the political power. No doubt in the beginning, we shall have to fight for little economic demands and privileges of these classes. But these struggles are the best means for educating them for final struggles to conquer political power.

Apart from these, there shall necessarily be organized a military department. This is very important. At times its need is felt very badly. But at that time you cannot start and formulate such a group with substantial means to act effectively. Perhaps this is the topic that needs a careful explanation. There is a very great probability of my being misunderstood on this subject. Apparently I have acted like a terrorist. But I am not a terrorist. I am a revolutionary who has got such definite ideas of a lengthy programme as is being discussed here. My "comrades in arms" might accuse me, like Ram Prasad Bismil, for having been subjected to certain sort of reaction in the condemned cell, which is not true. I have got the same ideas, same convictions, same zeal and same spirit as I used to have outside, perhaps-nay, decidedly-better. Hence I warn my readers to be careful while reading my words. They should not try to read anything between the lines. Let me announce with all the strength at my command, that I am not a terrorist and I never was, except perhaps in the beginning of my revolutionary career. And I am convinced that we cannot gain anything through those methods. One can easily judge it from the history of the Hindustan Socialist Republican Association. All our activities were directed towards an aim, i.e., identifying ourselves with the great movement as its military wing. If anybody has misunderstood me, let him amend his ideas. I do not mean that bombs and pistols are useless, rather the contrary. But I mean to say that mere bomb-throwing is not only useless but sometimes harmful. The military department of the party should always keep ready all the war-material it can command for any emergency. It should back the political work of the party. It cannot and should not work independently.

On these lines indicated above, the party should proceed with its work. Through periodical meetings and conferences they should go on educating and enlightening their workers on all topics.

If you start the work on these lines, you shall have to be very sober. The programme requires at least twenty years for its fulfilment. Cast aside the youthful dreams of a revolution within ten years of Gandhi's utopian promises of Swaraj in one year. It requires neither the emotion nor the death, but the life of constant struggle, suffering and sacrifice. Crush your individuality first. Shake off the dreams of personal comfort. Then start to work. Inch by inch you shall have to proceed. It needs courage, perseverance and very strong determination. No difficulties and no hardships shall discourage you. No failure and betrayals shall dishearten you. No troubles imposed upon you shall snuff out the revolutionary will in you. Through the ordeal of sufferings and sacrifice you shall come out victorious. And these individual victories shall be the valuable assets of the revolution.

LONG LIVE REVOLUTION
2 February 1931

OUR OPPORTUNITY

Indian freedom is not perhaps any longer a far distant dream; events are moving apace and it may become a reality sooner than we expect. British Imperialism is admittedly in a tight corner. Germany is about to topple down, France is tottering, even the United States shaky. And their difficulty is our opportunity. Everything points to that long prophesied eventuality – the ultimate and inevitable breakdown of the Capitalistic order of Society. Diplomats may agree to save themselves and Capitalistic conspiracy may yet keep the wolf of Revolution away from their doors. The British budget may be balanced, the moribund mark granted some hours of respite and King Dollar may retain his crown; but the trade depression if continued, and continued it must be, we know the members of unemployed being multiplied daily as a result of the Capitalistic race in production and competition is bound to throw the Capitalistic system out of gear in the months to come. The Revolution is, therefore, no longer a prophecy and prospect – but "practical politics" for thoughtful planning and remorseless execution. Let there be no confusion of thought as to its aspect or as to its immediacy, its methods and its objective.

Gandhism

We should not have any illusion about the possibilities, failures and achievements of Congress movement, which should be, as it is today, be better stamped Gandhism. It does not stand for freedom avowedly; it is in favour of "Partnership"

– a strange interpretation of what "complete independence" signifies. Its method is novel, and but for the helplessness of the people. Gandhism would gain no adherent for the Saint of Sabarmati. It has fulfilled and is fulfilling the role of an intermediate party of Liberal Radical combination fighting shy of reality of the situation and controlled mostly by men with stakes in the country, who prize their stakes with bourgeoisie tenacity, and it is bound to stagnate unless rescued from its own fate by an infusion of Revolutionary blood. It must be saved from its friends.

Terrorism

Let us be clear on this thorny question of terrorism. The cult of the bomb is old as 1905 and it is a sad comment on Revolutionary India that they have not yet realized its use and misuse. Terrorism is a confession that the Revolutionary mentality has not penetrated down into the masses. It is thus a confession of our failure. In the initial stages it had its use; it shook the torpor out of body politic, enkindled the imagination of young intelligentsia, fired their spirit of self-sacrifice and demonstrated before the world and before our enemies the truth and the strength of the movement. But by itself it is not enough. Its history is a history of failure in every land – France, in Russia, in Balkan countries, in Germany, in Spain everywhere. It bears the germ of defeat within itself. The Imperialist knows that to rule 300 million he must sacrifice 30 of his men annually. The pleasure of ruling may be bombed out or pistoled down, but the practical gain from exploitation will make him stick to his post. Even though arms were as readily available as we hope for, and were it pushed with a thoroughness unknown anywhere else, terrorism can at most force the Imperialist power to come to terms with party. Such terms a little more or less, must fall short of our objective – complete independence. Terrorism thus hope to wring out what Gandhism bids fair to attain – a compromise and an instalment of reforms – a replacement of a white rule at Delhi by a brown rule. It is aloof from the life of the masses and once installed on the throne runs the risk of being petrified into a tyranny. The Irish parallel, I have to warn, does not apply in our case. In Ireland it was not sporadic terroristic activities she witnessed; it was a nation-wide rising, the rank and file were bound by an intimate knowledge and sympathy with the gunmen. Arms they could have very easily, and the American–Irish poured out their money.

Topography favoured such a warfare, and Ireland after all had to be satisfied with an unaccomplished movement. It has lessened the bonds but not released the Irish proletariat from the shackles of the Capitalist, native and foreign. Ireland is a lesson to India and a warning – warning how nationalistic idealism devoid of Revolutionary social basis although with all other circumstances in its favour, may (be?) lost itself in the shoals of a compromise with Imperialism. Should India, if she could imitate Ireland still?

In a sense Gandhism with its counter – revolutionary creed of quietism makes a nearer approach to the revolutionary ideas. For it counts on mass action, though not for the masses alone. They have paved the way for the proletariat revolution by trying to harness them, however crudely and selfishly to its political programme. The Revolutionary must give to the angle of non-violence his due.

The devil of terrorism needs, however, no compliments. The terrorist has done much, taught us much and has his use still, provided we do not make a confusion of our aims and means, at desperate moments we can make of terrorist outrages our best publicity works but it is none the less fireworks and should be reserved for a chosen few. Let not the revolutionary be lashed round and round the vicious circle of aimless outrages and individual self-immolation. The inspiring ideal for all and sundry workers should not be that of dying for the cause but of living for the cause, and living usefully and worthily.

Needless to point out, that we do not repudiate terrorist activities altogether. We want to assess its proper value from the standpoint of proletariat Revolution. The youth, who is found not to fit in with the cold and silent organization work, has another role to play- he is to be released from the dry work and allowed to fulfil his destiny. But the controlling body should always foresee the possible reaction of the deed on the party, the masses and on the enemy. It may divert the attention of the first two from militant mass action to the stirring sensational action and it may supply to last with clues for striking at the root of the whole party. In either case it does not advance the cause.

Secret military organization is, however, not an anathema. Indeed it is the front line, "the firing line" of the Revolutionary party; must be linked with the "base" formed by a mobile and militant mass party. Collections of arms and finances for organization are therefore to be under taken without any scruple.

Revolution

What we mean by Revolution is quite plain. In this century it can mean only one thing -the capture of the political power by the masses for the masses. It is in fact The Revolution. Other risings attempt a mere change of your lordships, trying to perpetuate the rotting capitalistic order. No amount of profession of sympathy for the people and the popular cause can ultimately hoodwink the masses about the true nature and portent of such superficial replacement. In India too, we want nothing less than the regime of the Indian proletariat in the place of the Indian Imperialists and their native allies who are barricaded behind the same economic system of exploitation. We can suffer no black evil to replace the white evil. The evils have a community of interest to do any such thing.

The proletariat revolution is the only weapon of India to dislodge the Imperialist. Nothing else can attain this object. Nationalists of all shades are agreed on the objective- Independence of the Imperialists. They must realise rebelliousness of the masses is the motive force behind their agitation and militant mass action alone can push it to success. Having no recourse to it easily, they always delude themselves with the vision of what they consider a temporary remedy but quick and effective remedy, viz, overthrowing the foreign rule by an armed opposition of a few hundreds of determined idealist nationalists and then reconstructing the State on Socialistic lines. They should see into the reality of the situation, arms are not in plenty, and in the modern world the insurrection of an untrained body isolated from the militant masses stands no chance of success. The nationalists to be effective must harness the nation into action, into revolt And the nation are not the loud- speakers of the Congress-it is the peasants and the labourers who formed more than 95 per cent of India. The nation will stir itself to action only on assurance of nationalisation. i.e., Freedom from slavery of Imperialist – capitalists.

What we need to keep in mind is that no revolution can succeed or is to be desired, but the proletariat revolution.

The Programme

The need of hour is therefore for a clear, honest programme for the revolution, and determined action for realization of the programme.

In 1917 before the October Revolution had come off Lenin, still in hiding in Moscow, wrote that for a successful revolution three condition are essential:

1. A political-economic situation
2. A rebellious mass mind, and
3. A party of revolutionaries, trained and determined to lead the masses when the hour of trial arrives.

The first condition has been more than fulfilled in India; the second and third yet await finally and completeness. To mobilise them is the work before all workers of freedom and the programme should be farmed with that end in view. We propose to discuss its outline in the following and our suggestions on each section are to be detailed out in the Appendix A and Appendix B.

(1) *The base work:* The foremost duty before workers is to mobiles the masses for militant mass action. We need not play on his blind prejudices, sentiment, piety or passive idealism. Our promises to him are not mere sops or half a loaf. They are complete and concrete, and we can be with him sincere and plain, and should never create in his mind any miasma of prejudices. The revolution is for him, for to name only the prominent heads:

1. Abolition of Landlordism.
2. Liquidation of the peasants' indebtedness.
3. Nationalization of land by the Revolutionary State with a view finally to lead to improved and collective farming.
4. Guarantee of security as to housing
5. Abolition of all charges on the peasantry except a minimum of unitary land tax.
6. Nationalization of the Industries and industrialization of the country.
7. Universal education.
8. Reduction of the hours of work to the minimum necessary.

The masses are bound to respond to such a programme – we have only to reach them. It is the supreme task. Enforced ignorance on their part, and apathy of the intelligent classes on the other, have created an artificial barrier between the educated revolutionary and his less-fortunate comrade of the sickle and the hammer. That must be demolished by the revolutionary and for that purpose.

1. The Congress platform is to be availed of.
2. The Trade Union are to be captured and new Unions and bodies shaped and modelled on aggressive lines.
3. Ryat Union are to be formed to organize them on the issues indicated.
4. Every social and philanthropic organization (even the cooperative societies) that offers an opportunity to approach the masses should be secretly entered into and its activities controlled so as to further the real objective.
5. The Unions are Committees of artisans workers as well as intellectual workers and are to be set up everywhere

These are the lines of approach for the educated and trained revolutionary to reach the masses. And once they are reached, they can be moved easily by a training, at first in aggressive assertion, of their rights, and later on, by militant offensives like strikes combined with sabotage.

The Revolutionary Party

It is on the active group of Revolutionary that the main task of reaching the masses as well as preparing them for the action rests. They are the mobile, determined mind which will energise the nation into a militant life. As circumstances arise they come and will also come for some time longer from the ranks of the revolutionary intelligentsia, who have broken away from their bourgeois or petty bourgeois traditions. The revolutionary party will be composed of these souls and they will gather around them the more and more active recruits from the labour, peasant or small artisan classes. It will be mainly a body of revolutionary – intellectuals, men and women – and on them will devolve the duty of planning and executing, publicity and propaganda, initiating and organizing, or coordinating the activities and linking up the different unions into an offensive, of seducing the army and the police and forming the army of revolution with themselves and these forces, of offering combined and organised armed resistance in the shape of raids and risings, of mobilising forces for mass insurrection and fearlessly guiding them when that hour comes. In fact they are the brains of the movement. Hence what they will require is character, i.e., capacity for initiative and revolutionary leadership and above all it should be disciplined and strengthened by an intensive study of politics, economic problems, of history and social tendencies, and current diplomatic relations, of the progressive sciences and the science and art of modern warfare. Revolution is the creation of hard thinkers and hard workers. Unfortunately, the intellectual equipment of the Indian Revolutionaries is often neglected, but this has made them lose sight of the essential of revolution as well as the proper bearing of their actions. So a revolutionary must make of his studies a holy duty.

The party, it is clear, can in certain matters act openly and publicly. It should not be secret in so far as it can help it. This will disarm suspicion and will bestow on it prestige and power. The Party will have to shoulder high responsibilities, so it will be convenient to divide it into certain committees for every area with special tasks allocated to each of them. The division should be flexible, and according to the needs of the hour or on the study of the possibilities of a member, he should be assigned duties under any such local committee. The local committees are subordinate to the Provincial Boards, and they in their turn to the Supreme Council. The work of liaison "linking" within the province should be the concern of the PB and inter-provincial liaison is to be maintained by the Supreme Council. All sporadic actions or disintegrating Factors are to be checked but over centralisation is not feasible, and hence better not be attempted yet.

All the local committees should work in close cooperation having on each one representative of other committee. The Committee should be small, composite and efficient, never allowed to degenerate into discussion clubs.

The local Revolutionary Party in each area should have –

(a) General Committee: Recruitment, propaganda amongst military, general policy, organization. Co-ordination of the popular Unions (See Appendix A)

(b) Committee of Finance: This Committee may be composed with a majority of Women members. On it rests the most difficult of all takes and hence it should have ungrudging help from the others. The source of Finance are – Voluntary contribution, Forced contribution (Govt money), Foreign capitalist and Banking houses, native one in order of precedence, outrages on private personal wealth (however repugnant

to our policy reacts against the party and should not be encouraged), Contraband sources (embezzlement).
(c)   Committee of action: Its composition – A secret body for sabotage, collection of arms. Training for insurrection.
(d)   Groups (a) Younger: Espionage, local military survey (b) Experts: collection of arms, military training etc.
(e)   Committee of Women: Through no artificial barrier is recognized between men and women, yet for the sake of convenience and safety of the party there should be for the time being such a body entirely responsible for its own members. They may be put in entire charge of the (b) F. C.and of the considerable activities of the (a) G. C. Their scope on (c) is very limited. Their primary duties will be to revolutionise the women folk and select from them active members for direct service.

It might be concluded from the programme outlined that there is no short cut to Revolution or freedom. It cannot "dawn on us one fine morning", that would, were it possible, be a sad day. Without the base work, without the militant masses and the party ready in every way, it would be a failure. So we have to stir ourselves. And we have to remember all the time that the capitalistic order is drifting ahead for a disaster – the catastrophe will come off perhaps,in course of two or three years. And if we still dissipate our energies or do not mobiles the revolutionary forces the crisis will come and find us wanting. Let us be warned and accept two and three year's plan of Revolution.

APPENDIX A.

Duties of the General Committee.

Recruiting groups: A country-wide youth league chain which is almost complete. It has be linked together and most closely co-operate with the other Schools, Colleges, Gymnasiums, Clubs, Libraries, Study circles, Welfare association and even Ashrams – every inch of it are to be nabbed by the Youth Movement.

Propaganda

The Press is the best medium, but in rural areas the platform is to be utilized. Nothing is so helpful for workers and the masses as cheap, plainly written periodicals, books or leaflets. A warning is to be given against the present supply – the stuff we consume. It is not an easy art to say what one has to say and make other hear him. Special duty of seducing the military should be assigned to tried workers, e.g., 27 per cent of the army of the Punjabi Musalman are to be tampered by their Punjabi kinsmen. The Gurkhas are a problem, the Sikhs, Marhattas and Rajputs are not so.

General policy

Substitution of the bureaucratic authority by that of the masses. The Union of labourers, ryots, artisans, in their aggressive struggle to enforce their own right must be trained for the revolutionary offensive for capture of the political power.

Co-ordination

Calling for representatives of the local union, to form the local general Committees, calling for representatives to form the central committee of the party, and for delegates from time to time to meet in conferences for deciding on policy or programme.

Organization

Besides the forgoing, the selection of the personal and members of other committees.

APPENDIX B.

Duties of the Committee of Action.

Two classes of members (1) Junior & Women (ii) Senior. It is to be in charge of the underground work.

(1) Composition: Its membership is bound to be not large but efficient. It should insist on a rigorous discipline. It will supply the leaders for the Revolutionary "Red" Army, hence, extreme care and caution should be taken in its composition, and its existence and activities are to be kept secret from the ordinary members of the party.

Duty of the Junior & Women.

(1) Espionage and intelligence supply (2) Collection of Arms; to the present method should be added the method of direct acquisition through international sources;

(3) Members should be a sent to Western Countries for the purpose and the for learning the use of arms, e.g., Lewis and Vickers guns, preparation of hand-grenades, etc.; (4) Action - Survey of the locality. (The Government maps are to be spotted showing routes, canals possible shelters for members.) The model is indicated below from "Field notes, Afghanistan, 1914."*)

> Chapter 1. Physical Features, General Boundary, Rivers, Flood seasons, Bridges, Forts and Ferries, Navigability, Waistes.
> II. Populations, Religion; Language, Tribes, Castes, Distinctive dress and character.
> III. Supply - Fodder, firewood, grain transport, Ponies, Mules, Bullocks, Donkeys, Horses, Camels, Motors and Buses.
> IV. Forces - Police, Military Police - Military their strength, their activities if tempered, Outpost stations, cantonments. Distribution of Police, of the military police, of the infantry, cavalry or artillery - of arms and magazines, guns, pistols, rifles, small arms and big arms. Possible fighting men from the locality - hostile and friendly.

Roads: Description and a chart as follows

1. Form ....to ....Miles
2. Stages: ....stop ....Miles
3. Nature: Metalled - Motorable - Kutcha, etc.
4. Obstacles; Difficult in rains, etc.
5. Water supply, fuel, fodder connection, with remarks.

Training In volunteer corps - University corps, etc. Thorough study of the Field Service Regulation Vol. I and Vol. II is bound to be profitable. This knowledge is essential. Study of more military Literature and acquaintance with wherever possible, Soldiers in barracks and cantons to be encouraged.

Duty of the Seniors

Action of Finance: To be undertaken at the request of FC and GC with their sanction. To be limited to public money and Foreign capitalistic gains, for the present The effect on popularity and unpopularity, should be final test for such action.

SABOTAGE

On behalf of the Unions at the direction of GC
COLLECTION OF ARMS.

See foregoing.

ACTIONS FOR TERRRORISING

Against individual only in very extreme cases when his offence is against the public, not against mere groups or individual. Generally to be discouraged unless forced circumstances.

INSURRECTION

When the Supreme Council directs. Group rising essential. Raids for arms.

SKETCHES OF INDIAN REVOLUTIONARIES IN *KIRTI, MAHARATHI, PRATAP* AND *PRABHA*

Bhagat Singh wrote sketches of Indian revolutionaries many times over and in many languages: Hindi, Punjabi and Urdu; so some of his sketches are actually repetition with minor variations. He wrote the first of such sketches when he was in Kanpur and working in Ganesh Shankar Vidyarthi's Hindi paper *Pratap* under a fictitious name. Later on, he wrote such sketches in the Hindi-language *Maharathi* and *Prabha*, the Punjabi/Urdu *Kirti* and finally in the 'Gallows' issue of *Chand* published in November 1928. All such sketches have been put into this section with the details available.

1. Drops of Blood on the Day of Holi; 1926 (Originally in Hindi.)

Bhagat Singh came to Kanpur in 1923 after he ran away from home. There he worked on the editorial board of Ganesh Shankar Vidyarthi's weekly, *Pratap*. It was in Kanpur that he formed a close relationship with the revolutionary party. He discussed India's future with Shiv Verma, Jaidev Kapoor, Batukeshwar Datt, Bejoy Kumar Sinha, and the other comrades in the revolutionary party. During this time, he read Kazi Nazrul Islam's Bangla poems. In this period, Bhagat Singh also took part in flood relief activities in Kanpur and also served as the headmaster of National School at Shadipur village in Aligarh district, which was established by Congress activists of the area. Ganesh Shankar Vidyarthi had sent Bhagat Singh to the school when he realized Kanpur police had suspicions about him.

During this time, the Babbar Akali Agitation was underway in Punjab. This essay, 'Drops of Blood on the Day of Holi', was published in *Pratap* on 15 March 1926, to report the hanging of six activists from the agitation. Not only do we learn about the agitation from this essay, but the thoughts of an eighteen- year-old Bhagat Singh are also reflected in this essay.

On the 27 February 1926, on the day of Holi when the rest of us were busy in our merriment, a terrible event was unfolding in one corner of this vast province. When you hear of it, you will tremble! You will shudder! That very day, in the Lahore Central Jail, six brave Babbar Akali men were hanged to death. The contempt and lightheartedness that these people had demonstrated for nearly two years during their trial proved how earnestly Shri Kishan Singhji Gadgajj, Shri Santa Singhji, Shri Dilip Singhji, Shri Nand Singhji, Shri Karam Singhji and Shri Dharam Singhji had been waiting for just such a day. The Honourable Judge pronounced his verdict after months. Death by hanging for five, exile and long sentences the Cellular Jail in the Andaman Islands for many more in large numbers. The brave defendants thundered. The sky reverberated with their enthusiastic victory cries. An appeal was filed. Six, instead of five, became the recipient of the death sentence. That day the news came

From left to right: S. Kishen Singh (father), Bibi Amar Kaur (sister), social worker Sarla Devi and Rajguru's mother Parvati Bai

Bhagat Singh at eleven; this is the first of the four photographs of Bhagat Singh ever found

From left to right: Hukam (aunt), Vidyawati (mother), Jai Kaur (grandmother), Harnam (aunt), Amar (sister, sitting)

The Khatkar Kalan residence of Bhagat Singh; photograph taken circa 1858

Blood-soaked sand collected by Bhagat Singh from Jallianwala Bagh, Amritsar, in April 1919 (source: Supreme Court exhibition, 2008)

Bhagat Singh (standing fourth from right) photographed with the theatre group of his college

A photograph of Bhagat Singh during his first incarceration

Cells of the Delhi District Jail in which Bhagat Singh and B.K. Dutt were lodged

One of the bombs used in the bombing of the Delhi Assembly

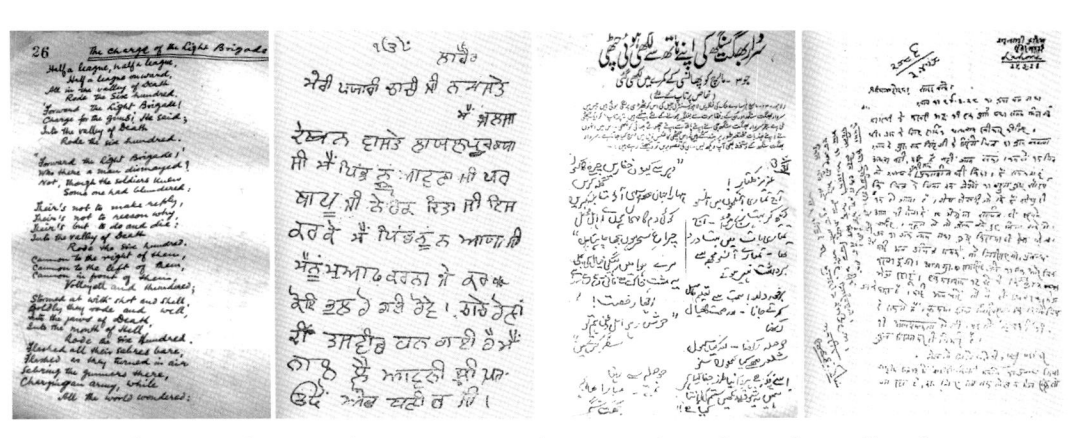

A prolific writer, Bhagat Singh wrote numerous letters, articles and even the profiles of fellow freedom fighters; these are writing samples from the four languages he wrote in: English, Punjabi, Urdu and Hindi

The only four photographs of Bhagat Singh ever found

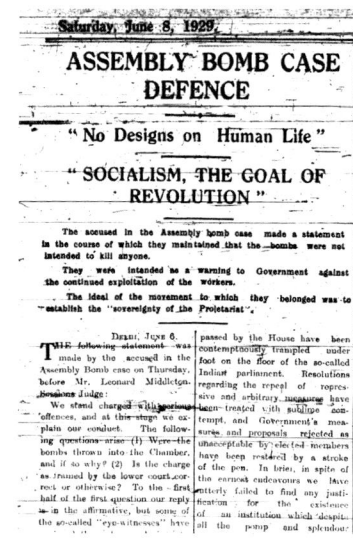

News reports about the cases against Bhagat Singh in various newspapers; from left to right: *The Hindustan Times*, India, and *The Pioneer*, London, on 8 June 1929

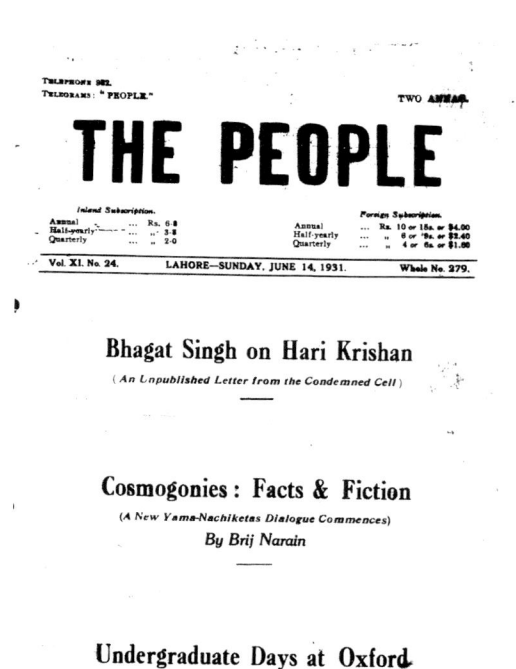

Articles and pieces written by Bhagat Singh in various publications; from left to right: Bhagat Singh profiles fellow freedom fighter Hari Krishan in *The People*, Lahore, 14 June 1931; *The People* carries 'Why I am an Atheist' by Bhagat Singh in its 27 September 1931 edition

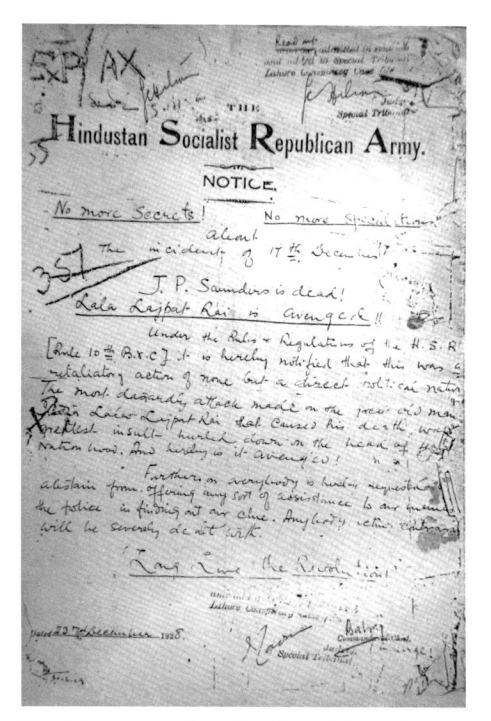

The Hindustan Socialist Republican Army issues a notice declaring that the murder of JP Saunders was an act of retaliation against the killing of Lala Lajpat Rai

The Tribune, Lahore, carries a report about the Dussehra bomb, 28 October 1926

Bhagat Singh, Rajguru and Sukhdev, the Assembly Bomb Case accused who were hanged to death on 23 March 1931

A poster displaying all the accused in the Lahore Conspiracy Case

A report in *The Tribune*, 27 March 1931, details how the bodies of Bhagat Singh and his comrades were disposed of

The telegram ordering the execution of Bhagat Singh and his comrades

Thousands gather at the cremation site near Hussainiwala on 24 March 1931 to bid farewell to the martyrs (source: *My Brother Sukhdev* by Mathuradas Thapar)

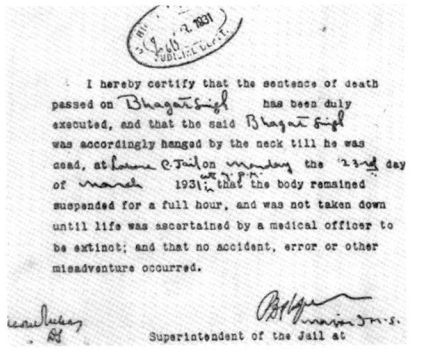

The death certificate of Bhagat Singh, issued by the superintendent of Lahore Jail

Edmonton Journal, Canada, carries an article about the unrest in the assembly after Bhagat Singh, Rajguru and Sukhdev were executed

The Tribune, 25 March 1931, carries news of the secret execution

Bhagat Singh's signature in one of his books

that a mercy petition had been filed; the Punjab Secretary declared that the hanging would not take place immediately.

There was a period of waiting, but suddenly we saw a small group of people accompanying the dead bodies to the cremation ground on Holi. Quietly their last rites were conducted.

The city was filled with festivities. People were throwing colour on the passers-by as usual. What terrible disregard! If they were misguided, so be it; if they were crazy, so be it. They were fearless patriots. Whatever they did was for this unfortunate country. They could not endure injustice; could not see the country in this fallen state; the oppression inflicted upon the weak became intolerable for them, they could not bear the exploitation of the common man; they challenged it and jumped into the fray. They were alive, they were visionaries. O, the mercilessness of the battlefield! Blessed are you! All friends and foes are equal after death; this is the principle of human beings. Even if they had done anything unpleasant, they should be worshipped because of how bravely and unhesitatingly they sacrificed their lives for the country. Despite being in the opposition, Mr Teggart could offer condolences upon the death of Jatin Mukherjee, a brave Bengali revolutionary, and praise his courage, patriotism and commitment; but we cowardly, beastly men cannot pause in our pursuit of pleasure even for a moment to dare to heave a sigh at the martyrdom of such brave men. How disappointing this is! These poor souls got 'adequate' punishment for their crime in the eyes of bureaucracy; another chapter in this tragic play came to a close. But the climax is still to come. Some more terrible scenes are yet to be played out. It is a long story; one will have to go further back in time to hear the story.

The Non-Cooperation Movement was at its peak. Punjab was not to be left behind. The Sikhs also rose in Punjab; they awoke from deep slumber and rose with a mighty roar. The Akali Agitation began. A string of sacrifices were made. The ex-Schoolmaster, Master Mota Singh of Khalsa Middle School, Mahalpur, District Hoshiarpur, gave a speech. A warrant was issued for him. But the Emperor's 'hospitality' was not acceptable to him. Even otherwise they were opposed to going to jail. He continued to give speeches. A huge meeting took place in Kot Fatuhi; the police surrounded it, but Master Mota Singh continued to speak. At the end, the audience rose to their feet with the President's permission. No one knew where Masterji disappeared. This hide-and-seek went on for a long time. The government was unable to handle this. Ultimately, an associate betrayed him and after a year and a half, Master Sahib was caught. This was the first scene of this horrible play.

The agitation for 'Guru Ka Bagh' began. Hired goons would fall upon unarmed brave men and beat them to a pulp. Could anyone who witnessed this or heard about it remain unaffected? All around there was a spate of arrests. A warrant was issued for Sardar Kishan Singh Gadgajj too. But he too belonged to the same group of people who did not believe in voluntary arrest. The police pursued him relentlessly, but he kept managing to evade arrest. He had also organized a small revolutionary band. He could not bear the brutal attacks on unarmed crowds. Along with pursuing peaceful ways of agitation, he considered the use of weapons necessary as well.

On one side, police dogs were set to sniff him out, on the other side, it was decided that the sycophants be 'reformed'. Sardar Kishan Singhji felt that though they needed to be armed for their own protection, they should try not to precipitate the issue. But the majority was of the other opinion. Finally it was decided that three people would announce their names, and take the entire responsibility upon them and begin to 'reform' (annihilate in reality) the sycophants. Shri Karam Singh, Shri Dhanna Singh and Shri Uday Singhji came forward. For a moment, keep aside the issue whether this was appropriate or inappropriate and try to imagine the scene when these brave men took the oath:

'We shall sacrifice everything for the love of our country; we take an oath that we shall die fighting, but never go to jail.'

What a beautiful, sacred scene it must have been in which these people who had sacrificed their families took their oaths! What is the limit of self-sacrifice? Is there any limit to courage and fearlessness? Can one ever reach the peak of idealism?

A Subedar was the first victim near a station on the Sham Churasi, Hoshiarpur railway branch line. After that these three people announced their names. The government tried very hard to arrest them, but could not succeed. In Rurki Kalan, Sardar Kishan Singh Gadgajj was surrounded. Another youth who was with him was also injured and arrested. But

Kishan Singh managed to escape with the help of his weapons. He met an ascetic on the way, who told him that he had a special herb with the help of which anything that he wanted could be done. He fell into his trap, and, leaving his weapons behind, went to see the ascetic. The ascetic gave him some medicine to grind and left, ostensibly to fetch the herb. He brought the police back with him. Sardar Sahib was arrested. That ascetic was a Sub-Inspector in the C.I.D. Babbar Akali braves had started their work in earnest. Several police informers were killed. The area between Doaba Beas and Sutlej, Jalandhar and Hoshiarpur district had been well known on the political map of India even earlier. Even in 1915, most of the martyrs had been from this region. This is where the maximum action was taking place now as well. The police department expended all its energy, but could not lay hands on anyone. There is a small stream a little distance away from Jalandhar. 'Chaunta Sahib' Gurudwara is located in a village on its banks. Shri Karam Singhji, Shri Dhanna Singhji, Shri Uday Singhji, and Shri Anoop Singhji were sitting with a few other people while tea was being made. Shri Dhanna Singh said, 'Baba Karam Singhji! We should leave this place this very instant. I feel something bad is going to happen.' The 75-year old Karam Singh did not pay heed to this. But Shri Dhanna Singh and the 18-year old Dilip Singh left. Baba Karam Singh peered carefully towards Shri Anoop Singh and said, 'Anoop Singh, you are not a good man.' But he himself did not pay too much attention to his own words. They were conversing when the police landed there. All the bombs were in Shri Anoop Singh's custody. All these people hid themselves in the village. The police searched everywhere, but it was futile. Finally, the police made an announcement. 'Hand over the traitors, or the village will be set on fire.' But still the villagers did not weaken.

Baba Karam Singh himself came forward when he realized the situation. Anoop Singh ran towards the police with all the bombs and surrendered. The other four people stood surrounded. The English police officer said, 'Karam Singh! Surrender and you shall be pardoned.' The brave man challenged the police, 'We will die for our country like true revolutionaries but will never surrender.' He encouraged the other three comrades as well with his words. All of them roared like lions. Both sides began to fire. When the ammunition of the patriots was exhausted, they jumped into the river. But the heavy firing went on and finally these four were martyred.

Shri Karam Singh was 75 years old. He had lived in Canada. He had an unblemished and pious character. The government thought that they had finished off Babbar Akalis, but they were rising steadily. 18-year old Dilip Singh was an extremely handsome, determined, robust but illiterate youth, and he had joined a band of robbers. Dhanna Singhji's education turned him from being a robber into a true revolutionary. Moreover, Sardar Banta Singh and Waryam Singh and several other dreaded robbers also abandoned robbery and became revolutionaries.

None of them feared death. They wished to cleanse their past sins. Their numbers rose steadily. One day while Dhanna Singh was sitting in village Manhaana, the police was called in. Dhanna Singh was heavily intoxicated and was arrested. His loaded pistol was snatched and he was handcuffed and brought out. Twelve plainclothes policemen and two English officers surrounded him. That very moment, a bomb exploded. It was Dhanna Singh's handiwork. He died, along with an English officer and ten soldiers. The others were injured badly.

Similarly, in village Munder, Banta Singh, Jwala Singh and several others were besieged. They were sitting on a terrace. There was an exchange of fire for some time, and then the police sprinkled kerosene oil with a pump and set the house on fire. Even so, Waryam Singh escaped, but Banta Singh was killed.

It would not be inappropriate to mention a couple of incidents that occurred earlier. Banta Singh was a very courageous man. Once, perhaps in Jalandhar Cantt, he had snatched a horse and a rifle from a soldier standing guard. During this time, when police parties would be searching for him high and low, he happened to accidentally bump into one such search party in the jungle. Sardar Banta Singh immediately challenged them. 'Come and fight if you dare!' On one side were mercenaries, and on this side, a person willing to do or die. How could there be any comparison? The police party left quietly.

A special force had been appointed to deal with these people. And this was the state of affairs! Anyway, there were plenty of arrests. In village after village police posts were set up. Gradually the power of the Babbar

Akalis began to wane. So far they had ruled virtually unchallenged. Wherever they went, they were welcomed happily and affectionately, and with a little fear and dread, too. The informers of the government were defeated. They didn't even dare to step out of their houses before dawn or after sunset. These people were regarded as heroes. They were brave, and it was considered auspicious to worship them. But gradually their influence began to ebb. Hundreds were arrested, and cases were filed against them.

Only Waryam Singh managed to stay alive. Upon realizing that there was greater police presence in Jalandhar and Hoshiarpur, he decided to leave for Lyallpur. One day, he was completely surrounded there but he managed to escape by fighting heroically. However the fight had exhausted him. And he had no companion. It was a difficult situation. One day he went to village Desiyan to visit his maternal uncle. His weapons were kept outside. After his evening meal, he was just about to pick up his weapons when the police came there. He was surrounded again. The English officer caught him from behind. But Waryam Singh managed to wound him grievously with his kirpan. Then he fell down on the ground. All attempts to handcuff him were in vain. After two full years of attempts to suppress the Akali group, it came to an end. A case was filed, the result of which has already been written above. That day these people had expressed a desire to be hanged quickly. Their wish was granted. They were granted eternal peace. Eik Punjabi Yuvak[82]

2. Introduction to the Heroes of Kakori; 1927 (Originally in Punjabi.)

On 9 August 1925, martyrs Ram Prasad Bismil, Ashfaqullah, and some other revolutionary comrades stopped a train near Kakori, near Lucknow, and robbed it to collect funds for their revolutionary party. Except for the martyr, Chandra Shekhar Azad, all the other

---

82   A Punjabi youth

revolutionaries were arrested. Bhagat Singh, too, by that time, had joined the Hindustan Republican Association during his stay in Kanpur. In his own words, 'Then came the time to shoulder the entire responsibility.' He took a great leap ahead from being a romantic revolutionary, and in his own words, 'I began to study.'

Bhagat Singh's essay, 'Introduction to the Heroes of Kakori', was published in Punjabi under the pseudonym of 'Vidrohi' (Rebel) in the May 1927 issue of *Kirti*. Bhagat Singh was arrested immediately after the essay was published, and the famous photograph taken of a handcuffed Bhagat Singh sitting on a charpoy was taken at this time. Before this, Bhagat Singh had returned to Punjab and got a Punjabi translation of Sachindra Nath Sanyal's book *Bandi Jeevan* (Enslaved Life) published.

Something has already been written about Kakori in *Kirti*. Today, we shall write about the Kakori Conspiracy and the heroes who were awarded harsh sentences in that case.

On 9 August 1925, a passenger train started from a small station, Kakori. This station is eight miles away from Lucknow. The train had gone barely a mile or a mile and a half when it was stopped by three young men travelling in the second-class compartment, and the money of the government treasury was looted by their other comrades. Right at the outset these men told the passengers in a loud voice not to be afraid, because their aim was not to harm them, but only to rob the cache of money. Anyway, they fired continuously. A passenger, who got off the train, was caught in the cross-firing and died.

A C.I.D. officer, Horton was put in charge of the investigation. He was sure right from the very beginning that the robbery was the handiwork of some revolutionary group. He began to investigate all the suspects. In the meantime, it was decided that a meeting of the state committee of the revolutionary group would be held in Meerut. The police got wind of it. Intense investigation was carried out.

Then towards the end of September, Horton issued warrants for arrests of these various people, and many searches were carried out on 26 September and a number of people were arrested. However, a few escaped arrest. One of these, Shri Rajindra Lahiri was arrested in connection with the Dakshineshwar Bomb Case and he was given a ten-year sentence. Later Ashfaqullah and Sachindra Bakshi were caught and a separate case was filed in the court.

The judgement pronounced by the judge makes it clear that the patriotic youth of the country no longer believed in a peaceful mode of agitation after the suppression of the Non-Cooperation Movement and they established a group, Yugantar Dal. Shri Jogesh Chandra Chattopadhyay came to the United Provinces from Bengal to help in the establishment of this group, and after setting things in place, he returned to Bengal in September 1924. At that time, an Ordinance had been passed in Bengal, and he was arrested on the Howrah Bridge as soon as he reached there. Upon being searched, his pocket yielded a piece of paper that had details of some meeting of the state committee of UP. Anyway, work had begun, and several dacoities took place. According to the judge, the leader of this group was Shri Sachindra Nath Sanyal.

Who does not know the name of Shri Sachindra Nath Sanyal! He is the author of the wonderful and famous book, *Bandi Jeevan*. He was a resident of Banaras and worked tirelessly in the Ghadar Movement of 1915. He was also the leader in the Banaras Conspiracy and the right-hand man of Shri Ras Bihariji. He was given life imprisonment but was released in 1920. Then he went back to his previous work and in 1925, his pamphlet 'The Revolutionary' was distributed throughout the entire country in a single day. Even the English newspapers heaped praise on it for its use of language and noble ideas. He was arrested in February. A case was filed against him and he was given a two-year sentence. He was dragged into the Kakori Case. He was very jovial person. He always remained cheerful in court and kept everyone else in a good mood also. He argued his own case. The judge believed him to be the leader. *Bandi Jeevan* has been translated into Gujarati and Punjabi.

He was a good writer in English and Bangla. Now he was awarded two life sentences. His younger brother, Bhupindra Nath Sanyal was also dragged into the case. He was an undergraduate student. He was arrested and sent behind bars for five years.

After Shri Sachindra, Shri Ram Prasad was the next famous brave. It was difficult to find such a handsome, strong youth. A very able man and an eminent Hindi writer. He wrote several books like *Katherine*, *Bolshevikon ke Kaam Man ki Leher* etc. He was also a reputed Urdu poet. He was 28 years old. First a warrant for his arrest was issued in 1919 in the Mainpuri Conspiracy, and he had a difficult time there. He ploughed the field all day long, tilled it, toiled and sweated over it, and got only an anna and a half for all his pains which was not sufficient to buy even one square meal a day. He even had to eat grass to survive. And yet, he would sit and compose poetry and cry for his beloved motherland and sing songs. Where can one find such young men now? He was very adept in the knowledge of warfare, and this was largely the reason he was given the death sentence. He laughed when the death sentence was pronounced. Such a fearless and handsome youth, an able and good writer and a fearless warrior is difficult to find.

The third brave is Shri Rajinder Lahiri. A handsome youth of 24, he was a student of a postgraduate programme at the Banaras Hindu University. The judge called him one of the pillars of the Yugantar Dal. He was among those who used to hold up trains. He looked weak and thin. He was caught in the Dakshineshwar bomb factory near Calcutta and given a ten-year sentence. He was filled with joy and even gained some weight. His body had filled out considerably during the Kakori Conspiracy Case and now he was given the death sentence.

The brave Roshan Singh was also given death by hanging. Earlier he had helped the police nab several dacoits. He was also caught. But he wasn't a dacoit. The judge also noted that this youth was a true patriot. We offer our obeisance to such a patriot!

Now it is the turn of Shri Manmath Nath Gupta. He was an undergraduate student in Kashi Vidyapeeth. Eighteen years old. He learnt Bangla, Gujarati, Marathi, Oriya, Hindi, English, French, and several other languages. The judge held him guilty for the dacoities as well, and pronounced a fourteen-year rigorous jail sentence. He was very fearless and laughed out loud when the sentence was pronounced. These days he is on a hunger strike in jail. A non-government member came to the jail to ask him why he was not eating, and he answered that he was a human being. And that they should be treated like human beings. He said that he didn't think he could endure treatment given to animals and survive fourteen years like that. It's better to die at once than die a tiny bit every moment. Earlier, he had gone to jail even during the Non-Cooperation Movement.

Now if we call the youth that we are about to talk about, a Mahatma, we wouldn't be lying. That brave man is Shri Jogesh Chandra Chatterjee. He was a resident of Comilla (Dhaka). He was an undergraduate philosophy student. His Professor considered him a very bright student and was happy with his work. However he not only spurned the college, but the entire philosophy of the world and, leaving everything, joined the Yugantar Dal. He was arrested under the Defence of India Act and was brutally tortured. One day faeces were thrown on his head and he was kept locked up in a cell for four days. He was not even given water to wash his face and his entire body was black and blue with bruises from severe beatings. But he did not utter a word.

When he was released in 1920, he began to work like an ordinary party worker in the Congress Party. He belonged to a poor family but, without bothering about that, gave up everything to serve the world. In 1923, he came to U.P. and laid the foundation of Yugantar Dal there. In 1924, he returned to Bengal and was arrested. First he was arrested under the Ordinance, and later he was brought to Kakori. He was given a ten-year sentence. He was an extremely handsome youth. The judge heaped praise on him.

Shri Govind Charan Kar, also known as D.N. Chaudhary, was arrested in Lucknow. He is a veteran revolutionary. In 1918 or 1919 the police came to arrest him in Dhaka. He returned fire and managed to escape, but his ammunition was exhausted and he was injured. He was arrested and sent to the Cellular Jail in Andaman Islands. In 1922, he fell seriously ill and was released. In 1925, he was arrested again, and this time he was sent behind bars for ten years.

Now we shall write something about Shri Suresh Chandra Bhattacharya. He also belonged to Banaras. At the time of the Banaras Conspiracy he was about 16 years old, and he was caught. But he was released as there was no evidence against him and then he was placed under house arrest in Bundelkhand. He was a well-known writer in Hindi. He was the assistant editor of the famous newspaper *Pratap* in Kanpur. He was also a wonderful singer. And he would practice yoga in jail.

Shri Raj Kumar lived in Kanpur. He was an undergraduate student of Banaras Hindu University. He was caught. Two rifles were confiscated from his room. He was a wonderful singer and quite a good looking young man. He was full of enthusiasm. When Sri Damodar Swarup was summoned to court despite being very ill, he got very agitated and verbally bashed up the judge. The judge threatened him, saying that he would pay for it when the judgement was pronounced. The brave youth was sentenced for ten years. In a way, his life was finished, but he only laughed. God bless such brave men and the brave mothers who gave birth to them.

Shri Vishnu Sharan Dublish was a resident of Meerut. He was the Superintendent of the Vaish Orphanage. He participated in the Non-Cooperation Movement while still in his undergraduate course and he made a second Bardoli out of Meerut. He was prepared for civil disobedience. He was an eloquent speaker. The Yugantar Dal met at his house. He was sentenced to seven years of jail.

Shri Ram Dulare was also given a seven-year sentence. He lived in Kanpur. A Scout-Master, he was an energetic party worker in the Congress.

The judgement was pronounced on the 6 April, and all these brave lads entered singing:

Sarfaroshi ki tamanna ab hamare dil me hai,
Dekhna hai josh kitna baazue kaatil mein hai!

The desire to die now suffuses our hearts
Let us test the might of the enemy!

They heard the punishment with smiling faces and laughed. Then came the sorrowful moment! These braves who were set to sail in the seas together were to be parted. "Ordinary people caught in their mundane lives cannot experience the boundless and fervent love that revolutionaries have." We cannot even fathom the meaning of this sentence by Shri Ras Bihari. How can inferior people like us understand the greatness of these people who had 'put their head on their palm in the lane of love'; were ready to either do or die. We cannot even dream of how deep their love for each other was. For a year and a half, they had been sitting together in anticipation of a dark future. That moment came – death by hanging to three of them, life imprisonment for one, a fourteen-year sentence for another, a ten-year sentence for four of them, and five to ten years rigorous sentences for the rest of them – and after pronouncing the judgement, the judge began to pontificate, "You are true devotees and selfless. But you have chosen a wrong path." It is only in a poor India that true patriots meet this fate. The judge left after advising them to reconsider their actions, and then... then what? Why do you ask? Moments of separation are very painful. We cannot understand what must have gone through the minds of those who were hanged; those who were thrown in jails for the rest of their lives. Indians, prone to bursting into tears at every step, quaking with fear for no reason – the cowardly Indians – what can you think about them? The younger bowed at the feet of the older ones. The older gave their blessings to the younger, embraced them warmly and could only heave a sigh. They were sent away. As he was leaving, Shri Ram Prasad said in a very poignant manner,

> '*Daro diwar pe hasrat se nazar karte hain*
> *Khush raho ahle vatan hum to safar karte hain*'

'We cast a yearning glance at the door and the wall
May our sweet country be happy; we embark upon a journey.'

With these words, he set off on a very long journey. As he came out of the door, he heaved a sigh that broke the terrible silence that shrouded the courtroom and said,

> '*Hai, hum jis pur bhi tayyaar themar jaane ko*
> *Jeeteji humse chhuraaya usi kaashaane ko*'

'Oh! Our beloved home that we were ready to die for

Has been snatched from us even while we live.'

People like us heave a deep sigh and think that we have done our duty. Our body doesn't feel on fire, we don't writhe in pain; this is how corpse-like we have become. Today they are sitting on a hunger strike and are groaning in pain and we sit quietly and watch the show. May God grant them strength and power that they may complete their term bravely and their sacrifice may bear fruit.

3. The Conditions under Which the Braves of Kakori Were Executed; 1928 (Originally in Punjabi.)

Bhagat Singh wrote another article about the martyrs of Kakori, 'Conditions under Which the Braves of Kakori Were Executed' in the January 1928 issue of *Kirti,* under the pseudonym of 'Vidrohi'. He also wrote an article titled 'The Last Message of Martyr of the Nation – Ram Prasad Bismil' in same issue.

We have told the readers about the Kakori Case in an earlier issue of *Kirti*. Now we shall narrate the conditions in which these four braves were hanged to death.

Shri Rajinder Nath Lahiri was hanged to death in the Gonda Jail on 17 December 1927 and Shri Ram Prasad Bismil in Gorakhpur Jail on 19 December 1927, Shri Ashfaqullah in the Faizabad Jail, and Shri Roshan Singhji in Allahabad Jail.

The judge in these cases, Mr Hamilton said while pronouncing judgement, that these youths were patriots and they did not do anything for personal gain and if these gentlemen repented their actions, their punishment could be mitigated. The four braves even made such a declaration, but how could the bureaucracy rest without hanging them? The sentences of many were even raised when their appeal came up. Neither the Governor, nor the Viceroy paid any heed to their extreme youth and the Privy Council dismissed their appeal even before hearing it. Many members of the U.P. Council, members of the Assembly, Council and State pleaded with the Governor to take pity on their tender age, but what was to come of it? All their efforts came to naught. The leader of the Swaraj Party of the U.P. Council, Shri Govind Vallabh Pant, was clamouring to send his arguments regarding their case to the Viceroy and the Governor. At first, the Honourable President dithered about granting permission, but when several members raised a united voice, they got permission to discuss the matter on the following Monday, but then, the English Vice-President, who was the officiating President at that time, announced a holiday for the Council on Monday. The council members took their petition to the doors of Nawab Chhatari, but he paid no heed, and not a single word could be said about their case in the Council, and the men were hanged finally. A similar anger raged in the hearts of the Russian Tsars and the French Emperor Louis, who assuaged it by hanging young men, but the foundations of their rule kept getting hollow, and they were overturned. The same immorality is being used again today. Let us see if they can fulfil their desire this time. We present below the circumstances of all the brave four men, which tell us that these priceless gems laugh in the face of death.

Shri Rajinder Lahiri

He was a post-graduate student at the Hindu University in Banaras. In 1925, the Dakshineshwar bomb factory near Calcutta was discovered by the police, and he was arrested and given a seven-year sentence. He was brought to Lucknow from and then given a death sentence in the Kakori Conspiracy Case. He was lodged in the Barabanki and Gonda Jails. He did not fear the approaching death, in fact, he was always smiling. He was a very cheerful and fearless man. He would mock death. Two of his letters will always remain with us. One was written on 6 October after the Viceroy had rejected the mercy petition. He wrote:

After spending six months in the cells of Barabanki and Gonda Jails, today I have been informed that I shall be hanged within a week, because the Viceroy has rejected the petition. I consider it my duty now to go to thank my friends (their names are given here) who have made efforts on my behalf. Please accept my final Namaskar. For us, life and death is nothing more than changing of old clothes. [The jail authorities censored the letter so a section is illegible] Death is approaching, and I shall embrace it with all my heart, eagerly and happily. As per the jail regulations, I cannot write anything else. A Namaskar to you and a Namaskar to the oppressed people of the country, Bande Mataram!

Yours,
Rajinder Nath Lahiri

When after this letter, he could not be hanged because an appeal had been filed in the Privy Council. He wrote the second letter to a friend:

Yesterday, I came to know that my appeal has been rejected by the Privy Council. You people tried very hard to save us, but it seems that the altar of our country needs the sacrifice of our bodies. What is death? Nothing but a different direction of life. What is life? The name for the other direction of death. Then why be afraid? This is a natural fact, as natural as the sunrise at dawn. If what we think is right that history turns full circle, then I think our sacrifice will not have been in vain.

My Namaskar to everyone – final Namaskar.

Yours
Rajinder Nath Lahiri

How innocent, how beautiful and fearless is this letter, and how simple is the writing! Then he was hanged to death two days before the others. When they prepared to handcuff him before the hanging, he asked what the need for that was. 'Tell me the way, and I'll walk there by myself.' A procession was taken out with his martyred body and the last rites were conducted with great fanfare. Building a memorial there is under consideration.

Shri Roshan Singhji

He was hanged to death on 19 December in Allahabad. His last letter was written on 13 December. He wrote:

The hanging will take place this week. I pray to God that your love bears fruit. Don't grieve for me. My death is a happy one. What one wants is that one should not die after committing a bad deed or earning a bad name and should think of God in one's last moments. So these two things are there. That is why there should be no sadness. For two years, I have been separated from my family and children. I got plenty of opportunities to pray to God. So I have severed myself from this web of earthly relationships. Now no desire remains. I believe that my agonizing journey of life is coming to an end and I shall go to a happier place. The scriptures say that those who die in battlefield are reborn as great souls. [Some text is illegible]

Zindagi zindadili ko jaaniye roshan! ('Know life as liveliness of spirit, Roshan!') Otherwise countless are born and die. A final Namaskar!

Shri Roshan Singh worked in Rai Bareilly. He had gone to jail in the Peasant's Agitation. Everyone was convinced that his death sentence would be commuted by the High Court because there was nothing against him. But even then he fell prey to British imperialism and was hanged. The words he uttered as he stood on the platform of the gallows were, "Bande Mataram!"

His dead body was not allowed to be taken in a procession. A photograph of the corpse was taken and he was cremated in the afternoon.

Shri Ashfaqullah

This passionate poet also went to the gallows with amazing cheerfulness. He was a handsome, well-built strong young man. He lost some weight in the jail. During visiting hours he said that he hadn't lost weight because he was unhappy, but because he ate very little as he was lost in his thoughts. A day before the hanging was to take place, he dressed up very well for a visit. His long tresses were well groomed. He talked cheerfully. He said, 'I'm getting married tomorrow'. The next day he was hanged at six in the morning. With a satchel containing the Quran Sharif slung on his shoulder, he strode confidently murmuring his prayers like a Haji. He moved forward to kiss the noose. And there he said,

"I don't have anyone's blood on my hands, and God will be my judge. All the accusations against me are false." The noose was pulled, and with God's name on his lips, he left for his heavenly abode. His relatives had to plead and beg to take his dead body, and they brought him to Shahjahanpur. Some people got an opportunity to pay their last respects to him as he was carried in a goods train at the Lucknow station. His face glowed even after ten hours of death. He seemed to have just dropped off to sleep. But Ashfaq had gone into such a deep slumber that he would never waken. Ashfaq was a poet and his pen name was 'Hasrat'. He said the following two couplets before he died.

Fanaa hain hum sabke liye, hum pey kuchh nahin mauokof!
Vaka hai ek fakat jaane ki briya ke liye.

Destruction is for each one of us; we are not the only ones
It is God alone who does not die

And

Tang aakar hum unke zulm se bedaad se,
chal diye sooye adam zindaane faizabaad se.

Tired of enduring their oppression, their cruelty
We are setting off for the beyond from the Faizabad.

A mercy petition was published, purportedly from Ashfaq; and Shri Ram Prasad has made the position clear regarding this in his final speech. He said that let alone a mercy petition, Ashfaq was not even willing to file an appeal. He had said that he did not want to bow before anyone except God. He had written all that only on the bidding of Ram Prasad. Otherwise, he had no fear or dread of death. The reader can also gauge as much after reading the above account. He was a resident of Shahjahanpur and was the right-hand man of Shri Ram Prasad 'Bismil'. Despite being a Muslim, he dearly loved the hardcore Arya Samaj activist (Bismil). Both these ardent souls sacrificed their lives for a noble cause and became immortal.

Shri Ram Prasad 'Bismil'

Shri Ram Prasad 'Bismil' was a very promising young man. A wonderful poet. Very handsome to look at. Very talented. Those who knew him said that had he been born in another place, or country or another era, he would have been an army chief. He has been considered the leader of the entire conspiracy. Even though he was not very educated, he would beat a public prosecutor like Pandit Jagat Narayan. He wrote his appeal in the Chief Court himself, upon which the judges commented that a very intelligent and competent person had a hand in the writing of that appeal.

He was hanged on the evening of the 19 December. When on the evening of 12 December, he was offered milk, he declined saying that now he would drink only his mother's milk. He met his mother on 18 December. When he met her, tears streamed from his eyes. His mother was a very strong lady. She said to him, "Sacrifice your life with courage for dharma and country like elders such as Harish Chandra, Dadhichi, etc. There is no need to worry or regret anything." He burst into laughter, said, "Ma! What worry and what regret would I have? I have not committed any sin. I am not afraid of death. But Ma! Ghee/Oil kept near the fire is bound to melt. Our relationship is such that tears welled in my eyes; otherwise I'm very happy." As he was taken to the gallows, he proclaimed loudly, "Bande Mataram!', 'Bharat Mata ki Jai!', and walked ahead calmly, saying:

Maalik teri raza rahe aur tu hi tu rahe
baaki na main rahun, na meri aarzoo rahe.
Jab tak ki tan mein jaan ragon mein lahu rahe
Tera hi zikreyaar, teri justujoo rahe.

Lord! May your will prevail and may you prevail
Neither I nor my desire may remain.
Till there is life in the body and blood in my veins
May you be remembered, and longed for.

As he stood on the platform, he declared:

'I wish the downfall of the British Empire.' (Originally in English.)

And then he recited:

Ab n ahle valvaley hain aur n armaanon ki bheed,
ek mit jaane ki hasrat, ab dile-bismil mein hai!

Now are there no sweet desires, nor do hopes throng,
Just a desire to die now lives in the wounded heart!

Then he began to pray to God and chant a prayer. The rope was pulled. Ram Prasadji was hanged. Today, that brave is no longer in this world. The English government considered him a formidable enemy. The popular notion is that his only fault was that he was born in this colonized country, but had become a heavy burden to bear and was well versed in warfare. A brave warrior like the leader of the Mainpuri Conspiracy, Shri Genda Lal Dixit had trained him. During the Mainpuri Case he had escaped to Nepal. Now that very training became a cause of his death. His dead body was handed over at seven and a huge procession was carried out. His mother said in her love for the freedom of the country, 'I'm happy at such a death for my son, not sad. I wanted a son like Shri Ram Chandra. May Shri Ram Chandra live long!'

His procession was bedecked with flowers and wreaths. Shopkeepers showered money from rooftops. At eleven they reached the cremation ground and the last rites were conducted.

The concluding part of his letter is presented here for you:

"I'm very glad. I'm ready for what has to happen on the morning of the 19th. God will grant me strength. I have faith that I shall be reborn very soon to serve people again. Please say my Namaskar to everyone. Kindly do one thing more for me – say my final Namaskar to Pandit Jagat Narayan.[83] May he sleep in peace with the money from our blood on his hands! May God grant him wisdom in his old age!"

All Ram Prasadji's desires remained locked in his heart. He made a grand declaration that we are presenting separately. Two days before

---

83 The Public Prosecutor who had tried so hard to get a death sentence for him

the hanging, Mr Hamilton from the C.I.D. tried to get information out of him, saying that five thousand rupees would be given to him and he would be sent abroad on a government scholarship to study for a Barrister's degree. But what did he care for such things! He was among those few who are born once in a lifetime and have the courage to reject the rulers. During the case, the judge asked him, "What degree do you have?" He had laughed and answered, "Kingmakers do not need any degrees; even Clive didn't have a degree." Today that brave man is no longer amongst us! Oh!

In the same issue of *Kirti*, Bhagat Singh wrote another piece, 'The Last Message of Martyr of the Nation Shri Ram Prasad Bismil', which is translated here for the first time. Bhagat Singh has written an autobiographical sketch, which was published in *Swadesh*, a Gorakhpur-based paper. The abridged form of the article is carried here, so that they can know the last thoughts of the revolutionary.

He wrote on 16 December 1927:

The time of execution is fixed for 6.30 a.m. on 19 December. Nothing to worry, I shall be reborn again and again due to God's grace and my aim will be to ensure complete freedom for the world. That nature's gifts should be equally shared by all and no one shall rule others. Everywhere people should have their democratic institutions. I now think it necessary to mention those things also, which happened with Kakori prisoners after 6 April 1927 Sessions Court judgement. There was an appeal in Avadh Chief Court on 18 July. That was only on behalf of four persons sentenced to death. But police filed counter appeal for enhancing the sentence. Then others also filed appeals, but Sh. Sachinder Nath Sanyal, Sh. Bhupender Nath Sanyal and approver Banwari Lal did not appeal. Then Pranvesh Chatterjee became approver and withdrew appeal. The death sentence remained unchanged, but the ten year sentence of Sh. Jogesh Chatterjee, Gobind Charan Kar and Mukandi Lal was enhanced to life imprisonment.

The seven year sentence of Sh. Suresh Chander Bhattacharya and Sh Vishnu Sharan Dublish was enhanced to ten years. Ramnath Pandey's sentence was reduced to three years and Pranvesh Chatterjee to four years. Prem Krishan Khanna's dacoity sentence was reduced to five years. Other appeals were dismissed. Ashfaq's death sentence remained unchanged and Sachinder Nath Bakshi did not file any appeal.

Before filing an appeal, I had already sent an application to the Governor that 'I have not taken part in any secret conspiracies nor will I have any links with these'. This application was mentioned in mercy petition also. But judges did not pay any attention to it. I sent my own arguments from jail to Chief Court, but the judges said that it is not the writing of Ram Prasad, but has been written with the help of a very competent person. Rather they negatively said that 'Ram Prasad is a dangerous revolutionary and if released, would do the same activities'.

After appreciating intelligence, ability etc, they said that 'he is a merciless murderer, who can even shoot them with whom he has no enmity'. Anyway, they had the pen, whatever they may write! But the decision of Chief Court shows that we have been sentenced to death due to vengeance only.

Appeal was dismissed, and then mercy petitions were filed with the Governor and Viceroy. Almost all the elected members of the U.P. Legislative Council made a signed appeal to remission the death sentence of Ram Prasad Bismil, Sh. Rajinder Nath Lahiri, Sh. Ashfaqullah and Sh. Roshan Singh. With my father's efforts, two big landlords and 250 honorary Magistrates gave a separate application. Assembly and Council of State's 108 members gave an application to the Viceroy to change our death sentence. They also said that the judge had said that 'if they repent then sentences would be radically reduced'. There were calls from all sides, but they were our blood seekers on all sides and Viceroy also did not listen to us.

Pandit Madan Mohan Malviya met the Viceroy with many people. Everybody thought that now the death sentence would be remitted. But what was to happen. Quietly, two days before Dussehra, all jails were sent telegrams that the date of executions has been fixed. When I was told about this telegram by the jail superintendent, I also said now you do your job, but on his insistence sent a mercy telegram to the emperor. That time, the idea of filing an appeal in the Privy Council also struck. Sh. Mohan Lal Saxena, an advocate was given the wire, and when he was told that the Viceroy had rejected all the applications, nobody believed it. Convincing him, the appeal was filed in the Privy Council; the result was known, and it was dismissed prematurely.

Now the question will arise that knowing everything beforehand, why did I send an apology, a mercy petition, and appeal after appeal? The only reason seems to me is that politics is a game of chess. The government has said forcefully in the Assembly about Bengal ordinance prisoners that there is strong evidence against them, which we don't present in open court for the safety of witnesses, though the Dakishneswar Bomb and Shobha Bazaar Conspiracy Cases were heard in open court. Killing of C.I.D. Superintendent Case was also held in open court and Kakori Case also took one and half years. 300 prosecution witnesses were produced, none had any problem, though it was also said that the root of the Kakori Case is in Bengal only. To expose the chinks in government declarations, I did all these things. I gave an apology too, sent appeals also, but what was to happen? The reality is that the oppressor kills and does not allow to even cry!

No revolt was going to take place by our remaining alive. Till now such strong appeals were never made for revolutionaries in India. But what has the government got to do with it? It is proud of its power. It has the arrogance of its oppression. **Sir William Maurice had himself remitted the death sentences of Shahjahanpur and Allahabad riots. And these sentences were remitted when riots were taking place every day. If reducing the sentence would have emboldened others then the same thing could be said about communal riots too. But here the issue was different** (emphasis added).

I am not disappointed at this time of giving up my life that this is wasted. Sacrifices never go to waste. Maybe because of our sighs that the idea of sending royal commission came to the mind of Lord Birkenhead, for whose boycott Hindu- Muslims got together again. God may give some wisdom to them fast and they become united again. **I had told advocate Mohan Lal Saxena, after our appeal was dismissed, that at least** to commemorate us this time Hindu-Muslim leaders should be united (emphasis added).

Government had mentioned that Sh. Ashfaqullah Khan is the right-hand man of Ram Prasad. **If a devoted Muslim like Ashfaq could be right-hand man of Arya Samaji like Ram Prasad in the revolutionary movement, then why can't other Hindus and Muslims unite forgetting their petty interests?** (emphasis added) Ashfaq is first such Muslim, who is being executed in connection with Bengal revolutionary party. God has listened to my prayer. My task is over. I have shown Hindustan by getting one Muslim youth for sacrifice that the **Muslim youth can also sacrifice their life for the country even more enthusiastically than Hindu youth** (emphasis added) and he had passed all the tests. Now no one shall dare say that Muslims should not be trusted. This was first experiment which succeeded.

Ashfaq! May god give peace to your soul. You have saved the honour of mine and all Muslims and also showed that like in Turkey and Egypt, one can also find such Muslim youth in India.

Now my only request to countrymen is that if they had even an iota of sorrow at our death, then, with whatever means, they must establish Hindu–Muslim unity; that was our last wish and this only can be our memorial (emphasis added). All religions and all parties should consider Congress as a representative. Then the day is not far, when Britishers have to bow before Indians.

Whatever I am saying, same is the opinion of Sh. Ashfaq ullah Khan Warsi. At the time of making appeal, I had talked to him in Lucknow; Ashfaq was not agreeable for giving a mercy petition. Only on my insistence, he had done so.

I had even told the government that till it is not ready to trust me, it can keep me in jail or exile to some other country and not allow me to return to India. But what was the government to do? Government only wanted to hang us, to sprinkle salt on Hindustanis raw wounds, to make them writhe in pain. Some things may get balanced and by the time we are reborn and get ready to work, the condition of country should have improved.

Now my clear advice is that neither one should give any statement before British courts nor make any defence. One reason for making an appeal was to get the execution date postponed and see the strength of youth and countrymen's help! I was really disappointed in this. I had thought of breaking out of the jail, if it had happened, other three's death sentence would also had been remitted. If government had not done it, I would have got it done. I knew its methods very well. I tried my best to break out of jail, but got no help from the outside. No youth turned up to help me. **My request to youth is that till many people get educated; don't pay attention to secret organisations. If they have desire to serve the country, they should work openly** (emphasis added). Just listening to empty rhetoric and imagining green pastures, they should not put their lives in trouble. **There is not yet time for secret work** (emphasis added). We had a lot of experiences during this trial, but the government did not give us any opportunity to avail these. But both Indian and Britain's governments will regret this.

At the time of interview, he said this also that 'revolutionaries lack courage and people don't have sympathy for them yet and they have regionalism among them a lot. They don't trust each other fully, so because of this, their desires remained suppressed. **I was offered rupees five thousand and promised to be sent to England for doing Bar at law, just on verbal assurance; but I treated it as a deep sin and paid no attention to it** (emphasis added). But regrettably many trusted and self-sacrificial considered comrades deceived the party for their personal comforts and behaved treacherously with us'.

(Signed off with 'Vidrohi', the fictitious name Bhagat Singh, used for writing many articles. He used many other fictitious names.)

4. Kuka Revolt; 1928 (Originally in Hindi.)

This essay, 'Kuka Revolt', was written by Bhagat Singh under the name of BS Sindhu. In this, he gives information about the history of the Kuka Revolt, and published this in the Delhi-based *Maharathi* in February 1928.

There is a sect in Sikhism that is known as 'Naamdhaari' or 'Kuka'. It doesn't have an ancient history. It emerged in the last half of the previous century. Today it seems to be a narrow religious sect, but its founder, Shri Guru Ram Singh was a true revolutionary. A famous devotee of God, he turned into a revolutionary social worker when he saw the flaws of society, and like a true servant of the people, he jumped into the fray when he realized that for the progress of the nation it was essential to cut off the shackles of slavery. A huge agitation was planned to revolt against foreign rule. Whatever disturbances took place during the run-up to the revolt gave ample opportunity to the rulers to crush the agitation and all those efforts bore no fruit except failure.

The history of the Kuka Agitation is still not known to people. No one has considered it important enough. We declare the Kukas to be misguided and foolish, and think we have dealt with them. Had these people laid down their lives for selfish gain, we could have shown contempt, but the spirit of patriotism suffused even their 'foolishness'. They would laugh even when being tied to the mouths of cannons. They would rend the skies with their happy yet thunderous slogans of 'Sat Sri Akal!' No line of pain, worry or regret ever showed on their brow. Is it right to forget them? Their only crime was perhaps that they did not succeed. But the Scottish revolutionary William Wallace also got the death punishment after failing in his mission. England adores him today. Then why should our heroes alone be consigned to such dense darkness? Anyway!

We think it gross ingratitude to forget those selfless people who laid down their lives for the country. If we cannot build a big stupa to honour their memory, then should we hesitate even to give them some place in our hearts? Inspired by this thought, this is an attempt to write a brief history of these 'foolish' and impatient optimists. If this helps people to know the truth about these people and inspires a desire in them to know more about them, I shall consider my attempt successful.

We can divide this mini-history into three parts:

1. The Character of Guruji
2. Kuka Revolt
3. After the Revolt

The Life History of Guru Ram Singhji

Shri Ram Singhji was born in 1824 in a village called Bhaini in the Ludhiana district of Punjab in the house of a carpenter. It is said that Guru Gobind Singhji had once prophesized, "I shall be born in the twelfth year and appear and achieve fame under the name of Ram Singh." That is why his devotees consider him to be an avatar of the ten Gurus. But the rest of the Sikh community holds the view that Guru Gobind Singhji bestowed all the rights of a Guru on the *Guru Granth Sahib* and brought the Guru system to an end. Thus, Guru Ram Singh cannot be called a Guru.

We are not concerned with such issues. As a young man, Guru Ram Singh enrolled in the army of Punjab Kesari Maharaja Ranjit Singh. He was a pious man and spent a large amount of time in his prayers. And that is the reason he quickly gained popularity in the army. As a result of spending too much time in his prayers, he would not be able to complete his duties as a soldier; and though he was retained in the army, he was relieved of all his tasks. One day, it is said, Guru Gobind Singh visited him in a dream and asked him to take up Baba Balak Nath's place as the Guru in Hazara (a border district). The very next day he left for that place with twenty - odd followers. Baba Balak Nath welcomed him warmly and baptized him. After returning from there, he resigned from the army and returned to the village to lead a quiet life there.

Many years passed. Many changes came. There was a succession battle after the death of Maharaja Ranjit Singh. The English won Punjab and it too was shackled in slavery like the rest of India. All this happened and along with this the 1857 Sepoy Mutiny also took place and the English began to rule in peace over India, but Guru Ram Singh continued spending a quiet life in his village. However, he was known far and wide for his religious devotion. People came to pay their respects from all over the district.

At first, he preached only devotion to God, but later he began to speak about social reforms. He vociferously opposed the sale and buying of girls, consumption of alcohol or meat products, etc. His followers, too, led simple lives and remained occupied in their devotion to God. He ran a community kitchen where everyone was served food free of cost. But soon all this changed.

It is said that an unknown sanyasi called Ram Das came and told him, "At this time the primary duty is to liberate the country from foreign rule." And from that very moment, his agenda became political. This anecdote about the sanyasi is only hearsay. It is possible that no such incident took place, but one will have to acknowledge that from this moment onwards Guru Ram Singh began to chafe at the country's slavery. He realized that not only did we lack physical freedom but the souls of our countrymen were dying too. People had forgotten even the idea of attaining freedom. Only recently had he learnt about the Sepoy Mutiny and its failure, and the untold and unspeakable cruelties inflicted upon Indians after it. That must have shocked him as well. Whatever it may have been, he studied the hollowness of foreign rule in great depth and set to work after outlining a programme. Till now there had only been preaching, now training and organization also commenced.

From that very moment, he began to preach non-cooperation that Mahatma Gandhi preached much later in 1920. His non-cooperation went beyond Mahatmaji's non-cooperation in some respects. Rejection of the courts, establishment of our own panchayats, boycott of British education along with a complete rejection of the foreign government, boycott of railways, telegraph and postal services was proposed. In those days our country had not yet become as dead as it has today; it had not become so totally dependent on these things that it could not even imagine rejecting them. Rather, they made such excellent arrangements for an alternative postal service that 'their mail reached more quickly than the government post did'.[84] In addition to this a strong message was given to always present a simple appearance and be clad in home-spun cloth. This

---

84   This observation is based on an essay by Bhai Parmanand.

message had not been taught for long before the government's sharp gaze fell upon this agitation. They began to plot to suppress this fiery agitation.

TD Forsythe, who was the Chief Secretary in the Punjab Government, and later Commissioner, Ambala Division in 1872 during the Kuka Revolt, wrote in his autobiography:

"In 1863 itself I had delved deep into the layers of this agitation and had realized what terrible consequences it could lead to. That is why I imposed a lot of restrictions on their propaganda, which led their propaganda work to slow down somewhat."

When the government prevented people from going to Bhaini in large numbers, or staying there for too long, Guru Ram Singh thought of a plan to counter this and continue with his work. He divided the entire community into 22 parts and appointed 22 capable men to organize them. They were known as 'Subas'. The work went on very smoothly. All the Naamdhaari Sikhs would give a tenth of their incomes to the Guru. All of it would be sent to Bhaini. While this went on, revolt was propagated secretly as well. The external fervour was toned down. So much so that the suspicion of the government abated considerably and it lifted all the restrictions in 1869.

Being released from the restrictions added to the enthusiasm of the people. So much so that it became difficult to contain it. And a half-baked revolt brewed up in 1872, which led to the suppression of the entire revolution. But before writing about that main event, it would not be inappropriate to reveal some interesting things about Shri Guruji's personal character.

Guru Ram Singh was a very noble-spirited and inspiring personality. Several incidents are popular about his unusual strength of character. It is said that anyone in whose ear he would chant the mantra of initiation, would become his devotee and follower for life. When this rumour about his power spread, two sly Englishmen came to test his power. They challenged him, 'We'll see what effect the Guru has on us!' But after the initiation, they became staunch devotees and even their personal flaws vanished from that day. In a similar vein, Dr Gokul Chand, PhD, writes in an essay that his paternal grandmother's brother was a very depraved man and was addicted to the hookah. Only one meeting with Guru Ram

Singh changed his life forever. He immediately gave up the hookah and was devoted to God for the rest of his life. Then there is the incident of another person, who had once committed a murder, who also took initiation from Guruji. He surrendered in court and confessed to his crime. When the judge asked in astonishment, "No one even knew you and there was nothing to link you with the murder, then why did you suddenly confess to the crime and invite death?" he answered, "This is the command of my Guruji."

Even the government wanted to test him. They sent a Sub-Inspector. He was also pleased at the assignment. He hoped to extract some secrets and win rewards. He met with Guruji. Returned. Gave in his resignation. The officers asked, "What does Ram Singh say?" He answered, "I don't have permission to say." He was asked, "Why are you submitting your resignation?" He answered, "This is Guruji's command. He says, don't work for foreign rulers."

There are several such incidents. Whatever may be the case, one will have to agree that Guruji was a great soul due to his devotion to God and noble character. So the above-mentioned incidents are not impossible. Anyway! The government became anxious to suppress this agitation. This was also natural.

The Beginning of the Half-Baked Revolt

In 1869 all the restrictions imposed earlier were lifted. Hundreds of people began to come to Bhaini. Some Kukas were travelling through Amritsar in 1871. They heard that Muslim butchers killed countless cows daily in front of the Hindus to taunt them. The Hindu community was distressed. Staunch cow-worshippers like Kukas could not endure this. They attacked the abattoir and killed all the butchers and set off for Bhaini. All the reputed Hindus of Amritsar were arrested. Guruji had already heard about the incident and the Kukas related the entire story to him as soon as they reached there. Guruji ordered, "Go, go and confess your crime and save those innocent people from catastrophe." The command was obeyed. The innocent were released and these brave men went to the gallows smiling cheerfully. A similar incident happened in

Raikot. Several Kukas had been hanged there as well. But there the rest of the Sikhs felt that their innocent fellow men had been hanged. The desire to retaliate with violence sharpened, but nothing in particular happened. On 13 January 1872, a Maghi Mela, the fair of the Maghi, was to be held in Bhaini. People began to arrive in thousands from far and near. One Kuka Naamdhaari brave was travelling through Malerkotla, the capital city of the Muslim-majority district. There he saw a Muslim riding an ox laden with a huge amount of load. He was beating the ox. The ox could barely move. When he saw this, the Kuka said to the Muslim, "Bhai! Don't be so cruel. He's already lugging so much load, why don't you get down and walk?" But that Muslim only cursed and swore at him. The Kuka-Sikh wasn't a coward or a faint heart; he retaliated. It led to fisticuffs. The officer of the Muslim kingdom, intoxicated with his own power, arrested him and bore him off to the police station, where the poor man had to undergo all kinds of torture and humiliation; and he was made to witness the killing of that ox. This was unbearable for him. As soon as he was released, he went to Bhaini. He narrated this heart-rending tale of vindictiveness in a crowded congregation. The people were already angry about the Raikot incident, and then this incident happened! It was like adding a spark to a smouldering fire, and it burst into flames. A decision was taken to take revenge on the basis of sheer brute power. Guruji became somewhat uneasy as he saw this immense enthusiasm. He wore his prayer clothes and pleaded, "Khalsaji! What calamity are you about to inflict? Just reflect with a cool head and patience. At least give a thought to what you seek to achieve by this. You'll ruin everything." Once Guruji explained to them the consequences of the action they proposed, a lot of them calmed down, but 150 men still remained bent on revenge. Their ardour didn't cool. Guruji tried everything but the insult to one of their brethren became unendurable for them.

The situation was grave. The work was incomplete and no preparations had been made. In such a situation, supporting these 150 men might have ruined the entire agitation. What was to be done? Everyone wondered how to resolve this dilemma and looked up to Guruji to show the path. What would another person have done in such a position? We don't know nor do we care. The far-sighted Guru thought at that time that those angry people could not be appeased, the revolt was not in a state of sufficient preparation and they had still not managed to get as organized as they wished to. If they could let go of those people and pretend as if they didn't have any connection with them, at least the rest of the agitation would be saved. The plan seemed good but the significance of political moves is dependent on their success. Guruji made this move, but it proved unsuccessful. The tables turned. This was a grave error that Guruji committed. He immediately informed the police that certain persons were preparing to go against his express command and going to kick up trouble in their passionate frenzy. 'I wish to inform the police immediately to alert them. Let the police deal with them. I don't wish to be responsible for any devastation.'

The Deputy Commissioner in Ludhiana at that time, Mr Cowan, wrote to the Ambala Commissioner about this incident in a letter dated 15 January:

"He (a police reporter) stated to me that Ram Singh, the leader of the kookas, went to those men, with a turban around his neck, and entreated them not to create a disturbance; and they would not listen to him; and that Ram Singh then came to the Deputy Inspector and reported to him that these men were upto mischief, and that he had no control over them." (Originally in English.)

But the government and the police deliberately kept quiet at that time. They passively allowed them to enter the state through territory controlled by the English. Why were those people not arrested immediately? Their ardour would have cooled down in a few days. But no, the government actually wanted an opportunity to crush the agitation. Now they had got a much-awaited opportunity. People also say that in fact the government had a hand in aggravating the situation. Anyway, even without saying anything more about this, we can accuse the government of keeping quiet deliberately. So, those 150 Kuka braves camped outside a village called Rabbon on the border of Patiala. They rested there all night and stayed there the next day as well. Perhaps they were waiting for more people to join them.

On 14 January 1872, they attacked a fort called Malaudh belonging to some Sikh chieftains. Why was this fort attacked? About this the District

Gazetteer record indicates that they were hopeful of the chieftains joining them in the revolt. It is possible that this may have been planned in the larger revolt that was being organized and they may have now refused help seeing the half-baked nature of the revolt. Anyway, the Kukas attacked the fort and carried off some weapons, horses and cannons. Both sides lost two men each and some were injured.

The next day they reached Malerkotla at seven in the morning. The government had already warned the kings of Patiala and Malerkotla. Special preparations had been made to protect Malerkotla, but this fearless force attacked with such formidable ferocity that they invaded not just the town but the palace as well. They attempted to rob the treasury. They would have succeeded but for a door which they wasted a lot of time in breaking open, and which revealed nothing but some worthless papers. And they had to make their escape hurriedly. They killed eight, injured fifteen and ran off with some weapons and horses. They lost seven men, five were arrested or wounded. The armed soldiers of Kotla pursued them and 'a sort of running fight was kept along, shots fired, and many more kookas were wounded, till both parties reached the village of Ruir in the Patiala State; the kookas carrying most of the wounded with them.' (Originally in English.)

They hid in the forests around Ruir village. The Deputy Administrator of Shivpur attacked them again. A battle was fought, but the Kukas were tired and weary, hungry and thirsty, and injured with no access to first aid. They were caught. In all, 68 people were caught and out of them 28 had been injured.

This incident is referred to as 'Revolt'. Mr Cowan writes in a letter:

'It looks like the commencement of an insurrection ...'

And at another place, he writes:

'I propose to execute at once all who were engaged in attacks on Malaudh and Malerkotla, I am sensible of great responsibility in exercising an authority which is not vested in, but the case is an exceptional one. These men are not ordinary criminals. They are rebels, having for their immediate object the acquisition of plunder, and ulteriorly the subversion of order. It is certain that had their first attempts been crowned with success, had they succeeded in arming themselves with horses and treasures, they would have been joined by all abandoned charities in the country and their extinction would not be effected without much trouble.' (Originally in English.)

These 68 people were brought to Malerkotla on 17 January. Two of these were women. They were residents of Patiala State. They were handed over to the State and of the remaining 66, it was decided that 50 would be tied to the mouth of a cannon and blown up. They were tied to the mouth of the cannon amid slogans of 'Sat Sri Akal' as their turn came. A loud boom and that Kuka brave left this world for another. Those 'fanatics' did not dread death; they did not quake with fear at the mere thought of dying like we 'intelligent' people do. Where else can one find such 'foolish' men in such numbers? It seems impossible that people dying for selfish ends could be as happy or embrace death as cheerfully. They had become victors over death with their self-respect, patriotic fervour, the desire to attain freedom and other such noble thoughts as inspiration. That is why we are compelled to bow our heads to them rather than consider them either over-zealous or impatient. Anyway, 49 men became cannon fodder but when it was the turn of the fiftieth, a lad of thirteen, a dispute rose. Mr. Cowan wrote in a letter:

'It was my intention to have had 50 men blown away, and to have sent the remaining 16 rebels to Malaudh to be executed there tomorrow, but one escaped from the guards and made a furious attack on me, seizing me by the beard and endeavouring to strangle me; and as he was a very powerful man, I had considerable difficulty in releasing myself ... The officials whom he attacked drew their sword and cut him down.'(Originally in English.)

What is commonly heard about this incident is that the fiftieth person was a thirteen-year-old boy. Mrs Cowan took pity on him. She asked her husband to release him. Mr Cowan acceded to his wife's request, and bent to say to the boy, 'Hey, you rascal, abandon the company of that rogue Ram Singh and say, "I am not his follower" and you will be let off.' The brave lad could not bear such insulting words for his Guru. He became enraged and grabbed Cowan's beard and did not let go till both his hands were hacked off and he was killed with a sword. In this manner, another chapter in this tragic drama came to an end.

To blow these people off at a cannon's mouth without a trial; this 'summary execution' seems completely improper. In the meantime, the Commissioner of the Ambala Division, Mr Forsyth sent a letter that clearly stated that no one was to be executed without a proper trial, but Mr Cowan did as he pleased, and when later a case was filed against him, he showed the Commissioner's letter written the next day, in which his action had been praised. But Mr Forsyth's statement had only said that he considered the matter to be a sensitive one and thought it was important that any difference of opinion between the officers should not be evident. So he had praised his previous work and asked him not to carry out 'summary executions'. But the rest of the 16 people were also hanged to death the very next day.

Even the officers were impressed with the lack of fear for death that these heroes exhibited. Mr E Perkinson, Deputy Superintendent of Police, wrote about two of these men in his report dated the 17 January:

'Both Hira Singh and Lehna Singh – the leaders – taken. They are generally well-dressed and well-to-do men; but have the appearance bold and determined-looking fellows.' (Originally in English.)

While this was going on, the Deputy Commissioner called Guru Ram Singh and asked him to go home because he was considered to be innocent as he had warned the police about the inflamed passions of the Kukas beforehand. The Punjab government recorded his innocence in its report to the Indian government in the following words:

'No direct evidence against Ram Singh in this case is sufficient to put him on trial.' (Originally in English.)

But on 17 January, the cavalry and other policemen surrounded Bhaini under the command of Colonel Baillie as per the directions of the Commissioner. The people were astonished to see the police, but when they learnt that the government wanted to arrest them, they surrendered peacefully. Along with Guru Ram Singh, four other people from four different districts – Shri Sahib Singh, Shri Jawahar Singh, Shri Gurdit Singh, and Shri Tannu Singh were caught. First they were sent to Allahabad and later to Rangoon. This arrest was as per the 1818 Regulation. This is when Guru Ram Singh's move turned wrong. Had he escaped arrest, the situation would have been brought under control.

As the news of the revolt spread in the state, people from all over began to march towards Bhaini. Everyone thought that the day they had waited for had come. The police also became alert. They would arrest on the spot any Kuka that they saw. During this, Colonel Baillie met a band of 172 Kukas. Four of them were people from other subas – Shri Brahm Singh, Shri Kahan Singh, Shri Pahad Singh, and Shri Hukum Singh were immediately sent first to Ludhiana and then to Allahabad to Guruji. 120 were sent back home and the rest of the 50 – having no homes and no ostensible means of living, being in fact, a dangerous clan of this sort who having sold all they possessed, hold themselves in readiness to perform any act that their leaders may order – were locked up in jail. In this manner, things quietened down in a few days. (Originally in English.)

After that:

Everything had happened. The main event of the drama had been enacted. Now only the conclusion remains to be narrated. Mr Cowan and Mr Forsyth were charged with 'summary execution'. They left no stone unturned to paint a thrilling picture of the terrible condition of Punjab and expressed a hope of collecting a reward. Mr Cowan was dismissed and sent back to England and Mr Forsyth was transferred to Awadh from Punjab at the same post. 50 blown off at the head of cannon and 16 hanged to death – and all that without a single case being filed; without allowing those people a chance to offer a defence – and this was the punishment meted out! In the words of Sir Henry Cotton, this punishment was grossly inadequate and unsatisfactory. But the Anglo-Indian press raised a hue and cry at even this mild punishment.

Here the rest of the Kuka community was being oppressed. Guru Hari Singh took over from Guru Ram Singh. He was placed under house arrest in Bhaini. A police post was set up right outside the gurudwara. For six years Bhaini was besieged as if by an enemy. No one was allowed in nor was anyone allowed to leave. Then the situation eased somewhat. Hari Singh could still not move freely, but others were allowed to move in and out of the village. Visitors would be harassed. They would be insulted, their arms would be tied and they would be left in the sun where they would sweat for hours. String cots would be placed on the palms of these men and some people would sit on top of the cots. Dirty, putrid water from the hookah would be poured on them. The people carrying out this torture were also citizens of this very country and the ones to endure these quietly were also unfortunate fellow citizens. And now this was reduced to a mere religious sect. But the history of Punjab is a very strange one. It was in Punjab that an entire community was outlawed; it was in Punjab that all the members of a particular community endured terrible oppression; it was in Punjab that an entire agitation of an entire community was declared unlawful. And that is what happened this time as well. Each Kuka was under house arrest in his own house. He could not go outside without permission from the police. To go to seek permission meant suffering unspeakable torture at the hands of the police and enduring insults and finally return home after being kept hungry and thirsty for several days; and still being denied permission to go. This went on for a long time and the restrictions have been lifted only now in 1920 during the days of the non-cooperation movement. So be it!

Guru Ram Singh stayed under house arrest in Burma. The District Gazetteer records, "Finally he died in Burma in 1885." But in 1920, Shri Alam Singh Engineer, a resident of Daska refuted this statement in an essay. He wrote that he and two other friends were travelling in Lower Burma from some port to Laasat Island. That port was called Bholmein. There they saw a man with a noble demeanour strolling under the eye of a policeman and after making some inquiries, they learnt that he was Kuka Guru Ram Singhji. One of his officers, Lakkha Singh was with him at the time. They conversed with each other and they learnt that he had permission to walk anywhere within a radius of five miles. So be it! The government never refuted the essay. Whatever the case may be, it seems clear that Guruji is not in this world today, but the Kuka people believe that he is alive even today. So be it!

Even today the Kuka community is present in Punjab. They continue to give the greatest importance to devotion to God. Their daily routine is to get up very early in the morning, have a bath and wash their hair, and spend hours in prayers. They are staunch opponents of alcohol and non-vegetarianism. A simple turban, a long kurta and long shorts – this is their dress. A blanket, a large drum-shaped tumbler, and an axe-like sharp weapon that they call 'safajang' – this was the sum total of their belongings. A beautiful cotton thread is tied around their throats. Even among them there is a special mendicant group. They forget their very being while singing hymns. Everyone who hears them experiences a sense of bliss and joy. One feels gripped by fervour of faith and eyes fill with tears of love and devotion.

Due to a belief in the eleventh and the twelfth guru, and staunch opposition to alcohol and non-vegetarianism, they are distinct from the rest of the Sikh community. But they have a strong sense of equality. They have festivals on Holi, etc., where they have a huge sacrificial fire. The rest of the Sikh community is not in favour of this. Kukas think of themselves as Hindus, not other Sikhs. During the days of the Akali agitation of yore, they had opposed the Akalis, which put them in a difficult position. But they are a unique community. They remind one of a budding flower that is crushed before it can blossom fully. Guru Ram Singhji's desires remained buried in his heart. The self-sacrifice of his followers also has been cast into oblivion. God alone knows what the fruit of the sacrifice of those anonymous people was. But keeping the issue of their success or failure aside, we bow in reverence to their selfless sacrifice.

5. Picture Introduction; 1928 (Originally in Hindi.)

An essay on the Kuka Revolt was published in February 1928 in *Maharathi*. Bhagat Singh wrote two picture-portraits along with the essay. This picture portrait has also been taken from *Maharathi*.

This time the colourful portrait is of Guru Ram Singh. He has already been introduced in detail in the last issue and also in this one. That is sufficient. However, there are two colourful pictures worth mentioning. One is of the Italian young men – every child aspires to become Mussolini. Even in India, a Scouts' Group, Mahavir Group, Swayam Sewak Dal became briefly, spaces were created but it was merely a temporary fad, like the boiling over of milk. It would be better for the leaders to make these sensitive young leaders into something rather than spout rhetoric in the Council.

The other picture is of Hunar Nagar (Craft Colony), which was organized in a special way in Bombay. We are struck with shock when we compare this huge Hunar Nagar and the condition of the poor, illiterate crafts persons. Even a fraction of the huge amount of money spent on craft exhibitions is not spent on the actual betterment of the condition of the craftspeople. We demand to know how many craftspersons are given money and basic rights by society and the government to aid them and enable them to progress. In how many mohallas, bazaars, towns and cities are craft workshops being opened? How many craftspersons are encouraged to participate in competitions? And how many young people are given stipends to encourage them to learn different crafts? Instead of opening Hindu Sabhas and Congress Mandals, we should expend all our energies in opening craft schools. It is craftwork that can save us from unemployment, slavery and poverty.

6. Kuka Revolt-II; 1928 (Originally in Punjabi.)

In the September–October 1928 issues of the Punjabi *Kirti*, Bhagat Singh again wrote on the Kuka revolt in an article titled 'Kuka Revolt'. The first two pages of this article have been reproduced and translated in English for the first time; these pages were left out in the earlier reproductions of the article in different volumes of Bhagat Singh's writings.

Today we present the history of the awakening of political consciousness and the anti-government agitation in Punjab. The political activity in Punjab begins with the Kuka Revolt. Although the Revolt appears to be communal, yet if we look a little more carefully, we realize that it was a huge political agitation with religion mixed in it, just as on earlier occasions, religion and politics were mixed in the Sikh agitation. Anyway, we see that our mutual sense of communalism and narrow-mindedness has the effect of making us forget great souls as if they had never been born. This is the situation that we see happening in the case of our great, great soul, 'Guru' Ram Singh. 'We cannot refer to him as "Guru" and they call him "Guru"; that is why we have no relation with them' – we wash our hands off the whole thing by saying such things. This is the biggest shortcoming of Punjab. All the great men born in Bengal have their anniversaries celebrated there, every newspaper has articles on them, *but we are always looking for pushing away our great men!*

If we start judging 1860 ideals of them in 1928, it will not fulfil the touchstone. But does it anyway lessen its significance? No! We have moved ahead and we should have. Our ideals should have been higher. But how their foundations were laid, to know this, knowing history is a must, and we shall bring to fore before people our old movements in their true colour. This shall include all movements – Arya Samaji, Islamic. Sikh gentlemen should not look at it with narrow communal glasses. Here political history is being written. (Editor, Kirti[85])

Maharaja Ranjit Singh was holding his court. The map of Hindustan was before the Maharaja. Hari Singh Nalwa was a brave general. He requested with folded hands, 'Maharaj[86] I have a request, if you will acced to!'

Maharaja said, 'Tell me, Hari Singh. What is it?'

He said, 'There is enough of rule now. Please order for including for merging two pilgrimage centres – Haridwar and Prayagraj – to the kingdom.' The King said with a long sigh, 'Hari Singh, all those places are red in colour. That is British territory. I apprehend the same colour roaming on Punjab too.' There was complete silence. The lion of Punjab knew what is going to happen after him. Days passed. Months and years too passed. The king left the world forever. The lion slept for ever. Leaving his dear Punjab as an orphan, he slept never to be woken. It was a hard life of wars. His whole life was a hard struggle of uniting Punjab into oneness. Now he departed, leaving everything.

Hari Singh Nalwa had already passed away. There was no inheritor of Punjab. The death of the lion made even jackals bold and there was fratricide. All the men of royal family were exterminated one by one.

---

85 Could be Bhagat Singh's note, as he was part of editorial team of *Kirti*
86 King

So in the end there were internecine wars among the Khalsa (Sikh royalty). The lion of Attari, Sher Singh Attariwala, fought with courage, but there were Lal Singh – and Teja Singh – like traitors of nation and country. In Gujrat and Chelian Wale, the Khalsa army showed its bravery for the last time, but due to Dhyan Singh and Gulab Singh, Punjab got drenched in red. Punjab was gobbled up. Maharaja Dalip Singh was sent to England, and what happened to Queen Zinda, who does not know?

Having suffered the oppression and with the idea coming to mind that their religions are being violated, kingdoms being snatched, common people, kings, Nawabs, armymen, every one got organised. There was preparation to throw the British out. Baji Rao Peshwa's adopted son Nana Dhundhupant, was a mature politician. Preparations were made throughout India secretly. It was a big organisation. Finally instead of 1 June, on 10 May, the struggle for independence began from Meerut. It was a movement to throw out the British from all over India. Everyone thought that Punjab is freshly trapped, after a brave fight; Punjab has been taken away from them. Lot of oppression has been committed on King Dalip Singh and Queen Mother Zinda. So everybody thought that Punjab was always ready to fight. Nana Dhundhupant returned from Ambala. It was thought enough to send envoys to Sikh states. But what turned out, nobody expected.

Sikhs were told that these Purbis (Easterners) had fought many battles against Sikhs and their kingdom was snatched. So by defeating their present movement, revenge should be taken. Poor Sikhs! What the army groups know about politics? Now there was no wise man like Maharaja Ranjit Singh among them. Everyone got trapped in this situation.

Once they jumped into war, they committed so many atrocities on freedom fighters that can't be described. Delhi was captured by the rebel forces. Sikhs were told that, it is the word of Guru Sahib that Khalsa will smash Delhi once and now is the time. Guru Sahib's word should be proved true by capturing Delhi. But this was also told that Khalsa will not rule in Delhi itself, but will hand it over to 'Sikh with hat'!

Innocent people got trapped. Slowly the war of independence was crushed, now it was called Ghadar-the revolt. This is considered one of the stigmas on Punjab. Given the chance, it will be discussed again and whatever material is found, will be shared with readers.

The above italicized part of Bhagat Singh's essay was edited out in the Punjabi and Hindi reproduced versions, and is being presented for the first time in English. It was probably left out due to Bhagat Singh's leaving out of Punjab's role during the Indian rebellion of 1857 against British rule. But even if someone disagrees with Bhagat Singh's analysis – one could counter it with facts as some people have done later – one cannot take the liberty of 'editing' his writing. In any case being printed, it is in the public domain, though not much in the public eye.

Punjab had been asleep only for a short while, it was a deep slumber, though it is beginning to regain consciousness now. A huge agitation rose. An attempt was made to suppress it. God also created a situation somewhat like this, and this movement was also suppressed. This agitation was the Kuka Agitation. A little religious, with some elements of a social revolution, this was an agitation not just for a change of rulers, but the change of an epoch.

Because now the history of all these movements tells us that a separate category of people is created who fight for freedom that neither care for the world nor abandon it like hypocritical ascetics. Those who were soldiers, but not those who fight for money, rather only for their duty or for some work, they fought and died selflessly. This is what Sikh history was, and this is what Maratha history tells us. The Rajputs with Rana Pratap were also similar warriors. The companions of Bundelkhand's brave hero were also like this.

It was to create a group of people like this that Baba Ram Singh began his preaching and organization. Baba Ram Singh was born in 1824 in village Bhaini in Ludhiana district. He was born to a carpenter. He served in Maharaja Ranjit Singh's army in his youth. Since he spent all his time in devotion to God, he left his job and returned to the village. He began to give discourses there.

Witnessing the tyranny inflicted upon the people in the name of the Mutiny of 1857 and the betrayal by Punjab certainly had some impact on him. The story is that Baba Ram Singh began to preach. And along with that, he began to speak about how necessary it was to free Punjab from the clutches of the firangis, the British. Even in those days he preached non-cooperation, which Mahatama Gandhi did only in 1920. In his programme, not only English education, jobs, courts, etc., and foreign goods were boycotted, but also the railways and telegraph services.

At first, only the name of God was preached. Religious sermons were delivered, though a great deal of emphasis was laid on completely giving up alcohol and non-vegetarianism. There was discourse against social evils like selling girls, but later the discourse took on a political hue.

In the old documents of the Punjab government, there is a mention of a Swami Ram Das, who was considered to be a political being by the English government and on whom the latter kept a close watch. After 1857, there is information about his sudden departure for Russia. Later, there is no mention of him. It is also said that this person one day told Baba Ram Singh that there was a need for a political programme and education in Punjab. It was thought necessary to liberate the country at that point of time. Henceforth, he included non-cooperation as part of his teaching.

TD Forsythe, the Chief Secretary of Punjab in 1863, has written in his autobiography that in 1863 itself, he could sense that this religious kind of agitation would create a huge furore some day. That is why he prohibited people from gathering in large numbers and going to the gurudwara in Bhaini. Upon this Babaji changed his tactics. He divided the state of Punjab into 22 parts. A person was appointed to be in charge in every district, which was referred to as 'suba'. Now he began the work of propaganda and organization in these subas. He even kept the propaganda for freedom of the country secretly. The organization grew and every Namdhari Sikh began to pay one-tenth of his income for the community. The government's suspicion was lulled as the external upheaval had died down and all restrictions were removed. And as soon as the restrictions were lifted, the enthusiasm of the people multiplied.

One day some Kukas were travelling through Amritsar in 1871. They heard that some butchers were killing cows in front of the Hindus to taunt them. They were staunch cow-worshippers. That night itself they killed all the butchers and set off for Bhaini. Many Hindus were arrested. Guruji heard the entire story. He asked them all to return and confess to their crime. The command was obeyed and these men went to the gallows. A similar incident happened in Ferozepur district. The hangings only incited people further. These people had an ideal before their eyes – to establish a Sikh rule in Punjab and they considered the protection of cows their greatest dharma. They continued to work to fulfil their duty.

On 13 January 1872, a Maghi Mela, the fair of the Magh (Hindu lunar month), was to be held in Bhaini. People began to arrive in thousands from far and near. One Kuka was travelling through Malerkotla. He fell into a fight with a Muslim, and was taken to a police station and beaten mercilessly and accused of killing an ox. He went to Bhaini and narrated his heart-rending tale. The people were inflamed. The desire to take revenge spread. The revolt that had been preached secretly was raging to find an outlet. But the preparations for a revolt were not adequate. What could Baba Ram Singh do in such a situation? If he had refused to let them vent their anger they would not have agreed, and if he supported them, then all their efforts would have gone waste. What should they do? Finally, when 150 men set off, he informed the police that those people were creating a disturbance and may cause some destruction, and that he was not responsible for it. The calculation was that if a hundred odd people out of thousands get killed and the rest of the organization remains intact, the absence of those people would be made up and soon they would be fully prepared to revolt. But we see that in the world, the principle of the end justifying the means works in the political field. If one is successful, then moves are considered to be well-intentioned and far-sighted, and if one fail even once, then nothing! The leaders get titles such as foolish, malintentioned etc. This is what we witness here. The move that Baba Ram Singh made to save his agitation resulted in his being called a coward, weak-willed, ill-intentioned and pathetic – all because his tactic failed.

We understand that it was a political move. He informed the police so that the damage could be controlled, but the government had been deeply suspicious of his great agitation and had been in search of an opportunity to crush them. They abstained from taking any action and let these men carry on.

But in his letter dated 11 January, Mr Cowan, the Deputy Commissioner of Ludhiana, wrote to the Commissioner that Ram Singh had informed them of his dissociation with the events and even warned them to take precautions against repercussions. Anyway, those 150 Namdhari Singhs set off in great enthusiasm.

When those 150 persons set off with the idea of taking revenge, the police had already been informed about it, but the government did nothing. Why? Because they wanted these men to create a disturbance so that they would get an opportunity to crush the agitation. And now they had found such a chance.

Those Kuka braves halted in a village called Rabbon on the border of Patiala State that day. The next day also they stayed there. On 14 January 1872, they attacked the fort of Malaudh. This fort belonged to some Sikh chieftains, so why did they attack? Regarding this, the *District Gazetteer* says that they hoped that the Malaudh government would lead their revolt, but since they refused, the Kukas attacked them. It is very possible that the Malaudh government may have promised to support Baba Ram Singh's effort, but refused when they realized that the revolt was taking place ahead of schedule, that even Baba Ram Singh was not with them, and that even the whole community had not been summoned. Anyway! Whatever it may have been, a pitched battle took place. They made away with some horses, weapons and cannons. Both sides lost two men each and some were injured.

They reached Malerkotla the next day at seven in the morning. The English administration had already informed the Malerkotla government about it. Preparations had been made. The army was armed and prepared but these people attacked with such ferocity that the army and the police were powerless. They entered the village and even attacked the palace. Even there the army couldn't stop them. They tried to rob the treasury. They would have succeeded, but for the enormous amount of time they wasted in trying to break open a door, which really didn't yield much. The army attacked with a great deal of intensity. Finally, they had to retreat. They killed 8 soldiers and injured 15 in that battle. Seven of their men were killed. They escaped with some weapons and horses. They managed to escaped, with the Malerkotla army in hot pursuit, and –

"A sort of running fight kept along. Shots fired and many more Kookas were wounded till both the parties reached the village of Ruir in the Patiala State, the Kookas carrying most of the wounded with them." (Originally in English.)

That is, they were retreating and fighting as they retreated. Many of their comrades were wounded and they would carry them as they retreated. Finally they reached Ruir village in Patiala State and hid in the jungles. After a few hours, the administrator of Shivpur launched another attack. A battle ensued, and by now these poor people were tired and weary. Finally 68 people were arrested. Two of them were women, and they were handed over to the Patiala State.

This incident is known as the revolt. Mr Cowan, the Deputy Commissioner of Ludhiana, wrote in a letter,

'It looks like the commencement of an insurrection ...' (Originally in English.)

That is, this appears to be a revolt.

The next day, a cannon was installed in Malerkotla and 50 Kukas were tied to their mouths and blown off. Each one of them would stride towards the cannon and bend down and utter 'Sat Sri Akal' as he was blown off. Then no one knew to which world they went. Forty-nine persons were blasted in this manner. When the turn came for the fiftieth, it turned out to be a thirteen-year-old boy. The Deputy Commissioner bent to whisper in his ear, asking him to abandon the foolish Ram Singh and seek pardon. But the boy could not bear this, and he leapt and grabbed Cowan by the beard and did not let go till both his hands were hacked off. The remaining 16 men were taken to Malaudh and hanged to death. And Baba Ram Singh along with four of his officers had already been arrested and sent to Rangoon. This arrest was made as per the 1818 Regulation.

When the news of this incident spread throughout the country, people were really surprised at what had occurred. They wondered why Babaji had not summoned them when he had started the revolt and set off towards Bhaini in large numbers. One group of 172 people met Colonel Wyllie. He was the Superintendent. He immediately got them arrested. One hundred and twenty of them were sent back home but 50 people were such who had no home or family. They had sold off all their land and property and set off to fight. They were thrown into jail. In this manner, the agitation was suppressed and Baba Ram Singh's entire mission came to naught. Later, all the Kukas in the country were placed under house arrest. They were asked to report their presence. People were no longer allowed to travel freely to or from Bhaini Sahib. These restrictions were lifted only in 1920.

This is a brief history of the first battle for independence in Punjab.

7. Madan Lal Dhingra March; 1928 (Originally in Punjabi.)

Bhagat Singh wrote a series called 'Azadi ki bheint Shahaadatein (Sacrifices for Liberty)' in *Kirti* between March-October 1928. While the people of Punjab were acquainted with Indian martyrs through these essays, at the same time, these essays help one gauge the questions arising in the minds of Bhagat Singh and his friends. The series of essays were written under the author name as 'Vidrohi'. In August 1928, the aim of this series of essays was described in these words: "Our aim is to write a chronological narrative of the agitations by the leaders even while publishing their biographies so that our readers can understand how consciousness was born in Punjab, and how the was work carried on and to what purpose, and what was the ideology for which those martyrs gave up their lives." A summarized version of this essay was published in *Chand* in the 'Phansi' issue in November 1928.

There is no need to reiterate the fact that no other state made as many sacrifices for the freedom of the country as did the state of Punjab. As the twentieth century dawned, a new wave of unrest spread through India which manifested itself in the form of agitation for 'Swadeshi'. Even then it was Punjab that was able to match Bengal. When the pain of watching the chains of slavery tighten day by day grew too intense, a large number of young men, inflamed with a passion for patriotism, were no longer satisfied with mere lectures and proposals; and some ardent souls launched a movement to change the epoch. This agitation succeeded in attracting patriotic young men and these moths hovering around the flame of liberty even gave up their lives; and by showing fearlessness towards death, revived memories of their elders.

In his poem 'Vidrohi', Bengal's revolutionary poet, Nazrul Islam describes how unique such epoch-changing rebels are. He has painted a wonderful picture of the hearts, minds, temperaments, and desires of these rebellious braves who go hand in hand with death, helpers of the poor, soldiers of freedom, enemies of slavery, foes of tyrants, oppressors and wilful rulers. At the very beginning he says –

Speak up, warrior! Say – My head is held high,
The Himalayan peak bows its head
As it gazes at my head held high!

Then he has described his firmness and gentleness. At places, he dances with death; at times, he is bent upon destroying the entire world in one blow. He crackles like lightning. He is sweet as music. He weeps in the midst of widows, slaves, the destitute, poor, hungry and the wretched. While describing the wondrous greatness of such wondrous lives, he makes the rebel say at the end –

I, the rebel, am now weary of battle; I shall find peace
Only the day the cries of the oppressed don't rend the sky,
When the tyrant's terrible sword no longer slices the battleground,
That is the day I shall find peace.

Such great rebels, who take on the entire world and throw themselves into the fire, forget all personal comfort and ease, they enhance the beauty of the world and adorn it further; and it is with their sacrifice that the world becomes a better place. Such brave souls are present in every country in every age. Even in Hindustan these Gods who deserve to be worshipped have always taken birth, are being born and will continue to do so. In Hindustan, it has been Punjab that has produced a greater number of such gems, and the first such martyr of the twentieth century was Shri Madan Lalji Dhingra.

He was not such a leader that his biography would be published while he was alive and distributed and sold for a couple of *annas*. He was not an avatar either, one whose 'greatness' was predicted. So many of the events in his life are not even known to us; so that we are able to shout, 'Talented ones show some early signs'.

He was a poor and unfortunate rebel. His father refused to recognize him as his son. Patriots and sycophants alike, even the popular leader in those days, Bipin Chandra Pal, abused him roundly in the newspapers. Then tell me, how in those circumstances, can one be successful in stringing together any facts regarding his life?

We have sat down to write his life-story in such difficult circumstances. Over a period of time we might even forget their names; that is why we are presenting this narrative with the few facts that are available.

He was perhaps a resident of Amritsar. He belonged to a good family. He went to England for further studies after his graduation. It is said that there he indulged in pleasures of life. This cannot be stated with certainty, but it is not inconceivable either. He was of a very romantic and sensitive temperament; that we do find evidence of. A famous detective of Scotland Yard in England, Mr ET Woodhall, published his diary in the weekly newspaper *Union Jack*. In the March 1925 issue, he wrote about Mr Madan Lal Dhingra. This detective had been assigned to watch him. He writes,

"Dhingra was an extraordinary man. Dhingra's passion for flowers was remarkable." (Originally in English.)

He further writes that Dhingra would go and sit in a beautiful corner in a garden and gaze like a poet at a flower for hours and sometimes a very keen glint would flash in his eyes. Noticing this, E.T. Woodhall writes,

'There is a man to keep an eye on. He will do something desperate someday." (Originally in English.)

We mentioned earlier that he might have gotten trapped in the pleasures of life. The story ahead is that the impact of the Swadeshi movement reached England and as soon as Mr Savarkar reached there, he started an organization by the name of India House. Madan Lal also became a member of that.

In the meantime, in India the epoch-changing people had established secret societies because open revolt was being crushed. So much so, that in 1908, a case was filed as the Alipore Bomb Conspiracy. Mr Kanhai and Mr Satyendra Nath were given death by hanging. Dhirendra and Ulhaskar were also sentenced to death by hanging at that time. These items of news reached England and these hot-blooded young men were inflamed. It is said that Shri Savarkar and Madan Lal Dhingra discussed these issues till very late into the night. To test his courage to give up even his life for the country, Savarkar asked Madan Lal to place his hand on the ground and stabbed his palm with a poker, but this Punjabi brave did not even let out the slightest squeal. The poker was pulled out. The eyes of both of them filled with tears. They embraced each other. Ah! What a beautiful time that was! How invaluable and rare were those tears! How beautiful a union! What greatness! How would we mere mortals know, we who are afraid of even the idea of death, how can we understand how noble, pure and heroic are those who sacrifice their lives for the sake of their country and community!

From the next day Dhingra did not go to India House or Savarkar's organization, and went and joined the Indian students' organization, run by Sir Curzon Wyllie, who organized both the Indian students and a special secret police to crush the puny efforts of the Indians to attain liberty. This Sir Wyllie was also the aide-de-camp of the Secretary of State for India. This incited the men in the India House and they began to call them traitors, conspirators, but Savarkar managed to pacify their anger by saying that after all was said and done, they had made great efforts to run their organization as well, so they should thank them. Anyway, some time passed without much happening.

There was a meeting in the Jahangir Hall of the Imperial Institute on 1 July 1909. Sir Curzon Wyllie was also attending it. He was talking to a couple of people when suddenly Dhingra whipped out a pistol and aimed it at his head. Curzon Sahib let out a scream in fear, but before anything could be done, Madan Lal pumped two bullets straight into his heart and put him to eternal sleep. He was caught after a struggle. And this was a sensational act in the eyes of the entire world. Everyone began to curse and abuse him. His father sent a telegram from Punjab saying that he refused to recognize such a traitor, rebel and killer as his son. Indians held many meetings. Tall speeches were given. Many resolutions were passed; all of them against Dhingra. But even at that time, there was a brave man, Savarkar, who supported him unreservedly. First, he did not allow the resolution against him to be passed saying that the case was sub-judice and that they could not blame him in the existing circumstances. Finally they began to vote on this resolution, and when the President, Shri Bipin Chandra Pal asked if it could be taken as passed unanimously, Savarkar Sahib stood up and began his oration. Just then an Englishman punched him in the face and said, "Look! How straight the English fist goes." He had barely finished speaking when an Indian youth struck him a blow with a club on the Englishman's head and said – "Look! How straight the Indian club goes." There was a furore. The meeting was suspended. The resolution could not be passed. Anyway!

The case was in the court. Madan Lal was very pleased. He seemed very much at peace. He was smiling in the face of death. He was fearless. Ah! He was a brave rebel. The speech that he gave at the end is proof of his goodness, patriotism and ability. We present it in his words. It was published in the *Daily News* dated 12 August.

I admit the other day; I attempted to shed blood as a humble revenge for the inhuman hangings and deportation of patriotic Indian youth. In the attempt I have consulted none but my own conscience; I have conspired with none but my duty."

"I believe that a nation held down by foreign bayonet is in a perpetual state of war. Since open battle is rendered impossible to disarmed races, I attacked by surprise, since guns were denied to me I drew forth my pistol and fired."

"As a Hindu, I felt that wrong to my country is insult to God. Her cause is the cause of Shri Rama; her service is the service of Shri Krishna. Poor in wealth and intellect, a son like me has nothing else to offer but his own blood, and so I have sacrificed the same on her altar."

"The only lesson required in India at present is to learn how to die, and the only way to reach is by dying ourselves. Therefore I die and I glory in my martyrdom."

My only prayer to God is – "May I be reborn of the same mother and May I redie in the same sacred cause, till the cause is successful, and she stands free for the good of humanity and to the glory of God – Bande Mataram." (Originally in English.)

History shall remember 16 August 1909. That day, the brave Dhingra, the one that made the voice of the Indian epoch-changing party in England resound, walked blithely to the gallows. Mrs Agnes Smedley mentions this incident and writes, "He walked to the scaffold with his head high and shook off the hands of those who offered to support him, saying that he was not afraid of death." (Originally in English.)

Ah! He shrugged off the hands of those trying to offer him support and said, "I am not afraid of death." Ah! Glory be to the immortal victory over death!

"As he stood on the scaffold he was asked if he had a last word to say. He answered – "Bande Mataram." (Originally in English.)

Such love for his mother! As he stood on the gallows, he was asked – 'Do you wish to say anything?' And the answer given was "Bande Mataram! Mother India, I salute you." The brave warrior went to the gallows; his corpse was buried inside itself, and the Indians were not given permission to cremate his body and perform the last rites. Glory to his memory is blessed. Many salutes to the priceless diamond of a dead country!

THIRTY-FIVE SKETCHES FROM PHANSI ANK (GALLOWS ISSUE) OF *CHAND*, ALLAHABAD; NOVEMBER 1928 (ORIGINALLY IN HINDI.)

The next thirty-five sketches are from the November 1928 issue of 'Phansi ank' (Gallows issue) of the Allahabad-based Hindi journal *Chand*. This special issue was edited by the well-known Hindi fiction writer Acharya Chatursen Shastri.

'Offerings to the Sacrificial Pyre of the Revolution'

Forty-eight word-portraits of patriotic revolutionaries were published in the issue 'Phansi' (Gallows) of *Chand*, titled 'Offerings to the Sacrificial

Pyre of Revolution'. Bhagat Singh's niece, Veerendra Sindhu published them in 1977, under the title 'My Revolutionary Comrades -Writer: Bhagat Singh'. She explained that most of these essays had been written by Bhagat Singh in *Kirti* in the Punjabi language, especially those related to Punjabi revolutionaries. The editor of the issue, Acharya Chaturen Shastri, who is also a famous Hindi writer, corroborated that most of these essays had been written by Bhagat Singh under different pseudonym. Shiv Verma, a co-author of these sketches, later clarified that out of the total of forty-eight sketches, twenty-eight were authored by Bhagat Singh. He (Shiv Verma) along with Jai Gopal translated many sketches from the Punjabi journal *Kirti*. Two essays of Bhagat Singh were taken directly from Hindi journals. However, nine essays related to the Punjabi martyrs of Babbar Akali and other movements, which were also written or drafted by Bhagat Singh, were in poor form. Shiv Verma, probably improvised these nine essays. So, as it turns out, twenty-eight out of the forty-eight sketches have been written by Bhagat Singh himself, nine were drafted or jointly written by Bhagat Singh and Shiv Verma, while the rest have been written by Shiv Verma under different pen names. The last nine sketches included here are the ones written by Bhagat Singh and Shiv Verma together. Two out of the thirty-seven, have been included above as they were directly taken from other Hindi journals in *Chand*, and therefore, the remaining thirty-five have been attached here. One sketch was ascribed by Shiv Verma to Ram Prasad Bismil. It must be noted that the order of the sketches has been maintained, as was in *Chand*. Special attention may be paid to Kartar Singh Sarabha's sketch, which has two versions; one published in the April-May 1927 issue of *Kirti*, and the other is perhaps improvised from *Chand*. Sarabha was very special to Bhagat Singh; he had seen Sarabha since his early childhood days at his home and always kept his picture in his pocket. Both versions of this sketch are included in the volume; the *Kirti* version is the first ever translation of the sketch!

8. Master Amir Chand (1928)

The sketches of Master Amir Chand, Avadh Behari and Basant Kumar Biswas have been published in the Punjabi journal, *Kirti*, in September 1928. In translation from Punjabi, these seem to have gone through minor changes by Shiv Verma and Bhagat Singh himself.

Shri Amir Chand was a teacher at the Mission High School in Delhi. At that time, he was a devotee of Swami Ram Teerth, but after he was exposed to the speeches of Lala Hardyal, he became his follower instead. Soon, he began helping in disseminating Hardyal's message. He was a good writer in both languages, Urdu and English, and when Lala Hardyal left India in 1908, the responsibility of the entire group fell upon Shri Amir Chand's shoulders.

Chand was robust and loved the spirit of freedom. He would laugh at himself and joke that if anyone came to Delhi and asked about the 'Monkey Master', that person should be directed to his home.

It was unclear who had lobbed the bombs in Delhi and Lahore. Only after the police had searched high and low did they manage to find a clue about Avadh Bihari's whereabouts from a house-search in the Raja Bazaar area of Calcutta. He was living in Amir Chand's house during that time. The police were already suspicious, and thus, a search was conducted and the cap of a bomb was discovered in the house. A letter signed 'M.S.', which was sent from Lahore, was also confiscated. Upon interrogation, it was revealed that the letter had been written by Deena Nath. As a result, several people by the name of Deena Nath were arrested. But later, the real Deena Nath was identified. He was also searched and arrested, and he disclosed the entire plot.

Amir Chand was charged with having written a leaflet 'Liberty'. The following lines were found to be especially objectionable:

We are so many that we can seize and snatch from them their cannons", and "Reforms will not do. Revolution and general massacre of all the foreigners, especially the English will and alone can serve our purpose. (Originally in English.)

When a death sentence by hanging was pronounced in the court, he laughed. He was fifty years old that time. Reputed people of Delhi vouched for his noble character in his defence. As a result of that, the judge wrote in his verdict on the appeal:

It must be borne in mind that 'patriots' of Amir Chand's type are often, except in regard to the monomania possessing them, estimable men and of blameless private life.(Originally in English)

In court, it was his adopted son, Sultan Chand, who became the witness for the prosecution and testified against him. Someone has rightly said:

"When my caretaker himself burnt my nest

The very leaves I had rested upon fanned the fire."

That day, even Master Amir Chand finally gave in, and tears flowed from his eyes in the court. A human being can endure everything but betrayal by those whom one holds dear; those who are closest to one's heart. That day, even such a simple and courageous personality as Masterji, could not hold back his tears. Sultan Chand, the adopted son, enjoys a life of pleasure even today.

Master Amir Chand may have shed tears over his son's betrayal, but the death sentence filled him with pride and joy. He was far above ordinary mortals. He proved this by embracing the noose cheerfully. He's not with us today, but his name, fame and rebellion lives on. Whenever the nation is free, this great soul will be venerated.

- Gautam

9. Shri Avadh Behari (1928)

After clearing his B.A. examination, Shri Avadh Behari cleared B.T. from Lahore Central Training College. He was a clever and intelligent young man. Even the judge present in the court proceedings of Amir Chand, wrote in his verdict:

Avadh Behari is only 25 years of age but he is a highly educated and intelligent man. (Originally in English.)

After a clue about his whereabouts had been discovered in Raja Bazaar in Calcutta, he was arrested at Amir Chand's house itself. At that time, he was responsible for leading the revolutionary activities in Uttar Pradesh and Punjab. Sachindra Babu has heaped praises for him in *Bandi Jeevan* (*Enslaved Life*). He used to often sing the following lines:

"Not I will take the obligation of the boatman
I'll leave the boat to God, and break the anchor"

Behari was charged with a total of thirteen crimes in court. It was said that he had capped the bomb in the Lahore Lawrence Garden along with Basant Kumar, and that he was fully involved in the incident.

He was sentenced to death by hanging. The day he was to be hanged, an Englishman asked him – 'What is your last wish?', to which he replied, 'Only that British imperialism is completely destroyed!' The Englishman said, 'Be quiet. At least be at peace in these last moments; what's the use of such talk now?' Upon this, he had answered, 'How can there be peace today? I want the fire to rage; rage on all sides. It should burn you and us, and our slavery; and finally Bharat shall emerge like gold from the dross.'

He put the noose around his neck himself, and bid a cheerful goodbye with 'Vande Mataram', his last words, on his lips.

Vidrohi

10. Bhai Bal Mukund (1928)

In the August 1928 issue of the Punjabi *Kirti*, the sketch of Bhai Balmukand is published with the note in the beginning which says, 'Till now we have been publishing the life sketches of Punjabi martyrs without any order. Sometimes we published sketches of martyrs of Babbar Akali and sometimes of 1914–5 Ghadar Party martyrs. Once we also published Madan Lalji's sketch. Now we wish to write an account of these movements chronologically. The sketch published in *Kirti* here is more or less the same as presented in the Hindi *Chand*. But this note indicates that Bhagat Singh did write sketches of Punjab martyrs in different movements, in Punjabi magazines like *Kirti*. Not all issues of *Kirti* have been traced yet, but this does confirm that most of the sketches included in Hindi journal, *Chand* were translated from Bhagat Singh's original Punjabi sketches.

This happened a long time ago. Aurangzeb reigned over Delhi. What can be said about the skirmishes of those days? Once a Hindu leader, Shri Guru Tegh Bahadur, was summoned. When he refused to convert to Islam, he was sentenced to death. His trusted aide and devotee, Shri Bhai Mati Das, was with him. Bahadur was brutally assassinated; hacked to pieces with a saw. Seeing his fortitude and courage, even the enemy was impressed by him. Since then, his descendants have been given the title of 'Bhai'.

Even in the twentieth century, this same revolutionary family has sacrificed two more jewels for the country. Who is not familiar with the name of Bhai Parmanandji, M.A.? And Shri Bal Mukundji was the son of his paternal uncle.

Bhai Bal Mukund was born in a village near Chakwal, in the district of Jhelum, in Punjab. He received his schooling there and then went to D.A.V. College in Lahore. After completing his graduation, he took a vow to dedicate his life to the service of the nation. He began to work in the programme spearheaded by Lala Lajpat Rai, which dealt with the upliftment of the untouchables. Despite many inconveniences, he persevered by working in distant hilly regions, where there was total ignorance. He worked with great enthusiasm and courage. His co-workers still sing his praises of his commitment and energy. In the meantime, the organization's work of the revolutionary party had begun in 1908, after the agitation launched by Sardar Ajit Singh and Sufi Amba Prasad in 1907. In 1909, an escaped revolutionary from Bengal came to them. Then, work to establish a consolidated group began. Around that time, in 1908, Lala Hardyalji, M.A. had left his studies midway and returned from England. He immediately began to promote the idea of a revolution. Within a short period of time, many idealistic youths became his followers. However, he had to leave for Europe midway.

Some time later, Sufi Amba Prasad and Sardar Ajit Singh were also constrained to leave for Iran. The youth continued to receive political education from Delhi's venerated martyr, Shri Master Amir Chandji. In

1910, Shri Ras Bihari Bose had begun to work at the Forest Department in Dehradun, and the onus of the organization of the revolutionaries outside Bengal fell upon Bhai Bal Mukund. He organized all the revolutionaries in Lahore and also constituted a working committee. Shri Bal Mukund was entrusted with the task of looking after the Lahore group. Revolutionary pamphlets by the name of 'Liberty' used to be distributed by members of this group.

In 1912, Sir Michael O'Dwyer became the Governor of Punjab. He was informed that a volcano was simmering in Punjab and that it could explode any moment. He was taking up his responsibilities with the specific brief of dealing with this problem when a bomb was tossed on 23 December, in Chandni Chowk in Delhi, at then Viceroy Lord Hardinge. This led to chaos all around, but despite their best efforts, the police could not lay their hands on the person responsible for throwing the bomb. The police were very frustrated.

In May 1913, all the British civilian officers were gathered in Lahore's Lawrence Garden. A bomb had been planted to blow up all of them. However, barring an Indian peon, no one died in the bomb explosion. But yet again, the culprit could not be traced. Bhai Bal Mukund was serving as the prince's teacher in Jodhpur at the time of this incident.

In Raja Bazaar, Calcutta, the police had managed to track some information about Avadh Bihari. The search also yielded Deena Nath's address. Several men by the name of Deena Nath were arrested. But they were let off for lack of evidence. However, finally the right Deena Nath was nabbed. This righteous gentleman was always immersed in God's worship, began weeping copiously upon being arrested. God knows why, the courage he had exhibited for so long deserted him suddenly. It is said that when he looked into the fiery eyes of the Deputy-Superintendent Sardar Sukha Singh, Deena Nath trembled and blurted out – 'All right, I'll tell you everything I know; but please don't look at me like that.' He gave a statement that ran for hundreds of pages. He divulged each and every detail. Bhai Bal Mukund in Jodhpur and a student of post-graduation, Shri Balraj, were arrested, along with several others. As per the statement recorded by Deena Nath, Shri Bal Mukund was still in possession of two bombs. The floor of his house in the village was dug two metres deep to search for them. All the roofs were taken apart as well, but nothing was found.

The case was filed.

Those were strange days. To sympathize with revolutionaries was no less than playing with fire. Several great leaders even threw out the revolutionaries' relatives who had come to them to seek advice. No one wanted to help them under such circumstances. Bhai Parmanand made all the necessary arrangements for the case of Bhai Bal Mukund, but this extraordinary soldier took everything as play. Upon hearing his death sentence he only said cheerfully – 'I am extremely happy today that I am also sacrificing myself at the feet of the Mother, in the same place where our ancestor Shri Bhai Mati Ramji had sacrificed his life for freedom.'

He was hanged at the beginning of 1915. His family was in dire straits. Bhai Parmanand had managed to scrape together a tiny amount to send a telegram to the advocate for the Privy Council. One gentleman asked – 'Bhaiji! What is happening in the case of Bal Mukundji?' He answered – 'We are trying to file an appeal in the Privy Council.' He was again asked – 'And what about you?' The answer was – 'I'm also ready.' By the time the telegram stating the rejection of appeal arrived from England, Bhai Parmanand had also been arrested. By then, all the efforts of the great revolution of 1915 had been unsuccessful. He was also arrested in that connection.

In the meantime, Bhai Bal Mukund was hanged to death. It is said that he was very elated that day. He shook off the policemen and went to stand on the platform by himself. Oh! Where else can one find such courage but in these revolutionaries! Mere mortals cannot show such disdain for death.

His sacrifice became even more poignant when his wife committed Sati upon his death. She loved him dearly. They had not been married very long; and she went to meet him in jail. She asked him – 'What kind of food do you get in the jail?' He showed her what they got to eat. She returned home and began to cook the same kind of food. She met him again. She asked him – 'Where do you sleep?' The answer was – 'Even in this hot weather, with two blankets in this pitch-dark cell.' She began to live exactly like him. One day, she heard noises and crying outside and understood what it meant. She got up, bathed, dressed well and wore her jewellery and sat down on a plinth inside the house to meet her beloved. She never got up again. Far, far away – as far as the eye can see, beyond the brutal rule of tyrants, far away from that – ahead of where there is no jail, no hanging, no revolution, no oppression, just love, it is there that she went to continue to live eternally with her beloved Bal Mukundji.

– Ramesh.

11. Shri Basanta Kumar Biswas (1928)

Shri Basanta Kumar Biswas lived in the Nadia district of Bengal, and he stayed as a servant under the alias of 'Haridas' with Shri Ras Bihari Bose as long as the latter stayed in Dehradun. Later, in 1912, he became a compounder in a clinic in Lahore.

He used to help in the organization of the revolutionary group in Punjab along with Bhai Bal Mukund. It is said that when the bomb planted in Delhi in 1912 exploded, he vanished from Lahore.

It is believed that the bomb in the Lawrence Garden of Lahore was also placed by him with the help of Avadh Bihari. Later, he brought two more bombs, which were kept with Bhai Bal Mukund as per Deena Nath's statement.

He left for Bengal in December 1913, and was arrested there in 1914 and brought to Lahore. Biswas was given a life imprisonment sentence in the Cellular Jail at the Andaman and Nicobar Islands. But then, Sir O'Dwyer, who at that time was extremely frustrated about not being able to nab the culprit of the Delhi bombing, appealed that the death sentence be given to Shri Basanta Kumar as well. He had acknowledged as well. And there was no doubt that the appeal filed by the police, with a recommendation from Sir Michael O'Dwyer, would be accepted. So, Shri Basanta Kumar was also condemned to death.

The judge had this to say about him:

He looked to me a man of some force of character, with none of the familiar marks of weakness in his face. (Originally in English.)

He was only 23 years old when he was hanged.

– Vidrohi

12. Bhai Bhag Singh (1928)

It may be common to find examples of well-educated people born in prosperous households, who dedicate their lives to the service of their nation and their community, but only a rare example might be found in history, of a person born in an ordinary village, schooled in an average manner, yet one who has astonished the world with his heroic deeds.

Such people are rare enough to be counted on one's fingers. Bhai Bhag Singh is one example of this kind. He was born in 1878, in the village of Bhikhiwind in the Lahore district, to Sardar Narain Singhji. His mother's name was Maankunwari. He stayed at home till the age of twenty and looked after the farming there. He learnt a smattering of Gurmukhi during this time and that is the extent of his education. Right from his childhood, he had the temperament of a soldier. And thus, he joined the army when he turned twenty. He was known for his independent spirit, and wasn't one to endure a reprimand or any advice from anyone. Even in the army, he would be wrangling with somebody one day, and scolding another the next. Everyone, especially the officers, found him utterly tiresome. Due to such behaviour, he could not get promoted to a higher rank from an ordinary constable, despite working for five years in the job.

Later, he left the army, and without returning home, went off to China and joined the Hong Kong police. After working there for two and a half years, he had a disagreement with his superior officer and went to Shanghai. After working for another two and a half years in the Municipal Police there, he decided to go to Canada as he saw a large number of Indians bound for America. And this is where his public life was to begin.

It doesn't take long for hearts to meet if one's thoughts and temperaments converge. So he became fast friends with Bhai Balwant

Singh, Bhai Sunder Singh, Bhai Harinam Singh and Arjun Singh, upon reaching Canada. During that time, the Canadians treated the Indians that had settled in Canada very poorly. This was done to the extent that even after toiling very hard, the Indians were not able to find a foothold anywhere. They were also prone to infighting. They only thought about their own selves. This above-mentioned group of friends extended a hand in these tough times. They had only begun work and things quickly gained momentum; in a place where there had not been a single gurudwara, now, there were several. All the dispersed energy was given a focal point and work soon began to establish a strong organization. Indians in Canada did not have the liberty to live like themselves, like Indians. They were not allowed to cremate their dead and perforce had to bury them instead. These people bought some land and made a cremation ground there. In fact, Bhai Arjun Singh was the first to be cremated there.

It was difficult for the Immigration officers to tolerate this progress made by the Indians. On one hand, they began to attempt to send the Indians to Honduras, and on the other, a new law was enacted. According to this law, no *new* Indian could come to Canada. Bhai Bhag Singh raised his voice against this with the help of his friends. Two people were sent to Honduras to assess the situation there. They returned, reporting that Honduras was in a terrible state, worse than that of Canada. Seeing their plan fail, the Immigration officers felt frustrated and were furious with them.[87] In the meantime, to oppose the new law, it was decided that those people who had been already living in Canada could go to India and bring their families, but this decision had to be given a more practical shape. So, our hero Bhai Bhag Singh and two other friends, left for India.

They came to India but were clueless about where to bring the families from. Singh's wife had died and he had no children, so he remarried a woman from Peshawar and headed back. At Hong Kong, he learnt that it was not possible to buy a ticket to Canada. Despite his best efforts, he had to stay in Hong Kong for a very long time and this is where his son, Joginder Singh, was born. Finally, he was allowed to disembark at Vancouver after overcoming many hurdles.

---

87   The two Indians who were sent to Honduras.

Till then, he had largely been involved only in religious matters, but the experience of this voyage altered his outlook. He became increasingly convinced that there was no corner of the world where colonized people were welcome, and till India did not attain independence, they would have to face trouble at every step. During this time, the newspaper *Ghadar* began to be published from America. Bhag Singhji helped the paper with utter devotion and financially supported it. Interestingly, even though the *Ghadar* paper was published from the United States, its policies were mainly propagated in Canada.

The quarrel between the Immigration officers and the Indians was still going on, when the Komagata Maru ship landed in Canada. Untold miseries were heaped upon the passengers. The dastardly ruses that were used to torture those valiant souls cannot be described here, but I am narrating one of those which is related to our hero. When the Immigration officers did not allow this ship to dock anywhere, Bhai Bhag Singh arranged for a harbour to be bought and the ship was docked there. Another stratagem was employed by the Immigration office. They persuaded the owner of the ship to side with them and made him demand the entire amount of his fare in advance instead of accepting instalments. The people on the ship were caught in a bind. They did not have enough money for that. They had not even been able to sell anything so far, so what were they to do? But Bhag Singh and his friends managed to collect the money and pay the instalments, and also got the charter of the ship in their name.

After making all these arrangements, Singh left for South British Columbia with some of his friends to cogitate over matters. This is when he was arrested along with Harnam Singh and Balwant Singh; however he and Balwant Singhji were soon free to go. The ship was ready to return. Most of the people were left with hardly any money to buy provisions, and after returning, it was Bhai Bhag Singh who made all the arrangements to help them.

Singh was a thorn in the eyes of the immigration officers due to the help he rendered to the ship and for his propagation of the message of independence. They had also openly declared on numerous occasions, that they would get him shot. But Bhai Bhag Singh laughed off the threats at that time and others also did not pay much attention to them. They thought that it was mere bluster, and that it would require a singularly courageous person to do that.

One day, Bhai Bhag Singh returned to the gurudwara, after assisting in the last rites of a Sikh. The prayers had begun and Bhai Bhag Singh sat down to read the *Guru Granth Sahib*. Everything progressed peacefully, but when Bhai Bhag Singh bent down to place his forehead on the ground in obeisance after the 'ardas', Bela Singh, who was sitting behind him, shot him with a pistol. The bullet pierced through Bhai Bhag Singh's back and lodged itself in his lungs. In a vain attempt to nab the assassin, even Bhai Vatan Singh was killed. (His biography is given below.)

Bhag Singh was brought to the hospital. He was fully conscious even during the operation and continued to cheer the people around him. When his son was brought before him, he said – 'This is not my son; but the son of the entire community. Take him to the darbar. Why have you brought him to me?' Scores of people were present in the hospital to meet him. Finally he took his last breath with the following words on his lips – 'I had wished to die fighting for independence, but fate had a death on a bed in store for me. Anyway, God had willed it this way.' He was only 44 years old at the time of his death.

Ultimately, the assassin was let off in court when he admitted that whatever he had done, had been at the behest of the Immigration officers. He claimed to be a loyal subject, and stated that he would have given evidence of his patriotism by enlisting in the army to fight the war had he not been arrested at that point of time, etc. One can only bemoan this slave mentality.

– Natwar

13. Bhai Vatan Singh (1928)

People did not realize what Bhai Vatan Singh truly was till after his death. He led a very ordinary life and never had the good fortune to be called a leader. However, his heart was filled with love for his country. He only knew how to die; and that, like a true soldier.

The only thing known about his childhood is that he was born in a village called Kumbadwal in Patiala, and that his father was Bhai Bhagel Singh. Vatan Singh was very fond of rearing cattle and that's why the people in Canada referred to him as Vatan Singh 'Maiyyan wala' which translates to, 'the one with the buffaloes'.

He spent the first twenty-two or twenty-three years of his life at home and then enlisted in the army. Till then he had spent most of his time in Burma. After five years he left that job and returned home, only to work on his fields for the next ten years. But he was to become an example and a role model for the Indians; how could have stayed home for long! Wearying of his work in the fields, he left for Hong Kong. He worked as a jail guard for five years there and then went to Canada.

He reached Vancouver, but now where could he go? He was in a foreign country and he didn't know a single soul. He somehow managed to discover the whereabouts of the gurudwara after a great deal of effort, and went there. No one knew at that time, least of all Vatan Singh himself, that one day he would preach a lesson in courage to humanity, and sacrifice his life in that very place. Anyway, after staying there for a few days, he started work in a timber factory. Bhagel Singh used to work in the same place during that time.

The wave of the independence struggle had not reached its crest as yet, so most of the Sikhs' attention was mostly drawn to the propagation of ideas among themselves. Our hero would also converse about these matters whenever he found time.

Vatan Singh came back to Vancouver in 1911. He began working in another place and saw a golden opportunity to get immersed in devotional singing, and so he began to visit the gurudwara daily. He even served as a member on the gurudwara committee for a year. People came to hold him in high esteem due to the dedication he showed in his work.

The same old story repeated itself after this. A quarrel with the Immigration officers – brutality, agitation; and the conspiracy to assassinate Bhai Bhagel Singh and Balwant Singh. People were returning to India in large numbers at the time. It is believed that this conspiracy was hatched so that any noteworthy Sikh leader could not advocate the same things in India after returning home. Anyway, whatever it may have been, the day Bela Singh fired a pistol at Bhai Bhag Singh, Vatan Singhji was sitting beside him. When he saw Bhag Singh injured, he challenged the assassin. And then ... The second bullet buried itself into the bosom of this heroic man instead of wounding Balwant Singh. A brave man's courage is roused upon being injured. He roared like a true Singh, a lion, and charged towards the assassin. The next bullet also went through his chest. Undeterred, Vatan Singh continued to advance and seven bullets were fired at him point-blank before he could finally grab the assassin by the throat. But as his strength and his life ebbed out of him, Bela Singh succeeded in shaking himself free, and Vatan Singh fell into an eternal slumber. The people in the gurudwara were in a state of complete shock, but now they were galvanized into action. The gurudwara was turned into a battleground. There was chaos all around. The people had barely come to terms with the loss of one of comrades, and now they had lost two more gems.

Bhai Vatan Singh is no more. But the example that he's left in history by sacrificing his life like a true brave-heart at the age of fifty, will be etched forever.

– Chakresh

14. Shri Mewa Singh (1928)

There are some people who are always in the midst of difficulties and work diligently in the background, not because they are afraid, but because the desire to step into the limelight to get accolades has never been present in them. Had astrologers been able to predict at the time of their birth that they would one day become staunch revolutionaries and sacrifice everything they had, or that some day they would go dancing to the hangman's noose, singing 'Death is fated, yet we fight!', then perhaps their life stories would have been written fully. But who knows from which corner of the world they sprung up, dedicated their entire being to the service of humanity, and left, just as suddenly. That moment is when people looked up at them in astonishment. They even offered bouquets to mark their devotion and reverence. But even then, no one bothered to gather details about any incidents of their lives and publish them. If today one sits down to pen the life history of such idealists, there is very little to write.

The birth of our unsung hero, Shri Mewa Singh took place in an ordinary village Lopoke of the Amritsar district. And that is the sum total of the information available about his family and his childhood. They were simple peasant folk and they cultivated land. Seeing a lot of people leave for Canada, he decided to migrate as well. He was extremely religious and devoted himself almost exclusively to God and prayers.

He was terribly hurt to see the cruelty, injustice and abhorrent behaviour meted out to the Indians in Canada. When Shri Bhag Singhji and Balwant Singhji had left for the South accompanied by some comrades as they deliberated over the Komagata Maru incident, the Immigration department had arrested them and incarcerated them in the 'Subhash' Jail; he was among them. But he was let off when he said that he'd wandered off only casually in that direction. Later, he became a shareholder in the Guru Nanak Mining Company.

The prayers were taking place in the gurudwara. Shri Bhag Singh was reading the *Guru Granth Sahib* and Shri Vatan Singh was sitting next to him. Suddenly, the tranquillity of the congregation was shattered when shots rang out and within a few moments, Shri Bhag Singh and Shri Vatan Singh lay there, dead. Mewa Singh was aghast as he witnessed this contemptible act of the traitor, Bela Singh. He could not endure the heart-rending sight. He was shocked that they had been killed so brutally even while the holy book, the *Guru Granth Sahib* was being read. At the time of prosecution, the murderer stated that he was asked by immigration officials to commit the act.

Tears filled Mewa Singh's eyes when he beheld the miserable, bloodied condition of the colonized Indians. They were despised only because they were enslaved by another nation. Injustice was heaped upon them everywhere because they were not a free people, and their leaders could be killed without any repercussions because they were foreign slaves. This deeply saddened his heart. He immersed himself deeper into his prayers to bury his inner sorrow. But even so then, unhappiness would reflect in his words that he said often – 'Now this debased and enslaved life; rejection at every step had become unbearable.' No one paid any attention to his words then.

This was the zenith of the revolutionary movement. People had begun to practise shooting with a rifle and a revolver. It is said that our hero also used up Rs 100-worth of shots. No one paid much attention to this either. One day he went to get a photograph clicked of himself. This was the last valuable gift he brought for his family.

There was a court hearing that day. The Chief Immigration officer, Mr Hopkinson was also present to make a statement. The proceedings were going on smoothly when a shot rang out suddenly, and before anyone could realize who had fired the shot, Mr Hopkinson fell dead to the ground. The shot had found its mark unerringly. The killer was one hundred percent successful. The judges went hiding under the chairs and lawyers ran out helter skelter out of the court. As Mewa Singh saw Hopkinson fall, he placed the revolver judge's table and said loudly – 'I do not want to run away. Please calm down. I am not a madman. I shall not shoot at anyone else. I've accomplished my task.' Then he called the policemen and surrendered quietly. He could have escaped in the ensuing chaos had he wished to, but that brave revolutionary had no wish to live any longer. He wanted to prove that the spark of life continued to smoulder in the humiliated, enslaved and trampled India. He gave up his life only to prove that they could still react to an insult; they could still take revenge for a national insult.

After his arrest, when he was asked the reason for having killed Hopkinson, he asked – 'Is Hopkinson really dead?' He laughed out loud when he heard the answer in the affirmative, and said – 'Today I feel truly happy.' When he was questioned further, he said – 'Hopkinson has been killed deliberately. This is revenge for the insult to the nation and the community; this is revenge, for the killing of two of our jewels. I wanted to kill Mr Reid (Hopkinson's associate) also, who has escaped because he isn't there.'

Upon hearing about her husband's killing, Hopkinson's widow is believed to have expressed a desire to meet the brave man who had killed her husband in a full court and then surrendered with such composure.

After this incident, no one in Canada referred to the Indians with contempt. He confessed to his crime courageously when he was prosecuted in court. After the death sentence was pronounced, he seemed almost intoxicated with joy, he was elated. By the time he had to be hanged, his weight had gone up by 13 pounds.

A sea of humanity, including the immigrant Indians settled in Canada, descended upon the jail on the day he was to be hanged to take a last look at this great soul. There were a great number of white people as well. As per the regulations, a visit by a priest was mandatory. Thus, Bhai Mitt Singh entered the jail. After saying the prayers, Mewa Singh gave his last message. The language was simple, but the thought was noble and patriotic. He said, 'Go outside and tell all Indians, and especially those who work for the nation, that they must try their best to throw off this curse of slavery and colonial rule. But this task can be accomplished only when regionalism and communalism are completely eradicated. No issue of Majha, Malwa and Do-aab[88] should arise, nor of Hindu, Muslim and Sikh. This is a special request to all my fans and friends.'

Mitt Singh's eyes filled with tears as he heard these words. Shri Mewa Singh immediately reprimanded him. He said, 'You came to give me courage; not shed tears yourself. At least give it a thought, what else could be our condition? And one attains such a death with great good fortune, and it is absolutely unseemly to express grief rather than elation and delight.'

Finally it was time for him to be hanged. Ah! See how that madman goes merrily to the noose. Fear and worry dare not approach him. Finally, singing 'Sing the glory of God, sing for Him, who is your companion ...' he went to stand on the platform. The reader can imagine what happened next – Guru Govind Singh's devotee entered the lane of love with his head placed on his palm and so, sacrificed himself.

---

[88] Do-aab is in middle of the river Sutlej and Beas. Malwa lies to the east of Sutlej, while Majha is falls in the middle of Lahore and Amritsar, between the rivers Ravi and Beas. There has been some dispute among Sikhs of about these regions.

The undulating wave of humanity was ready to receive the dead body; and a grand procession was taken out. Lord Indra could not control himself either, and it rained heavily. But the crowd did not disperse. Even English women could not help admiring such a hero. After the last rites had been observed, the gurudwara commemorated his sacrifice for one whole week.

– Kovid

15. Shri Kashi Ram (1928)

Shri Kashi Ram is one of the anonymous seven revolutionaries, who were arrested by the so-called justice-loving government for the murder of a police officer near a village in Ferozepur district and plucked from the lap of India forever. After a confession by the real culprit when he was finally arrested, the government shrugged off its liability in just a few words 'The seven people who have already been hanged to death, were not the culprits and the real culprit is this one, whom we are now going to hang.' That was all!

Pandit Kashi Ram was born to Shri Pandit Ganga Ram in the village of Badi Mandauli, in the Ambala District. He was born in 1881 (1938 in the Hindu calendar), on the twelfth day of Bhadon (the sixth month as per the Hindu calendar) he was married off at the age of 10, but those who are intoxicated with a desire for independence, cannot be bound by ties of affection for their wives and children. So, after clearing his Intermediate examination in Patiala, he left his home and returned for just a few hours in 1914. His wife had passed away during this time.

After completing his education, he took some training in telegraphy and was employed in the district office at Ambala on a salary of Rs 30 per month initially; and then in Delhi at Rs 60 per month. Later, he went to Hong Kong and finally he went to America where he was employed in a dynamite factory for Rs 200 per month. However, he even regarded this as slavery, and took a contract for gold-digging on an island.

During this time, there was a wave of people who were returning to India from America, and he also joined one group and returned to India on 25 or 26 November, 1914. Inspired by a desire to see the place where he'd spent his childhood playing in the dust, he went to his village. This news spread like wildfire in the village and a considerable crowd gathered to meet him. Finding a golden opportunity, he delivered a lecture about the activities of the revolutionary party, Ghadar Party.

After a few hours, he left his home saying that he had deposited a sum of thirty thousand rupees in Lahore National Bank, and that he was going to withdraw that. This was the last time the villagers got a glimpse of him. He never returned.

Upon arriving in Lahore, he was sent to Ferozepur with some comrades. They had an encounter with the police there. In the firing, the inspector was killed, and later seven out of the thirteen comrades were arrested in the jungle. Some were killed, some escaped. Our hero was among the seven who had been arrested.

After a farcical trial that stretched up to five months in Ferozepur, all the seven were sent to different places. But later, they were also accused of the robbery that had taken place near Mishri village, murder, etc., and all seven of them were hanged to death.

The same people for whom he had sacrificed everything he had, for whom he had left his aged mother desolate and weeping, for whom he had taken to asceticism, the same villagers celebrated his hanging by saying that the British government had performed a noble service by hanging the robbers. But this is something that happens quite frequently in the lives of revolutionaries. Their motto is to die, *'unwept, unhonoured and unsung'* (originally in English). They have no time to bother about what names they are given by the world; nor do they have time to worry themselves about it. They have not trod on this path to get accolades from the world. They only try to satisfy their own calling.

Panditji was lodged in the Lahore Central Jail. His father came and lamented – 'Son, don't you have the slightest bit of pity for my elderly state? Your mother is already losing her mind in her grief for you. I had thought you'd give us some comfort when you grow up, but I didn't know you were so unemotional. You have not bothered to find out how we are doing. Now what do we have to look forward to in our old age?'

The ascetic heaved a deep sigh and said – 'Respected father, what is the use of this futile mortal world? No person is a son nor is anyone a father in this world. This is only a feeling of one's mind, so don't distress yourself for nothing. As far as survival is concerned ... Well! Nature, that has given birth to us, will nurture us, and takes care of her sons all the time. All the Indians my age are your sons; have faith in them.'

When Kashiram saw his brother, he said – 'I forbid you to fill your eyes with tears. I have not committed any sin, and I shall find a place at the feet of patriots if I die like this. I consider this my supreme good fortune.'

Ultimately, his family was still not convinced and filed an appeal, but he was hanged before it could be decided.

– Bandi

16. Shri Gandha Singh (1928)

Shri Gandha Singh was born in the Kachcharbhann village of Lahore district. People used to call him Bhai Bhagat Singh. After his baptism as a Sikh, he was named Bhai Ram Singh; however, he was always known to all as Bhai Gandha Singh. He went to America when he was still a child, and he was the leader of the Ghadar Party there in 1914 and 1915. And when it was finally decided to return to India to propagate the ideology of the Ghadar Party, he was the first one to set off for India with a friend. Within a few days of his return, a firing took place on the Bajbaj Ghat and the police were on alert to keep a strict watch on those who were returning from abroad with a ticket to Calcutta. It became not just difficult, but well-nigh impossible for Indians to return to their native soil from America. Anyway, seeing the situation worsening, he and his friend left for Hong Kong. There, due to the close monitoring by the police, they were compelled to get the tickets of all Calcutta-bound Indian passengers changed to Bombay and Madras. Whatever little revolutionary activity took place in Punjab in 1914 and 1915, was due to the Sikhs that were saved by this hero.

After his return from Hong Kong, Bhai Gandha Singh began to propagate revolutionary ideas with all his might. He walked tirelessly all day, from place to place, even on hot summer days. He never allowed himself to despair. Perhaps this was because he had learnt the lesson of death even before stepping into the field of work. He often said that when he was about to set off for India from America, he spent many nights convincing his heart that he was going to get executed, and when his heart still remained determined about coming to India despite repeated warnings, only then had he bought the ticket. This sums up that he was a living embodiment of enthusiasm, and had infinite courage.

Once, when he was going on a road near the 'Ghalkhurd' village of Ferozepur with ten or fifteen other comrades, they found themselves surrounded by the police. Since the Inspector enjoyed the patronage of the British government, in this intoxication, he abused and slapped one of Gandha Singh's comrades. At home, parents had never even scolded the youth, and hence, he could not bear being slapped, and his eyes filled with tears. Brought up in a free country and having sacrificed home and heart to wander like a madman from place to place for the freedom of the country, how could a self respecting man swallow this insult? The next moment, the Inspector fell to Gandha Singh's shot. A Revenue Collector was also killed. Due to the dispersal of comrades in the jungle after this incident, some of them encountered the police again. These people had left home after a vow of sacrificing their lives for their country, so there was firing from both sides, and finally the ammunition was all spent. Some died there, while seven were arrested by the police. All of them were sentenced to death by hanging after a farcical trial, and in the winter of 1914 all seven of them went far away – very far away – to their God, to narrate all this drama.

The citizens of the country – the country that these people loved madly and wandered in from place to place, and even finally laid down their lives in their attempt to free her – did not even know their names, nor when, why or in which country they had disappeared.

Din younhi ghulami men basar hote hain sare
Ek aah tum jaison ke liye bhi nahin bharte

Days pass in subjugation,
Not even a sigh
Do they heave for (patriots) like you?

Our hero, Gandha Singh, had yet to see something more of the world. So, he managed to escape the police net this time. He resumed his work of propagating revolutionary ideas from place to place. The police was so intimidated by his mere name this time, that even when an opportunity to arrest him would present itself, they would not dare to do so.

There was a meeting in progress, in a village near Khanna. Singh met a teacher there called Giani Natha Singh, who worked in the Ludhiana Khalsa High School. He took Gandha Singh with him. On the journey there, they found a crowd of people standing in their way. Once they were close, the traitor, Natha Singh grabbed Gandha Singh from the rear. Other people also attacked him. Gandha Singh was helpless and unable to fight off so many men. The teacher said – 'Now you have been arrested.' He was brought to the village and thrown into a hovel with his hands tied behind his back.

The warrior who would strike terror in the hearts of the police, whom no one dared to look in the eye, who was so formidable that the police feared arresting him, was now locked in a small hut due to the treachery of his own fellow men, hands tied, rolling on his stomach in the dust. He was a trapped prisoner that day, not a free warrior.

He lay like that all night in the hut and the next morning, the police chief came and got the door opened. Narrating his condition about this night to his comrades in jail, he said – 'My hands swelled and became thick as a thigh, and even the noose seemed an easier option than that.'

He was prosecuted for the crime of having killed the police inspector and received a death penalty. The judge wrote in his verdict – 'The seven men who were hanged earlier were not the culprits. This man whom we are sentencing to death by hanging today is the real culprit.' What justice!

He was overjoyed to receive the death sentence. An English sergeant said to his associate – 'Today we saw Gandha Singh. He's very happy and is speaking with his head swaying as if he's intoxicated.'

It was 8 March 1916, 5 a.m. The man who brought water for his bath said – 'Do you know that you are going to be hanged today?' He answered simply – 'The noose is not something new for me. I was hanged the day I left America for India.'

The Warden said after the hanging – 'In my thirty years of service, I have hanged 125 men with my own hands. There have been all kinds of men but the courage, the passion, and the enthusiasm I have seen in Gandha Singh, I have not seen in anyone else.' Even the jail employees wept to see his courage.

– Lakshman

17. Shri Kartar Singh 'Sarabha' (1928)

In the April–May 1927 issues of the Punjabi monthly *Kirti* from Amritsar, Bhagat Singh wrote the life sketch of Kartar Singh Sarabha in two installments with the title, 'Bhai Kartar Singh Sarabha' as part of the Martyr series no.7. He had probably, already written on six martyrs of either the Ghadar Movement or other revolutionary movements martyrs. Addressing one as 'Bhai', is a respectable form of address, just like 'Shri' in Hindi. While reproducing many of sketches from *Kirti*, which were in Punjabi, to Hindi in *Chand*, 'Bhai' is used as a form of address for Sikh Ghadarite martyrs; in some cases it has been changed to 'Shri' as has been done here in this improvised version of *Chand*. Since these sketches from *Chand* are approved by Bhagat Singh himself, being part of his writings in collaboration with Shiv Verma, the original Punjabi versions are no more being reproduced. There is anyhow very little difference between the two version in terms of content and style.

This heroic devotee of the deity of battle – the rebel Kartar Singh Sarabha – was not even 20 years old when he sacrificed his life on the altar of freedom. He appeared from nowhere like a whirlwind, lit a flame and tried to rouse the deity of battle from slumber. He conducted the *yajna* (the ritual fire oblations) of revolution and finally offered himself to its flames. We were unable to fathom what he was, from which world he suddenly appeared and where he suddenly disappeared.

It is astonishing to see how much he accomplished at the young age of 19 years. Such courage, such self-confidence, such a spirit of sacrifice, and such devotion is extremely rare to find. Very few people have been born in India who can be called revolutionaries in the true sense of the word; but Kartar Singh Sarabha's name would feature at the top among these few. The spirit of revolution suffused every pore of his body. There was only one ambition, one desire, and only one hope – revolution; this is what he was born for, and this is for what he ultimately laid down his life.

He was born in 1896 in village Sarabha in Ludhiana district. He was the only son of his parents. His father passed away while he was still very young. However, his paternal grandfather took great pains to raise him well. His father's name was Mangal Singh; one of his uncles was a police sub-inspector in the United Province and another uncle was a high official in forest department of Orissa. After his initial education at village school, he took admission in Khalsa High School Ludhiana. Academically, he was an average student, too mischievous, he would play pranks on others and was termed 'Aflatoon' by classmates. He was loved by all and had a separate group in school, was a sportsman and had all the qualities of a leader. After passing Class 9 at Ludhiana, he went to his father's younger brother in Orissa. After clearing his matriculation there, he took admission in a college. This was in 1910-1911. Here, he got an opportunity to read a number of books beyond the narrow boundaries of school and college syllabi. This was the age of revolutionary movements and his patriotism was fostered in this environment.

Kartar Singh expressed a desire to go to America after his college. His family did not raise any opposition to it. He was sent to America.

He reached the San Francisco coast in the year 1912. He was subjected to rigorous questioning by immigration authorities. He told them that he had come there for his education. On being asked why he did not study in India, Sarabha told that he had come for higher studies and intend to join California University. Being asked about being denied admission, Sarabha instantly responded-'That will be a grave injustice. If hurdles are created in the path of students, the progress of the world will stop. Who knows the education here might empower me to achieve some great deed for the betterment of the world. In case I am not allowed to land here, won't the world suffer due to the lack of that great deed?' Officers were impressed and he was allowed to land.

After stepping on that free soil, the humiliation faced at every stage began to hammer upon his tender heart. He would go mad with anger upon hearing 'Damn Hindu' and 'Black Man' etc. on the lips of the whites. He began increasingly to feel that the honor and respect of his country was in danger. Whenever he felt homesick, the vision of a helpless country in shackles would swim before his eyes. His tender heart began to harden gradually and his resolve to sacrifice his life for the freedom of his country began to deepen. How can we understand what went on in his heart at that time!

It was impossible for him to remain unaffected by the events around him. He was constantly tormented by the question of how the country would attain freedom if the path of non-violence failed. Then, without further ado, he began to organize Indian workers together. He was able to inculcate a spirit of independence in them. He would spend hours talking to each worker to impress upon him that death was a thousand times preferable to a life of humiliation and slavery. Once he had begun, other people joined in too. They held a special meeting in May 1912, in which some nine Indians took part. They decided to sacrifice everything they had – wealth, mind and life – for the freedom of their country. It was during this time that the exiled patriot Bhagwan Singh also reached there. There was a flurry of meetings, processions, lectures. The need for was felt, so *Ghadar* was published. The first issue of the paper was published in November, 1913. Kartar Singh Sarabha was on the editorial board. There was infinite enthusiasm in his pen. The printing of the paper was manually done on a hand press by the editorial board. Kartar Singh would hum songs to keep him going when he got tired during his work.

Seva desh di jindadiye badi aukhi
Gallan karnian dher sukhllian ne
Jinhan is seva vich pair paya
Uhnan lakh musibtan jhallian ne

Service to the nation is very difficult, O life!
It is easy to converse.
One who serves the nation
Faces a million hardships.

Kartar Singh's zeal inspired the others who saw him work so hard. One doesn't know whether others had thought about how to free India, or whether to keep their work a secret or not, but Kartar Singh was deeply involved in this issue. In the meantime, he took employment with an aircraft company in New York and began to learn the ropes wholeheartedly.

In September 1914, the Komagata Maru ship had to return without completing its mission after undergoing untold suffering at the hands of the white imperialists. Then, our Kartar Singh came to Japan along with Gupta, who advocated revolutions, and an American revolutionary. They met Baba Gurdit Singh in Kobe to discuss these issues. *Ghadar*, *Ghadar di Goonj* and several books were published in the Yugantar Ashram Printing Press in San Francisco. The net of their propaganda spread wider. Their enthusiasm grew. In February 1914, the flag of freedom was unfurled in a public meeting in Stockton and pledges were made in the name of equality and freedom. Kartar Singh was among the chief speakers in this meeting. All of them declared that they would lay down their lives in the struggle for freedom of the country. Time passed. Suddenly they received news of the outbreak of the First World War. They were delighted. All of them began to sing –

Come; let us go to fight for our country,
This is our last oath and decree.

Kartar Singh exhorted people to return to their motherland. He himself boarded a ship and reached Colombo in Sri Lanka. In those days, those who returned to Punjab from America often found themselves arrested under the Defence of India Rule (D.I.R). Very few would reach home safe and sound. Kartar Singh was among those who did. He launched his plans with fervor. There was a problem of organization, but that was somehow sorted out. The Maratha youth, Vishnu Ganesh Pingle also joined him in December 1914. They made efforts to ensure that Shri Sachindra Nath Sanyal and Ras Behari Bose came to Punjab. Kartar Singh would manage to attend all the meetings everywhere. Today there is a secret meeting in Moga; and he's here. Tomorrow there is a lecture for students there, and Kartar Singh is in the first row. The next day, the soldiers in the Ferozepur Cantonment are being organized. Then he is leaving for Calcutta to procure weapons. When they faced a problem of insufficient funds, he suggested dacoity as an answer. Most people were stunned at the suggestion, but he said that there was nothing to fear, and even said that Bhai Parmanand, too, was in favor of this idea. Kartar Singh was asked to get approval from him. The next day he reported, though without meeting Bhai Parmanand, 'I've asked; he's agreeable.' He could not bear the thought that they should delay the revolution, merely due to a paucity of funds.

One day he went to a village to commit a dacoity. Kartar Singh was the leader of the gang. The house was being looted. There was an extremely beautiful girl in the house. One of the Ghadarite cast an evil eye upon the girl. He grabbed the girl's hand. The girl raised an alarm. Kartar Singh rushed to her rescue, aimed a revolver at the man's temple and disarmed him. Then he roared, 'Sinner! You have committed a heinous crime. You deserve a death sentence, but you are pardoned due to the exigencies of the situation. Fall at the girl's feet *immediately* and beg forgiveness. Say, "Sister! Forgive me." Then touch her mother's feet and say, "Mataji, I am sorry for this lapse." If she forgives you, your life will be spared; otherwise you'll be shot dead.' The man did as he was told. Kartar managed to save the situation before it deteriorated too far. Both mother and daughter were touched. The mother said affectionately to Kartar Singh, 'Son! How did a saintly and well-mannered youth like you get involved in something like this?' Kartar

Singh's heart, too, overflowed with emotion and he said, 'Maji! We aren't doing this because of greed. We've put everything at stake to commit this robbery. We need money to buy weapons. Where can we get it from? Maji, it is only for this noble work that we are forced to do such jobs.' This was a very poignant scene. The mother said again, 'We have to marry this girl off. We'd be grateful if you could leave something for her.' Kartar placed all that they had gathered in front of the mother and said, 'Take whatever you want.' The mother took a little money and gave the rest to Kartar Singh with a blessing, 'Go, son! May you achieve success!' How sensitive, pure and large-hearted Kartar Singh was, even when involved in something like dacoity, is clear from this incident.

Before contacting the Bengal group, Sarabha had already planned the attack on the magazine of the Lahore cantonment. Once he met with an army soldier in charge of the magazine in a train, he promised him to give the keys. On 25 November, Sarabha went there with some daring comrades, however soldier was transferred to some other place a day earlier. Whole plan collapsed, yet disheartenment or anxiety was not in the genes of such revolutionaries.

Preparations for a revolution were complete in February 1915. A week before the appointed date, Kartar Singh, Pingle and a few other comrades went to Agra, Kanpur, Allahabad, Lucknow, Meerut and several other places to discuss the details of the revolution with people at large. Finally the much-awaited day drew near. 21 February 1915 had been decided as the day of revolution in India. Preparations for making it a success were underway. But at that very time, a rat was gnawing at the roots of the tree of their hopes. Four or five days prior to the day, they got suspicious of Kirpal Singh and feared that his treachery would ruin all their plans. Due to this suspicion, Kartar Singh and Ras Behari Bose suggested advancing the date of the revolution to 19 February. But Kirpal Singh managed to get information regarding this change of date as well. The presence of a traitor in this group of revolutionaries proved to have fatal consequences. Ras Behari and Kartar Singh were also unable to hide their identity due to lack of preparedness. What could this result in, but misfortune for India?

Kartar Singh reached Ferozepur with about fifty-sixty people as per the original plan. He met a comrade, an army havildar and discussed the revolution with him. But Kirpal Singh had already ruined everything. The Indian soldiers had, by now, been disarmed. A frantic round of arrests took place. The Havildar refused to help. Kartar Singh's attempt failed. Disappointed, he returned to Lahore. A round of arrests was made all over Punjab. People began to succumb to pressure.

Ras Behari Bose, disappointed with this situation, was lying on a bed in a house in Lahore. Kartar Singh also came there and lay down on another charpoy with his face turned towards the other side. They did not utter a word but understood the state of each other's hearts. We can gauge their condition, too.

> Our fate is to bang our head on Lady Fortune's door
> But the means to test our fate slipped from our hands.

They decided to leave Punjab by crossing the western border. The three who crossed the border were Sarabha, Jagat Singh and Harnam Singh Tunda. After crossing a desert mountain, they reached a picturesque spot. A beautiful stream was flowing, they sat at its bank and started eating roasted gram. Then Kartar Singh began to sing:

> Why should the lions run in the face of dire straits?

Poet Kartar wrote this poem in US, he sang this in melodious voice repeatedly and suddenly stopped to ask his companion, 'Jagat Singh, was this poem written for others? Should not we be responsive to our comrades in dire straits?' They looked at each other and decided to return to India, knowing well that death was awaiting them.

Kartar Singh's only desire was for a revolutionary war to attain freedom so that he could lay down his life for his country. Then he came to Chak No. 5 near Sargodha. Again, he began to preach revolution. He was arrested there and shackled. The fearless revolutionary, Kartar Singh, was brought to the Lahore Railway Station. He said to the Police Officer, 'Mr Tomkin, please bring us some food.' How carefree he was! Friend and foe alike would be glad to meet this charismatic personality. He was happy even when he was arrested and would often say, 'Bestow the title of 'Rebel' upon me after I die a brave and courageous death. If anyone remembers me, let it be as, Kartar Singh, the Rebel.'

Sarabha's restless soul was not pacified even behind bars. One day, he managed to get some tools to cut through bar and contacted 60-70 prisoners, they planned to escape by jail break and attack Lahore cantonment to snatch weapons and revolt again. In times of dejection and failure, this hope was just a mirage. One prisoner got wind, which made all to be searched and shackled. Tools were recovered and all efforts to break jail came to a naught!

His case was brought to trial. Kartar Singh was merely 18-and-half years old at that time. He was the youngest among the accused, but the judge wrote about him :

He is among the most dangerous criminals amongst the accused. There is not a single part during his journey from America and the conspiracy in India in which he has not played a pivotal role.

When it was his turn to record his statement, he accepted all the charges. He continued to speak the language of revolution. The judge, with his pen between in his teeth, watched him and didn't write a single word. Later he said, 'Kartar Singh, we have not recorded your statement yet. Think about what you want to say. Do you know what consequences your statement can have?' Those who witnessed the trial say that upon hearing these words, Kartar Singh answered cheerfully, 'At the most you can give me the hangman's noose. What else? I am not afraid of that!' The proceedings of the court were adjourned till the next day. The next day again began with Kartar Singh's statement. The previous day the judges had been under the impression that Kartar Singh had given the statement under the influence of Bhai Parmanand, but they were unable to plumb the depths of the heart of the revolutionary Kartar Singh. Kartar Singh's statement was even more hard-hitting, more passionate and radical in spirit than the previous day. He admitted to all the charges as he had on the first day. He concluded his statement, saying, 'I'll get either life imprisonment or death for this. But I shall prefer death, so that I can be reborn till Hindustan is liberated, and go to the gallows again and again. This is my last wish ...'

The judge was extremely impressed with Kartar Singh's courage, but unlike a large-hearted enemy who would have called this courage, he labelled it as shamelessness. Kartar Singh was not only awarded abuses, but a death sentence as well. He thanked them smilingly. While Kartar Singh was locked up in the cell awaiting his death, his paternal grandfather visited him and asked, 'Kartar Singh, you are dying for the sake of those who abuse you. One can't even fathom how your nation will benefit from your death.' Kartar Singh asked in a soft voice, 'Dadaji, where is that relative of ours, Mr so-and-so?'

'He died in the plague.'

'And he?'– mentioning another relative

'He died of cholera.'

'So do you want that Kartar Singh should be bedridden in illness for months and die a painful death? Is this death not a thousand times better?' Dadaji had nothing more to say.

Even today this question is relevant: What benefit did his death have? Who did he die for? The answer is absolutely clear. He died for the country. His ideal was to die in the service of his nation. He wanted nothing more than that. He was content to die unknown and unsung.

Only he labours in the garden of love,
Who values labour for the sake of labour.
One does not arrange flowers on display,
One strews pearls in the garden in the dark night.

The case continued for a year and a half. It was 16 November 1915, when he was hanged to death. He was as happy as ever on that day. His weight increased by ten pounds. With 'Bharat Mata ki Jai' (Hail Mother India!), on his lips, he embraced the noose.

– Balwant

There was another sketch written on Kartar Singh in *Kirti*; this is the first-ever translation of the sketch.

Martyrdom serial no. 7
Bhai Kartar Singhji Sarabha in *Kirti*, April 1927

There would hardly be any unfortunate in Punjab, who has not heard something about Bhai Kartar Singh. The bravery, boldness and courage with which he achieved martyrdom in very young age, it created love and sympathy in every heart for him, besides created a movement to liberate the country. Bhai Kartar Singh's name is very famous and even a child is aware of it.

There are lot of tales of his bravery, which are spread in common people and which need to be collected. Here we present Bhaiji's brief life sketch.

Brave Kartar Singh was born in year 1896. He was the only son of his parents. His father loved him a lot, but the will of the God! His father died, when he was too young. For poor Kartar, the parting away from his father at such young age was very painful. But his grandfather brought him up and was like a father to him.

This talented boy grew up in his village Sarabha, which is a middle-level village in Ludhiana (District). His family was of peasants. His father's name was Sardar Mangal Singh. His two uncles were in government job. One was a sub inspector in United Province and another was in service of forest department in Orissa. After his father's demise, his grandfather wished that his grandson should get good education and get a high-status job. His grandfather did not want to put him into peasantry profession.

There was school up to primary level in village, our Kartar was admitted there. He was not so good in education; he was more interested in sports. But his grandfather did not back him much. He could not sit idle. He was very agile and clever. Village boys called him 'Aflatoon' (Plato).

Anyway! He passed out primary school in six years, and then he was admitted to Khalsa High School Ludhiana. There he gained education up to ninth class. Peasant boys grow up fast. He came out to be a handsome young man. He has a height of about five-feet eight inches. He had very beautiful eyes. The colour of his face was reddish like apple. His teeth were like pearl.

He was very good in sports. Teachers loved him a lot. He was ahead of others in every activity of the school. He was a born leader of boys and he had all the qualities of a leader. He could maintain discipline very well.

He was neither very good, nor very bad at studies, yet everyone liked and loved him.

He held very free ideas in school. He had his own group and they enjoyed a lot. He was cheerful by nature and humorous, every boy was very happy to be associated with him.

He left Khalsa School in ninth class itself and went to his uncle in Orissa, where he passed his matriculation. He got good experience in English conversation there and he started reading good books of English.

Bengal-Orissa at that time was much awakened. Some by reading books and some by watching those regions movements carefully, his views became freer and he got the seed of serving the nation.

After his Matriculation, family decided to send Kartar Singh to America. He already wished to see the outside world, and what happens there! After coming to Orissa, he had learnt a lot, and now, his desire to see more countries grew stronger. It wasn't just his family's wish, he himself desired to go to America. Finally, he got the passport made and Kartar Singh left for America.

He arrived in 1912 on the San Francisco coast. The Immigration Department would especially interrogate Indians then, before allowing them to enter America. He was also stopped with his associates and the interrogation began. He came to know that this interrogation is done only to 'Hindis' (Indians) and only to harass them. He felt quite hurt by this fact. For the first time, he realised what was India's place in the 'Family of Nations' and how Hindustan was viewed. He felt sorry at the lowly status his country enjoyed and started worrying about India!

Kartar Singh had the following conversation with head of the Immigration Deparment:

Officer: For what purpose you have come here?

Kartar Singh: I have come to study.

Officer: You did not get any place in India to study?

Kartar: There are lot of places in India to study, but I have come to join California University to acquire a good education of modern times.

Officer: If you are not allowed to land, what will you do?

Kartar Singh: This will be a great injustice. If students also face such hurdles, how will the world progress? If I am not stopped and I acquire education, then it is possible that I might do something for the betterment of the world, which may not be done, due to my remaining uneducated. So world shall suffer a big loss.

What a beautiful reply! What can one say after this? The officer was speechless and he got the permission to land.

After landing he went to Yulo County to live with his Sikh brothers. Sikhs often got jobs in the gardens there, plucking fruit. He joined them and became acquainted with the lives of his brothers.

He came to know many things there. How Indians are looked at and how 'well-respected' they were – he became well aware of that. Then he saw how black Hindustanis were treated vis-à-vis a white – who is a 'black coolie', how the toadies of British government looked at Indians. These things opened the eyes of young Kartar Singh, and he started shedding tears over their miserable conditions. A slave does not realise his slavery at his own home; it is only when he comes out of his home and sees how free people live that he realises his bondage. Then the slave feels the impetus to break the shackles of his slavery and wishes to break free instantly. But how would those who bind him with these shackles allow them to break? That is how the strife takes place.

When Kartar Singhji went to America, he went here from slavery. When he saw the movements of free men there, he remembered his home. Home, where his countrymen were rotting and from which he had just left. He felt his mind burning at the misery of India. The more he contrasted India with America, the more inflamed he felt. Where in America, even the President could be told the bitter realities, whereas in India, even to tell a policeman the real thing would be to invite death! Where in America, every man could keep whatever arms he wishes, whereas in India, even to hold a hatchet could invite prosecution and being sent to jail! Where in America, everybody could take part in choosing a government, whereas in India, even to raise such demand was to be tagged a rebel!

These things overturned the ideas of Kartar Singh. He was young and the youth feel such things more. He had enthusiasm; he decided to change the mission of his life. He decided that now his life is dedicated to the nation and the country. So he prepared himself to fulfil this mission.

He thought that it was not time to make calculations, it was the time for action. He began by spreading political awareness among his brothers in America. He narrated the misery of his country's slavery and said that they also have some duty towards their country and nation. 'We shall also improve the conditions of our brothers and our country should be freed from the curse of slavery' he said.

There were already many men, who were burning with passion to change their conditions. They already wanted that some such thing should begin, so that they could also burst out their heart's burning. Finally nine more persons joined and they all took pledge to serve the nation with body, mind and money!

This happened in May 1912.

A meeting was planned in June 1912, and it was given much publicity. The main reason for this meeting was to think of ways to free India. Many eminent personalities attended this meeting and it was decided to bring out the *Ghadar* journal. The resolution was passed and money started pouring in instantly! One hand press (A press run manually) was bought and patriots began working hard. They were so enthused and loved their work so much, that they ran the machine with their hands only. When they got too tired by the work, they would joke with each other and say:

It is too hard to serve the nation, but too easy to chat!
Those who took the path to serve, they suffered millions of calamities!

In the early days, this paper was published in Gurmukhi. Its bigger writer was our brother Kartar Singh. The main aim of it was to bring complete freedom to Hindustan and to establish its own government.

This paper attracted much attention within days of its publication. Within very little time, this paper became so popular that everywhere slogans of 'Ghadar!'[89] were raised and people were filled with enthusiasm and fervour. The spirit of sacrifice roused the people, so much so, they were ready to give up their body, soul and money for freedom!

After sometime, the resolution to install a bigger (printing) machine was passed. Without any demand being raised, people began coming and contributing money. A big lithographic machine was bought and installed in a very beautiful house in a crowded market in San Francisco. To run it an electric motor was also purchased.

This paper grew so much that organisers received demands to print it in Urdu, Gujarati and Hindi. They happily accepted the demand of the people and began printing it in other languages too.

These papers were published in the thousands and were sent free of cost to everyone. No subscription was ever asked from anyone. In this whole task, much of the hard labour was of Bhai Kartar Singh's. He used to work with love and devotion. And he always worked with a smile on his face. It was due to his efforts that wherever there was an Indian, a paper was sent there. There was no subscription for the paper, but for its support, paying Rs 100 or Rs 200 for its admirers was a little trivial matter.

This Ghadar Movement became so popular that patriots felt fully assured that they were about to win the game! It is not in the power of words to describe their love for the country, the spirit of sacrifice and their joy of service. They were an embodiment of service, models of sacrifice and used to sacrifice surpassing each other!

The paper was doing well for itself. Then, an idea struck Kartar Singh why not learn the functioning of aeroplanes! Just as the idea struck him, the lion became ready to learn this as well!

To this end, the man joined an American aircraft company. And in a short time, he learnt flying, repairing and making an aeroplane. The same Kartar Singh, who was mediocre in studies here, proved to be very able there. People used to appreciate his intelligence and many would say, 'Kartar Singh you are real Aflatoon.' When the Komagata Maru ship was

---

89   Rebellion

sent back from Vancouver, Kartar Singh along with two more associates flew to Japan and held discussions there.

By now, the First World War began. The same war, which people in the West said was being fought for freedom. But people with vision knew that this word was used just to trap people. In reality, the imperialists were fighting this war for their selfish motives – for trade, for searching new markets! India also fell for this bait and got trapped, but American-Indians living among them knew their motives and understood their cleverness. They knew that the outcome of this war would not be freedom, but a worse form of slavery than before. So they thought it better that when Britain had joined the war, let Hindustan decide about its freedom and, till the decision is taken, Indians should not step out for any other task! (Incomplete) – To be continued.

Martyrdom serial no. 7
Bhai Kartar Singhji Sarabha in Kirti, May 1927
(Continued from last issue)

For the cause of freedom hundreds of Sikhs and many Hindu–Muslims got ready to go to Hindustan. They left all their work mid-way. Such was the passion for freedom surging in them that they did not think of any sacrifice for the country as something too big. To free the country, the birds of freedom from San Francisco, Vancouver and Shanghai, dancing in ecstasy, jumping, playing, and singing songs of freedom, sailed to liberate the country. Who can describe their excitement and yearning in words? Who can understand their heart's desires? Who can even guess their heart's aspirations? How could Bhai Kartar Singh, who was the leader of this movement, have stayed behind? He had not learnt the art of 'body forward and mind backward'. He wanted to find a time, an occasion, when he could offer his head at the altar of freedom. He got this beautiful occasion. Oh no, no! He had no fewer roles in bringing this beautiful occasion closer! Our brave Kartar Singh got into the Nippon Maru ship and began his journey towards freeing the country from the clutches of oppressors.

This is now an open secret that these men, who returned from America by spending thousands and lakhs of rupees, had not come to sit idle. The clear purpose of their coming was to throw out the British Government from India, one way or another, and establish an Indian government instead. To achieve this task, they had made following programme:

1. There should be one paper in India like the *Ghadar* paper and whose aim should be to achieve complete freedom.
2. To hold public meetings of every type to spread hatred for the British government and such a movement should be built in a manner that common people should become determined to throw away the yoke of the government.
3. Agitation should be launched against sending armed forces from India to fight outside and till the country gets complete freedom, this agitation must not stop.
4. Propaganda should be done in Hindustani armed forces that they should not be used against India when the occasion arises; rather, they should help freedom fighters in all possible ways.
5. The devotion for freedom of the country should be aroused especially among youth and they should be turned towards the service of nation and country.
6. By bringing out pamphlets and small posters, falsehoods of the foreign government should be exposed and people should be aroused against the government.

It is true that they resorted to dacoities sometimes to collect funds and many people felt bad about it. They said that for the pious cause of freedom, they should not have resorted to such means. But we should consider their state of mind at that time and see how distressed they were and how much they had suffered at the hands of a foreign government. And what misery they had seen abroad and what oppression the British government had committed in Hindustan; all this had hardened their hearts against the government and they were ready to use any weapon to bring it down.

Apart from this programme, magistrates have written in their judgements that after coming here they: (1) wanted to raise the flag of revolt (2) Break the jails (3) Murder the toadies (4) Loot the treasuries (5) Wanted to tie-up with foreigner enemies (6) Commit dacoities (7) Brought arms from abroad and made bombs here (8) Established secret societies (9) Looted police stations and (10) Wanted to destroy rail and telegram links.

Maybe some of the men in the movement wanted to do all of this, but this statement cannot be applied to all men. Because there were so many men among them who did not want to do it! Those poor innocents were just crushed by the justice-claiming British government. Though they had admitted everything very bravely in their statements and had stated whatever was truthful, still those poor voices were not heard. But where in the world is the voice of the poor heard? And they were hanged, not in dozens, but hundreds!

Those who know law used to tell us that law demands that if a criminal gets acquitted, so be it; but no innocent should be punished. Our courts are 'accounts of casualness', one could see at least a thousand times here that innocents get punished and thieves get acquitted. Oh Wajid, 'who has to tell the ruler – don't do this way, do this way?'

At that time, the British government was adamant, because these freedom lovers had created trouble for them. So people were blindly hanged at that time. How can one hope for justice from special commissions! They just play 'throw dice and finish', what justice could be expected from these?!

Anyhow! Bhai Kartar Singh reached Punjab, hale and hearty. Those days, reaching Punjab was no child's play. The British government had made many laws to keep away fighters, by which just saying 'disappear', at Calcutta like ports, freedom fighters were held and sent straight for a round to 'big house' (jail).

What rest was there for lion-hearted Kartar Singh? Those who have a passion for freedom, where is rest for them? Their disease increases with treatment. He immediately created turmoil upon arriving and did such daring acts that a rare 'mother's child' can do it!

He gave two great statements in the court. In those, he very bravely and courageously admitted everything. Kartar Singh was a brave man and he did not know to die like cowards. He said, 'I was assigned the task to establish an ashram like Yugantar Ashram in India, whose aim should be the same and, if need be, propaganda should be done through distributing literature. I went to Kapurthala, Pingle Amar Singh and Parmanand (also known as Pandit Parmanand Jhansi) was with me. There was discussion with Ramsaran Das and he was told to support the scheme of bringing out the paper, but he declined. Pingle, Parmanand and I went to Sant Gulab Singh Dharmshala. There, we planned to bring out a paper. In January, I met Ras Behari Bose; Pingle has introduced him to me. We met to discuss publishing a paper in Bengali. I took part in the Sahnewal and Mansooran dacoities also. And bought cloth for the flag too, as the flag was a sign of the Yugantar Ashram and meant "Liberty, Fraternity and Equality". I was arrested from Chak no. 5 with Jagat Singh and Harnam Singh Tunda, but I never saw Parmanand before! I met Pirthi Singh and Labh Singh in Ladowal, but this meeting was only in context of the paper. I had told a constable in a train that the government was oppressing us. I was related to the Ghadar Party and I knew Lala Hardyal too. Whatever speeches I have made, these can't be considered seditious in America!'

From the statements made above we learn how courageous Bhai Kartar Singh was! Fear or terror could not stand near him. He never learnt to be scared of death! Whatever he did, he truthfully stated! This statement was not made to seek release or to reduce his punishment, rather they were made to make the world aware of the truth and world could not stay in darkness.

In the Lahore Conspiracy Case, the magistrate writes, 'It can be seen how very far his own statement goes to prove the truth of the evidence of the prosecution witnesses! There are no defence witnesses; there was practically no cross-examines throughout the trial; and before us the accused did not wish to argue his own case, nor allow the Counsel appointed for him to argue. It only remains to be said that the guilt of this accused has been proved to the hilt. He is a young man, no doubt; but he is certainly one of the worst of these conspirators; and he is a thoroughly callous scoundrel, proud of his exploits, to whom no mercy whatever can or should be shown.'

Many of us say with pride, 'Oh, I did not cooperate at all in my case! And I proved that I don't accept these so-called courts!' But Bhai Kartar Singh did complete non-cooperation in his case, when nobody knew about the word 'non-cooperation'. And this at a time, when not two or three years of ordinary imprisonment, rather death, was standing before him laughing and was saying, 'Just a moment and you will be in my lap.' But buck up, Kartar Singh! Glory to you and glory to your courage! Darlings like only you take the ship of nation across through storms!

From these words of magistrate, it is clear that he considered Kartar Singh to be very dangerous and somehow wanted to finish him off. That is why they did not think of even his young age and just hanged him.

Judges have written about his age, 'The accused has given his age as eighteen-and-a-half years; but he is certainly older than that and probably over twenty years of age! In spite of his age, he is one of the most important of these sixty-one accused; and has the largest dossier of them all. There is practically no department of this conspiracy in America, on the voyage, and in India in which this accused has not played his part!'

All thirty witnesses were presented in the Bhai Kartar Singh Case, six out of whom had become approvers, and gave maximum evidence against him.

Judges wrote while pronouncing the judgement:

'In view of above evidence, we sentence the accused under following sections:

Section 121(To help in war), section 121 A, 122, 124A, 395, 396,397,398,131, and 132 of Indian Penal code!

"We sentence him to be hanged till death! We order that his property, which can be confiscated, be confiscated by the government"

Kartar Singh! Darling of his parents and dear of his nation and country, Kartar Singh! Hanged but spread seeds of freedom in the country! When will these seed become fruit, only age can tell.

Along with him, many of his friends, such as Pingle, Pirthi and Harnam Singh Tunda etc. were hanged!

About Kartar Singh, this is said that the judges told him, 'Kartar Singh, you are yet too young, don't give such statements. See some of the world. These statements will take you to the gallows!' He replied, 'Whatever statement I give, I give truthfully. I am not afraid of hanging. Rather I wish that I should be hanged quickly, so that I could be born again in India and start my work again. If I am born as a boy, I will start the same programme and if I am born as a girl, I will give birth to such lion children, such freedom lovers, who will not rest till achieving freedom!'

It is told that once Kartar Singh came to know about the weakening of one of his associates and he was about to speak out on everything. He cycled to the village where that man was held by the police. He took permission to meet him and emboldened him. Only later, the police came to know the man on the cycle was none other than Kartar Singh. Warrants were issued against him, but the police just rubbed their eyes and could not do anything except say, 'Oh he is gone ... he is gone!'

One gentleman tells the story of how once Kartar Singh's grandfather came to see him. Kartar Singh was sentenced to death by that time. His grandfather asked him, 'Kartar Singh, what did you get out of doing these things? Just dying for nothing; what will people give you?' Kartar Singh started asking casually, 'Babaji, how is that Singh of our village?' 'He died long ago of plague,' his grandpa replied. Kartar Singh then said, 'Tell me about that Singh?' This time, Babaji said he died of fever.

Kartar Singh started telling his grandfather, 'if I also had died with fever or plague, where I would have been counted? Now I am getting executed for the country and the nation, and in whole world you and our family will be honoured for Kartar Singh being lion-hearted, who had gone by doing something! But if I had died just like that, then it was a meaningless death. Now my life is successful and you shall feel proud that your family has sacrificed itself for the country. So it is not time to condole, rather it is occasion for joy and celebration.'

Kartar Singh's heart was full of concern for poor people. When he used to see the miseries of peasants and workers, he could not control his tears. Then he was filled with enthusiasm and used to be furious. Subjection is a big curse. Subjugated people always go through miseries.

Kartar Singh's ideal was to establish a Republic in Hindustan. But everything remained in his heart.

In the Lahore Conspiracy Case, many were executed and many homes were left shattered because of this. It was terror in the world.

So! Finally Kartar Singh was just Kartar Singh. Mothers have given birth to innumerable sons, but Kartar Singh was given birth by a rare one!

18. Shri V.G. Pingle (1928)

The one to step forward to sew Mother's torn hem
Congratulations, for living even after death, O madman!

Having taken birth in the house of Shri Ganesh Pingle in the hilly region of Poona, he had not yet spent his childhood when his sensitive heart cried out at the slap of slavery. His family sent him to America to study engineering. It is there that he was baptised as a revolutionary and he returned to India. That restless heart did not tolerate wasting even a second of his time now. Instead of going home upon his return to India, he went straight to Bengal. He informed the revolutionaries there about the turmoil in Punjab and established an association with them. The coming together of Punjab and Bengal led to the work being carried out with much enthusiasm and gusto. Arrangements were made to make as many bombs as possible and the organization vastly expanded.

After meeting Ras Behari's group, Pingle went to Kashi. After he had spent two-three days there, some people pleaded with him to go to Punjab. So, instructing them to send as many bombs as possible, Pingle came to Punjab and within one week, after learning about the entire organization, he returned to Kashi. This time he had come to take Ras Behari to Punjab, but due to some reason Sachindra Nath Sanyal had to take his place. Pingle took Sachindra in the garb of an ordinary Hindustani to a Gurudwara in Amritsar. He was conversant in Punjabi. So, staying there for a few days, they worked to strengthen the organization. At that time, Pingle and Kartar Singh were the life of the movement in Punjab. When everything was fine, Ras Behari also came to Punjab. Preparations for the revolt were underway with great fervour. Sachindra Babu was entrusted with the responsibility of Banaras. 21 February was the day of the revolt. But India had yet to suffer some more setbacks. So, this task could not be accomplished against fate's will; that is, one police informer ruined all their hard work. After arrests, the whole group got scattered. Those who were comrades of life and death started to die one after the other in jail.

While returning to Banaras with Ras Behari, Pingle again entered Meerut Cantonment, for propagating the revolution. One Muslim gave him a lot of hope and he came with them to Banaras. Ras Behari tried to dissuade him for trusting such constables, but he was not to be moved, so finally he had to allow him. Pingle was sent with ten big bombs.

Ras Behari's apprehensions proved to be true; the havildar got him arrested at the Merrut Cantonment. The Rowlett report mentions, 'One bomb was sufficient to annihilate half a regiment.' (Originally in English.)

Ras Behari later wrote in his diary, 'If I had known that I would not meet Pingle again then I would not have let him go, even if he had insisted to go a million times! The words of that indomitable fair-skinned young brave who said with pride, "As a brave solider, I only know how to work" continue to ring in my ears and one cannot forget those large eyes of his that reflected his sharp intellect.'

The court gave him the death sentence. It was 16 November. He was brought to the gallows with his comrades, early in the morning. He was asked. 'Do you wish to say something?' He answered, 'I should get two minutes to offer prayers to God.' His handcuffs were removed and he folded his hands and said –

'O God! You know our hearts. The responsibility to protect the noble task for which we are sacrificing our lives today is now yours. India should be free; this is the only wish.'

After this, he himself put the noose around his neck and as the rafter was pulled away, with the first tug his breath left his body.

– Virendra

19. Shri Jagat Singh (1928)

Nothing is known about Jagat Singh's birth or dwelling place, but what is known is that he left for America during the great wave of people migrating there. And once the talk of Ghadar had begun, the desire to join the struggle to end the slavery of his country pulled him back to India. He was an extremely well-built and robust man and towered over the rest as he was probably the tallest among his peers.

That day due to the treachery by Kirpal Singh, all efforts for a revolution had come to naught. Work had to begin anew as if to test their faith. All the associates of Ras Behari Bose had been arrested. State repression continued unabated. Every step could mean danger and death. Anyway, Jagat Singh and two other associates were sent on an errand.

The police came and surrounded the three Sikhs on a tonga, and forced them to go to the police station. These brave men knew that to go into the police station meant walking into the jaws of death, and that they would not be able to give verifiable antecedents. So they decided to try their luck in a do-or-die effort and all three of them started firing.

One of them managed to escape during the firing; another one was arrested by the police. The third person, Jagat Singh managed to escape but later, when he was drinking water at a tap and wiping his hands, a more powerfully built Muslim youth came up from behind and grabbed his feet so tightly that he was unable to move.

As he fell down, he was arrested. He was also given a death sentence in the trial along with other people, and thus ended his role as the curtain fell upon another scene of the drama of revolution.

– Surender

20. Shri Balwant Singh (1928)

Shri Balwant Singh was a God-fearing soul. He was made a Sikh priest due to his devotion to his creed. A votary of peace, Balwant's nature was very gentle. He was a very soft-spoken gentleman. At first he was immersed in the service of God. Then he tried to bring others into the fold of God. Later, he constantly confronted the white British colonizers in order to help people, and finally, he willingly gave up his life and was hanged to death.

Shri Balwant Singh was born in village Khurdpur, in the Jalandhar district on a Friday, the first day of Ashvin, the seventh month of the Hindu calendar. His father's name was Sardar Budh Singh.

He belonged to a prosperous family. His father was a well-respected man due to his temperament and other qualities. He was admitted to the Adampur Middle School as soon as he was old enough to attend it. He was married while still a student, but his wife died soon after the wedding. He left school without completing his education and enlisted in the army. He met Sant Karam Singh in the platoon. The company he kept drew Balwant towards God through devotional songs and literature. He managed to hold on to the job for a period of ten years, then he suddenly left the job and went back to the village to lead a life devoted to God. He had also remarried while in the army. There was a cave near the village. He began to meditate inside this cave. He stayed inside the cave for eleven months, and as soon as he came out in 1905, he took an impulsive decision to immediately leave for Canada.

Once he was in Canada, he began the task of constructing a gurudwara with the help of another friend, Shri Bhag Singh, who was later shot dead by a traitor. It was with his help that the first gurudwara in Vancouver was established. At that point of time there was no unity among the Indians there. The white people would harass them, but when Balwant Singh went there, he tried his best to address these issues.

In those days, the Hindu and Sikh diaspora faced a great deal of difficulty in carrying out the last rites of the dead. They were not allowed to cremate the dead bodies. They suffered tremendous mental anguish and physical hardship in such circumstances. At times, they had to take the bodies into the jungle, in rain or snow, gather up a few logs and sprinkle some oil and set the body on fire and run away. Even then, there was always the danger of being shot at by the Canadians. Shri Balwant Singh made arrangements to solve this problem. He bought some land. In addition, he sought, and was granted, permission to cremate the dead. He formed an organization of Indian workers in the gurudwara. He would preach good behaviour and devotion to God. The gurudwara came about with a great deal of effort, in which his efforts were the greatest; and that is why everyone decided unanimously to make him the priest, the *granthi*. He demurred, but was finally persuaded to take up the post.

The Sikhs are a very robust and hardworking people. The white labourers lost some of their value when the Sikhs arrived there. And the Sikhs would be paid a lower wage than white workers. The white labourers began to create a disturbance as soon as the first group of Sikhs reached the shore. But the brave Sikhs were not going to be deterred by such things. This enraged the whites further. The establishment of the gurudwara helped in uniting the people. Fresh arrivals began to get all kinds of facilities. The white government sought ways to stop these people from coming there. The immigration officers tried to convince the Indian labourers through persuasion to go to the island of Honduras. The island was praised in exaggerated terms. But Bhai Balwant Singhji was fully aware of the hoax that the white were trying to perpetrate. He sent a trusted aide to go and inspect that land. This gentleman was Shri Nagar Singh. The immigration officers promised him approximately five acres of land and five thousand dollars to persuade the Indians to take up land in the Honduras. However, he returned and exposed the truth. The immigration officers also came out in the open. Now it was an open war between the two parties. The Immigration Department abandoned any pretence of behaving in a fair and civilized manner. The matter became more complicated and Shri Balwant Singh went further ahead.

The immigrant Indians wished to return to India to bring their families. This tussle continued for a long time. Finally, a strategy was planned. It was decided that Shri Balwant Singh, Shri Bhag Singh and Bhai Sunder Singh would return to India and bring back their families. Accordingly, all three gentlemen returned to India.

In 1911, they set off again with their families. They had to stop at Hong Kong as they did not get the tickets to travel further. They stayed there and continued consultation through correspondence with the people at the Vancouver gurudwara. Finally, the three gentlemen set off. Shri Sunder Singh went towards Vancouver and the other two set off with all three families towards San Francisco. Bhai Sunder Singh reached Vancouver, but the United States of America was also, after all, a country of the whites and these were slave Indians; the two gentlemen did not get permission to disembark with their families. They returned to Hong Kong once again. Then they got tickets for Vancouver for their families after a great deal of hardship. Both gentlemen got permission to disembark in Vancouver, but the families did not get permission to do the same. The issue became more complicated. Finally, the families were granted permission to disembark only for the number of days it would take to get a final order from Ottawa, the central immigration office. So the families did manage to land, but upon certain conditions. Two days after the period of grace was over, the immigration officers came to fetch the families, but the Sikhs were prepared to fight. The officers also lost their cool but ceded space when they saw the fire in the eyes of the warriors. What strength, what determination, what resolution was it that forced the government of Canada and its Immigration Department to bow down and allow the families to stay? This was not something that colonized Indians could then appreciate. Their frog-in-the-well attitude, their narrow-mindedness could not tell them what moments, what events shape the destiny of nations. Independent India would remember these unparalleled incidents of its freedom struggle. The recorders of her history would be granted an opportunity to write about them realistically. Section no. 124A would not be forever be at their throats, stifling them till their eyes popped out and did not allow them to breathe. Those families were allowed to stay but the other Indians were still not permitted to take their families with them. There was no solution even after a struggle of two years. It was finally resolved that their demands be placed before the British government, the Indian government and their citizens, and their help be sought to solve the issue.

A deputation went to both England and India. One of the three members of the deputation was our hero, Shri Balwant Singh. They went to England. They met all the top officials. They were told, 'The matter should be routed through the Indian government.' They returned to India, disappointed. An agitation was launched. At that time, even the popular leader of the time, Lala Lajpat Rai gave a curt reply and washed his hands off the business. However, some people offered support. Public meetings were held. There was anger, frustration and deep disappointment. Everything that could pour out of wounded hearts was said, and then? Sir Michael O'Dwyer wrote in his book *India As I Knew It* – At this stage I sent a warning to the delegates that if this continued, I would be compelled to take serious action ... The delegates on this asked for an interview with me. I had a long talk with them and repeated my warning. Two of them were ... and spacious; the manner of third seemed to be that of a dangerous revolutionary. They wished to see the Viceroy, and in sending them on to him. I particularly warned him about this man. (Originally in English.)

This third gentleman, the one on whom this peer has heaped such words, was Shri Balwant. That tender heart was wounded deeply. His self-respect had repeatedly been hurt. They came to the conclusion that it was the prime duty of every Indian to try to free his country by every means possible.

The deputation returned home at the beginning of 1914 without achieving anything. It was in these days that the Indian revolutionary, Shri Bhagwan Singh and Shri Barkatullah arrived in America. Moreover, the work of Hindustan Association was moving at a rapid pace in the United States of America. The Ghadar Party, Ghadar Press, and *Ghadar* newspapers were issued. But so far, the members of the above-mentioned deputation had no relation with them. But Sir Michael O'Dwyer called them the representatives of the Ghadar Revolutionary Party. So be it.

Till then the accusations made by the Indians had not been placed before the other nations. But this delegation met politicians in Japan and China as well, and tried their best to win the sympathy of these people towards India. Shri Balwant Singh gave a moving speech after his return to Vancouver about their unsuccessful effort. Such speeches find a special place in the histories of nations. After deep contemplation, he could only hear one voice; his inner being also gave rise to only one voice, 'The panacea to all of India's ills is independence.' In his speech he narrated his personal experiences and the deduction that emerged out of his deep contemplation.

People would see his sincerity, serenity, courage, earnestness and fearlessness – 'It is difficult to decide if Balwant Singh is the priest or the General of the Sikhs.

They had not really got an opportunity to decide what to do in the immediate future, when another problem raised its head before them – the arrival of the Komagata Maru ship. The ship did not get permission to dock, and on top of that, untold miseries were heaped on the passengers. For as many days as the ship remained docked, Indians were immersed whole-heartedly in its help. The leadership was yet again in the hands of our hero. He worked day and night tirelessly. One can't say if anyone else would have been able to work as hard. The penalty that the whites had imposed due to a default in payment of an instalment of rent, too, had to be borne by him. A sum of eleven thousand dollars was needed. The speech that he made in a meeting in an appeal for eleven thousand dollars was so moving and was filled with so much earnestness that it is difficult to describe it in words. Eleven thousand dollars were collected. After fulfilling their economic needs, he went deep into the South to discuss things with the people there. He went right up to the border of America. The white government arrested him. They said – 'You have come from America and have entered Canada illegally.' This baseless accusation also became the cause of a long tussle, but finally it was resolved, and they reached Vancouver. A few days later, even the Komagata Maru ship was forced to return.

Along with this, all the hopes of India were squashed. This was the first step taken by India towards commerce and these rulers, so 'concerned' about India, tried to squeeze this to the maximum so that no one would dare to try anything like that in the future. This is not the place to write an evocative account of the barbaric behaviour that the passengers of the ship were forced to endure as long as it was docked at Canada. But its memory is enough to drive one mad or move one to tears. The responsibility of the entire incident was on the shoulders of Mr. Hopkinson, the Chief of the Immigration Department. These people were very angry with him, but there's more. Shri Balwant Singh and Shri Bhag Singh were the two gentlemen who had fought the immigration officials bravely right from day one. And it was these two gentlemen who did all the work on the Komagata Maru ship. They were the thorns in the sides of the Immigration Department. They found a traitor they could buy. There was a gathering in the gurudwara. That traitor shot at point-blank range at Bhag Singh and Balwant Singh while they were deep in meditation. Shri Bhag Singh died on the spot but Shri Balwant Singh survived. The bullet hit another patriot, Shri Vatan Singh, instead of Shri Balwant. He was also martyred on the spot. The assassin managed to escape the people present there, who were too stunned to react immediately. Even the Canadian law did not punish him. He is still alive. He has been the blue-eyed boy of the Punjab government. Why he committed such a dastardly act, and what good he saw in it is something only he knows!

So, many months passed in these activities. It was towards the end of 1914. The World War had begun. All the Indians living in America began to make preparation to return to India. So how could our hero stay there? He left with his family. He went to Shanghai where he was blessed with a son. There he had to change his plans to return home due to some work. He sent his family home with Shri Kartar Singh and stayed back himself. After accomplishing whatever he had to do there, he arrived in 1915 in Bangkok.

He was asked to stay to work to organize and supervise those who were trying to inspire a revolution in the Far East. This is not the place to write a moving account of all those unsuccessful attempts. With the help of Imperial Japan and the heavily armed armies of France, the English won the week-long brutal war that was played out in Singapore. India's attempt at independence was defeated. The Eastern plot came to an end. These were the conditions in which Shri Balwant reached Bangkok. Unfortunately, he fell ill. His condition became serious and he had to be admitted to the hospital. An inexperienced doctor operated upon him and that too without chloroform. His body was debilitated with pain. He had still not developed enough strength to walk about, when the hospital asked him to leave. His acute weakness was also not taken seriously. He was discharged from the hospital. And there is a story behind why he was discharged so unceremoniously. The police were waiting for him outside the hospital to arrest him. He had barely come out of the hospital gate when was arrested. All efforts at getting a bail were futile.

The independent government of Siam quietly handed over Shri Balwant Singhji and his other comrades to the British government. And why? The sole reason being that India was a colonized nation. Who would invite trouble for the sake of a colonized nation?

Shri Balwant Singhji was brought to Singapore. He was given every threat and enticement under the sun to persuade him to reveal the secrets, but he offered nothing except silence. Finally, he was included in the second list of the Lahore Conspiracy of 1916. The crime was the same, in which one gets a death sentence upon failure to prove one's innocence. He was accused of treason. The drama went on for twenty-four days. Bela Singh Jaind and several other witnesses testified against him. The drama was tragic. It was decided that the accused be sacrificed at the altar of imperialism. Even God would have been thunderstruck at the verdict. A death sentence to this great soul? A fiendish laughter must have shaken the demons and ogres.

He was locked in a tiny cell; and being a Sikh, could not wear the cap. He wrapped the blanket around his head. To malign him, someone tied a sachet of opium to one corner of his blanket and alleged that he had wanted to commit suicide. He answered with infinite serenity – 'Death is standing before me. I'm ready for its embrace. I shall not mar the face of beautiful death by committing suicide. I am proud to be given death sentence for treason. I shall offer my life courageously at the noose.' Upon interrogation, the truth came out. Some convicts and the warden who were responsible were punished. Everyone lauded his patriotism and courage.

This was during 1916. There were a spate of death sentences and life-term sentences to the Andaman and Nicobar Cellular Jail, notorious as the 'Kaala Paani' in those days. The entire region of north India was in a state of turmoil. A massive secret rebellion was underfoot, but the people of India were unaware of it. The leaders did not dare to even glance at those people. A majority of the public believed that the government had launched such terrible charges only to terrorize the people. Whatever it may have been, even after its grand failure, its memory is beautiful. It is beautiful, because it has been written with the pious blood of the idealistic youth of India. It still lingers because the sacrifices made, never go in vain.

Shri Balwant Singh's wife went to meet him on 18 March of the same year. She was handed some clothes and books and informed, 'He was hanged to death yesterday on the 17 March'. His wife was shocked to hear that.

The news of the day of Shri Balwant Singh's hanging was revealed later. He took a bath in the morning, and along with six other comrades (who were hanged the same day) he offered a final salute to his motherland. They sang a patriotic song. They went to the gallows cheerfully. And what happened then? Why do you ask? The same hangman, the same noose! Oh! The same hanging and the same sacrifice of life!

Today, Balwant is no more with us, only his name, his country, his revolution.

– Mukund

21. Doctor Mathura Singh (1928)

Despite having suffered the maximum cruelties, despite having sacrificed gems of its youth at the altar of freedom, today Punjab is considered to be backward in the political sphere. Shri Khudi Ram Bose embraced the noose in Bengal. He was acclaimed so highly that his name is known in every corner of the region today. He is famed in the whole country. There are numerous jewels in Punjab who bestowed their lives for the sake of the nation, there are several heroes who cheerfully embraced the gallows, or took a bullet in their chests. But how many people know about them? Let alone other areas, how many people in Punjab know about them? It is not as if just any ordinary anonymous rebel swung from the hangman's noose and the people forgot all about him. Such people worked tirelessly, with unfailing enthusiasm, and incomparable courage to strive for their country that, even today, just listening to their exploits leaves one astounded. Had these priceless jewels been born in any other nation, they would have been revered and worshipped like Washington, Garibaldi and William Wallis. But they committed the unforgivable crime of being born in India. They have been punished by being consigned to the realm of the forgotten. Neither their work, nor their sacrifice is mentioned;

neither their heroism, nor their courage is famous. But how can a nation that shows such ingratitude, progress?

The place of the staunch idealist, Dr Mathura Singh is indeed very high. He was born in 1883 in a village called Dudhiyal, in the Jhelum district of Punjab. His father was Sardar Hari Singh. After his initial education in his village, he went to Chakwal High School. His sharp intelligence set him apart from his classmates. After clearing his Matriculation exams there, he began to learn medicine privately. There was a shop in Rawalpindi run by Messres Jagat Singh and Brothers. That is where he began his training. He worked very hard. Within three or four years, he had mastered the subject. Then he opened his own clinic in Naushehra Cantonment. He would procure medical journals from as many countries that he could. He decided to go to America for specialized study. He had not even succeeded in sorting out the business of his shop when his wife and daughter passed away. But that did not discourage him. He departed for America in 1913. He had to make a halt in Shanghai due to a paucity of funds. He started his practice there itself and was hugely successful. But he intended to go to Canada; and he reached there with some other Indians. But he faced many hardships there. At first, only he and another man got permission to disembark there, but the others were not allowed to get off. He, too, decided not to get off there. However, he was persuaded by the other people in the group to get off. He did so and immediately got into a quarrel with the immigration officers. This even led to his prosecution. But the law and the court are for the powerful; not for the citizens of a colonized nation. These people were forced to return on the pretext that they had not come by ship directly to Canada.

Dr Mathura Singh returned to Shanghai. He narrated the miserable condition of the Indians there and exhorted Shri Baba Gurdit Singhji to buy an entire ship that would go straight to Canada. Acting upon this advice, Babaji hired the Komagata Maru ship and named it Guru Nanak Ship. Dr Mathura Singh, in the meantime, had to return to Punjab. The ship was readied for his voyage; but he was unable to reach there in time to board it. He, along with about thirty five other people, started in another ship from Singapore, so that they could catch the Komagata Maru at Shanghai and board it. Upon their arrival in Hong Kong, they learnt that the ship had already left Shanghai. So he decided to stay there. By now he had made up his mind to dedicate his life to striving for the independence of India.

Dr Mathura Singh began propagating his ideas in Hong Kong. The newspaper *Ghadar* issued by the Ghadar Party in America used to be brought there. He also began to secretly publish a similar paper and distributed it. And he also received constant intimation about the untold viciousness that was heaped on the Komagata Maru. When it became clear that the Komagata Maru would be forced to return, then his propaganda touched new heights. At that time, a Sikh inspector in Canton was trying very hard to suppress this agitation. After Dr Mathura Singh met him, he too became their supporter.

Dr Mathura Singh had to go to Shanghai for some work. As he was leaving, he advised everyone that they should all board Komagata Maru ship and return to India. But the government got wind of his plan and so they did not allow the ship to dock at Shanghai. A day or two later, all of them returned to India on different ships; Komagata Maru was also docked at Hoogly when they arrived in Calcutta. The government gave them tickets and put them on trains to Punjab. Even before they reached Amritsar, the Budge Budge incident had taken place. They heard the news and were enraged. A violent desire for revenge raged in their hearts. However, Dr Mathura Singh managed to somehow pacify his comrades, exhorted them to engage themselves in disseminating information and immersed himself in the organizational work of the agitation. In this huge attempt, he was entrusted with the task of making bombs. He was quite adept at it. Hundreds of ardent patriots began to stream in from America to help ignite the rebellion. All preparations were underway. Such a massive group of revolutionaries was ready that there were rumours of one massive revolt all over India and even the date was fixed. But within a short time, all the effort; all the arrangements came to naught. Kirpal's treachery undid everything. A round of arrests followed, but Dr Mathura Singh managed to escape. A government spy tried to lure him into becoming a witness for the prosecution and win a huge reward and be granted a pardon. He rejected the offer without the slightest hesitation. Once, a secret agent managed to approach him. The agent knew fully well that Dr Mathura Singh was a fearless revolutionary and he did not dare to arrest him by himself. On the contrary he spun a tale about his coming, saying that the government had pardoned him and had promised him a reward. Dr Mathura Singh realized that his talk was to hide his pusillanimity in arresting him. So he pretended to be inclined to take up the offer and got rid of him. This also made him realize that it was well-nigh impossible for him to stay free in the country, so he set off for Kabul. He was arrested by the police at Wazirabad station but managed to bribe the policeman and get away. He left for Kohat. The police also got this information so they posted a large contingent of policemen at the Kohat railway station. A large number of policemen boarded the train, and without a warning, they carried out a search in all the compartments, but he did not fall into their hands. After staying there for a few days, he left for Kabul. He soon acquired a name for himself there. He was nominated the Chief Medical Officer in Kabul due to his ability.

Even if all hopes of a revolution in India had been dashed, the people abroad were still trying their best to achieve it. At that time, there was the Provisional Government of India in Kabul that was engaged in striving for Indian independence with the help of the Germany Committee. At this time, Indian revolutionaries – Hindu, Muslim, and Sikh – in the Arab world, Egypt, Mesopotamia and Iran, were busy in trying to foment revolution in India. Dr Mathura Singh also put all his energies to this end. He even had to go to Germany for this purpose. Then a decision was taken that a '*swaran patr*', a gilded testament, would be issued in the name of the Provisional Government directed to the Tsar of Russia with the hope that he would support the cause of Indian freedom. Dr Mathura Singh was seen off with great pomp and show. Several bearers and camels laden with goods accompanied him. But even as the preparations were being made, a traitor was informing the British about Dr Mathura Singh's movements, unknown to him. Dr Mathura Singh was arrested in Tashkent. He was brought to Iran to be identified and he was prosecuted. Many people tried to prevent his being handed over to the Indian government, but when all the efforts till date had been unsuccessful, this was not likely to succeed either.

Dr Mathura Singh was brought to Lahore. O'Dwyer's rule was paramount those days. A farce of a court case was carried out for some time. He was sentenced to death. He heard the pronouncement of the sentence with extreme pleasure. His younger brother went to meet him in jail. Dr Mathura Singh asked him – 'So, brother, I hope you are not worried about my dying!' The young lad started to cry. Dr Mathura Singh addressed him in a sharp but heartening voice – 'Vaahji! This is a time to celebrate. Do Sikhs cry upon laying their lives for the nation? I am filled with extreme joy that I've done whatever I could have to make the Indian revolution a success. I shall hang with great serenity.' This is the way he exhorted his brother.

And then? On 27 March 1917, the drama began again. There was only a single scene in the drama of that day – and that too just for a few minutes. God knows from where these extraordinary people had come – who neither feared death nor loved life; they remained cheerful in their work, laughed at the battlefront, and even smiled at the hangman's noose. They were great souls.

'The angels themselves were in love with them, such were these men!'

– Vrajesh

22. Shri Banta Singh (1928)

Even in these thoroughly rotten times, when Indians have degenerated to the extreme end, some adventurous youths who revived the sweet memories of the ancient times have been born. These people lived such a daring and fearless life that it gave rise to hope again, even in this time of cowardice; some people do take birth, who can sacrifice their very existence for the country. This offers hope for the revival for this degenerate country. Such brave people are found only in the more radical or revolutionary parties.

Shri Jatindranath Mukherjee and Nalini Bagchi from Bengal, Shri Genda Lal Dikshit from UP, Kartar Singh and Babbar Akali martyrs can be counted among these people. Shri Banta Singhji Sangwal was also one such revolutionary. The Punjab police used to tremble with fear at the mere mention of his name. The way Shri Jatindranath Mukherjee was considered as the 'terror of Bengal police', so was Banta Singh considered the 'terror of Punjab police'!

Banta Sigh was born in 1890 in Sangwal village of district Jalandhar. Shri Buta Singh was his father. He was admitted to school at the age of five. He was good at studies. He cleared both Class 7 and 8 in one year. When he was a student in DAV High school of Jalandhar, in 1904-5, Kangra experienced a severe earthquake, which inflicted a lot of damage. Banta Singh also went for relief work to Dharmshala with a group of fellow students. Looking at his competence and eagerness, every one became enamoured of him.

Those days he organised a new group; and he led that group. Its aim was to help the poor. He used to do a great deal of service to the people with the help of this group. After completing his school education, he went abroad. First he went to China and then to America from there.

His American stay had a great impact on him. He realised his slavery at every step. So he resolved to fight for the freedom of the country after his return. He opened a school when he returned from abroad and formed a democratically elected body, a Panchayat as well. Everyone held him in great esteem. He was made the head of the panchayat too. All the people of the village gladly honoured the decisions taken by the Panchayat. Once, it even went on to change the decision of the chief court and both parties were satisfied with the decision. However, this was not such a simple matter; this reached the higher functionaries as well. They were very annoyed and offended. On the other hand, his house was a centre for Indians returning from America. This report also reached the officers. This was a good opportunity for them to interfere. One day, the police suddenly raided Banta Singh's house. He was not at home; but they confiscated a lot of papers, which included many tracts written by him. After scrutinising the material, an arrest warrant was issued against him. But he could not be arrested. Later, a reward was also announced for anyone who helped to get him arrested.

One day, he was going to Anarkali Bazar in Lahore, along with his comrade, Sh. Sajjan Singh Ferozepuri, to attend an underground meeting. He had to confront a police sub-inspector on the way, who insisted on conducting a body search. Banta Singh argued with him, asking him to behave like a gentleman and go away as he had no reason to search him. But why would that Sub-Inspector leave him? When he did not listen, Banta Singh said, 'All right then, go ahead and search me!' When the sub-inspector advanced to search him, he quietly took out his pistol and saying, 'It would have been better had you not searched me as I have just this; so here you are!' Banta Singh fired at him. The sub-inspector collapsed and they ran away. They had not covered much ground when his comrade stumbled and fell down. Banta Singh kept the police and the crowd at bay by firing at them to scare them away and helped his comrade to rise. But due to being injured quite seriously he could not run, so Banta Singh escaped alone. This incident happened at noon.

He escaped and reached Mianmir station. The police were already waiting for him there. But somehow, he managed to climb onto a train, and many policemen also boarded the same compartment of that train. He understood his situation, but what could be done now? When the train was about to stop at the Attari station, he jumped down. The policemen were left, rubbing their palms. From there, Banta Singh made to Jalandhar in Doaba.

At that very time, Zaildar Chanda Singh of Nangal Kalan in Hoshiarpur had got a Ghadar Party activist, Bhai Pyara Singh arrested. Banta Singh decided to take his comrades along and punish these traitors. He took Bhai Buta Singh and Bhai Jiwand Singh with him, and killed Chanda Singh in his house. Then he got down to action. He destroyed a bridge in Amritsar district using dynamite.

After that, there were many encounters with the police, but he was such a terror that the policemen used to run away and try to hide themselves the moment they spotted him. Once, the cavalry police gave him a chase. He kept running for sixty miles in front of them. The readers would think this to be somewhat implausible, but they should keep in mind that these activists from the American Ghadar Party were quite extraordinary. Punjabi Jats (peasants) are quite handsome and well-built, and then these people had returned from America after acquiring a special practice of running. Among them, Sh. Banta Singh was especially strong and well-built. The Bengali revolutionary, Nalini Bagchi too, ran for eighty miles continuously after escaping from a confrontation with the police in Guwahati. Nothing is impossible for adventurous people. That day, his feet were injured and he felt sick, so went home and rested for many days.

He somehow believed that he would get arrested due to the treachery of some of his own relatives, but could not do anything due to the deterioration of his health! The main case of the Lahore Conspiracy was going on. For another big case, there was a spate of arrests being made. The whole organization of the party was in a shambles. There was no other option other than self-dependence. So, even in a poor state of health, he had to return to his own home. For many days he stayed there, but later a relative insisted on taking him to his place in order to provide better treatment and take greater care of him. After taking him to his place, the same relative quickly called the police. The Superintendent of Hoshiarpur arrived with a large contingent of armed police.

The police surrounded Banta Singh from all sides. Opening the door of the room, he laughed heartily at seeing the police and addressed his relative, 'Brother, if you had to call the police, why did you disarm me? If not a pistol or a revolver, you could have at least left me one lathi or stick. I would have given up my life like a brave soldier, fighting.'

At these words, the police chief said, 'Sir! You think yourself to be brave. Are we all cowards?'

He answered smilingly, 'Great! You are daring to advance to arrest me after disarming me. Let me go out and then let us see who can arrest me.'

That brave fellow wished to die like a soldier, fighting the battle, but his wish was not fulfilled. He was arrested and brought to Hoshiarpur. He was produced in the court of the Deputy Commissioner. For nearly one hour, he conversed with him. The Deputy Commissioner was almost enamoured at his courage and fortitude. On the other hand, the news of his arrest spread like wildfire in Doaba. People started gathering in hundreds to take a look at him. The courtyard was milling with people.

When he came out, the people surged ahead to see him. In such a situation, he could not leave without saying something to his brothers. He asked for the Deputy Commissioner's permission to speak, who did not refuse. Banta Singh appealed the surging sea of people to calm down and made a short speech:

"Dear brothers, don't be saddened at seeing us today in chains and shackles. Do not get upset at our certain death. We are sure that our sacrifices will not go waste. The day is not far when India will be completely free and the arrogant British will fall at your feet. xxxx[90] all of you should be ready to give up your life at the altar of freedom."

He was taken to Lahore from there. He was put on trial, along with Shri Balwant Singh. Though everywhere the play of justice is played with the slaves, yet in those days, O'Dwyer-ism was at its peak. It was a wonderful justice; there could be no appeal! Everything was through in few days. He was handed out a death sentence. He said cheerfully, 'Thank you, God; you have given me a golden opportunity to sacrifice my life for the nation.' He was overjoyed when he heard the death sentence, and from that day to the day of execution, his weight increased by eleven pounds!

Finally one day he was taken to the gallows. He was as happy as ever at that time. The scaffold was lowered; the rope was already put around his neck. His life snapped in just one stroke and so one more human gem from Punjab sacrificed his life at the altar of India's freedom!!

– Girish

23. Shri Ranga Singh (1928)

Shri Ranga Singh was one of the hundreds of jewels who sacrificed his mortal life in the Lahore Central Jail during the unsuccessful attempt at attaining independence for India in 1914-15. He was born to Shri Gurudatt Singhji probably in 1885, in Khurdpur village in Jalandhar

---

90   Text struck out in original.

district. After acquiring some learning in school, he joined the army to get military training. After working in Battalion No. 30 till he was 23, he went to America in 1908.

Henceforth, it is the same old story. The Ghadar Party was established, the paper was published, there was dissemination of the revolutionary ideas, and his views were transformed. When the Sikhs were returning to India in large numbers in 1914, he too returned to India to fight the British.

He stepped on Indian soil on 21 December 1914 after being abroad for six years. He stayed at home for about a month in which he made all arrangements for his household and then began to travel from village to village to propagate the ideas of Ghadar.

It is believed that when the news of the revolution planned for the 19 February was leaked to the police and a lot of leaders were arrested and thrown into Lahore Central Jail, there was also a plan to rescue them. It was decided that the armoury of the Kapurthala State would be looted for this purpose. Shri Ranga Singh was among the leaders of this plan. Later, due to a lack of adequate strength, it was decided that first the policemen posted at the Bala Bridge would be overpowered and their weapons seized, and then these would be used to attack the armoury.

Some of the men present were chosen to carry out this job, and our hero was among them. But when the policemen were found to be vigilant, and the ambush was postponed by the revolutionaries, he was very angry. He said – 'If we go on quitting like this fearing a lack of strength, then nothing will get done. We have to face them with these handfuls of men itself.'

Finally the police got a clue about his whereabouts and captured him on 26 June 1915, as he was sleeping in a sweet drinks shop. After his arrest, a case was registered against him for carrying out treasonable activities against the government and he was awarded the death sentence. Thus the curtains came down forever on another act of the tragedy of the Lahore Central Jail.

– Ghanshyam

24. Shri Veer Singh (1928)

Shri Veer Singh was born in Bahowal in the Hoshiarpur district. His father's name was Sardar Boota Singh. Shri Veer Singh left for Canada in 1906. A free country on one hand, and a rapidly spreading agitation on the other – he too could not remain untouched by the wave. Dissemination of ideas had already taken place. The incident of the Komagata Maru ship, the failure of the deputation and the outbreak of the war led to voices of the Ghadar to resound from all directions. People began to spend their hard-earned money on Ghadar activities and their return to India. There was hardly a soul that remained untouched by all these activities. Everywhere, the cries of 'Return to the homeland' and 'Fight for the independence of the country' could be heard. Shri Veer Singh was also influenced by these calls and returned to India, and he began to go from place to place to propagate the Ghadar ideology.

It was 6 June 1915. He was bathing at a well in Chiththi village when he was surrounded by the police. He was arrested and brought to Lahore, and along with another 100 people, he was prosecuted in the second case. He was accused of having attacked and robbed the armoury, and was sentenced to death by hanging.

Apart from him, five of the other 100 accused were given death sentence by hanging and 42 were given life imprisonment in the Cellular Jail in Andaman and Nicobar Islands. All his property was confiscated.

The Lahore Central Jail shall, indeed, always have a special significance in the historic independence struggle of India.

– Yadav

25. Shri Uttam Singh (1928)

Shri Uttam Singh was one of the people possessed by the frenzy of getting freedom for their country, and he lit the sacrificial fire of revolution and sacrificed his own life in it. He was born in a village called Hans in the

Ludhiana district. His father's name was Shri Jeet Singh. Shri Uttam Singh was also known by the name of Shri Ragho Singh.

No one has researched where and till what level was he educated yet, or till what age did he stay in the country, or when he went to America. What has come to light is that he was an active member of the Ghadar Party in America and as per the decision of the party, he returned to India in 1914 with some other comrades to propagate the Ghadar ideology. He began his task on the journey itself by preaching Ghadar to soldiers and other Indians.

He was already known to the revolutionary Kartar Singh Sarabha. He was introduced to Gandha Singh, Boota Singh, Arjun Singh, Pingle, etc., and he began his work enthusiastically.

The frenzy of these people also had a synergy in it. There was a breath of freshness in it. He was among the 50 men who, enthused by this fresh energy, had the courage to attack the strongest of strongholds – the Ferozepur Cantonment – on 19 February 1915, along with the young Kartar Singh Sarabha. Even though they did not succeed due to adverse circumstances, his courage, his enthusiasm, his dedication and self-confidence can be gauged from this incident.

After the failure of the plan of the massive revolt on the 19 February, there was a frantic round of arrests. A warrant was issued in the name of Uttam Singh as well, but he was successful in evading the police at that point of time. He did not lose heart even when he stood witness to the destruction of his cherished mission. Most of the leaders, barring a very few, had been arrested at that time, so he began to amass weapons anew to free them from the jail. At first there was a plan to loot the Kapurthala State Armoury, but then a mere 7-8 armed revolutionaries snatched 750 cartridges, 15 rifles from 15 soldiers from Bala Bridge. Shri Uttam Singh had a role to play in this incident as well. He knew how to make bombs and once, when he had no other ingredients; he used brass utensils to make bombs.

They were still planning the raid on the jail when he was arrested on 19 September 1915, along with a comrade from an ascetic's hut in Mana-Bhagwana village in Faridpur State. He said at that time – 'The only thing I regret is that I did not have a revolver or a pistol in my hand.' Both the comrades burst into the national song when they were caught by the police. He was sentenced to death by hanging in the third Conspiracy Case of Lahore and, in just a few days, another sacrifice had been made to the sacrificial pyre.

– Pathik

26. Dr Arur Singh (1928)

These people sacrificed everything to the tongue of the burning flame of patriotism like an enamoured moth. For them:

> Life was incomplete after all
> I chose the coffin
> I had heard, this is where
> Total bliss lay

Doctor Sahib was born in a village called Sagwal in the Jalandhar district. The martyr Banta Singh also belonged to this town and both of them worked together. They were especially gifted in ferreting out information and in spying activities. They often went to the police station and managed to get information even from there. Singh could walk more than 40 miles without tiring. His full black beard and prominent eyes made him an awe-inspiring personality. But he was a very simple and gentle soul. He led a very simple life. He did not like to live and work outside Punjab; so much so that even when the police was searching high and low for him, he continued to move from village to village in Punjab, disseminating his message, and narrowly escaped arrest several times. He prayed to God every morning – 'O Lord! Let me die like a brave patriot – either shot by a bullet or the hangman's noose.'

He was very closely associated with an American. He considered the latter to be his mentor. Once, he learnt that the American had been arrested and lodged in the Lahore Central Jail. Despite a strict guard kept by the police, he managed to enter the jail, meet him and get all the information from him. It was ironic that on the one hand, a poster with his picture was plastered on the walls everywhere, and on the other, he coolly walked into the jail and escaped after accomplishing his task.

When he began to visit the Lahore jail frequently, one spy informed the police. Once, he was standing near the gate of the jail, when one police officer asked him:

'What is your name?'
'I am Arur Singh.'
'Arur Singh who?'
'The one whom you're tired of searching for.'

The officer did not believe his ears and he turned to leave. No one knows what came into his mind at that moment; but Arur Singh called the officer back and surrendered.

He confessed to everything during the court case. When the police officer Sukhha Singh said something cutting to him, Arur Singh shot back – 'Coward! All of you are sitting ducks for me. I could have wrung your neck in an instant had I wished to, but I think it a sin to stain my hands with the blood of cowards.' On another occasion, an inspector asked him if they had met earlier, and Arur Singh had answered – 'Met? Not only that, all that you've done is recorded in my diary.'

He was given a death sentence. He spent his time in jail narrating tales and anecdotes to the other inmates and gained considerable weight in those days. He was the epitome of a carefree soul. The fear that the word 'death' evokes in people was nowhere in his demeanour, which remained unchanged. The morning, on which he was to be hanged, he was in deep sleep. The officer came and woke him up, saying – 'Come, you are to be hanged.' He stood up and uttered 'Vande Mataram' in a loud voice and walked cheerfully to the gallows.

After that, the same gallows, the same platform, the same hangman, the same noose and the same last tug, and then …

– Pathik

27. Babu Harinam Singh (1928)

Ravi Babu wrote a poem about the Sikhs during Guru Gobind Singh's time. In that he wrote – 'They owe nothing to anyone and have death at their feet; such are the fearless and fierce Sikhs.'

Harinam Singh is one of these fearless and fierce gems. He was born in Sahri village of the Hoshiarpur district. His father's name was Shri Laabh Singh. He was a very clever student, but as soon as he reached high school, he quit and joined the army. He had a separate group there in which they sang devotional songs. He often used to say – 'What a life we have! We have stooped so low that we have to struggle for mere ten or eleven rupees and actually collude with our oppressors in tightening our own chains and that of other slave races. It is better to starve rather than keep this job, and death is preferable to this life!' His friends would laugh and ask him – 'So why don't you leave your job if that's the way you feel?' He would smile and answer – 'You know that I don't work for money. My family has property; I can spend a leisurely life, but ...'

How long could a man who harboured such ideas keep a job? After a year and a half, he quit his work and returned home. He was very fond of Shri Balwant Singhji in the army. Their ideas coincided and so did their time of quitting the army.

After spending some time at home, he went to Burma and then onwards to Hong Kong where he joined a tram company. A large number of Indians who came here to go to America or Canada used to be disappointed when the Immigration officer refused them permission. They would be left with nothing, and found it difficult even to scrape something to buy food. Harinam Singh would often help them out and try to boost their morale.

He began to realize that people in America led a good life and that even the most ordinary Indian began to dream of India's independence in that environment. Therefore, he began to encourage the Indians in Hong Kong to leave for America. He would even help them do so.

Finally, on 1 December 1907, when he was not even 20 years old, he also left for the States. He lived in Victoria for a year and began to earn money to send to India to be used for education in schools.

On 1 January 1908, he went to the USA from Canada and began to study in a school in Seattle. He studied very hard for three years. It was during these days, that the Canadian-Indians collected Rs 1.5 lakh and opened an Indian Trading Company and even kept a white manager. Harinam Singh was one of the partners of the company. The company did very well. Its success rankled with the white capitalists. They colluded with the white manager of the company who began to cheat. Harinam Singh began to suspect him of deception and began to keep a watch. When the issue got ugly, Harinam Singh became a sore point for the whites. They tried to trap him. But one of his friends, Ramisburg, who was a Magistrate, took him in with him. This gentleman lived in the US and Harinam Singh stayed with him for three years and continued his education.

Singh soon returned to Canada and began to publish an English newspaper, the *Hindustan*. He was an inspiring writer. He made a special impression on Canadian Indians. The government was not too pleased with this and he was accused of manufacturing bombs and treasonable propaganda and asked to leave Canada within 48 hours. It was a very difficult situation. He immediately wired a message to Ramisburg, who sent a wire to the Canadian government asking that Harinam Singh not be ordered to leave, and that he would personally come to take him and he fetched him in his private boat. Singh was granted permission again to go to Canada in a few days. On 20 March 1911, he began studying at Berkeley University. He also helped in every way he could in bringing out the *Ghadar* newspaper.

In the meantime, the two gentlemen, Bhai Gurdit Singh and Bhai Dilip Singh were arrested in connection with a bomb blast and the Komagata Maru ship came to the dock. Harinam Singh went with some other people to Bhai Gurditt Singh to discuss the matter, and he was arrested there. Though the others were let off, Harinam Singh was not. He was again ordered to leave the country. After fighting a lost battle for a few days, he boarded a ship to India. After carrying out activities of the Ghadar Party in China, Japan and Siam, he reached Burma. This was in 1915. After the suppression of revolutionaries in Singapore, a large number of Ghadar leaders had gone to Burma. The intention was to revolt on the day of

Bakrid in October 1915, and make sure that it was the white rulers who were sacrificed instead of lambs, but later, 25 December was fixed as the date. He was working day and night to achieve as much as he could when one day, suddenly he was arrested in Mandalay. He was prosecuted and given the death sentence. He was put in jail but he managed to escape. However, he was caught again very soon and hanged with as little delay as possible.

As per his wishes and local custom, his widow married his younger brother. Babu Harinam Singh was a man of a very independent nature and determined mind. He would often hum the songs *Hindi hain hum vatan hai Hindustan hamara* (Hindi are we, and our country is Hindustan) and *Marna bhala hai uska Jo apne liye jeeye* (It is better for him to die who lives for himself).

Shri Bhag Singh, Shri Harinam Singh, and Shri Balwant Singh loved each other dearly. They lived, ate and worked together. They were the life and soul of the Ghadar Party at that time. All three of them laid down their lives one by one in their attempt to win freedom for their country. They lived for their country and died for their country. What a beautiful idea of love!

– Anonymous

28. Shri Sohan Lal Pathak (1928)

This incident is from 1914. People were being sent to all the countries by the Ghadar Party in America to spread the idea of Ghadar. In this manner, Shri Pathak was also sent to Burma by this very party for propaganda. At the beginning of 1914, he came to Bangkok and after a few days of carrying out the Ghadar work, came to Burma. Here, establishing a centre in an organized manner, with the futile hope that the entire India would be in the grip of a revolution, he began his task of propaganda among the armies with great fervour.

21 February came and went by. Due to the plot being revealed, the revolution could not be initiated and a round of arrests took place. But

this was nothing new in the life of the revolutionaries. They were used to dealing with failures. They had come to this field with the motto of doing their duty without any expectation of reward, as is our culture. As a result, Sohan Lal did not get disheartened even upon this. He began preparations for revolt again with renewed enthusiasm.

One day in August 1914, when he was disseminating his ideas of Ghadar in the armoury of Memeo, one police officer got him arrested. Despite having three pistols and 270 cartridges, one doesn't know why Sohan Lal did not use them at that time.

Shri Pathak was kept in jail. When officers visited the jail, the prisoners would bow and scrape to greet them, but Sohan Lal was of a different temperament. He said – 'When I consider the English, the Raj, to be unjust and brutal, why should I accede to the rules of their prison?'

Perhaps it was not a part of his programme to stand up upon the arrival of the officers. But one thing was certain – he was never uncivilized in his behaviour. If anyone came to him and talked to him while standing, he too would rise. Once the Governor of Burma visited the jail. The jailor requested Sohan Lal to rise when the officer came. But when Sohan Lal did not agree, the jailor employed another stratagem. Just before the Lord came to the jail, the jailor went to stand beside Sohan Lal and engaged him in conversation. Sohan Lal too rose to his feet to talk, so he was not required to stand up when the Lord came there. In two hours of conversation, the Lord tried his best to persuade Sohan Lal to plead forgiveness and be granted a reprieve from the death sentence, but he did not agree.

Finally on the day of the hanging, an English magistrate again came and requested him to ask for forgiveness. Death stood before him with its jaws wide open. The platform and the noose had been readied. All the employees working in the jail began to look at Sohan Lal to listen to his reply. After a moment of silence, this mad devotee smiled and said, 'As far as begging for forgiveness is concerned, it is the British who should ask for my forgiveness. I have not committed any crime. They are the real culprits. But there is one thing. If you promise to let me go unconditionally, then I may consider your offer.'

The reply was – 'This is beyond our power.'

'Then why delay? Fulfil your duty and let me fulfil mine.'

Within moments, the platform was pulled away from under his feet, the noose jerked and this scene came to an end.

– Subodh

~

29. Patriot Sufi Amba Prasad (1928)

How many people in India today are familiar with the name of Sufi Amba Prasad? How many would shed tears for him, even if they remember him with sorrow? Ungrateful India has forgotten about countless such precious jewels without feeling an iota of remorse.

Sufi Amba Prasad was a true patriot. His heart was filled with anguish for his country. He wanted to see India achieve glory; he wanted to see India at the peak of progress, yet very few Indians even know his name. If he has ever been venerated, it has been in Iran, where the name of Aaka Sufi is becoming increasingly popular.

Sufiji was born in 1858 in Moradabad. He was born with his right hand missing. He would joke about it, 'Well, brother! We fought a war against the British in 1857. I lost my hand. I died. Then I was reborn, and the missing hand has followed me into this life.'

He was educated in several towns like Moradabad, Bareilley and Jalandhar. After clearing his F.A. exams, he studied law, but did not practise. He was also an influential Urdu writer, and this is where his calling lay.

In 1890, he published an Urdu weekly called *Jamyul Ilum*. Each word in it reflected the state of his mind. Though he was a well-known humourist, there was a great deal of underlying seriousness in his writing. He was a staunch supporter of Hindu–Muslim unity and denounced the divide-and-rule policy of the British in no uncertain terms.

In 1897, he was sentenced to one-and-a-half of imprisonment after being prosecuted for the charge of sedition. Upon his release in 1899, he found that the British were interfering in the affairs of some of the small principalities of Uttar Pradesh. Sufiji publicly exposed the policies of the

British government and the British residents there. He was charged with perjury and sentenced to six years imprisonment; and all his property was confiscated. He had to endure unspeakable torture in the jail, but not for a moment did he falter in following his path.

In jail, Sufiji was incarcerated in a filthy cell. He fell ill but was not given any medical assistance; nor was there any arrangement for any drinking water. The jailor would come and jeer at him – 'Still alive, Sufi?' However Sufiji managed to survive the jail term and was finally released in 1906.

Sufiji had a very close relationship with the Nizam of Hyderabad, and went to him immediately upon his release from jail. The Nizam got a beautiful house constructed for him. Once it was ready, he told Sufiji, 'This house is ready for you.' Sufi answered, 'I'm ready, too.' He packed his bags and left for Punjab. There he began to work in the newspaper, *Hindustan*. It is said that the government was impressed with his cleverness, eloquence and intelligence, and offered him a job as an informer at a salary of one thousand rupees a month. But he preferred jail and penury to that. Later he fell out with the editor and resigned from the job.

It was in those days that Sardar Ajit Singh laid the foundation of Bharat Mata Society and launched an agitation against the New Colony Bill of Punjab. Sufiji also began to associate with him, and their relationship developed.

In 1906, a round of arrests again began in Punjab, and Sufiji left for Nepal along with Sardar Ajit Singh's brother, Sardar Kishan Singh and Mehta Anand Kishore, a Secretary of the Bharat Mata Society. In Nepal, Sufiji met the Governor of Nepal, Shri Jang Bahadurji, who was very gracious. Later Shri Jang Bahadurji was removed from office for offering asylum to Sufiji and his property was confiscated. Sufiji was arrested and brought to Lahore. He was tried for his essays that had been published in Lala Pindi Dasji's newspaper, *India*, but was later acquitted of the charge and released.

Sardar Ajit Singh was also released soon after and the foundation of Bharat Mata Book Society was laid in 1909. Most of the work associated with it was done by Sufiji. He published a book, titled either *Baagi Masih* or *Vidhrohi Masih (The Rebel Christ)*. This book was later confiscated.

The same year, Lokmanya Tilak was tried in court and was convicted and sentenced for a period of six years. Then all the members of Deshbhakt-Mandal became ascetics and took to the Himalayas. One devotee accompanied them as they were trekking up the mountains. When the ascetics sat down to rest, the devotee came and bowed to Sufiji. He was a very well-dressed gentleman. He placed his forehead at Sufiji's feet and asked – 'Babaji, where do you live?'

Sufi answered brusquely, 'On your head.'

'Sadhuji, why are you annoyed?'

'You fool! Why did you bow to me alone? There are so many ascetics; why didn't you greet them?'

'I thought you were the sadhu.'

'Anyway, go and get some food.'

The gentleman left and returned soon with great quantities of food. After the meal, Sufiji called him closer and said – 'Are you going to stop following us or not?'

'How do I bother you?'

'Don't try to be too clever. Trying to spy on us! Go, go and tell your boss that Sufi is going to the mountains to start a revolution.'

He fell at Sufi's feet, 'Sir, a person is forced to do all these things to fill one's belly.'

Sufi brought out the newspaper, *Peshwa* in 1909. The movement had picked up momentum in Bengal in those days. The government was worried lest the fire of revolution spread to Punjab as well. Ergo, the wheel of repression began. Then Sufiji, Sardar Ajit Singh and Zia-ul-Haq went to Iran. Zia-ul-Haq became a turncoat there. He calculated that if he informed against his comrades, he would benefit doubly – escape punishment as well as get a reward. But Sufiji guessed his intention. He asked Zia-ul-Haq to go on ahead. As a result, it was he who was arrested, and the other two escaped.

How these people lived in Iran; what happened there, are things that may unfold at some later date; however this is a narration of what came to be heard about those days. The British searched high and low for them in Iran and they had to endure many hardships. It is said that they were surrounded by the British once. It was well-nigh impossible to escape from there. A group of traders was staying there. A great many boxes were being loaded on camels. They were filled with cloth material etc. Sufiji and Ajit Singh were packed in two boxes on one camel and herded out.

Then they stayed at the house of a rich man. The information leaked out somehow and they were surrounded. Both of them were dressed in burqas and made to sit in the zenana. All the men were searched, and in the end even women were searched. The veils of a couple of women were even lifted, but the Muslims became aggressive and did not allow any other woman's veil to be lifted. So the two of them escaped even from there.

Later they published a paper called *Aab-e-Hayat* from there and began to participate in the national struggle. After Sardar Sahib left for Turkey, the entire responsibility fell upon Sufiji's shoulders and this is when he became popular as Sufi. In 1915, there was some unrest again when the British tried to establish complete control over Iran. Shiraz was besieged. Sufiji faced them boldly with a revolver in his left hand, but the British finally overpowered him. He was court-martialled. The decision to execute him the next morning was taken.

Sufiji was locked up in a cell. In the morning, he was found in a trance; a state of deep meditation. He had already passed on to the next world. Countless Iranians accompanied his bier and there was deep mourning. The whole city mourned his demise for several days. A tomb was erected in his memory. Till date, a function is held at his tomb every year. People bow their heads in reverence upon hearing his name.

There are several interesting anecdotes about him. He could grip a pen between his toes and write with his foot. One man narrated how Sufiji had written down the name of a medicine with his foot once. There is another tale that his friends narrate about him. One doesn't know how much truth there is in it, but it seems quite probable. It is believed that when the Resident in Bhopal or some other state was fomenting trouble with a view to annex it, *Amrit Bazaar Patrika* dispatched Sufiji there to expose the truth. This incident is believed to have taken place around 1890. A slightly crazy-looking individual came to the bearer of the Resident for a job and was finally employed upon the condition that he wouldn't be paid any wages, but would be given his meals. When this fellow would sit down to wash the utensils, he'd be coated in dirt. He would smear mud even on his face. But since he would fetch excellent bargains, he would be sent to bring the goods.

In the meantime, article after article was published in the *Amrit Bazaar Patrika*, criticizing the Resident. He was finally so defamed that he was removed from office. After he had left the state, he was approached by a dark, well-dressed man in a suit and shoes and hat, at a railway station. The Resident was amazed to see him. 'He's the fellow who used to wash the utensils! He doesn't appear mad today!' The man came near and began to converse in English. The Resident was stunned. Finally he asked – 'You've already been rewarded; so what have you come to me for?'

Sufi replied, 'You said that you would offer a reward to any man who helps in nabbing the spy who exposed you.'

'Yes, I did say that. Have you got him?'

'Yes. Yes … give me my reward. I'm that man.'

The Resident started trembling with anger. He said – 'Had I learnt about your true identity while I was within the state, I would have got you hacked to pieces.' Anyway, he gave him a gold watch and said – 'I can get you a job with a salary of one thousand rupees as an informer if you wish.' But Sufiji said, 'If a salary is all that I had to earn, why I would have washed your utensils?'

Today Sufiji is not in this country. But even the mere memory of such a patriot is inspiring. May God grant him eternal peace!

– Anonymous

30. Bhai Ram Singh (1928)

Bhai Ram Singh was born in village Tuletan in the Jalandhar district. His father's name was Shri Jeevan Singh. He left for Canada at a tender age in 1907 or 1908. Here he was quite successful in his business and he began to be counted among the wealthiest Indians. But even then his behaviour was very simple, and he referred to his wealth as the wealth of his country and community. He was very generous when it came to giving alms. The 'langar', i.e. the community kitchen for the gathering, was run on his money.

In 1914, Indians living in Canada had to face many difficulties. The Komagata Maru episode, reverses in business, the killing of two leaders in a gurudwara, etc., transformed the prevailing circumstances. Unable to endure any more wounds of slavery, people began to return to their country. Ram Singh came to the United States from Canada with the same intention. Here, he was exhorted by the people to continue to live and work there.

In those days, the responsibility of the Ghadar Party was in the hands of a person called Pandit Ram Chandra. He had set norms aside and had overshadowed the party with his personality. Everything was dependent only on his wishes. He was always worried lest someone doing good work should come and settle down in America. With this at the back of his mind, he tried a ruse to make Ram Singh leave. He sewed a piece of paper in a shoe and gave it to Ram Singh, saying, 'Take this to that particular person in India. It is so important, that none other than you can be entrusted with it.' Well! Ram Singh set off for India. On the way, he met some old co-workers in Manila. They revealed Ram Chandra's true colours and also told him that he would be walking into a death trap by going to India at that time. When the boot was taken to pieces, there was nothing except an ordinary, printed paper. So he returned to America via China and Japan.

In the meantime, the rift between Ram Chandra and other people had widened considerably. When, after a great deal of effort also there seemed to be no hope of ending the quarrel, he held a meeting in 1916 in Sacramento in California, elected a new leader and began the work of the party. Ram Chandra called it irregular and called another meeting, but even in this, Ram Singh's committee was considered supreme and three members were added. It was also decided that within seven days, the old group would hand over the charge to the new committee. If this was not done, then the committee would take charge of everything by force. Despite this, they were not given the charge. While establishing their charge over the press, they called the police. Ram Singh narrated the whole sequence of events to the police; after all, it was the police of a free nation. So, the police itself broke open the lock on the press and handed over the charge to the new committee.

After this, Ram Singh completed the task of the organization, carrying its name to great heights. The people wanted to make him President of the Central Committee, but he refused the position, saying that it would be inappropriate for him to have first made the committee and then to himself become the leader of it. But even so, all his time would be spent in working for it.

During this time, America announced its participation in the World War and along with it, specific workers of the Ghadar Party were arrested. It was said that there was a change in the non-aligned status of America towards the British due to these people. Well, whatever it might have been, Ram Singh was arrested for this very reason. A few days later, Pandit Ram Chandra was also caught. At that time, Ram Singh told Ram Chandra that whatever their internal differences might have been, it would be right to work together there. But the latter did not agree, and finally this is what gained prominence. During the trial, the newspapers magnified the entire episode to great proportions, printing charges and countercharges by Ram Chandra's party and the other side. Seeing that the party was getting a bad name, Ram Singh made another effort to erase internal differences so that the case for all of them could be conducted at the same time, but he did not succeed even this time.

The case was handed to a jury, and when the judges went for lunch, Ram Singh pulled out a revolver in the court itself and fired at Ram Chandra. As Ram Chandra fell and Ram Singh lowered his arms, the police officer seated in the front shot at Ram Singh. In this manner, this scene of martyrdom came to an end in the middle of a court room in America.

Whatever may have been hidden in the layers of this episode, one has to agree that Ram Singh committed this act only because he could not endure the bad name given to the Ghadar Party.

– Bhanu

31. Shri Bhan Singh (1928)

If those revolutionaries who embrace the hangman's noose and give up their lives are a source of pride for a nation, then the significance of those people who continuously endure great tortures by the oppressors and die a slow, torturous death is no less. The common public does not learn their names, it is their secret work that is so important and it is their sacrifice that is so intensely heartbreaking.

Shri Bhan was one such hero. He was born in village Sunet in Ludhiana district. He first joined a cavalry unit, but later quit his job and left for America. Living in California, he began to participate enthusiastically in political activities in 1911.

The rest is an old story. Ghadar Party was formed, the newspaper *Ghadar* was published, it was organized, and finally when the World War began, people began to return home to India. The first to come were the Korea and Toshamaru ships. Shri Bhan Singh was on board one of these. He fell prey to the Immigrants Ordinance as soon as he landed. He had been carrying out propaganda on the way and therefore, this had to happen.

He was arrested as soon as he landed in Calcutta on 29 October 1914. After being incarcerated in the Montgomery Jail till the end of November, he was suddenly released one day. Due to this, some of his companions began to suspect him, but he was able to regain everyone's trust with his enthusiasm for his work. The work went on, but in the end, all the preparations were wasted. As soon as the plan for revolution failed, arrests were made in great numbers. Despite the fact that no charge of dacoity or murder could be proved against him, he was given life-imprisonment in the Cellular Jail in the Andaman Islands.

In jail over there, the jailor and the other officers prided themselves on their mercilessness, and as a result, there was a constant tussle between the prisoners and the officers. Once, some festival was being celebrated, and sweets were distributed. They were offered to the political prisoners as well. Some of them partook the treat. Bhan Singh accosted them and expressed his displeasure. It was because of their commitment to revolution that they were so unhappy with their companions, and they bore everything quietly. They all begged for forgiveness. The officers came to know about this. Bhan Singh was abused by some officer and he could not put up with it. He was locked in a cell that day and had to quietly bear it. The next day he refused to work. The jailor locked him up in a dark dungeon in chains with a staff tied to his shoulders. Moreover, his rations were reduced by half. Such a prisoner was not even given sufficient water to drink. Can we even imagine how unbearable such a punishment must have been on an island in severely hot conditions?

Who knows in what fervour revolutionaries can endure such unspeakable torture so cheerfully! What noble ideal enables them that not even worldly comforts lure them to stray from their path? Bhan Singh, more than forty years of age, bore the punishment of inadequate food and insufficient water in that severe summer so cheerfully. That brave man was maddened in the intoxication of love. One day, he began to hum, 'Tell my dear friend (God), the state of the devotee!' The jailor asked him to stop. But who had given him the right to prevent someone praying to God? Why would Bhan Singh follow his command? He continued to sing. He was locked in a cell on the second floor. Now he was locked in a cell on the third floor. Hardly a cell even, it was no bigger than a narrow trunk. What can a cell of two-and-a-half square feet be? But the singing did not stop. The heartless officers then beat him up brutally. They broke his bones. But what could it do? These inhuman brutalities inflicted on political prisoners were unbearable for them, and these people wanted to create a powerful movement by dying at their hands.

Seeing that the singing still did not stop, the officers went again to beat him up. This time the rest of the group also got to know about it. It was time for a meal. All of them ran towards that cell. But the gates of the barracks were shut and that jewel was beaten badly. This time, that lion was locked in a cage, shackled with chains. He had to endure everything. The brave man who had come with great enthusiasm to participate in the freedom struggle of the country was today helpless, imprisoned, and being beaten! How can we people understand what must have gone through his heart at that moment? He finally got only that half rations, murky cell, and staff-and-chain shackles. Other prisoners also gave up work and met with the same fate.

Bhan Singh had been beaten badly. His condition was serious. He couldn't even swallow water. There was no hope for his survival. He was sent to a hospital, so that he would not die inside the jail. After a few days there, his journey of life came to an end and he went to narrate the story of the 'devotee' to his 'dear friend'.

– Dhanesh

32. Shri Udham Singh (1928)

Udham Singh was born in a village called Kasel in the Amritsar district. Revolutionaries usually come before the world only during the final moments of their life. That is why not much could be learnt about the childhood of Udham Singh. The only thing that is known is that he went to America for business and when the newspaper *Ghadar* announced the war of India's independence, he joined the struggle. In 1914, Indians in America began to return to the country once the World War began. Once, all 350 Indian travellers aboard a ship sailing from America to India were arrested as soon as they landed on Indian shores. Born and brought up in India, these few Indians were deprived of the free environment of their own country; the government threw them in different jails in Punjab to be stifled to death. Among these 350 was our hero, Udham Singh.

In April 1915, after the large-scale plan for revolution came to naught in Punjab, the First Lahore Conspiracy Case began. This was justice meted out. Udham Singh, who had been arrested even before setting foot on Indian soil, was also dragged into this case. Awarded life imprisonment in the Andaman Jail, he was kept there for a few years; and then, towards the end of 1921, he was brought to Bellary Jail in Madras. Kept apart from the other political prisoners of Punjab in a solitary cell in a different compound, Udham Singh was passing his days, when one morning the officials came to the cell and discovered that Udham Singh had disappeared. Frantic efforts were made to locate him, but even after a great deal of effort, no one could find Udham

Singh nor could anyone explain how, when and where Udham Singh had escaped from a locked cell despite strict vigilance by the police.

Udham Singh reached Kabul after escaping, but as a poet has said, 'the fire in one's heart can take one to any limit', he was not able to rest there and returned to India, then worked for some time before leaving again. Even the police could not give up the search for him. A manhunt was launched and notices were pasted everywhere. After tricking the jaws of death several times, once when he was again returning to India, he was shot dead at the border and he could not return. Who fired that shot is a mystery even today.

– Pancham

33. Shri Khushi Ram (1928)

The year 1919 will always remain important in the history of India. A massive agitation had erupted in the country upon getting the Rowlatt Act as a reward for the War, and that resulted in the Jallianwala Bagh tragedy and the imposition of martial law. The people had lost their patience during those days. They didn't know that suddenly they would have to face so much brutality. But even in those wretched days, brave men such as our hero, Shri Khushi Ram, didn't care for their lives and made themselves immortal.

He was born into a poor family, in the month of Shravan, according to the Hindu calendar in 1957 (1900). His father's name was Lala Bhagwan Das. They were Aroras by caste. His father passed away just a few days after his birth. His birthplace was Pindi-Saidpur in district Jhelum. After his father's demise, he was brought up in an orphanage in Lahore Nawakot. He had a beautiful, chubby body. He was very powerful. The astrologer who prepared his astrological chart said at that time that the child would be strong as an elephant and his name would be immortal. He was named Bhimsen, but later he was known as 'Khushi Ram'.

He was student of DAV College, Lahore. After appearing in the Shastri examination in 1919, he had gone to Jammu for his vacations.

Here, everywhere there was talk of a strike to be held all over India after 30 March, on 6 April. So, he did not stay there and immediately returned to Lahore to lead the processions of college students.

A massive assembly was held in the Badshahi Mosque of Lahore on 12 April. Countless people had gathered; there were lectures, and enthusiasm ran high. The meeting came to an end, and the people proceeded towards the town in a procession. The banner was held by our hero. The Heera Mandi market was just a furlong ahead. This is from where they wanted to enter the town. The army was posted ahead. The person in charge of the army was Nawab Mohammed Ali (Barkat Ali). The order was given to the people – 'Disperse. You will not be allowed to carry out a procession.' The leader of the procession, Shri Khushi Ram said – 'The procession shall be carried out most definitely; and it will proceed from this very road.' The Nawab asked his soldiers to fire in the air. People began to run helter skelter, and Khushi Ram roared like a lion and said – 'Why needlessly behave like cowards by running? One has to die one day, then why not die like a hero? It is shameful that all of you are running hither thither like jackals to save your skins. You should be ashamed of yourselves!' And so on. The people stopped running. The Nawab again warned, 'Stop this procession!' Khushi Ram thundered again – 'No, that will not happen. Our procession will carry on like this only.' He moved forward and a shot was fired. This time it was not in the air. It went straight to Khushi Ram's chest. He took two steps forward. Another bullet struck him; he still went forward. In this way, seven bullets – one after the other – pierced his chest, but that brave man continued to step forward. The eighth bullet struck him on the right side of his forehead; the ninth on the left side. Now it was difficult for him to keep his balance and he fell into eternal slumber, never to wake any more.

That day a huge crowd of people swelled to accompany his corpse. Contemporary newspapers reported that the numbers were more than fifty thousand people.

Khushi Ram achieved immortality; he is not in this world today, but his name, his work and courage is alive even today.

– A Spectator

34. The Four Martyrs of the Battle of Bomeli (1928)

Out of the many jewels in the famous Babbar Akali Dal who played with death are Shri Karam Singh, Shri Uday Singh, Shri Bishan Singh and Shri Mahendra Singh. After making a mark in their field of activity, these people didn't even express a desire to look back. Watching their beloved country suffer one indignity after another, they were not able to control themselves. They could not endure the oppression inflicted upon Indians in Canada, the Komagata Maru incident, the killings of Budge Budge, the heart-rending scene of Jallianwala Bagh, the imposition of martial law, the caning of unarmed people in the Guru's Bagh, etc. This story is a mere reflection of the path that they chose to tread at that time, as they were impatient to break the chains of slavery.

Out of the above-mentioned four brave men, Karam Singh belonged to Daulatpur, Uday Singh to Ramgarh Jhuggian, Bishan Singh to Mangat and Mahendra Singh Pindori lived in Gung Singh. When Kishan Singh Gadgajj laid the foundation of Babbar Akali Agitation, then all four of them left the non-violent agitation and began to participate in this. They were a match for each other in courage; and these people always preferred to do the most difficult and complicated tasks. After a few days, Karam Singh and Uday Singh began to be counted among the chief workers of the movement.

After being baptized in the faith of the Akalis, Karam Singh began to go from village to village, propagating the message. He would attend meetings and explain to people how the cruelties inflicted upon them every day were due to their own weakness and till the time they became self-reliant and eliminated slavery, they would continue to be kicked around, etc. He had worked only for some time before he became fodder for arrests. He disappeared when a warrant was issued for him, and the police could not nab him even though he continued to carry out his work till the end.

Karam Singh was not merely a soldier; he was also a good orator and could sing. The periodical *Babbar Akali* was also edited by him. Like a devoted lover, if he worried about anything at all, it was his work. He could work day and night and yet not tire of it. Today, it is a lecture in a meeting, another day planning the system to punish a traitor is being laid out; and yet another day, plans are afoot to carry money and go to a far off place to procure weapons.

The police too was eager to nab him. Policemen were posted in many places, a reward for his arrest was fixed, but he still evaded them.

He had a deep relationship with Udham Singh. The two of them would usually be together. Both of them disappeared together and even died fighting the British together. What a shining example of love and friendship!

On 14 February 1923, Udham Singh killed the Diwan of Hyatpur for the crime of betraying the Babbar Akalis to the police. He said that he could have forgiven an enemy but not a traitor. After this, on 27 March 1923, the two friends, along with some other comrades, killed Baibalpur's Hazara Singh for the same reason. They punished several other traitors of the country. Punishment did not mean only death. If the crime was less serious, the offender's property would be confiscated or his nose or ears would be chopped off before letting him go.

One day when these four were passing close to Bomeli village in Kapurthala state, some traitor informed the Police Superintendent, Mr Smith. Immediately he set off in pursuit with some members of the infantry and the cavalry. Additional Police Sub-Inspector Fateh Khan was sent from the other side with fifty men. These people, seeing Mr Smith in pursuit, decided to take refuge in the Chaunta Sahib Gurudwara, which was close by. But since there was firing from the rear as well, these men tried to move towards the gurudwara while returning fire. Fateh Khan's men were lying hidden till now, and upon hearing the gunfire, they also came out of hiding. A nullah ran on all four sides of the gurudwara, and these four brave youths reached close to it, all the while facing the armed forces of Mr Smith bravely. They had barely stepped into the water when Fateh Khan's men, standing a little further away, also began to fire at them. The four men were trapped from all sides by a fully armed group of soldiers. How long could they have held out? So, after managing to ward off the attack for some time, Udhay Singh and Mahendra Singh fell into the water after being shot.

Karam Singh managed to cross the nullah somehow and began to fire at the enemy from that side. Fateh Khan called out from the other side – 'Surrender!' But that brave man had taken a vow to do or die. He refused and shot at Fateh Khan. Unfortunately he missed and the next moment, that brave man was shot in the forehead and he fell into the water.

In the meantime, Karam Singh had pulled the attention of the army towards him on the other side, and Bishan Singh who was still on the opposite side, got an opportunity to hide in the bushes. The rustle alerted the police and two men were sent to investigate. As soon as they came close, with a cry of '*Sat Sri Akal*', Bishan Singh attacked them with a sword and first wounded one man's hand. When the other soldier retreated, Bishan Singh tried to cross the nullah, but the other soldier shot at him, and he too, like his three companions, fell into the nullah.

This incident happened on 1 September 1923.

– Madhu Sen

35. Shri Dhanna Singh (1928)

Dhanna Singh's childhood was spent in a village called Baibalpur, in Punjab. He was a very stout and beautiful child. Courage and enthusiasm was filled in every pore of his body and fear itself feared him. After seeing the cruelties inflicted on the Akalis in the Guru's Bagh, he became opposed to the non-violent movement. Several people who shared similar ideas those days, cogitated about following a different path to liberate the country from the burden of colonialism. And when Babbar Akali was founded, Dhanna Singh also decided to participate in it.

He played an important role not only in propaganda and organizational work, but also in punishing the traitors. He had a considerable hand in both the attempts on the life of Patwari Arjun Singh who had colluded with the police to torment the Akalis. Later, on 10 February 1923, he along with three comrades, killed Zaildar Bishan Singh, of Rani Police Station, for being an informer. Sant Singh, who was hanged later, was also one of the accomplices in this. Later, even a notice was issued that Bishan Singh was killed only for 'reform'.

He was involved even in the killing of Lambardar 'Boota' by Banta Singh Dhamiyan. It is said that this Lambardar had ensnared several innocent Akali fighters in the police net and these people had committed this act only to bring about 'reform'.

Just a few days later, on 23 March 1923, Dhanna Singh and three comrades 'reformed' Mistri Labh Singh. And then, on 27 March 1923, with another set of three comrades, he 'reformed' a man called Hazara of Baibalpur village, who had revealed a great deal of information about the group to the police; they killed him and posted a notice in this manner – 'Reward xx today on 27th March Hazara Singh of Baibalpur village has been given three feet of land, i.e. three bullets.' *(The reference is to the space needed to bury a person).*

This is the manner in which he rewarded traitors and spies for their crimes, and carried on propaganda for their movement. One day, on 25 October 1923, he was caught in the net of the police. Till date, all the revolutions that have been attempted in India, have failed due to defection by one's own brothers. Dhanna Singh had gone to Jwala Singh to ask about the arrest of a youth, Dalipa. How was he to know that it had been because of Jwala Singh that Dalip Singh had been caught? Jwala Singh asked Dhanna Singh to wait in a sugarcane field and informed police sub-inspector Gulzar Singh about his whereabouts. Then, the both of them went to Hoshiarpur to inform the Police Superintendent Mr Horton. Mr Horton asked Jwala Singh to bring Dhanna Singh to Mananhaana village in Hoshiarpur and put him up on the terrace of Karam Singh's house. Jwala Singh did as he was told. The next night, both of them were sleeping on cots in the cattle enclosure. At midnight, Jwala Singh saw the police approach and ran away. The police was drawing closer to the enclosure, when Dhanna Singh got up and started off in the direction Jwala Singh had gone. The police, that had let the first man escape deliberately, surrounded Dhanna Singh. There were a total of 40 men. Dhanna Singh was just about to take out his revolver, when Gulzar Singh struck him with a staff. Dhanna Singh lost his balance and fell down as he tried to duck this sudden attack. The men swooped down upon him and were able to overpower him after great difficulty. He tried to free himself even after he was handcuffed. He was made to sit in one place and a couple of men clutched the chain to his handcuffs and kept both his hands high. Fear is a terrible thing. Not satisfied with this, one man even grabbed both his wrists from behind.

What a strange rhythm time has! Dhanna Singh, who had been dreaming of the founding of a new nation just a few hours ago, now had to wait like a criminal for his fate to be decided. So did Dhanna Singh get arrested? No! Could it be possible? He had taken an oath to die, not to be arrested. So while the policemen had caught hold of him, he gave one mighty heave and pulled his arms down so that his elbow could nudge the bomb hidden at his waist to detonate it.

There was chaos all around, and the place where Dhanna Singh had sat was now only a pile of blood, flesh and bones. Five policemen also died in the blast and three were badly injured, out of whom Mr Horton and a constable died later in the hospital; and this is how this brave warrior ended his life.

– Chaturanan

36. Shri Banta Singh Dhamiyan (1928)

One of the main and most interesting incidents of the Babbar Akali Agitation was the famous Battle of Munder. Three Babbar Akali youths were besieged in a house but fought successfully to keep at bay countless armed soldiers for several hours. Two of them died in the battle and the third managed to escape despite the heavily guarded house. His name was Shri Waryam Singh. The two who were martyred were Shri Banta Singh Dhamiyan and Shri Jwala Singh Kotla.

Shri Banta Singh was a resident of Dhamiyan Kalan. He was born sometime around 1900. Right from his childhood, he was very mischievous. He was very good at sports too. He was sent to the village school where he was a student for four or five years after which, he became busy in household work. Later, he joined the army and served in the Sikh

Battalion No. 55 for three years. There too, he was ahead of everyone else at sports, and he was especially unmatched in running. He fell into bad company and started robbing people. But, he had not travelled far on that path, when the Babbar Akali agitation appeared on the scene. He was profoundly moved by the statements of Babbar Akalis like Shri Karam Singh of Daulatpur, Shri Uday Singh of Ramgarh etc. He joined the group.

He became convinced that the only way to atone for his past misdemeanours would be to lay down his life in the service of the nation. He had stepped into the fray with this determination to wash his past sins with his own blood. Even after adopting this path, he was compelled to abet a couple of dacoities, but his temperament had changed completely. On 2 or 3 March 1923, a dacoity had taken place in the house of the stationmaster of Jamsher. He[91] was the leader of the group. It is said that one wicked fellow tried to touch a woman in the house. But Shri Banta Singh addressed the lady from a respectful distance – 'Mother, please take off your ornaments yourself and hand them over. We shall not touch you.' She began to weep, and narrated the previous encounter with the earlier robber. She asked sarcastically – 'What's the use of showing such nobility now?'

Banta Singh was furious upon hearing about his companion's misbehaviour. He picked up an axe to hack him down but another member held his hand. They all begged him for mercy and finally his rage subsided. He said – 'Such depraved men will earn a bad name for our Swaraj movement. First we are forced to rob; and then to commit such shameful behaviour! What will we be able to accomplish like this?' This is an indication to how his character was transformed once he became a revolutionary.

Then he worked as per the programme of the Babbar Akali and put many traitors to death. On 11 or 12 March he attacked the house of Boota Singh and killed him. Boota Singh was a confidant of the police and rendered them possible help in suppressing the national agitation. These kinds of activities went on in those days. In the meantime, the police was

---

91 Banta Singh

hunting all over the Doaba to arrest these people. A handsome reward had been announced. But it was not easy to arrest him. One day, some cavalry soldiers encountered him in a nearby forest. These soldiers had been appointed for the sole purpose of capturing these Babbar Akali bravehearts. Banta Singh challenged them all by himself. But the soldiers promptly ran away, saying, 'We neither wish to capture you nor kill you. It's thanks to you that we have also acquired a status and our salaries have been doubled and tripled.' Many such incidents can be found that relate to the bravery of this hero. It is said that one day, he entered a cantonment all by himself and snatched the mare and the rifle from the guard of the battalion.

These cat-and-mouse games continued for a long time. But he was captured finally on 12 December 1923. The truth was that a man named Jagat Singh was arrested on suspicion from Sham-Churasi village, which was about 10 or 12 miles away from Jalandhar. The police failed to muster any evidence against him, so he was threatened and forced to accede to a demand to aid in capturing the Babbar Akalis, and was let off on this condition. That rogue extended a hand of friendship to the Babbar Akalis. He boasted about the time spent in the jail, projecting it as proof of his patriotism and courage. But he was no better than an animal. He called Banta Singh, Jwala Singh and Waryam Singh to stay over at his house one day and sent information to the police. Within hours the police surrounded the entire village.

When these people learnt that the enemy had surrounded the village, they immediately climbed onto the terrace. They were prepared to die, but wanted to die fighting bravely. Strategically they were on a higher and superior location than the police, and these three men were successful in harassing the police for hours. There was heavy firing from both sides. The machine guns and rifles of the soldiers seemed to be in vain. They placed the machine gun on the terrace of a house facing Jagat Singh's house. But they were not able to breach the defences of these patriots.

Then the 'benevolent' white masters showed their unparalleled 'compassion'! The house was doused with petrol with a pump and set on fire. Shri Jwala Singh also received a bullet wound. He was badly wounded. Shri Banta Singh tried to escape from the house. He was also shot and fell there, wounded. He did not even have the strength left in him to go to the window and shoot at the enemy. He said pitifully – 'Waryam Singh! At least you should go. Bhai, save yourself if you can! Then you can avenge our death later. But we have one last wish. Take this revolver and shoot either at the head or the heart. I don't wish to be captured alive by the enemy. I would rather die once than die every moment at the hands of the enemy.' Waryam Singh's beloved companion, through thick and thin, was now writhing in pain before his very eyes. Moreover, he had expressed his last wish. Would he hesitate to fulfil the last wish of his dear friend? But how terrible and difficult it would be! It is not easy to put a bullet through one's dear friend. But it was equally difficult to leave him to the enemy who would not let him die in peace and would certainly resort to torture him to make him talk. Then Waryam Singh loaded a revolver and handing it over to Banta Singh, bid farewell in a choked voice and said – 'Bhai! God knows how many I have killed till date. How many times have I shot unhesitatingly at people? But I'd never bargained for shooting at my dearest friend. No, I cannot do this. Take this revolver, and shoot yourself when you need to.' Tears streamed down his face. His friend and comrade were dying in front of his eyes and his own death was staring him in the face. Outside there was heavy shooting. Waryam Singh held Banta Singh close to his bosom for the last time and left. That brave man managed to escape quite easily with a revolver in his hand. A couple of policemen tried to seize him. He shot at them, and they fell, wounded. Then they could not muster the courage to follow this brave soldier.

The house began to go up in flames. And the firing went on relentlessly. One doesn't know if Banta Singh died due to a bullet or in the fire. He must not have been more than 22 or 23 years old at that time.

– Senapati

37. Shri Waryam Singh Dhugga (1928)

Waryam Singh was born in a village named Dhugga in the Hoshiarpur district, in 1892 or '93. He was a very energetic and powerful person. He was physically strong and tough. He enlisted in the army. For a long time he received military education and worked there. During this time, in order to take revenge upon a personal enemy, he recorded his evening attendance and left the place. He ran for twenty miles. He murdered the man, declared his name and returned to the unit before the morning attendance. So no action could be taken against him. After all the army attendance register could not lie, could it? Later, he became a dacoit. He was notorious in the Doaba region. His fame had spread far and wide.

But as soon as the Babbar Akali group was formed, he joined it and ably supported Banta Singh in all the work.

That day, on 12 December 1923, when Banta Singh was surrounded in Munder village, Waryam Singh was with him. But when the house caught fire, he mustered the courage to escape the siege. The soldiers used to dread him.

After this, he left for the far off district of Lyallpur. He was staying at a relative's house, who raised him from his childhood. But greed and self-interest destroys the humanity of a human being. Waryam Singh was told, 'Leave your weapons in the fields outside the village so that no one suspects you.' He was taken to the village and given a meal. The night was dark. As soon as he finished his food, he said, 'I think I'll leave; I don't feel comfortable without my arms.' He returned to the place where he had left his weapons. But the army was already waiting for him. The police superintendent, Mr D Gayle had been a soldier. He was very courageous and gutsy. He intended to arrest Waryam Singh alive. But Waryam Singh had already made up his mind to sacrifice his life. The soldiers advanced upon him from all sides. He realized their intention. He stood his ground and wondered what he should do next. Mr D Gayle announced in a loud voice, 'Waryam Singh, surrender!' Waryam Singh answered, 'What? If you have guts, just let me take my weapons once; then we will fight each other.' But the British were hardly likely to show such nobility. Mr D Gayle caught him from behind and restrained his arms. Waryam Singh pulled out his kirpan and wounded his arms badly and pushed him to the ground. The lion was surrounded by hares. The enemy wanted to take him alive, but they all feared his kirpan. Several times a couple of soldiers moved forward, but had to retreat, wounded.

Finally, Mr D Gayle gave the order to fire at him. A shower of bullets rained upon him from all sides. In this way, he breathed his last, taking the bullets on his chest.

His corpse was taken to Lyallpur. Hundreds of men and women gathered to get a last glimpse of him. This incident took place on 8 June 1924.

– Bhushan

38. Shri Kishan Singh Gadgajj (1928)

Shri Kishan Singh Gadgajj was a resident of Waring village in Jalandhar district. His father's name was Shri Fateh Singh. After basic school education, he enlisted in the army and then, till March 1921, he worked as a Hawaldar in Sikh Battalion No. 35.

After the Jallianwala Bagh incident, a wave of non-cooperation spread through the entire nation and, influenced by that, he resigned from his job. In his written statement at the time of his arrest he wrote, 'While I was serving in the army, incidents such as the house arrest of Sardar Ajit Singhji, the demolition of the wall of Delhi's Rakabganj Gurudwara, the incident of firing at innocent travellers in Bajbaj, the Rowlatt Act, the Jallianwala Bagh tragedy and the imposition of the martial law etc. had already created hatred in my heart and finally, not being able to bear the burden of slavery any more, I resigned from service to the government to take part in the national movement.'

Even the old wounds had not healed, when another great blow left the heart trembling. After the tragedy at Nankana Sahib on 20 February 1921, he began to take part in the activities of the Akali Dal and was even elected a secretary in the party. But he could not endure this silent beating at the hands of the police and began preparations for a secret organization.

The work had barely begun when carelessness on the part of two persons partially revealed the secret. Six people were arrested, but Kishan Singh escaped with four other comrades. He stayed in a place called Mastuana in Jind, in the Malwa region, and then returned to the Doaba region in the winter of 1921. As soon as he returned, he announced the founding of the 'Chakravarty-Group' that later became famous as Babbar Akali-Dal, and began to go from village to village to give lectures. Kishan Singh was a good orator and, therefore, people were greatly influenced by his words. It is said that by the time he was arrested, he had given a total of 327 lectures in various places.

It was at the time Kishan Singh was expanding his work in the Kapurthala state and Jalandhar district, that Daulatpur's Karam Singh and Uday Singh, who later died fighting the police near Bomeli, were spreading exactly the same message in Hoshiarpur district. In the end, the uniting of both these parties saw the work gather further momentum. Bombs, revolvers and guns were amassed and centres were established in several places. They had thought that with this accumulation of arsenal, they would be able to free India through a revolution with the help of the military as in 1857. These people never let any traitor go.

Babbar Akalis referred to the killing of the traitors as 'reforming' them. After 'reforming' a large number of people and managing to spread the work far and wide, finally the conspiracy was unearthed and a round of arrests was made. Kishan Singh was also arrested and brought to Lahore. During the case, he admitted to all the charges and said, 'I was a bitter enemy of the government and because of this, whatever I did was done to oust the British from India by whatever means.' The court gave him a death sentence and one day, he was hanged by the now familiar noose in the Lahore Central Jail.

– Mohan

39. Shri Santa Singh (1928)

Shri Santa Singh was a resident of a village called Haryon Khurd in the Ludhiana district. His father was known as Suba Singh. There is not much known about his childhood and early education. However, in February 1920, he enlisted in Sikh Battalion No. 54 and after serving for two years, he resigned on 26 January 1922. Before serving in the army, he had also worked as a fee clerk at Khalsa High School, Ludhiana.

After resigning from his job, moved by the sacrifice and determination of the Akalis, he also began to participate in their activities and very soon began to be ranked among the top leaders of the movement due to his cleverness and commitment to work. While pronouncing his judgement in his case, the judge had remarked, 'Apart from a few jobs carried out by the Akalis, this accused has participated in all of them and in the conspiracy, he had the largest hand after Kishan Singh and Karam Singh.'

Finding Zaildar Bishan Singh creating hurdles in the path of the mission, he went alone and killed him. Apart from this, he also took part in punishing traitors like Boota, Labh Singh, Hazara Singh, Rala and Dittu, Subedar Gainda Singh and the Nambardar of Naungal Shama.

Finally, he was arrested due to the betrayal by one of his own relatives. Upon being examined in court, he said, 'I have no hopes of any justice from this government, so I don't wish to respond to a single question.'

In the end, he confessed to the charges. He said, 'Though I am fully aware that confessing to these crimes will ruin my chances in this case I did whatever I did for righteousness. So I don't want to hide a single thing.'

The court pronounced a death sentence and on 27 February 1926, he, along with five of his friends, was hanged to death in the Lahore Central Jail.

– Veer Singh

40. Shri Dalip Singh (1928)

Youthful Dalip! In what universe did you suddenly disappear after enthusing the base life of a slumbering India in that age of cowardice? In what frenzy did you do all this at the tender age of seventeen? From where did you acquire that ability at work, that courage, that enthusiasm, and that commitment so quickly? Perhaps we cowards of today cannot understand all these things even after a great deal of effort.

This brave fighter was born at Labh Singh's house in Dhamia Kalan, in the Hoshiarpur district. He began to prove his ability as soon as he was sent to school upon growing a little older. Despite not being very good at his studies, he was popular among his schoolmates. Getting them to do what he wanted them to do, was an easy task for him.

It was in 1922. The games of his youth had not yet been left behind when his soft heart suffered a harsh setback. The tragedy at Nankana Sahib and the cruelties inflicted upon the Akalis destroyed the equanimity of his mind. Sacrificing his home, where he was brought up with much love and pampering, that child Dalip was baptised in the Akali party in 1923.

After that, to describe what all he achieved, I think it is only appropriate to repeat the judge's words in the court when the decree was pronounced. He said, 'This accused, young as he is, appears to have established a record for himself second only to that of Santa Singh accused, as to the offences in which he has been concerned in connection with this conspiracy. He is implicated in the murders of Buta Lumberdar, Labh Singh Mistri, Hazara Singh of Baibalpur, Ralla and Dittu of Kaulgarh, Ata Mohammad Patwari, in the second and third attempts on Labh Singh of Dhadda Fateh Singh, and in the murderous attack on Bishan Singh of Sandhara.' (Originally in English.)

Working in this manner and distributing pamphlets in Kandi village with Santa Singh, one day he was surrounded by the police. On 12 October 1923, the tender Dalip was brought to Multan jail in chains. Thinking him to be a child, some people thought that they could extract some information out of him by intimidation, but seeing their hopes belied, their anger knew no bounds. How could they tolerate a young boy's impertinence? They began to beat him, interspersing the blows with some allurements, but in the end they achieved nothing but the same silence.

It is said that Dalip Singh was a very innocent and handsome young man. He was only seventeen years old. The Sessions Judge, Mr Tapp was bowled over by his tender years and innocence. He did not want to pronounce a death sentence for him. But after listening to the statements of all the witnesses, he was very frustrated and tried by various means not to write anything too damaging against Dalip Singh. This tussle went on for several days, and finally one day, Dalip Singh folded his hands and stood before the judge and said. 'I thank you for your graciousness, but first, kindly record my statement. I have done all these things and if I am released today, I shall do all these things all over again. But why are you so keen to keep me alive? I'm ready to be hanged and sacrifice my life. The reason is that by God's grace I have been given such a rare thing as a human being's body. I have not polluted it in any way as yet and I want to offer it in its pure state to my mother (land). Who can predict if this purity will be maintained if I stay alive longer, and then the entire significance and beauty of this sacrifice will be worn away.'

The judge was astounded and stared at his face. Finally, death by hanging was pronounced to be Dalip Singh's fate.

It was 27 February 1926 – with the first crimson ray of dawn – God put His seal on the pure life of that youthful saint.

Your life be written in words of blood
Oh! Never shall I forget this poignant tale!

— Kapil

41. Shri Nand Singh (1928)

Shri Nand Singh was born in the Ghudial village of Jalandhar district, in 1895. His father's name was Ganga Singhji. Since his parents died when he was too young, he was taken care of by his elder brother in Rawalpindi. He was very smart from his childhood and was more interested in playing. After being married at the age of 15 years, he worked as carpenter for some time at his house, then left for Basra.

The Akali movement gained momentum after the Nankana Sahib tragedy and Nand Singh returned to his country to participate in it. That time, he too had to serve a six-month sentence for participating in the Guru's Bagh's Satyagraha. He also suffered a great deal in jail, as he was beaten up severely on multiple occasions. This is where his thoughts began to change. That self-respecting young man realized that there was no point in being beaten up by the merciless police. So, he joined the

Babbar Akalis as soon as he was released from prison. He took the oath to either kill or die, instead of being beaten up.

Upon his arrest during the Satyagraha, his brother advised him to plead for forgiveness and get released. He said, 'The elder brother has passed away. The son has to be married. In such a situation if you also go to jail, nothing will be done.' He answered, 'If the marriage can take place without the elder brother, it can take place without me as well. I don't wish to stop the work of the community for the sake of personal matters like a wedding.'

After participating in the Babbar Akali movement, the Subedar of the village, Genda Singh, began to harass him a lot. He would keep the police informed about Nand Singh's movements, but one day, Nand Singh killed him. The police harassed the villagers for 11 days, and then Nand Singh said to them, 'Whatever has been done, is done by me. Why do you harass these people needlessly?'

He was arrested and charged; and sentenced to death. After the pronouncement of the judgement, he said to his family, 'Don't worry about me. I'm not dying a bad death. I'm happy that my life is being offered for the sake of my country. I have laid the foundation of the building. Now it is the country's responsibility to build a house on this foundation if she wants to be free.' He also said that after they were killed, all of them should be burnt on one pyre and the ashes strewn into the river Ravi.

Finally on 27 February 1926, he was hanged to death along with five comrades in the Lahore Central Jail and his relatives cremated them on a single pyre.

– Nat Nath

42. Shri Karam Singh (1928)

Shri Karam Singh's father's name was Shri Bhagwan Das. He belonged to the community of goldsmiths and lived in a village called Manko in the Jalandhar district. His childhood was spent in playing, and despite being poor, he was quite divorced from worldly matters. Right from the beginning, he was very naughty and never tolerated any harsh words from anyone.

He learnt the lesson of independence during the Non-Cooperation Movement and joined the Babbar Akali movement.

He was also involved in the killing of Subedar Genda Singh. After that, he continued to carry out propaganda work for a while till he was arrested on 12 May, 1923.

During the trial he said, 'The entire proceedings of the court are like a drama and the judges are puppets in the hands of the police. So, I don't wish to present any statement or defence.' He was severely coerced to issue a statement in jail and was forced to narrate the entire tale to the police. But, he refused to answer any question.

The court awarded him the death sentence and on 27 February 1926, he was hanged in the Lahore Central Jail along with five comrades.

– Prabhat

SECTION – 5

THE JAIL NOTEBOOK

Edited and first annotated by
Bhupender Hooja
Annotations updated by
Sudhanva Deshpande and *Chaman Lal*

A SHORT HISTORY OF THE PUBLICATION OF THE JAIL NOTEBOOK

Chaman Lal

Even though today, every admirer of Bhagat Singh knows about his Jail Notebook, before 1981 hardly anyone other than Bhagat Singh's family members knew about its existence. It was only in 1981, which was also the fiftieth martyrdom anniversary of Bhagat Singh, Rajguru and Sukhdev, that Bhagat Singh's younger brother, Kulbir Singh, allowed microfilms to be made by the National Archives of India and the Nehru Memorial Museum and Library (NMML), on the condition that it was not to be published or reproduced the *Jail Notebook*, along with other documents from India's revolutionary movements, was put on exhibition in the National Archives of India. After the exhibition, both institutions kept the notebook for consultation in their records. The copy of the *Jail Notebook* then went through many hands as soon after Kulbir Singh's younger son Abhey Sindhu shared it with the Gurukul Kangri in Inderprastha. Later, through its journey, it would reach Bhupender Hooja, the brother of the vice chancellor of the Gurukul Kangri, GB Kumar Hooja, who encouraged Hooja to publish the book. This was also based on fact that the *Jail Notebook* was demanding serious attention. This was primarily due to the writings of Russian scholar LV Mitrokhin, who specialized in Indian history. Mitrokin in his many visits to India, took parts of the *Jail Notebook* back to Moscow and wrote extensively about them. His writings on the book grabbed the attention of Indian scholars all around. I, too, saw the notebook for the first time when the microfilms were displayed at the Nehru Memorial Library and Museum in 1984, and then started writing about it in various newspapers and journals.

During his incarceration, Bhagat Singh handed over two bags of documents and books to various people – a bagful of documents to

Kumari Lajjawati, who was the secretary of the Bhagat Singh Defense Committee then and later the Principal of KMV College in Jalandhar, and another bagful of books and some documents to his younger brother, Kulbir Singh, as per Bhagat Singh's instructions to him in a letter dated 16 September 1930. Bhagat Singh had asked Kumari Lajjawati to hand over the bag to Bejoy Kumar Sinha on his release from jail – transported for life in the Lahore Conspiracy Case, Sinha was released in 1938. But before the bag could be handed over to Sinha, Lajjawati showed the contents of the bag to Lala Feroze Chand, editor of the *People*. A committed socialist himself, Lala Feroze Chand published a few documents from the papers, including 'Letter To Young Political Workers', which was published on 2 February 1931 in an abridged form, 'Letter about Harikishan's Case', who was executed after Bhagat Singh for shooting the Punjab Governor in Punjab University Lahore's convocation, and 'Why I am an Atheist', which was published on 27 September 1931 on the first birthday of Bhagat Singh after his execution. Though the essay, 'Why I am an Atheist' was lost during Partition, I have reproduced the *People*'s first printed version of this essay in my book, *Understanding Bhagat Singh*. The publication, in its editorial, had ascribed copyright of the essay to Bhagat Singh's father, S Kishan Singh.

It is Veerendra Sindhu, who authored the most authoritative biography in Hindi on Bhagat Singh's whole family in 1968. Bhagat Singh's writings have been getting published in various Hindi, Punjabi, Urdu, and English papers, since his lifetime. It was only in 1974, that they were first put together into a Punjabi volume by Amarjit Chandan as *Likhtan* (Writings). Later in 1977, Veerendra Sindhu, Bhagat Singh's niece and the daughter of S Kultar Singh, published *Patr aur Dastavez* (Letters and Documents) in Hindi. In 1985, Jagmohan Singh, another nephew of Bhagat Singh collected more documents written by his uncle, and put them in a volume in Punjabi, *Bhagat Singh ate Unah de Saathiyhan dian Likhtan* (Writings of Bhagat Singh and his Comrades).

Bhupender Hooja belonged to a family of freedom fighters, and after his retirement as an IAS officer in the Rajasthan Government, he took over a mammoth project – that of serializing Bhagat Singh's jail notebooks. In fact, Hooja took over the *Indian Book Chronicle* from Dr Amrik Singh, who expressed his inability to bring this journal further. In 1992, Hooja started serializing the 'Jail Notebooks' in the monthly *Indian Book Chronicle*. Hooja got a copy of Bhagat Singh's jail notebook from his elder brother, GB Kumar, who in turn got it from the Gurukul Inderprastha. Hooja's efforts were further made easy with the availability of a typed copy of the book, courtesy Prakash Chaturvedi who brought it from the Moscow archives, which made Hooja's task of printing it easier. After consultation with me and other local sources regarding the authenticity of the *Jail Notebook*, and the tremendous labour that went into annotating the sources of the books, writers, and quotations mentioned by Bhagat Singh, Hooja brought out the first printed edition of Jail Notebook in 1994, released in a grand manner at the Jaipur Raj Bhavan by the then Governor of Rajasthan, DP Chattopadhyaya. I complimented Hooja in his efforts; in fact in his acknowledgements, apart from others, Hooja acknowledged three of us – Dr Kamlesh Mohan from Chandigarh, and Shiv Verma, a comrade of Bhagat Singh, both who wrote on his ideology, and me. *Jail Notebook* got good reviews in papers like the *Tribune* and the *Times of India*, including my write-ups in the Kolkata-based *Frontier*, and the *Indian Book Chronicle*. But despite good reviews, the book did not reach a large reader base as its publisher had no network of distribution. Later more translations of the book came about, in different languages like Hindi, Punjabi and others.

It can be assumed that the notes were written by Bhagat Singh in the latter half of 1929. While in jail, the authorities gave him a notebook used by school children in those days, on 12 September 1929, just a day before their comrade, Jatinder Nath Das passed away after being on a hunger strike for 63 days. Bhagat Singh and B.K. Dutt continued their hunger strike till 4 October 1929. This means that the actual use of the notebook may have started by October 1929, as on 16 September 1930 Bhagat Singh wrote to his younger brother Kulbir Singh asking him to collect documents and other items from the jail office due to his impending death sentence. So literally, Bhagat Singh's jail notebook contains extracts and notes from the duration of one year or even less. One can only wonder at Bhagat Singh's talent, who apart from continuously struggling against the British even when in jail, resorted to hunger strikes, got beaten up for being a revolutionary, wrote petitions and articles, and yet read and took notes from the most significant books of human history!

After I joined Jawaharlal Nehru University in 2005, I convinced Leftword Press to bring out a new edition of the *Jail Notebook*, and with Bhupender Hooja's permission, we managed to bring it out in 2007– which also happened to be the birth centenary year of Bhagat Singh. It was updated with my introduction and new additions in the form of a few articles written by Bhagat Singh and some written on him by authors like Periyar. Since then, it has been translated in Marathi from my Hindi book *Bhagat Singh ke Samupran Dastavez*, and in 2009 and 2012, two new editions, one in Bengali were released. More translations in Urdu and Kannada followed, while another scanned and print edition was released.

By 2007, this jail notebook was part of the Government of India's publication division, titled *Shaheed Bhagat Singh: Dastavezon ke Aiene Men*. The book was released by Kuldip Nayar in the presence of Abhey Sindhu and Kiranjit Sindhu, two nephews of Bhagat Singh on 19 December 2007, which also happens to be the martyrdom day of Ram Prasad Bismil and Ashfaqualla Khan. The function was presided over by then Minister for Information Shri Priyaranjan Dasmunshi, who has passed away now. This volume is edited by me; and later, an Urdu version was also produced.

Since then, more editions of the *Jail Notebook* have come out. One in Kannada in 2016, one more by Yadwinder Sindhu, which was also translated into Marathi, and another edited by Harish Jain from Chandigarh. But none gave credit to late Shri Bhupender Hooja – his *Jail Diary*, published in 1994, is a pioneering work. Only the versions that were translated by me gave him due credit.

I understand that many more editions of the notebook have been brought out by publishers and individuals. There is no harm in multiple editions of such inspiring books. For example, there are many editions out there of Ram Prasad Bismil's autobiography in Hindi – in fact, Swami Agnivesh brought out an edition at just five rupees per copy, which his organization distributes to school students almost free of cost.

One may bring out editions of such inspiring books from as many institutions or persons, but without making the false claim that this is 'going to be first-ever publication' of this jail notebook and thus denying credit to the wonderful work done by the late Bhupender Hooja; for he was the first person to get this document into the public domain, after it remained hidden for six decades!

In the meantime, the first two pages from the *Jail Notebook* have been put on display at the Bhagat Singh Museum at Khatkar Kalan, his ancestral village near Banga. Those two pages have also been included in this edition. In addition, three more loose papers in Bhagat Singh's handwriting have been found; a few of these are with the museum at Khatkar Kalan. These three pages have been added at the end of the *Jail Notebook*.

Jagmohan Singh, Bhagat Singh's nephew, copied the text by hand from Bhagat Singh's hand-written pages probably written during the period he was in jail. These notes were written on loose pages and are titled as 'Miscellaneous Notes', posted on his website, shaheedbhagatsingh.org. Nine pages out of these notes seem to be in the pattern of notes taken on a notebook formally provided by the jail officials, but the original copy of these is not available in the public domain. Whether it is with some family member of Bhagat Singh or somewhere else is not known. Interested readers can look at these notes on the website, which are not included in this edition.

The original copy of the *Jail Notebook* is still with Yadwinder Sindhu, the grandson of Bhagat Singh's younger brother, Kulbir Singh. Microfilm copies of the notebook are with the National Archives, NMML, and the Supreme Court. The present copy of the notebook has been permitted to be reproduced by the Supreme Court Museum.

A MARTYR'S NOTEBOOK: ABOUT THE BOOK

Bhupender Hooja[92]

Having spent the greater part of my days during the last four years and more with the 'Prison Days' notebook of Bhagat Singh – editing it, adding reference notes, and seeing it through all the stages of printing – I feel so relieved that the work is now over. It has indeed been a unique experience of 'living' with Bhagat Singh and his comrades, so to say, at least in mind and spirit, if not in actual physical proximity. In the process of editing this book, I also had some insights into the workings of Bhagat Singh's mind, the books he read, and the deep concerns and commitments he experienced as he completed the last phase of his journey along the revolutionary path. I owe it to his memory to share a compilation of extracts and notes that reflect his thoughts.

I

The spring of 1989 was one full of fear and growing tensions between various communities, especially in Northern India and Punjab. On 23 March 1989, to foster communal peace and harmony, and restore mutual trust between the estranged communities, the Hindustan Manch was formed by a small group of people. Through this, they wanted to spread the two-fold message of '*Hindustaniyat*' (Indianess) and '*Insaniyat*' (humanity). It's inception also happened to be the day of Bhagat Singh's martyrdom. It was in one of the early meetings of the Manch that GB Kumar Hooja, who was also a former civil servant and Vice Chancellor of the University of Gurukul at Haridwar, brought to our notice that he had in possession a diary which contained the writings of Bhagat Singh. He had come across this diary during an

---

92 This is the introduction to the *Jail Notebook* by Bhupender Hooja, who first published this notebook in 1994.

inspection visit at the Gurukul Inderprasatha, near Delhi, a few years ago. The premises of the Gurukul had been used by a generation of revolutionaries as their meeting and hiding place. More background of the place was explained by the in-charge of the Gurukul and the fact that the diary was kept at the Martyr's Memorial Museum verified its authenticity. And since this diary had not been published so far, the Manch decided to bring it out as a book.

II

I was associated with the project as an editor, along with Sardar SS Oberoi, General Secretary of the Hindustan Manch, Professor RP Bhatnagar, and Professor RP Bhartiya. However, when the costs of bringing out the book was worked out, we realized that that the Manch, still in its infancy, could not hope to raise the amount needed – the project had to be shelved.

At the same time, another set of notes – a typed copy this time – was handed over to Dr Bhartiya by a local scholar, Dr Prakash Chaturvedi. Dr Chaturvedi had come across the copy in a Moscow library and had brought the photostat copy home. On comparison, we found that the typed copy from Moscow was word-for-word similar to the diary Hooja had found. This further spurred us on and stoked our enthusiasm. We also realized that having a typed version now saved us the extra time, energy, and additional cost of preparing a neat and legible copy for the press.

Faced as we were with the challenge of giving the diary the form of a book, it occurred to me that perhaps there was another way to get the contents of the diary to readers. The readers of the *Indian Book Chronicle* (IBC), a journal I have been editing since 1985-86, would be interested in knowing about this unpublished document or the Diary (as the notebook was known at that time). We wrote an introductory piece for the March 1991 issue of the *Indian Book Chronicle*. Later, May onwards, we began to carry installments from the Notebook as a regular monthly feature. The effort received appreciation from several quarters and we got many queries about it.

The required funds for the proposed book were still nowhere in sight, but our keenness was unabated. I tried and succeeded in cajoling a printer, Hazara Singh of M/s. Indo-Burma Printers at Jaipur, to publish the notebook in a book format from the proofs composed and set for the IBC journal. And so the process began.

However in 1992, we had another setback when our printer took up the task of printing and publishing the voters' lists for one or two constituencies, and hence could not carry on with the printing of either the IBC or the book. The work was at a standstill, as at that stage we could not go to another printer. The project could only be revived in the middle of 1993.

III

All of us at the Hindustan Manch can now share with an immense sense of satisfaction, notes or extracts from several books which Bhagat Singh would read during his days in prison, these no longer remain 'lost' or 'forgotten' like some of his other valuable manuscripts. As his friend and comrade, Shiv Verma has confirmed, at least four manuscripts by Bhagat Singh had been smuggled out of the jail – all were intact until 1942, but were lost later. However, these notes and extracts compiled and published here should give us some clue to the possible contents of the lost manuscripts.

The term 'diary' has been used rather loosely to describe this compilation. As a matter of fact, these 'notes' are not autobiographical nor are they pages from a personal diary. How could that be? How could the revolutionaries commit to writing their innermost thoughts and emotions when they knew that the police, the jail wardens and other agents or stooges of the government were all out to get such information on them. Yet, these notes do reveal a discerning and sympathetic soul, and a lot about the personality and psyche of the young Bhagat Singh and his contemporaries.

IV

Through testimonies from various colleagues and his *gurus* like Chhabil Das from the National College Lahore, and Rajaram

Shastri, the librarian at Dwarkadas library, we know that the young Bhagat Singh had developed a serious interest, almost a passion for reading. Thus, besides being an activist and an organizer of young revolutionaries in the folds of Naujawan Bharat Sabha and the Hindustan Socialist Republican Army (HSRA), he was also a serious student of human society, the Indian polity, social and political revolutions in different parts of the world, and the age-old institutions of family and the state. Is it surprising then that the first few pages of Bhagat Singh's prison notebook are replete with extracts from and references to Frederick Engels's *The Origin of Family*, philosophers like Bertrand Russell, and even poet-philosopher Omar Khayyam who, given the chance would also have loved to change the scheme and order of things entirely?

In this very context, a rather enlightening and scintillating evening comes to mind. Some members of the *Hindustani Manch* and the editorial team for the book met with the philosopher Professor DP Chattopadhyaya, then Governor of Rajasthan, at Raj Bhavan. As we presented him the copies of *Indian Book Chronicle* with extracts from Bhagat Singh's prison notebook, the question came up: How could the revolutionary youth of that generation find time from their activism and have the inclination to read such a variety of books? And to what purpose?

For nearly an hour or more, Chattopadhyaya talked about the various revolutionary movements in Bengal, Bihar, U.P., and Punjab, giving us a detailed and eloquent exposition of the lives, ideals, and interests of these brave revolutionaries. So many young heroes of the Indian resurgence were mentioned, their social and family backgrounds, the influences and inspirations which guided them, and what shaped their aspirations. They were a generation apart! They were not just trigger happy, young adventurers or social anarchists, as they were often maligned. They were perhaps the best of the Indian youth, the torchbearers, path-finders, and seekers of new freedoms. Their commitment lay in their search for new social and political horizons for India, in aiming at an all-round political and socio-economic revolution. And that evening, as we left Raj Bhawan, we wondered, when will we have a breed like that again? That evening also, once more, sealed our determination to complete this project.

V

The publication of Bhagat Singh's notes in the *Indian Book Chronicle* also brought some encouraging response from the readers. Among these, I must mention the keen interest and support of Dr Chaman Lal of the Punjabi University at Patiala, who wrote to us to confirm that he, too, had come across a similar 'notebook' in the Nehru Museum and Library. Chaman Lal, is the co-author of the book *Bhagat Singh aur unke Sathiyon ke Dastavez* (Documents and Writings of Bhagat Singh and his Comrades) with Dr Jagmohan Singh, who is a nephew of Bhagat Singh. His letter of support helped to further confirm the 'authenticity' of the document we were publishing. We also received additional support from Dr Kamlesh Mohan from Punjab University, who authored *Militant Nationalism in Punjab* and a monograph on Bhagat Singh, *The Man and His Ideology*.

VI

As several contemporaries and close associates of Bhagat Singh have confirmed in their respective writings, Bhagat Singh was, by and large, a self-taught and self-trained 'revolutionary', and if one may add, a 'thinker' and an 'ideologue'. Most of the clarity and direction in his thinking came during the last 4-5 years of his young life. We see glimpses of his activities and his thought process in several of these memoirs or tributes. For example, Raja Ram Shastri has described Bhagat Singh's reading interests and habits, and how they secretly published Veer Savarkar's *First War of Independence* in his book *Amar Shaheedon ke Sansmarn (1981)*. Similarly, Hindi writer Yashpal has given us some sketches and profiles of Bhagat Singh as a student of National College and as a revolutionary journalist, in his book *Simhavalokan* (three volumes) and *Fansi ke Phande Tak* (two volumes). Yashpal also mentioned the titles of several books which these young revolutionaries read at that time; in an account of the police raid on a bomb factory at Agra, Yashpal listed more than a score of such books including nationalist and revolutionary literature.

Shiv Verma has mentioned the names and titles of a few books and manuscripts written by Bhagat Singh, all survived for almost a decade after at the Kanya Mahavidyalya, Jalandhar, and elsewhere. During the uncertain times of the political movements of 1942, these were lost or destroyed. What a pity! No amount of literature on or about Bhagat Singh and his comrades can fill the vacuum left by these lost manuscripts. Yet, we have some references and specimens of these writings here and there in the records of the court cases, in scraps of communications exchanged, and in the various memoirs and reminiscences of Bhagat Singh's companions and contemporaries. But none of these can substitute for the lost originals.

VII

Bhagat Singh in Prison

Perhaps we should briefly recapitulate the two occasions Bhagat Singh was in police custody and in prison. He was first arrested in Lahore in May 1927. As he subsequently wrote in his article, 'Why I am an Atheist', he was suddenly surrounded by the police while passing through a garden, and taken into custody for questioning. There was a warrant for his arrest because of an article he had written under the pseudonym 'Vidrohi', titled 'Kakori ke Veeeron ki Pehchan' (Introduction of Kakori Braves) about the band of revolutionaries who had taken part in the looting of the government treasury at the Kakori railway station. Kept in the railway police lock-up for almost a month, Bhagat Singh was questioned for his association with the other accused in the Kakori Case and subjected to the third-degree police treatment, as well as tempted with 'rewards' if he confessed or turned approver.

He was also charged in the case of a bomb explosion at the Lahore Dussehra fair the previous year, when about a dozen innocent people lost their lives and three scores were injured. However, since nothing concrete could be found against him, he was let off against a heavy security of Rs 60,000 and on account of good behaviour. It was later discovered to be the work of a C.I.D. agent to discredit the revolutionaries and create communal tension in the community. As Bhagat Singh would reflect later, '… It was absolutely false … Persons like me do not throw bombs at innocent people …' Recounting how police officials tried to elicit his confession or their suggestions that he should take recourse to prayers in this hour of difficulty, Bhagat Singh came to the conclusion that he could neither put his faith in God, nor take to praying just to save his own life.

About the Kakori Case, Bhagat Singh would recall later that the episode was instrumental in converting him from being a romantic revolutionary to a socialist revolutionary. He began a serious study of the revolutionary movements and studied communist and Marxist literature. 'Study', as he was to say, 'so that you can understand the real forces of change. Study, so that you may be able to answer the arguments or questions of your opponents.' Kakori, thus, became a turning point in his awareness.

VIII

Almost two years later, Bhagat Singh was again in police custody, this time after they threw bombs on the floor of the Central Assembly Hall – he and comrade Batukeshwar Dutt, though armed with pistols, surrendered themselves to the momentarily terrified (even petrified) security police. They could have made their escape, they had done so before at Lahore in the winter of 1928 in the Saunders Case. But, on this occasion, their aim was different – they wanted rouse the consciousness of the people at large, especially the youth. They threw the bombs, raised slogans of 'Down with Imperialism' and '*Inquilab Zindabad*', distributed handbills, explaining both their action and their cause; and surrendered without resistance.

While in police custody from 8–22 April, both accused refused to give any statement and were sent to the Delhi jail.

First Trial – The bombing of the Assembly

As planned, during the trial Bhagat Singh and Batukeshwar Dutt availed every opportunity to give publicity to their cause. They did this through their statements before the court, accepting responsibility for throwing the bombs and stressing the point that, '[they] bore no ill will towards anyone', and that their 'aim was to express protest in a practical way against the institution ... [which]represents the oppressive power of an irresponsive and arbitrary rule'. They further explained that in their view, 'the use of force is unjust only when it is aggressive in form, which we consider to be violence; but when force is used to achieve some inherent (or socially approved) objective, it becomes morally just...'

The trial opened in the Delhi on 7 May, with restricted entry to close relatives of the accused and a few selected persons. On Bhagat Singh insisting that they would only give their statement before the Sessions Court, the case was moved, where the proceedings resumed on 4 June, Here, after the preliminary arguments (as partially noted before) Bhagat Singh expounded on his concept of revolution, and said, 'Revolution is not the culture of bombs and pistols. By revolution, we mean that the existing order based on oppression and injustice must be changed.' He went on to mention how workers, peasants, weavers, and artisans were all being exploited and condemned to live in slums while the capitalists thrive. 'This enormous inequality and indiscrimination imposed by force is bound to lead to mutual confrontation. Such a situation cannot continue for long. It is obvious that the existing social system, which is flourishing because of the helplessness of some, is sitting on the mouth of a volcano...' Therefore, a 'radical change is needed... to reorganize society on the basis of socialism... Unless this is done, all talk of avoiding war and establishing peace in the world is nothing but hypocrisy. By revolution, we mean the establishment of a society which will not be in danger of disintegration, and where the supremacy of the proletariat is recognized... Only then will it be possible to free humanity from the shackles of capitalism and protect it from the destruction imperialist war...' Further... 'Revolution is the birthright of mankind. Man cannot be deprived of the right to freedom...'

The young revolutionaries were ready to sacrifice their youth and their lives for the cause of such a revolution. No wonder their courageous act and bold taking to the revolutionary path electrified the whole subcontinent.

IX

The Sessions trial ended on 10 June, and on 12 June, Bhagat Singh and his comrades were both awarded life imprisonment. From Delhi, Bhagat Singh was sent to Mianwali Jail in west Punjab and Batukeshwar Dutt to the Lahore Central jail. Facilities being given to them previously in Delhi Jail, on par with the British offenders, were now withdrawn. This led to their historic hunger strike, which started on 14 June and continued till the first week of October. Other political prisoners also joined them from time to time; and outside the prison there were fasts and protests in sympathy and support. In a letter to the Home Member of the Government of India, Bhagat Singh outlined eight demands on behalf of the political prisoners – ultimately these demands had to be conceded after the great suffering the prisoners experienced and the death of Jatinder Nath Das on 13 September 1929. This not only won the revolutionaries a new status of dignity and better facilities for political prisoners, but also galvanized the whole country in support of the revolutionaries and other political workers.

After the judgement was passed, an appeal was filed before the High Court at Lahore. Here again, Bhagat Singh used the occasion once more to vindicate their revolutionary stand and to point out some patent flaws in the Sessions Court proceedings. But the High Court, ignored their plea and confirmed the judgement on 30 January 1930. Perhaps the minds of the authorities, including the judges, had by now been hardened in view of the patent threats which these young accused and their colleagues had suddenly posed for the British rulers in India by their relentless determination.

X

Second Trial – The Saunders' Murder Case trial

We have reasons to believe that it was as a result of the long hunger strike and its fallout, that writing material was made available to the political prisoners. That is perhaps how Bhagat Singh was given the notebook, which bears his initials and date mark of 12 September 1929 on its first and last page. From then onwards, Bhagat Singh could use his notebook to record extracts and notes from the books he would read.

Needless to add that most of their time and energy was taken up by the new trial in the Saunders' Murder Case. A committee of three – Bhagat Singh, Sukhdev, and Bejoy Kumar Sinha – came into being to see and ensure how the forum of the trial could be used to the utmost advantage for their revolutionary cause. There were daily battles of wits and clashes of will in the court room where the prisoners on trial would raise slogans and often interrupt the proceedings; often the magistrate would lose his cool and order the accused to be handcuffed or otherwise restrained. Scuffles ensued in the court and Pathan policemen came down heavy upon them, especially on Bhagat Singh. This rather horrid, cat-and-mouse game went on for some time, but nothing could break the will of the revolutionaries, nor weaken their united stand.

Meanwhile, as the hunger strike progressed, Bhagat Singh had been brought to the Lahore Central Jail, where he was now to stand trial as the principal accused in the Saunders' Murder Case. Other co-accused had also been hauled up. That trial started on 10 July 1929 in a Magistrate Court, where Bhagat Singh was brought on a stretcher. He had become quite weak and had lost a lot of weight due his hunger strike. The jail authorities adopted all manners of stratagems, including forced feeding, and in some cases actual use of force, to break the will of strikers, but to no avail.

There was some improvement in the diet given to them, and also the practice of feeding milk was continued; but for Jatinder Nath, these ameliorative measures had come too late. Even a last-minute personal visit by Bhagat Singh to successfully persuade him to give up his fast-unto-death could not save him, and Jatinder Nath died on 13 September 1929. As the Government-appointed jail reforms sub-committee submitted its report, in addition to the improvement in diet, already partially conceded, the demands of the revolutionaries as 'political prisoners' was accepted and they became entitled to better, more civil and humane treatment. For the the revolutionary prisoners, it was a major victory, in addition to the bonus of widespread publicity for their cause. Their well-coordinated hunger strike was called off on 5 October 1929 after 114 days, perhaps the longest such strike in the history of the Indian freedom struggle.

In May 1930, the exasperated government, not quite happy with the prolonged trial, brought forth a special ordinance to constitute a Special Tribunal to proceed with the trial, without the presence of the accused in the court. In a well-reasoned statement, while recapitulating what had happened and why undertrials had to resort to hunger strike Bhagat Singh had declared, 'You may be able to suppress a few persons, but remember, you cannot suppress this nation ...' He continued, '... We have been trying to point out from the beginning that your law is a beautiful deception. It is not capable of administrating justice ... [you must] clearly state that the political prisoners cannot be given any opportunity to defend themselves." That was the gist of Bhagat Singh's communication to the Governor-General of India.

Out of the 24 revolutionaries in the list of accused, sixteen were put on trial (B.K. Dutt's name was later deleted). When the Special Tribunal met, the accused resisted the order of the Chief Judge to be produced in handcuffs, which led to their resistance. The judge not only abused them (and Indians, at large), but had also ordered Bhagat Singh to be beaten with lathis. The episode got widespread publicity; and the case had to be adjourned until a fresh tribunal was constituted on 12 June 1930. Thus, the trial continued to receive wide coverage; the fearless stand of the revolutionaries giving fresh impetus to a movement which might have otherwise died its slow death. The judgement, running into 281 pages, came out on 7 October 1930. Bhagat Singh, Sukhdev and Rajguru were ordered to be hanged to death; seven other accused were to be imprisoned for life in the Andaman Jail, two were given prison sentences with hard labour for seven and five years respectively; while three others were ordered to be released. In spite of the government trying to impose Section 144 and a veil of secrecy over the judgement, there were widespread protests, processions, demonstrations, and *hartals* (strikes) not only in Lahore, but other major towns and cities in the country. Initiatives and movements were launched to save the lives of the condemned trio. A defence committee was set up to appeal to the Privy Council. What lent strength to their case were the patent flaws in the proceedings in which neither the accused, nor their defence lawyers had appeared before the Special Tribunal, nor had the prosecution witnesses been cross-examined. It had been an ex-parte proceeding all along, and an ex-parte judgement.

XI

Bhagat Singh and his comrades remained undeterred, unafraid, and brave to the end. He did not approve of appeals or mercy petitions as he had made sufficiently clear to all concerned, including his defence counsel and his father. Thus, on 23 March 1931, with revolutionary songs and slogans on their lips, he and his two brave companions mounted the gallows. The authorities, once again, showed their panic and lack of humanity by hanging them in the darkness of dusk, rather than in the dawn of a new day. Their bodies were taken away surreptitiously under the cover of darkness to the distant banks of the Sutlej, to be hastily cremated. But, as usual, the news had leaked out, and the youth of Lahore swarmed the streets in their anger and anguish, and raced to the cremation grounds in the thousands. The brave ones who had become living legends in their life time became the three martyrs.

There were loud protests against the actions of the government, and the 'inaction' on the part of the national leadership, including Gandhi, for not having bestirred themselves in time to save the martyrs; the Gandhi-Irwin pact – or 'compromise' as Bhagat Singh would have called it, as he had done on some earlier occasions – had been ominously silent about the fate of the three martyrs. But the popular feelings were so deeply aroused that there were loud and prolonged black-flag protest demonstrations to greet Mahatma Gandhi when he reached Karachi for the Congress session few days after the national tragedy.

It may be seen that the supreme sacrifice of Bhagat Singh and his two comrades had a purpose behind it, for they had spoken to the nation, especially the youth. A few days before his sacrifice, he had sent a rousing message to the youth of India – they had given the call for a total political, economic, and social transformation of the Indian polity, and to transform India into a socialist republic. *Inquilab* or revolution was their motto, their goal for which no price or sacrifice was too great. Not only was their goal or vision clear, their ideology and the pursuit of their aims had a clarity, as well as dedication and a meeting of minds, which is rare; and has been a shining example of devotion and unflinching courage ever since.

XII

Studies and Writings

Two small points before we close. First, to show Bhagat Singh's devotion to study. In a letter from the prison to his childhood friend Jaidev Gupta, dated 30 July 1930, Bhagat Singh had asked for about a dozen books to be borrowed from the Dwarkadas Library in his name, and also from the Lahore Public Library. Almost all of these related to what may be called socialist and Marxist streams of thought. Thus, as many others have testified, his mind was set on a serious study of society, the state, the various revolutions, and similar themes. 'Equip your ideology with supporting arguments ... Logic and freethinking are the twin qualities that a revolutionary must necessarily possess ...' as he was to write in his tract 'Main Nastik Kyon Hoon' (Why I am an Atheist).

We have had no chance to delineate the role of Bhagat Singh as a nationalist or a revolutionary journalist. He has been credited with having contributed a large number of articles in *Kirti* and other contemporary newspapers of his time, besides his apprenticeship with *Pratap* and *Vir Arjun*. Once again, there was not much time at his disposal; not much free time, that is, because for a greater part of 1926–29 he was a revolutionary activist, on the run from the authorities and deeply engrossed in various organisational or political activities at the same time. Perhaps there needs to be some thorough research on Bhagat Singh as a journalist to do full honour to his work in this field.

XIII

In his Prison Notebook, we had a clear reflection of Bhagat Singh's interest in revolutionary literature, not only in its political or ideological format, but also in the form of poetry and fiction. Whenever he would come across a poem or a verse or a passage that seemed to be in tune with his own emotional makeup or mental experience, or some extract that gave him clarity and support in his deep reflections and commitments, he would note it down. That is how we know what he, and others, must have felt being locked up in a prison, cut-off from the outside world; and how he and his comrades managed to keep up their morale and accept with a brave face and stout heart their inevitable fate.

But perhaps what gives a greater meaning and purpose to these notes is the manner in which Bhagat Singh tried to organize his reading (and note-taking) into something like a systematic and planned study of politics, the nature of society and state, nationalism, the urge for freedom, and a search for the meaning of revolution and the goal of socialism. There are enough notes on these varied but interlinked topics and themes, which bear testimony to his search for an ideology and his commitment to the path of revolutionary action. These extracts also make somewhat clear what Bhagat Singh had in mind when he coined and gave to the nation his new, bold, and lasting slogan, *Inquilab Zindabad* or 'Long Live Revolution'. He and his colleagues wanted to wake up a slumbering nation into the new game of revolutionary mass action. Revolution for them was not just change or transfer of power. It meant a complete overhaul, a total transformation of the state and society; of all the political, economic, social, cultural, educational, and administrative institutions. But since Bhagat Singh had only short time at his disposal, all he could do was to sound the kettledrums of revolution, and give it a new theme song with a new direction.

Who can deny that there was a 'significant' and revolutionary change in the goals and directions of the freedom movement in India, after these brave birds of passage had spread their wings, soared high, and then gone their way! But can we, more than sixty years later, say with confidence that the revolutionary goals of total transformation of state and society in the Indian subcontinent have since been reached? Therein lies the challenge of our time.

Here also is some justification of bringing out this collection of Bhagat Singh's notes in the present volume. We hope that admirers of the revolutionary movement, the scholars and historians of our national struggle will approach and examine this compilation in a proper historic context and in the context of our present-day predicaments in the Indian polity.[93]

THE JAIL NOTEBOOK

As we open the notebook, on the first page, there are some jottings which say, 'For Bhagat Singh Four hundred and four pages (404 pages)' with some initials and the date 12/9/1929 jotted down. This is an entry duly initialed by the concerned jail authority to the effect that the book was given to Bhagat Singh on that date.

According to jail procedure, when any prisoner would ask for some writing material, etc., the jail authorities would note the fact in a similar fashion, both at the beginning and at the end of the notebook. The prisoner or undertrial would also initial an entry to confirm the receipt of the writing material. This practice was followed in this case also and at the end of the notebook there are initials of Bhagat Singh dated 12/9/1929. The notebook was of the usual size of a school or college exercise book, approximately 6.75 x 8.50 inches or 17.50 cm x 21 cm.

Besides these entries; on the right-hand top corner of the title page, there is a signature of Bhagat Singh. At the lower left-hand corner there is an entry: 'Copy by Abhey Kumar Singh, nephew of Shaheed Bhagat Singh.'

---

93   Editor's note: edited and abridged from the original

Explanatory notes and numbers, found in the corner of the pages[94]

Page 2 (**Blank**)

Page 3[95]
'Lover, lunatic and poet are made of the same stuff'
Inductive – from particular to general
Deductive – from general to particular
Centrifugal – tending from the centre
Centripetal – tending to the centre
'My strength is the strength of oppressed, my courage is the courage of desperation'
Kureh Khak hai Gardash main Tapash se Meri, Main Voh majnu hun Jo Jindan men Bhee Azad Raha
Every tiny molecule of ash is in motion with my heat,
I am such a lunatic that I am free even in jail
'Money is the honey of mankind–'
Dostoevsky

Page 4[96]

Currency rates of various countries:
Rouble (Russian) [Silver] : 100 copeks:2 Sh. 1½ d
Crown silver: 5 shilling 1 Lira (Italian): 1 france (Divided into 100 centesimal): 9/1/2d

---

94 Annotations in the notebook were improvised by Sudhanva Deshpande in the LeftWord edition of the book; and these are further improved in the present edition due to the availability of more information in regard to the books quoted by Bhagat Singh in these notes.

95 This page was found later and is kept at Bhagat Singh's ancestral village, the Khatkar Kalan Museum.

96 This page was found later and is kept at Bhagat Singh's ancestral village, the Khatkar Kalan Museum.

Mark [English coin now quite out of use was worth 13 sh. 4 d]
Mark [German coin existing and in use] :1 sh. 4 d
Drachma: Greek coin
Agnosticism: The idea that we can know nothing of God
Agnosticism might be tolerated, but materialism is utterly inadmissible; (in England) - Engels

Land Measurements:

German 20 hectares - 50 acres i.e. 1 hectare : 2 ½ acres[97]

Page 6

Freedom from Property

The 'freedom of property' ... as far as the small capitalist and peasant proprietors are concerned, became 'freedom from property.'

Marriage itself remained, as before, the legally recognied form, the official cloak, of prostitution ...

(S'ism Scientific and Utopian)[98]

Mental Bondage

'An eternal being created human society as it is today, and submission to "superior" and "authority" is imposed on the "lower" classes by divine will.'

This suggestion, coming from pulpit, platform and press, has hypnotised the minds of men and proves to be one of the strongest pillars of exploitation.

---

97 This short and odd entry in the notebook seems to be continuation of the page 4 entry on currency.

98 *Socialism, Utopian and Scientific* by Frederick Engels

Page 7

The Origin of the Family by Engels[99]

Morgan was the first to make an attempt at introducing a logical order into the history of primeval society.

He divides it into three main epochs:

(1) Savagery, (2) Barbarism, (3) Civilization

1. Savagery, re-divided into three stages:

1. Lower 2. Middle 3. Higher.

1. Lower Stage of Savagery: Infancy of human race. Living in trees.

(2) Fruits, nuts and roots serving as food (3) The formation of articulated speech is the principal result of that period.

2. Middle Stage: (1) Fire discovered. (2) Fish being used as food.

(3) Hunting stone implements invented. (4) Cannibalism comes into existence.

4. Marginal note in the original: Venison: animal flesh taken by hunting

3. Higher Stage: (1) Bow and arrow, No pottery. (2) Village Settlements. (3) Timber used for building. (4) Cloth weaved.

Bows and arrows were for the stage of savagery what the iron sword was for barbarism and the fire arm for civilisation, the weapon of supremacy.

Page 8

2. Barbarism:

1. Lower Stage

1. Introduction of pottery. At first wooden pots were covered with layers of earth, but afterwards earthen pots were discovered.

---

99   Translator's Preface to Origin of the Family in *The Origin of the Family, Private Property and the State* by Frederick Engels. The notes on the evolution of society and marriage below are from here.

2. Human races divided into two distinct classes: (i) Eastern who tamed animals and had grain; (ii) Western who had only 'corn'.

2. Middle Stage

1. (a) Western hemisphere: i.e. in America they grew food plants, (cultivation and irrigation), and baked bricks for house-building.

(b) Eastern: They domesticated animals for milk and flesh. No cultivation in this stage yet.

3. Higher Stage:

1. Melting of iron ore.

2. Invention of letter script and its utilisation for writing records. This stage is richer in inventions. This is the period of Greek heroes.

3. Iron ploughs are drawn by animals to grow corn on a large scale.

4. Clearing of forests, and iron axe and iron spade used.

5. Great attainments: (i) Improved iron tools, (ii) the bellows, (iii) hand-mill, (iv) Potter's wheel, (v) Preparation of oil and wine, (vi) fashioning metals, (vii) wagon and chariot, (viii) ship building,

Page 9

(ix) Artistic Architecture, (x) Towns and forts built, (xi) Homeric Epochs and entire mythology.

With these attainments, Greeks enter the third stage – the 'civilisation'!

To sum up:

1. Savagery: Time of predominating appropriation of finished natural products; human ingenuity invents mainly tools useful in assisting this appropriation.

2. Barbarism: Time of acquiring knowledge of cattle raising, of agriculture and of new methods for increasing the productivity of nature by human agency.

3. Civilisation: Time of learning a wider utilisation of natural products, of manufacturing and of art.

We have, then, three main forms of the family corresponding in general to the three main stages of human development:
1. For savagery: "group marriage"
2. For barbarism: the pairing family
3. For civilisation: monogamy supplemented by adultery and prostitution. Between the pairing family and monogamy, in the higher stage of barbarism, the rule of men over female slaves and polygamy is inserted.

Page 10

Defects of Marriage
Especially a long engagement is in nine cases out ten, a perfect training school of adultery.

Socialistic Revolution and Marriage Institution!
We are now approaching a social revolution, in which the old economic foundations of monogamy will disappear just as surely as those of its complement prostitution. Monogamy arose through the concentration of considerable wealth in one hand – a man's hand – and from the endeavour to bequeath this wealth to the children of this man to the exclusion of all others.

This necessitated monogamy on the woman's, but not on the man's part.

Hence this monogamy of women in no way hindered open or secret polygamy of women.

Now the impending social revolution will reduce this whole case of the heritance to a minimum by changing at least the overwhelming part of permanent and inheritable wealth – the means of production – into social property. Since monogamy was caused by economic conditions, will it disappear when these causes are abolished?

Page 11

'Ah, my Beloved, fill the cup that clears
Today of past Regrets and future Fears—
Tomorrow? - Why, Tomorrow I may be
Myself with Yesterday's Sev'n Thousand Years.

Here with a loaf of Bread beneath the Bough,
A Flask of Wine, a Book of verse - and you
Beside me signing in the Wilderness—
And Wilderness is Paradise now!
Umar Khayyam

State
The State presupposes a public power of coercion separated from the aggregate body of its members.
(Engels) pp. 116

Origin of State
Degeneration of the old feuds between tribes - a regular mode of existing by systematic plundering on land and sea for the purpose of acquiring cattle, slaves and treasures. ... In short, wealth is praised and respected as the highest treasure, and the old gentile institutions are abused in order to justify the forcible robbery of wealth. Only one thing was missing: an institution that not only secured the newly acquired property of private individuals against the communistic tradition of the gens, that not only declared as sacred the formerly so despised private property and represented the protection of this sacred property as the highest purpose of human society, but that also stamped the gradually developing new forms of acquiring property of constantly increasing wealth with the universal sanction of the society. An institution

Page 12

That lent the character of perpetuity not only to the newly rising division into classes, but also to the right of the possessing classes to exploit and rule the non-possessing classes.

And this institution was found. The State arose.
pp. 129-130

Definition of a Good Government
'Good government can never be a substitute for self-government.'
Henry Campbell Bannerman
5. The Rt. Hon. Sir Henry Campbell-Bannerman (1836-1908), British liberal statesman who served as Prime Minister between 1905 and 1908.
'We are convinced that there is only one form of Government, whatever it may be called, namely, where the ultimate control is in the hands of the people.'
'Earl of Balfour'[100]

Religion
'My own view of religion is that of Lucretius. I regard it as a disease born of fear, and as source of untold misery to the human race. I cannot, however, deny that it has made some contributions to civilisation. It helped in early days to fix the calendar and it caused the Egyptian priest to chronicle eclipses with such care that in time they became able to predict them. These two services, I am prepared to acknowledge, but I do not know of any other.'
Bertrand Russell[101]

---

100 Probably Arthur James, 1st Earl of Balfour (1848-1930) British Statesman & Prime Minister (1902-1905).

101 Bertrand Arthur William Russell, 3rd Earl Russell (1872–1972), well-known British philosopher and pacifist spokesman. Awarded Nobel Prize for Literature (1950).

Page 13

Benevolent Despotism

Montagu-Chelmsford Reforms called the British Government a 'benevolent despotism' and according to Ramsay MacDonald, the Imperialist leader of the British.

Labour Party, 'in all attempts to govern a country by a "benevolent despotism", the governed are crushed down. They become subjects who obey, not citizens who act. Their literature, their art, their spiritual expression go.'

The Montagu-Chelmsford Report (1918) for constitutional reforms in India led to diarchy under the Government of India Act, 1919. Edwin Samuel Montagu (1879-1924) was the Secretary of State in the India Office (1917 to 1922), while Lord Chelmsford - Frederick John (Napier Thesiger, 3rd Lord and 1st Viscount (1868-1933) - was the Viceroy of India (1916-1920) during a hectic period of political strife.

James Ramsay MacDonald (1866-1937), British politician and labour leader who helped form the British Labour Party (1900) and led its Parliamentary wing in the House of Commons (1911-1914, and again from 1923 and in 1929). Was Prime Minister twice (from January to November 1924, and from 1929-1935). Author of several books on socialism and allied themes, which came out between 1905 and 1921.

Government of India

Rt. Hon'ble Edwin S Montagu, Secretary of State for India, said in the House of Commons in 1917: 'The Government of India is too wooden, too iron, two metallic, too antediluvian, to be of any use for modern purposes. The Indian Government is indefensible.'

British Rule in India

Dr Ruthford's words: 'British Rule as it is carried on in India is the lowest and most immoral system of government in the world - the exploitation of one nation by another.'

10. Identity not clear.

Liberty & English People

'The English people love liberty for themselves. They hate all acts of injustice, except those which they themselves commit. They are such liberty-loving people that they interfere in the Congo and cry, "Shame" to the Belgians. But they forget their heels are on the neck of India.

–An Irish Author

Page 14

Mob Retaliation

... Let us therefore, examine how men came by the idea of punishing in this manner. They learn it from the Governments they live under, and retaliate the punishment they have been accustomed to behold. The heads stuck upon spikes, which remained for years upon Temple Bar, differed nothing in the horror of the scene from those carried about upon spikes at Paris; yet this was done by the English Government. It may perhaps be said that it signifies nothing to a man what is done to him after he is dead; but it signifies much to the living; it either tortures their feelings or hardens their hearts, and in either case, it instructs them how to punish when power falls into their hands.

Lay then the axe to the root, and teach Governments humanity. It is their sanguinary punishments which corrupt mankind ... The effect of these cruel spectacles exhibited to the populace is to destroy tenderness or excite revenge, and by the base and false idea of governing men by terror instead of reason, they become precedents.'

pp. 32, *Rights of Man* by T. Paine[102]

---

102 Thomas Paine, English author and publicist (1737–1809) known for his significant contributions to the American War of Independence and the French Revolution.

Page 15

Monarch and Monarchy
It was not against Louis XVI, but against despotic principles of government that the Nation revolted. The principles had not their origin in him, but in the original establishment, many centuries back, and they were become too deeply rooted to be removed, and the Augean stable of parasites and plunderers too abominably filthy to be cleaned by anything short of a complete revolution.

When it becomes necessary to do a thing, the whole heart and soul should go into the measure, or not attempt it ... The Monarch and the Monarchy were distinct and separate things; and it was against the person or principals of the former, that the revolt commenced and the Revolution has been carried. (p. 19)[103]

Natural and Civil Rights
Man did not enter into society to become worse than he was before, but to have those rights better secured. His natural rights are the foundation of all his civil rights.

Natural rights are those which appertain to man in right of his existence (intellectual-mental, etc.)

Civil rights are those that appertain to man in right of his being a member of society.

(p. 44)[104]

Page 16

King's Salary
It is inhuman to talk of a million sterling a year, paid out of the public taxes of any country, for the support of an individual, whilst thousands

---

103 From Thomas Paine's *The Rights of Man*. Source not indicated in notebook however.
104 *Ibid.*

who are forced to contribute thereto, are pining with want and struggling with misery.

Govt does not consist in a contract between prisons and palaces, between poverty and pomp; it is not instituted to rob the needy of his mite and increase the worthlessness of the wretched.

– p. 204
14. Underlined in the original

'Give me Liberty or Death'
It is in vain, Sir, to extenuate the matter. Gentlemen may cry, peace, peace – but there is no peace. The war is actually begun. The next gale that sweeps from the North ... to our ears the clash of resounding arms. Our brethren are already in the field. Why stand we here idle? What is it that gentlemen wish? What would they have? Is life so a dear or peace so sweet as to be purchased at the price of chains and slavery? Forbid it, almighty God! I know not what course others may take. As for me, give me 'liberty or death'.
Patrick Henry[105]

Right of Labour
'Whoever produces anything by weary labour does not need revelation from heaven to teach him that he has a right to the thing produced.'
Robert G. Ingersoll[106]

Page 17

'We consider it horrible that people should have their heads cut off, but we have not been taught to see the horror of life-long death which is inflicted upon a whole population by poverty and tyranny.'

---

105 Patrick Henry (1736–1790), American politician, orator and legislator.
106 U.S. lawyer, public speaker and author (1832–1899).

Mark Twain[107]

Anarchists

'... The Anarchists and the apostles of insurrection are also represented; and if some of the things seem to the reader the mere unchaining of furies, I would say, let him not blame the faithful anthologist, let him not blame even the writer – let him blame himself, who has acquiesced in the existence of conditions which have driven his fellowmen to extremes of madness and despair.'

Upton Sinclair, Preface, *Cry for Justice*[108]

The Old Labourer

'... He (the old labourer out of employment) was struggling against age, against nature, against circumstances; the entire weight of society, law and order pressed upon him to force him to lose his self-respect and liberty ... He knocked at the doors of the farms and found good in man only – not in law and order, but in individual man alone.'

– Richard Jefferies, (80)

19. English naturalist and novelist (1848–1887).

Page 18

Poor Labourers

'... And we, the men who braved this task were outcasts of the world. A blind fate, a vast merciless mechanism, cut and shaped the fabric of our existence. We were men despised when we were most useful, rejected when we were not needed, and forgotten when our troubles weighed upon us heavily. We were the men sent out to fight the spirit of the wastes, rob it of all its primeval horrors and batter down the barriers of its world-old

---

107 Pen name of Samuel Langhorne Clemens (1835–1910), American novelist and radical humorist. Source of this quote unclear.

108 U.S. journalist, novelist and radical, author of over 90 books; (1878–1968). The following several quotes appear to be from this work.

defences. Where we were working, a new town would spring up some day; it was already springing up, and then, if one of us walked there, "a man with no fixed address," he would be taken up and tried as a loiterer and vagrant.'

From *Children of the Dead End* by Patrick Macgill, C. J., 48[109]

Morality

'Morality and religion are but words to him who fishes in gutters for the means of sustaining life, and crouches behind barrels in the street for shelter from the cutting blasts of a winter night.'

Horace Greeley, 128[110]

Hunger

'It is desirable for a ruler that no man should suffer from cold and hunger under his rule. Man cannot maintain his standard of morals when he has no ordinary means of living.' - p. 135, Konko Hoshi, Buddhist Monk of Japan, 14th century.

Page 19

Freedom
Men! – Whose boast it is that ye
Come of fathers, brave and free,

If there breathe on earth a slave,
Are ye truly free and brave?
If you do not feel the chain
When it works a brother's pain,
Are ye not base slaves indeed,
Slaves unworthy to be freed?
Is true Freedom but to break
Fetters for our own dear sake,

---

109 Patrick Macgill (1889–1963), Irish journalist, poet, novelist.
110 American journalist and statesman (1811–1872).

And, with leathern hearts, forget
That we owe mankind a debt?
No! True Freedom is to share
All the chains our brothers wear,
And, with heart and hand, to be
Earnest to make others free!
They are slaves who fear to speak
For the fallen and the weak;
They are slaves who will not choose
Hatred, scoffing and abuse,
Rather than in silence shrink
From the truth they needs must think;
They are slaves who dare not be
In the right with two or three.

p. 189, James Russell Lowell[111]

Page 20

Full many a gem of purest ray serene
The dark unfathomed caves ocean bear;
Full many a flower is born to blush unseen,
And waste its sweetness on the desert air.
From 'Elegy written in a Country Churchyard' by English poet Thomas Gray (1716-71).

Invention
'Hitherto it is questionable if all the mechanical inventions yet made have lightened the day's toil of any human being.'

---

[111] James Russell Lowell (1819–91), American poet essayist and editor of *Atlantic Monthly*. Wrote several memorial odes after the Civil War; was also the American Minister in Spain (1877–80) and England (1880–85).

p. 199, J. S. Mill, 199[112]

Alms
'There is no one on earth more disgusting and repulsive than he who gives alms. Even as there is no one so miserable as he who accepts them.'
p. 204, Maxim Gorky (1888-1936), Russian writer; author of several books, including *Mother*; pen-name of Alexey Maximovich Penshkov.

Liberty
Those corpses of youngmen,
Those martyrs that hang from the gibbets—
Those hearts pierced by the grey lead,
Cold and motionless as they seem, live elsewhere
With unslaughtered vitality.
They live in other youngmen, O kings!
They live in other brothers again ready to defy you!
They were purified by death—
they were taught and exalted!

Page 21

Not a grave for the murder'd for freedom,
but grows seed for freedom, in its turn to bear seed.
Which the winds carry afar and re-sow, and the
rains and the snows nourish.
Not a disembodied spirit can the weapons of
tyrant let loose
But it stalks invincibly over the earth, whispering,
counselling, cautioning.

---

112 J.S. Mill (1808–73), essayist and philosopher, founder of the Utilitarian Society and author of several books on philosophy, political economy and reform.

p. 268 Walt Whitman[113]

Free thought
'If there is anything that cannot bear free thought, let it crack.'
p. 271, Windell Phillips, 271[114]

State
'Away with the State! I will take part in that revolution. Undermine the whole conception of a state, declare free choice and spiritual kinship to be the only all important conditions of any union, and you will have the commencement of a liberty that is worth something.'
p. 273, Henrik Ibsen[115]

Oppression
'Surely oppression maketh a wise man mad.'
p. 278[116]

Page 22

Martyrs
'The man who flings his whole life into an attempt, at the cost of his own life, to protest against the wrongs of his fellow-men, is a saint compared to the active and passive up-holders of cruelty and injustice, even if his protest destroys other lives besides his own. Let him who is without sin in society cast the first stone at such a one.'

---

113 Walt Whitman (1819–92) had a humble start with little education and worked his way through to win recognition late in life. Now acknowledged as a great and popular poet, especially for his masterpiece, *Leaves of Grass*.
114 Wendell Phillips (1811–1884), American orator and reformer; also active in the anti-slavery movement.
115 Henrik Johan Ibsen (1828–1906), Norwegian playwright acknowledged as a founder of modern prose drama.
116 *Ecclesiastes*, Chapter 7, Verse 7.

p. 287, Emma Goldmann (1869-1940), Lithuania-born American anarchist.

Lower Class
While there is a lower class, I am in it.
While there is a criminal element, I am of it.
While there is a soul in jail, I am not free.
p. 144, Eugene V Debs, 144[117]

One against all **(Charles Fourier: 1772-1837)**

The present social order is a ridiculous mechanism, in which portions of the whole are in conflict and acting against the whole. We see each class in society desire, from interest, the misfortune of the other classes, placing in every way individual interest in opposition to public good. The lawyer wishes litigation and suits, particularly among the rich; the physician desires sickness.

(The latter would be ruined if everybody died without disease, as would the former if all quarrels were settled by arbitration.) The soldier wants a war, which will carry off half of his comrades and secure him promotion; the undertaker wants burials; monopolist and forestallers want famine, to double or treble the price of grain; the architect, the carpenter, the mason want conflagration, that will burn down a hundred houses to give activity to their branches of business.

p. 202,[118]

---

117 31. Eugene Victor Debs (1855–1926), American socialist leader. On June 16, 1918, Debs made an anti-war speech in Canton, Ohio, protesting World War I, and was arrested under the Espionage Act of 1917. He was convicted, sentenced to serve ten years in prison and disenfranchised for life. Debs made this memorable statement at his sentencing hearing.

118 Francois Marie Charles Fourier (1772–1837), French socialist writer. Quote probably from *The Cry for Justice*.

Page 23

New Gospel
'Society can overlook murder, adultery or swindling; it never forgives the preaching of a new gospel.'
 - p. 327, Frederic Harrison[119]

Tree of Liberty
'The tree of liberty must be refreshed from time to time with the blood of patriots and tyrants. It is its natural manure.'
 p. 332, Thomas Jefferson[120]

Chicago Martyrs
Say, then, that the man erred grievously, if his error had been ten times as great, it ought to have been wiped from human recollection by his sacrifice ...

Granted freely that their idea of the best manner of making a protest was utterly wrong and impossible, granted that they went not the best way to work. But what was it that drove them into attack against the social order as they found it? They and thousands of other men that stood with them were not bad men, nor depraved, nor blood thirsty, nor hard hearted, nor criminal, nor selfish, nor crazy. Then what was it that evoked a complaint so bitter and deep seated ...

No one ever contemplated the simple fact that men do not band themselves together to make a protest without the belief that they have something to protest about, and that, in any organised state of society, a widespread protest is something for grave inquiry.

---

119 Frederic Harrison (1831–1923), Professor of jurisprudence and international law to the Inns of Court (1877–89). Author of many books on historical, political and literary subjects.

120 Thomas Jefferson (1743–1826), a great liberal and the third President of the United States of America. From a letter to W.S. Smith, 13 November 1787.

– p. 333, Charles Edward Russell[121]

Page 24

Will of Revolutionary

'I also wish my friends to speak little or not at all about me, because idols are created when men are praised, and this is very bad for the future of the human race ... Acts alone, no matter by whom committed, ought to be studied, praised or blamed. Let them be praised in order that they may be initiated when they see to contribute to the common weal; let them be censured when they are regarded as injurious to the general well-being, so that they may not be repeated.

'I desire that on no occasion, whether near or remote, nor for any reason whatsoever, shall demonstrations of a political or religious character be made before my remains, as I consider the time devoted to the dead would be better employed in improving the conditions of the living, most of whom stand in great need of this.'

– Will of Francisco Ferrer,

Spanish educator (1859–1909)[122]

Charity

'Come follow me', said Jesus to the rich young man ... To stay in his own set and invest his fortune in work of charity, would have been comparatively easy. Philanthropy has been fashionable in every age. Charity takes the insurrectionary edge off of poverty. Therefore, the philanthropic rich man is a benefactor to his fellow magnates, and is made to feel their gratitude, to him all doors of fashion swing. He denied the legitimacy of alms-giving as a plaster for the deep-lying sore

---

121 From Upton Sinclair, *The Cry for Justice*.
122 Francesc Ferreri Guardia (1859–1909), Catalan free thinker, anarchist and educationist. He was arrested, charged and executed without any proof in a trial which was widely condemned as judicial murder.

in social tissue ... Philanthropy as a substitute or justice – he would have none of it ...

Page 25

Charity is twice cursed – it hardens him that gives and softens him that takes. It does more harm to the poor than exploitation, because it makes them willing to be exploited. It breeds slavishness which is moral suicide. The only thing Jesus would permit a swollen fortune to do was to give itself to revolutionary propaganda, in order that swollen fortunes might be forever after impossible.
– p. 353, Bouck White,(1874–1951), American socialist and author. From, *The Cry of Justice* by Upton Sinclair.

Fight for Freedom
The power of armies is a visible thing
Formal, and circumscribed in time and space;
But who the limits of that power shall trace
Which a brave people into light can bring
Or hide, at will, – for freedom combating.
By just revenge inflamed? No foot may chase,
No eye can follow, to a fatal place
That power that spirit whether on the wing
Like the strong wind, or sleeping like the wind
Within its awful caves – from year to year
Spring this indigenous produce far and near;
No craft this subtle element can bind,
Rising like water from the soil, to find
In every nook a lip that it may cheer.
W. Wordsworth[123]

---

123 William Wordsworth (1750–1850), popular English poet among the early Romantics and also a poet of nature; radical and pro-republican in his youth.

Page 26

The Charge of the Light Brigade
Half a league half a league,
Half a league onward,
All in the valley of Death
Rode the six hundred.

'Forward the Light Brigade!
Charge for the guns!' He said;
Into the valley of Death,
Rode the six hundred.
'Forward the Light Brigade!'
Was there a man dismayed?
Not, though the soldiers knew
Some one had blundered;
Their's not to make reply,
Their's not to reason why.
Their's but to do and die;
Into the valley of Death
Rode the six hundred.
Cannon to the right of them,
Cannon to the left of them,
Cannon in front of them,
Volleyed and thundered;
Stormed at with shot and shell,
Boldly they rode and well
Into the jaws of Death,
Into the mouth of Hell,
Rode the six hundred.
Flashed all their sabres bare,
Flashed as they turned in air
Sabring the gunners there,
Charging an army, while
All the world wondered:

Page 27

Plunged in the battery-smoke
Right through the line they broke,
Cossacks and Russians
Reeled from the sabre stroke
Shattered and sundered.

Cannon to the right of them.
Cannon to the left of them,
Cannon behind them
Volleyed and thundered;
Stormed at with shot and shell,
While horse and hero fell
They that had fought so well
Came through the jaws of Death,
Back from the mouth of Hell,
All that was left of them,
Left of six hundred.
When can their glory fade?
O the wild charge they made!
All the world wondered.
Honour, the charge made!
Honour, the Light Brigade!
Noble six hundred.

Lord Tennyson[124]

Dilde tu is mizaaj kaa Parvardigaar de
Jo gham ki gharhi ko bhi khushi se guzaar de

---

124 Lord Alfred Tennyson (1809–1892), English poet. Several generations of Indian students grew up reading Tennyson, and this poem in particular.

Give me a (stout) heart of such temperament, O Protector
That it may pass the hour of sorrow also as a happy hour

Sajaa kar mayyiat-e-umeed naakaami ke phoolon se
Kisi hamdard ne rakh di mere toote hue dil mein

The bier of (my) hope, bedecked with the flowers of failure
Some fellow-sufferer (friend) has placed it in my broken heart!

Chherh naa ai farishte tu zikre ghame-Jaanaanaan
Kyon yaad dilaate ho bhulaa huaa afsaanaa

Do not start O Angel, with the sad tale of the dear beloved
Why must you remind (me) of that forgotten episode (tale)?

Page 28

Birth-right
We're the sons of sires that baffled
Crowned and mitred tyranny;
They defied the field and scaffold
For their birth-rights – so will we!
T. Campbell[125]

Glory of the Cause
Ah! not for idle hatred, not
For honour, fame, nor self applause
But for the glory of the cause,
You did, what will not be forgot.

---

125 43. Thomas Campbell (1777–1844), Scottish poet. Earlier editions of the Notebook misread the 'T' as 'J' and identified this as Joseph Campbell (1879–1944), whose lyrics and ballads were based on Irish legends and folklore.

Arthur Clough[126]

Immortality of Soul
'For you know if you can once get a man believing in immortality, there is nothing more left for you to desire; you can take everything in the world he owns – you can skin him alive if you please – and he will bear it with perfect good humour.'
– p. 403, Upton Sinclair from *Cry for Justice*.

God's Tyrants?
A tyrant must put on the appearance of uncommon devotion to religion. Subjects are less apprehensive of illegal treatment from a ruler whom they consider god-fearing and pious. On the other hand, they do less easily move against him, believing that he has the gods on his side.[127]

Page 29

Soldiers and Thought
'If my soldiers were to begin to reflect, not one of them would remain in the ranks.'
p. 562, Frederick the Great[128]

The Noblest Fallen
The noblest have fallen. They were buried
obscurely in a deserted place.

---

126 Arthur Hugh Clough (1819–61), an English poet. A pupil of Thomas Arnold at Rugby, a Fellow of Oriel. Principal of University Hall, London and an examiner at the Education Office.
127 From Aristotle.
128 Frederick of Prussia (1712–86), administrator, military genius and a man of culture, who gave nationhood to Prussia.

No tears fell over them.
Strange hands carried them to the grave.
No cross, no enclosure, and no tomb stone tell
their glorious names.
Grass grows over them, a feeble blade
bending low keeps the secret.
The sole witness were the surging waves,
which furiously beat against the shore,
But even they the mighty waves could
not carry farewell greetings to the distant home.
V.N. Figner[129]

Prison
There were no stars, no earth, no time,
No check, no change, no good, no crime,
But silence, and a stirless breath,
Which neither was of Life nor death.
The Prisoner of Chillon[130]

Page 30

After Conviction
'During the moments which immediately follow upon his sentence, the mind of the condemned in many respects resembles that of a man on the point of death. Quiet, and as if inspired, he no longer clings to what

---

129 Vera Nikolaevna Figner (1852–1942), Russian revolutionist and martyr. 'One of the first women to declare war on Tsarism' (E. Yaroslavsky in her obituary note). Her memoirs were published in seven volumes.
130 Lord Byron published this in 1816 and describes the imprisonment of a patriot Francois de Bonnivard (1496–1570) in the castle of Chillon on the Lake of Geneva. Lines 245–258.

he is about to leave, but firmly looks in front of him, fully conscious of the fact that what is coming is inevitable.'
V.N. Figner

The Prisoner
It is suffocating under the low, dirty roof;
My strength grows weaker year by year;
They oppress me; this stony floor,
This iron chained table,
This bed-stead, this chair, chained
To the walls, like boards of the grave,
In this eternal, dumb, deep silence
One can only consider oneself a corpse.[131]

Naked walls, prison thoughts,
How dark and sad you are,
How heavy to be a prisoner inactive,
And dream of years of freedom.
Morozov

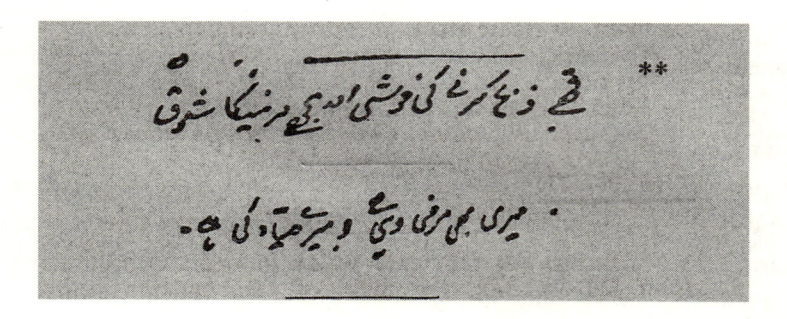

---

[131] Nikolai Alexandrovich Morozov (1854–1946), professional revolutionary, writer, poet and scientist. Met Karl Marx in London in 1880 and was handed the *Communist Manifesto* for translation into Russian. Studied and wrote about the Sciences (28 volumes on Chemistry, Physics, Mathematics and Astronomy) while in prison for nearly 25 years (1875–78 and 1881 to 1905). Also wrote poetry and fiction.

Tujhe zabaah karne ki khushi, mujhe marne kaa shauq,
Meri bhi marzi wohi hai, jo mere sayyaad ki hai

You delight in slaughter, I have a craving for death
I have the same wish as has my executioner

Page 31

Everything here is so silent, lifeless, pale,
The years pass fruitless, leaving no trace;
The weeks and days drag on heavily,
Bringing only dull boredom in their suite.
– Morozov

Our thoughts grow dull from long confinement;
There is a feeling of heaviness in our bones;
The minutes seem eternal from torturing pain,
In this cell, four steps wide.
Entirely for our fellowmen we must live,
Our entire selves for them we must give,
And for their sakes struggle against ill fate!
– Morozov

Came to Set me Free
At last men came to set me free;
I ask'd not why and reck'd not where,
It was at length the same to me,
Fetter'd or fetterless to be;
I learn'd to love despair.
And thus when they appeared at last,
And all my bonds aside were cast,
These heavy walls to me had grown
A hermitage – and all my own.

The Prisoner of Chillon[132]

Page 32

And from on high we have been honoured with a mission!
We passed a severe school, but acquired higher knowledge.
Thanks to exile, prison, and a bitter lot,
We know and value the world of truth and freedom!
Prisoner of Schlusselburg[133]

Death and Suffering of a Child
'A child was born. He committed consciously neither bad nor good actions. He fell ill, suffered much and long, until he died in terrible agony. Why? Wherefore? It is the eternal riddle for the philosopher.'

Frame of Mind of a Revolutionary
'He who has ever been under the influence of the life of Jesus, who has borne, in the name of an ideal, humiliation, suffering and death; he who has once considered Him as an ideal and his life as the prototype of a disinterested love – will understand the frame of mind of the revolutionary who has been sentenced and thrown into a living tomb for his work on behalf of popular freedom.'
Vera N. Figner

Rights
Don't ask for rights. Take them. And don't let anyone give them to you. A right that is handed to you for nothing has something the

---

132 Lord Byron, XIV, Lines 370–378.
133 Schlusselburg, a town in the Leningrad area. On an island opposite is a fortress built by the army of Peter the Great. The fortress was later converted into a prison whose inmates included Marshal Dolgoruki, Tsar Ivan VI, many Decemberists (revolutionaries), the anarchist Bakunin, Polish patriot Lukasovislag, and Lenin's brother, who was hanged there.

matter with it. It's more than likely, it is only a wrong turned inside out.[134]

Page 33

No Enemies?
You have no enemies, you say?
Alas! my friend, the boast is poor;
He who has mingled in the fray
Of Duty, that the brave endure,
Must have made foes! If you have none,
Small is the work that you have done.
You've hit no traitor on the hip,
You've dashed no cup from perjured lip,
You've never turned wrong to right,
You've been a coward in the fight.
p. 747, Charles Mackay[135]

Child Labour
No fledgling feeds the father bird,
No chicken feeds the hen;
No kitten mouses for the cat—

This glory is for men
We are the wisest, strongest Race—
Loud may our praise be sung!
The only animal alive
That lives upon its young!

---

134 Torn sheet. Source not given.
135 Charles Mackay (1814–1889), British poet and journalist. Edited *Cavalier Songs and Ballads of England from 1642 to 1684*.

Charlotte Perkins Gilman[136]

Page 34

No Classes! No Compromise!!
(George D. Herron)

Under the Socialist movement there is coming a time, and the time may be even now at hand, when improved conditions or adjusted wages will no longer be thought to be an answer to the cry of labour; yes when these will be but an insult to the common intelligence. It is not for better wages, improved capitalist conditions or a share of capitalist profits that the Socialist movement is in the world; it is here for the abolition of wages and profits, and for the end of capitalism and the private capitalist. Reformed political institutions, boards of arbitration between capital and labour, philanthropies and privileges that are but the capitalists' gifts – none of these can much longer answer the question that is making the temples, thrones and Parliaments of the nation tremble.

There can be no peace between the man who is down and the man who builds on his back. There can be no reconciliation between classes; there can only be an end of classes. It is idle to talk of goodwill until there is first justice, and idle to talk of justice until the man who makes the world possesses the work of his own hands. The cry of the world's workers can be answered with nothing save the whole product of their work.

George D. Herron[137]

---

136 Charlotte Perkins Gilman (1860–1935), American novelist, writer, lecturer and social reformer. Source illegible; bottom part of page is torn.
137 George D. Herron (1862–1925), who was at one time a Christian Socialist minister, a founder of the Rand School of Social Science, and member of the Socialist Party (USA). Quoted in *The Cry for Justice*.

Page 35

Wastes of Capitalism
Economic estimate about Australia by Theodore Hertzk[138]

Every family: 5-roomed 40 ft. sq. House to last for 50 years.
Workers' workable age: 16-50.
So we have 5,000,000.

Labour of 615,000 workers is sufficient to produce food for 22,000,000 people: 12.3% of labour.

Including labour cost of transport, luxuries need only 315,000 : 6.33% workers' labour.

That amounts to this-that 20% of the available labour is enough for supporting the whole of the continent. The rest 80% is exploited and wasted due to capitalist order of society.

Page 36

Tsarist Regime and the Bolshevist Regime
Frazier Hunt tells that in the first fourteen months of their rule, the Bolsheviks executed 4,500 men, mostly for stealing and speculation.

After the 1905 Revolution, Stolypin, minister of Tsar, 59- Pyotr Arkodyevich Stolypin (1862-1911) was Chairman of the Council of Ministers and Minister for the Interior from 1906 to 1911 under the Tsar.

Caused the execution of 32,773 men within twelve months.
- p. 390, Brass Check[139]

---

138 Theodor Hertzka (1845–1924), Hungarian-Austrian economist and journalist, author of *Freeland: A Social Anticipation*. Quoted from *The Cry for Justice*.

139 Source uncertain. Probably Upton Sinclair.

Page 37

Permanency of the Social Institutions
It is one of the illusions of each generation that the social institutions in which it lives are, in some peculiar sense, 'natural', unchangeable and permanent. Yet, for countless thousands of years, social institutions have been successively arising, developing, decaying and becoming gradually superseded by others better adapted to contemporary needs ... The question, then, is not whether our present civilisation will be transformed, but how it will be transformed?

It may, by considerate adaptation, be made to pass gradually and peacefully into a new form. Or, if there is angry resistance instead of adaptation, it may crash, leaving mankind painfully to build up a new civilisation from the lower level of a stage of social chaos and disorder, in which not only the abuses but also the material, intellectual and moral gains of the previous order will have been lost.

P.I. *Decay of Cap. Civilisation*[140]

Page 38

Capitalism and Commercialism
Rabindra Nath's address to an assembly of Japanese students:

You had your own industry in Japan; how scrupulously honest and true it was, you can see by its products – by their grace and strength, their conscientiousness in details where they can hardly be observed. But the tidal wave of falsehood has swept over your land from that part of the world where business is business and honesty is followed merely as the best policy. Have you never felt shame when you see the trade advertisements, not only plastering the whole town with lies and exaggerations, but invading the green fields, where the peasants do their honest labour, and to hilltops which greet the first pure light of the morning?

---

140 Source uncertain. Probably Sidney Webb.

... This commercialism with its barbarity of ugly decorations is a terrible menace to all humanity, because it is setting up the ideal of power over the perfection. It is making the cult of self-seeking exult in its naked shamelessness. Its movements are violent, its noise is discordantly loud.

It is carrying its own damnation because it is trampling into distortion ... the humanity upon which it stands.

62. Nationalism lecture in Japan – Rabindranath Tagore (1861–1941) poet, philosopher and educationist; founded Shantiniketan (1901) as a forerunner of Vishwa-Bharati. Awarded Nobel Prize for Literature (1913). Visited Japan and the United States in 1916–17.

Page 39

It is strenuously turning out money at the cost of happiness ... The vital ambition of the present civilisation of Europe is to have the exclusive possession of the devil.

Capitalist Society
'The foremost truth of political economy is that everyone desires to obtain individual wealth with as little sacrifice as possible.'
Nassau Senior[141]

Page 40

Karl Marx on Religion
Man makes religion; religion does not make man. Religion, indeed, is the self-consciousness and the self-feeling of man who either has not yet found himself, or else (having found himself) has lost himself once more. But man is not an abstract being squatting down somewhere outside the

---

141   Nassau William Senior (1790–1864), English economist.

world. Man is the world of men, the state, society. This State, this society, produces religion, produces a perverted world consciousness, because they are a perverted world.

Religion is the generalised theory of this world, its encyclopaedic compend, its logic in a popular form ... The fight against religion is, therefore, a direct campaign against the world whose spiritual aroma is religion.

Page 41

Religion is the sight of oppressed creature, the feelings of a heartless world, just as it is the spirit of unspiritual conditions. *It is the opium of the people.*

The people can not be really happy until it has been deprived of illusory happiness by the abolition of religion. The demand that the people should shake itself free of illusion as to its own condition is the demand that it should abandon a *condition which needs* illusion.

The weapon of criticism cannot replace the criticism of weapons. Physical force must be overthrown by physical force; but theory, too, becomes a physical force as soon as it takes possession of the masses.

Page 42

A Revolution not Utopian
A radical revolution, the general emancipation of mankind, is not a utopian dream for Germany; what is Utopian is the idea of a partial, an exclusively political, revolution, which would leave the pillars of the house standing.

'Great are great because
We are on knees

Let us Rise!"[142]

⁓

Page 43

Herbert Spencer on State
'Whether it be true or not that man was born in equity and conceived in sin, it is certainly true that Government was born of aggression and by aggression.'[143]

Man and Mankind
'I am a man,
and all that affects mankind concerns me.'
Roman Dramatist[144]

England's Condition Reviewed
'Good people, things will never go well in England, so long as goods be not in common, and so long as there be villains and gentlemen. By what right are they, whom we call lords, greater folk then we? On what grounds have they deserved it? Why do they hold us in serfage? If we all come of the same father and mother, Adam and Eve, how can they say or prove that they are greater or are better than we? If it be not that they make us gain for them by our toil what they spend in their pride. They are clothed in velvet and are warm in their furs and ermines, while we are covered with rags. They have wine and spices and their bread; and we oatcake, and straw, and water to drink! They have leisure and fine houses;

---

142 At several places in the notebook, such as this, Bhagat Singh writes quotations or captions in the margins or diagonally across the page. All such instances are not noted here. In many cases, it has not been possible to ascertain the source of the quote. Probably written by James Connoly.

143 Herbert Spencer (1820–1903), English philosopher who applied evolutionary theory to philosophy. Works include *The Principles of Psychology* (1855) and *First Principles* (1862).

144 Other details not given.

we have pain and labour, rain and wind in the fields, and yet it is *of our toil that these men hold their state.*'

– Alfred Barton[145]
67. *Friar of Wat Taylor's Rebellion* by Alfred Barton

⁓

Page 44

Revolution and Classes
All classes striving for power are revolutionary, and talk of Equality. All Classes, when they get into power, are conservative and are convinced that Equality is an iridescent dream. All classes but one – the working class, for as Come has said, 'The working class is not properly speaking, a class at all, but constitutes the body of society. But the day of the working class, the Fusion of all useful people, has not even yet arrived.'

⁓

Page 45

Sir Henry Maine has said:
'That most of the land of England has passed to its present owners by the Mistake of lawyers – mistakes that in lesser criminals were punished by Hanging.'
'The law convicts the man or woman
Who steals the goose from of the Common?
But lets the greater felon loose
Who steals the Common from the goose.'[146]

⁓

---

145 Alfred Barton, *World History for Workers*, p. 47
146 Perhaps Sir Henry James Sumner Maine (1822–88), English historian and comparative jurist. Also legal member of Council in India from 1863 to 1869 and Vice Chancellor, Calcutta University.

Page 46

Democracy

Democracy is theoretically a system of political and legal equality. But in concrete and practical operation it is false, for there can be no equality, not even in politics and before the law, so long as there is glaring inequality in economic power. So long as the ruling class owns the workers' jobs and the press and the schools of the country and all organs for the moulding and expression of public opinion; so long as it monopolise(s) all trained public functionaries and disposes of unlimited funds to influence elections, so long as the laws are made by the ruling class and the courts are presided over by members of the class; so long as lawyers are private practitioners who sell their skill to the highest bidder, and litigation is technical and costly, so long will the nominal equality before the law be a hollow mockery.

In a capitalist regime, the whole machinery of democracy operates to keep the ruling class minority in power through the suffrage of the working class majority, and when the bourgeois govt. feels itself endangered by democratic institutions, such institutions are often crushed without compunction.

p. 58, From Marx to Lenin, by Morris Hillquit[147]

Democracy does not secure 'equal rights and a share in all political rights for everybody, to whatever class or party he may belong'. (Kautsky) It only allows free political and legal play for the existing economic inequalities.

... Democracy under capitalism is thus not general, abstract democracy but specific bourgeois democracy... or as Lenin terms it – democracy for the bourgeois.[148]

---

147 Morris Hillquit (1869–1933), socialist lawyer from New York.
148 Quoted by Morris Hillquit

Page 47

Term 'Revolution' defined

'The conception of revolution is not to be treated in the police interpretation of the term, in the sense of an armed rising. A party would be mad that would choose the method of insurrection on principle so long as it has at its disposal different, less costly, and safer methods of action. In that sense, social democracy was never revolutionary on principle. It is so only in the sense that it recognises that when it attains political power, it can not employ it for any purpose other than the abolition of the mode of production upon which the present system rests.'

Karl Kautsky[149]

Some facts and figures about United States

5 men can produce bread for 1000
1 man can produce cotton cloth for 250
1 man can produce woollens for 300
1 man can produce boots and shoes for 10
Iron Heel (p. 78)[150]

15,000,000 are living [in] abject poverty who cannot even maintain their working efficiency.

3,000,000 child labourers.[151]

Re: England Pre-war estimates

---

[149] Bhagat Singh had first attributed this quote to Eduard Bernstein, but then crossed it out and wrote Kautsky's name. Karl Johann Kautsky (1854–1938), German politician who influenced the adoption of Marxist principles in Erfurt Programme (1891) for Social Democrats.

[150] *Iron Heel* (published in 1908) by Jack (John) Griffith London (1876–1916), American novelist who, growing up in poverty, became a socialist essayist, journalist and author of several books.

[151] *Ibid.*

Total Production of England (per annum) £ 2000,000,000
Gains through foreign investments £ 200,000,000
£ 2200,000,000
1/9th part of the population took away ½ £ 1100,000,000
2/9th part of the population 1/3 of the Rest £1100,000,000
i.e. £ 300,000,000

Page 48

Internationale
Arise, ye prisoners of starvation!
Arise ye wretched on earth,
To justice thunders condemnation,
A better world's in birth.
No more traditions chains shall bind us.
Arise, ye slaves! no more in thrall!
The earth shall rise on new foundations,
We have been naught, we be all.
[Refrain]
It is the final conflict,
Let each stand in his place,
The Internationale Party
Shall be the human race.
Behold them seated in their glory,
The kings of mine and rail and soil!
What would you read in all their story
But how they plundered toil?
Fruits of people's work are buried
In the strong coffers of a few;
In voting for their restitution,
The men will ask only their due.
[Same Refrain]
Toilers from shops and fields united,
The party we of all who work;

The earth belongs to us, the people,
No room here for the shirk,
How many on our flesh have fattened?
But if the noisome birds of prey,
Shall vanish from our sky some morning
The blessed sunlight still will stay.
[Same Refrain again][152]

Page 49

Marseillaise
Ye sons of toil, awake to glory!
Hark, hark, what myriads bid you rise;
Your children, wives and grand sires hoary,
Behold their tears and hear their cries!
Shall hateful tyrants mischief breeding,
With hireling hosts, a ruffian band—
Affright and desolate the land
While peace and liberty lie bleeding?
[Chorus]
To arms, To arms! Ye brave!
The avenging sword unsheathe
March on, March on, all hearts resolved,
On Victory or death.
With luxury and pride unsounded,
The vile insatiate despots dare,
Their thirst for gold and power unbounded
To meet and vend the light and air;
Like beasts of burden would they load us,
Like gods would bid their slaves adore,
But man is man and who is more?

---

152 Eugene Pottier's revolutionary song, first sung in France in 1871, and since then a popular song of workers and communists. Adopted as a 'national anthem' by several Communist countries.

Then shall they longer last and goad us?
[The same Chorus again]
Oh liberty! Can man resign thee,
Once having felt thy generous flame?
Can dungeons bolts and bars confine thee,
Or whips thy noble spirit tame?
Too long the world has wept bewailing,
That falsehood, daggers tyrants wield;
But freedom is our sword and shield,
And all their arts are unavailing?
[Same Chorus again][153]

Page 50

Growth of Opportunism
'It was the possibility of acting within law that reared opportunism within the labour parties of the period of Second Internationale.'
– Lenin vide Collapse of II Int.N.

Illegal Work
'In a country where the bourgeoisie, or the counter revolutionary Social Democracy is in power, the Communist Party must learn to coordinate its legal work with illegal work, and the legal work must always be under the effective control of the illegal party.'
Bukharin[154]

---

153 The French National Anthem, composed by Claude Joseph Rouget de Lisle, French Captain of Engineers, and a musical amateur, on 24 April 1792, in response to a call by the Mayor of Strasbourg for a patriotic song. It was adopted and sung with enthusiasm by troops on their march from Marseille to Paris.

154 Nikolai Aleksandrovich Bukharin (1888–1938), Soviet leader, a leading Marxist theorist after Lenin. Executed during the Stalinist purges of the Communist Party.

Betrayal of II Int.N.'s Cause

The vast organisation of socialism and labour were adjusted to such peace time activities, and when the crisis came, a number of the leaders and large portion of the masses were unable to adapt themselves to the new situation.

... It is this inevitable development that accounts largely for the betrayal of II International.

P. 140, Marx to Lenin, by Morris Hillquit

The Cynic's Word Book (1906)

Ambrose Bierce writes:

'Grape shot (n.) – An argument which the future is preparing in answer to the demands of American Socialism.'[155]

Page 51

Slavery

Religion a supporter of the established order:

In 1835, the General Assembly of the Presbyterian Church resolved that: 'Slavery is recognised in both Old and New Testaments, and is not condemned by the authority of God'.

The Charleston Baptist Association issued the following in 1835:

'The right of masters to dispose of the time of their slaves has been distinctly recognised by the Creator of all things, who is surely at liberty to vest the right of property over any object whomsoever He pleases.'

The Revd. ED, Simon, Doctor of Divinity, a professor in Methodist College of Virginia wrote:

"Extracts from Holy Writ unequivocally assert the right of property in slaves, together with the usual incidents to that right. The right to buy and sell is clearly stated. Upon the whole, then, whether we consult the

---

[155] Also known as *The Devil's Dictionary*, this satirical book by Ambrose Bierce has inspired dozens of imitations. Bierce (1842–1914) was an American journalist, short-story writer and satirist.

Jewish policy instituted by God Himself, or the uniform opinion and practice of mankind in all ages, or the injunctions of the New Testament and the moral law, we are brought to the conclusion that slavery is not immoral. Having established the point that the first African slaves were legally bought into bondage, the right to detain their children in bondage follows as an indispensable consequence. Thus we see that the slavery that exists in America was founded in right."

Capitalism Supported
'Henry Van Dyke writes in 'Essay in Application' (1905):
'The Bible teaches that God owns the world. He distributes to every man according to His own Good pleasure, conformably to the general laws.'

Page 52

Statistics about United States
Army was 50,000 strong
It is now 300,000 strong.

Plutocracy owns 67 billion of wealth.
Out of the total persons engaged in occupations, only 9/10% belong to Plutocracy
Yet they own 70% of the total wealth.

Out of persons engaged in occupations 29% belong to Middle Class
They own 25% of the total wealth : 24 billion

Remaining 70% of the men in occupations belong to the Proletariat and they only (have)
4% of the total wealth i.e. 4 billion.[156]

---

156 From Jack London's novel *Iron Heel*.

According to Lucian Saniel, in 1900:
Out of total people engaged in occupations
: 250,251 belonged to Plutocrats
Out of total people : 8,429,845 to Middle Class
Out of total people : 20,395,137 to Proletariat
(Iron Heel)

Rifles

You say you will have majority in the Parliament and State offices, but
'How many rifles have you got? Do you know where you can get plenty of lead? When it comes to powder, the chemical mixtures are better than mechanical mixtures. You take my word.'
Iron Heel p. 198

Page 53

Power

A socialist leader had addressed a meeting of the plutocrats and charged them of mismanaging society and thereby thrown the whole responsibility on their shoulders, the responsibility for the woes and misery that confronts the suffering humanity. Afterwards, a capitalist (Mr. Wickson) rose and addressed him as follows:

'This, then, is our answer. We have no words to waste on you. When you reach out your vaunted strong hands for our palaces and purpled ease, we will show you what strength is. In roar of shell and shrapnel and in whine of machine guns will our answer be couched. We will grind you revolutionists down under our heel, and we shall walk upon your faces. The world is ours. We are its lords and ours it shall remain. As for the host of labour, it has always been in the dirt since history began, and I read history aright. And in the dirt it shall remain so long as I and mine, and those that come after us, have the power.

'There is the word. It is the king of words - Power. Not God, not mammon but Power. Pour it over your tongue till it tingles with it. Power.'

"I am answered." Earnest (the socialist leader) said quietly. "It is the only answer that could be given. Power. It is what we of the working class preach.

We know, and well we know by bitter experience, that no appeal for the right, for justice, for humanity can ever touch you. Your hearts are hard as your heels with which you tread upon the faces of the poor. So we have preached power. By the Power of our ballots, on election day, will we take your government away from you..."

"What if you do get a majority, a sweeping majority on election day," Mr Wickson broke in to demand. "Suppose we refuse to turn the Government over to you after you have captured it at the ballot box?"

―

Page 54

"That also, have we considered," Earnest replied. "And we shall give you an answer in terms of lead. Power, you have proclaimed the king of words. Very good! Power, it shall be. And in the day that we sweep to victory at the ballot box, and you refuse to turn over to us the government we have constitutionally and peacefully captured, and you demand what we are going to do about it – in that day, I say, we shall answer you; and in roar of shell and shrapnel, in whine of machine guns shall our answer be couched.

"You cannot escape us. It is true that you have read history alright. It is true that labour has, from the beginning of history, been in the dirt. And it is equally true that so long as you and yours and those that come after you, have power that labour shall remain in the dirt. I agree with you. I agree with all that you have said. Power will be the arbiter, as it always has been the arbiter. It is a struggle of classes. Just as your class dragged down the old feudal nobility, so shall it be dragged down by my class, the working class. If you will read your biology and your sociology as clearly as do your history, you will see that this end I have described is inevitable. It does not matter whether it is in one year, ten or a thousand – your class shall be dragged down. And it shall be done by power. We of the labour host have conned that word over, till our minds are all a-tingle with it. Power. It is a kingly word."

– p. 88, *Iron Heel* by Jack London[157]

Page 55

Figures
England:
1922 – Number of unemployment (?) : 1,135,000
1926 – it has oscillated to 1 ¼ and 1 ½ million i.e. 1,250,000 to 1,500,000.

Betrayal of the English Labour Leaders

The years 1911 to 1913 were times of unparalleled class struggles of the miners, railwaymen, and transport workers generally. In August 1911, a national, in other words a general, strike broke out on the railways. The vague shadow of revolution hovered over Britain in those days. The leaders exerted all their strength in order to paralyse the movement. Their motive was 'Patriotism'; the affair was occurring at the time of the Agadir incident, which threatened to lead to a war with Germany. As is well known today, the Premier summoned the workers' leaders to a secret council, and called them to the salvation of the fatherland. And leaders did all that lay in their power, strengthening the bourgeoisie, and thus preparing the way for the imperialist slaughter.

p. 3, Leon Trotsky, *Where is Britain Going*[158]

---

157 This long extract of an argument from Jack London's novel can perhaps give some indication of Bhagat Singh's mind and his philosophy of revolution.

158 Leon Trotsky (1879-1940) a Russian revolutionary, was with Lenin during the 1917 October Russian Bolshevik Revolution, expelled from Communist party after Lenin's death and went in exile to Mexico, where he was assassinated in 1940. Author of many other books apart from *Where is Britain Going* (1926).

Page 56

Betrayal
Only after 1920, did the movement return within bounds, after 'Black Friday', when the Triple alliance of miners, railwaymen and transport leaders betrayed the general strike. (p. 3)

For Reform a Threat of Revolution is Necessary
... The British bourgeoisie reckoned that by such means (reform) a revolution could be avoided. It follows, therefore, that even for the introduction of reforms, the principle of gradualness alone is insufficient, and that an actual threat of revolution is necessary. (p. 29)

Social Solidarity:
... It would seem that once we stand for the annihilation of a privileged class, which has no desire to pass from the scene, we have therein the basic content of the class struggle. But no, Macdonald desires to "evoke the consciousness of social solidarity. With whom? The solidarity of the working class is the expression of its internal welding in the struggle with the bourgeoisie.

The social solidarity which Macdonald preaches, is the solidarity of the exploited with the exploiters, in other words, the maintenance of exploitation.

Revolution a Calamity
"The revolution in Russia", says Macdonald, "taught us a great lesson. It showed that revolution is a ruin and a calamity and nothing more."[159]

Page 57

Revolution leads only to calamity! But the British democracy led to the imperialist war ... with the ruin of which the calamities of revolution

---

[159] James Ramsay MacDonald (1866–1937), a British statesman and Prime Minister (1924, 1929–35).

cannot, of course, be compared in the very least. But in addition to this, what deaf ears and shameless face are necessary in order, in the face of a revolution which overthrew Tsarism, nobility and bourgeoisie, shook the church, awakened to a new life a nation of 130 million, a whole family of nations, to declare that revolution is a calamity and nothing more.

p. 64

Peaceful?

When and where did the ruling class ever yield power and property on the order of a peaceful vote – and especially such a class as the British bourgeoisie, which has behind it centuries of world rapacity?

p. 66

Aim of Socialism – Peace

It is absolutely unchallenged that the aim of socialism is to eliminate force, first of all in its most crude and bloody forms, and afterwards in other more concealed forms.

p. 80 *Where is Britain Going?*, Trotsky

Aim of the World Revolution:

1. To overthrow capitalism.
2. To control the nature for the service of humanity.

This is how Bukharin defined it.

Page 58

Man and Machinery

The United States Bureau of Labour tells:

12 lbs. package of pins can be made by a man working with a machine in

1 hour and 34 minutes.

The same would take 140 hours and 55 minutes, if man works with tools only, but without machine.

(Ratio – 1.34: 140.55 minutes)
100 pairs of shoes by machine work take 234 hrs. 25 min.
By hand it will take 1,831 hrs. 40 minutes.
Labour cost on machine is $ 69.55
Labour cost by hand is $ 457.92
500 yards of gingham checks are made by machine labour in 73 hours.
By hand labour, it takes 5,844 hours.
100 lbs. of sewing cotton can be made by machine labour in 39 hrs.
By hand it takes 2,895 hours.

Agriculture
A good man with a scythe can reap 1 acre a day (12 hours)
A machine does the same work in 20 minutes
Six men with flails can thresh 60 litres of wheat in half an hour.
One machine thresher can do 12 times as much.
"The increased effectiveness of man-labour, aided by the use of machinery... varies from 150% in the case of rye, to 2,244% in the case of barley..."

Page 59

The Wealth of U.S.A. and Its Population
1850–1912
Per capita T. Population
In 1850 total wealth was $ 7,135,780,000 $ 308 : 23,191,876
1860 $16,159,616,000 $514 : 31,443,321
1870 $30,068,518,000 $780 : 38,558,371
1880 $43,642,000,000 $870 : 50,155,783
1890 $65,037,091,000 $1,036 : 62,947,714
1900 $88,517,307,000 $1,165 : 75,994,575
1904 $107,104,202,000 $1,318 : 82,466,551
1912 $187,139,071,000 $1,965 : 95,400,503
Due to the use of machinery.

The machine is social in nature, as the tool was individual.

"Give us worse cotton, but give us better men" says Emerson.

"Deliver me those rickety perishing souls of infants, and let the cotton trade take its chance."

p. 81, *Past and Present*, Book 4, 'The One Institution', Thomas Carlyle

The man cannot be sacrificed to the machine. The machine must serve mankind, yet the danger to the human race lurks, menacing, in the Industrial Regime.

p. 81, *Poverty & Riches*, Scott Nearing[160]

Page 60

Man and Machinery

p. 88, *Payday* by C. Nanford Henderson,

'This institution of industry, the most primitive of all institutions, organised and developed in order to free mankind from the tyranny of things, has become itself the greater tyranny, degrading a multitude into the conditions of slaves – slaves doomed to produce, through long and weary hours, a senseless glut of things and then forced to suffer for the lack of the very things they have produced.'

Pov. Riches p. 87[161]

Man is not for Machinery

The combination of steel and fire, which man has produced and called a machine, must be ever the servant, never the master of man. Neither the machine nor the machine owner may rule the human race.

p. 88

---

160 Scott Nearing (1883–1983), American economist, conservationist, peace activist, and writer. *Poverty and Riches* was published in 1916.

161 Identity not clear.

Imperialism

Imperialism is capitalism in that stage of development in which monopolies and financial capital have attained a preponderating influence, the export of capital has acquired great importance, the international trusts have begun the partition of the world, and the biggest capitalist countries have completed the division of the entire terrestrial globe among themselves.

– Lenin

Page 61

Dictatorship

Dictatorship is an authority relying directly upon force, and not bound by any laws. The revolutionary dictatorship of the proletariat is an authority maintained by the proletariat by means of force over and against the bourgeoisie, and not bound by any laws.

– p. 18, *The Proletarian Revolution and the Renegade Kautsky*, Lenin[162]

Revolutionary Dictatorship

Revolution is an act in which one section of the population imposes its will upon the other by rifles, bayonets, guns, and other such exceedingly authoritarian means. And the party which has won is necessarily compelled to maintain its rule by means of that fear which its arms inspire in the reactionaries. If the Commune of Paris had not relied upon the armed people as against the bourgeoisie, would it have maintained itself more than twenty four hours? Are we not, on the contrary, justified in reproaching the Commune for having employed this authority too little?"

– F. Engels[163]

---

162 *The Proletarian Revolution and the Renegade Kautsky* (1918), Lenin.

163 Friedrich Engels on the Paris Commune, quoted by Lenin in *The Proletarian Revolution*. The subsequent quotations, till Engels' letter to Babel, are all from this work.

Bourgeois Democracy

Bourgeois democracy, while constituting a great historical advance in comparison with feudalism, nevertheless remains, and cannot but remain, a very limited, a very hypocritical institution, a paradise for the rich and a trap and a delusion for the exploited and for the poor.

p. 28, Lenin

Page 62

Exploitation of Labour and State

"Not only the ancient and feudal, but also the representative state of today is an instrument of exploitation of wage-labour by capital."
Engels

Dictatorship

"Since the state is only a temporary institution which is to be made use of in revolution, in order forcibly to suppress the opponents, it is perfectly absurd to talk of about a free popular state; so long as the proletariat still needs the state, it needs it not in the interest of freedom, but in order to suppress its opponents, and when it becomes possible to speak of freedom, the state, as such, ceases to exist."
Engels in his letter to Babel. 28 March 1875

The Impatient Idealists

The impatient idealist – and without some impatience, a man will hardly prove effective – is almost sure to be led into hatred by the oppositions and disappointments which he encounters in his endeavour to bring happiness to the world.
Bertrand Russell[164]

---

164 Bertrand Russell (1872–1970), British philosopher and peace activist, author of numerous books.

Page 63

Leader
"No time need have gone to ruin" writes Carlyle, "could it have found a man great enough, a man wise and good enough; wisdom to discern truly what the time wanted, valour to lead it on the right road thither; these are the salvation of any time."

Arbitrariness
Kautsky had written a booklet with the title *Proletariat Dictatorship* and had deplored the act of Bolsheviks in depriving the bourgeoisie people from the right of vote. Lenin writes in his *Proletarian Revolution*: (pp. 77)

'Arbitrariness! Only think what a depth of meanest subservience to the bourgeoisie, and of the most idiotic pedantry, is contained in such a reproach. When thoroughly bourgeois and, for the most part, even reactionary jurists of capitalist countries, have in the course of, we may almost say, centuries, been drawing up rules and regulations and writing up hundreds of volumes of various codes and laws, and of interpretations of them to oppress the workers, to bind hand and foot the poor men, and to place a hundred and one hindrances and obstacles in the way of the simple and toiling mass of the people – when this is done, the bourgeois Liberals and Mr Kautsky can see no "arbitrariness"! It is all Law and Order! It has all been thought out and written down, how the poor man is to be kept down and squeezed. There are thousands and thousands of bourgeois lawyers and officials able to interpret the laws that the worker and average peasant can never break through their barbed wire entanglements. This, of course, is not any arbitrariness. This, of course, is not a dictatorship of the filthy or profit-seeking exploiters who are drinking the blood of the people. Oh, it is nothing of the kind! It is "pure democracy", which is becoming purer and purer.

Page 64

Everyday. But when the toiling and exploited masses, for the first time in history, separated by Imperialist War from their brothers across the frontier, have constructed their Soviets, have summoned to the workers of political construction, the classes which the bourgeois used to oppress and to stupefy, and begun themselves to build up a new proletarian State, begun, in the midst of raging battles, in the fire of Civil War, to lay down the fundamental principles of 'a State without exploiters', then all the scoundrels of the bourgeoisie, the entire band of blood suckers, with Kautsky, singing "obliger to", scream about arbitrariness!'

pp. 77-78, Lenin[165]

Party

But it has become clear that no revolution is possible unless there is a party able to lead the revolution. (p. 15, 'Lessons of October', 1917).

A party is the instrument indispensable to a proletarian revolution. (p. 17, ibid by Trotsky)[166]

Page 65

The upper-half of this page is blank, except the (slanting) signature of B.K. Dutta with the date 12.7.30 written twice. The quotation from Karl Marx is given below the signature.

---

165 Karl Kautsky (1854–1938), leading social democratic theoretician. Author of numerous works, among which *The Dictatorship of the Proletariat* (1918) is the most pertinent in the context of Bhagat Singh's readings of Lenin.

166 The *Lessons of October* was written in 1924 as a preface to Trotsky's – whose name Bhagat Singh sometimes spells 'Trotzky' – writings of 1917. Except for some intervening quotes from *The Communist Manifesto*, all the subsequent quotes, till Bhagat Singh's notes on sociology, are from this work.

Law, morality, religion are to him (the working man) so many bourgeois prejudices, behind which lurk in ambush just as many bourgeois interests.
 — *The Communist Manifesto*, Karl Marx[167]

~

Page 67

Pages 66 and 68 are missing. Page no. 67 has B.K. Dutta's signature, with the following text below it:

Autograph of Mr. B.K. Dutta taken on 12 July '30, in Cell No.
137 Central Jail Lahore four days, before his final departure from this Jail.

Bhagat Singh

~

Page 69

Aim of Communists
"The Communists disdain to conceal their views and aim. They openly declare that their ends can be attained only by the forcible overthrow of all existing social conditions. Let the ruling classes tremble at a Communist revolution. The proletarians have nothing to lose but their chains. They have a world to win. Working men of all countries, unite!"

Aim of Communist Revolution
"We have seen above, that the first step in the revolution by the working class, is to raise the proletariat to the position of ruling class, to win the battle of democracy to wrest, by degrees, all capital from the bourgeoisie, to centralise all instruments of production in the hands of the

---

167 From *The Communist Manifesto* by Karl Marx and Friedrich Engels, 1848. The subsequent quotations are also from this work.

State, i.e., of the proletariat organised as the ruling class, and to increase the total of productive forces as rapidly as possible."
Communist Manifesto

Page 70

To point out the mistakes of Karl Marx
... And it certainly looks as if Trotsky belonged to what Germans called the school of 'real politics' and was as innocent as Bismarck of any ideology at all. And it is, therefore, rather curious to note that even Trotsky is not revolutionary enough to say that Marx had made a mistake; but feels obliged to devote a page or so to the task of exegesis – that is, proving that the sacred books meant something quite different from what they said.
Preface to the 'Lessons of October' 1917 by Trotsky: preface by A. Susan Lawrence

Voice of the People
The governments we know have all ruled, in the main, by indifference of the people; they have always been governments of a minority, of this or that fraction of the country which is politically conscious. But when the giant wakes, he will have his way, and all that matters to the world is whether he will wake in time.
Ibid., Preface

Page 71

"It so often happens," wrote Lenin in July, 1917, "that when events take a sudden turn, even an advanced party cannot adapt itself for some time to the new conditions. It goes on repeating yesterday's watchwords, watchwords which, under the new circumstances, have become empty of

meaning and which have lost meaning 'unexpectedly', just in proportion as the change of in events has been "unexpected".'
p. 17, *Lessons of October*

Tactics and Strategy
In politics as in war, tactics means the art of conducting isolated operations; strategy means the art of victory that is the actual seizure of power.
p. 18

Propaganda and Action
And it is an extremely sudden change, when the party of the Proletariat passes from preparation, from propaganda and organisation and agitation, to an actual struggle for power and an actual insurrection against the bourgeoisie.

Those in the party who are irresolute, or sceptical, or compromising, or cowardly ... oppose the insurrection, they look for theoretical arguments to justify their opposition, and they find them, all readymade, among their opponents of yesterday.
p. 19, Trotsky[168]

Page 72
'It is necessary to direct ourselves, not by old formulas, but by new realities.'
p. 25, Lenin[169]

He always fought for the future against the past.
Ibid., p. 41

---

168 Quoted from Leon Trotsky's *Lessons of October*
169 Quoted from Leon Trotsky's *Lessons of October*

... But a moment comes when the habit of thinking that the enemy is stronger becomes the main obstacle to victory.
Trotsky 48[170]

... But in such circumstances not every party will have its Lenin ... What does it mean to lose the moment? ...
All the art of tactics consists in this, to match the moment when the combination of circumstances is most favourable ... (Circumstances had produced the combination and Lenin said) The crisis must be settled in one way or another. 'Now or never' repeated Lenin.
p. 52

Page 73

The strength of a revolutionary party grows to a certain point, after which the contrary may happen ...[171]

"To hesitate is crime" wrote... (Lenin)... in the beginning of October,
"To wait for the Congress of Soviets is a childish playing with formalities, a disgraceful playing with formalities, it is betraying the revolution.'

Opportune Moment
Time is an important factor in politics; it is thousand times more so in war and revolution. Things can be done today that cannot be done tomorrow. To rise in arms, to defeat the enemy, to seize power, may be possible today, and tomorrow may be impossible. But, you will say, to seize power means changing the course of history; is it possible that such a thing can depend on a delay of 24 hours? Even so, when it comes to an armed insurrection, events are not measured by the long yards of politics but by short yards of war. To lose a few weeks, a few days, sometimes even one day, may mean giving up the revolution, may mean capitulation.

---

170 Quoted from Leon Trotsky's *Lessons of October*
171 Last words are indistinct.

Political cunning is always dangerous, especially in a revolution. You may deceive the enemy, but you may confuse the masses who are following you.

~

Page 74

Hesitation
Hesitation on the part of the leaders, and felt by their followers, is generally harmful in politics; but in the case of an armed insurrection, it is a deadly danger.

War
... War is War; come what may, there must be no hesitation or loss of time.

The Inefficient Leaders
... There are two kinds of leaders who incline to drag the party back at the moment when it should go fastest. One kind always tends to see overwhelming difficulties and obstacles in the way of revolution, and looks at them – consciously or unconsciously – with the desire of avoiding them. They alter Marxism into a system, for explaining why revolutionary action is impossible.

The other kind are mere superficial agitators. They see never any obstacles until they break their heads against them. They think they can avoid real difficulties by floods of oratory. They look at everything with supreme optimism, and, naturally, change right over when something has actually to be done.

p. 80[172]

~

---

172   Pages 75 to 100 are missing. The next page number is 101 (74) and starts with 'Sociology', which may be treated as a distinct section of the notebook.

Page 101

Sociology
Value

1 quarter corn : X/cost of iron. What does this question tell us? It tells us that in two different things – in 1 quarter of corn and X cost of iron – there exists in equal qualities something common to both. The two things must therefore be equal to a third, which in itself in neither the one or the other ... Let us now consider the residue of each of these products; it consists of the same unsubstantial reality in each, a mere congelation of homogenous human labour, of labour power expended without regard to the mode of its expenditure. All these things now tell us that human labour power has been expended in their production, that labour is embodied in them. When looked at as crystals of this social substance, common to all, they are '*values.*'

–(pp. 3-4, 5), *Capital*, English Translation by Karl Marx.

Law

'Society, however, does not rest upon law. This is a legal fiction. Rather the law must rest on society. It must be the expression of the interest and needs of society which result from the social and invariably material method of production as against the arbitrariness of the industrial. As for Napoleon Code, which I have in my hand, that has not engendered modern civil society.

'The society which arose in the 18th century and developed in the 19th finds in the Code only a legal expression. As soon as that no longer corresponds to social conditions, it is merely so much waste paper ... The law necessarily changed with the changing conditions of life. The maintaining of the old law against the new needs and demands of the social development is at bottom nothing but a hypocritical assertion (in accord with the spirit of the age) of special interest against the common interest.'

Marx (Before the Court of Jury of Cologne)[173]

---

[173] *The Trial of the Rhenish District Committee of Democrats* by Karl Marx, February 1849.

Masses

'The people is a fat and motley beast, ignorant of its prowess and hence enduring burdens, lash and cudgel. Driven it is by a feeble child, whom it can shake off in an instant. But it fears that child and so serves all its whims and fancies, never realising how much it itself is feared by that child ... Marvellous thing! They hang themselves with their own hands and send themselves to jails and bring upon themselves war and death for a single farthing, paid to them out of the many that they themselves have given to the King. Everything between heaven and earth belongs to them, but they do not know it, and should anyone tell them that, they would knock that man down and kill him.'

Tommasso Campanella[174]

Page 102

Marxism versus Socialism by Vladimir G. Simkhovitch
PhD, Columbia University (1908-12)
He criticises all the Theories of Marx one by one and refutes all:
1. Theory of Value
2. Economic Interpretation of History
3. Concentration of Wealth in fewer hands, i.e., the capitalists, and elimination of middle class altogether and swarming of the Proletariats class
4. Theory of increasing misery, leading to the
5. Inevitable crises of the Modern State and social order.

He concludes that Marxism solely rests on these fundamental theories and refutes them one by one, concluding that all the vague apprehensions about the hurrying avalanche of the Revolution has proved futile till now.

The middle class is not diminishing but growing. Rich class is growing in number, and the mode of production and consumption is also changing along with the circumstances, hence the reforms in the condition of the

---

174 Tommaso Campanella (1568–1639), Italian poet and philosopher. Author of *City of Sun* (1623), describing a utopian society.

workers can avoid any sort of friction. It is not the growing poverty that is the cause of the social unrest, but it is the concentration of the poor classes in Industrial Centres that the class consciousness is growing. Hence all this hue and cry.[175]

Page 103

Preface to Les Miserables

So long as there shall exist, by virtue of law and custom, a social damnation artificially creating hells in the midst of civilisation, and complicating the destiny which is divine with a fatality which is human; so long as three problems of the age - the degradation of man through poverty, the ruin of woman through hunger, the crippling of children through ignorance - are not solved; so long as in certain regions, social asphyxia is possible - in other words, and from a still wider point of view - so long as ignorance and wretchedness exist on the earth, books like this cannot be useless.

Victor Hugo[176]

A Judge Defined

'A judge callous to the pain he inflicts loses the right to judge.'
Rabindranath Tagore[177]

'But what unresisting martyrdom fails to do, righteous and resisting force does and renders tyranny impotent to do further harm.'[178]

'Rather get killed than converted' was the cry prevalent amongst the Hindus then. But Ram Das rose and exclaimed 'No! Not thus! Better get

---

175 Vladimir G. Simkhovitch (1874–1959), author of *Towards the Understanding of Jesus* and *Marxism versus Socialism* (1913). It is a short review of the book by Bhagat Singh.
176 Victor (Marie) Hugo (1802–85), French poet, dramatist and novelist, and a leader of Romanticism. Wrote his classic *Les Miserables* in 1862.
177 From 'The Mother's Prayer' from *The Fugitive and Other Poems* (1921).
178 Source and other details not available. Could be from *Hindu Pad Padshahi*

killed than converted is good enough; but it would be better so to strive as neither to get killed nor violently converted, by killing the forces of violence itself. Get killed if that must be, but get killed while killing to conquer - conquer in the cause of Righteousness.'

p. 181-82, Hindu Pad Padshahi[179]

Page 104

All Legislators Defined as Criminals

'All legislators and rulers of men commencing with the earliest down to Lycurgus, Solon, Mahomet, Napoleon, etc., etc., have, one and all, been criminals, for, whilst giving new laws, they have naturally broken through older ones which had 'been faithfully observed by society and transmitted by its progenitors.

pp. 205, *Crime and Punishment*, Dostoevsky[180]

'A true politician,' says Burke, 'always considers how he shall make the most of the existing materials of his country.'[181]

---

179 This is probably a quotation from Vinayak Damodar Savarkar, *Hindu Pad Padshahi;* or from *A Review of the Hindu Empire of Maharashtra* (Madras, 1925).

180 Fyodor Mikhailovich Dostoevsky (1821–81), author of *Crime and Punishment* (1866). His other well-known books include *The Idiot* (1868) and *The Brothers Karamazov* (1879–80). Dostoyevsky has apparently used the term 'criminals' for law breakers, and suggested that all law-givers tend to break the existing laws or codes of society.

181 Edmund Burke (1729–97), British statesman and writer. Born in Dublin, he also became a prominent Whig orator and pamphleteer. In *Thoughts on the Present Discontents* (1770), he advocated less concern in American Colonies and instigated the trial of Warren Hastings (1785–94). Denounced the French Revolution in *Reflection on the French Revolution in France* (1780).

Page 105

Jurisprudence
Law:
1. Legal exposition as it exists.
2. Legal History as it developed.
3. Science of Legislation as it ought to be.

1. Theoretical (i) Philosophy. Supplying foundation for the science
2. General Jurisprudence

1. Analytical
2. Historical Jurisprudence
3. Ethical

1. Analytical jurisprudence explains the first principles of Law. It deals with:
(a) Conception of Civil Law
(b) Relation between Civil and other Laws
(c) Various constituent ideas that constitute the idea of Law viz. State, Sovereignty and administration of justice.
(d) Legal sources of Law and Theory of Legislation, etc.
(e) Scientific arrangements of Law
(f) Legal rights
(g) Theory of Legal (civil and criminal) liability
(h) Other legal conceptions.

Page 106

2. Historical Jurisprudence deals with the general principles governing the origin and development of Law; legal conceptions. It is the history.
3. Ethical Jurisprudence: is concerned with the theory of justice in its relation to Law.

Law and Justice
The total disregard of the ethical implications of the law tends to reduce analytical jurisprudence to a system rather arid formation.

In England
Two different words, 'Law' and 'justice' are a constant reminder that these are two different things and not the same thing. And their use tends to hide from view the real and intimate relation which exists between them.

and in Continent
(Rechet: Right : Droit: Law)
Continental speech conceals the difference between 'law' and 'right', whereas
English, speech conceals the connection between them.

Page 107

Law
'We term any kind of rule or canon whereby actions are framed a law.'
– Richard Hooker[182]

'Law in its most general sense signifies a rule of action, and is indiscriminately to all kinds of action whether rational or irrational, animals or inanimate.
'Thus we say, the Laws of motion, of gravitation, of optics, of nature and of nations.'
William Blackstone[183]

---

182 Richard Hooker (1554–1600), English theologian who codified principles of Anglicanism in *Of the Lawes of Ecclesiastical Politie*.
183 Sir William Blackstone (1723–80), English Jurist, author of *Commentaries on the Laws of England* (1765–69), an authoritative book on English legal doctrine.

Kinds of Laws
1. Imperative Law
2. Physical Law or Scientific Law
3. Natural or Moral Law
4. Conventional Law
5. Customary Law
6. Practical or Technical Law
7. International Law
8. Civil Law or the Law of the State.

Page 108

1. Imperative Law means a rule of action imposed upon men by some authority which enforces obedience to it.

The sanction of Imperative Law-1-Punishment, Wars etc.
'A Law is a command which obliges a person or persons to a course of conduct.'
Austin[184]

Positive morality in society also amounts to the Imperative Laws.
Hobbes' View:
It is men and arms that make the force and power of the Laws.
Hobbes[185]

2. Physical Law is an expression of actions as they are. (Moral Law or the Law of Reason is an expression of actions as they ought to be).
3. Natural or Moral Law means the principles of natural right and wrong – the principles of natural justice including all rightful actions.

---

184 John Austin (1911–1960), British philosopher who investigated linguistic use for knowledge. Author of *How to Do Things with Words*.
185 Thomas Hobbes (1588–1679) English philosopher, author of the celebrated *Leviathan* (1651; on the social contract theory) and several other works.

Justice being of two kinds – the Positive and Natural.
Natural justice is justice as it is indeed and in truth.
Positive justice is justice as it is conceived, recognised and expressed.

Page 109

4. Conventional Law: is any rule or system of rules agreed upon by persons for the regulation of their conduct. Agreement is a law for the parties to it.

5. Customary Law: is any rule of action which is actually observed by men – any rule which is the expression of some actual uniformity of voluntary action.

Custom is law of those who observe it.

6. Practical or Technical Law: consists of rules for the attainment of some practical end. In games, there are both 'Conventional Laws' and 'Practical Laws', the former being the rules agreed upon by players, the latter being the rules to make the play a success or for the successful playing of the game.

7. International Law: consists of those rules which govern sovereign states in their relations and conduct towards each other.

(i) Express Laws (Treaties, etc.)
(ii) Implied Laws (Customary)

Again divisible into two kinds:

(i) Common Laws (between all nations)
(ii) Particular Laws (between two or more particular nations).

8. Civil Law: Law of the State or of the land; is applied in the courts of justice.

Page 110

Punishment
Political Crimes

'We agree with the great body of legislators in thinking, that though, in general a person who has been a party to a criminal design, which has not been carried into effect, be not severely dealt with, yet an exception to this rule must be made with respect to high offences against the State; for State crimes, and especially the most heinous and formidable State crimes, have this peculiarity, that, if they are successfully committed, the criminal is almost always secure from punishment. The murderer is in greater danger after his victim is despatched than before. The thief is in greater danger after the purse is taken than before; but the rebel is out of danger as soon as he has subverted the Govt. As the penal law is impotent against a successful rebel, it is consequently necessary that it should be made strong and sharp against the first beginning of rebellion ...'

p. 120, LCC Judgement 1916[186]

Page 111

Punishment

Dream that merited Capital Punishment

When Marsyas dreamed that he had cut Dionysius's throat, the tyrant put him to death, arguing that he would have never dreamt of such a thing by night, had he not thought of it by day.[187]

Capital Punishment and Draco's Law

The Laws of Draco affixed the penalty of death in almost all crimes alike, to petty thefts, for instance, as well as to sacrilege and murder; and the only explanation Draco is said to have given of that is, that minor offences deserve that penalty, and he could find no greater for more

---

186 Details not available on the Second Lahore Conspiracy Case, 1916
187 Dionysius the Elder (*c.* 430–367 BC), Greek political leader in Sicily, became the tyrant of Syracuse (406 BC) and resisted Carthage.

heinous. *Punishment* is thought by many philosophers to be a *necessary evil*.[188]

State and Man
The State is not really an end in itself and man is not here for the sake of Law or the State, but that these rather exist for man.[189]

Page 112

Justice
The maintenance of right within a political community by means of the physical force of the State.

It has replaced the personal vengeance, when men avenged their own wrongs by themselves or with the help of their kinsmen. In those days, the principle of 'Might is Right' worked.

Civil and Criminal Justice
Civil Justice enforces rights. Criminal justice punishes wrongs.

A man claims a debt that is due to him, or the restoration of property wrongfully detained from him. This is Civil. In a Criminal Case, the defendant is accused of a wrong. Court visits the accused with a penalty for the duty already disregarded and for a right already violated as where he is hanged for murder and imprisoned for theft.

Page 113

Both in civil and original proceedings, there is a *wrong* complained of

---

188 Draco (Dracon) 7th century BC, statesman of Athens who codified the previously unwritten laws. The word 'draconian' is derived from his name, since his laws were rather severe, with the death penalty for even minor offenses.

189 Unclear if this is a quote.

In civil it amounts to a claim of right;
In criminal it amounts nearly to an accusation of wrong
Civil justice is concerned primarily with the plaintiff and his rights;
Criminal with defendant and his offence.

The Purposes of Criminal Justice

Punishment
1. Deterrent: Chief end of the Law is to make the evil-doer an example and a warning to all that are like-minded with him. It makes every offence, *'an ill bargain to the offender.'* (Changing motive)

Then this cannot be useful in cases of disinterested 'offenders' such as politicals.

It can be an evil bargain for him!

2. Preventive: In the second place, it is preventive or disabling. Its special purpose is to prevent a repetition of wrongdoing by the disablement of the offender.

Justification of Capital Punishment
We hang murderers not merely that it may deter others, but for the same reason for which we kill snakes, namely because it is better for us that they should be out of the world than in it.

3. Reformative: Offences are committed through the influence of motives upon characters, and may be prevented either by a *change of motives* or *by a change of character*.

Deterrent punishment acts in the former event while *Reformative* deals with the second.[190]

Page 114

Advocates of 'Reformative theory' admit only such forms of penalty as are subservient to the education and discipline of the criminal, and reject all those which (are) profitable only as deterrent or disabling. Death is

---

190 Words unclear.

in their view no fitting penalty; *'we must cure our criminals not kill them.'* Flogging and other corporal punishments are condemned as relics of barbarism. Such penalties are considered by them to be degrading and brutalising both to those who suffer and to those who inflict them.

Result of severe punishment. Dangerous and desperate class of criminals springs up.

The more efficient the coercive action of the State, the more successful it is in restraining all normal human beings from the dangerous paths, and the higher becomes the proportion of degeneracy among those who break the law.

4. Retributive Punishment: The most horrible theory! People thinking in these terms are really maintaining the barbaric faculties of ancient and pre-civilisation times.

It gratifies the instinct of revenge or retaliation, which exists not merely in the individual wronged, but also by way of sympathetic extension in society at large.

According to this view, it is right and proper that evil should be returned for evil. An eye for an eye and a tooth for a tooth is deemed a plain and self-sufficient rule of natural justice. *Punishment becomes an end in itself.*[191]

Page 115

Punishment – an evil

Punishment is in itself an evil, and can be justified only as the means of attaining a greater good.

But the supporters of Retributive theory argue this way, 'Guilt plus punishment is equal to innocence.'

'The wrong whereby he has transgressed the law of right, has incurred a debt. Justice requires that the debt be paid … the first object of punishment is to satisfy the outraged law.'

Peine forte et dure: was death with torture … judgement for which was delivered as follows:

---

191 This page probably has Bhagat Singh's own comments.

'That you be taken back to the prison whence you came, to a long dungeon into which no light can enter; then you be laid on your back on the bare floor, with a cloth round your loins, but elsewhere naked, that there be set upon your body a weight of iron as great as you can bear, and greater; that you have no substance save, on the first day, the morsels of the coarsest bread; on the second day, three draughts of stagnant water from the pool nearest to the prison door; on the third day again three morsels of bread as before, and such bread and such water alternately from day to day until you die.'

This punishment was inflicted on people of both the sexes alike, for all sorts of offences not extraordinary.

Page 116

Foreign Subjugation
'Subjection to foreign yoke is one of the most potent causes of the decay of nations.'
Professor EA Ross[192]
Domination of a democracy and Foreign Nations
No rule over a foreign people is so exacting and so merciless in its operations as that of a democracy.
Lalaji[193]

---

192 Identity unclear. Lala Lajpat Rai quoted in *Unhappy India*
193 Lala Lajpat Rai (1865–1928), known for his radical leanings in the Indian National Congress along with his contemporaries Bal Gangadhar Tilak and Bipin Chandra Pal. Deported with Ajit Singh (Bhagat Singh's uncle) in 1907 to Mandalay (Burma) for his part in an agitation of canal settlers in the Canal Colonies. During his externment and extended visit to USA, he became a mentor to many Indians, including M.N. Roy; and authored *Arya Samaj* (1915), *Young India* (1917), and *National Education in India* (1917/20). Later wrote *Unhappy India* (1928) and *England's Debt to India: A Historical Narration of Britain's Fiscal Policy*.

Marriage

Dr Tagore holds that the marriage system all over the world – and not only in India – from the earliest ages till now, is a barrier in the way of the true union of man and woman, which is possible only when society shall be able to offer a large field for the creative work of woman's special faculty, without detracting in the creative work in the home.[194]

Page 117

Citizen and Man

The Spartan Pedarctes presented himself for admission to the council of the Three Hundred and was rejected; he went away rejoicing that there were 300 Spartans better than himself. I suppose he was in earnest, there is no reason to doubt it,

That was a citizen.

A Spartan mother had five sons with the army. A Helot arrived; trembling she asked his news. "Your five sons are slain."

"Vile slave, was that what I asked thee?"

"We have won the victory". She hastened to the temple to render thanks to the gods.

That was a citizen.

– p. 8, Emile

121. Novel by Jean Jacques Rousseau (1712-1778), French philosopher, regarded as founder of Romanticism. His book on political theory *The Social Contract* (1762) described an ideal state in which sovereignty vested with the people as a whole and individuals would retain freedom by submitting to the "general will". His novel *Emile* (1762) dealt with the theme of education. Also wrote his *Confessions* in several volumes.

Life and Education

People think only of preserving their child's life; this is not enough, he must be taught to preserve his own life when he is a man, to bear the

---

194 Tagore quoted in *Unhappy India*.

buffets of fortune, to brave wealth and poverty, to live at need among the snows of Iceland or on the scorching rocks of Malta. In vain you guard against death; he must die; and even if you do not kill him with your precautions, they are mistaken.

Teach him to live rather than to avoid death! Life is not breath, but action! The use of our senses, our mind, our faculties, every part of ourselves which makes us conscious of our being. Life consists less in length of days than in keen sense of living. A man may be buried at a hundred and may never have lived at all. He would have fared better had he died young.

p.10, Emile

Page 118

Truth

'Truth however does not lead to fortune, and the people confer neither embassies, nor professorships nor pensions.'
Rousseau[195]

Crime and Criminals

'... With readymade opinions one cannot judge of crime. Its philosophy is a little more complicated than people think. It is acknowledged that neither convict prisons, nor the hulks; nor any system of hard labour ever cured a criminal. These forms of chastisement only punish him and reassure society against the offences he might commit. Confinement, regulation, and excessive work have no effect but to develop with these men profound hatred, a thirst for forbidden enjoyment and frightful recalcitrations. On the other hand, I am convinced that the celebrated cellular system gives results, which are specious and deceitful. It deprives a criminal of his force of his energy, energates his soul by weakening and

---

195 Rousseau, *Social Contract* (1762). This quotation appears at the end of chapter 2.

frightening it, at last exhibits a dried up memory as a model of repentance and amendment.'

p.17, *The House of Dead,* Fyodor Dostoevsky[196]

⁓

Page 119

Desire vs. Contentment

A conscious being whose powers were equal to his desires would be perfectly happy ... The mere limitation of our desires is not enough, for if they were less than our powers, part of our faculties would be idle, and we should not enjoy our whole being, neither is the mere extension of our powers, enough, for if our desires were also increased, we should only be the more miserable.

True happiness consists in decreasing the difference between our desires and our powers.

p. 44, *Emile*

⁓

Page 120

Bourgeois revolution is germinated by the circumstance already existing in its predecessor regime.[197]

"The bourgeois revolution usually ends with the seizure of power. For the proletarian revolution the seizure of power is only a beginning; power, when seized, is used as a lever for the transformation of the old economy and for the organisation of a new one."

---

196 Fyodor Mikhailovich Dostoevsky (1821–81), is counted among the greatest Russian novelists. *The House of Dead* is a novel published in 1862, and is based on his own experience of spending four years in a Siberian prison.

197 Some of the following passages from Lenin are hard to trace. It is possible that some are in fact not exact quotations, but Bhagat Singh's paraphrasing of Lenin.

p. 20

"There still remain two gigantic and extremely difficult tasks – (even after the overthrow of the existing regime in one country – say Russia).

"First of all comes the internal organisation.

"The second crucial problem is that of the world revolution ... the need to solve international problems, the need to promote the world revolution– (without which communist regime cannot be quite safe from the international capitalist threat.)

p. 21–22

❦

Page 121

I. If the proletariat is to win over the majority of the population, it must first of all overthrow the bourgeoisie and seize the powers of the State.

II. Next, it must establish the Soviet authority breaking up the old State apparatus, and thus at one blow counteracting the influence which the bourgeoisie and the petty-bourgeoisie apostles of class collaboration exercise over the working (though non-proletariat) masses.

III. Thirdly, the proletariat must completely and finally destroy the influence which the bourgeoisie and petty-bourgeoisie compromisers exercise over the majority of the working (though non-proletarian) masses; it must do so by the revolutionary satisfaction of the economic needs of these masses at the cost of the exploiters.

p. 23, Nikolai Lenin[198]

"Dictatorship of the proletariat means the masses guided and directed by the Communist Party. Though party exercise substantial influence or control, still it is not all. Apart from its guidance, the "will" of the masses is necessary for the achievement of any particular object.

"We have to admit that the broad masses of the workers must be led and guided by the class conscious minority. And that is the Party. Party

---

198 Lenin, 'The Constituent Assembly Elections and the Dictatorship of the Proletariat', December 1919, *Collected Works*, volume 30.

has Trade Unions to link the Party with proletariat labour ... "Soviets" to link it with all the labouring masses in the political field, "Cooperatives" in the economic field

Page 122

especially to link the peasantry, "League of Youth" to train communists from amongst the rising generation. Finally, Party itself is the sole guiding force within the Dictatorship of the Proletariat.'

Page 123

Figures
Inequality of incomes:
Production:
Pre-war United Kingdom's (England's) annual production amounted to £ 2000,000,000
Gained through foreign investments £ 200,000,000
Total £ 2200,000,000

Distribution:
1/9th of the whole population i.e. capitalist or bourgeois took away 1/2 of the total production - i.e. £ 1100,000,000
(Least average income annual £ 160)

2/9th of the whole population i.e. petty bourgeoisie took away 1/3 of the remaining half or 1/6th of the whole - i.e. £ 300,000,000
(Average income less than £ 160 a year)

2/3rd of the population i.e. manual labour or proletariat got the rest - i.e.
£ 800,000,000
(Average income £ 60 yearly)

United States America: in 1890
40% of total production was received by the owners of means
60% of total production was given to all workers.[199]

Page 124

Aim of Life

'The aim of life is no more to control mind, but to develop it harmoniously, not to achieve salvation hereafter, but to make the best use of it here below, and not to realise truth, beauty and good only in contemplation, but also in the actual experience of daily life; social progress depends not upon the ennoblement of the few but on the enrichment of the many; and spiritual democracy or Universal Brotherhood can be achieved only when there is an equality of opportunity in the social, political and industrial life.'[200]

Page 165[201]

Science of the State:[202]

Ancient Polity; Rome and Sparta; Aristotle and Plato:

Subordination of the individual to the state was the dominant feature of these ancient polities, Sparta and Rome. In Hellas or in Rome, the citizen had but a few personal rights; his conduct was largely subject to public censorship, and his religion was imposed by State authority. The

---

199 Source not given.
200 Source of quotation unclear.
201 There are no page numbers from 125 to 164 in the notebook. In the next pages, we find an outline of Bhagat Singh's proposed study of Science and the State.
202 No source or reference has been indicated for this section. These appear to be Bhagat Singh's notes, rather than quotations.

only true citizens and member of the Sovereign body being an aristocratic caste of freemen, whose manual work is performed by slaves possessing no civil rights.

Socrates[203]

Socrates is represented as contending that whoever, after reaching man's estate, voluntarily remains in a city, should submit to the Govt. even when he deems its laws unjust; accordingly, on the ground that he would break his *covenant* with the State by escaping from prison into exile, he determines to await the execution of an unjust sentence.

Social Contract, Plato[204]

He traces the origin of society and the State to mutual need, for men as isolated beings are incapable of satisfying their manifold wants. He, while depicting a kind of idealised Sparta says, "In an ideal State, philosophers should rule; and to this aristocracy or government of the best, the body of citizens would owe implicit obedience." He emphasises on the careful training and education of citizens.

Aristotle[205]

He was the first to disentangle politics from ethics, though he was careful not to sever them. "The majority of men", he argued, "are ruled by their passions rather than by reason, and the State must therefore, train them to virtue by a life-long course of discipline, as in Sparta. Until political society is instituted, there is no administration of justice ... (but) it is necessary to enquire into the best constitution, and best system of legislation ...'

---

203 Socrates (*c.* 470–399 BC), Greek philosopher, tried and condemned for 'corrupting' the youth.

204 Plato (*c.* 427–347 BC), Greek philosopher, disciple of Socrates. Author of numerous works, and founder of the Assembly in Athens (387 BC) where Aristotle was a student.

205 Aristotle (384–322 BC), Greek philosopher, pupil of Plato and tutor of Alexander the Great. Works include *Metaphysics, Nicomachean Ethics, Politics and Poetics.*

Page 166

The germ of the State is found in the family or household. From the union of many households arose the village community ... members being subject to *patriarchal government*.

By the association of several villages *was formed the State*, a natural, independent, and self-sufficing organisation.

But while the household is ruled monarchically, in constitutional governments, the subjects are free and on equality with their rulers.

Natural sociability and mutual advantage implements union. Man is by nature a political (*social*) animal.

The State is much more than an alliance which individuals can join or leave without effect, for the independent or city-less man is unscrupulous and savage, something different from a citizen.

Plato: Plato had anticipated this conception of the State as a body whose members *combine harmoniously for a common end*.

Aristotle: Aristotle held that where freedom and equality prevail, there should be alternate rule and subjection, but it is best, if possible, that the same persons should always rule.

In opposition to *Plato's communism* he argued in favour of duly *regulated private property*, considering that only a moral unity is possible or desirable in the State.

Kinds of Government

He divided governments into monarchies, aristocracies, and republics and their respective perversions, tyrannies, oligarchies and democracies, according as the supreme power is in the hands of one or a few or the many, and according as the end is the general good or the private interests of the rulers, regard also being paid to freedom, wealth, culture and nobility.

Each polity consists of three parts: (1) the deliberative, (2) the executive, and (3) the judicial bodies. Citizenship is constituted neither by residence, nor by the possession of legal rights, but by participation in judicial power and public office.

The many, having attained a certain standard of morality, should rule, for though individually inferior, they are collectively wiser and more virtuous than a select few. But, while undertaking all deliberative and judicial functions, they should be excluded from the highest executive offices. The *best Polity* is that in which the middle class between the very rich and the very poor controls the govt., for that class has most permanent life, and is the most conformable to reason, as well as the most capable of constitutional action. This is virtually an affirmation that sovereignty should reside in the majority of the citizens, slaves of course being ignored.

Page 167

Democracies agree in being based on equality in respect of personal liberty, which implies the eligibility of all citizens to hold, or elect to the offices of State, and the rule of each over all and of all over each in turn.

Aristotle, like Plato, treated democracy as a debased form of Government, and held that it is more suitable to large states than any others.

Epicureans: "Justice", said Epicurus "is nothing in itself, but merely a compact (as the basis of justice) of expediency to prevent mutual injury."[206]

Stoic(ism): A disciple of the philosopher Zeno (340-260 BC) who opened his school in a colonnade called the 'Stoa Poikile' (painted porch) at Athens.[207]

Later Roman stoics were Cato the Younger,[208]

---

206 Epicurus (341–270 BC), Greek philosopher, founder of Epicureanism, and an atomic materialist.
207 Zeno of Citium (333–264 BC), Hellenistic Stoic philosopher, who believed that "tranquility can best be reached through indifference to pleasure and pain."
208 Mareus Porcius Cato (95–46 BC), known as Cato the Younger, Roman politician and statesman, a follower of Stoic philosophy.

Seneca,[209]
Marcus Aurelius[210]
The word stoic literally means 'one indifferent to pleasure or pain'.

Stoicism is a school of ancient philosophy strongly opposed to Epicureanism in its view of life and duty; indifferent to pleasure or pain.

Cynicism: A sect of philosophers founded by Antisthenes of Athens (born c.444 BC) characterised by an ostentatious contempt for riches, arts, science and amusements. They are called Cynics because of their morose manners.

Cynicism is sometimes used to denote the contempt for human nature.[211]

Epicureans: Epicurus (341-270 BC) was a Greek philosopher, who taught that pleasure was the chief good. Epicurean is used to denote one devoted to luxuries of the table or given to sensual enjoyment.

Page 168

Roman Polity

'Little of direct importance was added to political theory by the Romans, but in a closely allied department viz jurisprudence - they made contributions of deep interest and value.'

Jus Civik, Jus Gentium

---

209 Lucius Appaeus Seneca (*c.* 4 BC–AD 65) Roman writer and statesman, tutor of Nero, wrote essays on Stoicism, also wrote tragedies *Medea, Phaedra, Oedipus.*

210 Marcus Aurelius Antoninus, originally Marcus Annius Verus (AD 121–180), Roman philosopher, and Emperor (AD 161–180). Also wrote *Meditations*, a classic Stoic interpretation.

211 Antisthenes (*c.* 444–365 BC), founder of the cynic school of philosophy, studied rhetoric in his youth and came under influence of Socrates.

Under the Republic, there had grown up, beside the "Civil Law" (Jus Civik) a collection of rules and principles called Jus Gentium (Law of Nations), which represented the common features prevailing among the Italian tribes.

Jus Naturale

The great Roman juris-consults (experts in the science of Law) [deriving the idea from the Stoics] came gradually to identify the Law of Nature (Jus Naturale) with the Jus Gentium. They taught that this Law was divine and eternal, and that it was superior in majesty and validity to the laws of particular States. *Natural Law* was supposed to be actually existent and bound up with Civil Law.

In the Antonian Era, when Roman Law attained a high development and Stoic doctrines were most influential, the jurists formulated as juridical but not as political principles the maxims that:

"*all men were born free*" and that, by the Law of Nature, "*All men are equal*" – the implication being that although the Civil Law recognised class distinction, all mankind were equal before the Law of Nature.[212]

Social Contract in Roman Polity

Though the Roman jurists did not postulate a contract as the origin of Civil Society, but there is a tendency to deduce recognised rights and obligations from a supposed, but non-existent contract.

With regard to sovereignty, the citizens assembled in the Comitia Tributa exercised the supreme power during the golden days of the Republic.

Under the Empire, the sovereign authority was vested in the Emperor, and according to the later juris consults, the people, by the Lex Regia, delegated the supreme command to each Emperor at the beginning of his reign, thus conferring on him all their rights to govern and legislate.

---

212 After Antonius Pius (AD 86–161) Roman Emperor (AD 138–161). His reign was marked by peace and sound administration.

Page 169

Middle Ages

Thomas Aquinas: (1226-1274) is said to be the chief representative of the middle ages political theory. He following Roman jurists, recognised a natural law, the principles of which have been divinely implanted in human reason, together with positive laws that vary in different States.

He held that the legislative power, the essential attribute of sovereignty, should be directed to the common good, and that, for the attainment of this end, it should belong to the multitude or to their representative, the prince. A mixed government of monarch, nobles, and people, with the Pope as final authority, seemed to him the best.[213]

Marsilio of Padua (died in 1328)

Idea of Contract

In his *'Defensor Pacis'*, Marsilio of Padua advocated the doctrine of Popular Sovereignty, and combated the papal pretensions to temporal power that had been based on *the Falso Decretals*.[214]

Sovereignty of the People

Since men adopted civil life for their mutual advantage, the Laws ought to be made by the body of citizens; for laws are not likely to be the best possible, nor to be readily obeyed, unless enacted by those whose interests are directly affected and who know what they need.

He affirmed that the legislative power belongs to the people, and that the legislature should institute the executive, which it may also change or depose.

---

213 St. Thomas Aquinas (1225–1274) philosopher and theologian, whose major work was *Summa Theologiae* (1267–73). Bhagat Singh's given date is incorrect.

214 Marsilius of Padua (1270–1342), Italian political theorist, author of the extraordinary *Defensor Pacis*, on separation of Church and State, written for Emperor Louis IV in his struggle against the Pope. Bhagat Singh's given date is incorrect.

Renaissance – Reformation

In Renaissance, all departments of knowledge were vitalised and the circumscribed philosophy – having served as a hand-maid of theology for a thousand years, rapidly gave place to a new philosophy of *Nature and man*, more, liberal, more profound, and more comprehensive.

Bacon recalled man from metaphysics to nature and actuality.[215]

Philosophy must begin with universal scepticism. But one fact is soon found to be indubitable: The existence of a thinking principle in man. The existence of consciousness.

Cartesian Philosophy

The appeal to subjective conviction, to the authority of the individual, which was so strongly emphasised in the Reformation, thus becomes the very basic of Cartesian philosophy.

Cartesian: Relating to a French Philosopher Rene Descartes (1596–1650 AD) and his Philosophy.[216]

Page 170

New Period

After Reformation, the Papal authority having been shaken off, a wave of freedom swept minds of both the rulers and the people. But there was confusion.

To settle new situation, great many thinkers began to meditate over the question of State. Different schools grew up.

---

[215] Roger Bacon (*c.* 1214–1294), English scholar who placed considerable emphasis on empiricism, he was one of the earliest advocates of the modern scientific method in the West. Was imprisoned for heresy.

[216] René Descartes (1596–1650), French philosopher and mathematician, after whom is named the Cartesian school of philosophy, based on distinction between spirit and matter, as expressed in his dictum: "I think therefore, I am", in his *Discourse on Matter* (1673).

Machiavelli

Machiavelli, the famous Italian political thinker thought the Republican form of Government to be the best one, but doubting the stability of such a form of government, he inculcated maxims of securing a strong princely rule and hence he wrote *The Prince*.

His advocacy of centralised government had greatly affected political theory and practice in Europe.

Machiavelli was perhaps the first writer who treated "politics" from a purely secular point of view.[217]

Other Thinkers
Pact and Contract

Majority of others favoured the theory of pact or contract. (In Roman Law, a pact was the product of an agreement among individuals and fell short of a contract, which was a pact plus an obligation).

There were two different sects of these thinkers. The first one expounded the theory based on the Hebrew idea of covenant between God and man supplemented by the Roman idea of contract. It postulated a tacit contract between the government and the people.

The second or modern form, relates to the institution of Political Society by means of a compact among individuals. Prominent thinkers of this school were Hooker, Hobbes, Locke and Rousseau.[218]

Defenders of Popular Liberty

---

217 Niccolò di Bernardo dei Machiavelli (1467–1527), political philosopher, musician, poet, and romantic comedic playwright. A key figure of the Italian Renaissance, most widely known for his treatises on political theory (*The Prince*) and republicanism (*Discourses on Livy*).

218 John Locke (1632–1704), English philosopher, leading empiricist, social contract theorist and author of several influential works, including *Two Treatises on Government* (1689) and *An Essay Concerning Human Understanding* (1690).

Huguenot[219]

The *Vindiciae contra Tyrannos* (1579), ascribed to Huguenot Languet, contended that kings derive their power from the people's will, and that if a king violates the compact to observe the laws which he and the people promise conjointly at the institution of royalty, the latter are absolved from allegiance.[220]

Buchanan

(2) Buchanan also held that the king and people are mutually bound by a pact, and that its violation by the former entails forfeiture of his rights.[221]

Page 171

Jesuits[222]

---

219 In the 16th and 17th centuries, the name Huguenot was applied to a member of the Protestant Reformed Church of France, historically known as the French Calvinists.

220 Hubert Languet (1518–1581), French Huguenot, writer and diplomat. *Vindiciae contra tyrannos* which brought him fame, upheld the doctrine of resistance against tyranny, so long as it came from a properly constituted authority.

221 George Buchanan (1506–1582), Scottish historian and humanist scholar, author of *De Jure Regni apud Scales* (1579). In this work, composed in the form of a dialogue, Buchanan lays down the doctrine that the source of all political power is the people, that the king is bound by those conditions under which the supreme power was first committed to his hands, and that it is lawful to resist, even to punish, tyrants.

222 Jesuits are members of the Society of Jesus, a Catholic Religious Order founded by St. Ignatius Loyola in 1540. A mendicant order whose members rely on alms for their support, and seek the spiritual perfection of all humans.

(3) Even the Jesuits Bellarmine[223]

Juan de Mariana (1536-1624): Spanish historian and Jesuit. Went to Rome (1561) to teach theology, where Roberto Bellarmine was among his pupils. After service in Sicily, he was sent to Paris in 1569, where his exposition of Thomas Acquinas' writings drew attention. Returned to Spain in 1674. He considered it lawful to overthrow a tyrant andargued that kings derived their authority from the people, but they are subject to the Pope.

King James I (1609): James I admitted this theory in a speech to Parliament in 1609, saying that "every just king in a settled kingdom is bound to observe that paction made to his people by his laws, in framing his government agreeable there unto."[224]

Convention Parliament (1688)

Convention Parliament declared in 1688 that James II, "having endeavoured to subvert the constitution by breaking the original contract between the king and people", had rendered the throne vacant.[225]

'The first comprehensive political philosopher of modern times', Bodin, author of the *Republic* (1577 and 1586) says that '*force and not a contract is the origin of a commonwealth*'. Primitive patriarchal governments were overthrown by conquest and natural liberty was thus lost.

In his opinion "Sovereignty was the supreme power over citizens." He regarded "Sovereignty as independent, indivisible, perpetual, inalienable

---

223 Roberto Francesco Romolo Cardinal Bellarmine (Italian: Bellarmino) (1542– 1621), Italian theologian, entered the Society of Jesus in 1560, and was chosen in 1576 by the Pope to lecture on controversial theology in the new Roman College.

224 James I, King of England, Scotland, Wales and Ireland (1566–1625). He succeeded to the throne of Scotland (as James VI) on the abdication of his mother, Mary, Queen of Scots, and to the English throne on the death of Queen Elizabeth I. He was in conflict with the Parliament when he asserted the Divine Right of Kings. A scholar, earlier tutored by George Buchanan, he also wrote several books.

225 James II (1633 to 1701), King of England, Scotland, Wales and Ireland. He alienated his subjects by his pro-Catholic policies and assertion of arbitrary rule. Fled to France after the Glorious Revolution of 1688.

and absolute power." He confused his idea of sovereignty with the then existing kingship.[226]

Althusius (1557-1638)
He is notable for clearly asserting that sovereignty resides in the people alone.

Kings being only their magistrates or administrators; and that the sovereign rights of the community are inalienable.[227]

Grotius (1625)
In his work, *De Jure Belli et Paris* (1628), Grotius holds that man has a strong desire for a peaceable and ordered society. But he inculcates the theory of non-resistance and denies that the people are always and everywhere sovereign, or that all government is established for the sake of the governed.

Sovereignty arises either from conquest or from consent; but he lays emphasis on the idea that sovereign is the indivisible power.

Hugo Grotius (1583-1645), Dutch jurist and statesman, laid the foundations for international law.

Hooker
He, in his *Ecclesiastical Polity* – Book I (1592-3), postulates an original state of nature in which all men were equal and subject to no Law. Desire for a life suitable to man's dignity, and aversion to solitude, impelled then to unite in 'politic societies'. 'Natural inclination' and an order expressly or secretly agreed upon touching the manner of their union in living together, were the two foundations of the present 'politic societies'. It is the latter that we call 'the Laws of a Commonwealth'.

---

[226] Jean Bodin (1530-1596), French philosopher, author of *Six Livres da la Republique* (1956), advocated that the power of the sovereign should be modified by a democratic parliament.

[227] Johannes Althusius (1557-1638), a Calvinist philosopher and theologian. Often considered the intellectual father of modern federalism and an advocate of popular sovereignty.

Page 172

Origin of State

Sovereignty: Legislative power controlling the Executive as well 'To take away all mutual grievance, injuries and wrongs, the only way was to ordain some kind of government, or common judge'. He admitted with Aristotle that the origin of government was in kingship. But he says 'Laws not only teach what is good, but also have a constraining force, derived from the consent of the governed, expressed either personally or through representatives'.

'Laws human of what kind so ever, are available (i.e., valid) by consent'. 'Laws they are not which public approbation hath not made so.'

Sovereignty of the people

Thus he clearly affirmed that sovereignty or legislative power resides ultimately in the people.

1620: Famous Declaration of the "Pilgrim Fathers" on board the Mayflower

(1620): "We do solemnly and mutually in the Presence of God and of one another covenant and combine ourselves together into a civil Body Politic."[228]

1647: The Agree of the People of England: (another famous Puritan document, which emanated from the Army of the Parliament) (1647) also indicates the same tendency of mind.

1649: Milton: In his *Tenure of Kings and Magistrates* (1649), also propounds similar principles. He affirms that "all men naturally were born free". They "agreed by common league to bind each other from mutual injury and jointly to defend themselves against any that gave disturbance or opposition to such agreement. Hence came towns, cities and commonwealths! This authority and power of self-defence and preservation being originally and naturally in every one of them and

---

228 Pilgrim Fathers (1620), a group of Puritan objectors in the Church of England who sailed away in the Mayflower to escape persecution and settle in North America.

unitedly in all, was vested, in kings and magistrates as deputies and commissioners!

"The Power of kings and magistrates is nothing else but what is only derivative, transferred, and committed to them in trust from the people to the common good of all, *in whom the power yet remain(s) fundamentally* and cannot be taken from them without a violation of their natural birth-right.

'Hence nations may choose or depose kings, merely by the right and liberty of freeborn men to be governed as seems them best.'[229]

Page 173

Theory of Divine Rights of Kings

[Patriarchal Theory]

In this very age when great many thinkers were thus propounding these principles of 'Sovereignty of the People', there were other theorists, who tried to prove that kingdom(s) being enlarged families, the patriarchal authority of the head of a household was transferred by primogenitary descent to the representative of the first sovereign who could be proved to have reigned over any nation. Monarchy was therefore presumed to rest on an indefeasible right, and the king was held responsible to God alone! This was known as *'Divine Rights of Kings!'* This was known as the 'Patriarchal Theory!'[230]

Thomas Hobbes: In his various works written in 1642, 1650, 1651, he combined the doctrine of the unlimited authority of the sovereign, with

---

229 John Milton (1608–74), English poet who wrote great epics in blank verse like *Paradise Lost* (1667) and *Paradise Regained* (1671) despite having become blind after 1652. During the Protectorate (1653 onwards) he acted as Oliver Cromwell's Latin secretary.

230 In all likelihood, these are not quotations, but Bhagat Singh's own observations.

the rival doctrine of an original compact of the people. Hobbes' defence of absolutism – passive obedience – was secular and rationalistic rather than theological. He regarded the happiness of the community (as a whole) as the great end of government.

Man an unsociable animal!
Perpetual danger forces them to form state!

Hobbes' philosophy is cynical. According to him a man's impulses are naturally directed to his own preservation and pleasure and he cannot aim at anything but their gratification. Therefore man is unsociable by nature! He says in the natural state every man is at war with his fellows; and the life of everyone is in danger, solitary, poor, unsafe brutish and short.' It is the fear of this sort of life that impelled them to political union. Since mere pact wouldn't do, hence the establishment of supreme common power the government.'[231]

'Conquest' or 'acquisition' and 'institution' the only basis of all states
Society is founded by 'acquisition', i.e., by conquest or 'institution' viz. By mutual contract or compact. In the latter case once the sovereign authority is established all must obey. Anybody rebelling must perish. He should be destroyed.

Unlimited Authority of the Sovereign!
He gives the rights of Legislature, Judicature and Executive – one and all to the sovereign. To be effective, he writes, 'the sovereign power must be unlimited, irreclaimable and indivisible. Unlimited power may indeed give rise to mischief, but the worst of these is not so bad as civil war or anarchism.'

---

231 While the second part of the quote is from *Leviathan*, the first is Bhagat Singh's (or someone else's) paraphrasing. The *Leviathan* itself does not contain these words.

Page 174[232]

In his opinion, monarchy, aristocracy or democracy do not differ in their power. Their achievement towards general plan and security rests on the obedience of the public or people they command. Anyhow he prefers 'Monarchy'! 'Limited Monarchy' is the best in his opinion. But he prefers [?] that the sovereign must regulate ecclesiastical as well as civil affairs and determine what doctrines are conducive to peace.

Thus he holds a clear and valid doctrine of sovereignty, while retaining the fiction of a social contract to generate the King or Sovereign.

Spinoza (1677)
'Unsociability of man!'
In his work *Tractatus Politicus*, 1677, regarded men as originally having equal rights over all things; hence the state of nature was a State of War.

Men, led by their reasons, freely combined their forces to establish Civil Government. As man had absolute power, hence the Sovereign authority thus established had the absolute power. In his opinion, 'Right' and 'Power' are identical. Hence, the sovereign being rested with the 'power' had all the 'rights' ipso facto. Hence he favours 'absolutism'.[233]

Puffendorf
Of the Law of Nature and Nations (1672). In his opinion man is a sociable animal, naturally inclined towards family and peaceful life.

Experience of injuries that one man can inflict on another leads upto Civil Government, which is constituted (1): by a unanimous mutual covenant of a number of men to institute a Common wealth, (2) by the resolution of the majority that certain ruler shall be placed in authority,

---

232 Page 174 has a line on top, which is illegible and presumably a continuation of this line.

233 Benedictus de Spinoza or Baruch de Spinoza (1632–1677), Dutch philosopher of Jewish origin, one of the great rationalists of 17th-century philosophy and, by virtue of his magnum opus *Ethics*, one of the definitive ethicists. Considered to have laid the groundwork for the 18th-century Enlightenment.

(3) by a covenant between the Government and the subjects that the former shall rule and the latter shall obey lawful commands!²³⁴

Page 175

Locke

Two Treatises of Civil Government – 1690
'No man has a natural right to govern.'
He portrays the state of nature – a state of freedom and equality in respect of jurisdiction and dominion, limited only by natural law or reason, which prohibits men from harming one another in life, health, liberty and possessions, the punishment requisite by way of restraint or reparation being in everyman's hands.

State of Nature
"Men living together according to reason without a common superior on earth with authority to judge between them is properly the State of Nature!"

Private Property
'Every man has a natural right of property in his own person and in the product of his own labour exercised on the material of nature. As much land as a man tills, plants, improves, cultivates, and can use the product of, so much is his property.'

Property and Civil Society
According to him 'property' is antecedent to 'civil society'!

---

234 Baron Samuel von Pufendorf (1632–1694), German jurist, political philosopher, economist, statesman, and historian. Wrote commentaries and revisions of the theories of Thomas Hobbes and Hugo Grotius. Bhagat Singh misspells his name, with 'ff'.

Origin of Civil Society

But it appears men were in some sort of dangers and fears, and therefore, they renounced their natural liberty in favour of civil liberty. In short, necessity, convenience, and inclination urged men into society.

Definition of Civil Society

Those who are united into one body, and have a common established Law and judicature to appeal to, with authority to decide controversies between them and punish offenders, are in a civil society.

Consent

Conquest is not an 'original' of government. Consent was, and could be the sole origin of any lawful government.

The legislature assembly is not absolutely arbitrary over the lives, liberties and property of the people, for it possesses only the joint power which the separate members had prior to the formation of the Society, and which they resigned to it for particular and limited purposes.

Law

'The end of Law is not to abolish or restrain but to preserve or enlarge freedom.'

Legislative

The legislative being only a fiduciary power for certain ends, the people may remove or alter it, when it violates the trust reposed in it.

Ultimate Sovereignty of the People!

Thus the community always retains the supreme power or ultimate sovereignty, but does not assume it until the government is dissolved.

Page 176

Legislative and Executive

To prevent the sacrifice of the general welfare to private interests, it is expedient that the legislative and executive powers should be in different hands, latter being subordinate to the former.

Where both powers are vested in an absolute monarch, there is no civil government, for there is no common judge with authority between him and his subjects.

The forms of different commonwealths in free societies are Democracy, oligarchy, or elective Monarchies together with mixed forms.

'Right of Revolution'!

'A Revolution is justifiable when the government ceases to fulfil its part of contract – the protection of personal rights.'

Rousseau[235]
Equality

No one should be rich enough to buy another nor poor enough to be forced to sell himself. Great inequalities pave the way for tyranny.

Property and Civil Society

The first man who, having enclosed a piece of land, thought of saying 'this is mine', and found people simple enough, to believe him, was the true founder of Civil Society.

What wars, crimes, and horrors would have been spared to the race, if someone had exposed this imposture, and declared that the earth belonged to no one, and its fruits to all.

Page 177

"The man who meditates is a depraved animal"

---

235 The following are Bhagat Singh's notes from Rousseau's *Social Contract*.

Civil Law

Pointing to the oppression of the weak and the insecurity of all, the rich craftily devised rules of justice and peace, by which all should be guaranteed their possessions, and established a Supreme ruler to enforce the Laws.

This must have been the origin of Society and of the Laws, which gave new chains to the weak and new strength to the rich, finally destroyed natural liberty, and, for the profit of a few ambitious men, fixed for ever the law of property and of inequality, converted a clever usurpation into an irrevocable right, and subjected the whole human race hence-forward to labour, servitude and misery.

Re: Inequalities

But it is manifestly opposed to natural law that a handful of people should gorge superfluities while the famished multitude lack the necessities of life.

Page 178

Fate of his Writings

Emile and *Social Contract*, both published in 1762, the former burnt in Paris, Rousseau narrowly escaping arrest, then both being publically burnt in Genoa, his native place whence he expected greater response.

Sovereignty of Monarch to that of the People

Rousseau retains the French ideas of unity and centralisation; but while in the seventeenth century, the State (or sovereignty) was confounded with the monarchy. Rousseau's influence caused it in the 18th Century to be identified with the people.

Pact

By pact men exchange natural liberty for civil liberty and moral liberty.

Right of First Occupancy
Right of Property:

Its justification depends on these conditions: (a) that the land is uninhabited; (b) that a man occupies only the area required for his subsistence; (c) that he takes possession of it not by an empty ceremonial, but by labour and cultivation.

Page 179

Religion
Rousseau places even religion under the tyranny of the sovereign.

Introductory Note
I wish to enquire whether, taking men as they are and laws as they can be made, it is possible to establish some just and certain rule of administration in civil affairs...

... I shall be asked whether I am a prince or a legislator that I write on politics. I reply that I am not. If I were one, I should not waste time in saying what ought to be done; I should do it or remain silent.

Man is born free, and everywhere he is in chains.

Shaking off the Yoke of Slavery by Force
I should say that so long as a people is compelled to obey and does obey, it does well; but that, so soon as it can shake off the yoke and does shake it off, it does better; for, if men recover their freedom by virtue of the same right (i.e., force) by which it was taken away, either they are justified in resuming it, or there was no justification for depriving them of it.

Page 180

Force
"Power which is acquired by violence is only a usurpation, and lasts only so long as the force of him who commands prevails over that of those

who obey; so that if the latter become the strongest in their turn and shake off the yoke, they do so with as much right and justice as the other who had imposed it on them. The same law (of force) which has made the authority then unmakes it; it is the law of the strongest."

– *Encyclopaedia*, Diderot[236]

"Authority"

Slaves lose everything in their bonds, even the desire to escape from them.[237]

The Right of the Strongest

'Obey the powers that be. If that means, yield to force, the precept is good but superfluous; I reply that it will never be violated.'[238]

Right of Slavery

'Do subjects, then, give up their persons on condition that their property also shall be taken? I do not see what is left for them?'

'It will be said that the despot secures to his subjects civil peace. Be it so; but what do they gain by that, if the wars which his ambitions bring upon them, together with his insatiable greed and the vexations of his administration, harass them more than their own dissensions would?'[239]

Page 181

To say that a man gives himself for nothing is to say what is absurd and inconceivable.

---

236 Denis Diderot (1713–84), French philosopher and Chief Editor of *Encyclopaedia*. He also wrote the first French 'bourgeois' drama, *Le Neveu de Rameau*. He was anti-clerical and was imprisoned because of his works like *Lettres sur les Aveugeles* (1749).
237 Rousseau, *Social Contract*, chapter 2, 'The First Societies'.
238 Rousseau, *Social Contract*, chapter 3, 'The Right of the Strongest'.
239 Rousseau, *Social Contract*, chapter 4, 'Slavery'.

Whether addressed by a man to a man, or by man to a nation, such a speech as this will always be equally foolish: 'I make an agreement with you wholly at your expense and wholly for my benefit, and I shall observe it as long as I please, while you also shall observe it as long as I please.'

Equality

If then you wish to give stability to the State, bring the two extremes as near together as possible; tolerate neither rich nor beggars. These two conditions, naturally inseparable, are equally fatal to the general welfare; from the one class spring tyrants, from the other, the supporters of tyranny; it is always between these that the traffic in public liberty is carried on; the one buys the other sells.

Page 182

'Hail lays waste a few cantons, but it rarely causes scarcity. Riots and civil wars greatly startle the chief men; but they do not produce the real misfortunes of nations, which may be abated, while it is being disputed who shall tyrannise over them. It is from their permanent conditions that their real prosperity or calamities spring; when all is left crushed under the yoke, it is then that everything perishes; it is then that the chief men, destroying them at their leisure, where they make a solitude, they call it peace.'

p. 176

Page 183

French Revolution[240]

---

240 It is not clear which book, if any, on the French Revolution had reached Bhagat Singh's hands. It is however apparent from his notes that he was more interested in the conflict between the authority of the King or the

America

American war of Independence had great effect on the French situation (1776).

Taxes

Court or ministry acting under the use of the name 'The King', framed the edicts of taxes at their own discretion and sent them to the Parliament to be registered; for until they were registered by the Parliament, they were not operative.[241]

The court insisted that the Parliament's authority went no further than to show reasons against it, reserving to itself the right of determining whether the reasons were well or ill founded and, in consequence thereof, either to withdraw the edict as a matter of choice, or to order it to be enregistered as a matter of authority.

The Parliament, on the other hand, insisted for having the right of rejection.

M. Calonne.[242]

---

old regime on one hand and the new 'popular' forces which appeared on the scene to challenge that authority. Also, Bhagat Singh did not seem to have much time at his disposal for a more serious or in-depth study of all the events. His notes seem to be cursory but factual. Perhaps he was conscious that time was running out.

241 *Parlement* was a body of the King's counsellors, not an elected body as today. Under pressure from the nobles and in a mood of appeasement, King Louis XVI had restored the 'dormant' parlement in 1776.

242 Charles Alexandre de Calonne (1734–1802), French statesman, who became controller-general of finance (1783). The State coffers being empty, he sought to raise loans but the parliament resisted. He then proposed to the King to suppress internal customs and duties, and tax notables and the clergy. An 'Assembly of Notables' was called in January 1787, but his proposal to curtail their privileges was opposed. He was dismissed, and went to England in exile; only allowed to return to Paris in 1802, he died soon after.

It was not a States-General which was elected, but all the members were nominated by the King and consisted of 141 members. Even then he could not get the majority support. He divided it into 7 committees. Every committee consisting of 20 members. Every question was to be decided by majority votes in committees and by majority committee votes in Assembly. He tried to have 11 members whom he could trust in each of/any four committees, thus to have a majority. But his devices failed.

Page 184

M. de Lafayatte was Vice President of a second committee. He charged M. Calonne for having sold crown land to the amount of two millions of livres. He gave it in writing too. Sometimes afterwards, M. Calonne was dismissed.[243]

The Archbishop of Toulouse was appointed the Prime Minister and Finance Minister. He placed before the Parliament two taxes - Stamp Tax and a sort of land tax. The Parliament returned for answer, That with such a revenue as the nation then supported, the name of taxes ought not to be mentioned but for the purpose of reducing them and threw both the edicts out. Then they were ordered to Versailles, where the King held, 'A Bed of Justice' and enregistered those edicts. Parliament returned to Paris. Held a session there. Ordered the enregistration to be struck off. Declaring everything done at Versailles to be illegal. All were served with 'letter de cachets' and exiled. And afterwards they were recalled. Again the same edicts were placed before them.

---

243 Marie-Joseph-Paul-Yves-Roch-Gilbert Du Motier, Marquis de La Fayette (or Lafayette) (1757–1834), French aristocrat and military officer. La Fayette is considered a national hero in both France and the United States for his participation in the American and French revolutions.

Page 185

Then arose the question of calling a States-General. The King promised with the Parliament. But ministry opposed. They put forth a new proposal for the formation of a 'Full Court'. It was opposed on two grounds: Firstly, for principle's sake, government had no right to change itself. Such a precedent will be harmful. Secondly, on the question of form; it was contended that it was nothing but an enlarged Cabinet.

The Parliament rejected this proposal. It was besieged by armed forces. For many days, they were there. Still they persisted. Then many of them were arrested and sent to different jails.

A deputation from Brittany came to remonstrate against it. They were sent to Bastille.

'Assembly of Notables' again recalled, decided to follow the same course as adopted in 1614 to call States General.

Parliament decided that 1200 members should be elected, 600 from commons, 300 from clergy and 300 from nobility.

States General met in May 1789. Nobility and clergy went to two different chambers.[244]

Page 186

The third estate or the Commons refused to recognise this right of the clergy and nobility and declared themselves to be the 'Representatives of the Nation' denying the others any right whatsoever in any other capacity than the national representatives sitting along with them in the same chamber. Hence the States General became the 'National Assembly'. They sent invitations to the other chamber. Majority of Clergy came over to

---

244 States-General met in May 1789, after a long gap of nearly 175 years (since after 1614). King Louis XVI was compelled to call the representatives of the nobility, the clergy and the bourgeoisie because of the bankruptcy of his treasury.

them. 45 of the aristocracy also joined them; then their number increased to eighty and afterwards still higher.[245]

Page 187

Tennis Court Oath

The malcontents of Nobility and Clergy wanted to overthrow the National Assembly. They conspired with the ministry. The doors of the chamber were shut in the face of the 'Representatives of the Nation' and were guarded by militia.

They then proceeded to a tennis court in a body, and took an oath never to separate until they had established a constitution.

Bastille

The next day the chamber was again thrown open to them. But secretly thirty thousand troops were mobilised to besiege Paris. The unarmed Parisian Mob attacked Bastille; and Bastille was taken.

14 July 1789

Versailles

5 October 1789 – Thousands of men and women proceeded towards Versailles to demand satisfaction from 'Garde du Corps' for their insolent behaviour in connection with national cockade. It is known as Versailles expedition. As a result of further developments, the King was brought to Paris. Members each of the first two ranks and twice the number of the third category attended. It soon became the epicentre of a new kind of political struggle, popular representatives grabbing the initiative and then setting the course of future events.

The storming of the Bastille, the much-hated symbol of tyranny and oppression, on July 14, was one such expression of the people's mood, as

---

[245] As these extracts show, Bhagat Singh was keenly interested in how the people's representatives came to influence the course of the Revolution.

was the march of Paris citizens on Versailles, and the enforced return of the King and his retinue, as their hostages.

Page 188

The wisdom of every country when properly exerted, is sufficient for all its purposes.
p. 112, *Rights of Man*[246]
House of Lords. Minister Earl of Shelburne[247]

Page 189

King:
If there existed a man so transcendently wise above all others, that his wisdom was necessary to instruct a nation, some reason might be offered for monarchy; but when we cast our eyes about a country and observe how every part understands its own affairs; and when we look around the world and see that, of all men in it, the race of kings are the most insignificant in capacity, our reason fails to ask us – What are these men kept for?

Libeller
'If to expose the fraud and imposition of monarchy and every species of hereditary government to lessen the oppression of taxes – to propose plans for the education of helpless infancy, and the comfortable support of the aged and distressed – to endeavour to conciliate nations to each

---

246 This, and the following quotes, are from *The Rights of Man* by Thomas Paine. Some of the earlier notes on French Revolution also seem to be taken from *The Rights of Man*.
247 It is hard to say why this name is written here, since the preceding quote is from Paine. Paine may have quoted this name.

other – to extirpate the horrid practice of war – to promote universal peace, civilisation and commerce – and to break the chains of political superstition, and raise degraded man to his proper rank – if these things be libellous, let me live the life of a libeller, and let the name of "Libeller" be engraven on my tomb.'

Xi[248]

Page 190

But when principle and not place, is the energetic cause of action, a man, I find, is everywhere the same.

Death
If we were immortal we should all be miserable; no doubt it is hard to die, but is sweet to think that we shall not live for ever.
p. 45, *Emile*[249]

Socialistic Order
'From each according to his ability, to each according to his need.'
Karl Marx, from *Critique of Gotha Programme*
Audacity is the soul of success in Revolution.
'Action, Action. Power first discussion afterwards,' said Danton.[250]

---

248 From Thomas Paine.
249 *Emile,* Rousseau.
250 George Jacques Danton (1759–94), French revolutionary, drawn to liberal, republican ideas after he came to Paris (1780) to study law. He became a powerful orator and one of the leaders of the radical Cordeliers group during the early phases of the Revolution. He helped organize the overthrow of the monarchy (1792); became head of the Provisional Government, and set up the Committee of Public Safety (1793) which became an instrument of 'revolutionary terror'.

Page 191

Russian Experiment[251]
1917-27

The philosophy of the Bolsheviks is utterly, aggressively materialistic, whose one redeeming feature even their bitterest enemies will have to recognise, viz. the utter absence of any illusion.

They held firmly to the faith of their founder that 'Everything can be explained by natural laws or, in a narrower sense, by Physiology!'
p. 30[252]

1. *Face and Mind of Bolshevism* by Rene Fulop-Miller[253]
Fulop-Miller's dates are 1891–1963.
2. *Russia* by Makeev-O' Hara
3. *Russian Revolution* by Lancelot Lawton[254] (Macmillan)
4. *Bolshevist Russia* by Anton Karlgreen[255]
5. *Literature and Revolution* by Trotsky
6. *Marx-Lenin and Science of Revolution* by Anton Karlgreen[256]

"Philosophers," said Marx, "have merely interpreted the world in many ways; the really important thing is to change it."

---

251 It is unclear if this refers to a book or not. Some books are listed on this page. It is not certain how much time he got to read these. At any rate, the notes are now somewhat less detailed.

252 Source of this quotation unclear. Could be from one of the books mentioned next.

253 Subtitle of the book: 'An Examination of Cultural Life in Soviet Russia', published in 1927.

254 Subtitle of the book: '1917–1926', published in 1927.

255 Translated from Swedish by Anna Barwell, published in 1927. Karlgreen lived between 1882–1973.

256 Further details not available.

Page 192

Religion and Socialism
"Religion is opium for mankind" said Marx.

"All idealistic considerations lead in the end to a kind of conception of Divinity, and are, therefore, pure non-sense in the eyes of Marxists. Even Hegel saw in God the concrete form of everything good and reasonable that rules the world; the idealist theory must put everything on the shoulders of this unfortunate grey beard, who, according to the teachings of his worshippers, is perfect, and who, in addition to Adam, created fleas and harlots, murderers and lepers, hunger and misery, plague and vodka, in order to punish the sinners whom he himself had created, and who sin in accordance with his will

... From the scientific standpoint, this theory leads to absurdity. The only scientific explanation of all the phenomenon of the world is supplied by absolute materialism.

p. 32, Bukharin[257]

According to them, in the beginning, Nature; from it, life; and from life, thought and all the manifestations we call mental or moral phenomenon. There is no such thing as Soul, and Mind is nothing but a function of matter, organised in a particular way.

p. 33[258]

Page 193

Marx on Insurrection
Firstly: "Never play with insurrection, if there is no determination to drive it to the bitter end (literally - to face all the consequence of this play). An insurrection is an equation with very indefinite magnitudes,

---

257 Bukharin, quoted by Rene Fulop-Miller, *The Mind and Face of Bolshevism*, p.53.
258 Source unclear. Possibly from one of the books referred to above.

the value of which may change every day. The forces to be opposed have all the advantages of organisation, discipline and traditional authority.

"If the rebels cannot bring great forces to bear against their antagonists, they will be smashed and destroyed."

Secondly: "The insurrection once started, it is necessary to act with the utmost determination and pass over to the offensive. The defensive is the death of every armed rising; it perishes before it has measured forces with the enemy. The antagonists must be surprised while their soldiers are still scattered, and new successes, however small, must be attained daily; the moral ascendancy given by the first success, must be kept up. One must rally to the side of insurrection the vacillating elements, which always follow the stronger, and which always look out for the safer side ... In one word, act according to the words of Danton – the greatest master of Revolutionary policy yet known – Audacity ... audacity ... and yet again audacity!"[259]

Page numbers 194 to 272 in the notebook are blank. The *Jail Notebook* mainly contains quotes and extracts from the books read by Bhagat Singh. Only from page number 165 to 193 are Bhagat Singh's own personal notes on his projected study of 'The Science of the State'. Had he got the chance to complete his project, it could have been a major contribution to Marxist theory!

Page 273

"... Do you want an expansion of the Legislative Councils? Do you want that a few Indians shall sit as your representatives in the House of Commons?

---

259 It is unclear why Bhagat Singh attributes the above quotes to Marx. They are from Frederick Engels' *Revolution and Counter-Revolution in Germany*, 1852. Many of Marx and Engels writings have great similarity, possibly Marx was quoted in some other book, from where Bhagat Singh noted this quotation.

Do you want a large number of Indians in the Civil Service? Let us see whether 50, 100, 200 or 300 civilians will make the government our own ... The whole Civil Service might be Indian, but the civil servants have to carry out orders – they cannot direct, they cannot dictate the policy. One swallow does not make the summer. One civilian, 100 or 1000 civilians in the service of the British Government will not make the government Indian. There are traditions, there are laws, there are policies to which every civilian, be he black or brown or white, must submit; and as long as these traditions have not been altered, as long as these principles have not been amended, as long as that policy has not been radically changed, the supplanting of Europeans by Indian agency will not make for self-government in this country ...

'If the Government were to come and tell me today. "Take Swaraj", I would say thank you for the gift, but I will not have that which I cannot acquire by my own hand ...

'We shall in the imperative compel the submission to our will of any power that may set itself against us.

'... The Primary thing is the prestige of the Government.'

Page 274

Is really self-government within the Empire a practicable ideal? What would it mean? It would mean either no real self-government for us, or no real overlordship for England. Would we be satisfied with the shadow of self-government?

If not, would England be satisfied with the shadow of overlordship?

In either case, England would not be satisfied with a shadowy, overlordship, and we refuse to be satisfied with a shadowy self-government. And, therefore, no compromise is possible under such conditions between self-government in India and the over-lordship of England ... If self-government – (real) – is conceded to us, what would be England's position not only in India, but in British Empire itself? Self-government means the right of self-taxation; it means the right of self-control; it means the right of the people to impose protective and prohibitive tariffs on foreign imports. The moment we have the right of self-taxation, what shall we do? We shall not try to be engaged in this uphill work of industrial boycott. But we shall do what every nation has done. Under the circumstances in which we live now, we shall impose a heavy, prohibitive, protective tariff upon every inch of textile fabric from Manchester, upon every blade of knife that comes from Leeds. We shall refuse to grant admittance to a British soul into our territory. We would not allow British capital to be engaged in the development of Indian resources, as it is now engaged. We would not grant any right to the British capitalists to dig up the mineral wealth of the land and to carry it to their own isles. We shall want foreign capital. But we shall apply for foreign loans in the open markets of the whole world, guaranteeing the credit of the Indian Government, the Indian Nation, for the repayment of the loan ... And England's commercial interests would not be furthered in the way these are being furthered now, under the condition of

Page 275

Popular self-government, though it might be within the Empire. But what would it mean within the Empire? It would mean that England would have to enter into some arrangements with us for some preferential tariff. England would have to come to our markets on the conditions that we would impose upon her for the purpose, if she wanted an open door in India; and after a while, when we have developed our resources a little and organised our industrial life, we would want the open door not only to England, but to every part of British Empire. And do you think, it is possible for a small country like England with a handful of population, although she might be enormously wealthy, to compete on fair and equitable terms with a mighty continent like India with immense natural resources, with her teeming population, the soberest and abstemious population known to any part of the world?

If we have really self-government within the Empire, if 300 millions of people have that freedom of the Empire, the Empire would cease to be British.

It would be the Indian Empire ...
New Spirit, Bipin Chandra Pal[260]

Page 276

Hindu Civilization

It may seem to us to present in many of its aspects an almost unthinkable combination of spiritualistic idealism and of gross materialism, of asceticism and of sensuousness, of overweening arrogance when it identifies the human self with the universal self and merges man in the Divinity and the Divinity in man, and of demoralising pessimism when it preaches that life itself is but a painful allusion and that the sovereign remedy and end of all evils is nonexistence.

p.26, *Indian Unrest*, Chirol[261]

Education Policy

The main original object of the introduction of Western Education into India was the training of a sufficient number of young Indians to fill the sub-ordinate posts in the public offices with English-speaking natives.

p. 34

193. Valentine Chirol, *Indian Unrest*.

---

260 Bipin Chandra Pal (1858–1932), first came to the forefront in the Swadeshi and boycott campaigns in Bengal and outside, in the wake of the popular upsurge against the Partition of Bengal (1905). He was associated with the 'extremist' trio of Pal, Bal and Lal. A journalist of repute, he was the editor of *New India* (1901) and *Bande Mataram* (1906); also edited *Swaraj* from London for some time.

261 Sir Valentine Chirol (1858–1929), journalist and author of *Indian Unrest* and *India Old and New*. Was in charge of the *Times* foreign Department from 1890 to 1912, besides being a member of the Indian Public Service Commission (1912– 1914).

Page 277

How many of the Western educated Indians who have thrown themselves into political agitation against the tyranny of the British bureaucracy have ever raised a finger to free their own fellow countrymen from the tyranny of those social evils? How many of them are entirely free from it themselves, or, if free, have the courage to act up to their opinion?
p. 107, India Old & New
194. Valentine Chirol, *India Old and New*.

Page 278

No Indian Parliament Conceivable!
The Indian National Congress assumed unto itself, almost from the beginning, the function of a Parliament. There was and is no room for a Parliament in India, because, so long as British rule remains a reality, the Government of India, as Lord Mosley has plainly stated, must be an autocracy – benevolent and full of sympathy with Indian ideas, but still an autocracy.
p.154, *Indian Unrest*, Valentine Chirol[262]

Aim or Goal of the Congress
"The objects of the Indian National Congress are the attainment by the people of India of a system of government similar to that enjoyed by the self-government members of the British Empire and a participation by them in the rights and responsibilities of the Empire on equal terms."
Malviyaji from the Chair, Lahore Session of the Congress, 1909

---

262 Valentine Chirol, *Indian Unrest*. This book is referred to again and again by Bhagat Singh, from page 273/130 onwards.

Page 279

Re. Constitution of Free India

No one but the voice of the Mother herself will and can determine when once she comes to herself and stands free what constitution shall be adopted by Her for the guidance of Her life after the revolution is over ... Without going into detail we may mention this much, that whether the head of the Imperial Government of the Indian Nation be a President or a King depends upon how the revolution develops itself ... The mother must be free, must be one and united, must make her will supreme. Then it may be that she gives out this

Her will either wearing a kingly crown on her head or a Republican mantle round her sacred form.

Forget not, O Princes! That a strict account will be asked of your doings and non-doings, and a people newly born will not fail to pay in the coin you paid. Everyone who shall have actively betrayed the trust of the people, disowned his fathers, and debases his blood by arraying himself against the Mother – he shall be crushed to dust and ashes ... Do you doubt our grim earnestness? If so, hear the name of Dhingra[263] and be dumb. In the name of that martyr, O Indian princes, we ask you to think solemnly and deeply upon these words. Choose as you will and you will reap what you sow. Choose whether you shall be the first of the nation's fathers or the last of nation's tyrants.

p. 196, *Indian Unrest,* Valentine Chirol
'Choose O Princes'[264]

---

263 Madanlal Dhingra (1887–1909), was a young revolutionary with the Indian Home Rule Society and the India House Centre, and associate of Shyamji Krishnavarma, Lala Hardayal, and V.D. Savarkar. On 1 July 1909, Dhingra shot dead Sir Curzon Wylie at a function at the Imperial Institute in London 'in humble protest against the inhuman transportation and hangings of Indian youth.' Dhingra was hanged on 17 August 1909.

264 From a leaflet then in circulation – 'Choose, O Indian Princes' – a 'characteristic document' sent by the 'extremists' to the rulers of the

Untouchables

From the political point of view the conversion of so many millions of the population of India to the faith of their rulers would open the prospects of such moments that I need not expatiate upon them.

p. 184[265]

Page 280

Hatyanoy Jagna[266]

Tempted by gold, some native devils in form of men, the disgrace of India – the police – arrested those great men Birendra Ghose[267] and others who worked for the freedom of their country by sacrificing their interests and dedicating their lives in the performance of the sacred ceremony of 'Jagna', preparing bombs. The greatest of these devils in human form, Ashutosh Bishwas[268] began to pave for these heroes the way to the gallows.

Native States. One chief gave it to Chirol who has given two extracts from it on pages 196–197 of his book, with his interlinking comments.

265 These are the concluding comments Valentine Chirol, in context of whether the British should take in hand 'the elevation of the depressed castes …'

266 'Not Murder but Sacrifice'. This long extract is from Chirol's *Indian Unrest*, pp. 341–342, and is a reproduction of an appeal that was issued in Calcutta. This refers to some incidents of violence, bomb explosions and attacks on (or attempts on the life of) government dignitaries, police officers and informers.

267 Bindra (Barendra) Ghose was involved and convicted in the Alipore Conspiracy Case (May 1909).

268 'On 10 February 1909, Mr Ashutosh Biswas the Public Prosecutor and a Hindu of high character and position, was shot dead outside the Alipur Police Court…'

Bravo Charu! (the murderer of Biswas)[269] all honour to your parents. To glorify them, to show the highest degree of courage, disregarding the paltry short span of life, you removed the figure of that monster from the world. Not long ago, the Whites, by force and trick, filched India from Indians.[270] That mean wretch Shamasul-Alam[271] who espoused the cause of Alamgir Padsha, who put a stain on the name of his forefathers for the sake of gold – today you have removed that fiend from the sacred soil of India. From Nuren Gossain[272] to Talit Chakravarti, all turned approvers through the machinations of that fiendish wizard Shamasul-Alam and by his torture. Had you not removed that ally of monsters, could there be any hope for India?

Many have raised the cry that to rebel is a great sin. But what is rebellion?

Is there anything in India to rebel against? Can a Fering hee be recognized as the King of India, whose very touch, whose mere shadow compels Hindus to purify themselves?

These are merely Western Robbers looting India ... Extirpate them, ye good sons of India! where ever you find them, without mercy, and with them their spies and secret agents. Last year, 19 lakhs of men died of fever, smallpox, cholera, plague and other diseases in Bengal alone. Think yourself fortunate that you were not counted amongst those, but

---

269 Charu Chandra Guha, a daring teenager (handicapped from birth, without his right palm and fingers) shot prosecutor Biswas dead from close range, because, as Charu later confessed, "he was an enemy of the country." Charu was hanged in the Alipore Central Jail on 10 March 1909.

270 Chirol's original text has the term 'the Mohammedans'.

271 In the words of Chirol, Shemas-ul-Alam was "a Mohammedan Inspector of the Criminal Investigation Department in the High Court itself of Calcutta" who was gunned down on 24 January 1910, by young Birendra Nath Datta, a nineteen-year-old who was caught and executed on 21 February 1910.

272 Narendranath Gosain had turned approver in the Bomb Case following an attack aimed on Mr Kingsford, the Magistrate of Muzaffarpur, when Mrs and Miss Kennedy fell victims (April 30, 1908).

remember that plague and cholera may attack you tomorrow, and is it not better for you to die as heroes?

Page 282

When God has so ordained, think you not that at this auspicious moment, it is the duty of every good son of India to slay these white enemies? Do not allow yourselves to die of plague and cholera, thus polluting the sacred soil of the Mother India. Our Shastras are our guide for discriminating between virtue and vice. Our Shastras repeatedly tell us that the killing of these white fiends and of their aiders and abettors is equal to a great ceremonial sacrifice (Ashwamedh Yagna). Come, one and all! Let us offer our sacrifice before the alter in chorus, and pray that in this ceremony all white serpents may perish in its flames as the vipers perished in the serpents slaying ceremony of Jamajay Yagna. Keep in mind that it is not murder but Jagna – a sacrificial rite.

p. 342, Notes
I. U.[273]

"Total electors in India 62, 00,000 viz. 2-3/4% of the total population throughout India under direct British administration, excluding the areas to which the 1919 Act was not to be applied."

194. I.O.N.[274]

Page 283

India Old and New: Chirol V.
'The British people will have to beware that if they do not want to do justice, it will be the bounden duty of every Indian to destroy the Empire.'
Mahatmaji (Nagpur Congress)
191

---

273   Valentine Chirol, *Indian Unrest*.
274   Valentine Chirol, *India Old and New*.

Rural and Urban Question

Some official ingenuity had been displayed in grouping remote towns together without any regard for geography, in order to prevent townsmen undesirably addicted to advanced political view from standing as candidates for the rural constituencies in which many of the smaller towns would otherwise have been naturally merged. This was a last effort based on the old belief that the population of the Punjab could be divided into goats and sheep, the goats being the 'disloyal' townsmen and the sheep being the 'loyal' peasantry.

208. Valentine Chirol, *India Old and New*.

Khalsa College was opened in 1892

Page 284

India as I Knew it![275]

Truly the path of a 'Mahatma' is difficult, and it is not surprising that Gandhi has recently tried to repudiate the title – and its responsibilities. His influence in India is steadily waning, but his ascetic pose and the vague impracticable Tolstoyan theories which he so skilfully enunciates as great moral truths, seem to have deluded many well-meaning but weak-minded people in sentimental England and some even in logical France, who are on the lookout for a new light from the East.

P. 65.

Informer[276]

---

275 Sir Michael O'Dwyer, *India as I Knew it: 1885–1923*, (London, Macmilan 1925/28). O'Dwyer was Lt. Governor, Punjab, during the years of the First World War, when he mobilized 'support' for the war effort and recruited soldiers from Punjab.

276 In this extract, O'Dwyer drew attention to a parallel situation from the annals of the Irish revolutionary movement, and to his own role in dealing with Punjab revolutionaries.

The failure of the authorities in that case to conceal and protect the informer (or James Carey who betrayed the Invincible gang of the revolutionaries and due to whose evidence Brady, Fitzherbert and Mullen were hanged for the Phoenix Park double 211 murder, i.e. of Chief and Under-Secretaries. The informer was shot dead on board at Durban by a young revolutionary, O'Donnell) even though his assassin was brought to justice, was I believe, one of chief reasons why the supply of that *contemptible but useful class*, previously so common in Irish Conspiracies, ran dry at the source. As Lt. Governor of Punjab, before and during the Great War, I had to deal with many revolutionary conspiracies, in unravelling which the genus informer played a considerable role, and our precautions were so thorough that not in a single case did an informer come to any injury.

211. Phoenix Park Murders and their references relate to the well-known activities of the Irish Revolutionaries. The brave and daring deed of Patrick O'Donnell who had shot dead James Carey, the approver in Phoenix Park murders, case was much admired in India end emulated by young Bengali revolutionaries.

Page 285

One can imagine how thoroughly the Indian conspirator, with his low cunning, abnormal vanity, inborn aptitude for intrigue, and capacity for glossing over unpleasant facts, was at home in this atmosphere.

p. 187, *India as I Knew It*

Through often coercive methods, and who was also there when the Jallianwalla Bagh massacre took place. He was known and disliked for his 'Jabardust' or strong and imperious ways. Even a moderate leader like Annie Besant was forced to condemn (in 1912) the 'harsh and oppressive rule of Sir Michael O'Dwyer, his press-gang methods of recruitment, his forced war-loans and his cruel persecution of all political leaders'. His book was a justification or vindication of his conduct and of other authorities or British rulers.

Arya Samaj

In fact the Arya Samaj is a nationalist revival against Western influence; it urges its followers in the Satyarth Prakash, the authoritative work of Dayanand, who was the founder of the sect, to go back to the Vedas, and to seek the golden future in the imaginary golden past of the Aryas. The Satyarth Prakash also contains arguments against non-Hindu rule, and a leading organ of the sect, a few years ago, claimed Dayanand as the real author of the doctrine of Swaraj.

However, the Arya Samaj in 1907, thought it wise to publish a resolution to the effect that as mischievous people here and there spread rumours hostile to them, the organisation in reiterating its old creed, declared that it had no connection of any kind with any political body or with any political agitation in any shape. While accepting this declaration as disassociating the Samaj *as a body* from extremist politics, it should be noted in fairness to the orthodox Hindus that while the Samaj does not include perhaps more than 5% of the Hindu population of the Punjab, an enormous proportion of the Hindus convicted of sedition and other political offences from 1907 down to the present day are members of the Samaj.

p. 184

Page 286

Statistical Figures About India

In England and Wales 4/5 of people live in towns.

Standard of urban life begins when 1000 people live together. Only then Municipal drainage, lighting and water supply can be organised.

India (British)
Out of total 244000,000, 226000,000 live in villages
England – In normal times gives to
Industry 58% of people to Industry 8% to Agriculture

India gives 71% to Agriculture
12% to Industry

5% to Trade
2% to Domestic Service
1 ½ % to independent Professions
1 ½ % to Government Service, including Army.

In whole of India, 226 million out of 315 million are supported by soil. 208 million out of them live or depend directly upon agriculture.

Montford Report[277]

Page 287

Total area – 1,800,000 square miles
20 times of Great Britain 700,000 square miles, or more than 1/3, are under States' control. Indian States are 600 in number.
Burma is greater than France.
Madras and Bombay are greater than Italy separately.
Total population of India (1921 census) – 318,942,000
i.e. l/5th of the whole human race.
247,000,000 are in British India and 71,900,000 in States.
2 1/2 million persons were literate in English. – 16 in every thousand males and 2 in every thousand females.
Total Number of *vernaculars is* 222
Total Number of *villages* 500,000.

---

277 The Montford Report of 1918 was on Indian constitutional reforms by Secretary of State Montague, and Governor-General Chelmsford. Shortly after Edwin Montague, a former Under-secretary of State for India, had made a scathing criticism of the system of Government in India in 1917, he was appointed the Secretary of State. In that capacity, Montague made his historic announcement (on 20 August 1917) about "increasing the association of Indians in every branch of administration" with a view to "progressive realization of Responsible Government in India". See also *An Indian Diary* by E.S. Montague (Hienemann, London, 1930). Many of the following figures are also from this report.

Page 288

Suez Canal Opened in 1869
Total Export of India at that time was:
Rs. 80 crores : £ 80,000,000
1926-27 and preceding two years, the average was:
Rs. 350 crores i.e. about £ 262,500,000
Total population : 319 million, out of which 32 ½ million i.e. 10.2% live in towns and cities (urban) while in England the percentage is 79%

And the most difficult part of the task will be to instil into the minds of slum dwellers themselves the desire for something better.
p.22

Simon Report[278]

There are no entries from page numbers 289- 303 in the diary. The last page of the notebook has Bhagat Singh's initials with this date (as did the first page) by way of acknowledging the receipt of the notebook. The number of pages mentioned on the top page is 404. Here we have only 304 pages, as numbered with a rubber stamp, of which Bhagat Singh used a total of 145. We do not know what happened to the remaining 100 pages.

∽

Page 304

Initials of Bhagat Singh
Dated: 12.9.1929

∽

---

278 Simon Report: Report of the Indian Statutory Commission (London, 1930). The Commission was set up on November 8, 1927 by the British Cabinet to enquire into the working of the 1919 Reforms under a provision of the Government of India Act, 1919. The seven-member Commission had no Indian representative, and this led to widespread protests wherever the Commission went.

Page 1[279]

6. Life of Robespierre
French Revolution 4 vols.– 944. A: 3
7. *Garibaldi and the making of Italy* – by G. M. Trevelyan
8. *Under Fire* – Henri Barbusse
Idiot- Dostoevsky
Underworld – James C. Welsh
Majesty of Justice – Anatole France
Revolt of the Angels – do –
9. *What Then We Must Do* – Tolstoy
Slavery of our times – do –
The Great Iniquity – do –
Social Evils and their Remedy – do –
Death of Ivan the Terrible
Unto This Last – Ruskin
10. *Illegible*

※

Page 2

Cash only
Due to Smith   £10,000 Loan to Jones   £10,000
Due to Smith   £10,000   Cash in hand   £10,000
Notes outstanding   £10,000   Loan to Jones £10,000
Due to Smith £10,000 Cash in hand £10,000
Notes outstanding £10,000 Loan to customers £10,000

£50,000 £50,000

Bank Act of the UK (England)

---

279   It seems Bhagat Singh was making a list of books to be sent to him in jail from a library outside, as was his usual practice. First page or later pages are not found of this possible book list.

Notes upto £14, 000, 000 against Govt. Securities can be issued 2/3 of that country notes lapsed. Total now approximately 181/2 millions. Any notes above these limitations can be issued only if full value is preserved in treasury in GoI.

Page 3

Two deaths are impossible and one is unavoidable
American gold reserve 900 million pounds
England gold reserve 150 million pounds only

REFERENCES

1. Gupta, Manmath Nath, *Bharat Ke Krantikari* (Delhi: Hind Pocket Books, 1969).
2. Singh, Jagmohan and Chaman Lal, eds., *Bhagat Singh aur Unke Sathiyon ke Dastavez* (New Delhi: Rajkamal Prakashan, 1986).
3. Sindhu, Veerendra, *Bhagat Singh aur Unke Mrityuanjay Purkhe* (Varanasi: Bhartiya Gyanpeeth, 1968).
4. Dutta, V.N., *Gandhi and Bhagat Singh* (New Delhi: Rupa & Co., 2008), pp. 73–4.
5. Singh, Bhagat, *Mere Krantikari Saathi*, compiled by Veerendra Sindhu, (Delhi: Rajpal & Sons, 1977).
6. Lal, Chaman, *Bhagat Singh* (Delhi: Medha Books, 2009), pp. 236–45.
7. *Hindu Panch* (1931).
8. Shastri, Acharya Chatursen, ed., *Chand ka Phansi Ank* (Delhi: Radhakrishan Prakashan, 1988).
9. Sinha, Srirajyam, *Bejoy Kumar Sinha: A Revolutionary's Quest for Sacrifice* (Bombay: Bhartiya Vidya Bhavan, 1993), pp. 46–52.
10. Noorani, A.G., *The Trial of Bhagat Singh: Politics of Justice* (Delhi: Konark Publishers, 1996), p. 33.
11. Singh, Namvar, ed., *Aalochana*, Issue Number 67 (1983), p. 28.

APPENDICES

MANIFESTOS DRAFTED IN CONSULTATION WITH BHAGAT SINGH[280]

Two documents – the manifestos of the Naujawan Bharat Sabha (NBS) and the Hindustan Socialist Republican Association (HSRA) – are the most important ideological texts to understand Bhagat Singh and his comrades' struggle for Indian freedom from British colonialism. The drafts of both were written by Bhagwati Charan Vohra, with Bhagat Singh being consulted before they were finalized for publication. While the manifesto of NBS was written when Bhagat Singh was not yet in jail, the HSRA manifesto was drafted after his incarceration.

According to Ramchander, founder–president of the Naujawan Bharat Sabha, the organization was formed in 1924–25. The Sabha was an open organization of the party. Bhagat Singh was the founding General Secretary of the NBS and Ramchander its founder–president. Bhagwati Charan Vohra was the founder–propaganda secretary.

The HSRA – a reorganized and renamed version of the Hindustan Republican Association or HRA, founded in 1923 – was formed in September 1928.

MANIFESTO OF NAUJAWAN BHARAT SABHA (NBS)

YOUNG COMRADES,

Our country is passing through a chaos. There is mutual distrust and despair prevailing everywhere. The great leaders have lost faith in the cause and most of them no more enjoy the confidence of the masses. There is no programme and no enthusiasm among the 'champions' of Indian independence. There is chaos

---

280 Source: Verma, Shiv (edited by), *Selected Writings of Shaheed Bhagat Singh*, National Book Centre, Delhi, 1986

everywhere. But chaos is inevitable and a necessary phase in the course of the making of a nation. It is during such critical periods that the sincerity of the workers is tested, their character built, real programme formed, and then, with a new spirit, new hopes, new faith and enthusiasm, the work is started. Hence there is nothing to be disgusted of.

We are, however, very fortunate to find ourselves on the threshold of a new era. We no more hear the news of reaching chaos that used to be sung vastly in praise of the British bureaucracy. The historic question "Would you be governed by sword or pen", no more lies unanswered. Those who put that question to us have themselves answered it. In the words of Lord Birkenhead, "With the sword we won India and with the sword we shall retain it." Thanks to this candour everything is clear now. After remembering Jallianwala and Manawala outrages it looks absurd to quote that "A good government cannot be a substitute for self-government." It is self-evident.

A word about the blessings of the British rule in India. Is it necessary to quote the whole volumes of Romesh Chandra Dutt, William Digby and Dadabhai Naoroji in evidence to prove the decline and ruin of Indian industries? Does it require any authorities to prove that India, with the richest soil and mine, is today one of the poorest, that India, which could be proud of so glorious a civilisations, is today the most backward country with only 5% literacy? Do not the people know that India has to pay the largest toll of human life with the highest child death rate in the world? The epidemics like plague, cholera, influenza and such other diseases are becoming common day by day. Is it not disgraceful for us to hear again and again that we are not fit for self-government? Is it not really degrading for us, with Guru Govind Singh, Shivaji and Hari Singh as our heroes, to be told that we are incapable of defending ourselves? Alas, we have done little to prove the contrary. Did we not see our trade and commerce being crushed in its very infancy in the first effort of Guru Nanak steamship co-started by Baba Gurdit Singh in 1914; the inhuman treatment meted out to them, far away in Canada, on the way, and finally, the bloody reception of those despairing, broken-hearted passengers with valleys of shots at Bajbaj, and what not? Did we not see all this? In India, where for the honour of one Dropadi, the great Mahabharat was fought, dozens of them were ravaged in 1919. They were spit at, in their naked faces. Did we not see all this? Yet, we are content with the existing order of affairs. Is this life worth living?

Does it require any revelation now to make us realise that we are enslaved and must be free? Shall we wait for an uncertain sage to make us feel that we are an oppressed people? Shall we expectantly wait for divine help or some miracle to deliver us from bondage? Do we not know the fundamental principles of liberty? "Those who want to be free, must themselves strike the blow." Young men, awake, arise; we have slept too long!

We have appealed to the young only. Because the young bear the most inhuman tortures smilingly and face death without hesitation. Because the whole history of human progress is written with the blood of young men and young women. And because the reforms are ever made by the vigour, courage, self-sacrifice and emotional conviction of the young men who do not know enough to be afraid and who feel much more than they think.

Were it not the young men of Japan who come forth in the hundreds to throw themselves in the ditches to make a dry path to Port Arthur? And Japan is today one of the foremost nations in the world. Were it not the young Polish people who fought again and again and failed, but fought again heroically throughout the last century? And today we see a free Poland. Who freed Italy from the Austrian yoke? Young Italy.

Do you know the wonders worked by the Young Turks? Do you not daily read what the young Chinese are doing? Were it not the young Russians who sacrificed their lives for Russia's emancipation? Throughout the last century hundreds and thousands of them were exiled to Siberia for the mere distribution of socialist pamphlets or, like Dostoyevsky, for merely belonging to a socialist debating society. Again and again they faced the storm of oppression. But they did not lose courage. It were they, the young only, who fought. And everywhere the young can fight without hope, without fear and without hesitation. And we find today in the great Russia, the emancipation of the world.

While, we Indians, what are we doing? A branch of peepal tree is cut and religious feelings of the Hindus are injured. A corner of a paper idol, tazia, of the idol-breaker Mohammedans is broken, and 'Allah' gets enraged, who cannot be satisfied with anything less than the blood of the infidel Hindus. Man ought to be attached more importance than animals and, yet, here in India, they break each other's heads in the name of 'sacred animals'. Our vision is circumscribed by....

There are many others among us who hide their lethargy under the garb of internationalism. Asked to serve their country they reply: "Oh Sirs, we are cosmopolitans and believe in Universal Brotherhood. Let us not quarrel with the British. They are our brothers." A good idea, a beautiful phrase. But they miss its implication. The doctrine of Universal Brotherhood demands that the exploitation of man by man and nation by nation must be rendered impossible.

Equal opportunity to all without any sort of distinction. But British rule in India is a direct negation of all these, and we shall have nothing to do with it.

A world about social service here. Many good men think that social service (in the narrow sense, as it is used and understood in our country) is the panacea to all our ills and the best method of serving the country. Thus we find many ardent youth contending themselves with distributing grain among the poor and nursing the sick all their life. These men are noble and self-denying but they cannot understand that charity cannot solve the problem of hunger and disease in India and, for that matter, in any other country.

Religious superstitions and bigotry are a great hinderance in our progress. They have proved an obstacle in our way and we must do away with them. "The thing that cannot bear free thought must perish." There are many other such weakness which we are to overcome. The conservativeness and orthodoxy of the Hindus, extra-territorialism and fanaticism of the Mohammedans and narrow-mindedness of all the communities in general are always exploited by the foreign enemy. Young men with revolutionary zeal from all communities are required for the task.

Having achieved nothing, we are not prepared to sacrifice anything for any achievement; our leaders are fighting amongst themselves to decide what will be the share of each community in the hoped achievement. Simply to conceal their cowardice and lack of spirit of self-sacrifice, they are creating a false issue and screening the real one. These arm-chair politicians have their eyes set on the handful of bones that may be thrown to them, as they hope, by the mighty rulers. That is extremely humiliating. Those who come forth to fight the battle of liberty cannot sit and decide first that after so much sacrifice, so much achievement must be sure and so much share to be divided. Such people never make any sort of sacrifice. We want people who may be prepared to fight without hope, without fear and without hesitation, and who may be willing to die unhonoured, unwept and unsung. Without that spirit, we will not be able to fight the great two-fold battle that lies before us – two-fold because of the internal foe, on the one hand, and a foreign enemy, on the other. Our real battle is against our own disabilities which are exploited by the enemy and some of our own people for their selfish motives.

Young Punjabis, the youth of other provinces are working tremendously in their respective spheres. The organisation and awakening displayed by young Bengal on February 3, should serve as an example to us. Our Punjab, despite the greatest amount of sacrifice and suffering to its credit, is discribed as a politically backward province. Why? Because, although it belong to the martial race, we are lacking in organisation and discipline; we who are proud of the ancient University of Texila, today stand badly in need of culture. And a culture requires fine literature which cannot be prepared without a common and well developed language. Alas, we have got none.

While trying to solve the above problem that faces our country, we will also have to prepare the masses to fight the greater battle that lies before us. Our political struggle began just after the great War of Independence of 1857. It has passed through different phases. Along with the advent of the 20th century, the British bureaucracy has adopted quite a new policy towards India. They are drawing our bourgeoisie and petty bourgeoisie into their fold by adopting the policy of concessions. Their cause is being made common. The progressive investment of British capital in India will inevitably lead to that end. In the very near future we will find that class and their great leaders having thrown their lot with the foreign rulers. Some round-table conference or any such body will end in a compromise between the two. They will no more be lions and cubs. Even without any conciliation, the expected Great War of the entire people will surely thin the ranks of the so-called champions of India independence.

The future programme of preparing the country will begin with the motto: "Revolution by the masses and for the masses." In other words, Swaraj for the 90%; Swaraj not only attained by the masses but also for the masses. This is a very difficult task. Though our leaders have offered many suggestions, none had the courage to put forward and carry out successfully a concrete scheme of awakening the masses. Without going into details, we can safely assert that to achieve our object, thousands of our most brilliant young men, like the Russian youth, will have to pass their precious lives in village and make the people understand what the Indian revolution would really mean. They must be made to realise that the revolution which is to come will mean more than a change of masters. It will, above all, mean the birth of new order of things, a new state. This is not the work of a day or a year. Decades of matchless self-sacrifice will prepare the masses for the accomplishment of that great work and only the revolutionary young men will be able to do that. A revolutionary does not necessarily mean a man of bombs and revolvers.

The task before the young is hard and their resources are scanty. A great many obstacles are likely to block their way. But the earnestness of the few but sincere can overcome them all. The young must come forth. They must see the hard and difficult path that lies before them, the great tasks they have to perform. They must remember in the heart of hearts that "success is but a chance; sacrifice, a law". Their lives might be the lives of constant failures, even more wretched than those which Guru Govind Singh had to face throughout his life. Even then they must not repent and say, "Oh, it was all an illusion."

Young men, do not get disheartened when you find such a great battle to fight single-handed, with none to help you. You must realise your own latent strength. Rely on yourselves and success is yours. Remember the words of the great mother of James Garfield which she spoke to her son while sending him away, penniless, helpless and resourceless, to seek his fortune: "Nine times out of ten, the best thing that can happen to a young man is to be thrown overboard to swim or sink for himself." Glory to the mother who said these words and glory to those who will rely on them.

Mazzini, that oracle of Italian regeneration, once said: "All great national movements begin with unknown men of the people without influence, except for the faith and the will that counts neither time nor difficulties." Let the boat of life weigh another time. Let it set sail in the Great Ocean, and then:

> Anchor is in no stagnant shallow.
> Trust the wide and wonderous sea,
> Where the tides are fresh for ever,
> And the mighty currents free.
> There perchance, O young Columbus,
> Your new world of truth may be.

Do not hesitate, let not the theory of incarnation haunt your mind and break your courage. Everybody can become great if he strives. Do not forget your own martyrs. Kartar Singh was a young man. Yet, in this teens, when he came forth to serve his country, he ascended the scaffold smiling and echoing "Bande Mataram". Bhai Balmukund and Awadh Bihari were both quite young when they gave their lives for the cause. They were from amongst you. You must try to become as sincere patriots and as ardent lovers of liberty as they were. Do not lose patience and sense at one time, and hope at another. Try to make stability and determination a second nature to yourselves.

Let young men think independently, calmly, serenely and patiently. Let them adopt the cause of Indian independence as the sole aim of their lives. Let them stand on their own feet. They must organise themselves free from any influence and refuse to be exploited any more by the hypocrites and insincere people who have nothing in common with them and who always desert the cause at the critical juncture. In all seriousness and sincerity, let them make the triple motto of "service, suffering, sacrifice" their sole guide. Let them remember that "the making of a nation requires self-sacrifice of thousands of obscure men and women who care more for the idea of their country than for their own comfort and interest, than own lives and the lives of those who they love".

MANIFESTO OF THE HINDUSTAN SOCIALIST REPUBLICAN ASSOCIATION (HSRA)

"The food on which the tender plant of liberty thrives is the blood of the martyr."

For decades, this life blood to the plant of India's liberty is being supplied by revolutionaries. There are few to question the magnanimity of the noble ideals they cherish and the grand sacrifices they have offered, but their normal activities being mostly secret, the country is in dark as to their present policy and intentions. This has necessitated the Hindustan Socialist Republican Association to issue this manifesto.

This association stands for revolution in India in order to liberate her from foreign domination by means of organised armed rebellion. Open rebellion by a subject people must always in the nature of things be preceded by secret propaganda and secret preparations. Once a country enters that phase the task of an alien government becomes impossible. It might linger on for a number of years, but its fate is sealed. Human nature, with all its prejudices and conservatism, has a sort of instinctive dread for revolution. Upheavals have always been a terror to holders of power and privilege. Revolution is a phenomenon which nature loves and without which there can be no progress either in nature or human affairs. Revolution is certainly not unthinking, a brutal campaign of murder and incendiarism; it is not a few bombs thrown here and a few shots fired there; neither is it a movement to destroy all ramnants of civilisation and blow to pieces time-honoured principles of justice and equity. Revolution is not a philosophy of despair or a creed of desperadoes. Revolution may be anti-God, but is certainly not anti-Man. It is a vital, living force which is indicative of eternal conflict between the old and the new, between life and living death, between light and darkness. There is no concord, no symphony, no rhythm without revolution. 'The music of the spheres' of which poets have sung, would remain an unreality if a ceaseless revolution were to be eliminated from the space. Revolution is Law, Revolution is Order and Revolution is the Truth.

The youths of our nation have realised this truth. They have learnt painfully the lesson that without revolution there is no possibility of enthroning order, law and love in place of chaos and legal vandalism and hatred which are reigning supreme today. Let no one, in this blessed land of ours, run with the idea that the youths are irresponsible. They know where they stand. None knows better than their own selves, that their path is not strewn with roses. From time to time they have paid a fairly decent price for their ideals. It does not, therefore, lie in the mouth of anybody to say that youthful impetuosity has feasted upon platitudes. It is no good to hurl denunciatory epithets at our ideology. It is enough to know that our ideas are sufficiently active and powerful to drive us on aye even to gallows.

It has become a fashion these days to indulge in wild and meaningless talk of non-violence. Mahatma Gandhi is great and we mean no disrespect to him if we express our emphatic disapproval of the methods advocated by him for our country's emancipation. We would be ungrateful to him if we do not salute him for the immense awakening that has been brought about by his Non-Cooperation Movement in the country. But to us the Mahatma is an impossible visionary. Non-violence may be a noble ideal, but is a thing of the morrow. We can, situated as we are, never hope to win our freedom by mere non-violence. The world is armed to the very teeth. And the world is too much with us. All talk of peace may be sincere, but such false ideology. What logic, we ask, is there in asking the country to traverse a non-violent path when the world atmosphere is surcharged with violence and exploitation of the weak? We declare with all the emphasis we can command that the youths of the nation cannot be lured by such midsummer night's dreams.

We believe in violence, not as an end itself but as a means to a noble end. And the votaries of non-violence, as also the advocates of caution and circumspection, will readily grant this much at least that we know how to suffer for and to act up to our convictions. Shall we here recount all those sacrifices which our comrades have offered at the altar of our common Mother? Many a heartrending and soul-stirring scene has been enacted inside the four walls of His Majesty's prison. We have been taken to task for our terroristic policy. Our answer is that terrorism is never the object of revolutionaries, nor do they believe that terrorism alone can bring independence. No doubt the revolutionaries think, and rightly, that it is only by resorting to terrorism alone that they can find a most effective means of retaliation. The British government exists, because the Britishers have been successful in terrorising the whole of India. How are we to meet this official terrorism? Only counter-terrorism on the part of revolutionaries can checkmate effectively this bureaucratic bullying. A feeling of utter helplessness pervades society. How can we overcome this fatal despondency? It is only by infusing a real spirit of sacrifice that lost self-confidence can be restored. Terrorism has its international aspect also. England's enemies, which are many, are drawn towards us by effective demonstration of our strength. That in itself is a great advantage.

Indian is writhing under the yoke of imperialism. Her teeming millions are today a helpless prey to poverty and ignorance. Foreign domination and economic exploitation have unmanned the vast majority of the people who constitute the workers and peasants of India. The position of the Indian proletariat is, today, extremely critical. It has a double danger to face. It has to bear the onslaught of foreign capital on the other. The latter is showing a progressive tendency to join forces with the former. The leaning of certain politicians in favour of dominion status shows clearly which way the wind blows. Indian capital is preparing to betray the masses into the hands of foreign capitalism and receive, as a price of this betrayal, a little share in the government of the country. The hope of the proletariat is, therefore, now centred on socialism, which alone can lead to the establishment of complete independence and the removal of all social distinction and privileges.

The future of India rests with the youths. They are the salt of the earth. Their promptness to suffer, their daring courage and their radiant sacrifice prove that India's future in their hands is perfectly safe. In a moment of realisation, the late Deshbandhu Dass said: "The youths are at once the hope and glory of the Motherland. Theirs is the inspiration behind the movement. Theirs is the sacrifice. Theirs is the victory. They are torch-bearers on the road to freedom. They are the pilgrims on the road to liberty."

Youths, ye soldiers of the Indians Republic, fall in: do not stand easy, do not let your knees tremble. Shake off the paralysing effects of long lethargy. Yours is a noble mission. Go out into every nook and corner of the country and prepare the ground for future revolution which is sure to come. Respond to the clarion call of duty. Do not [be a] vegetable. Grow! Every minute of your life you must think of devising means so that this ancient land may arise with flaming eyes and fierce yawn. Sow the seeds of disgust and hatred against British imperialism in the fertile minds of your fellow youths. And the seeds shall sprout and there shall grow a jungle of sturdy trees, because you shall water the seeds with your warm blood. Then a grim and terrible earthquake having a universally destructive potentiality shall inevitably come along with portentous rumblings, and this edifice of imperialism will crash and crumble to dust, and great shall be the fall therefore. And then, and not till then, a new Indian nation shall arise and surprise humanity with the splendour and glory, all its own. The wise and the mighty shall be bewildered by the simple and the weak.

Individual liberty shall be safe. The sovereignty of the proletariat shall be recognised. We court the advent of such revolution. Long Live Revolution!

Kartar Singh,
President

LANGUAGE-WISE DETAILS OF BHAGAT SINGH'S WRITINGS

Documents of Bhagat Singh in English

1.	Letter to Postmaster, Lahore	1 November 1926
2.	Letter to Secretary, Punjab Government, Lahore	17 November 1926
3.	Letter to Secretary, Punjab Government, Lahore	28 November 1926
4.	Letter to SSP, Lahore	1927
5.	Letter to District Magistrate, Lahore	9 May 1928
6.	Letter to Superintendent CID, Lahore	19 June 1928
7.	Poster on Saunders' Killing (signed by Balraj, Chandra Shekhar Azad)	18 December 1928
8.	Notice on Saunders' Killing (signed by Balraj, Chandra Shekhar Azad)	23 December 1929
9.	Leaflet in Central Assembly (signed by Balraj, Chandra Shekhar Azad)	8 April 1929
10.	Letter to District Magistrate, Delhi	25 April 1929
11.	Letter to CID, Lahore	31 May 1929
12.	Statement in Session Court (signed by Bhagat Singh and B.K. Dutt)	6 June 1929
13.	Letter to IG Jails for transfer	17 June 1929
14.	Notice for hunger strike	17 June 1929
15.	Letter to Jail Superintendent	19 June 1929

16. Letter to Home Member
    (signed by Bhagat Singh and B.K. Dutt)   24 June 1929
17. Letter to Chairman, Punjab Jail Enquiry Committee
    (Bhagat Singh, on behalf of all hunger strikers)   6 September 1929
18. Message to Punjab's Student Conference
    (Signed by Bhagat Singh, B.K. Dutt)   19 October 1929
19. Letter to Special Magistrate   21 October 1929
20. Letter to Special Magistrate   October end–November-
                                                      beginning 1929
21. Letter to Special Magistrate   4 November 1929
22. Letter to Special Magistrate   16 December 1929
23. Letter to the Editor, *Modern Review*   22 December 1929
24. Statement before High Court
    (Signed by Bhagat Singh, B.K. Dutt)   13 January 1930
25. Telegram to Home Secretary, Government of India
    (Bhagat Singh, on behalf of all)   20 January 1930
26. Telegram to the Third International on Lenin Day
    (Bhagat Singh, on behalf of all)   24 January 1930
27. Memorandum to Home Ministry, Government of India
    (Signed by Bhagat Singh, B.K. Dutt, and others)   28 January 1930
28. Letter to Special Magistrate, Lahore
    (Bhagat Singh, on behalf of all)   11 February 1930
29. Telegram to the Kakori Case Prisoners
    (Bhagat Singh, on behalf of all)   1930
30. Telegram to the Hindustan Committee, Berlin
    (Bhagat Singh, on behalf of all)   5 April 1930
31. On Special Tribunal (Bhagat Singh, on behalf of all)   2 May 1930
32. On Exposing Special Tribunal (Bhagat Singh, on behalf
    of Jitender Nath Sanyal, Mahabir Singh, B.K. Dutt,
    Dr Gaya Prasad, and Kundan Lal)   5 May 1930
33. To Special Tribunal   8 May 1930
34. On Special Tribunal   19 June 1930
35. On Reconstitution of Special Tribunal
    (Signed by Bhagat Singh, B.K. Dutt)   25 June 1930
36. To Special Tribunal   11 August 1930
37. To Lahore High Court   11 August 1930

38. To Punjab High Court	16 August 1930
39. To Special Tribunal	18 August 1930
40. To Special Tribunal	22 August 1930
41. To Special Tribunal	26 August 1930
42. To Special Tribunal	30 August 1930
43. Letter to Jaidev Gupta	24 February 1930
44. Letter to Jaidev Gupta	28 May 1930
45. Letter to Jaidev Gupta	3 June 1930
46. Letter to Jaidev Gupta	24 July 1930
47. Letter to Promila	17 July 1930
48. Letter to B.K. Dutt	October 1930
49. Why I am an Atheist	October 1930
50. Ideal of the Indian Revolution	1930
51. On Political Trials (Harikishan Case)	January 1931
52. Second letter on the Harikishan Case	February 1931
53. Introduction to Dreamland	January 1931
54. Letter to Young Political Workers	2 February 1931
55. Letter to Governor of Punjab	
(Signed by Bhagat Singh, Rajguru, and Sukhdev)	20 March 1931
56. Jail Notebook	(1929–1931)

Documents of Bhagat Singh in Urdu

1. Letter to grandfather, Arjun Singh	22 July 1918
2. Letter to grandfather, Arjun Singh	27 July 1919
3. Letter to grandfather, Arjun Singh	14 November 1921
4. Letter to father, Kishan Singh	1923
5. Letter to friend Amar Chand (USA)	1927
6. Letter to father from Delhi Jail	26 April 1929
7. Letter to younger brother Kulbir	16 September 1930
8. Letter to younger brother Kulbir	25 September 1930
9. Letter to father, Kishan Singh	4 October 1930
10. Letter to younger brother Kulbir	3 March 1931
11. Letter to younger brother Kultar	3 March 1931
12. 'The First Rise of Punjab in Freedom	
Struggle', *Bande Matram*	31 January 1931
13. Letter to Comrades	22 March 1931

Documents of Bhagat Singh in Hindi

1.	Problem of Punjab's Language and Script	1923
2.	Vishav Prem (*Matwala*)	November 1924
3.	Yuvak (*Matwala*)	16 May 1925
4.	Holi Ke Din Rakat Ke Chhinte (*Pratap*)	15 March 1926
5.	Letter to Editor (*Maharathi*)	22 February 1928
6.	Kuka Vidhroh (*Maharathi*)	February 1928
7.	Chitra Parichey (*Maharathi*)	February 1928
8.	Letter to Sukhdev	5 April 1929
9.	Letter to Sukhdev	September–October 1930
10 to 46.	37 Sketches of Revolutionaries in *Chand*	November 1928

Documents of Bhagat Singh in Punjabi

1.	Letter to aunt Hukam Kaur	24 October 1921
2.	Letter to aunt Hukam Kaur	15 November 1921
3.	About Kakori Martyrs (*Kirti*)	May 1927
4.	About Kakori Martyrs, Hanging (*Kirti*)	January 1928
5.	Religion-oriented Riots and Their Solution (*Kirti*)	June 1927
6.	Kuka Revolt II (*Kirti*)	September–October 1928
7.	On Religion and Our Freedom Struggle (*Kirti*)	May 1928
8.	Issue of Untouchability (*Kirti*)	June 1928
9.	On Satyagraha and Strikes (*Kirti*)	June 1928
10.	Students and Politics (*Kirti*)	June 1928
11.	New Leaders and their Different Ideas (*Kirti*)	July 1928
12.	Lala Lajpat Rai and the Youth (*Kirti*)	August 1928
13.	What is Anarchism I (*Kirti*)	May 1928
14.	What is Anarchism II (*Kirti*)	June 1928
15.	What is Anarchism III (*Kirti*)	July 1928
16.	The Revolutionary Nihilists of Russia (*Kirti*)	August 1928

While all the fifty-six documents in English and the thirteen in Urdu are confirmed to be from Bhagat Singh's pen; the languages of nine documents in Hindi and sixteen in Punjabi are also confirmed. The confusion is regarding the many life sketches of revolutionaries, which Bhagat Singh wrote in all three languages – Punjabi, Hindi and Urdu. While a few of these sketches are likely written in Punjabi first for *Kirti* magazine and later translated, rewritten, improvised by Bhagat Singh himself, at times by Shiv Verma or his other comrades in Hindi and Urdu. Due to the improvisation of some sketches by Shiv Verma, these can be put under joint authorship. As many files from the Urdu *Kirti* are missing, about thirty-five such sketches cannot be clearly defined in terms of what language they were originally written in.

Details of forty-eight sketches of revolutionaries in the 'Phansi' (Gallows) issue of *Chand*, November 1928

There are forty-eight articles and sketches in total, attributed to Bhagat Singh in *Chand*. Out of these, some were written in collaboration, while others were written by his comrades and compatriots.

Sketches by Ram Prasad Bismil

1. Genda Lal Dikshit

Sketches by Shiv Verma

1. Chaphekar Bandhu
2. Kanhai Lal Dutt
3. Satyender Kumar Basu
4. Jatinder Nath Mukhrejee
5. Nalini Vakchaya
6. Gopi Mohan Saha
7. Ram Prasad Bismil
8. Rajender Nath Lahiri
9. Roshan Singh
10. Ashfquallah

Sketches by Bhagat Singh

1. Kuka Vidroh ke Balidan
2. Madan Lal Dhingra
3. Amir Chand
4. Awadh Behari
5. Bhai Balmukund

6. Basant Kumar Biswas
7. Bhai Bhag Singh
8. Watan Singh
9. Mewa Singh
10. Kashi Ram
11. Gandha Singh
12. Kartar Singh
13. V.G. Pingle
14. Jagat Singh
15. Balwant Singh
16. Maura Singh
17. Banta Singh
18. Ranga Singh
19. Veer Singh
20. Uttam Singh
21. Dr Arur Singh
22. Babu Harnam Singh
23. Sohan Lal Pathak
24. Sufi Amba Prasad
25. Bhai Ram Singh
26. Shri Bhan Singh
27. Udham Singh
28. Khushi Ram

Sketches written jointly by Bhagat Singh and Shiv Verma; many of them were drafted by Bhagat Singh and improved by Shiv Verma.

1. Bomeli Yudh ke Char Shaeed
2. Dhanna Singh
3. Banta Singh Dhamian
4. Waryam Singh Dhugga
5. Kishan Singh Gadgajj
6. Santa Singh
7. Dalip Singh
8. Nand Singh
9. Karam Singh

LIFE EVENTS OF BHAGAT SINGH

1. 1907– Bhagat Singh was born on 28 September at about 9 a.m. at village Chak no. 105, Lyallpur Bange, district Lyallpur, now known as Faisalabad in Pakistan. After the partition of India in 1947, Bhagat Singh's mother, Vidyawati, and father, Kishan Singh, moved to their ancestral village, Khatkar Kalan, which, at that time, came under the district of Jalandhar, but now is in Nawanshahr (later renamed as Shaheed Bhagat Singh Nagar), in the district of East (Indian) Punjab.
2. 1911– Went to primary school in the District Board Primary School, Chak no. 105, till 1917.
3. 1917– Later attended DAV High School Lahore till Class 9 till 1921.
4. 1919– Visited Jallianwala Bagh in Amritsar in April just after a peaceful gathering on 13 April was interrupted by the British police led by General Reginald Dyer, leading to a deadly massacre.
5. 1921– Joined National College Lahore for his undergraduate studies. This was the first time when a student without a matriculation degree – the minimum eligibility condition – was admitted into college.
6. 1923– Cleared the Intermediate examination, and joined the revolutionary organization Hindustan Republican Association (HRA) while still in college.
7. 1923– Left for Kanpur mid-year, after being pressurized by his family for marriage. This was also the end of his academic life.
8. 1923– Over the year, he worked with journalist and revolutionary Ganesh Shankar Vidyarthi, and he worked in the Hindi journal *Pratap* under the pseudonym 'Balwant'. Also, served as the headmaster at the National School in Shadipur, Aligarh, during this time.
9. 1924– Attended the Congress session at Calcutta. Unconfirmed reports say that Bhagat Singh also attended a Congress session in Belgaum (now Belgavi, Karnataka) with his father Kishan Singh in 1924. This was also the only session of the Congress party which was presided over by Mahatma Gandhi.
10. 1926– In March, formed the Naujawan Bharat Sabha (Young India Association), inspired by Young Italy, a revolutionary underground organisation formed by Guiseppe Mazzini and Garibaldi. Bhagat Singh served as the General Secretary of the party.

11. 1927– Arrested for the first time on 29 May, in connection with the Dussehra Bomb Case at Lahore, which took place in October 1926. He was kept in police custody for five weeks.
12. 1927– Was granted bail on the security of Rs 60,000 on July 4. Later, the case was also closed.
13. 1927– During his bail-bound period, he worked at the dairy farm which his father had set up at Khwasarian village near Lahore. At the same time, he wrote for multiple magazines and newspapers such as *Kirti, Akali, Maharathi, Prabha,* and *Chand.*
14. 1928– On 8–9 September, at a historic meeting held at Feroz Shah Kotla grounds in Delhi the name the Hindustan Republican Association was changed to the Hindustan Socialist Republic Association. The more militant wing of the organisation was headed by Chandra Shekhar Azad and Bhagat Singh was made the coordinator for different states of the political wing of HSRA.
15. 1928– On October 30, Bhagat Singh and his comrades ask leader Lala Lajpat Rai to lead the anti-Simon Commission procession in Lahore. Lala Lajpat Rai was injured when the DSP of Lahore, John Saunders, orders lathi charge.
16. 1928– On November 17, Lala Lajpat Rai died in Lahore due to the grave wounds he suffered at the hands of the police at the rally.
17. 1928– On 17 December 1928, to avenge the death of Lala Lajpat Rai, John Saunders is shot dead in front of the SSP office at Lahore in broad daylight.
18. 1928– Bhagat Singh, disguised as a British officer, escapes from Lahore accompanied by Durgawati Devi, also known as Durga Bhabhi, who posed as his wife.
19. 1929– Between 3–6 April, the now iconic photo of Bhagat Singh wearing a hat, along with with B.K. Dutt, was taken by photographer Ramnath at Kashmiri Gate, Delhi.
20. 1929– On 8 April, they threw bombs and leaflets from the visitor's gallery in the Central Assembly at Delhi, now known as the Indian Parliament, while it was in session.
21. 1929– From 8 April to 14 June, they were imprisoned at Delhi. Later Bhagat Singh was shifted to Central Jail at Mianwali in Punjab, while B.K. Dutt was moved to Lahore Jail.

22. 1929– On 6 June, the now-historic statement by Bhagat Singh and B.K. Dutt was read at the Delhi Sessions Court by their lawyer, Asaf Ali, on their behalf.
23. 1929– On 12 June, both Bhagat Singh and B.K. Dutt are found guilty in connection with the Delhi Assembly Bomb Case and sentenced to transportation for life, which under East India Company law meant to send a convict into exile.
24. 1929– On 15 June, Bhagat Singh and B.K. Dutt start a hunger strike to advocate for status of 'Political Prisoners'.
25. 1929– On 10 July, Bhagat Singh is brought to Lahore to face trial in the Saunders Murder Case.
26. 1929– The hunger strike ends on 4 October, after their demands were partially accepted and also the death of their comrade, Jatinder Nath Das, who died on 13 September after sixty-three days of fasting. By then, Bhagat Singh and B.K. Dutt had completed about 110 days on their hunger strike.
27. 1929– Between 21–23 October, Bhagat Singh and his comrades are badly injured as they were repeatedly beaten by the police in court and in jail.
28. 1930– On 14 February, another two-week hunger strike commences, this time to get all their demands met.
29. 1930– On 1 May, British Viceroy, Lord Irwin, issued an ordinance to establish a Special Tribunal for the trial of the Lahore Conspiracy Case. The case is transferred from Special Magistrate to the Special Tribunal.
30. 1930– On 5 May, the trial of the Lahore Conspiracy Case officially begins at the Special Tribunal.
31. 1930– On 12 May, during a session at the court, Bhagat Singh and others are beaten up again. The only Indian judge on the three-member jury, Justice Agha Haider, disassociates himself from the Tribunal President's order. Other revolutionaries begin their boycott of the tribunal.
32. 1930– On 21 June, the Special Tribunal is reconstituted, but this time without Justice Agha Haider.
33. 1930– On 10 July, formal charges are framed against the accused.
34. 1930– Protests begin, and a three-week hunger strike begins from 28 July.
35. 1930– On 7 October, Bhagat Singh, Shivaram Rajguru, and Sukhdev Thapar are sentenced to death, with the date of execution fixed as 27 October. Bhagat Singh later filed an appeal in the Privy Council.

36. 1931– The appeal is heard and dismissed by the Privy Council on 11 February.
37. 1931– On 23 March, 3 p.m., the Punjab High Court dismisses the appeals lodged against the Privy Council and Tribunal Court, and the execution order is passed.
38. 1931– On 23 March, between 7 p.m. and 7.33 p.m., Bhagat Singh, Shivaram Rajguru, and Sukhdev Thapar are executed. Their bodies were cut up and filled into sacks, and burnt at Gandiwand village near Hussainiwala, in Ferozepur district.
39. 1931– On 24 March, the remains of the bodies were brought back to Lahore and were properly cremated in the evening at the banks of the river Ravi in Lahore, with thousands of people in attendance. Tributes were paid to the fallen heroes at Minto Park.
40. 1932– On 23 March, the song 'Ghori of Bhagat Singh' (a folk song in Punjabi), written by poet Mela Ram Tair was sung on the roads of Lahore as a tribute to Bhagat Singh.

The above facts are based on the following:
Bhagat Singh aur unke Mrityunjay Purkhe' (Bhagat Singh and His Immortal Ancestors*)* by Veerendra Sindhu, Bhagat Singh's niece
The Trial of Bhagat Singh by A.G. Noorani
The Hanging of Bhagat Singh edited by M.J.S. Waraich
Reports from the *Tribune, Abhyuodey* and *Bhavishya*

GENEALOGY

Family Tree

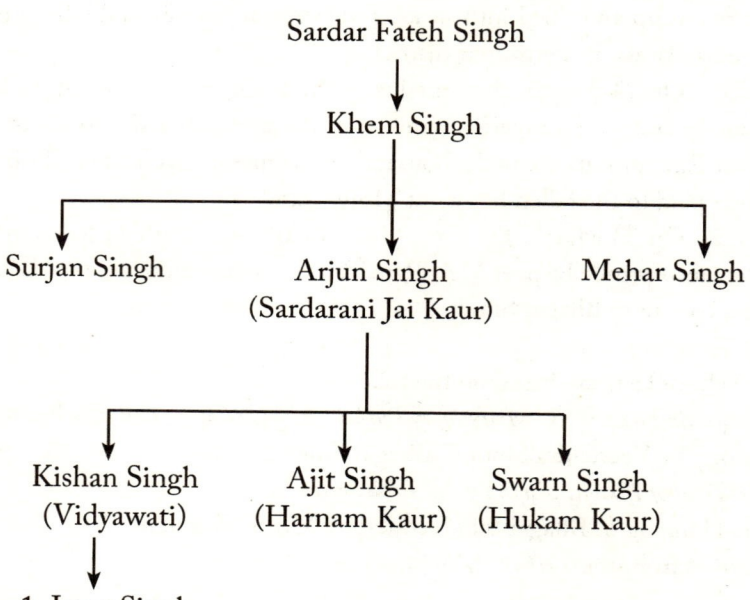

Sardar Fateh Singh
↓
Khem Singh

- Surjan Singh
- Arjun Singh (Sardarani Jai Kaur)
- Mehar Singh

Children of Arjun Singh:
- Kishan Singh (Vidyawati)
- Ajit Singh (Harnam Kaur)
- Swarn Singh (Hukam Kaur)

Children of Kishan Singh:

1. Jagat Singh
2. **Bhagat Singh**
3. Bibi Amar Kaur
4. Kulbir Singh
5. Kultar Singh
6. Bibi Sumitra (Prakash Kaur)
7. Bibi Shakuntla
8. Ranbir Singh
9. Rajendra Singh

ORDINANCE BY VICEROY ISSUED ON 1 MAY 1930 (ORIGINALLY IN ENGLISH.)

Ordinance No. III of 1930

An Ordinance to make provision for the trial of the persons accused in the Lahore Conspiracy Case.

Whereas an emergency has arisen which makes it necessary to provide specially for the trial of the accused in the cases known as the Lahore Conspiracy Case; now, therefore, in exercise of the power conferred by section 72 of the Government of India Act, the Governor General is pleased to make and promulgate the following Ordinance:

Short Title

1. This Ordinance may be called the Lahore Conspiracy Case Ordinance, 1930.

Definitions:

2. In this Ordinance –
   (a) the "Code" means the Code of Criminal Procedure, 1898; V of 1896
   (b) the "High Court" means the High court of Judicature at Lahore; and
   (c) the "said cases" mean the cases specified in section 3.

Trial of Lahore Conspiracy Cases by Special Tribunal

3. Notwithstanding anything contained in the Code, all cases pending in the Court of Rai Sahib Pandit Sri Kishan, Magistrate of the First Class, Lahore, against any or all of the persons named in the Schedule shall be tried by the Tribunal to be constituted under section 4.

Constitution of the Tribunal:

4. (i) As soon as may be after the commencement of this Ordinance, the Chief Justice of the High Court shall constitute a Tribunal for the trial of the said

cases consisting of three persons who at the time of such constitution are Judges, Additional Judges or officiating Judges of the High Court.

(ii) The Chief Justice shall appoint one of the members of the Tribunal to be President of the Tribunal.

Appointment of a new member where a member is unable to attend:

5. (i) If, for any reason, any member of the Tribunal is unable to discharge his duties, the Chief Justice shall appoint another Judge, Additional Judge, or officiating Judge of the High Court to be a member of the Tribunal.

(ii) Notwithstanding any change in the composition of the Tribunal, it shall not be incumbent on the Tribunal to re-call or re-hear any witness who has already given evidence, and it may act on any evidence already recorded by or produced before it.

Procedure of the Tribunal:

6. (1) When the Tribunal has been constituted, it shall take cognizance of the said cases and the jurisdiction of the aforesaid Magistrate shall cease.

(2) The Tribunal shall, subject to the provisions of this Ordinance, follow the procedure prescribed in Chapter XXI of the Code for the trial of warrant cases by Magistrates.

(3) In matters not coming within the scope of sub-section (2), the provisions of the Code, so far as they are not inconsistent with this Ordinance, shall apply to the proceedings of the Tribunal; and for the purpose of applying the said provisions, the proceedings already taken before the aforesaid Magistrate shall be deemed to be proceedings under Chapter XVIII of the Code, where under the accused persons have been committed to the Tribunal for trial, and the Tribunal shall be deemed to be a Court of Session to whom the accused persons have been duly committed by the aforesaid Magistrate.

(4) In the event of any difference of opinion among the members of the Tribunal, the opinion of the majority shall prevail.

Conduct of the prosecution

7. (1) The Local Government may appoint a person to be prosecutor for the conduct of the prosecution of the said cases, and such other persons to assist him as it may think fit.

(2) The prosecutor appointed under this section shall have the powers and shall discharge the duties of a Public Prosecutor under the Code.

Power of the Tribunal:

8. The Tribunal may pass upon any person convicted by it any sentence authorized by law for the punishment of the offence of which such person is convicted and no order of confirmation shall be necessary in respect of any sentence by it.

Special Powers of the Tribunal:

9. (1) The Tribunal shall have powers to take such measures as it may think necessary to secure the orderly conduct of the trial; and where any accused by his voluntary act has rendered himself incapable of appearing before the Tribunal, or resists his production before it, or behaves before it in a persistently disorderly manner, or in any other way wilfully conducts himself to the serious prejudice of the trial, the Tribunal may, at any stage of the trial, dispense with the attendance of such accused for such period as it may think fit and proceed with the trial in his absence.
(2) Where a plea is required in answer to a charge from an accused whose attendance has been dispensed with under sub-section (1), such accused shall be deemed not to plead guilty.
(3) An order under sub-section (1) dispensing with the attendance of an accused shall not affect his right of being represented by a pleader at any stage of the trial.

Special Rule of Evidence:

10. Notwithstanding anything contained in the Indian Evidence Act, 1872 (1 of 1872), when the statement of any person has been recorded by a Magistrate, such statement may be admitted in evidence before the Tribunal if such person is dead or cannot be found or is incapable of giving evidence, and the Tribunal is of opinion that such death, disappearance or incapacity has been caused in the interests of any accused.

Finality of Proceedings of Tribunal:

11. The judgement of the Tribunal shall be final and conclusive and, notwithstanding the provisions of the Code or of any other law for the time being in force, or of anything having the force of law by whatsoever authority made or done, there shall be no appeal from any order or sentence of the Court, and the High Court shall not have authority to revise any such order or sentence or to transfer any case from the Tribunal or to make any order under section 491 of the Code or have any jurisdiction of any jurisdiction of any kind in respect of any proceedings under this Ordinance.

Power of the President in Ancillary Matters:

12. (1) The President may make all necessary orders for the transfer to the custody of the Tribunal of all records, documents, exhibits and other things connected with the said cases.

(2) The President may also, from time to time, make orders consistent with this Ordinance to provide for the place and conduct of the trial, and all other ancillary matters which he may deem necessary to carry into effect the provisions of this Ordinance.

Schedule

1. Sukh Dev alias Dyal alias Swami alias Villager, son of Ram Lal, Thapar Khatri, of Mohalla Arya Samaj, Lyallpur.
2. Agya Ram alias Masterji, son of Nand Lal, Brahman, of Lalla, police station Killa Sobha Singh, District Sialkot.
3. Kishori Lal Rattan alias Deo Datt Rattan alias Mast Ram Shastri, son of Raghbar Dutt, Brahman, of Dharampur, police station Hajipur, District Hoshiarpur.
4. Des Raj, son of Ram Kishan, Khatri, of Balgan, police station Sambrial, District Sialkot.
5. Prem Dutt alias Master alias Amrit Lal, son of Ram Datt, Khatri, of Gujrat.
6. Surindra Nath Pandey alias Stone, son of Hira Lal Pandey, Brahman, resident of Mohalla Sabzimandi, Cawnpore.
7. Jai Dev alias Harish Chander, son of Babu Salig Ram, Khatri Kapur, Sadar Bazaar, Hardoi.
8. Sheo Varma alias Parbhat alias Harnarain alias Ram Lal alias Ram Narain Kapur, son of Kanhiya Lal Varma, Khatri, of Hardoi.

9. Gaya Parshad alias Dr B S Nigam alias Ram Lal alias Ram Nath alias Desh Bhagat, Kurmi, resident of Khajuri Khurd, Police station Billhaur, District Cawnpore.
10. Mahabir Singh alias Partab, of Shahpore Tehla, post office Raja ke Rampur, District Eta.
11. Bhagat Singh, son of Kishan Singh of Khawasrian, Lahore.
12. Batukeshwar Dutt alias Battu alias Mohan, son of GD Dutt, of Bedwan, Bengal.
13. Ajoy Kumar Ghosh alias Negro-General, Son of Dr Ghosh, of Cawnpore.
14. Jatin Sanyal (Jatindra Nath Sanyal), son of Hira Nath Sanyal, of Allahabad.
15. Bijoy Kumar Sinha alias Bachu, son of Markando Kumar Sinha of Mohalla Karachi Ganj, Cawnpore.
16. Shivram Rajguru alias "M", son of Hari Raj Guru, of Sadashiv Peth, Poona.
17. Kundan Lal alias Partap alias Partap alias No. 1, of Fyzabad.
18. Kanwal Nath Trivedi, alias Kanwal Nath Tewari, son of Pandit Surej Nath Tewari, of Sarya, police station Govindagunj, Champaran (student Vidya Sagar College, Calcutta).
19. Bhagwan Dass alias Gunthala, of Jhansi.
20. Chander Shekar Azad alias Panditji, son of Baij Nath Ram alias Sita Ram, Brahman, of Baij Nath Tula, Police station Bhilopur, Benares.
21. Kailashpati alias Kali Charan, son of Harde Narain, Kayasth, of Mongranwan, police station Chamirpur, District Azamgarh.
22. Bhagwati Charan alias B.C. Vohra, son of Rai Sahib Shiv Charan Dass, Brahman, of Lahore.
23. Yashpal, son of Hira Lal, Khatri, of Nidhon, police station Hamirpur, District Kangra, and of Wachhowali, Lahore.
24. Satgurdyal, son of Pandit Sukhbasi Lal Avasthi, Brahman, of Mohalla Bama Khori, Cawnpore.

Simla, IRWIN, 1 May 1930.
Viceroy and Governor General.

Statement

1. On 11 July 1929, the enquiry in the proceedings known as the Lahore Conspiracy Case commenced before a Magistrate, who was for this purpose relieved of all other duties. The accused are in the case number

24, of whom 5 are still absconding. The offence alleged against the accused are both in their own nature and in their relation to the public security of unusually serious character. They include the murder of Mr Saunders, Assistant Superintendent of Police, and head Constable Chanan Singh in Lahore, on 17 December 1928, the establishment of bomb factories at Lahore and Saharanpur, the conspiracy leading to the throwing of two bombs in the Legislative Assembly on 8 April 1929, and various other revolutionary activities. For the purpose of establishing these charges which were concerned with many different places and with events occurring over a considerable period of time, the prosecution considered it would be necessary to produce about 600 witnesses.

2. Two of the accused had resorted to hunger strike before the commencement of the enquiry. A number of other followed the same course shortly afterwards, with the result that by 26 July 1929, the case had to be adjourned owing to some of the accused being unfit to attend the Court. The case had to be successively adjourned on the same ground until 24 September. It was then resumed, but there were numerous interruptions owing to defiant and disorderly conduct by some of the accused or demonstrations by members of the public. On 14 February 1930, most of the accused again went on a hunger strike, and the case was on this account adjourned from 8 February till 8 March.

3. The enquiry has now been in progress for more than 9 months and during that time it has been possible to examine about 230 witnesses, only out of a unprecedented delays, and repeatedly disturbed by disorderly conduct and revolutionary demonstrations, has tended to bring the administration of justice into contempt, and it is impossible to count upon obtaining a conclusion by the normal methods of procedure within any calculable period.

4. After anxious consideration, I have come to the conclusion that neither the ends of justice nor the interests of the accused are served by allowing these proceedings to drag out to a length which cannot at present be foreseen. Public policy clearly demands that the grave charges against the accused should be thoroughly scrutinized and finally adjudicated upon with the least possible delay, by a tribunal of indubitable impartiality and authority, and that the preliminary proceedings which have already extended over nine months and the end of which is not yet in sight should be terminated. It is also necessary to ensure that obstructions shall not further interrupt the course of justice. I have accordingly decided to avail myself of the authority

conferred upon the Governor General under section 72 of the Government of India Act and to issue an Ordinance which has the effect of entrusting the trial of this case to a tribunal to be constituted by the Chief Justice of the High Court Judicature at Lahore, consisting of three Judges of the High Court, and to invest this tribunal with powers to deal with willful obstruction. By these means the accused will be assured of a trial before a court of the highest possible authority and it may be expected that a final and just decision will be reached with no unnecessary delay. I am convinced that the action which I have thought it right to take will best secure the achievement of the true ends of justice and re-establish respect for the administration of the law.

Simla IRWIN
1 May 1930. Viceroy and Governor General.
(From the book *Bhagat Singh: On the path of Liberation*)

SIGNIFICANT PART OF LAHORE CONSPIRACY CASE JUDGEMENT, 7 OCTOBER 1930 (ORIGINALLY IN ENGLISH.)

Accused No. 11, Bhagat Singh, as proved in the Lahore Conspiracy Case

Bhagat Singh was arrested in the Assembly Hall at Delhi on the 8 April 1929, by Sergeant Terry (P.W.18), after he and Bhatkeshwar Dutt had thrown a bomb in that building.

The important feature of the evidence regarding Bhagat Singh is his ubiquity[281] which may be taken to be in part, a result of the fact that at the Delhi meeting of September 1928 he was appointed to be a link between the various provinces. Thus, he is found at Lahore, Rawalpindi, Ferozepur, Delhi, Jhansi, Agra, Allahabad, Bettiah, and Calcutta, and his presence in Amritsar is

---

281 Exactly the same word had been used by judges of the Tribunal earlier, in 1914–15, for Kartar Singh Sarabha.

also mentioned by the approvers. He was arrested before the Saharanpur centre became important.

Both Jai Gopal and Hans Raj Vohra speak of meeting Bhagat Singh at the Lachhman Gali house in Gowalmandi, Lahore, towards the end of 1927, but of this there is no direct corroboration. Mahabir Singh in his confession states that he first met Bhagat Singh at Ferozepur, in November 1928, while Prem Dutt does not appear to have met him until the beginning of 1929. Phonindra Nath Ghosh and Man Mohan Bannerji, first saw Bhagat Singh at the Delhi meeting in September 1928, while Prem Dutt does not appear to have met him until the beginning of 1929. Phonindra Nath Ghosh and Man Mohan Bannerji first saw Bhagat Singh at the Delhi meeting in September 1928, while Lalit Kumar Mukerjee met him at Allahabad in the same month.

When Jai Gopal went to Rawalpindi in January 1928, both he and Hans Raj Vohra depose that Bhagat Singh accompanied him. Of this there is corroboration in the evidence of Head Constable Kharak Singh, (P.W.139), who has identified Bhagat Singh at a magisterial parade and in Court as having stayed with Jai Gopal at the Hamilton Bazar house.

Jai Gopal has deposed that when living at Rawalpindi in the house in Nawan Mohalla, Bhagat Singh paid him a visit and gave him Rs. 30 and told him to stay at Rawalpindi until further order, but of this visit there is no corroboration.

Thus Bhagat Singh's visit to Rawalpindi at the beginning of 1928 is proved but, owing to lack of corroboration, the second visit to that place is not satisfactorily proved.

According to Lalit Kumar Mukerjee, Bhagat Singh came to Allahabad in September 1928, and again in January 1929. The visit in January 1929 is corroborated by the evidence of Ragho Nath Mittra, (P.W.352), and should be taken as sufficiently proved.

Regarding Bhagat Singh's presence at the Delhi meeting of September 1928, and his appointment to the Central Committee on that occasion, there is the evidence of Phonindra Nath Ghosh and Man Mohan Bannerji corroborated in an important manner by the testimony of the Chaukidar of the Feroz Shah Tughlak Fort, Bara Singh, (P.W.420), who spoke to Bhagat Singh at the time of the meeting and subsequently identified him in the Court of the Special Magistrate as well as a magisterial parade. That this witness, being the chaukidar of the fort, should have been present on that particular occasion is a natural circumstance and there is no suspicion attaching to his evidence, which should be taken, when coupled with the evidence of two approvers, as fully proving Bhagat Singh's presence at the Delhi meeting.

Bhagat Singh's visits to Gaya Parshad's house at Ferozepur are proved by Jai Gopal's evidence, corroborated by the confession of Mahabir Singh who also met him there, as well as by the confession of Gaya Parshad and the evidence of one other witness, Diwan Chand, (P.W.200), who picked out Bhagat Singh at the magisterial parade and also in Court as having been seen by him at that house. It was during one of these visits, shortly after the Delhi meeting of September 1928, that Bhagat Singh had his hair and beard cut in accordance with a decision made at Delhi, and on this particular matter the confession of Gaya Parshad which mentions it is sufficient proof in corroboration of Jai Gopal's evidence on the point.

Next there was the visit of Bhagat Singh along with Panditji to Bettiah towards the end of September 1928; the object of which was to arrange a dacoity in Bihar and thus acquire funds for the party, another matter which had been discussed at Delhi. The particular journey proved abortive at that time as no dacoity was arranged, but the presence of Bhagat Singh on that occasion is proved by the evidence of Phonindra Nath Ghosh and of Man Mohan Bannerji ,coupled with the corroborating testimony of Raghuni, (P.W.17), who has satisfactorily identified Bhagat Singh and who was present when a meal was brought for Bhagat Singh and his companions by Man Mohan Bannerji from the latter's house, the witness Raghuni being employed on that occasion by Man Mohan Bannerji to carry a lantern.

The next scene of action in which Bhagat Singh is proved to have participated is the projected raid on the Punjab National Bank at Lahore early in December and the visits of Bhagat Singh to the Mozang House in Lahore at the same time. The evidence on these points is that of Jai Gopal and Hans Raj Vohra, coupled with the confession of Mahabir Singh; all whose confession proves Bhagat Singh's part in the Bank raid and is admissible against Bhagat Singh under section 30 of the Indian Evidence Act. General corroboration of the truth of Mahabir Singh's statement on these points is also provided by the taxi driver, Barkat Ali, (P.W.87), and the tonga driver, Feroz Din, (P.W.449), neither of whom however, could identify Bhagat Singh. Further, Bhagat Singh's presence at the Mozang House in those days is proved by four witnesses who corroborate the approvers on this point, namely, Hussain Baksh (P.W.60), Bura (P.W.72), Budhu (P.W.73), and Fakir Chand (P.W.86) all of whom identified Bhagat Singh at magisterial parades and also in Court.

Bhagat Singh's participation in the Saunders murder is the most serious and important fact proved against him, and it is fully established by ample evidence. That he was present at the Mozang House, at the meeting where the murder plot was elaborated, is proved by the evidence of Jai Gopal and by the confession of Mahabir Singh, while Hans Raj Vohra, mentions Bhagat Singh's presence in the Mozang House on that day. Jai Gopal also mentions that, on the 15 December Bhagat Singh showed him at the Mozang house some pink posters that read 'Scott is dead', and that Bhagat Singh and Panditji told him on that day about the decision to murder Mr Scott, while on the 17 December, the day of the murder at 11 a.m., Hans Raj Vohra saw Bhagat Singh copying similar posters with his own hand and at Bhagat Singh's request Hans Raj Vohra also copied three or four of them. The subsequent recovery of similar posters proved to be in Bhagat Singh's handwriting, which will be mentioned below, containing the heading 'Saunders is dead', proves the truth of Hans Raj Vohra's statement on this point.

The evidence that Bhagat Singh took part in the Saunders murder is threefold in character. There is first the evidence of various eyewitnesses who claim to have identified Bhagat Singh either as one of the men who committed the murder or as one of those who were retreating from the scene of murder soon after it had been committed.

Secondly, there is the evidence of two approvers, Jai Gopal and Hans Raj Vohra and especially that of Jai Gopal, who was himself a participator in the crime and whose presence at the scene of the crime has been well-proved by other evidence already referred to when dealing with the general corroboration of Jai Gopal, and certain corroboration of the evidence of Jai Gopal that Mr Saunders was actually shot at by Bhagat Singh, which is furnished by the testimony of Mr Robert Churchill, (P.W.31), the gun expert of London, who proves that a cartridge case found near the spot had issued from the automatic pistol, Ex. P. 480 which was recovered from the possession of Bhagat Singh by Sergeant Terry, (P.W.18), when he arrested Bhagat Singh on 8 April 1929, in the Assembly Hall at Delhi.

Thirdly, there are the posters; Exs. P.A.X., P.A.X./1, P.A.X/2, P.A.X/3, P.B.Q and P.B.S.; all of which are proved by the handwriting expert Mr Scott, (P.W.423), to be in the handwriting of Bhagat Singh and the contents of which are tantamount to a confession on the part of Bhagat Singh of complicity in the murder of Mr Saunders in the interests of the Hindustan Socialist Republican Army. A further admission of Bhagat Singh regarding his participation in the Saunders murder is proved by the confession of Prem Dutt who mentions that in his presence probably in January 1929, Bhagat Singh addressing Sukh Dev stated, 'Do you remember how endeavours were made by us to hit the mark accurately but we used to miss it? When we went to kill Saunders the bullet struck his head[282] and we thought that one of us would be arrested, but none was arrested'. This is quite a reliable piece of evidence. Another confession of Bhagat Singh is proved by Phonindra Nath Ghosh, Bhagat Singh having explained to him at Calcutta at the end of December 1928, that he and his party had murdered Mr Saunders and that Phonindra Nath Ghosh had not been asked to approve beforehand because he lived at a distance and also because Bhagat Singh had undertaken to take his consent.

Another alleged confession of Bhagat Singh to a fellow prisoner in the Mianwali Jail, Abdul Rehman Shah, (P.W.451), is not regarded as reliable and has been excluded from consideration.

The professed eyewitnesses of the actual murder are Abdullah (P.W.34), Muhammad Ibrahim (P.W.36), Faqir Sayed Wahid-ud-Din (P.W.47), Chaudri Habib Ullaha (P.W.101), Kamal Din (P.W.102), Ganda Singh (P.W.180) and Mr Fearn (P.W.46). Mr Fearn did not identify either of the assailants and the evidence of Wahid-ud-Din and Ganda Singh is disregarded owing to the fact that neither of these witnesses was prompt in giving information to the authorities about what has professed to have seen. Although the evidence of Muhammad Ibrahim, Constable, Habib Ullaha, and Kamal Din is not in itself unconvincing, there are certain discrepancies in the testimony of the other witnesses which give rise to some doubt whether these three men should be believed as measure of precaution their evidence also is disregarded.

The evidence of Abdullah, (P.W.34), is however, satisfactory and reliable. He was the motor driver whose motor arrived, while the firing was going on at the corner of Court Street near to the position which Jai Gopal had taken up. He afterwards took the body of Mr Saunders to the hospital in his car. He saw the attack upon Mr Saunders and he has identified Bhagat Singh satisfactorily both at a magisterial parade and also in Court as the taller of the two men who fired upon Mr Saunders. With this identification, there is no reason to doubt.

There are also witnesses who saw the murderers on their way from the scene of action passing through the D.A.V. College ground and leaving those grounds at the further end. These witnesses are Som Nath (P.W.144) student,

---

282 The Post Mortem Report does not support it, since there was no head injury on Saunders' body.

Abnash Chand (P.W.145) student, Aftab Ahmed (P.W.232) student, Ajmer Singh (P.W.181) student and Ata Muhammad (P.W.28) cycle merchant. Of these, Som Nath saw the three murderers coming down the staircase from Block B of the D.A.V. College Hostel and noticed that one of them was armed with a pistol. He satisfactorily picked out Bhagat Singh as one of those three men at a magisterial parade, but his identification of Bhagat Singh in the jail just before giving the evidence in this Court was not so successful. In the first instance he picked out another man but immediately corrected himself and picked out Bhagat Singh. His evidence should be regarded as good proof against Bhagat Singh. Abnash Chand, (P.W.145), saw the three members near the Botanical Garden of the D.A.V. College, one of them appeared to him to be carrying a pistol. He successfully picked out Bhagat Singh as one of those men at a magisterial parade by his back which was the only part of man in question that he had seen on the occasion referred to, but when he went to the jail shortly before giving the evidence he was unable to again pick out Bhagat Singh. His evidence, is therefore not very effective against Bhagat Singh. Aftab Ahmed, (P.W.232), was near the volleyball ground of the D.A.V. College and saw two of the murderers pass by, one having a pistol. He satisfactorily picked out Bhagat Singh both at a magisterial parade and in Court as the man who was carrying the pistol.

Ajmer Singh, (P.W.181), is the student from whom an attempt was made to take a bicycle. He did not succeed in identifying Bhagat Singh as one of the party who accosted him. Ata Muhammad, (P.W.48), is the cycle merchant from whose shop a bicycle was actually taken but abandoned when the witness gave chase. He deposed that one of the three men who passed his shop stopped at a turning while another one removed the bicycle from his shop. He has satisfactorily identified Bhagat Singh at a magisterial parade and also in Court as the man who stopped at the turning and his evidence is good proof against Bhagat Singh.

Thus, of the witnesses named in this group Som Nath (P.W.144), Aftab Ahmed (P.W.232) and Ata Mohammad (P.W. 48) provide good evidence of Bhagat Singh's participation in the Saunders murder.

Coming now to the evidence of Mr Robert Churchill, the gun expert which has been mentioned above, the recovery of the pistol Ex. P. 480 from Bhagat Singh when arrested at Delhi on the 8 April 1929 is adequately proved by Sergeant Terry (P.W.18). In this connection, it is explained by the evidence of Rai Bahadur Suraj Narain, (P.W.379), that when Bhagat Singh was tried at Delhi for the throwing of a bomb in the assembly hall, the pistol was intentionally not exhibited in the trial and there is no reason, therefore, doubt Sergeant Terry's evidence on the score that Bhagat Singh's possession of a pistol was not proved in that case. Ex. P. 864/1-1 is a bullet picked up by Muhammad Ibrahim, (P.W.150), from the spot where the body of Mr Saunders had been lying shortly after the murder and handed over by this witness to Inspector Bawa Mani Ram (P.W.78). (The statement of Muhammad Ibrahim, P.W.150, that he handed the bullet over to the Inspector Kundan Lal is taken to be a mistake and the statement of inspector Bawa Mani Ram, P.W.78, that it was to him Muhammad Ibrahim, P.W.150, had handed it over is taken as correct.) Inspector Bawa Mani Ram, (P.W.78), handed it over to Head Constable Jagan Nath, (P.W.105), who retained it until it was taken to Mr Churchill, (P.W.31), in London by Mr Jenkin, Superintendent of Police, (P.W.30). An empty cartridge case. Ex. P. 864/1-B, was picked up by Sub Inspector Bahadur Ali, (P.W.75), on 19 December 1928, together with other empty cartridge cases from near the spot where Mr Saunders was shot down. Bahadur Ali handed it over to Inspector Bawa Mani Ram, (P.W.78), who in turn handed it to Head Constable Jagan Nath, (P.W.105). This was also retained by Jagan Nath until Mr Jenkin took it to Mr Churchill in London. The evidence of Mr Churchill regarding these two exhibits as well as other exhibits examined by him is detailed and convincing and was supported by an ocular demonstration in Court to the Tribunal with the help of micro photographs and a pair of microscopes with one single eyepiece, in which eye piece half of each of two bullets to be compared could be simultaneously, showing whether or not they had been fired from the same weapon by relating the lines found on one bullet to those on the other. The comparison of Ex. P. 864/1-I made with a test bullet which was proved by the evidence of Mr Jenkin, (P.W.30), and a Magistrate, Mr Lewis, (P.W.264), to have been fired from the pistol Ex. P. 480. Similarly, an examination in the same manner of the marks on the empty cartridge case, Ex. P/864/1-B, with marks on a test cartridge case proved by the same witness to have been fired from the same pistol was also made by means of micro photographs and the pair of microscopes with a single eyepiece. The comparison proved conclusively to the expert and to this Court that the bullet Ex. P. 864/1-I and the empty cartridge case Ex. P. 864/1-B, had been fired from the automatic pistol Ex. P. 480. Had the pistol been recovered from Bhagat Singh immediately after the murder this piece of evidence would have proved by itself that he had fired on Mr Saunders. As it was recovered from Bhagat Singh nearly four months after, it cannot be said to amount to more that corroborative evidence of the statement of Jai Gopal but as corroborative evidence it has a very high value.

Coming now to the various confessions mentioned above, those which were made to Prem Dutt and to Phonindra Nath Ghosh are both important, but the most important of all is the evidence of the pink posters. The finding of the posters Exhibits, P.A. X. P.A.X. /1., P.A.X/2. and P.A.X./3 affixed in different public places of Lahore within a few days of the Saunders murder is proved by Khan Sahib Sheikh Muhammad Sadiq (P.W.81), Sub Inspector Amar Nath (P.W.82) and Rahmat Khan Constable (P.W.83), but it is really immaterial where these posters were found in as much as that wherever they were found they are proved by the evidence of Mr Scott, (P.W.423), to be in the handwriting of Bhagat Singh and having regard to the fact that the name of the murdered man is given as Saunders and not as Scott, it is highly improbable that they could have been written by Bhagat Singh before the murder. Mr Scott's evidence deals with Exhibits PA.X. P.A.X/1, P.A.X/2 and P.A.X/3 about which evidence is forthcoming as to where they were found and also with Exs. P.B.O and P.B.S. about which there is no such evidence on the record. In the case of Bhagat Singh, Mr Scott had ample material on the basis of which to work in the shape of documents proved beyond doubt to be in Bhagat Singh's handwriting, namely the documents Exhibits P.C.B., P.D.C., P.F.Y., P.F.Z., P.F.X. and P.G.B/1. His evidence is detailed and convincing and was assisted by an examination, which the Court itself could make, of juxtaposed photographs containing letters and words from the proved documents juxtaposed with letters and words from the posters. This evidence proves beyond all reasonable doubt that these posters were written by Bhagat Singh and a perusal of them shows that the writer must have been privy to the murder of Mr Saunders. The witnesses, by whose evidence those documents are proved on the basis of which Mr Scott made his comparison, are Chaudri Ghulam Rasul (P.W.152), Sheik Bashir Ahmed (P.W.153), Inspector Karam Singh (P.W.154), Zawwar Hussain (P.W.155), Sahibzade Mriza Aitzaz ud-Din Ahmed Khan, Superintendent of Police (P.W.165), Sheikh Murid Akbar (P.W.247) and Sub Inspector Charan Singh (P.W.313).

Taking all the above evidence together, it is conclusively proved that Bhagat Singh took part in the murder of Mr Saunders and actually fired at him with the pistol, Ex. P. 480.

After the murder Bhagat Singh went to the Mozang House and on 20 December 1928 he left Lahore for Cawnpore, travelling second class while Shivram Rajguru traveled as his servant. Both Jai Gopal and Hans Raj Vohra have mentioned this fact, Jai Gopal having been told by Sukh Dev about the end of March, 1929. The evidence is admissible against Bhagat Singh and Shivram Rajguru and it is well corroborated by the testimony of four Railway officials, Ram Saran Dass (P.W.114), Hari Chand (P.W.115), Niaz-ud-Din P.W.116) and Tej Singh (P.W.117), who prove that on 20 December 1928, one second-class ticket from Lahore to Cawnpore and one servant ticket were issued at Lahore and that similar tickets issued at Lahore were collected at Cawnpore on the following day on the arrival of the 14 Down Express from Lahore. This journey is, therefore, adequately proved.

At the end of December 1928 and in January 1929, Bhagat Singh was in Calcutta and was meeting Phonindra Nath Ghosh and JN Dass in connection with a proposal that JN Dass should come north and teach the members of the party bomb-making. In January also, a beginning was made in the quarters of Kanwal Nath Tiwari at Calcutta of the manufacture of guncotton for use in bombs and in this also Bhagat Singh assisted. The evidence by which these facts are proved is that of Phonindra Nath Ghosh corroborated by the statements of Balaio Lal Ghosh, (P.W.391), and Chander Shekhar Ghosh ,(P.W.392), both of whom saw Bhagat Singh in the company of Phonindra Nath Ghosh at Calcutta in those days and both of whom have satisfactorily identified Bhagat Singh at magisterial parades and also at the jail shortly before giving their evidence in this Court. While in corroboration of Phonindra Nath Ghosh evidence about the making of gun cotton at the quarters in Cornwallis Street there is the important witness Tulsi Ram (P.W.397), the jamadar of the Arya Samaj Mandir where Kanwal Nath Tiwari was living, who actually entered the room of Kawal Nath Tiwari on one occasion when both Phonindra Nath Ghosh and Bhagat Singh were there, and satisfactorily identified both of them at magisterial parades in addition to identifying Phonindra Nath Ghosh in Court and Bhagat Singh at the jail shortly before he gave his evidence in this Court. These activities of Bhagat Singh are thus adequately proved.

From Calcutta Bhagat Singh probably went to Agra, and was at Agra at any rate in February 1929 when bomb-making began at the Hing Ki Mandi House and when on 16 December the party left for Cawnpore to rescue Yogesh Chander of which party Bhagat Singh was a member of. It was at Agra also that the decision to throw a bomb in the Assembly Hall was made by the Central Committee at a meeting which Bhagat Singh attended. The proof of Bhagat Singh's presence at Agra and his participation in the above mentioned affairs is contained in the evidence of Phonindra Nath Ghosh and Lalit Kumar Mukerjee who had been sent for by Bhagat Singh from Allahabad to take part in the bomb making, while regarding the journey of rescue party to Cawnpore there is the corroborating evidence of Railway officials already referred to in discussing the case of Sheo Verma and, finally in regard to Bhagat Singh's presence in those days at the Hing Ki Mandi House, there is the evidence of Abdul Aziz Beg (P.W.239), Muhammad Irshad Ali Khan (P.W.240) and of Thakar Ram

Singh (P.W.371), all three of whom identified Bhagat Singh at a magisterial parade and also in Court . The evidence of both the approvers regarding these activities is in itself of a convincing character and the above mentioned corroborative evidence which is available coupled with their evidence furnishes proof of Bhagat Singh's participation in those events. His visit to Jhansi in March 1929 is an off-shoot of the Agra proceedings, the journey having been made from Agra at having been made in order to test one of the bombs that had been manufactured at Agra. In this Jhansi visit Bhagat Singh joined. The proof of Bhagat Singh's connection with that journey and with the experiment of exploding a bomb at lonely spot twenty two miles from Jhansi is contained in the evidence of Phonindra Nath Ghosh, who also took part in that journey and in the experiment which was its object and whose evidence on the point is very well-corroborated. Such corroboration is to be found in the first place in the evidence of railway officials, Rameshwar Dyal (P.W.268), Prabhu Dyal (P.W.269), Bijoy Singh (P.W.275), Sindohan Parshad (P.W.276), and Gobind Rao (P.W.277) who prove that four third-class tickets only were issued from Agra to Jhansi on 5 March 1929, and only two third-class tickets were issued from Jhansi to Raja Ki Mandi near Agra on 6 March 1929, and that on one of these two third-class tickets a bicycle was booked at Jhansi and taken delivery at Raja Ki Mandi. It is inconceivable that Phonindra Nath Ghosh when he first made his statement to a magistrate should have known that corroboration of this character concerning these two journeys and concerning the booking of a bicycle on the return journey would be available from the documents in possession of the Railway authorities and this evidence, therefore, provides a very valuable guarantee of the truth of his testimony. Apart from this there is also corroborative evidence of the visit of Bhagat Singh to Jhansi in the statement of Ram Dulare (P.W.288), Shiv Raj P.W.289) and Rama Nand (P.W.290), the taxi driver who drove the party to the scene where the bomb was exploded. All these three men satisfactorily identified Bhagat Singh at magisterial parades and also either in Court or at the Jail shortly before giving their evidence in this Court.

There remains the presence of Bhagat Singh at Delhi in March and April 1929, up to 8 April 1929, when he and B.K. Dutt threw a bomb in the Assembly Hall. The plan to throw the bomb was known to Phonindra Nath Ghosh and is mentioned in his evidence. It is also proved that Bhagat Singh travelled from Agra on 7 March 1929 and arrived at Delhi on 8 March taking with him a bicycle. On this point the evidence of the two railway officials Gobind Rao, (P.W.277), and Sham Manohar Lal, (P.W.280), is supported by a document Ex.

P.D.P., which is a risk note signed by Bhagat Singh with the signature "Ram Kishan" when he took delivery of the bicycle at Delhi. The signature on this document is satisfactorily proved by the handwriting expert Mr Scott ,(P.W.423), to have been made by Bhagat Singh and this journey of Bhagat Singh is thus clearly proved. The presence of Bhagat Singh at Mussamat Mukandi's house in Delhi is also proved by the evidence of Ms Mukandi (P.W.169), Ram Saran Das (P.W.172), and Nur Muhammad (P.W.174), all of whom identified Bhagat Singh at magisterial parades and also in Court. The same remark would apply to Banwari Lal, (P.W.170), and Harnam Singh, (P.W.171), but these two men are not regarded as reliable witnesses. Finally, the arrest of Bhagat Singh at the Assembly Hall, on 8 April is fully proved by Sergeant Terry, (P.W.18), and Sub Inspector Hans Raj (P.W.20). Regarding Bhagat Singh's intention to throw a bomb in Assembly Hall the letter, Ex.P.137, which he wrote to Sukh Dev and which was found in Kashmir Building, Lahore though it does not definitely mention such an intention gives an indication that Bhagat Singh had an intention of that character and that he had already discussed it with Sukh Dev. That this document is in the handwriting of Bhagat Singh is convincingly proved by the careful evidence of Mr Scott by means of juxtaposed photographs and detailed examination of the letter and words and form of writing. In the case of Bhagat Singh, Mr Scott had ample proved material upon which to work and his evidence of the subject is very convincing.

Another document proved by Mr Scott, (P.W.423), is the document, Ex. P.A.K. /7, which was found in the Saharanpur house when it was raided on 13 May 1929. This document is a rough list of books. The evidence that proves its recovery is that of Sher Ali, (P.W.228), and Khan Sahib Rehman Baksh Qadri,(P.W.204). Though Bhagat Singh never went to Saharanpur house, the finding of this document in that place proves a connection between Bhagat Singh and the three men who were arrested there.

To sum up, Bhagat Singh was a leader of the revolutionary party which was formed at Delhi in September 1928, and had already taken part in revolutionary activities before that party was formed. He was an active member of the Punjab branch, of which Sukh Dev was organizing member, and from the time of the Delhi meeting, Bhagat Singh was selected as a link between the various provinces and in this capacity was constantly travelling from place to place between the Punjab and Calcutta. As a member of the Central Committee he also took part in important deliberations and plans of the party and was generally found participating in the active side of the movement. He took part in the project to raid the Punjab National Bank in Lahore, he was a protagonist in the murder of

Mr Saunders, and it was he who entered into negotiations that JN Dass should teach bomb-making to the members of the party; he actually took part in the bomb-making at Agra, in the rescue party of Jogesh Chander Chatterji and in the journey to Jhansi to test a bomb and, finally, he was selected to throw the bomb in the Assembly Hall, Delhi, in April 1929.

Concluding part of the judgement

1. Bhagat Singh, Rajguru and Sukhdev sentenced to death under section 121 and section 302, section 4(b) of the Explosive Substance Act read with section 6 of the Act and section 120-B of the Indian Penal code.[283] Kishori Lal, Mahabir Singh, Bijoy Kumar Sinha, Sheo Verma, Gya Prasad, Jaidev and Kanwal Nath Tiwari sentenced to transportation for life under sections 120-B, 121 etc.
2. Kundan Lal sentenced to rigorous imprisonment for seven years without solitary confinement under section 121-A
3. Prem Dutt sentenced to five years rigorous imprisonment without solitary confinement under section 121-A and 120-B
4. Des Raj, Ajoy Kumar Ghosh and Jatindra Nath Sanyal acquitted.[284] (Five approvers–Jai Gopal, Phonindra Nath Ghosh, Man Mohan Bannerjee, Hans Raj Vohra and Lalit Kumar Mukherjee are discharged from custody.

Announced   GC Hilton
                                            Abdul Qadir
                                            JK Tapp
7 October 1930

Taken with thanks from *The Hanging of Bhagat Singh – Complete Judgment, and Other Documents,* edited by Prof. Malwinderjit Singh Waraich and Dr Gurdev Singh Sidhu.

---

283 Even though Sukhdev was not present at the site of assassination of Saunders.

284 Ironically, Jatindra Nath Sanyal was convicted for writing Bhagat Singh's biography in *Bhavishya* magazine later and sentenced to two years imprisonment in 1931–32.

PRIVY COUNCIL JUDGEMENT; 11 FEBRUARY 1931 (ORIGINALLY IN ENGLISH.)[285]

Bombay High Court
Bhagat Singh vs Emperor on 27 February 1931
Equivalent citations: (1931) 33 BOMLR 950
Author: V Dunedin
Bench: V Dunedin, Thankerton, Russell, G Lowndes, D Mulla

Judgement

Viscount Dunedin, J.

1. This case does not fall within the strict rule that has been again and again laid down that this Board does not and will not act as a tribunal of criminal appeal, because here the objection, if it were good, would go to the root of the jurisdiction. But it is subject to the ordinary criterion which is applied to all petitions for special leave to appeal, to wit, that leave will not be granted where upon the face of the application it is plain that on the merits it is bound to fail.

2. Now the only case that is made here is that Section 72 of the Government of India Act did not authorise the Governor General to make the order he did, constituting a special tribunal for the trial of the offenders who, having been convicted, are now petitioners here. The 72nd section is as follows:- 72. The Governor General may, in cases of emergency, make and promulgate ordinances for the peace and good governments of British India or any part thereof, and any ordinance so made shall, for the space of not more than six months from its promulgation, have the like force of law as an Act passed by the Indian legislature; but the power of making ordinances under this section is subject to the like restrictions as the power of the Indian legislature to make laws; and any ordinance made under this section is subject to the like disallowance as an Act passed by the Indian legislature and maybe controlled or superseded by any such Act.

---

285   Source: https://indiankanoon.org/doc/617286/

3. The petitioners ask this Board to find that a state of emergency did not exist. That raises directly the question who is to be the judge of whether a, state of emergency exists. A state of emergency is something that does not permit of any exact definition:--It connotes a state of matters calling for drastic action which is to be judged as such by someone. It is more than obvious that that someone must be the Governor General and he alone. Any other view would render utterly inept the whole provision. Emergency demands immediate action, and that action is prescribed to be taken by the Governor General. It is he alone who can promulgate the ordinance.

4. Yet, if the view urged by the petitioners is right, the judgement of the Governor General could be upset either (a) by this Board declaring that once the ordinance was challenged in proceedings by way of habeas corpus the Crown ought to prove affirmatively before a Court that a state of emergency existed, or (b) by a finding of this Board - after a contentious and protracted enquiry - that no state of emergency existed, and that the ordinance with all that followed on it was illegal.

5. In fact, the contention is so completely without foundation on the face of it, that it would be idle to allow an appeal to argue about it.

6. It was next said that the ordinance did not conduce to the peace and good government of British India. The same remark applies. The Governor General is also the judge of that. The power given by Section 72 is an absolute power, without any limits prescribed, except only that it cannot do what the Indian legislature would be unable to do, although it is made clear that it is only to be used in extreme cases of necessity where the good government of India demands it.

7. It was urged that there was repugnancy between the ordinance as passed and the constitution of the High Court of Lahore, and that the terms of Section 84 (1) make void the ordinance because of such repugnancy But, as soon as it is admitted, as counsel candidly did admit, that an Act might be passed by the Indian legislature under the powers of Section 65 in the same terms as the ordinance, the point as to repugnancy vanishes.

8. Their Lordships must add that, although the Governor General thought fit to expound the reasons which induced him to promulgate this ordinance, this was not in their Lordships' opinion in any way incumbent on him as a matter of law.

9. Their Lordships, for these reasons, have humbly advised His Majesty that this petition should be dismissed.

Bhagat Singh vs Emperor on 27 February 1931

The first trial of Bhagat Singh and B.K. Dutt for the Delhi Bomb Case was conducted by British Judge P.B. Pool, who handed over the case to Sessions Judge Leonard Middleton, who sentenced both Bhagat and Dutt to 'transportation for life'. The trial began on 7 May and got over on 12 June 1929. Their appeal in the High Court was dismissed in January 1930 by judges Forde and Addison.

The second trial, known as the Lahore Conspiracy Case, which dealt with the murder of Saunders, began in Lahore in Rai Saheb Pandit Sri Kishan's court from 10 July 1929 and was later handed over to a three-member High Court judge tribunal consisting of Justice Coldstream (the president of the tribunal), Justice Agha Haider and Justice Hilton. The trial began on 5 May 1930. On 22 June, the tribunal was reconstituted and independent judge Agha Haider was replaced by Justice Abdul Qadir, Justice Hilton was made president, and Justice Tapp was added to the tribunal. On 7 October 1930, this tribunal sentenced Bhagat Singh, Rajguru and Sukhdev to death.

The appeal to the Privy Council was dismissed by lords Viscount Dunedin and others on 11 February 1931. The date of execution was fixed as 24 March 1931, which was secretly advanced to the evening of 23 March.

NEWLY FOUND MATERIAL

Another letter found from Punjab archives, Lahore

A Special Tribunal of three High Court judges was notified by Chief Justice of Punjab High Court Shadi Lal, on 1 May 1930 for the trial of the Lahore Conspiracy Case. This tribunal consisted of Justice Coldstream as President of the Tribunal and Justice Agha Haider and Justice Hilton as members. While on 5 May, five comrades of Bhagat Singh wrote to the Tribunal regarding their decision to boycott the tribunal, ten other comrades, including Bhagat Singh, on 8 May 1930, wrote to avail legal help for the case. This letter was found for the first time in March 2018 and the Punjab Archives of Lahore, put up an exhibition of the 100-plus files relating to Bhagat Singh. Ammara Ahmad, a Lahore-based journalist, was kind enough to send the photograph of a few exhibits, which included this letter.

In the court of the Special Tribunal
Lahore Conspiracy Case, Lahore
Crown vs. Sukhdev & Others
Charged under secs 302, 120-B+121-A, IPC
This humble petition of the accused persons

Bhagat Singh & others most respectfully shweth:

(1) That the petitioners are charged with most serious offences including sec. 302 with 120B and 109 IPC
(2) That the majority of the petitioners have been lodged for the last eight or nine months in jail.
(3) That with one exception, all the petitioners as stated below belong to distant provinces and as such have no relative here to look after their defence.

    1. Ajay Kumar Ghosh – Allahabad, U.P
    2. Bejoy Kumar Sinha – Cawnpore, U.P
    3. Prem Dutt – Srinagar, Kashmir
    4. Kamal Nath Tewary – Betiah, Bihar
    5. Shiv Verma – Hardoi, U.P
    6. Jai Dev Kapoor – Hardoi, U.P
    7. S.N. Pande – Cawnpore, U.P.
    8. Kishori Lal – Quetta, Baluchistan
    9. Des Raj – Sialkot, guardian outside India

(4) That five of the petitioners are unrepresented accused defending their case themselves.
(5) That for the reasons stated above in paras 3+4, the petitioners can make arrangement for their defence only through their friends, attorneys and members of defence committee.

(6) That it is therefore prayed that in the interest of justice, the learned court be pleased to grant the petitioners following facilities-

1. Interviews with friends, attorneys, legal advisors and members of defence committee members and relatives in court during lunch hours or after the rising of the court during the one hour stay after accused for their mutual consultation
2. Instructions should be sent to the Supdts. of Borstal and Central jails for allowing interviews with the same.
3. Subject to accommodation the legal advisors of the unrepresented accused be given seats in the body of the court room.
4. Recognition of the defence committee and permission to two members of committee to sit in the body of the court subject to accommodation.

(7) That it is prayed that in view of the large number of prosecution exhibits of this case, one of the day of the week preferably Saturday be set for the examination of the exhibits by the accused and their counsels.

Hand written and signed by-

1. Bhagat Singh
2. Bejoy Kumar Sinha
3. Ajay Kumar Ghosh
4. SuPande
5. Jai Dev Kapoor
6. Kishori Lal Ratan
7. Prem Datt Varma
8. Shiv Varma
9. Kamal Nath Tewari
10. Des Raj

8th May 1930

(Official Stamp Lahore)

Specimen Signatures of Bhagat Singh, taken during trial

The court required specimen signatures of Bhagat Singh, which could be examined. This might have been the legal procedure to be followed during trials, as many posters produced as exhibits during the trial were hand-written by Bhagat Singh. It is interesting to note that even for a handwriting sample, the text chosen by Bhagat Singh was highly political.

The text written in Bhagat Singh's handwriting:

'Ours is a policy of sobriety which we can see through of nursing our trade E..

in to other better conditions of looking after education and health of our people and particularly of our women and children – a policy which goes in to every home and every cottage through throughout the country. From and to end is a policy which you know will be carried out to the the utmost of our ability and I will promise nothing more.

Mr Baldwin E

Sd./ Bhagat Singh

The above is the statement of Mr Baldwin which he has recently made in England, in connection with the election campaign.

Sd./Bhagat Singh

Witness
Sd./ Zawar Hussain, agent
Another signature
R.B. Boota Singh & Sons same company
20.4.29

BIBLIOGRAPHY

This is not a referral bibliography, meaning the list of books consulted or referred in this book. This is more of a comprehensive bibliography of books published in eighteen languages on Bhagat Singh, which include academic books, books related to the trial proceedings, popular standard biographies, banned books, and even children's books. The idea is to have an assessment of the popular fascination for Bhagat Singh. Some of the books listed might not even provide factual or authentic information, but have still been mentioned here since it is impossible to trace their existence or contents, and since references to them were found in broader publication lists. Despite our best efforts, the list is not exhaustive, as there were no resources to record all the publications on Bhagat Singh. All effort has been made to make the list as comprehensive as possible; however, it has not always been possible because of a lot of the literature being out of print or banned. So, the complete bibliographical details of books, especially from obscure sources and from the Internet – including crucial information like the name of the city of publication or year of publication, or even the name of the writer/editor – might not have been provided. Some books are only available as Kindle editions, and have been included as such.

The bibliography of Hindi books is somewhat different from that of other languages. The most numbers of books on Bhagat Singh were published in Hindi and the most to be banned were in the language too. In a study on banned literature on the freedom struggle, it was noted that the maximum number of books to be banned during the British colonial regime were on Bhagat Singh. In total, more than 125 books (in all languages) relating to Bhagat Singh were ordered to be taken off the shelves, mostly during 1931–33. This bibliography lists fifty-five banned books in Hindi.

1. English

1. Lal, Chaman (compilation and introduction), *Jail Notebook & Other Writings of Bhagat Singh*, Delhi, LeftWord, 2007

2. Lal, Chaman, *Understanding Bhagat Singh*, Delhi, Aakar Publications, 2013
3. Noorani, A.G., *The Trial of Bhagat Singh*, Delhi, Oxford University Press, 2005
4. Waraich, M.J.S., and GS Sidhu, *The Hanging of Bhagat Singh: Vol. I (Judgement)*, Chandigarh, Unistar, 2005
5. *Ibid., Vol. II (Proceedings)*, Chandigarh, 2008
6. *Ibid., Vol. III (Confessions, etc.)*, Chandigarh 2007
7. *Ibid., Vol. IV (Banned Literature)*, Chandigarh, 2007
8. Waraich, M.J.S., *Revolutionaries in Dialogue*, Chandigarh, Unistar, 2007
9. Verma, Shiv (edited by), *Selected Writings of Shaheed Bhagat Singh*, Delhi, NBC, 1986
10. Hooja, Bhupender (edited by), *A Martyr's Notebook*, Jaipur, IBC, 1994
11. Waraich, M.J.S., *The Eternal Rebel*, Delhi, Publication Division, 2007
12. Sanyal, Jitender Nath, *Shaheed Bhagat Singh* (Banned in 1932), Nagpur, Vishvabharti, 1983
13. Juneja, M.M., (edited by), *Selected Collections on Bhagat Singh*, Hisar, Modern, 2007
14. Sinha, Srirajayam, *A Revolutionary's Quest for Sacrifice*, Mumbai, Bhartiya Vidya Bhavan, 1993
15. Grewal, P.M.S., *Bhagat Singh: Liberation's Blazing Star*, Delhi, LeftWord, 2007
16. Habib, S Irfan, *To Make the Deaf Hear*, Delhi, Three Essay Collections, 2007
17. Habib, S Irfan (edited by), *Inquilab: Bhagat Singh on Religion and Revolution*, Delhi, Sage Publications, 2018
18. Moffat, Chris, *India's Revolutionary Inheritance: Politics and Praise of Bhagat Singh*, London, Cambridge University Press, 2019
19. Maclean, Kama, *A Revolutionary History of Interwar India: Violence, Image, Voice and Text*, London, Hurst and Company, 2015
20. Yadav, K.C., and Babar Singh, *Bhagat Singh, Contemporary Portrayals*, Gurgaon, Hope India, 2006
21. Dhawle, Ashok, *Shaheed Bhagat Singh: An Immortal Revolutionary*, Mumbai, CPM, 2007
22. Bardhan, A.B., *Bhagat Singh: Pages from the Life of a Martyr*, Delhi, PPH, 1984

23. Singh, Bhagat, and Bipin Chandra (introduction), *Why I am an Atheist*, Delhi, PPH/ National Book Trust of India (NBT), 1993, 2007
24. Comrade, Ram Chander, *NBS and HSRA*, Delhi, G-3, Anand Niketan, 1986
25. Comrade, Ram Chander, *Road to Freedom: Revealing Sidelights*, Delhi, Gitanjali Prakashan, 1980
26. Comrade, Ram Chander, *Ideology and Battle Cries of Indian Revolutionaries*, Delhi, G-3 Anand Niketan, 1989
27. Bharti, Balbhadra, *Shaheed Bhagat Singh*, Jaipur, 1993
28. Singh, Gulab, *Under the Shadow of Gallows*, Delhi, Rupchand, 1963
29. Gupta, Manmath Nath, *They Lived Dangerously*, Delhi, PPH, 1968
30. Mohan, Kamlesh, *Militant Nationalism in Punjab*, Delhi, Manohar, 1985
31. Mohan, Kamlesh, *Bhagat Singh: The Man & His Ideology*, Jaipur, 1993
32. Chatterji, Jogesh, *In Search of Freedom*, Kolkata, Firma KL, 1967
33. Gupta, D.N., *Selected Speeches and Writings of Bhagat Singh*, Delhi, NBT, 2007
34. Kalia, P.R. (edited by), *Bhagat Singh Today*, Canada, 2007
35. Govt. of Punjab, *They Died So That the Country May Live*, Chandigarh, 1981
36. Koonar and Sindhra, *Martyrdom of Shaheed Bhagat Singh*, Chandigarh, Unistar, 2005
37. Nayar, Kuldip, *Without Fear*, New Delhi, HarperCollins Publishers India, 2007
38. Gaur, I.D., *Martyrs as Bridgeroom: A Folk Representation of Bhagat Singh*, Delhi, Anthem Press, 2008
39. *Inqualaab Zindabad!* (banned), Lahore, 1930
40. Thakur, Gopal, *The Man & His Ideas*, Delhi, PPH, 1965
41. Majumdar, S.N., *In Search of Revolutionary Ideology*, Delhi, PPH, 1965
42. Bakshi, S.R., *Shaheed Bhagat Singh and His Ideology*, Delhi, Capital, 1981
43. Bakshi, S.R., *Bhagat Singh, Patriot and Martyr*, Delhi, Anmol 1997
44. Khullar, K.K., *Shaheed Bhagat Singh*, Delhi, Hem
45. Mathur, L.P., *Shaheed Bhagat Singh: Prince of Martyrs*, Jaipur, Avishkar
46. Sehgal, Omesh, *Shaheed Bhagat Singh, Legendary Martyr*, Delhi, Gyan Books, 2002
47. Ram, S, *Shaheed Bhagat Singh, Unique Martyr*

48. Ram, S, *Shaheed Bhagat Singh: Patriotism, Sacrifice and Martyrdom*, Delhi, Commonwealth 2005
49. Deol, G.S., *Shaheed Bhagat Singh*, Ludhiana, Deep Prakashan, 1977
50. Deol, G.S., *Bhagat Singh and his Ideology*, foreword by Emily C Brown, Nabha, Deep Prakashan, 1978
51. Ghosh, Ajay Kumar, *Bhagat Singh and His Comrades*, Bombay, PPH, 1945
52. Rana, Bhawan Singh, *Bhagat Singh*
53. Venu, C.S., *Bhagat Singh* (banned), Madras, 1931
54. Kanakasabai, T.S., *Bhagat Singh or Roar on Scaffold* (banned), Madras, 1931
55. Palnitkar, Shrichand Ramhari, *Life of Sardar Bhagat Singh* (banned), Akola, 1931
56. Ram, N, (edited by), *Celebrating Bhagat Singh* (*Frontline* Special Issue) Chennai, November 2007
57. Datta, V.N., *Gandhi and Bhagat Singh*, Delhi, Rupa, 2008
58. Gauba, Khalid Latif, *Famous and Historic Trials*, Lahore, Lion Press 1946
59. *Bhagat Singh: Path to Liberation*, Chennai, Bharti Pustakalayan, 2007
60. Grewal, J.S. (edited by), *Bhagat Singh and His Legend*, Patiala, World Punjabi Centre, Punjabi University, 2008
61. Singh, Colonel Raghvender, *Bhagat Singh: Symbol of Heroism for Indian Youth*, Delhi, Vijay Goel Publishers, 2008
62. Johar, K.L. (edited by), *Martyr Bhagat Singh: An Intimate View*, Yamunanagar, 2008
63. Sharma, Shalini, *Radical Politics in Colonial Punjab*, London, Routledge, 2009
64. Mohan, Krishan, *Revolutionary Politics and Indian Freedom Movement*
65. Singh, Chanderpal, *Bhagat Singh Revisited*, Delhi, Originals, 2011
66. Wilco Picture Library, *Bhagat Singh*, Mumbai, 2011
67. Singh, Veer (edited by), *The Life and Ideas of Shaheed Bhagat Singh*, Delhi, Originals 2010
68. Rahbar, Hans Raj, *Bhagat Singh: An Ignited History*, Delhi, Farsight Publishers, 2012
69. Dhillon, Harish, *Shaheed Bhagat Singh*, Delhi, Indus Source Books, 2011

70. Singh, Bhagat, *Words of Freedom*, Delhi, Penguin Books India, 2010
71. *Shaheed-e-Azam Bhagat Singh*, large print
72. Igen, B, *The Legend of Bhagat Singh*, Delhi, Manoj Publishers, 2003
73. Pasricha, Ashu, *The Political Thought of Bhagat Singh*, Delhi, Concept, 2008
74. Singh, M.K., and Ravi Ranjan, *Bhagat Singh*, Delhi, KK Publishers, 2009
75. Singh, Anil K, *Encyclopedia on Bhagat Singh*, Anmol, Delhi, 2008
76. Rao, Subba, *Bhagat Singh*, Amar Chitra Katha, 1981
77. Gusain, H.K., *Biography of Bhagat Singh*, Delhi, Cybertech Publications, 2011
78. Ambary, Shasi, *Bhagat Singh*, Prodigy, 2009
79. Shivaji, *Bhagat Singh and Tipu Sultan*, Maanu Graphics, 2008
80. Murthy, R.K., *Shaheed Bhagat Singh*, Macmillan India, 1997
81. *Bhagat Singh: Great Men of India*, Delhi, Sterling Publishers, 2006
82. Jadhav, R.P., and P.B. Relekar, *Bhagat Singh*, Adarsh Vidyarthi Prakashan
83. Pinney, Chirstopher, *Bhagat Singh (Pathfinders)*, Routledge, 2008
84. Paul, S, *Bhagat Singh*, Delhi, Learner Press, 1999
85. *Kumar, P. Bhagat Singh*, Mahaveer Press
86. Das, Shyam, *Luminous Life of Bhagat Singh*, Tinypot Publications, 2004
87. *Illustrated Biography of Bhagat Singh*, Delhi, Rohan Books, 2003
88. Puri, Harish, *Ghadar Movement to Bhagat Singh*, Chandigarh, Unistar, 2012
89. Massey, Reginald, *Shaheed Bhagat Singh and the Forgotten Indian Martyrs*, New Delhi, Abhinav Publications, 2013
90. Jaswal, Avtar, *The Legacy of Bhagat Singh and the Naxalite Movement*, Delhi, Anamika, 2011
91. *Know about Bhagat Singh*, Maple Press, 2014
92. Rico, Aka, *The Selected Works of Bhagat Singh*, CreateSpace Independent, 2009
93. Singh, Jupinderjit, *Discovery of Bhagat Singh's Pistol and his Ahimsa*, Chandigarh, Kalpaz, 2018
94. *Bhagat Singh: Shaheed-e-Azam*, Om Books International, 2011
95. Tewari, Vinod, *The Legend of Bhagat Singh*, Delhi, Manoj Publications, 2004

96. Singh, Ravinder, *Bhagat Singh: The Daring Youth of India*, Delhi, Navyug, 2007
97. Barrat, *Ultimate Revolutionary Bhagat Singh*, Delhi, Raja Pocket Books, 2015
98. Ana Books, *Bhagat Singh: The True Patriot*, Kindle edition
99. Ashraf, Mohammad Arslan, *Bhagat Singh: Pakistan's Unsung Hero*, Kindle edition
100. Simran, *Bhagat Singh*, Kindle edition, 2012
101. Patel, Dhirubhai, *Saheed Bhagat Singh*, Kindle edition, 2016
102. Sharma, C.P., *The Builder of Modern India: Bhagat Singh*, Delhi, Aavishkar, 2014
103. Pai, Anant, *Bhagat Singh*, Amar Chitra Katha, 2006
104. Alam, Firoz, *Great Indian Revolutionary Bhagat Singh*, 2013
105. Kaushik, Deepak, *Life and Works of Bhagat Singh*, 2015
106. Syed, M.H., *Bhagat Singh*, 2011

2. Punjabi

1. Chandan, Amarjit (edited by), *Likhtan: Shaheed Bhagat Singh Ate Saathi*, Amritsar, Balraj Sahni Yaadgar Pustakmala, 1974
2. Singh, Jagmohan (edited by), *Shaheed Bhagat Singh ate Unah de Saathiyan Diyan Likhtan*, Ludhiana, Chetna Prakashan, 2000
3. Waraich, M.J.S., (edited by), *Shaheed Bhagat Singh Dian Kujh Chonvian Likhtan*, Barnala, Tarakbhart, 2006
4. Waraich, Malwinderjeet Singh, *Jivani Shaheed Bhagat Singh*, Barnala, Tarakbharti, 2013
5. Waraich, M.J.J.S., *Bhagat Singh ate Saathi*, Barnala, Tarakbharti, 2013
6. Waraich, M.J.J.S., *Bhagat Singh Rajguru ate Chandershekhar Azad*, Chandigarh, Unistar, 2007
7. Lal, Chaman, *Bhagat Singh: Vicharvan Inqlabi*, Delhi, Navyug Press, 2009
8. Lal, Chaman (edited by), *Bhagat Singh de Syasi Dastavez*, New Delhi, NBT, 2011
9. Lal, Chaman, *Inqualaabi Itihas De Sunehari Panne*, Barnala, Taraksheel, 2005
10. Cheema, Zafar (edited by), *Punjab Rang* (quarterly), Lahore, Bhagat Singh Special issue, 2007

11. Cheema, Zafar, *Bhagat Singh Shaheed: Chonven Mazmun ate Kavitavan*, Lahore, Dayal Singh Foundation, 2007
12. Azad, S.S., *Shaheed Bhagat Singh: Jeevan ate Krantikari Marg*, Delhi, Manpreet Prakashan, 2007
13. Soomal, Mohindar, *Bhagat Singh di Soch Walio*, Ludhiana, Chetna, 2007
14. Daman, Devendar, *Chhipan Ton Pehlan* (play), Ludhiana, Chetna Prakashan, 2006
15. Sarhadi, Sagar, *Shaheed Bhagat Singh di Vapsi* (play), Jalandhar, Deepak Publishers, 1983
16. Sidhu, Charan Das, *Bhagat Singh Shaheed* (play), Delhi, Shilalekh, 1998
17. Komal, Jagjit, *Dhote Munh Chaped* (play), Amritsar, Literature House, 2004
18. Singh, Gursharn, *Inqualaab Zindabad* (play), Amritsar, Balraj Sahni Yaadgar Pustakmala, 1976
19. Singh, Didar, *Shaheed Bhagat Singh* (poetry), Ludhiana, Bhagat Singh Khoj Committee, 1984
20. Waraich, M.J.S., (edited by) and Didar Singh, *Kissa Shaheed Bhagat Singh*, Barnala, Tarakbharti, 1968, 2006
21. Singh, Gurdev (edited by), *Singh Garjna* (poetry), Patiala, Publication Bureau Punjabi University 1982
22. Sidhu, Gurdev Singh (edited by), *Sohile Shaheed Bhagat Singh* (poetry), New Delhi, NBT, 2008
23. Sidhu, Gurdev Singh (edited by), *Bandi Bol* (poetry collection), New Delhi, NBT, 2008
24. Sidhu, Gurdev Singh (edited by), *Bhagat Singh de Marathi Powade*, Delhi, NBT, 2011
25. Sidhu, Gurdev Singh (edited by), *Ghoriyaan: Shaheed Bhagat Singh*, Chandigarh, Lokgeet, 2006
26. Singhal and Badhan (edited by), *Shaheed-e-Azam Bhagat Singh Kav* (poetry), Delhi, NBT, 2005
27. Badhan, Baldev Singh, *Amar Shaheed Bhagat Singh: Kav Shardhanjli*, Ed. Patiala, Gurmat Parkashan, 2006
28. Badhan, Baldev Singh (edited by), *Bhagat Singh Kav Sangrah* (poetry), Jalandhar, Deepak Publishers, 2008
29. Ahluwalia Amarnath, *Virlap* (banned), 1931

30. Singh, Ajit, *Sutluj di Hawa* (novel), 2007
31. Singh, Baldev, *Satluj Vehnda Riha* (novel), Ludhiana, Chetna Prakashan, 2007
32. Mallunia, Jeet (translated by), *Karachi Congress ate Bhagat Singh di Shahidi*, Chandigarh, Lokgeet, 2007
33. Virli Tejinder, *Inqlab* (biography), Jalandhar, Kuknoos, 2006
34. Premi, Ram Lal, *Jithe Suraj Ugiya* (biography), Moga, Mukti Prakashan, 2006
35. Parwana, Balbir (edited by), *Shaheed Bhagat Singh Vichardhara Ludhiana*, Chetna, 2006
36. Deol, G.S., *Shaheed Bhagat Singh* (biography), Patiala, Punjabi University, 1973
37. Nayar, Kuldip, *Shaheed Bhagat Singh de Inqlabi Tajarbe*, Amritsar, Chatar Singh Jivan Singh, 2006
38. Josh, Sohan Singh, *Bhagat Singh Nal Merian Mulakatan*, Delhi, Aarsee, 1988
39. Singh, Pream, *Bhagat Singh te Sathi Jailan Vich*, People's Forum, 2007
40. Sindhu, Veerendra, *Yug Purush Bhagat Singh ate Unnah de Purkhe*, Patiala, Language Dept., 1975
41. *Taraksheel Bhagat Singh*, Taraksheel Society, Ludhiana, 1996
42. Singh, Tirlok, *Bhagat Singh*
43. Singh, Swarn, *Sardar Bhagat Singh*, Delhi, Wellwish Publishers, 1992
44. *Shaheed-e-Azam Bhagat Singh di Jail Diary*, Chandigarh, Punjab Government, 2007
45. Sufi, Amrjit, *Shaheed Bhagat Singh di Nastikata*, 2001
46. Duggal, Kartar Singh, *Bhagat Singh*, Delhi, Publication Division, 2001
47. *Bhagat Singh di Pahchaan*, Jalandhar, Desh Bhagat Yadgar Committee, 1988
48. Savyasachi, *Bhagat Singh*, Jalandhar, Kuknoos, 2002
49. Singh, Randhir, *Bhagat Singh nal Mulaquat*, Amritsar, 1963
50. *Jo Satluj Kandhae Sarh Gaye*, Jalandhar, Yuvak Kendar, March 1969
51. *Quami Lehar* (monthly), Bhagat Singh issue, Jalandhar, March 1971
52. Sukhindar (edited by), *Sanvad*, Bhagat Singh issues, Toronto, 2000–2006
53. Tarsem, S (edited by), *Bhagat Singh: Sangharsh te Shahadat*, Malerkotla, 2007
54. Tarsem, S (edited by), *Suraj, Suli te Shayar*, Malerkotla, Nazaria Prakashan, 2008

55. *Jagriti*, Bhagat Singh special issue, Chandigarh, Punjab Government, September 2007
56. Salim, Ahmad, *Bhagat Singh: Jiwan ate Adarsh*, Islamabad, 2008
57. Salim, Ahmad and Shabnam Ishaque (edited by), *Kehdi Maan ne Bhagat Singh Jammia* (poetry collection), Sanjh, Lahore, 2008
58. Sadiq, Mohamad, *Shaheed Bhagat Singh*, Chandigarh, Lokgeet
59. Singh, Rajinderpal (translated by), *Shaheed Bhagat Singh di Jail Notebook*, Chandigarh, Lokgeet, 2005
60. Johl, Lakhwinder, *Ek Sapna Ek Samvad* (poetry), 2007
61. Pali, Bhupinder Singh, *Main Bhagat Singh Han te Main Phir Awanga* (play), Ludhiana, Chetna, 2008
62. Sethi, Mohinder Singh, *Azadi da Parwana*, 1962
63. *Azad Hind da Pehla Quami Shaheed Sardar Bhagat Singh* (novel), Amritsar, Mehar Singh and Sons
64. Jawanda, Avtar, *Charhda Suraj Bhagat Singh*, Jalandhar, Deepak Publishers, 1983
65. Singh, Harcharn, *Masiha Suli te Muskraya* (play), Ludhiana, Lahore Book Shop, 1980
66. Nandan, Inderjit, *Shaheed Bhagat Singh: Anthak Jiwangatha* (epic), Ludhiana, Chetna, 2008
67. Sohinderbir, *Inqlab da Bani: Bhagat Singh*, Amritsar, Kasturi Lal & Sons, 2008
68. Inqlabi, Kirat Singh (edited by), *Shaheed Bhagat Singh Chintan*, Delhi, National Book Shop, 2008
69. Brar, Jangir Singh, *Quami Shaheed Bhagat Singh* (poetry), Mansa, Udaan, 2006
70. Dipti, Shyam Sunder, *Vihvin Sadi da Mahanaik – Shaheed Bhagat Singh*, Amritsar, Prerna Prakashan, 2008
71. Singh, Anup, and Shyam Sunder Dipti (edited by), *Shaheed Bhagat Singh di Vichardhara*, Amritsar, Prerna Prakashan, 2007
72. Singh, Anup, and Shyam Sunder Dipti (edited by), *Shaheed Bhagat Singh da Chintan*, 2007
73. Singh, Anup and Shyam Sunder Dipti (edited by), *Shaheed-e-Azam Bhagat Singh di Lodwandi*, Amritsar, Prerna Prakashan, 2011
74. Jagroop, *Paramguni Bhagat Singh*, Moga, Mukti Prakashan, 2007
75. Dandwindi, Balabir Sandha, *Shaheed Bhagat Singh: Jivani ate Kavitavan*, Jalandhar, Delite Publishers

76. Steno, Hem Raj, *Shahid Bhagat Singh: Vande Matram ton Inqlab Tak*, Barnala, Taraksheel Society, 2007
77. Mehraj, Chand Singh, *Qissa Shahide-Azam Bhagat Singh*, Lambra, Punjabi Sath, 2009
78. Rai, Jagtar Singh Giani, *Shaheed Bhagat Singh de Nanke Pind da Gauravmai Itihas*, Ludhiana, Swami Printers, 2001
79. Juneja, M.M., *Bhagat Singh di Kathni te Karni*, Zirakpur, Modern Publishers, 2011
80. Azad, Avtar Singh, *Bhagat Singh Shaheed*, Jalandhar, Hind Publishers, 1960
81. Sital, Dhanwant Singh, *Sardar Bhagat Singh Shaheed*, Amritsar, Sital Sahit Bhavan, 1960
82. Sangudhaun, Kanwarjit Singh, *Shaheed Bhagat Singh: Jivan ate Sanghrash*, Barnala, Tarakbharti, 2011
83. Brar, Surjit (translated by), *Shaheed Bhagat Singh: Kranti da Sipahi*, Barnala, Tarakbharti, 2016
84. Singh, Master Trilochan (edited by), *Hello Main Bhagat Singh Bol Rihan Han*, Jalandhar, 5Aab
85. Singh, Bhagat, *Achhut da Swal ate Main Nastik Kyon Han*
86. Sidhu, Charan Das (edited by), *Shaheed Bhagat Singh ate Dr Ambedkar di Sidhantak Sanjh*, Jalandhar, Navchetna, 2017
87. Rehbar, Hans Raj, *Bhagat Singh: Ekk Maghda Itihas*, Delhi, Shilalekh, 2010
88. Singh, Gulab, *Bhagat Singh te Usde Saathiyan da Inqlabi Jeevan*, Chandigarh, Unistar, 2013
89. Gill, Tejwant, and Jatinder Singh (edited by), *Filman ate Natkan Vich Bhagat Singh ate Hor Lekh*

3. Tamil

1. Chettiyar, K Sundarraju, *Bhagat Singh Thuku Alankaram* (banned), Tanjore, 1931
2. Pillai, W Nataraj, *Bahadur Bhagat Singh Pattu* (banned), 1931
3. Durairajan, T.K., *Desiya Geetangal* (banned), Madras, 1932
4. Manmargudi, *Sardar Bhagat Singh*, (banned), Madras, 1932
5. Mani, R.B.S., *Sutanandir Nadam* (banned), Madras, 1931
6. Pillai, K Tutralam, *Santamil Mairi* (banned), Madras, 1931

7. Chettiyar, V.A. Thiagaraja, *Congress Pattu* (banned), Madras, 1932
8. Parithapa, *Geetam – T.M. Thirumalai Swami* (banned), Madras, 1931
9. Chettiyar, K.V. Meenakshisundaram, *Congress Klerthanai or Swarajya Path* (banned), Madras, 1931
10. Pillai, V Nataraj, *Bhagat Singh Kirtanaurtam* (banned), Madras, 1931
11. *Sardar Bhagat Singh Charitaram*, Thruppathianpulian, 1931
12. Jeevanadam, P (translated by), *Na Nastheegan Ain? Sardar Bhagat Singh*, Erode, 1934; latest edition: Madras, 2005
13. Vellimalai, Ka, *Tukkile Pakatcin*, 1982
14. Pillai, V.R. Elumalai, *Bhagat Singh Keerthanamaritam*, Madras, 1981
15. Kannan, T.S., *Bhagat Singh*, Sebai, 1931
16. *Bhagat Singh: Thuppaki Vidu Thoothu*, Muthu Raman, Kizhakku Pathippagam, Chennai, 2007
17. Perumal, S.A., *Bhagat Singh Kalturaikal Katithankal*, Chennai, Paavai Publications, 2012
18. Perumal, S.A., *Bhagat Singhmarrum Thozharkal*, Chennai, Paavai Publications, 2012
19. Singh, Bhagat, *Oru Veera Varalaru*, Chennai, Bharti Pustkayan
20. Singh, Bhagat, *Viduthalai Vaani Jolikkum Tharakai*, Bharthi
21. *Vidudlai Pathaiyil Bhagat Singh*, Chennai, Bharthi
22. Hussain, Anwar A., *Bhagat Singh*, Bharthi
23. Verma, Shiv, *Vidutalaip Pathaiyil Bhagat Singh*, Bharthi
24. Singh, Bhagat, *Ilam Thozharkalurukku Lenin*, Bharthi
25. Grewal, P.M.S., *Bagath Singh: Indhiya Viduthaklaip Pozhic Muthal Ayutam Thangiya*, Chennai, Bharthi, 2007
26. Gurumurthi, V, *Vivar Bhagat Singh*, 1969
27. Ghosh, Ajai, *Bhagath Singhum Avarthu Thozargalum*, Chennai, New Century Book House, 2012
28. Vaaimenidhan, *Bhagat Singh Purtchi Kappiyam*, Chennai, New Century Book House, 2013
29. Singh, Bhagat, *Nan Nathigen Yen*, Kindle edition, Ethir Velvedu, 2017
30. Chokkan, N, *Biography of Bhagat Singh*, Kindle edition, 2018

4. Marathi

1. Lal, Chaman (edited by), Desai, Datta (translation), *Bhagat Singh: Samagra Vangmayaa*, Diamond Books, Pune, 2007, 2016

2. Chouslkar, Ashok, *Shaheed Bhagat Singh: Jeevan va Karya*, Kolhapur University, 2006
3. Mali, Sachin, *Bhagat Singh: Tarun Manacha Krantikaari Hunkaar*, Kolhapur, Nirmiti Vichaar Manch, 2006
4. Sakhavalkar, Krishna Madhav, *Amar Shahid sa Bhagat Simha*, 1968
5. Kasid, Girish (edited by), *Manza Krantii Swapan*, Kolhapur, 2005
6. Varvarkar, Sankar, *Bhagat Singhacha Povada*, Nashik, 1931
7. Narayan, Khandekar, *Bhagat Singhacha Powada* (banned), Bombay, 1932
8. *Bhagat Singhacha Povada* (ballad) (banned), 1931
9. Kumar, Ashwini, *Bhagat Singhacha Powada*, Bombay, 1932
10. Pandit, Bhgitha, *Sardar Bhagat Singhacha Powada*, Nasik, 1931
11. *Bhagat Singh, Rajguru va Sukhdev* (poetry)
12. Manmohan, *Sardar Bhagat Singh* (banned), Bombay, 1932
13. Sanjhgru, Prabhakar (edited by), *Jeevan Marg* (Bhagat Singh special issue), Mumbai, 2007
14. Joshi, Vishnu Shridhar, *Krantivir Chandershekhar Azad ani Sardar Bhagat Singh*, Mumbai, 1978
15. Joshi, Mrinalini, *Inqlab* (novel), Pune, Nehla Prakashan, 1993
16. Krishtanya, K, *Sardar Bhagat Singh*, Pune, 1955
17. Singh, Bhagat, *Mi Nastik Ka Ahe*, Pune, Lokayat, 2012
18. *Shaheed Bhagat Singhche Trunana Avahan*, Pune, Lokayta, 2014
19. Bhalerao, Abhit (translated by), *Shahid Bhagat Singhachi Jail Diary*, Mumbai, Jicanrang Prakashan, 2016
20. Gokhle, Hemant, *Krantikark Bhagat Singh*, Pune, Diksha Publishers, 2015
21. Bhatt, Vithalrai, *Krantiveer Bhagat Singh*, Pune, Manovikas Publishers, fourth edition: 2014
22. Nayar, Kuldip, and Datar Bhagwan (translated by), *Shaheed: Bhaymukta Houn Maranala Kavet Ghenarya Bhagat Singh Yancha Akherparyantcha Jeevanpravas*, Rohan Prakashan, 2015
23. Nahar, Sanjay, *Sardar Bhagat Singh*, Pune, Chinar Publishers, 2008

5. Urdu

1. Lal, Chaman (edited by), *Shaheed Bhagat Singh: Dastavezon ke Aaine Mein*, Delhi, Publication Division, 2014
2. Nayar, Kuldip, and Fahmida Riyaz (translated by), *Bhagat Singh aur Unki Inqlaabi Jaddojahad*, Karachi, Oxford University Press

3. Hasan, Sibte, *Bhagat Singh aur Uske Saathi*, Karachi
4. Salim, Ahmed, *Bhagat Singh Zindgii aur Khyalaat*, Karachi, Riktab, 1986
5. Bashir, Wahid, etc. (edited by), *Irtiqa*, Issue Number 44, Bhagat Singh Khasusi Karachi, 2007
6. Azad, Chaman Lal, *Bhagat Singh aur Datt ki Amar Kahaani*, Delhi, 1965
7. Mishra, Shambhu Dayal, *Sham-e-Aazadi ke Teen Parvaane* (banned), 1931
8. *Ghodi Bhagat Singh Shaheed*, Jalandhar
9. Hindi, Nazar Ahmad, *Shaheedan-i-Vatan urf Kurbanii Azam* (banned), Amritsar
10. Hussain, Sayyad Ali, *Naara-e-Jung* (banned), Lyalpur, 1932
11. Aflatoon, Bharat Bhushan, *Lutfe Shahadat ke teen Shaheed*, Lahore, 1932
12. Panchhi, M.S. Kavi, *Amulle Lal*, Sialkot, 1931
13. Prasad, Ram, *Qatliye-Begunah urf Shahidane Watan* (banned), Lahore, 1931
14. Bhajnik, Ashanand Mahasha, *Drama Bhagat Singh, Datt and Jatindar Das* (banned), Rawalpindi, 1930
15. Ashanand, Bhajnik, *Watan ke Shaheedan ka Bepanah Khoon* (banned), Rawalpindi, 1931
16. Seth, Bhai Shiv Prasad, *Inqlabi Lahar urf Toofan-e-Hind* (poetry) (banned)
17. Verma, Sukhdev, *Sardar Bhagat Singh* (banned), Lahore, 1931
18. Hindi, Meher Ilamuddin, *Pyara Bhagat Singh* (Banned), Lahore, 1931
19. Ahluwalia, Amarnath, *Virlap*, Lahore
20. Sehgal, Narayan Dutt, *Shama-e-Azadi ke Teen Parwane*, Lahore
21. Daler, Avtar Singh, *Shahid-e-Azam Bhagat Singh* (opera), 1962

6. Bengali

1. Das, Mahendra Nath, *Fansi* (banned), Calcutta, 1931
2. Mishra, Shambhu Prasad, *Sukhdev, Bhagat Singh aur Rajguru ki Faansi* (banned) Calcutta, 1931
3. Mishra, Shambhu Prasad, *Shaheed Bhagat Singh* (banned), Calcutta, 1931
4. Sengupta, Lokenderkumar, *Inqlab Zindabad*, 1970
5. Biswas, Bisva, *Shaheed Bhagat Singh*, 1971
6. Lal, Chaman (edited by), *Bhagat Singh Jail Notebook ani Anya Lekh*, National Book Agency, Kolkata, 2012,

7. Sarkar, Raghunath, *Shaheed-e-Azam Bhagat Singh*, Kolkata, 2007
8. Chattopadhyaya, Nrapender Krishan, *Bhagat Singh*, 1951
9. Adhikari, Santosh Kumar, *Santrasvad au Bhagat Singh*, 1979
10. Singh, Bhagat, *Keno Ami Nastik*, 1980
11. Bandopadhyaya, Tapan Kr. (translated by), *Bhagat Singh Jail Diary*, Kolkata, Shakti 2009
12. Gangopadhyay, Biswanath, *Amader Bhagat Singh*, Kolkata, 2013
13. Habib, S Irfan, *Bhagat Singh O Tara Sahjogira*, Sahitya Samsad, 2015

7. Telugu

1. *Naa Nethuru Vrudha Kadu*, Jana Sahiti Andhra Pradesh, 1986, 2004
2. Manikayan, M.R., *Sardar Bhagat Singh: Jivan Charitram*, 1931
3. Krishnaswamy, C, *Shaheed Bhagat Singh Jeevancharittar* (banned), Madras, 1935
4. Nirmlanand (edited by), *Jan Sahiti Bhagat Singh Shat Jayanti Ank*, Hyderabad, 2000, 2007
5. Reddy, K Pratap, *Bhagat Singh*, Hyderabad, Vishal Andhra, 2010
6. Ghosh, Ajoy, and Sohan Singh Josh, translated by Vasi Reddy, Bhaskar Rao, and K Rajeshwar Rao, *Bhagat Singh*, Hyderabad, Vishal Andhra, 1974, 2009
7. Sastri, M.V.R., *Bhagat Singh*, Durga Publications, 2016
8. Ravi, Thelkapalli, *Bhagat Singh Swiya Rachanalu – Sandesalu Jailu Dairy – Jeevita Ghatalu Smrutulu*, Prajasakti Book House, 2014
9. Shree, Malya, *Bhagat Singh*, Swathi Publications, 2012

8. Kannada

1. Ramakrishna, G, *Bhagat Singh: A Biography*, Navakannda Books, Bangalore, 1984, sixteenth edition: 2015
2. Gayathri, N (translated by), *Naaneke Nastika, Bhagat Singh*, Navkarnatka Publications, 2011
3. Anupama, H.S. (translated by), *Bhagat Singh: Jail Diary*, Ladai Prakashan, Gadag, 2016
4. Chidanandamurthy, *Bhagat Singh: Jeevana Sadhane*

5. Nayar, Kuldip, and Diwakar S (translated by), *Nirbhaya: Bhagat Singana Jeevna Jivana Mattu Horata*
6. Krishnamruthaya, Baabu, *Yougdrashtha Bhagat Singh*, Total Kannada, 2017
7. Bardhan, A.B., and Sau Diu Halimath (translated by), *Hutatma Bhagat Singh*, Bangalore, Navkarnatka Books, 2012
8. Murthy, B Rajsekra, *Devariddaaneye*, Total Kannada, 2013

9. Gujarati

1. Mehta, Chamanlal Ishwarlal, *Shaheed Bhagat Singh kee Jeevan Katha* (banned), Ahmedabad, 1931
2. Mehta, Chamanlal Ishwarlal, *Bhagat Singh Kaun?* (banned), Ahmedabad, 1931
3. Saran, Renu, *Shaheed Bhagat Singh*, Diamond Pocket Books, 2015
4. Rao, Subba, *Bhagat Singh*, Amar Chitra Katha Publication, 2010

10. Malayalam

1. Dhawle, Ashok and Yengad Raghvan (translated by), *Shaheed Bhagat Singh – Anaswara Viplavkari*, Thiruvananthapuram, Chintha Publishers, 2007/08
2. Grewal, P.M.S., and Vengad Raghvan (translated by), *Bhagat Singh*, Thiruvananthapuram, Chintha Publishers, 2008/2010
3. Habib, S Irfan, and Antony P.J. (translated by), *Badhirakarangal, Thurakkan: Bhagath Singhinteyum Koottalikaluteyum Prathyaya Sasthrayvum Pravrathalungam*, Kottayam, DC Press, 2012
4. Shihab, K.K., *Bhagat Singh*, Kindle edition, 2017

11. Sanskrit

1. Sudan, Krishan Lal Sharma, *Hutatma Bhkatsingh Charitarm*, Saharnpur
2. Shastri, Svayam Prakash Sharma, *Sri Bhakatsimhacharitarm*, Meerut, 1978
3. Sudan, Chuni Lal, *Bhagatsinghcharitamartam*
4. Shastri, Yageyeshwar, *Bharatrashtraratnam*

12. Sindhi

1. Ram, Ruchi, and Dwarkadas, *Inqlaab Zindabad!* (banned), Hyderabad, 1931
2. Hoondraj, Leelaram, *Fansi ke Geet* (banned), Larkana, 1931
3. Ayaz, Sheikh, *Bhagat Singh khe Phasi: Sangeet Nataku*, Niyu Fild, Hyderabad (Sindh), 1986

13. Odia

1. Rana, Bhavan Singh, *Bharat Ke Amar Krantikari Shaheed Bhagat Singh*

14. Manipuri

1. Kumar, Jatin, *Revolutionary Sahid Bhagat Singh*, 2010

15. French

1. Singh Bhagat, *Pourquoi Je Suis Athee*, Editions De L' Asmeterie, Paris, 2016

16. German

1. Paternoster, Julia, *Der Mythos Bhagat Singh in Hindi Film*, Grin Verla

17. Hindi

A. Collections of Writings/Documents

1. Salil, Suresh and Trinetar Joshi (edited by), *Mukti* (journal), Delhi, 1974
2. Sindhu, Veerendra (edited by), *Patar aur Dastavez*, Delhi, Rajpal & Sons, 1977
3. Sindhu, Veerendra (edited by), *Mere Krantikari Saathi*, Delhi, Rajpal & Sons, 1977
4. Singh, Jagmohan and Chaman Lal (edited by), *Bhagat Singh aur Unke Sathiyon ke Dastavez*, Delhi, Rajkamal Prakashan, 1986 (hardbound)
5. Singh, Jagmohan and Chaman Lal (edited by), *Bhagat Singh aur Unke Sathiyon ke Dastavez*, Delhi, Rajkamal Prakashan, 1987 (paperback)

6. Verma, Shiv (edited by), *Bhagat Singh ki Chuni hui Krityan*, Kanpur, Samajvadi Sahitya Sadan, 1987
7. Lal, Chaman (edited by), *Bhagat Singh ke Sampuran Dastavez*, Panchkula, Aadhar Prakashan, 2004
8. Lal, Chaman (edited by), *Bhagat Singh ke Rajnitik Dastavez*, New Delhi, NBT, 2007
9. Lal, Chaman (edited by), *Shaheed Bhagat Singh: Dastavezon ke Aaine Men*, New Delhi, Publication Division, Govt of India, 2007
10. Verma, Satyem, *Bhagat Singh ke Sampuran Uplabdh Dastavez*, Lucknow, Rahul Foundation, 2006
11. Vyas, Rajshekhar (edited by), *Main Bhagat Singh Bol Raha Hun (three volumes)*, Delhi, Praveen Prakashan, 2001
12. Breen, Dan, and Bhagat Singh (translated by), *Irish Swantantrta Sangram*, Kanpur, Pratap Press, 1928
13. *Dastavez Sankalan*, Hisar, Ekta Prakashan, 2012
14. Neeraj, Ved Swarup and Gian Kaur Kapoor (edited and translated by), *Bhagat Singh ki Jail Diary*, Jaipur, Raj Publishing House 1996
15. *Bhagat Singh ke Jail Notebook*, Chandigarh, Govt of Haryana, 2008
16. Mudgal, Puran, *Bhagat Singh: Jivani tatha Jail Notebook*, Kaithal, Akshardham Prakashan, 2016
17. Singh Jagmohan and Rahul Inqlab (edited by), *Shaheed-e-Azam Bhagat Singh ki Jail Notebook*, Indore, Elan-e-Inqlab, 2016

B. Banned Books (55)

1. Shastri, Chatursen (edited by), *Chand: Phansi Ank* (banned), Allahabad, November 1928
2. Sehgal, Ramrakh Singh (edited by), *Bhavishya: Bhagat Singh Visheshank* (banned), Allahabad, 16 April 1931
3. Malviya, Padam Kant (edited by), *Abhyuodey: Bhagat Singh Ank* (banned), Allahabad, 8 May 1931
4. *Amar Shaheed Bhagat Singh* (banned), Calcutta, Saraswati Book Agency, 1931
5. Chanderdev, Ramchander, *Azadi ke Chirag* (banned), Gaya, 1932
6. Upadhyay, Pandit Shiv Sampati, *Azadi ke Diwane* (banned), Banaras
7. Sharma, Chiranji Lal, *Azadi ki Aag* (poetry) (banned), Banaras
8. Shah, Ramnandan, *Azadi ki Tan* (poetry) (banned), Chhapra, 1932

9. Singh, Kale, *Azadi ki Tarang* (poetry) (banned), Sonepat, 1931
10. Yuvak Hridya, *Balivedi Par* (banned), 1931
11. Harshdatt, Pandey, *Bhagat Singh* (poetry) (banned), Kanpur
12. *Bhagat Singh ki Veerta* (poetry) (banned), Calcutta, Saraswati Book Agency, 1931
13. *Bhartiya Veer* (banned), 1931
14. Sao, Halwai Fagar, *Duniya ka Chand urf Gham ka Dhola* (banned), Calcutta, 1932
15. Nayar, Rajaram, *Fansi ke Shaheed* (poetry) (banned), Prayag, 1931
16. Mishra, Shiv Shambhu, *Jigar ke Tukde* (banned), Howrah, 1931
17. *Karachi Congress* (banned), Ajmer, Hindi Sahitya Mandir, 1931
18. Gujrati, Panna Lal, *Quami Parwana* (banned), Calcutta, 1931
19. *Khoon Ke Ansu* (banned), Calcutta, Saraswati Book Agency, 1931
20. Saraf, Ramchandra, *Kranti ki Chingari* (poetry) (banned), Banaras, 1931
21. Arman, Mohan Lal, *Kranti ka Pujari* (banned), Kanpur, 1931
22. Mukhrejee, Sumender, *Kranti Pushpanji* (banned), Dehradun, 1931
23. Mishra, Shambhunath, *Lahore ki Suli Arthat Bhagat Singh Mastana* (banned), Gaya, 1931
24. Swami, *Lahore ke Shaheed* (banned), Jabalpur, Azad Granthmala, 1931
25. Bamlat, N.L.A., *Lahore ki Fansi Arthat Bhagat Singh ka Tarana* (banned), Banaras, 1931
26. Sutantar, Shriyut Pratap, *Mardana Bhagat Singh* (poetry) (banned), Aligarh, 1931
27. Shukal, Mataprasad, *Matwala Gayan* (banned), Banaras, 1931
28. Markandey, *Nai Kajli Savan Bam Case urf Bhagat Singh ki Fansi aur Banaras ke Dange ki Nai Kajli* (Hindi songs) (banned), Banaras, 1931
29. Pathak, P.G. (edited by), *Prabhat Feri* (songs) (banned), Mumbai, 1931
30. Mishra, Surya Prasad, *Rashtriya Aalha Yani Bhagat Singh ki Ladai* (poetry) (banned), Kanpur, 1931
31. *Shaheedon ki Aahen* (banned), Mirzapur, 1931
32. Gupta, K.L., *Sardar Bhagat Singh* (banned), Agra, 1931
33. Gupta, K.L., *Sher Bhagat Singh* (banned), 1931
34. Gupta, Gopal, *Sardar Bhagat Singh ki Nai Kajri: Savan ke Singh* (songs) (banned), Banaras, 1931
35. Awasthi, Pandit Ram Bilas, *Sardar Bhagat Singh ke Gaane* (songs) (banned), Lucknow, 1931

36. Awasthi, Ram Bilas, *Sulah aur Rashtriya Pukar* (songs) (banned), Lucknow, 1931
37. Dhauria, Satya Narain, *Shaheedon ki Yadgar* (poetry) (banned), Allahabad, Abhyuodey Press, 1931
38. Mishra, Shambhu Prasad, *Shaheed Bhagat Singh* (banned), Calcutta, 1931
39. Mishra, Shambhu Prasad, *Shaheedon ka Tarana* (banned), Calcutta, 1931
40. Sharma, Vikal, *Shaheed-e-Navratan* (songs) (banned), Kanpur, 1931
41. Prabhakar, *Shaheed-e-Watan* (banned), Calcutta, 1931
42. Chander, Manohar, *Shaheedon ka Sandesh: Gandhi ki Jang* (poetry) (banned), Delhi, 1931
43. Arya, Dharam Singh, *Tarane Sardar Bhagat Singh* (banned), Delhi, 1931
44. Arya, Dharam Singh, *Veeron ke Gaane: Fansi ke Pujari* (banned), Delhi, 1931
45. Mishra, Pratap Narayan, *Lahore ki Suli* (banned), Banaras, 1931
46. Lal, Laxman, *Veeron ka Jhula* (poetry) (banned), Jhansi, 1931
47. Awasthi, D.D., *Shaheedon ke Gaane* (banned), Lucknow, 1931
48. Sharma, Fakira, *Swantantrta Bhagat Singh aur Jailon ki Basti* (banned), Muzaffarpur, 1931
49. Tiwari, Kashiram, *Yuvak Garjana* (poetry) (banned), Allahabad, 1931
50. Singh, Kunwar, *Lahore Shadyantar Arthat Bhagat Singh* (banned), Banaras, 1930
51. Dandewala, Prabhu Dayal, *Mardana Bhagat Singh* (banned), Delhi, 1931
52. Devi, Chandravati, *Shaheed Bhagat Singh*, Lahore, 1931
53. *Lahore ke Shaheed* (banned), Aligarh, Gokuldas Printing Press, 1931
54. *Bhagat Singh ki Varta* (banned), Calcutta, Radhesyam Prakashan, 1931
55. Prasad, Badri, *Amar Shaheed Sardar Bhagat Singh* (banned), Mathura, Hindi Sahitya Mandir, 1937

C. Books on Bhagat Singh – Biographies and Evaluation

1. Satyabhakat, *Krantiveer Bhagat Singh*, Kanpur, 1932
2. Trivedi, Ram Dulare, *Shaheed Bhagat Singh*, Kanpur, 1938
3. Sanyal, Jitender Nath, *Amar Shaheed Sardar Bhagat Singh*, Delhi, NBT, 1931, 2005

4. Chakarvrati, Tarini Shankar, *Bharat Mein Sashashatr Kranti ki Bhumika*, Mirzapur, Krantikari Prakashan, 1972
5. Aggarwal, Batuknath, *Viplav Yagya ki Aahutian*, Mirzapur, Krantikari Prakashan, 1971
6. Sehgal, R, *Azadi ke Parwane*
7. Shastri, Chatursen, *Yaadon ki Parchhayiyan*, Delhi, Rajpal & Sons
8. Sindhu, Veerendra, *Yugdrashta Bhagat Singh aur Unke Mrityuanjay Purkhe*, Banaras, Bhartiya Gyanpeeth, 1968
9. Sindhu, Veerendra, *Amar Shaheed Bhagat Singh*, Delhi, Prakashan Vibhag, 1974
10. Veerendra, *Ve Inqlabi Din*, Delhi, Rajpal & Sons, 1986
11. Raj, Sukhdev, *Jab Jyoti Jagi*, Mirzapur, Krantikari Prakashan, 1971
12. Shastri, Raja Ram, *Amar Shaheedon ke Samsmarn*, Kanpur, Sadhan Prakashan, 1961
13. Verma, Shiv, *Samsmrityan*, Delhi, Nidhi Prakashan, 1983
14. Verma, Shiv and Bhagwan Das Mahaur, Sadashiv Malkapurka, *Yash ki Dharohar*, Delhi, Atmaram & Sons, 1988
15. Sanyal, Sachindra Nath, *Bandi Jivan*, Delhi, Atmaram & Sons
16. Gupta, Manmath Nath, *Bharat Ke Krantikari*, Delhi, Hind Pocket Books, 1969
17. Gupta, Manmath Nath, *Bhagat Singh aur Unka Yug*, Delhi, Lipi Prakashan, 1985
18. Wariar, Rajenderpal Singh, *Eik Krantikari ke Sansmaran*, Lucknow, Shaheed Smarak
19. Thapar, Mathura Das, *Mere Bhai Sukhdev*, Delhi, Praveen Prakashan, 1998
20. Yashpal, *Simhavlokan*, Allahabad, Lokbharti Prakashan, 1994
21. Nayar, Kuldip, *Bhagat Singh: Kranti Men Eik Prayog*, Delhi, Diamond Prakashan, 2001
22. Rehbar, Hans Raj, *Bhagat Singh: Eik Jivani*, Delhi, Vaani Prakashan, 1988
23. Rehbar, Hans Raj, *Bhagat Singh Vichardhara*, Delhi
24. Lal, Chaman, *Bhagat Singh*, Delhi, Medha Books, 2009
25. Lal, Chaman (edited by), *Krantiveer Bhagat Singh: Abhyuodey aur Bhavishya*, Allahabad, Lokbharti Prakashan, 2012
26. Lal, Chaman, *Bhagat Singh ke Durlabh Dastavez aur Kranti ka Barahmasa*, Meerut, Samvad Prakashan, 2014

27. Lal, Chaman, *Navupniveshvad ke Khatre aur Bhagat Singh ki Krantikari Virasat*, Delhi, Udbhavna Prakashan, 2007
28. Waraich, M.J.S., *Amar Vidrohi*, Delhi, Prakashan Vibhag, 2013
29. Waraich, M.J.S., and Gurdev Singh Sidhu, *Bhagat Singh ko Fansi*, Delhi, Rajkamal Prakashan, 2007
30. Noorani, A.G., *Bhagat Singh ka Mukdma*, Delhi, Sahmat, 2015
31. Singh, Raghuvir Singh, *Swantantarta Sangram aur Bhagat Singh*, Delhi, Radha Publications
32. Singh, Raghuvir, *Shaheed Bhagat Singh: Eik Gambhir Adheyeta*, Delhi, Udbhavna, 2007
33. Singh, Raghuvir, *Shaheed-e-Azam Bhagat Singh: Krantikari Sanghrash ke Vaicharik Utkarsh*, Delhi, Confluence Prakashan, 2008
34. Satyashakun, *Shaheed-e-Azam Bhagat Singh*, Delhi, Sanmarg Prakashan
35. Bansal, R.L., *Teen Krantikari Shaheed*, Agra, Bharti Bhavan, 1962
36. Sinha, Sukhsagar, *Khun ki Holi: Krantikarion ke Romanchak Gathayen*
37. Suri, Naresh, and Ragini Mishra, and Mohini Gupta, *Bhagat Singh: Vyaktitav aur Vichar*, Delhi, Radha Publications
38. Nirmohi, Deepchand, *Suraj ka Safar: Bhagat Singh*, Allahabad, Itihas Bodh Prakashan, 2007
39. Rai, Vikas Narain, *Bhagat Singh se Dosti*, Allahabad, Itihas Bodh Prakashan, 2007
40. Mudrarakshash, *Bhagat Singh ke Hone ka Matlab*, Allahabad, Itihas Bodh Prakashan, 2008
41. Sultanpuri, Shankar, *Krantikari Bhagat Singh*, Delhi, Hind Pocket Books, 1969
42. Vidrohi, Ramesh, *Bhagat Singh*, Delhi, Bhavna Prakashan, 1982
43. Suresh, *Bhagat Singh*, Delhi, Hind Pocket Books
44. Dewan, Manorma, *Inqlabi Yatra: Chhabil Das/Sita Devi*, Delhi, NBT, 2006
45. Dewan, Manorma, *Azadi ki Basti*, Delhi, Raymadhav Prakashan, 2006
46. Rastogi, Subhash, *Krantikari Bhagat Singh*, Delhi, Suryabharti Prakashan, 2000
47. Juneja, M.M. (edited by), *Bhagat Singh par Chuninda Lekh*, Hisar, 2007
48. Juneja, M.M. and Raghuvir Singh (edited by), *Bhagat Singh par Durlabh Lekh*, Panchkula, Modern Publishers, 2012
49. Juneja, M.M., *Bhagat Singh ke Prati Rashtr Natmastak Kyon?*, Zirakpur, Modern Prakashan, 2012

50. Juneja, M.M., *Bhagat Singh ki Badhti Lokpriyta*, Zirakpur, Modern Prakashan, 2015
51. Prabhakar, Vishnu, *Amar Shaheed Bhagat Singh*, Delhi, Kitabghar Prakashan
52. Vyas, Rajshekhar, *Mrityuanjay Bhagat Singh*, Delhi, Granth Akademi, 2007
53. Kumar, Ajay (edited by), Bhagat Singh: *Smriti Mein Prerna Vicharon Mein Disha*, Delhi, Udbhavna Prakashan, 2008
54. *Krantikari Baikunth Shukal ka Mukdma*, Delhi, Rajkamal Prakashan, 2002
55. Shrivastav, Suresh Chander, *Shaheed-e-Azam Bhagat Singh*, Delhi, Sadhna Prakashan, 2005
56. Bakshi, Sachindernath, *Kranti ke Path Par*, Lucknow, Lokhit Prakashan, 2003
57. Saral, Shrikrishan, *Krantikarion ki Kahanian*, Ujjain, 1980
58. Sakhavalkar, Krishan Madhav, *Bhagat Singh: Brochure*, Chandigarh, Govt. of Punjab, 1981
59. *Amar Shaheed Bhagat Singh*, Delhi, All India Congress Committee, 1981
60. Singaria, Sohan Lal, *Shaheed Samrat Sardar Bhagat Singh*, Delhi, Samyak Prakashan
61. Joshi, Ratan Lal, *Krantikari Prerna Ke Sarot*
62. Joshi, Ratan Lal, *Mrityanjayi Bhagat Singh*
63. Mitrokhin, Vasili, *Lenin aur Bharat*, Moscow, Pragati Prakashan, 1987
64. Vidyarthi, Sudhir, *Inqlab ka Safar*, Bareilly, Jansulabh Prakashan, 2006
65. Vidyarthi, Sudhir (edited by), *Kranti Ka Sakshya*, Delhi, Rajkamal Prakashan, 2009
66. Bhattacharya, Dipankar, *Rashtar Nayak Bhagat Singh*, Patna, Samkaleen Janmat, 2006
67. *Bhagat Singh, Rajguru aur Sukhdev*, Delhi, Jan Natya Manch, 2006
68. *Shaheed-e-Azam Bhagat Singh*, Kolkata, Shaheed Yadgar Samiti, 2002
69. Hooja, Bhupender, *Shaheedon ki Vasiyat aur Virasat*, Jaipur, 2002
70. Savyasachi, *Shaheed-e-Azam Bhagat Singh*, Mathura
71. Baghele, Ram Singh, *Amar Shaheed Sardar Bhagat Singh*, Gwalior, 1982
72. *Yugdrashta Bhagat Singh*, Hyderabad, Shaheed Bhagat Singh Seva Samiti, 2007
73. Jagesh, Jagdish, *Kalam Aaj unki Jai Bol*, Banaras, Prachark Granthmala

74. Maheshwari, Sarla, *Shaheed-e-Azam Bhagat Singh*, Delhi, Udhbhavna, 2007
75. Sharma, Manoj, *Hava men Rahegi Mere Khayal ki Bijli*, Delhi, Udbhavna, 2007
76. Dhawle, Ashok, *Bhagat Singh*, Delhi, Udbhavna Prakashan, 2007
77. Sharma, Geetesh, *Bhagat Singh ka Raasta*, Howrah, Manav Prakashan, 2008
78. Ranjit, Anup Kumar, *Khayalat ki Bijlian*, Allahabad, Lokbharti Prakashan, 2008
79. Rai, Jharkhande, *Krantikarion ke Samsmaran*, Delhi, PPH, 1970
80. Rai, Jharkhande, *Bhartiya Krantikari Aandolan*, Delhi, PPH, 1970
81. Jain, Lalchand, *Shaheed Bhagat Singh*, Jaipur, Pustak Bhandar, 2000
82. Kamal, A.P., *Shaheed-e-Azam Bhagat Singh*, Delhi, Raj Pocket Books, 2002
83. Chakr, Sudarshan, *Bhagat Singh ka Aalha*, Kanpur
84. Dutt, Vishnu, *Kranti ka Devta*, 1962
85. Dayal, Brahmeshwar, *Bhagat Singh ke Gumshuda Patr*, Delhi, Prakashan Sansthan, 2007
86. Dayal, Brahmshewar, *Bhagat Singh ki Gupt Yatra*, Delhi
87. Rana, Bhavan Singh, *Shaheed Bhagat Singh*, Delhi, Diamond, 2006
88. Balley, L.R., *Shaheed Bhagat Singh ke Asli Varis Kaun?*, Jalandhar, Bhim Patrika Publications
89. Samal, Pratap, *Shaheed-e-Azam Bhagat Singh*, Delhi, AIDSO, 2015
90. Nath, Shambhu and Snehil Brahmchari, *Bhartiya Krantikari Andolan*, Delhi, Climax, 1991
91. Arya, Mange Ram, *Bhartiya Swantarta Andolan Mein Krantikarion ki Bhumika*, Delhi, 1991
92. Sahajwala, Prem Chand, *Bhagat Singh: Itihas ke Kuchh Panne*, Delhi, 2009
93. Vikal, Krishan, *Shaheed Bhagat Singh*, Delhi, Hind Pocket Books, 2002
94. Mrinal, *Bhagat Singh Hone ka Matlab*, Delhi, Shilpayan, 2011
95. Alok, Varsha, *Sardar Bhagat Singh: Swantarta Sangram Mein Yogdan*, Agra, Jaya Prakashan
96. Sharma, Mahesh, *Amar Shaheed Bhagat Singh*, Delhi, Prabhat Prakshan, 2010
97. Vishavprakash, and Mohini Gupt, *Sardar Bhagat Singh: Vyakti aur Vichar*, Delhi, Naman Prakashan, 2009

98. Kumar, Anil, *Main Bhagat Singh Bol Raha Hun*, Delhi, Prabhat, 2011
99. Ahsas, Ramesh, *Adhunik Bharat Ke Saput: Bhagat Singh*, Delhi, Shilalekh Prakashan, 2018
100. Sinhal, Meenu, *Bhagat Singh*, Delhi, Prabhat, 2011
101. Sharma, Rajender, *Kranti ka Surya: Bhagat Singh*, Delhi, Subodh Pocket Books, 2004
102. Rawat, Asha, *Chahiye Eik aur Bhagat Singh*, Hindi Sahitya Niketan
103. Tiwari, Vinod, *Shaheed-e-Azam Bhagat Singh*, Delhi, Manoj Pocket Books, 2004
104. Arya, Jagat Ram, *Sardar Bhagat Singh*, Delhi, Kitabghar
105. Hridya, Vyathit, *Bhagat Singh*, Penguin India, 2002
106. Jaswal, Avtar Singh, *Gandhi aur Bhagat Singh*, Delhi, Anamika, 2012
107. Manas, Mukesh, *Dalit Samsya aur Bhagat Singh*, Delhi, Aarohi, 2011
108. Panda, Chaynika, *Bhagat Singh: Vyaktitav, Vichardhara aur Prasangikta*, Delhi, Swaraj Prakashan, 2014
109. Pal, Rajiv Kumar, *Kalam, Tyag aur Talwar*, Delhi, Shivak Prakashan 2015
110. Sharma, Satyanarain, *Bhagat Singh aur Unke Sahyogiyon ke Mukadme*, Allahabad, Neelkanth Prakashan, 2017
111. Wahi, Tarun Kumar, *Yuva Krantikari Shaheed Bhagat Singh*, Delhi, Raj Pocket Books, 2015
112. Singh Vikram, *Bhagat Singh: Chetna ke Srot*, Mapple Press, 2014
113. Verma, Satyem, *Vicharon ke Saan Par*, Lucknow, Rahul Foundation, 2017
114. Raju, Raj, *Shaheed Bhagat Singh*, Delhi, Nai Sadi Prakashan, 2015
115. Nagar, Vishnu, *Bhagat Singh*, Delhi, Zi Prakashan, 2017
116. Verma, Sangita, *Bharat ke Nirmata: Bhagat Singh*, Delhi, Star Paperbacks, 2015
117. Goyal, Ram Gopal, *Amar Shaheed Bhagat Singh*, Delhi, Alka Prakashan, 2013
118. Singh, Tejpal Singh, *Rashtarputr Bhagat Singh*, Delhi, Raj Publishers, 2017
119. Bhasin, Sudhir, *Shaheed-e-Azam Bhagat Singh*, Delhi, Galaxy Prakashan, 2017

D. Creative Literature on Bhagat Singh

1. Sidhu, Gurdev Singh (edited by), *Fansi Lahore Ki* (poetry) (banned), New Delhi, NBT, 2006

2. Saral, Shrikrishan, *Sardar Bhagat Singh*, Ujjain, Rashtriya Prakashan, 1964
3. Thakur, Hira Prasad, *Veer Bhagat Singh* (poetry), Agra
4. Kusum, Shanti Swarup, *Amar Shaheed Bhagat Singh* (poetry), Delhi, Sahitya Vithi, 1996
5. Kusum, Shanti Swarup, *Krantikari Bhagat Singh* (poetry), Delhi, Sahitya Vithi, 1997
6. Joshi, Mrinalini, *Inqlab* (translated from the Marathi), Delhi, Prabhat Prakashan, 2005
7. Garg, Mridula, *Anitya* (novel), Delhi, National Publishing House, 2004
8. Singh, Bachchan, *Shaheed-e-Azam*, Delhi, Atmaram & Sons, 2006
9. Chauhan, Lal Bahadur Singh, *Krantiveer Bhagat Singh* (novel), Delhi, Atmaram & Sons, 2006
10. Vikal, Devi Prasad, *Sardar Bhagat Singh* (play), Kanpur, Chitnya Prakashan, 1952
11. Mahaur, Bhagwan Das, *Sardar Bhagat Singh* (play), Jhansi, 1980
12. Sidhu, Charan Das, *Bhagat Singh Shaheed* (play) (translated from the Punjabi), Delhi, Vaani Prakashan, 1998
13. Mishra, Piyush, *Gagan Damama Bajyo* (play), Allahabad, Itihas Bodh Prakashan, 2002

E. Special Issues of Journals on Bhagat Singh

1. Chaturvedi, Benarsi Das (edited by), *Smarika: Ardh Shatabadi*, Agra, 1981
2. *Bhagat Singh Smarika*, Mumbai, Sharmik Sangh, 1981
3. Savyasachi (edited by), *Utrardh: Bhagat Singh Visheshank*, Mathura, October 1988
4. Kavinder, Ram, and Subhash Gupt (edited by), *Bhagat Singh: Tab aur Ab*, Jamshepur, 2001
5. Nirmohi, Desh (edited by), *Pal Pratipal: Bhagat Singh Visheshank*, Panchkula, 2006
6. Vijay, Tarun (edited by), *Panchjanya*, Delhi, March 2007
7. Sinha, Preeti (edited by), Filhal: Shaheed Bhagat Singh Smriti Ank, Patna, April 2007
8. Mishra, G.P. (edited by), *Ujjwal Dhruvtara*, Allahabad, July–September 2007
9. Arun, A.K. (edited by), *Yuva Samvad: Bhagat Singh ka Bharat*, Delhi, November 2007

10. Suman, Sudhir (edited by), *Vicharon ki Saan Par: Bhagat Singh Smarika*, Aarah, 2007
11. Kumar Ajay (edited by), *Udbhavna: Bhagat Singh Visheshank*, Delhi, 2007
12. *Smarika: Shaheed Bhagat Singh*, Banaras, Gyan Vigyan Samiti, 2007
13. *Bhagat Singh: Durga Bhabhi Smarika*, Lucknow, Shaheed Smarak, 2007
14. Singh, Bharat (edited by), *Krantikari Mahanayak*, Godarn special issue, Aligarh, 2008

ACKNOWLEDGMENTS AND SOURCES OF DOCUMENTS

1. Grateful acknowledgement to the Nehru Memorial Museum and Library (NMML), New Delhi, popularly known as Teen Murti Bhavan, for providing copies of documents, original scanned letters and publications in different journals from their microfilms and other records.
2. Grateful acknowledgement to the National Archives of India (NAI), New Delhi, for copies of many documents, photographs, etc.; and particular thanks to Shri Rajmani Srivastava.
3. Grateful acknowledgement to the Supreme Court of India Museum, where 'The Trial of Bhagat Singh' exhibition was put up in the year 2008. A DVD of the exhibition items was graciously provided by the Supreme Court of India with due permission to use its material with acknowledgements. Through this collection, I had access to rare original letters and copies of the posters that were thrown in the Central Assembly, Delhi. The Supreme Court also provided a digital copy of Bhagat Singh's *Jail Notebook* from its records. Special thanks to Shri Noorul Hooda and Shri Rajesh Prasad, the former is assistant registrar at Jamia Millia Islamia and the latter is assistant director at the Supreme Court Museum
4. Grateful acknowledgement to Desh Bhagat Yaadgar Hall (Ghadar Memorial), Jalandhar, for providing photocopies of the Punjabi magazine *Kirti* for the years 1927 and 1928, with special thanks to Shri Charanji Lal Kangniwal.
5. Thanks and grateful acknowledgment to the family of the late Bhupender Hooja for allowing me to include the *Jail Notebook*, painstakingly annotated by Bhupender Hooja. Thanks also to Abhey Sindhu, nephew of Bhagat Singh, for bringing out multiple editions of the *Jail Notebook*, some of which are even distributed for free by the Punjab and Haryana governments.
6. Thanks also to the late Shri Kultar Singh, younger brother of Bhagat Singh, and his family, especially his daughter Veerendra Sindhu, who

collected and published *Bhagat Singh: Patra Aur Dastavez (Letters and Documents of Bhagat Singh)* in Hindi and wrote the best biographical account of Bhagat Singh and his ancestors in 1968. Some photocopies of the original letters were also sent by Shri Kiranjit Singh Sindhu from their family collection. The late Shiv Verma, a close comrade of Bhagat Singh, needs special mention for bringing out Bhagat Singh's documents in Hindi and English.

7. Thanks to Major General (Retd.) Sheonan Singh, nephew of Bhagat Singh, for providing copies of Bhagat Singh's correspondence with British officials in 1926 regarding the censoring of his mail. This correspondence includes five letters of Bhagat Singh, which were not discovered till 2018.

8. Thanks to M.J.S. Waraich and Jagmohan Singh, who published documents of Bhagat Singh in Punjabi through *Yuvak Kender*, Jalandhar, between 1969–73. Some documents of Bhagat Singh are included in *The Hanging of Bhagat Singh*, edited by M.J.S. Waraich, Gurdev Singh Sidhu and Harish Jain. This book has references to shaheed.bhagatsingh.org, with thanks to Professor Jagmohan Singh, who created the website. A special mention to the late playwright and publisher Gurshan Singh and Punjabi poet Amarjit Chandan for documents published under *Likhtan*, a Punjabi book that was published in 1974.

9. Thanks to Suresh Salil for providing a copy of relevant issues of the magazine *Mukti* in Hindi, which published some documents of Bhagat Singh in 1972.

10. Thanks to Dr Raghuvir Singh of Palwal and Ram Sharma from Beena, for providing the photocopy of *Hindu Panch*, a Calcutta-based magazine, which was published on 18 June 1931. This issue carried a long-lost letter of Bhagat Singh, and has been included for the first time in this volume.

11. Thanks also to Dr Hina Nandrajog, Associate Professor in English at the University of Delhi, who translated some of the documents into English. This volume has not used any previous translations of the documents and has made fresh translations to avoid copyright issues.

12. Last but not least, thanks to the editors at HarperCollins, who deserve appreciation for bringing out this long-delayed volume of Bhagat Singh's available writings in English, which may be updated as and when some more documents are discovered.